NO DIRECTION HOME

NO DIRECTION HOME

THE LIFE AND MUSIC OF
BOB DYLAN

Robert Shelton

BTB
BEECH TREE BOOKS
WILLIAM MORROW
New York

Library of Congress Cataloging-in-Publication Data

Shelton, Robert, 1926–
  No direction home.

  (Beech tree books)
  Discography: p.
  Includes index.
  1. Dylan, Bob, 1941–   . 2. Singers—United
States—Biography.   I. Title.
ML420.D98S5   1986   784.4'924   [B]   85-26781
ISBN 0-688-05045-X

Printed in the United States of America

First Edition

1 2 3 4 5 6 7 8 9 10

BOOK DESIGN BY RICHARD ORIOLO

The word "book" is said to derive from *boka*, or beech.
The beech tree has been the patron tree of writers since ancient times and
represents the flowering of literature and knowledge.

Dedicated to the memory and widows
of Geoff Ablett and Ralph J. Gleason.
How a twenty-eight-year-old London cop
and a fifty-eight-year-old California journalist
found their short lives deeply touched
by a writer of songs is part of the
mystery this book explores.

For my sisters and brother-in-law,
who lent support when it was most
needed. And for uncommon help and
inspiration from Gabrielle Goodchild,
Liz Thomson, and Clare Pedrick . . .
deep thanks.

—R.S., LONDON, 1986

CONTENTS

Prelude / Lifelessness, the Enemy   13
  1 / "Don't Raise Your Voice Around Here!"   21
  2 / The Wrong End of the Mississippi   62
  3 / Talking Greenwich Village Blues   87
  4 / Positively 161 West Fourth Street   127
  5 / Not a Puppet Laureate   159
  6 / Roll Over, Gutenberg   209
  7 / Several Seasons in Hell   239
  8 / Orpheus Plugs In   266
  9 / Inside the Coliseum   305
 10 / One Foot on the Highway . . .   340
 11 / Listening to the Silence   373
 12 / Running Free   410
 13 / Thunder, Hurricane, and Hard Rain   450
Coda: / Busy Being Born Again   476
    Acknowledgments   499
    Copyright Citations and Notes to Text 501
    Select Bibliography   511
    Song Index   517
    Discography   547
    Index   559

"Take care of all your memories
For you cannot relive them. . . ."

—DYLAN[1]

"Because he is part Orpheus, the poet . . .
is architect of myth, magician over
savagery, and pilgrim towards death. . . ."

—GEORGE STEINER,
 "SILENCE AND THE POET"

"The truth was obscure, too profound and
too pure; to live it you have to explode."

—DYLAN[2]

PRELUDE

LIFELESSNESS, THE ENEMY

"Could there be a more uncomfortable position intellectually than of floating in the thin air of unproved possibilities, not knowing whether what one sees is truth or illusion?"

—FROM CARL JUNG'S FOREWORD TO THE *I CHING*

"We've all got it within us, for whatever we want to grasp for."

—DYLAN, 1976

Where can I begin the story? I'd need a film camera's flashing chain of images: Dylan at London's Wembley Stadium in 1984 as 100,000 strangers sing his words . . . or Chicago, starting Tour '74 to a thunderclap ovation . . . at London's Albert Hall and the Olympia in Paris in May 1966, Dylan resisting hostility to his new music . . . or playing to Blackbushe in 1978, at Britain's largest-ever rock-concert audience . . . maybe back at Folk City in 1961, Dylan in his black Huck Finn corduroy cap, galvanizing us with intensity and gamesmanship . . . Dylan sitting at Jack Kerouac's grave in 1975, improvising a tribute to one of the writers who opened new roads to him . . . or his turbaned head on national TV in 1976, looking oppressed and singing oppression. Sometimes his whole life seems like a performance.

Perhaps I should begin at a midpoint, in 1971, about ten years after we had met. He visited me at the Henry Hudson Hotel on Manhattan's West Side. I hadn't seen him since the Isle of Wight Festival in England. I'd been living there, sifting the facts of his career.

I'd traveled so far and interviewed so many people. Most had said they knew only a fragment of the picture. They offered their bits toward my mosaic. Nearly everyone had a question about him, including his family. "How did he do it?" an English fan asked me. "Who do you think his Sad-Eyed Lady was?" Dylan's former Woodstock gardener/bodyguard asked that, and he knew Sara, Dylan's wife, well. A New York editor asked me if he took his name from Dylan Thomas or Matt Dillon. I often felt like that reporter in *Citizen Kane* looking for "Rosebud."

As my Kane sauntered up the hotel corridor, he looked as healthy as I'd ever seen him: color in his cheeks, fringe beard, heavy workman country boots, cords, an old shirt beneath his leather jacket. He was offstage now, but why should I be keyed up? How would he be today—mercurial, tense, playful, hostile? Which of his many pseudonyms would he be wearing: Elmer Johnson, Tedham Porterhouse, Bob Landy, Robert Milkwood Thomas, Big Joe's Buddy, Blind Boy Grunt, Keef Laundy, or Judge Magney?

Dylan began a minute examination of every detail of my room. "The things that must have gone on in this room," he remarked. He tried to guess whether a wall had been dented by a whiskey bottle or an ashtray during a lovers' quarrel. I recalled his brother's remark: "He has become like a fifty-year-old man . . . so calm, so peaceful and so dignified." That morning he looked like the album "New Morning" sounded.

He had moved back to New York City. "Woodstock turned into a bad joke," Dylan said. "Why, they were running tours up there. People were trying to pick up a piece of the earth, a piece of the lawn or of the shrubs." Why had he returned to the Village? "I'll be able to let you know about that better after we're not living in the Village anymore . . . we're just passing through. . . . A lot of time, you just have to go down many roads to get where you are going. . . . The important thing is to keep moving. . . . Or else to stop by the side of the road every once in a while and build a house. I guess that's about the best thing anyone can do." Was he looking for someplace to hide from fame? "No," Bob replied calmly, "I really don't want to hide from anything." He told me he was embattled again.

One self-styled "Dylanologist" had been systematically plundering his garbage pail for "clues" to the "real Dylan." Bob said with a sigh: "I guess that's just the price of fame. We all kept loading up the garbage pail with mousetraps . . . then . . . all the dog shit we could find. But he still kept going through the garbage, anyway." Not every superstar had to pay *that* price. Why was he still so worshiped and castigated? Dylan replied: "The media created the trouble for me. They blew me out of proportion. My thing was just for a crowd of people who were on the same wavelength I was on. What I was doing wasn't really for a mass audience. I'm not a Shea Stadium type of performer, I never was. The slogan that was going around was: 'The Beatles, Dylan, and The Stones were the kings.' *I* never said that. I never rejected the title of 'king' because I never accepted the title in the first place. . . .''

How depressing it was, I said, after he'd stamped intelligence onto pop music, that there was still so much Top Forty trivia. Dylan replied: "Changing the face of pop music is not necessarily changing its metabolism. I didn't change the metabolism. All I did was just open up a whole lot of doors. But, you have to admit my influence is there . . . all over . . . even in country music. Now you can hear the street sound in pop music almost anywhere. . . .''

We talked about some mutual friends we'd lost. He later tried to bring it all back home with the Rolling Thunder Revue in 1975–76. "Those were wonderful days, all right," Dylan said. "It was a movement then, a real movement. But it was probably the last movement. Say," he exclaimed, laughing, "that would make a good song title, wouldn't it?" Dylan resumed, sadly: "The dream is gone. It is meaningless to try to grasp what's passed. I see no similarity between today and what happened in the early 1960s. Those early days in the Village were great, and the days in Dinkytown [University of Minnesota] were even greater. Now, things are depressing. . . . The village is neon and cheapness. Today, it seems as if thousands of years of experience are being compressed into a year."

Could he find any encouragement in the New Left? "The New Left has no policy, no program, no philosophy. There really isn't a New Left. Those people who march for peace are just interested in peace, but that doesn't make them part of any New Left. Old Left had a program, and a policy, and a place, and some reason behind it. . . . When you come right down to it, there is no youth culture, and there is no New Left, and, as far as the music business is concerned, it's just a toy."

The words were cynical, but his tone wasn't. I asked him what he'd been reading lately. It was the sort of question he'd never answer when he arrived in New York, when he was devouring everything he could lay his eyes on. Even in the late 1960s, when he kept a large open Bible on a reading stand in Woodstock, he'd have thought it pretentious to tell anyone. (In early 1977, *The* [London] *Times Literary Supplement* asked Dylan, among many literary heavies, which books he regarded as the most underrated and overrated of the century. Dylan puckishly gave the same answer to both questions: "The Bible.")

He told me: "It's a very heavy responsibility for me to say what I'm reading, because too many people would regard that as some kind of endorsement. That happened once when I said I was interested in the *I Ching*." Relenting, he told me he was reading novels by Isaac Bashevis Singer and Chaim Potok. "They make a lot more sense to me these days

than all that Indian maharishi stuff." Bob was about to go on a private
visit to Israel, but it was to be publicized out of shape. "I went to a Hasid
wedding last week," Dylan told me, weighing my reaction.

Dylan knew I'd been interviewing his old friends. I told him I'd finally
tracked down a Hibbing pal, John Bucklen. Bob asked: "Where in the hell
did you find him?" I told him he was then a disc jockey in Wisconsin.
Dylan said: "John was really my best buddy." He regretted that when he'd
last seen Bucklen he "was terribly rushed, terribly busy." (Dylan has often
expressed regret that his rise wasn't graceful. He'd been thorny, said many
sharp things. I think what concerned him most was that his old put-down
"truth attacks" would come back to haunt him.)

"I went back to Hibbing for the class reunion." Of that tenth anniversary of high-school graduation, he continued: "When I was fifteen, I said
to myself: 'They treat me pretty low-down here now, but I'll be back one
day and then they'll all run up and shake my hand.' And it actually came
true, in the summer of 1969. I sat there in Hibbing and signed autographs
for an hour, more than an hour.... You've seen Hibbing," Dylan went
on. "You've seen that great ugly hole in the ground, where that open-pit
mine was. They actually think, up there, that it is beautiful. They think it
is a scenery place. Well, they are doing that now to the whole country....
I didn't really look at Hibbing, I just went back for the graduation party. I
don't need to be reminded of what it was like. I'll never forget it." His face
was impassive, but a shudder seemed to run through him. It reminded me
of his book *Tarantula,* where he said he'd make a Faustian pact with the
devil to get away from wasteland Middle America.

I told him that I'd be writing at great length about his albums; he
seemed impressed. When we talked about *Self Portrait,* his eyes narrowed
defensively. I told him I'd listen to that failed album again. Why hadn't
Nashville Skyline appeared on the country hit charts? Dylan: "I am just not
for the masses. The country people didn't buy that album in such great
numbers. It was the college people who bought it, the same people who
buy my other albums. There was a lot of shuck bullshit about that album.
The record was sold to country people as country music, but to sell to the
country people, you have to be out on the road with traveling country
shows every week. They have to expect to see you at the crossroads with a
live country show...."

I assured Dylan I aimed at a portrait in which he could retain respect as
an artist. He had known me long enough, I hoped, not to bracket me with
reporters who think denuding celebrities is a way to earn a living. Dylan
suggested some people I might try tracking down. A name or two from
Minneapolis came up and I asked how they might be helpful. Bob just
smiled and said: "It's just a clue."

Did he want to comment on drugs? "What sort of drugs?" he exclaimed. "I never had anything to do with glamorizing the drug thing,"
Dylan said. "That was the beat thing, not me. As for the hard drugs, that's

a question of trafficking. . . . But you have to realize that junk is not the problem in and of itself. Junk is the symptom, not the problem . . . as Dr. Freud would say."

Mellowness from the angriest of angry young men was startling. In the early years in New York he'd come on charming, then became tenser, warier, and more difficult. But here was the "moderate" man, about to sever his links with his longtime manager, Albert Grossman (Grossman died of a heart attack in February 1986 while on a flight to Europe. He was fifty-nine years old.) Dylan: "He had me signed up for ten years, for part of my records, for part of my everything. But I'll be out of that next month. Albert wanted it quiet and he settled out of court. A lot of people would go out of their way to run Albert down, but I wouldn't." (Dylan never used his considerable media power to vent his problems with Grossman, or Columbia Records, or the song publishers who held vital Dylan copyrights until 1965.) Dylan went on to tell me that a lot of deals he'd made with Grossman had proved better for Grossman than for himself. It had been a sticky, five-year, on-and-off divorce, painful to both parties. (Legal loose ends remained in 1986.) After Dylan's exhausting 1965–66 world tour, Grossman had scheduled more than sixty concerts for him. When, I asked, was the last time any manager said to his star: You're working too hard. Why don't you take off a year and enjoy what you've earned?

Dylan was one of the few music-makers who shifted partial control away from business fat cats to the artists themselves. He often told me of his troubles with record-company executives, box-office people. When things were going well with Grossman, Bob had lauded him to the skies; now he refused to attack, beyond saying, "Albert's got terrible taste, and you can quote that." He had his complaints, yet he wasn't vengeful. Even for him there's a limit to challenging authority. We both knew he'd been rudely ignored by Folkways, Vanguard, and Elektra before a producer who hadn't even heard him sing signed him to Columbia Records. He knew the rewards, defects, and hypocrisies of the international music business. He worked within it with detachment. He had no fan club; he didn't endorse products. During his retreats, he turned his back on several fortunes, while the American recording industry of the sixties grew from an annual gross on pop records of 250 million dollars to several billion dollars by the mid-1970s.

We talked on for hours. If I probed too deeply, he stood up and looked out the window, as if ready to split. If I released the pressure, he sat down again. Sometimes he spoke in aphorisms: "There's no place to go. There are guys in prison that just can't afford to get out." We joked about how he was never very organized. "I used to write songs on napkins, just like Woody did, and then I used the napkins to wipe my mouth with.

"I was doing new things in 1959. I was pretty raggy then, but I was doing things that haven't been heard since. Listen to my records before 1965, and you won't hear anything that sounds like that." Did the songs still flow quickly? "A few years ago, I would write a song in two hours, or maybe two days, at the most. Now, it can be two weeks ... maybe longer." (A few weeks later I saw one of those stories about Dylan at a studio session where he reportedly wrote a song in twenty-five minutes!)

We agreed that America was in trouble again, that the masters of war were still in power. Dylan did not say how, or if, he might remount the barricades. Yet, when he said to me, "They're not going to get away with it," there was a steely resolve in his voice. I didn't need to ask who "they" were.

Dylan and his wife, Sara, were flying to Israel in two days. I was refreshing memories of Greenwich Village and Woodstock. The New York in which Dylan had arrived late in 1960 was the proverbial concrete jungle of vitality and struggle—a lure to provincials who'd used up their hometowns. "Folk City is just a parking lot now," Dylan told me, and there at the corner it was, just torn down and paved over. The owner, Mike Porco, had moved the club to Third Street. I walked past Dylan's old apartment on West Fourth Street, across the street from the Bagel, then inched my way along to his new place down the road from the Hip Bagel. Sara Dylan, wearing sunglasses and wrapped in a raincoat, was just coming out the doorway, furtively looking both ways, walking her little white dog. Bleecker Street was slummy as ever—tired, dirty, sad cafés. Pizza shops and espresso joints thrived, but it had all slid downhill.

There had seemed so much hope back in 1960. John F. Kennedy had won the presidency from Nixon by a hairbreadth. Floyd Patterson was the boxing champion of the world. The soap opera *The Romance of Helen Trent* went down the drain, after twenty-seven sudsy years. In 1960, integration sit-ins began in Greensboro, North Carolina. Meanwhile, the cold war, which looked as if it might thaw, froze over again after the Russians shot down an American U-2 spy plane.

Americans were reading *To Kill a Mockingbird, Born Free,* and *The Rise and Fall of the Third Reich.* Many were preparing to celebrate the Civil War centennial. Broadway hits included *A Taste of Honey* and *Bye Bye Birdie.* Elvis made another dreary film, *G.I. Blues,* while Paul Newman emerged as a new screen hero. Hitchcock terrified us with *Psycho,* while a benign Frank Sinatra starred in *Can Can.* Emily Post died at eighty-six, and American manners haven't been the same. *Never on Sunday* was a global hit. Chubby Checker was about to turn Hank Ballard's "The Twist" into a dance craze. The biggest excitement in pop was coming from folk music.

Before the Cuban missile crisis, assassins' bullets, and Vietnam turned promise into sorrow, it was a great time to be young. Before the passive resistance of Martin Luther King, Jr., ran into a stone wall, it was even a time to be black and young.

The year 1960 was after Joe McCarthy, before Eugene McCarthy. After the beats, before the hippies. After the Old Left, before the New Left. After Campbell's soup, before Andy Warhol. After Dada, before camp.

After Batman, before the return of Batman. After *The Village Voice,* before *The East Village Other*. After Marshall Field, before Marshall McLuhan. After Trotsky, before Yippie.

The year 1960 was post-Thomas Wolfe, ante-Tom Wolfe. Post-Presley, ante-Beatles. After Bill Mauldin, before Jules Feiffer. After tea, before pot. After the lindy, before the twist. After the angry young men, before the protest singers. After the Red Cross, before the Red Guard. After Billy Graham, before Bill Graham. After momism, before popism. After the Establishment, before street people. After apathy, before cool.

World youth was beginning to breathe and stir after the dull fifties. Pope John XXIII was budging the Church into the twentieth century. Castro and Guevara were trying to galvanize a revolution that had turned bureaucratic and stifling. The Kennedy "Camelot" was bringing some youth, culture, and style to a Babbittized Washington.

The year 1960 was before Bob Dylan got to town. . . .

1

"DON'T RAISE YOUR VOICE AROUND HERE!"

"... where i live now, the only thing that keeps the
area going is tradition—it doesn't count very much—
everything around me rots ... if it keeps up, soon i
will be an old man—& i am only 15—the only job
around here is mining—but jesus, who wants to be a
miner ... i refuse to be part of such a shallow death—
everybody talks about the middle ages as if it was actually in the middle ages—i'll do anything to leave
here—my mind is running down the river—i'd sell my
soul to the elephant—i'd cheat the sphinx—i'd lie to
the conqueror ... tho you might not take this the right
way, i would even sign a chain with the devil ... please
dont send me anymore grandfather clocks—no more
books or care packages ... if youre going to send me
something, send me a key—i shall find the door to
where it fits, if it takes me the rest of my life. ..."[1]

—DYLAN, 1966

"... he not busy being born
Is busy dying. ..."[2]

—DYLAN, 1965

21

It's a long way home from the movies. The marquee of the Lybba Theater was dark as the plump, sandy-haired boy walked into the merciless cold. First Avenue was even colder by contrast with the heat of the Texas plains he'd felt from the screen inside. Even James Byron Dean couldn't have been a hero on First Avenue. He would have frozen in his tracks. Texas was rugged, but Minnesota was impossible.

Across the street was the sign of *The Hibbing Tribune*—stately Olde Englishe in flaming red neon. Out First Avenue were fainter neon signs, in Moderne American, offering miners quick credit and quick drinks. The boy glanced toward the pool hall, hesitated, then decided against the small talk. The film *Giant* was still in his head, with the shock that James Dean was really dead, more than a year now.

The boy turned onto Howard Street. He stood "at one end of Hibbing on the main drag and saw clear past the city limits on the other end."[3] There were red iron-ore mining dumps at nearly every fringe of town. "The richest village in the world" wasn't so rich anymore. They'd cut down the trees and dug the good ore out of the earth. He walked by storefronts, well stocked and confident, and others that had run empty when confidence and money gave out. Hibbing had dug its own grave with sixty years of mining shovels. Desolation Row, Take One.

Sinclair Lewis would have taken notes. The stores of Hibbing, 1956, and those of Gopher Prairie, 1926, must have all come from some factory assembly line. Montgomery Ward, J. C. Penney, and Woolworth patterned small-town America. Were the same shopfronts down in Macon, Georgia, where Little Richard was born? At least Georgia didn't have skin temperatures of 20 degrees below zero. The boy stepped into the doorway of Chet Crippa's Music Store. He scanned the record display. No Little Richard, no Hank Williams, no Buddy Holly. Bing Crosby was still dreaming about a white Christmas. So was Little Richard.

In front of the New Haven Lounge, he could hear the sputtering little band wheezing its way through "*Moja Decla*," the Slovenian national anthem. Or was it a lively polka of Whoopee John, or the "CIO Polka" for the union men? The wind from Lake Superior and the Canadian plains knew more songs, but who else listened, as the boy did, "when I first heard the ore train sing."[4]

No songs that night, as he approached Fifth and Howard, where the brick solidity of the Androy Hotel exuded permanence and prosperity for traveling salesmen and local Rotarians. A few hundred yards away, the Zimmerman Furniture and Appliance Company reposed in chrome and formica. ("A kitchen range for the Iron Range." "Absolutely no part ordered without a deposit.") I would rather be a miner than an appliance salesman, but Jesus, who wants to be a miner or an appliance salesman? As Howard Street tapered off toward the bush, the boy turned right onto Seventh Avenue. The darkness of the side street created a vacuum, which he filled with wide-screen Technicolor.

Time magazine, in October 1956, wrote:

James Dean, who was killed in a sportcar crash two weeks after his last scene was shot, clearly shows . . . a streak of genius. He has caught the Texas accent to nasal perfection, and has mastered the lock-hipped, high-heeled stagger of the wrangler, and the wry little jerks and smirks, tics and twitches, grunts and giggles that make up most of the language of a man who talks to himself a good deal more than he does to anyone else.

The fifteen-year-old moviegoer, who talked to himself a good deal more than he did to anyone else, filled Seventh Avenue with his own Actors' Studio. He pursed his lips, tried a line of dialogue, locked his hips, shambled like a wrangler, contorted his face to erase the North Country twang in his voice, slowing the words into an oozing drawl. As young Bob Dylan passed Hibbing High School, he halted his monologue-pantomime. The sprawling four-story pseudo-North Italian turreted castle brought one of its students back abruptly from Texas. The last few blocks, to 2425 East Seventh Avenue, were so familiar that in the dark Bob's feet led him past memorized breaks in the sidewalk. The corner house was ablaze with lights. Back to family life in a dying town.

He tiptoed through the back doorway and into the kithen. "Bobby, is that you?" His mother's voice was taut. He reported to the parlor. "I've told you a hundred times, if I've told you once," his mother began her litany. "How do you expect to grow up strong and healthy if you don't get your rest? What are the people in this neighborhood going to think of any boy of mine who is always out roaming the streets at night?" Why was she always so worried? Why did she talk so fast, leaving no room for answers?

"Your mother is absolutely right, Robert," his father broke in, his low and controlled voice somehow menacing beneath its even surface. The living room was so clean and orderly. Everything was in its place. Maybe that is what they expected of him, to be just another home appliance, to turn on and off. Bob tried to explain that it was a special James Dean movie that ran late. His voice began to rise with anger. "Robert, stop that shouting," his father said. "You know we don't tolerate shouting in this house." The argument spilled out of the room.

It wasn't just this lateness, his father told me in 1968. It was Bob's "attitude." One night he was late. The next night he neglected his schoolwork. He didn't show up at the store when they expected him. And soon it was going to be smashed-up cars, motorbikes, "that girl," and those "friends" of his. "Robert, you come back here," his father said. But he was gone, through the kitchen, down the stairs to the basement. The father followed, hurling recriminations: "We've given you a good home. We buy you the best of everything. What more do you want? I never had it so soft when I was your age. . . ."

In the basement den, Bob tried to explain that he had stayed to see part of the movie over again. He talked about James Dean and waved his hand toward the walls covered with pasted-up photographs of the dead actor.

"James Dean, James Dean," his father repeated. He pulled a magazine photograph of the actor off the wall. "Don't do that," Bob yelled. The father tore the picture in half and threw the pieces to the floor. "Don't raise your voice around here," he said with finality, stamping upstairs. Bob picked up the pieces of the photograph, hoping he might be able to paste them together. No, he wouldn't raise his voice around *there*.

Hibbing's a good ol' town
I ran away from it when I was 10, 12, 13, 15, 15½, 17 an' 18
I been caught an' brought back all but once . . .[5]

STOLEN MOMENT

Dylan didn't actually run away from "good ol' Hibbing" at all, except in his mind, where he kept running for years. He spoke about Hibbing rarely and wrote about it only fragmentarily. He had trouble coming to grips with his growing-up days, vacillating between nostalgia and repulsion. Hibbing was small-town Minnesota, his incubus and touchstone, home of provincialism, isolation, back-water Babbittry, and conservatism. Dylan could say, "Hibbing's got nothing to do with what I am, what I became," and yet sometimes reveal that his flight from small-town Philistinism had supplied motive, energy, ferocious drive, and will. His "North Country Blues," written in 1963, is an understated folk-epic of the history of Hibbing. His notes to *Joan Baez in Concert, Part 2,* dwell upon his early attitudes toward beauty in life and nature. On his third album, the second of his "11 Outlined Epitaphs" paints a dark portrait of his hometown, which had uprooted itself as it dug beneath for more precious ore. That had set him running as a refugee. Finally, in that epitaph, he dreams of accepting Hibbing (and his family and his childhood) without expecting what they could not offer him.

A more figurative retelling of his adolescence was his autobiographical "My Life in a Stolen Moment," written in spring 1963 as a program note for the tradition-hungry folk-music community that demanded roots, sources, and influences. Ringing with Woody Guthrie cadences, "Stolen Moment" was fine early page writing—rhythmic, sardonic, and self-revealing. Dylan took years to accept it. Ultimately, he decided to include "Stolen Moment" in *Writings and Drawings*. Before that he often denied it, saying others had "made" him write it, that it was just publicity. One problem was that his reference to running away pained his family. Perhaps the most revealing part was his refusal to examine the source of his music and writing creativity. "I never ever did take the time to find out why I took the time to do those things. . . ."[6]

If he wouldn't, or couldn't, take the time, I felt I had to try. Prior to my two visits to Hibbing, in 1966 and 1968, Dylan told me, "I didn't leave home because of my curiosity to see what was going on elsewhere. I just wanted to get away.... Yeah, get away. Hibbing was a vacuum. I just kept going because I was bored. I've always been very bored, only I've never accepted boredom.... I can lay on my bed for three hours and look at the ceiling, but, you know, that doesn't mean boredom.... You see, I don't come from what you would call a 'Great Society middle-class family in the suburbs.' Where I lived, there aren't any suburbs. There's no poor section and there's no rich section. There's no wrong side of the tracks and right side of the tracks.... As far as I knew, where I lived, nobody had anything that anybody else didn't have, really. All the people I knew had the same things...."

Reality is a prism for him, not a plate-glass window. Through that prism he would look back on Hibbing and his formative years, sometimes with anger, frequently with remorse, but sometimes with love and warmth. "My family?" Dylan repeated while he chose his response. "I never really had that much contact with them...." That is not quite the way his family remembered it.

HOME ON THE RANGE

History has left no record of what Franz Dietrich Von Ahlen's family thought about his decision to leave Hanover, Germany. Von Ahlen was a restless individualist, who decided, eighteen years after his birth in 1856, that Hanover was not where the action was. He packed his bags for the New World. He left behind his name and took instead an all-American moniker, Frank Hibbing. After farming and reading law, he became a timber cruiser, a prospector, and a woodsman. In 1885, hearing that the forest and mineral riches of northern Minnesota exceeded those of northern Michigan, he moved to Duluth as a land broker. He made and lost a fortune. When iron ore was discovered in 1890 on the Eastern Mesabi Range, largest of three iron ranges in Minnesota, Hibbing decided to prospect, and led some thirty men westward from Duluth to the area that would soon bear his adopted name.

Near what was to become the town center, Hibbing is reported to have stuck his head out of his tent one morning in January 1893. It was 40 degrees below zero. Three feet of snow mantled a frozen pine forest. Hibbing, a lean and determined man with a handlebar moustache, supposedly said: "I believe there is iron under me. My bones feel rusty and chilly." His men began to dig, and soon found ore. Hibbing helped form the Lake Superior Iron Company, leased lands and mineral rights, and became Hibbing township's first millionaire.

Before big money rolled in early in the 1900s, lumbering provided capital for mining, and supplied timber for local buildings. Most of the first 426 residents were lumberjacks earning forty dollars a month and all the pork, beans, and splinters they could take. The first main drag, Pine Street, had nearly sixty saloons to combat central-heating problems. A two-square-mile townsite was laid out in 1893, first called Superior, then changed to Hibbing. Mud streets, wooden sidewalks, saloon brawls, lumbering and mining accidents, and typhoid fever made Hibbing a frontier town. The German refugee advanced money to build a sawmill, a water plant, an electric generating station, roads, the first hotel, and a bank. He died at forty-one in 1897. For the next ten years, logging was the chief industry. While mining development continued, a slump, which may have been engineered by the big finance men, made the entire Mesabi Range available dirt cheap. John D. Rockefeller loaned a million dollars for the purchase of Iron Range land, and made a tidy fifty million. Through Rockefeller, the U.S. Steel Company gained a footing in the Mesabi.

Hungry mechanical mouths were invented to wolf out the ore. Wood-burning power shovels gulped like dinosaurs, and fed the cars of the Duluth, Missabe, and Northern railways. The big hole in the ground that haunts Dylan's memory was a "stripper," or open-pit mine. By 1964, the Hull-Rust pit covered 1,600 acres, measured 3¾ by 1 mile, and reached a depth of 535 feet. From this running sore was extracted a billion gross tons of earth—more than was dug for the Panama Canal—which yielded 500 million tons of iron ore. Great claims are made for Hibbing's mine— America might not have won both world wars without this high-grade ore, which supplied nearly one quarter of all the ore used in the nation. The shovels devoured the choice lode under the original township. "The razzle-dazzle village," "the iron ore capital of the world," "the center of the melting pot," and "the richest village in the world" became "the town that moved."

The transplanting took forty years, beginning in 1918. Nearly two hundred miners' homes and twenty business buildings were slid onto timbers, mounted onto steel wheels, tied to steam crawlers, and shunted to new resting places in Alice, first called South Hibbing. Countless more buildings were wrecked. The journey to Alice took nearly a month for the Colonia Hotel. The old Sellers Hotel never made it, ending up as debris. Property owners began complicated litigation with the mining interests, who still calculated that their cache of iron ore was worth it. The courts generally sided with the mines, and the relocation of Hibbing continued piecemeal until the late 1950s.

Dylan witnessed this curious social upheaval, and it left a strong impression on him. In his second epitaph, he reflected on the decaying courthouse and his mother's school left rotting like war wreckage.

POOR IMMIGRANTS

Hibbing was built mainly by Europeans. While urban bankers and financiers made big money, immigrant hands did hard labor. The Iron Range was Louis Adamic country, a melting pot. The loggers were mostly Scandinavian, primarily Finnish. Yugoslavs, Poles, Bohemians, Czechs, and Italians arrived. There was even a handful of Eastern European Jews.

Meanwhile, a pair of local drillers tapped another source of wealth. Andrew G. Anderson, a former blacksmith, and Carl Eric Wickham, a young Swedish immigrant, decided to use Andy's unsalable old Hupmobile car to transport passengers between Alice and Hibbing. In spring 1914, regular runs began; a two-mile trip cost fifteen cents. During the mine boom of World War I, the bus service expanded, and by 1916, the Mesabi Transportation Company had five buses, spreading to Duluth and Minneapolis. In the 1920s, following more mergers and purchases that added links to small companies as far away as California, the Greyhound Bus Company was formed.

Hibbing, fatter with war profits, boomed in the 1920s. Schools were built, and Howard Street was constructed. During that decade, the village reached an assessed valuation of ninety million dollars, the richest in the world. But during the 1930s, mining dropped off, and the village fathers issued scrip money. While Dylan was later taunted for "having invented his own Depression," he had only to listen to a few town elders to know what the slump was like. Thanks to the Works Projects Administration and World War II, prosperity returned. The Korean War in 1950 gave the local mines another short-term boost.

By 1953, the best iron ore had been eaten out. The taconite process, in which huge magnets and sifters separate out commercially usable ore, had been developed. But it did not bring economic stability to the Range until the 1960s. After 1953, the local Depression couldn't be ignored by anyone in Hibbing. Dylan mined that vein for "North Country Blues," which tells of the erosion of hope in a miner's family. The Iron Age along the Mesabi was over, and only the chamber of commerce held out hope for the taconite process. Miners' children began to drift away, for there was "nothing here now to hold them."[7]

Much as veterans rarely speak of combat, Dylan's family rarely spoke of its refugee past. Feelings of separateness, persecution, and landless insecurity do not disappear quickly. The strengths and fears of those who escaped the czars' tyrannies persisted. The life of Russian Empire Jews was not much better than that of black American slaves. Dylan's natural affinity with the descendants of black slaves was an extension of his background. To flee the czars, money was crucial. Pity the poor Jewish immigrant who arrived in America with about fifteen dollars, less than most refugees. Dylan's maternal forebears left Lithuania and Latvia, and his paternal grandparents fled from Odessa in the Ukraine.

The flood of immigrants, who went by way of Bialystok to Dutch or German ports, usually stayed around New York, but many moved on if a friend, a cousin, or even a rumor said that life elsewhere held promise. After hearing about Iron Range prosperity, Dylan's maternal grandfather, Ben D. Stone, made the trip to Hibbing from Superior, Wisconsin. In

1913, he opened a general store at Stevenson Location, a village twelve miles west of South Hibbing. There, about five hundred Finnish, Italian, and Slovenian miners worked, in clothes bought from friendly, outgoing Ben Stone. From the handful of Jewish families in the area, he chose a wife, Florence Edelstein, whose family operated a chain of Iron Range movie houses.

Movies came to Hibbing in 1906 in the form of twenty-minute, two-reel silents, followed by equally brief, silent westerns. Less than a decade later, Hollywood began to turn out five-reel features. By the 1920s, Julius Edelstein, Bob's great-grandfather's brother, was part owner of the Lyric Theater. Julius and B. H. Edelstein, Bob's great-grandfather, prospered and took over the Garden Theater in 1925. They renamed it the Gopher and in 1928 sold out to a larger chain. In 1947, the brothers built the Lybba Theater, named after Bob's great-grandmother. This family film link engendered Bob's early awareness of show business.

Ben Stone attended Range grade schools. He knew his market. Some say he was a backslapper. Ben earned a decent living and the respect of Hibbing. When times were hard, Stone's Clothing tried to help. If a pair of work pants cost $2.00, and a miner had only $1.10, Stone would settle. When the Stevenson Location mine dried up, he moved his family and reestablished his store at First Avenue and Howard Street in a former bank, keeping stock in an empty vault.

Ben and Florence had four children—Lewis, Vernon, Beatrice, and Irene. Beatrice, born in 1915, was Dylan's mother, a bubbly woman, blond, headstrong, nervous, volatile, and warm. She longed to get away. Some of Beatty Stone's restlessness was assuaged by her father's magnificent four-door Essex. When she was fourteen, her father offered her driving lessons. "I'll teach you," he said, moving the gearshift slowly. "You don't have to," Beatty replied. She had often watched him drive. To her father's astonishment, she got behind the wheel and drove off. "Bobby is very much like I am," she said years later. "You either do or you don't."

For Beatty, the original "rolling Stone," the car meant access to Duluth. She could drive down to clubs like the Covenant. She sought status, solidity, and the right marriage to a nice Jewish boy. To that end, she dressed impeccably in Iron Range high fashion, and kept the Essex highly polished. What others thought of her was important, material success meant security. In 1932, Beatty's dreams began to come true at a New Year's Eve party in Duluth. She was a popular girl, but one man she met that New Year's Eve had something beyond a sense of humor, quiet intelligence, and good looks. Abram Zimmerman had a job.

SWINGING DULUTH

Born in Duluth in 1911, Abe had some sort of a job since he was seven. His father, Zigman, had run a substantial shoe factory in Odessa, but in 1907 he traded it for a peddler's cart in Duluth. He then sent for his wife,

Anna, along with Abe's older brother and sister. Every member of what became a family of eight pitched in. Abe shined shoes and sold papers, and also became a semiprofessional ballplayer. Although Duluth had its Jewish ghetto "up on the hill," the Zimmermans grew up in a neighborhood with many Scandinavians. Abe took long walks to play ball with his fellow Jewish boys. He spoke Yiddish to his family, but English otherwise.

The Zimmermans lived in a six-room house on Lake Avenue. Abe's father finally parked his peddler's horse and buggy, having learned enough English selling fabric to farmers to sell shoes in the Fair Department Store. With everyone working, there was enough money to install a telephone. But whom could they call? They didn't know anyone else who had one! Abe's childhood was apparently uneventful, except for the great forest fire of 1918. Hundreds perished, but the fire was halted three miles outside Duluth.

By the time Abe was sixteen, the Zimmermans had moved to a nine-room house, and he was hired as a Standard Oil messenger boy for sixty dollars a month. He saved part, and contributed the rest to the family. "You wanted to do something for your parents *then*. You don't see parents working and suffering as hard as they did in those days. . . ."

Abe also wanted to do some things for himself, and began looking for a girl. At that party he sighted the bright and vivacious Beatty Stone, and made a mental note to see her again. She was snowed in in Hibbing for most of that winter. When did they start to get serious? "Weather permitting," replied Abe with characteristic sly humor. They were married two years later, in 1934, and Beatty escaped Hibbing for Duluth. By then, Abe was earning one hundred dollars a month. Abe and Beatty occupied the top floor of the two-family Overman frame house at 519 Third Avenue East. Abe knew that Standard Oil was no place for him to make a fortune, but it was secure. He rose through the seventy-five-employee office to junior supervisor.

One evening in mid-May 1941, Abe and Beatty were listening to the radio. Abe scanned the newspapers. The Nazis were on the rampage throughout Europe. Jews were being hunted again. The Battle of Britain had been won, but elsewhere Axis armies were triumphing. The radio and jukeboxes of 1941 incessantly played "The Hut Sut Song," a bit of nonsense in an unintelligible pseudo-Swedish dialect. (It was remarkably similar to a 1914 folk song, called "Hot Shot Dawson," sung by a blind Negro minstrel.) Minneapolis's own Andrews Sisters had sold their eight-millionth record, and their manager forbade them from taking music lessons for fear of spoiling their success. The radio broadcast family serials like *One Man's Family, The Goldbergs,* and *Fibber McGee and Molly. The Lone Ranger* was a favorite with kids.

Although it may not have been widely noted in Duluth, the literary world of 1941 mourned three of its giants. James Joyce died in Switzerland. F. Scott Fitzgerald and Sherwood Anderson, two of the writers whom critic Maxwell Geismar later numbered among "the last of the provincials," also died early in the year. Meanwhile, Beatty had a news bulletin of literary and musical significance. "Abe," she exclaimed. "Abe, I feel it! I think the baby is coming."

LABOR DAY

Beatty's bulletin was premature, but by nine P.M. on Saturday, May 24, she went into forced labor at St. Mary's Hospital, and delivered her first child, a hefty ten-pound boy. It was not an easy birth, because the baby had a very large head. The condition of her spine dictated that the obstetrician should operate. Beatty believed it nearly cost the life of the baby, if not her own. Abe bought cigars. He was proud to announce that he had a son, Robert Allen, and that mother and baby were doing fine!

Even the neighbors had to admit that Bobby Allen was a beautiful child. He had a golden head of hair, and Beatty would say to him: "You should have been a girl, you're so beautiful." She put colored ribbons in his hair and posed him for the camera. A picture at fifteen months showed a cherubic child, apple-cheeked and smiling, with that burst of golden blond hair. His father continued at Standard Oil, an essential job that exempted him from military service.

In the late 1930s, when the powerful John L. Lewis was organizing, Standard Oil had formed the Tri-State Petroleum Union, a company union. With about three hundred members signed up, all the new union needed was a leader, and they elected honest Abe. "Our personnel man felt that Standard Oil would fold up if Lewis came in with his demands," Abe explained. The company union was soon banned by the Wagner Act. The Duluth drivers entered the Teamsters Union. Standard Oil survived, and so did Abe.

When he brought his two-year-old son into the office, secretaries and clerks crowded around. When he was three years old, Bobby Allen gave his first public performances, perched atop his father's desk, talking and singing into a Dictaphone. The boy marveled at the recorded sound of his own voice. Sometimes Abe recorded him alone and would tease secretaries by slipping in a brief performance by Bobby between invoice numbers.

In 1946, there was a Mother's Day celebration in Duluth, where Bobby was taken with his grandmother Anna. "It was the talk of Duluth. . . . In fact, they still talk about it," Bob's mother recalled. "Everyone was getting up to perform, but nobody else but Bobby was listening to what was going on. They talked. Bobby just sat there and watched and listened. Then they called on him. This little four-year-old codger gets up with his tousled, curly hair and goes to the stage. He stamped his foot and commanded attention. Bobby said: 'If everybody in this room will keep quiet, I will sing for my grandmother. I'm going to sing "Some Sunday Morning." ' Well, he sang it, and they tore the place apart. They clapped so hard that he sang his other big number, 'Accentuate the Positive.' He didn't know much more than those two songs. Our phone never stopped ringing with people congratulating me. My mother and mother-in-law had lots of other grandchildren, but Bobby was the special apple of their eyes. He was the one they doted on, but he wasn't spoiled. How he remained unspoiled, I'll never know."

Within two weeks, Bob had another gig. Beatty's sister, Irene, had a lavish wedding reception at the Covenant Club. Bob's mother decked him out in a white Palm Beach suit. (In 1968, she still kept the collarless, three-button outfit handy in a front closet.) A fan club of relatives sponsored Bob's first paid performance. An uncle said, proferring a handful of bills, "You've got to sing." He refused. The pleading increased, although the fee remained the same. Bob turned to his father. "I told him," his father said, "that he should sing, because all those people had come to hear him. I told him that if he would sing we wouldn't pester him to sing publicly anymore."

"So he sang," his mother said, "but not until he had announced: 'If it's quiet, I will sing.' " It was not what you would call a boy soprano, but it was a thin, beguiling voice, and everyone was quiet as Bob's two-song repertoire was delivered. Again the audience cheered, and Bobby walked over to his uncle and took the twenty-five dollars. He approached his mother with his first gate receipts. "Mummy," he told her, "I'm going to give the money back." He returned to his uncle and handed him the money. He nearly upstaged the bridal couple.

His father recalled: "People would laugh with delight at hearing him sing. He was, I would say, a very lovable, a very unusual child. People would go out of their way to handle him, to talk with him. I think we were the only ones who would *not* agree that he was going to be a very famous person some day. Everybody would say: 'This boy is going to be a genius, or he was going to be this or that.' Everyone said that, not just the family. When he sang 'Accentuate the Positive' the way other children his age sang 'Mary Had a Little Lamb,' people said he was brilliant. I didn't pay too much attention to this, frankly. I figured any kid could learn a song like that from the radio—if he heard it often enough."

RETURN TO HIBBING

The end of World War II triggered a great migration. Abe and Beatty considered moving to Hibbing. He had lost his job at Standard Oil, which, by 1945, was a post equivalent to office manager, in charge of the stock and auditing division. Abe and Beatty had another son, David, in February 1946. Bobby was then attending kindergarten at Duluth's Nettleton School. On the first day, Bob simply refused to take the big step without his father. Abe escorted him, somewhat embarrassed to be the only father in a sea of mothers. Bobby seemed to fit in well at kindergarten.

Then Abe was stricken in the 1946 polio epidemic. He took the illness stoically. He stayed only a week in the hospital because it was short of help and equipment. "I had to crawl up the front steps like an ape." He remained home for six months, while Beatty was carrying or nursing David. Gradually he recovered, although left with one limp leg and weak muscles in the other.

The parents needed to be closer to their family while Abe recovered. Abe joined his two brothers in a furniture and appliance business. The Zimmermans moved in with Beatty's parents, on Third Avenue in Hibbing. Abe and his brothers Paul and Maurice had prospects: Consumer goods were rolling off assembly lines, and people were buying.

For Bob, the first two years in Hibbing was a period of bustling confusion. He started first grade at the Alice School right next door to the Stones' apartment. When the bell rang for recess, Bobby thought it meant the end of the day and returned home. After a few dropouts, he began to realize how long the school day was. Ben Stone took Bobby on deliveries and other store business. Ben, they say, was the first to perceive Bob's intelligence.

Before Ben's death in 1952, Beatty and Abe had already found their own home, a spacious corner house on Seventh Avenue. Three floors and nine rooms gave the boys plenty of space to explore and play in, even after their widowed grandmother came to live with them.

Their Fairview Addition neighborhood was an uncrowded middle-class section of about six houses, containing fifteen children. The families were friendly. Beatty: "I went to all their weddings, confirmations, and graduations. The neighbors were of all different faiths—Catholic and Lutheran and other Protestants—and we were the only Jewish family. But we absolutely respected each other. We have been better friends with our immediate neighbors than we have with some relatives. And our boys? No one ever called me to tell me they were touching their dogs or throwing rocks in the yard. They never stole anything. There was never anything but high regard in the whole neighborhood for my boys. They didn't go out of their way to be a nuisance. . . ."

THE CASE OF THE PURLOINED CRAB APPLE

"Bobby and I used to steal crab apples from the neighbors' trees all the time. Or we would steal carrots and onions. We just did the normal things that growing boys do," Larry Furlong told me in 1966. "We used to build backyard playhouses that looked just like outhouses. We used to go up to 'Pill Hill,' a few blocks away. Then it was just an old ore dump. They call it 'Pill Hill' now because so many doctors live there. But for Bob and me, and Luke Davich, and my brother Pat, and Bob Pedler, it was just a grand wilderness. We constructed forts and campsites and discovered little streams. The kids used to tease Bob, sometimes. They would call him

Bobby Zennerman because it was so difficult to pronounce Zimmerman. He didn't like that. Usually, he was fun to be with. He wasn't spoiled. He seemed no different than any of the kids in the neighborhood. But I do remember that his feelings could be hurt easily. He often went home pouting. Later, in high school, he wasn't so well liked, mostly because he stayed to himself so much. We're all very proud of Bob now. . . ."

"No artist can accept reality," Nietzsche said, and the same could be said of "no Zimmerman." Middle-class, small-town propriety impelled Beatty not only to say, but also to believe, her own version of reality. Abe freely admitted, with appropriate rising gestures of his hands, "I've got pride up to here and ego up to there." For the parents, their home life and their son's early years were a placid paradise of parental permissiveness and sagacity. For Bob, the Hibbing years were so limiting that he came to accept no limits.

As their son's career developed, the parents occasionally made light of his self-images, but their own image-making was nearly as prodigious. Abe wanted to impress the town Rotarians, and Beatty wanted to impress the "old lady judges," as Bob called them, of her family and community. Bob wanted to impress the world with a romantic flight to somewhere else. None of them was a liar. All of them were compelled to find their own realities.

Dylan used his personal mythology as armor while smashing and desecrating countless other myths around him. Knowing the value of myth, he also knew its potential danger, which he may have discovered the day his mother was told that her pride and joy had stolen the forbidden crab apple.

THE POET BEFORE THE ELECTRIC AGE

Abe was a short man with an appealing smile that revealed irregular teeth. Behind his strong glasses, his eyes were a soft boyish blue, until they hardened. His wavy black hair was flecked with gray. He dressed in sport shirts, slacks, and sweaters that suggested California more than Minnesota. He frequently sported a fine, thick cigar. Abe's speech was slow and deliberate, compared to Beatty's torrential flow. He peppered his talk with double negatives, yet he didn't sound unschooled. On his home turf, he was a big man and wanted to be in charge. When Abe said I *had* to see someone in town, it was imperative.

Abe and Beatty were clean and orderly, their house always ready for visitors. The social pivots of their large family, they were very proud to have retained many Duluth friends. At his mother's knee, Bob learned to expect and receive a great deal of attention from women. Beatty was warm, effusive, and outgoing. The other neighborhood kids called her Beatty. Abe enjoyed a good laugh himself. He wanted only what any man wanted—respect, especially from his sons.

Abe had belonged to the Golden Circle at Standard Oil, an executive group whose members "could do no wrong." He was active in various lodges of B'Nai B'Rith, a Jewish fraternal order, and designed basketball suits for one lodge's team. A loyal member of the Hibbing Rotary, Abe was delighted to have edged Bob into the Boy Scouts. Bob's membership lasted briefly. "He got the uniform and I was glad he joined," his father said. "But I didn't ask him if he liked it or not."

There were family rules: Be clean; put your things away; do your studies; be polite to everyone; don't play rough with your brother; brush your teeth—remember, you only got one set of teeth; don't play with matches. "We really only had two rules around here," Abe told me. "One was: Don't come and ask me for anything unless you are prepared to hear me say no. The other rule was: Do things for us because you like us, not because you are afraid of us. That's all. It worked pretty good." Mom amplified: "We were more like friends. We would tell the boys that they would have children of their own one day and they would want to be friends with them."

David's earliest recollection of his brother was the day Bob guided him, hand-in-hand, into their new Hibbing home, where carpets were mysteriously rolled up on bare floors of dark rooms. Bob remained the leader, although not always hand-in-hand. Bob was scrappy. Occasionally the parents returned home to find big brother firmly seated on little brother's stomach, pinning his shoulders to the floor. "This kid was so strong, he could lift a refrigerator," his mother put it. Beatty tried to show no favoritism, going so far as to put two soup bowls on the table at the same moment. The brothers generally got along well, trading *Illustrated Classics* comic books, roughhousing, going to Dad's store to play with a portable disk-recording machine.

Around the early 1950s, Bob began to spend an increasing amount of time in his upstairs room. Beatty will never forget her rapture when on one Mother's Day she saw his first poem. Written on notebook paper, it was carefully rhymed in twelve balanced stanzas of four or five lines each. The sentimental words told how his mother's face shone in the light, and described his fears that without her love he would be "six feet under." It concluded:

My dear mother, I hope that you
Will never grow old and gray,
So that all the people in the world will say:
"Hello, young lady, Happy Mother's Day."

Love, Bobby.

Beatty: "I had to read it to the women. I must have had about twenty of them just crying their eyes out. . . . We were going to frame some of those other poems, but I just kept them in a drawer. One of them I read over so often that the wording was nearly rubbed off the paper." By June 1951, Bob had brought another poem out of his room:

For Father's Day

This present is for my dad alone
To use when playing golf or sitting home.
He can use them after supper, or when riding in the car,
He can use them when relaxing or taking a trip far,
I know my dad is the best in the world.
Worth more to me than every diamond and peril [sic]
Though it's hard for him to believe
That I try each day to please him in every little way,
When sometimes he gets real mad at me
I think it best to keep quiet
So that he doesn't get more angry.
I keep his picture on my desk,
And also his handball medal above all the rest.
I'm very lucky to have a Dad this good
And if all the other kids only could,
You just can't beat him at any cost.
And without my dad, I'd be very lost.

Happy Father's Day ... Love, Bobby.

The poems Bob wrote at ten or eleven were a chance to "make something"; he was not especially interested in crafts or model-building. He wrote a great deal. "We thought he would get it out of his system, but he never did," his mother told me. For a time, the writing was eclipsed by an exciting diversion. In 1952, the family acquired the first TV set in Hibbing.

The new gadget delighted the boys. Bob and David were pioneer TV children, glued to the set for hours, watching everything from Milton Berle to *Kukla, Fran and Ollie*. Bob's superior muscles meant he generally chose the show. He liked music and variety shows, and preferred western adventure series. He loved the TV frontiersmen's name, which rang with earthy American directness. He could imagine himself as Wyatt Earp. Or, even more heroically, as the greatest frontiersman since Daniel Boone, that lean, laconic, fearless man of justice from Dodge City, named Matt Dillon.

WORDS AND MUSIC—TRADITIONAL

The emotional tethers of Judaism hold on for a long time. First- and second-generation offspring of Jewish immigrants found many powerful reasons for assimilating into the American grain. In the New World, the biblical-cum-medieval Jewish traditions had no apparent appeals and many obvious drawbacks.

"In Hibbing, the Finns hated the Bohemians and the Bohemians hated the Finns. Nearly everyone hated the Jews," a teacher at Hibbing High told me. "A lot has been done to break down the barriers, but it wouldn't be true to say that they have all broken down." The boy called Bobby Zennerman and Zimbo by his playmates before he called himself Bob Dillon (later, Dylan) sought assimilation. But before he drew his maps, he followed by rote his parents' traditions, which culminated when he was thirteen.

Bar Mitzvah means of an age to observe the commandments. The formal ceremony is rooted in antiquity but became a ritual during the Middle Ages. German Jews refined the formalities to celebrate a boy's attaining legal majority at thirteen by allowing him to join the public reading of the Torah, the Law of Moses. The festival that Abe and Beatty arranged for their eldest son was lavishly American. Beatty was delighted that out of the five hundred invited, four hundred attended.

To prepare, Bob studied Hebrew. With the nascent ear of the musician, he facilely mimicked the exotic sounds. His teacher, Rabbi Reuben Maier, of the only synagogue on the Iron Range, Hibbing's Agudath Achim Synagogue, was pleased at Bob's progress. At Friday night congregation meetings, he showed off the prodigy.

Confirmation day arrived, and Bob stood on the synagogue rostrum with his rabbi, his prayer book, and five thousand years of prophets and pogroms behind him. He was dressed in white, with a raised silken hat on his head and an ornate fringed shawl around his shoulders. He delivered the Hebrew scripture in a form of chanting known as cantillation. The elders told Bob he did a "tremendous" job at the crowded, ostentatious gathering afteward. Having attained manhood, having confirmed his belief in the God of his fathers, Bobby was ready to start living by no commandments but his own.

STRINGS OF FREEDOM

Although Abe never called himself a great music lover, music was important to him. He trooped Beatty off to a lodge dance at the drop of an invitation. He put a Gulbransen spinet piano in the front room for all to admire. Abe couldn't read a note, but he loved to fake a few chords. He brought home dance records and he particularly liked Billy Daniels's songs and Freddy Gardner's saxophone. When Bob was about ten, he started to peck out a tune. A cousin, Harriet Rutstein, gave piano lessons. David followed instructions, but Bob endured only one lesson. "I'm going to play the paino the way I want to," he declared impatiently. For a while he simply ignored the piano. But when he was about fourteen, music surged into his life. Amazingly, for a great musician and songwriter, he never learned to read music.

At Hibbing Junior High School, everyone who counted was playing in the school band. Bob started frequent visits to a Howard Street music store, which offered instruments on special rental/purchase plans. Bob first took home a trumpet, announcing he would master it soon. For two days, the air around the house ached. He couldn't seem to produce a single succession of clear notes. To general relief, Bob returned the trumpet.

Then he decided to play the saxophone. Two days later, he returned in defeat. He tried another brass instrument, then another reed. Neither responded. Finally, amid fears that he had worn out his welcome, Bob rented a crummy, little, cheap guitar, which he caressed like a Spanish heirloom.

Following the instruction sheet, he moved his hand gently across the six strings, cramping his fingers against the frets. It almost sounded like music. For hours he sat with the guitar cradled in his hands, experimenting and exploring. His fingers stung and ached. *Manoloff's Basic Spanish Guitar Manual* gave him some clues. But his own ear and fingers soon took the lead. He mastered one position after the other. He found the scale and he found the key.

> ... *send me a key—I shall find the door to where it fits, if it takes me the rest of my life* ...[8]

THE GUITAR PICKER

His guitar became his cane, weapon, status symbol, security blanket, and swagger stick. Around Hibbing, some remember him walking up and down the streets with his guitar slung over his shoulder on a leather strap. Chet Crippa recalls Bob having his guitar ready even in the coldest weather. As Dylan grew up, he grew inward, communicating less. He lavished attention on the friend he could fully trust, his guitar. Like a Delta bluesman, he treated the instrument as confidant and sidekick. "I didn't go hunting, I didn't go fishing, I didn't play on the basketball team," Dylan said later. "I just played the guitar and sang my songs. That was enough for me. My friends were like me—people who couldn't make it as the football halfback, the Junior Chamber of Commerce leader, the fraternity booster, the truck driver working his way through college. I couldn't do any of those things either. All I did was write and sing, paint little pictures on paper, dissolve myself into situations where I was invisible."

Dylan's "invisibility" was partly that of the alien assimilating. The thirty or forty Jewish families of Hibbing still had to huddle together against the cold. Abe, who loved to play golf, couldn't belong to the Mesabi Country Club.

But his son's invisibility also came from within. He started to want both personal privacy and public approval. A true Gemini, the introvert grappled with the extrovert, the shy boy turned brash, the kind lad became hostile, the studious boy went bad. There were two voices in him. From

Abe he inherited a slow and considered pattern of dealing out words, like an Indian, while from Beatty he inherited a constant flow of volatile emotions, a tongue that sometimes could not move as fast as his feelings. From Dylan's adolescence, his swings of attitude and mood were always extreme. "I hate to do the predictable," he told me, and he began to be unpredictable in his mid-teens, when the introvert set his high school on its ear with wild rock 'n' roll; the homebody turned motorcycle cowboy; the courteous youngster was as truculent as he could be; the antisentimentalist fell in and out of love; the son of the middle class spent most of his time with poor folk; the white boy studied black jargon.

"Where I lived," later Dylan told me, "was really hillbilly country. The radio stations I used to listen to weren't local, but came up from Louisiana, right up the Mississippi River. . . ." Hibbing's station, WMFG, was square before and after Bob's cousin, Les Rutstein, became its general manager in 1958. Bob often chided Les for not programming rock 'n' roll or rhythm and blues. In 1968, Les still held that "old standards" were what his housewives wanted. "We don't program for the youth," he told me. "Let Duluth do that!" In the early 1950s, WMFG played pop songs like "Too Young" by Frankie Laine, "The Song from Moulin Rouge" by Michel Legrand, "Love Is a Many-Splendored Thing" by The Four Lads, and middle-of-the-road Guy Mitchell, Doris Day, and Perry Como. Bill Haley and His Comets? Not on Hibbing radio!

Until eclipsed by Elvis Presley, Haley was the most successful white rock 'n' roll musician. As early as 1953, he had recorded black rhythm and blues hits. Haley's first rock hit was the cover version of Ivory Joe Hunter's "Shake, Rattle and Roll." He borrowed black R & B's choreography and visual games, country music's accent and stagemanship. Haley wanted his lyrical messages bright, cheerful, and escapist. He once said: "I personally have objected to protest . . . and crying songs. My idea in creating rock 'n' roll was to make kids happy. . . . Kids . . . have to face problems . . . when they get older, and I think it's wrong to make them face problems so young. . . ."

Haley's work, especially "Rock Around the Clock," became known around the world through the soundtrack of the 1955 film *Blackboard Jungle,* about a problematic city high school. The rock tide had been rising since 1951, when Alan Freed, the late disc jockey, had begun to push the new music on Cleveland radio. By 1954, rock 'n' roll had spread to major Coast stations, but WMFG ignored it. Dylan had to turn his radio on to a thin line that linked him with the farmers of Louisiana and the truck drivers of Tennessee. " 'Henrietta' was the first rock 'n' roll record I heard," Dylan says. He also calls Johnny Ray "the first singer whose voice and style I totally fell in love with."

Bob took most of his journeys down the Mississippi late at night, when the air was clearer. He often placed his radio under the covers to keep from waking anyone with sounds he caught from Shreveport or Little Rock.

Gatemouth Page, a voluble southern disc jokey, alternated country music with R & B. While Bill Haley was syncretizing the two musics, Dylan's radio fed him both. In 1954, *McCall's Magazine* editorialized about togetherness, an idyllic portrait of American family life updating *Saturday Evening Post* covers by Norman Rockwell, Andy Hardy films, *One Man's Family*. For Bob Dylan, who after he entered high school felt increasingly separate from his family, togetherness was a midnight radio show from the South that said white and black music got along very well.

> ... *I learned t' choose my idols well*
> *T' be my voice an' tell my tale*
> *An' my first idol was Hank Williams ...*[9]

Hiram "Hank" Williams was "the hillbilly Shakespeare" to millions of farmers, truck drivers, and factory workers. Born in an Alabama log cabin, he took his only musical instruction from Tee-tot, a black street singer. Williams wrote 125 songs, dozens of which wring pathos out of the simplest lyrics. "I'm So Lonesome I Could Cry," "Your Cheatin' Heart," "Cold, Cold Heart," and "Alone and Forsaken" embody a world of loss and loneliness. Hank Williams, making his sad songs sadder, died on New Year's Day, 1953, at the age of twenty-nine. Officially, he died of a heart attack. Unofficially, he died of too much living, alcohol, and drugs.

If Hank Williams was the poet of the early fifties, Little Richard was the pulse, a rhythm and blues John Henry. Richard Penniman, born in 1935 in Georgia, started to sing at the age of ten in churches and on street corners before going professional with Sugarfoot Sam from Alabam and Dr. Hudson's Medicine Show. His music, and life, swung from sacred to secular, from tabernacles to juke joints. Seemingly possessed, he shouted and pranced with demonic emotion that led John Lennon to describe him as the first primal screamer. He was a bridge between black gospel and modern soul. Elvis recorded his songs, The Rolling Stones and The Yardbirds liked his style, Paul McCartney was his devotee. In the mid-fifties, Dylan enrolled as a student of Little Richard in the radio university, heeding his raunchy sermon: "My music is the healing music that makes the dumb and deaf hear and talk. . . ." Little Richard briefly retired to become a theology student, then returned to show business in 1962. He worked with The Beatles at The Cavern in Liverpool, instructing them in the high falsetto wail, the "yeah, yeah, yeah" line. Dylan, who had not met Little Richard, assimilated his style seven years before The Beatles did. In his 1959 high-school yearbook, Bob listed his ambition: "To join the band of Little Richard."

Grateful for these early musical influences, but impatient with himself for not having understood more, Dylan once told me: "It was just like an adolescent, you know. When you need somebody to latch onto, you find somebody to latch onto. I did it with so many people, that's why I went through so many changes. I wrote a lot of stuff like Hank Williams, but I never grasped why his songs were so catchy or so classic. As for Presley, I don't know anybody my age that did not sing like him, at one time or another. Or Buddy Holly." Even as he was amassing musical idols, he shed them to rely on himself. As he later wrote:

> *In later times my idols fell*
> *For I learned that they were only men . . .*
> *But what I learned from each forgotten god*
> *Was that the battlefield was mine alone . . .*[10]

As time passed, however, the forgotten gods were remembered again. During his world tour of 1978, Dylan told me of his reaction to Elvis's death: "It was so sad. I had a breakdown! I broke down . . . one of the very few times. I went over my whole life, my whole childhood. I didn't talk to anyone for a week. If it wasn't for Elvis and Hank Williams, I couldn't be doing what I do today."

Soon after Dylan had learned his way around his first guitar, he wanted a bigger, flashier instrument. He saw it in a Sears, Roebuck catalog: turquoise with a little white wing by the strings. He saved toward the twenty-dollar down payment, and nineteen dollars more to pay it off. Fearing his father's annoyance, Bob hid the new guitar until he had paid for it. Abe had to admire Bob's resourcefulness. Bob bought as many records as he could afford without a weekly allowance. His first collection was of Hank Williams 78s. He went on to the new 45s by Little Richard, Buddy Holly, Hank Thompson. Bob gyrated from record player to guitar to the family piano, where he aped Little Richard, who danced from microphone to a standing slam at the piano keyboard. Now, all Bob needed was a band. In 1968, Le Roy Hoikkala, a shy, slight electronics technician, told me:

"I met Bob downtown one day and we got to talking about music. We were in eighth grade, and I was very much involved in playing drums. Monte Edwardson was guitar player, and the three of us got together, around 1955, in Bob's garage for some sessions. Monte played lead, Bob played rhythm and sang. We figured we had the makings of a band, and we decided to call ourselves The Golden Chords. Nobody was the leader. Bob really idolized Little Richard then. He could chord quite well on the piano. Rock was just starting then. Haley and Presley were just beginning to make it big. . . .

"We started to get some jobs, playing at some Moose Lodge meetings and a few PTA meetings. Whenever there was a talent contest, we would show up. I'll never forget the community talent contest at the Hibbing Memorial Building. The judges were chamber of commerce members, so you couldn't expect them to know too much about music. The Golden Chords won on audience applause, but the judges gave first prize to a girl who played classical piano. The kids booed the decision, because we only came in second."

The Golden Chords played some country songs, like Johnny and Jack's "I'll Be Home," but Bob soon led the trio toward Little Richard's extroversion. Le Roy was impressed by Bob's speed in putting together a song. "He would write a song right at the piano. Just chord it, and improvise on it. I remember that he sang one song about a train in R & B style. He could make sense with a song in an instant." Sunday afternoons, Bob slipped out to jam sessons at Van Feldt's little snack bar and barbecue, at Fourth Avenue and Nineteenth Street. For months, kids filled the place, making it "the scene" in Hibbing. The Golden Chords held public rehearsals, which the young people treated as a show. Dylan's other Hibbing bands were called the Shadow Blasters, Elston Gunn and the Rock Boppers. Because it was Sunday afternoon, no parents objected. After all, the boys would soon outgrow this nonsense.

BE IT EVER SO SQUARE

Bob's parents did not overtly discourage his music-making, but they certainly couldn't share his passion. He occasionally brought Le Roy and Monte home for rehearsals, generally when his parents were away. Only in hindsight did Abe and Beatty realize that from fourteen on, Bob was inexorably drifting away from all they held dear. "You understand," he told me, "I never was a kid who could go home. I never had a home, which I could just take a bus to. I made my way all by myself."

Abe still thought that inevitably Bob would complete his schooling and join the family business. Whenever he could, Abe found a chore to bring Bob into the shop. It was a losing battle. Bob would "run away" into his music, his writing, his reading behind his closed bedroom door. "Are you there, Bobby?" his mother often called up the stairwell. "It's all right, ma, I'm only reading," he could have replied.

"He was never detached from family or friends, but he dreamt a lot," his mother told me in 1966. "He was going to do something very different. He dreamed of what he was going to be . . . an architect, or an astronaut. . . . How often that boy told his grandmother: 'Grandma, someday I'm going to be very famous. You are never going to have to worry about anything.' He told her he would make a lot of money and that she would never have to want for anything." I repeatedly pressed the parents on the genesis of his writings:

Mother: "Bob was upstairs quietly becoming a writer for twelve years. He read every book there was. . . . He bought only comics that had some meaning, like *Illustrated Classics*. He was in the library a lot. We hardly ever discussed writers. . . . We would just be laughing and talking. . . ." Father: "I used to tell Robert that if he needed any help with his studies to let me know. I used to help him with math . . . history was always a problem with him. He just refused to get a good mark in history. I used to argue that history only required you to remember what you read. He said there was nothing to figure out in history.... I asked him why it was so hard, and he would just say: 'I don't like it.'" Mother: "I remember he said: 'I am not going to take physics, I don't like it.' I offered to get him a tutor. He said: 'I don't like physics. Please, please, let me drop it.'

"Bobby could write and he could draw. He was an artist. He was always drawing or painting the pictures that you put the colors in. I tried to push architecture. I figured at least he could make a living. From these poems, you are going to die and *then* be discovered. I said: 'Please go to school and make yourself a living. These poems aren't going to make you a living.' This was in the ninth and tenth grade. Those poems he wrote in high school, he wouldn't show to anybody, just to me and his dad. I said to Bobby that you can't go on and on and on and sit and dream and write poems. I was afraid he would end up being a poet! Do you know the kind of poet I mean? One that had no ambition, and wrote only for himself. In my day, a poet was unemployed and had no ambition. Here we would be at the back of him with a pitchfork. 'Bobby, you have to eat.' He still doesn't eat enough.... He eats to live. When he was planning to go to college, I would say: 'Bobby, why don't you take something useful?' He said: 'I'll take something in science, literature, and art for a year and then I will see what I want to do.' I told him: 'Don't keep writing poetry, please don't. Go to school and do something constructive . . . get a degree.'"

Only minutes after revealing their obliviousness to the import of his early passion for writing and music, Beatty and Abe turned to a painful subject. They couldn't understand why they had not then shared his success, even though he often sent them money. They were mystified at his saying that he ran away from their happy home. For a while they blamed his manager, Albert Grossman, for keeping them out of the picture. Beatty: "Did Albert really think that people all over the world thought Bob was an orphan?" Abe: "I told Albert: 'This can't go on forever, our hiding from the world.' I told Albert we have something to be proud of. We gave Robert his start, the encouragement he needed from the beginning."

THE TALENT CONTEST

The Golden Chords fell into disharmony as Bob became increasingly interested in black R & B while the other two drifted toward white rock 'n' roll. Bob soon was the key figure in another nameless band. This band featured Chuck Nara on drums, Bill Marinec on bass, and Larry Fabbro on electric guitar, with Bob on piano, guitar, and lead vocals. In autumn 1955, the four jammed often, exchanged recordings, and listened to Bob's plans for a life in music. To the others, music was just a hobby.

After this no-name band had been together a year, it appeared at Hib-

bing High's Jacket Jamboree Talent Festival. There were reciters and war-
blers and piano players—routine, boring stuff, until Bob's band came on.
He said so little in class, was such a quiet loner, that no one was prepared
for the onslaught from the band's piles of amplifiers and equipment. Bob
had also heightened the shock by insisting that his sidemen tell no one
what they were going to do. Even then his rule was: "Don't say what you
are going to do, just do it."

Bob wore his hair in mounds around his forehead, Little Richard–style.
The band worked with amplifiers at full roar, and when Bob began to sing,
in a hoarse, insistent, screaming wail, "it brought as much laughter as it
did applause," Fabbro told me. The songs came from Little Richard's and
Big Elvis's song bag. The one title everyone remembers was "Rock 'n' Roll
Is Here to Stay."

Not at Hibbing High, it wasn't! K. L. Pedersen, the principal, was
guiding around some touring education officials. The combined force of
the house mikes with the band's amplification was too much! He ran
backstage and cut the microphones. Seeing that he couldn't raise his voice
around there either, Bob seethed, but kept pounding his piano. Some say
he broke the pedal off and may have bruised a few strings. "African shrieking," remarked a startled teacher. Even Fabbro admitted that their performance was shocking, "for that time, for that town."

Another student eyewitness: "My first impression was embarrassment.
Our little community was unaccustomed to such a performance. I think a
lot of people were embarrassed too. I realize now, of course [in 1969], that
there was the young Bob Dylan in his very early form. He was a little bit
ahead of everyone, but he didn't seem to mind. Because he had such a fantastic confidence in his talent, he didn't care. He just said: 'Here I am.
Either you like it or you don't. I know that what I've got is great.' " The
eyewitness was John Bucklen, one year younger than Bob, who became a
smooth-voiced pop disk jockey in Fond du Lac, Wisconsin. "If a musical
opportunity came along, Bob wouldn't hesitate to go to the right person
and say what he wanted. He had an unusual way of winning people over."
Bucklen, and his mother and sister, were convinced that Bob had learned
something from his father. "We thought," said Bucklen, "that Bob would
make a very good salesman, of himself."

Tales of the talent contest rocked the school. Teachers laughed, students
sniggered, parents were alarmed. One teacher, Bonn Rolfsen, was upset
about the show, but struck by the difference between Bob onstage and in
class. Ten years later, Bonn told me that one key to understanding Dylan
was geographical: "If you go a few minutes from here in Hibbing into the
desolate bush, you'll know why we are so independent here."

Another teacher, Charlie Miller, who taught Bob social studies, always
remembered him as "different, from the viewpoint that he had a mind."
After the Jacket Jamboree, Bob slid back into his class chair quietly, although some recall that there was a difference. He seemed to be smiling to

himself. Bucklen thought he saw emerging "black humor," not like Lenny Bruce's mordant satire, but rather "the sort of put-on humor of a black person toward a threatening white." Bucklen saw a jokester protecting himself while taunting a differently colored world around him.

ACTORS' STUDIO MIDWEST

Before Elvis donned black leather, a small circle of Iron Range youths found their models in the Actors' Studio, by way of the movies. Brando's *The Wild One* and Dean's *East of Eden, Giant,* and, especially, *Rebel Without a Cause* stunned these isolated provincials.

Brando and Dean forged characters who eclipsed the western hero. The new folk hero didn't ride a horse; he drove a motorcycle through the stoplight of acceptable behavior. In a decade of soft American affluence with no visible frontier to challenge, nothing was better than a bike—unless it was a guitar—to symbolize the young man's dream of sexual potency, to defy his father in his "safe" car. Harley and Davidson were the Lewis and Clark of the 1950s.

The best rider in Hibbing was Dale Boutang, a cowboy on wheels and a seasoned weight lifter. He drove a Harley 74. Bob bought a Harley 45, the next smallest model. Le Roy quickly taught Bob how to drive it, out on the West Side. "You can't be *bad,* man, really *bad,* unless you have a motorcycle and a leather jacket," Bob used to tell his friends. One day, the gang drove out to a suburb called Brooklyn, divided from Hibbing by a level rail crossing. The four waited impatiently for a train to pass. Bob gunned his engine, ready to zoom off the instant the train went by. He started to move before he saw another train coming from the other direction on the track beyond. As he saw his error, he swerved sharply left, throwing himself off the bike. The other freight passed by only inches from him. Bob got up, heart pounding, hands trembling, and walked his bike back across the tracks. He could scarcely speak for two minutes. He drove the motorcycle home slowly, never telling his folks. For a few days he thought about selling his bike, but he was soon out riding again.

Bob wasn't content to ride, posture, and think like Dean-Brando-Presley; he wanted to be photographed like them. He enlisted his brother, David, with the family Polaroid. In their room upstairs, Bob, between the ages of fifteen and seventeen, learned how to pose. During one of their sessions, the boys used their bedroom window's long, heavy drapes as a stage curtain from which Bob peeked out, grinning or squaring his jaw. For action shots, Bob roared around the street corner on his Harley, bearing down hard toward his brother on the curb. As Bob swerved past, he yelled back: "Did you get it?"

Writing of Brando as an American prototype, film critic Pauline Kael drew a portrait that sounds like the one young Dylan was filling in with his own colors:

... Protagonists are always loners.... Brando represented a reaction against the post-war mania for security.... Brando had no code, only his instincts.... He was anti-social because he knew society was crap; he was a hero ... because he was strong enough not to take the crap.... Perhaps his special appeal was ... the conceit of tough kids. There was humor in it ... swagger and arrogance that were vain and childish.... He was explosively dangerous without being "serious" in the sense of having ideas. There was no theory, no cant in his leadership....

Because he had no code, except an esthetic one—a commitment to a style of life— he was easily betrayed by those he trusted. There he was, the new primitive, a Byronic Dead End Kid, with his quality of vulnerability.... We in the audience felt protective; we knew how lonely he must be in his assertiveness. Who even in hell wants to be an outsider? He was no intellectual who could rationalize it.... He could only feel it, act it out, be "The Wild One—" and God knows how many kids felt, "That's the story of my life."[11]

When Dylan was gunning his bike, posing in his own curbstone theater, James Dean was dead, and so was Hank Williams, but Brando was alive in Hollywood, and in Hibbing.

DON QUIXOTE AND SANCHO PANZA

At sixteen, Bob used to tell John Bucklen, "You are my main man"— high praise in 1950s patois. Bucklen's family was working-class, mainstream American, probably of English descent. John also had that sense of being *"bad,* man, *bad."*

Even with those nice middle-class boys from the Twin Cities whom Bob met at the Theodor Herzl summer camp near Webster, Wisconsin, he could find some "bad" guys to befriend. Beginning in 1954, Bob attended the Zionist camp run by a Hadassah Club for a few weeks each of four summers. He loved the swimming and didn't seem to mind speaking Hebrew. But by his sixteenth birthday, things were getting too tame. He had begun some singing around campfires there. To perk things up, Bob and six lads climbed to the roof of the shower house, pulling their ladders up after them. They sang, yelled, and taunted their counselors until the rabbi read them a sermon below the mount that got them back on the ground. "Bobby just about took over the whole camp that year," Abe recalled. "I thought they were going to send him home."

The more relaxed atmosphere around Bucklen's home appealed. Beatty insisted on a nine-thirty P.M. curfew on school nights. John's family seemed grittier. John and his mother, a seamstress, were dirt poor. His father, a railway man, had lost a leg in a rail accident, and was a semi-invalid until he died when John was fifteen. Bucklen told me that he was a born follower, while Bob was increasingly brash. Music bound the pair. They loved to ad-lib on tape. "We'd get a guitar and sing verses we made up as we went along. It came out strange and weird. We thought we'd send them in somewhere, but we never did."

John loved Bob's fanciful tales. On a trip to Highland Park, a suburb of St. Paul, Bob told his main man: "We're going to tell everyone here that we came to cut a record. I will tell everybody that you are my bass man."

They had some fine times with John's sister Ruth at her house out on Highway 165. John hears echoes in Dylan's "115th Dream" of their happy times of music, jokes, and games. Once, near a lover's lane, Bob donned a Frankenstein monster mask and scared several couples. Bob's put-ons extended to his music as well. "Come on over, I want you to hear something I just wrote." John: "I would say: 'No, you didn't write that!' Because it seemed too great. I could never quite understand why he did it. . . . He had the talent, and didn't have to fake it one bit. There really wasn't anything else like music for Bob to express in Hibbing what he felt. When he did express himself, even in music, people didn't really understand him."

Another passion of Bob's, from his sophomore year on, was girls. He ran through a lot, reportedly plump and large breasted. One of the first was Barbara Hewitt, a voluptuous girl he met in 1957. Bob was quite infatuated. Ten times a day Bob turned to his shadow and said: "I love Barb, John. I love Barb." Or he would say: "You know what, John?" and John replied: "I know, you love Barb." Barbara and her family drifted off to Minneapolis, and the first of several student flirtations cooled.

A restless quest for new people and ideas led Bob and John to Jim Dandy, a black disc jockey in his mid-twenties who lived in Virginia, a neighboring town. With so much cheap European immigrant labor, there were few blacks along the Iron Range. Bucklen: "We visited Jim Dandy so often because he was a refreshing change. He was a Negro, involved with the blues. He had a lot of records we liked." Jim Dandy and his wife and kids were the only blacks among Virginia's twelve thousand residents. Bob heard him broadcast on station WHLB in the summer of 1957, and searched for the man behind the voice. He and John were startled, but pleased, to discover that the DJ was black. Seeing he was with simpatico lads, Jim dropped his radio "white voice" for hip black slang. They spent hours playing old blues and R & B disks. The meetings went on sporadically for months. Through Jim Dandy, Bob discovered a new Iron Range that his family scarcely knew. That is why Dylan could say: "Where I lived . . . there's no poor section and there's no rich section. . . . There's no wrong side of the tracks and no right side of the tracks. . . ."

ECHO AND PAN: THE GIRL ON THE SWING

"One thing that always surprised me was that Bobby ever had anything to do with me, because I was from the other side of the tracks. He was a nice Hibbing boy and I was from out of town . . . he was rich folk and we were poor folk ... he was Jewish and we were German, Swedish, Russian, and Irish, all mixed together."

Echo Helstrom Shivers smoothed down a cascade of whitish blond hair with one well-manicured hand, took a long, calming puff of her cigarette, and settled into the sofa of her Minneapolis apartment. It was spring of 1968, eleven years after she had met Dylan. The day before, in a shack near Hibbing, Echo's mother, Martha Helstrom, a genial, matronly woman, had said to me: "Well, it's about time someone gave my Echo a little credit for what she did for Bob. She was hurt by the whole thing, but she loved Bob well enough to let him go. We always gave Bob the feeling he was welcome here and that Echo and I believed in him. He was restless and impatient. He didn't have enough time to get everything done. He was like a man in a hurry." When Echo and Bob were high-school juniors, Echo was sure that they would marry one day. Their plan was that whoever made it to the top first would help the other up the ladder. Bob was to be a pop-hero and Echo a movie star.

David referred to Echo as a nameless girl with whom Bob had been quite involved, but whom his parents did their best to persuade Bob to drop. "She was not Jewish and she was poor," David said, adding: "Bobby always went with the daughters of miners, farmers, and workers in Hibbing. He just found them a lot more interesting." In 1961, Bob said: "I dedicated my first song to Brigitte Bardot." Echo looked like a Minnesota Bardot, with a touch of Pat Neal. She had full lips, pouting round cheeks. The Helstroms named her Echo because she was born exactly fourteen years after her brother. Echo and her mother and older sister were all interested in mythology. But they were not aware that the nymph Echo had been one of the more celebrated conquests of the Greco-Roman wood-spirit, Pan, the musical, mischievous trickster god with a gift of prophecy.

In 1968, Echo was working in Minneapolis as a film-company secretary. She needed it to support a child from her brief marriage. The more she talked about the year when she was close to Bob, the more I thought that although she had left Hibbing, Hibbing had never quite left her.

"It was really funny how we met. I was in the L & B Café on Howard Street. Bob had been playing upstairs at the Moose Lodge and he and John Bucklen came downstairs. Bob started to talk to me. Right there in the street, he began to play his guitar and sing for me." In late winter of 1957, she was sixteen, he seventeen. Bob wanted to show her what he could do on piano, but the lodge was locked. "Bob slid a knife in the door and broke right in to play the piano. I was probably the only girl in Hibbing who could have known what Bob was talking about. I had always been very interested in music. I took some accordion lessons and sang in the school choir. We had a harmonium in the parlor. I had a record player at home, but my father wouldn't let me play it. I always listened to radio. I will never forget the first time I heard Chuck Berry's 'Maybelline' on the car radio. I got all excited, but my father turned the radio off. I had to go into one of the other little shacks behind our house to listen to the radio. Sometimes I stayed up to five o'clock in the morning listening to announcers like Gatemouth Page from Shreveport. In 1957, who had ever heard of rhythm and blues in Hibbing? They were still playing *waltzes!* So when Bob started talking about rhythm and blues, I knew what he was talking about. I was very happy when Bob said to me: 'Why don't you come over to my house and listen to some records?' "

The friendship blossomed. "I thought at first maybe he just liked me as a friend. This was the way it was always—even if we were sweethearts, we were still friends. The first time I met him I asked if he was Jewish. He just changed the subject." The Zimmermans were courteous to Echo, but they told Bob she wasn't good enough for him. After a few open, after-school visits, he always sneaked Echo in and out of his home. Once, Bob's grandmother came in suddenly. He hid Echo in a closet and rushed to greet his granny, telling her he was going to the library. Echo followed his instructions by crawling through an upstairs door to a porch over the garage. "With my skirt up to my neck, I hung from the railing until Bobby ran round the back of the garage to help me down. He really loved playing those little games."

Echo's mother was warm toward Bob, but Echo's father, Matt Helstrom, an ailing, embittered painter and welder, a keen hunter and woodsman, didn't approve. One evening, Echo was tending her nephew while John and Bob put on a cowboy and Indian show. "All of a sudden, my father's car drove up. John and Bob leapt out of the front door just as my dad walked in the back. You could hear them crunching on the gravel, and my father went chasing after the sound. 'Someone was here!' my father shouted. I said no one had been there. Bob could never be over when my father was around. Long after Bob had made a million dollars, my dad felt maybe he'd been a nice guy after all. My father had three guitars, one of them with an amplifier. Sometimes Bob would sneak over to play that one. One time, Bob told me that he had a test to prove if I would make a good wife. I had to bake something, so I made him a pizza. And I sewed a tear in a pair of his slacks. I don't remember if there were any other requirements," she added, smiling.

The Helstrom house was a box-like, tar-paper shanty on Highway 73, three miles southwest. Often, Bob hitchhiked out on Highway 73 from school. When he had his little blue Ford, they could ride south to the top of Maple Hill. There they looked out for thirty miles across the Iron Range. They drove or hiked along Fire Tower Road, a rutted lane, to the summit, dotted with white birch. At night, the air was crisp and heady, and stars lighted the sky. Mrs. Helstrom said later: "They had their dreams to get married and live on Maple Hill. They planned to call their child Bob, whether it was a boy or a girl. You know how teenagers are. They were so young, though. Girls are always ready to marry younger than boys are."

In the afternoon, if Helstrom was away, Echo and Bob would laze in front of the shack. Bob crouched on the wooden stairs with a guitar in his lap, while his golden-haired girl sat in a little wooden swing, gently keeping time with a pendulum motion. Bob improvised verses. "The songs he sang to me," recalled Echo, "were mostly rhythm and blues or talking blues. He didn't repeat the lyrics the way most singers did. His phrases were always different and they almost always told a story." By 1968, the swing was heavily rusted and weather-beaten, but it still swayed in the breeze from Maple Hill. I felt the swing was "Rosebud," the reporter's long-sought clue to lost childhood in *Citizen Kane*.

"John and Bob used to do a lot of talking blues. Sometimes they did a hillbilly takeoff of a song like 'Somewhere Over the Rainbow.' They were always trying to teach and learn from each other. I believed in him when nobody else did. When he was singing to me alone, you could see the talent, but whenever he would go out to perform, the amplifiers would be up so high that you couldn't hear him." Echo followed him from one performance to another. The Sunday jams at Van Feldt's moved to Collier's Barbecue. Other audiences were less enthusiastic. "One time they really booed Bob was at the St. Louis County Fair in Hibbing in the summer of 1958. There was a combination of laughing and booing." Did he tell her that he would spend his life in music? "That was the whole plan. He didn't tell that to anybody else because he didn't have anyone but John and me to talk to. He had casual friends, but he was always secretive like that. I remember when he decided what his name was going to be. It was 1958, and he was just a junior. He came over with John Bucklen one day and said: 'I know what I'm going to call myself. I've got this great name—Bob Dillon.' "

He didn't change his name legally until 1962, and didn't even begin to use it regularly until 1959. Ethel Merman, also saddled with the rather ungainly luggage of "Zimmerman," simply lopped off the first syllable, remarking: "Can you imagine the name Zimmerman in bright lights? It would burn you to death!"

Bob's new name probably had two sources. Although Matt Dillon is thought to be a real frontier hero, he was the fictional invention of television writer John Meaton and producer Norman Macdonnel for the adventure series *Gunsmoke*. The show began in 1952 on Columbia Broadcasting System radio, and premiered as a CBS-TV series on September 10, 1955.

Closer to Dylan's home frontier was a pioneer Hibbing family named Dillion. A James Dillion was the town's first drayman. Four families named Dillon were listed in the 1968 Hibbing phone book. Bob parried about the Dillions with a reporter from *The Chicago Daily News* in November 1965:

Q: What about the story that you changed your name from Bob Zimmerman to Bob Dylan because you admired the poetry of Dylan Thomas?

A: No, God, no. I took the Dylan because I have an uncle named Dillion. I changed the spelling but only because it looked better. I've
read some of Dylan Thomas's stuff, and it's not the same as mine.

Dylan reiterated this popular misconception to me: "Straighten out in
your book that I did not take my name from Dylan Thomas." Although
he registered at the University of Minnesota as Robert Zimmerman, students and friends there knew him as Dillon. He told a few friends that
Dillon was his mother's maiden name. Others heard that Dillon was a
town in Oklahoma. Only after he had achieved some early recognition in
New York did Minneapolis friends learn that Bob was spelling his name
Dylan. In the interim, he had become acquainted with the life and work of
Dylan Thomas.

Echo saw why Bob distanced himself from his family: "His family was
trying too hard to form him and he wasn't about to be formed in any
manner. I remember how much Bob hated having to sweep up in his dad's
shop. I know Bob was afraid of his father, although he never said he hit
him. I don't think his father gave him all that much money. I think I had
more money than he had. Sure, he had all the necessities, but no spending
money. That is why I had to buy him all those hot dogs."

Echo and John doted on Bob's humor. Echo: "He was always thinking
of something to laugh about." John: "He had a fantastic ability to put
people on. You never knew exactly when to believe him." One of the
boys' favorite games was hitchhiking. They parked Bob's car near Echo's
place and hitchhiked along Highway 73 to see how far they could get.
Echo patiently waited for them to return by a car or truck coming from
the opposite direction. Bob played a word game he christened Glissendorf.
They played it for Echo's cousin, a simple country girl, who nearly cried
because she couldn't understand it. They also played telephone mental telepathy. Bob would call Echo, tell her he had his mind fixed on some object in his house, and she had to guess what it was. If she guessed correctly,
he would say this confirmed his belief in telepathy and his ability to put
ideas into others' minds.

Bob often pretended to be musically precocious. "He called me and told
me he was going to play something he had recorded. He played Bobby
Freeman's 'Do You Want to Dance?' He said: 'That was us.' It couldn't
have been one of Bob's bands. He was always making up fantasies and
telling little fibs." One of Bob's games always ended seriously. He'd joke
with some itinerant musician, then start firing questions about work, life
on the road, arrangements, band discipline, pop trends, and got the musician to tell him all he knew.

Echo had no more affection for Hibbing than Bob did: "I couldn't wait
to get away. There is a terrible unfriendliness in Hibbing you don't find in
other small towns. I think other Iron Range towns are like that because of
similar economic problems. After we graduated, the mines almost closed
down. So we nearly all got out of town."

The three friends sympathized with working-class people. Mrs. Hel-strom remembered: "Bob seemed much more humble than his family. Both Echo and Bob seemed so sorry for the working people." She and Echo recalled how interested Bob was in John Steinbeck. In 1968, Echo kept his books on a shelf. "We used to talk a lot about Steinbeck. Bob was always reading something by him—*Grapes of Wrath, Cannery Row. Grapes of Wrath* gave him his strong feelings for the Depression Okies.

"I was also surprised that Bob had anything to do with me because I had originally thought that Jewish people had *nothing* to do with other people. Bob never talked about being Jewish. I really sensed that the Jew-ish people in Hibbing felt they were different from others, but I know that Bob didn't want to be separated from anyone. He really loved Negro peo-ple like Jim Dandy, even though there were so few around. Bob always used to come back from Minneapolis impressed by the way the colored people danced and made music."

For the junior prom at Hibbing High, Echo bought a pale-blue floor-length gown. She kept the corsage Bob brought her until the flowers turned dry and crumbling. In the 1958 Hibbing High yearbook, Bob de-clared: "Let me tell you that your beauty is second to none, but I think I told you that before. . . . Love to the most beautiful girl in school." They went to the prom, outsiders passing through the mainstream. Echo: "We were so different, we shouldn't have even been there. We really couldn't dance. Bob was a poor leader, and I am a poor follower. He would take little teeny steps and kept saying to me: 'What's wrong with you? What's the matter?' And I said: 'I can't dance with you.' It was just horrible. But we were just there together, with each other. Bob wasn't skinny then. He was more cheeky and had a little bit of a tummy. I thought he was really cute. He was really the clean-cut kid, well scrubbed with rosy cheeks. After the prom we didn't go to any of the parties. We just sat in Bob's car and fell asleep. We weren't like the other people at school in any way. I just couldn't stand being like other girls. I had to be different."

By summer 1958, they had moved in opposite directions emotionally. Echo wanted to marry; Bob wanted to travel and pursue his music, to date other girls. Echo became increasingly possessive; Bob was restless. When he wanted to go to the movies, he entered first, insisting Echo join him inside later. He spent as much time as he could in Duluth or the Twin Cities. By the time he inscribed her 1958 school yearbook, he was already alluding to "St. Paul girls."

John, a secret admirer of Echo, suffered divided loyalties. Echo pressed John to tell her if Bob was seeing other girls. John: "I told her it was prob-ably true." Echo decided the situation was painful and returned Bob's bracelet in a school corridor. "I can still see his eyes—they got so big. 'What are you doing?' he asked. I said: 'Goodbye.' He said: 'Don't do this here in the hall.' " Later, at her house, she demanded to know if Bob was dating others. He said no, but Echo chose to believe John. "Bob needs an awful lot of attention from females."

She spent the summer of 1958 reliving their moments together. She walked up to Maple Hill, but the view didn't look the same alone. She sat on that swing, remembering his voice singing. "He always said later that he couldn't marry because he had his career to think of. If he hadn't had that determination to make something big of himself, he probably would have married me. He would have ended up doing what his father wanted—working in the furniture store." A decade later, Mrs. Helstrom said: "When Echo plays Bob's records, she feels she is still talking with him." John Sebastian, formerly of The Lovin' Spoonful, once told me: "You can't get too close to Dylan. He burns with such a bright flame you can get burned."

Echo saw Bob briefly in Minneapolis in autumn 1969. When the Hibbing High School class of 1959 held its tenth reunion, two unexpected classmates appeared separately—Echo, and Dylan, who was there with his wife. Five years earlier, Bob had told Chris Welles of *Life:* " 'The teachers in school taught me everything was fine. That was the accepted thing to think. It was in all the books. But it ain't fine, man. There are so many lies that have been told, so many things that are kept back. Kids have a feeling like me, but they ain't hearing it no place. They're scared to step out. But I ain't scared to do it, man.' "

So Dylan, the school's most notable graduate since Francis Bellamy, author of *The Pledge of Allegiance to the Flag,* returned for a moment of quiet triumph. Bob was besieged by old friends demanding autographs. Bob signed an autograph for Echo too.

A WREATH FOR BUDDY HOLLY

During Bob's last year of school, he told Bucklen repeatedly, "It won't be long now." He slid off the honor roll three times. When Beatty chided him, he snapped: "The honor roll isn't everything." He experimented with drinking and smoking. Once, Bucklen recalled, Bob, who had been out drinking, telephoned: "John, I'm going to come over there and kick the hell out of you." John replied: "OK, let's go. I'll wait outside for you." His assailant hove into sight, weaving back and forth. "He swung and hit me in the jaw, but he was in such bad shape that the punch didn't hurt at all. I finally got him home safely. All of a sudden Bob had discovered what it was like to get drunk often."

By the time he went to Minneapolis, Bob preferred wine. In October 1964, he still thought wine was best for Joan Baez, Gregory Corso, Allen Ginsberg, Ornette Coleman, and the other guests at the party he gave after his Philharmonic Hall concert. Our genial host offered us bottled row upon row of Beaujolais. In his first years around the Village, Bob often gave the impression of being high on wine. Suze Rotolo (his sweetheart in the early New York days) told me: "I don't think I ever saw him sober for quite a while after our first meeting. But half of that was put on. He could watch and listen better to what was going on if people thought he was high."

Even cold sober, young Bob was prone to car accidents. Although his father could later make light of the car problem, it deeply wrenched their relationship. "Bob always had a standard answer for any damage he did to a car. He would call and say: 'I broke the fan belt.' " After one accident, Abe had to settle a claim out of court for four thousand dollars.

The worst accident occurred in 1958. Bob had decided to sell his motor-cycle, but wanted to take one final ride. As he slowly turned toward home, a three-year-old boy holding an orange ran into the street from between two parked cars and collided with the side of the motorcycle. Hibbing Hospital said the child needed further care, and Abe arranged for an ambu-lance to Duluth. The child recovered, but Abe regarded Bob and the mo-torcycle as a deadly mixture. The evening of the accident, Bob met Echo downtown and vowed he'd never ride a bike again. He told Echo several times: "I can still see that orange rolling across the street."

During senior year, Bob's career plans were crystallizing. He joined a cousin's little band, The Satin Tones, a rough-edged group that played one number on a TV station in Superior, Wisconsin, one dance at Hibbing Armory, and one tape on Hibbing radio. Bucklen: "He was always getting groups like The Golden Chords and The Satin Tones together. He had an uncanny talent for finding an opportunity and taking advantage of it." Bob began to admire Muddy Waters and Jimmy Reed, two Chicago bluesmen up from the South, and white country stars who went into "rockabilly." A new and lasting musical model emerged—Buddy Holly. Bob began to imitate Holly's sweet, naïve, almost childlike voice. The vocal quality of many Dylan recordings shows his debt to Holly.

Holly could sing in a belting style like Presley's, or in the sinuous, yearning, "little-boy-lost" voice that turned on 1950s teens. Charles Hardin Holly was born in Lubbock, Texas, in 1936, and by the age of fifteen, as Buddy Holly, was playing the West Texas club circuit. After a contract at Decca, where nothing happened, Holly and his band, The Crickets, signed on with Norman Petty, who ran a studio in Clovis, New Mexico. With Petty's expertise, they converted an earlier flop into a million-selling hit, "That'll Be the Day." By 1958, Holly's hits, such as "Peggy Sue," "Rave On," and "Early in the Morning," were sprinkled all over U.S.-U.K. charts. Holly's influence on The Beatles was probably close to that of Little Richard and The Everly Brothers. Dylan and his mates could identify eas-ily with Holly—another small-town boy, young, slight, vulnerable. Imag-ine the excitement on January 31, 1959, when Holly and musician Link Wray appeared at the Duluth Armory. (Dylan visited Wray in 1975 and told him: "Link, I was sitting in the front row when you and Buddy Holly were at Duluth, and you're as great now as you were then.") Onstage, Buddy Holly could have passed for Bob's older brother. Hank Williams and Dean were dead, Little Richard and Brando never came near Hibbing, but here was Buddy Holly right up in the North Country! Rockabilly, Tex-Mex, Little Richard songs, everything!

Only three days after Dylan had seen him, Buddy Holly was dead. Bob and his friends studied details of the tragedy. At one A.M. on February 3, 1959, a Beechcraft Bonanza, chartered in Mason City, Iowa, took off in light snow for Fargo, North Dakota. Trouble developed in minutes, probably because the twenty-one-year-old pilot couldn't cope with the weather and instruments. The left wing hit the ground first. Killed instantly were the pilot and three musicians, Holly, twenty-two; Ritchie Valens, seventeen, a Mexican-American whose biggest hit was "La Bamba"; and J. P. Richardson, twenty-four, who was called the Big Bopper. Bob's friends and family sensed a pervasive change in him. He seemed in a tremendous hurry; all the car and motorcycle accidents indicated that his time was limited. "I was burned with death around me," Dylan said in 1965. Gretel Whitaker, a friend from the University of Minnesota, said: "We never really expected Bobby to live past twenty-one." By the time Bob was nineteen, he had written a mournful blues, passed on to me by Minneapolis friends:

> *The queen of his diamonds*
> *And the jack his knave*
> *Won't you dig my grave*
> *With a silver spade?*
> *And forget my name.*
> *I'm twenty years old.*
> *That's twenty years gone.*
> *Can't you see my crying,*
> *Can't you see my dying,*
> *I'll never reach twenty-one . . .*[12]

There was a curious footnote to Buddy Holly's death. The Fargo concert manager desperately searched for a fill-in act for Holly. He found two brothers, Sidney and Bill Velline, in nearby Moorhead, Minnesota. The twenty-five hundred kids who turned out to hear Buddy Holly heard the Velline brothers' band. The Vellines let their kid brother, Bobby, sit in. Bobby Velline told the concert manager the band was called The Shadows—a name the high-school sophomore had just invented. Bobby Velline, his name shortened to Bobby Vee, soon became the bandleader. With five hundred dollars saved up from a few dances, The Shadows cut four sides for the Soma label in Minneapolis. One of those sides, "Suzy Baby," featured Bobby Vee, singing like Holly. The Shadows later searched around Fargo for a piano player. Someone suggested a kid who had spent the early summer of 1959 as a busboy at the Red Apple Café in Fargo. "There were very few rock piano players around," Vee told me in London in 1969. "We gave Bob Zimmerman a chance to work with us, and he played great—in the key of C. His style was sort of like Jerry Lee Lewis. Bob worked two dances with us in Fargo. But we decided that we weren't really making enough money to cut in another member."

Bobby Vee's "Suzy Baby" went on to be a hit in the Midwest. Bobby Dylan came home one night in the rain on a bus from Fargo, but told no one but his family that his first professional chance had failed. He told Bucklen and others that he was the star of the "Suzy Baby" record, and repeated the story in Minneapolis. No one took it too seriously, but no one could challenge it.

THE GRADUATE

Abe and Beatty were radiant at their son's graduation. Bob would go, it had been agreed, to the University of Minnesota. Beatty reluctantly admitted there was really nothing much to keep him. She gave the biggest graduation party in town. Arrangements moved along with only one hitch—the guest of honor wasn't coming. He was going out with the boys. His mother thought he should come round for fifteen minutes, at least, because she wouldn't call off the party. "To make a long story short, he came home with us."

There is a striking similarity between this party and the one that opened the Mike Nichols–Dustin Hoffman film, *The Graduate;* both were more for the parents than for the sons. Abe: "Robert just couldn't understand a party like this was customary. I told him: 'This is a milestone. You only graduate high school once, you only graduate college once.' He said: 'If I do come, I won't be here very long.' But he stayed, and he felt good that all these people had come." Were any of Bob's friends or fellow musicians invited? "No," Abe replied. "We had neighbors and family. During graduation, the kids have their own parties. All you expect the children to do is to make an appearance. Bob stayed around much longer than we expected. He didn't know half of the people who came to celebrate his graduation, but they knew him."

At midnight, Bob went out to walk Hibbing's streets. At two A.M. he returned, as Beatty and a cleaning woman were straightening up. "Wasn't it a nice party?" his mother asked. He admitted it had been. His mother's crowning recollection of her son, the graduate, was: "He was always a gentleman at all times. He might have been a little contrary sometimes, but he was always nice to people. We really loved that party, and we were so proud to have such a courteous boy." The dining-room table was heaped with gifts from strangers. Among them was a set of 78s of Leadbelly, the black songster who died in 1949. The forceful Louisiana bard, discovered in a southern jail by folk collectors John and Alan Lomax, was a revelation. With only his voice and his twelve-string guitar, Leadbelly filled Bob's head with "Rock Island Line," "Take This Hammer," "Green Corn," and "Midnight Special."

Bucklen: "Bob almost shouted over the phone: 'I've discovered something great! You got to come over here!' " They listened, and Bob was flabbergasted. " 'This is the thing, this is the thing,' he repeated. Leadbelly was too simple for me in 1959. There was another example of Bob's being way ahead of us all." Leadbelly was a bad man too. He had served time for murder. Bob's attraction to Leadbelly was just long enough to open his ears to folk music.

After graduation, Bob headed down to Minneapolis to play university student. He returned perhaps a half-dozen times, on school holidays, or on trips from New York with some new triumph to report. In spring 1964, Bob made a brief appearance when David graduated Hibbing High. Bonn Rolfsen was struck then by Bob's reserve in the same auditorium where he had outraged everyone with his music. Bonn: "He was so popular then that if he'd wanted, he could have torn the town apart. He sought no special attention. He appeared to be under a terrific amount of strain, smoking continuously and very nervous. He was wound up like a tight clock, because he had been doing nothing but driving himself."

After 1964, he returned only twice, to my knowledge. There'd been postcards, and telephone calls at all hours from stray places on the road, but Bob had nearly washed Hibbing out of his mind. In 1963, Walter Eldot, Sunday features editor of *The Duluth News-Tribune,* quoted Abe: " 'My son is a corporation and his public image is strictly an act,' says his father. . . . Playing around Minneapolis, usually without pay, he began to develop his present stage character—with the folk-style attire and accent that go with it. 'That is,' says his father, 'what we found so disturbing— and still do. But it's all part of the act.' . . . About that time, his father came to a definite understanding about Bobby's future. 'He wanted to have free rein,' says Zimmerman. 'He wanted to be a folk singer, an entertainer. We couldn't see it, but we felt he was entitled to the chance. It's his life, after all, and we didn't want to stand in the way. So we made an agreement that he could have one year to do as he pleased, and if at the end of that year we were not satisfied with his progress, he'd go back to school. . . .' "

Later in 1963, Eldot was legman for a *Newsweek* piece that drove Bob farther from his family. He raged over the telephone to his parents about the two articles. He warned them not to speak to anyone without his approval. This was too difficult for Abe. As late as spring 1968, he still had to tell his version. To Jules Siegel, for *The Saturday Evening Post,* Abe said: " 'I used to make him go out to the poor sections to make repossessions . . . knowing he couldn't collect any money from those people. I just wanted to show him another side of life. He'd come back and say: "Dad, those people haven't got any money." And I'd say, "Some of those people out there make as much money as I do, Bobby. They just don't know how to manage it." ' " The Helstroms, John Bucklen's mother, and Jim Dandy taught Bob more about poor people than Abe did. Abe, a likable fellow, couldn't help resembling George Babbitt.

THE ROTARY: WILL THE CIRCLE BE UNBROKEN?

By spring 1968, Abe was in much better spirits about Bob, but he still felt compelled to tell friends and neighbors that no one saw Bob because he flew his private jet into Hibbing late at night and took off early the next morning. Despite the fact that Bob hadn't been home in four years, the story of the night flights so took hold around Hibbing that some swore they knew someone who had seen the plane.

In the fall of 1967, Abe and Beatty visited Bob and his family in Woodstock, New York. Their famous son was no longer playing orphan. The fact that Bob had married and had a growing family was, by their standards, as much a success story as anything that had happened. Abe took me to dinner in New York a few days later, keen to let me know that there had been a rapprochement in Woodstock. Abe had already begun to rewrite his own history when I first met him in 1966. No longer was he the square father who thought pop music was nonsense. Behind his shop counter, awaiting the next customer, he would study the latest copy of *Billboard,* the music-trade weekly. "By all means, let's have dinner together tonight. And there's a Rotary luncheon tomorrow at the Androy. If you want to see the best of Hibbing, you have to see the Rotary in action." The manner was soft, but it was an offer I couldn't refuse.

Abe conducted me through a dozen introductions to pillars of the community. He had an easy conviviality, a personal comment to make to everyone, first-name regards to each wife. After lunch, Paul Harris, a leading lawyer in town, had a few thousand words to say about Rotary's objectives: "One: Service above self. You really should get to know your friends and neighbors. Two: High ethical standards in business. Be proud of what you do. Three: Involvement. Make time for as many community projects as you can."

Perhaps Hibbing looked a little different to you if you didn't belong to Rotary or Kiwanis. Perhaps the town was a vacuum if you didn't join the Moose Club, Odd Fellows, Veterans of World War I Auxiliary No. 2039, the Newcomers Club, the YWCA, Tenger Lodge of the Vasa Order of America, Bethel No. 4 Order of Job's Daughters, the Tuesday Musicale, The First Settlers of Hibbing, the Izaak Walton League, the Hibbing Figure Skating Club, the Wells-Woodland Garden Club, the Mesaba Rosarians, the Guglielmo Marconi Lodge No. 1164 of the Sons of Italy, the Hibbing St. Francis Court No. 610 of the National Catholic Society of Foresters, or the Bunker Willing Workers 4-H Club, B'Nai B'Rith, or the chamber of commerce.

Jim Hitchcock was chairman of the chamber of commerce in 1966 and publisher of *The Hibbing Tribune.* He admitted the town had seen hard times, but "we're on the comeback trail now. . . . Yes," he said, sadly, "the loss of our youth has been a major problem." According to Hitchcock, Hibbing had three prominent products besides iron ore: Jeno Paulucci, whose Chun King Corporation, packagers of pizza and Chinese food, had recently been sold for millions; Roger Maris, the ballplayer; and Bobby Dylan.

"I know that the town is a little mystified by Dylan. Roger Maris always says he is from Fargo, North Dakota, and gets mad when people say he's from Hibbing." People here are happy that Bob is from Hibbing, even if he is offbeat." Had the town fathers ever invited Bob to do a concert? "No formal invitation ever went out to Bobby, as far as I know. If we knew when he was coming, we'd ask him to perform." Had *The Hibbing Tribune* ever done a feature story about Bob Dylan? "No, I don't think so." In its ambitious seventy-fifth anniversary issue of August 10, 1968, *The Tribune* ran scores of articles about the virtues of Hibbing. Dylan's name never came up.

At Dylan's former home in the spring of 1968, there was Rotary talk, chamber of commerce talk, and "God Bless Our Home" talk. In retrospect, did Beatty and Abe know why Bob became the most renowned youth rebel of the 1960s? Dad: "He didn't really rebel. He convinced himself that he had something different to sell." Mom: "Yes, he convinced himself. We didn't. We certainly didn't." Did they think he left in anger? "Oh, no, he didn't leave in anger?" they replied. Abe and Beatty were not exceptionally old-fashioned. Mother: "We didn't rebel, we went along. We knew that our parents were doing the very best that they could for us." Father: "We were sometimes disappointed by what our parents made us do. We complained or cried a little bit, but eventually we did what we were told."

Abe took me around the house. In the basement recreation room, where Bob's James Dean collection once lined the walls, the parents now had a gallery of their own young rebel: posters, album covers, and publicity and magazine photographs of Dylan. His parents played me old practice tapes of his various high-school bands. Bob's young, harsh voice belted out "Rock and Roll Is Here to Stay." Piles of moldering 78s and 45s stood in a corner, a cross section of the 1950s. Here was "Dearest" and "There Ought to Be a Law" by Mickey and Sylvia on Vik, "Baby Blue" by Gene Vincent and the Hot Rods on Capitol, "Hank Snow Sings Jimmie Rodgers," The Clovers, and Nat "King" Cole. Then a flood of Hank Williams's lonesome blues, Haley, Pat Boone, Bobby Vee, Johnny Ace, Webb Pierce, and, inevitably, Buddy Holly's "Slippin' and Slidin'," Little Richard's "Tutti Fruitti," and Presley's "Heartbreak Hotel" and "Blue Suede Shoes."

Abe steered me up to Bob's room, passing on the stairway wall a picture of puffy-cheeked Bob with a neat tie—his graduation picture. Abe: "Both boys shared this room. We had twin beds in here. You would never know where either of them was sleeping. At first, we had a western motif on the walls, horses and saddles, but it's been painted over several times." Abe drew out several albums of family pictures. Almost startled at their number, he remarked: "I wonder if there is any money in these things."

Abe slowly leafed through the album. "Here's a picture of Bobby playing bullfighter, holding a bathroom towel as a cape. He was about twelve here. These are priceless now. . . . Here he is playing the bongo. . . . Here is the medicine he used to take for his asthma. He doesn't have too much trouble with that now. Here's the room when it had the cowboy wallpaper. . . . Bobby was fifteen when he posed with a cowboy hat on and a cigarette dangling out of his mouth. I sent the picture to him awhile ago with his photo from the ad for *Don't Look Back.* It had exactly the same expression. . . . Here we are at the Paul Bunyan site at the headwaters of the Mississippi. Yes, he liked those tall tales of Paul Bunyan. . . ."

What about Bob's fascination with badmen and outlaws? "Oh, yes, he was fascinated. That's true. Everyone was interested in those badmen. I was myself. . . . Here are all those *Illustrated Classics—Cyrano, The Hunchback of Notre Dame, The Corsican Brothers, The Pathfinder.*" Did he know Bob had done a series of drawings for Victor Hugo's *Les Miserables* when he was a boy? "No, I didn't know that. Wonder where they might be now?" Abe leafed through the memorabilia with a mixture of pride and sadness. So much time had passed and so much had happened since Bob left home.

Did Abe think that Bob would ever come back to Hibbing? There was a long pause, then: "Here's a picture of Bobby as a Boy Scout." "Do you think he will come back to Hibbing one day, or don't you know, Abe?" He went on leafing through the photographs. Three weeks later, Dylan went back to Hibbing for the first time in four years. Abe's son had returned to attend his father's funeral.

KADDISH

Abe suffered his first heart attack in summer 1966, shortly after Bob's motorcycle accident. It was a mild attack, but it forced him to cut down. However, no doctor could cure Abe of worry over his boys, of his public image as a father. In spring 1968, he had a new family problem: David's impending marriage to a Catholic. "When my boys make mistakes, they make big ones," Abe told me a few weeks before he died. The wedding, scheduled for the last week in May, was postponed.

On the morning of June 5, Abe awoke feeling weak and "strange." He stayed home, taking it easy. He was not feeling any better by the time Beatty returned from work. A little after five P.M., Abe suffered a fatal heart attack. At first, Bob was reluctant to appear, lest it charge the funeral's atmosphere. He flew in alone the next day on a commercial flight. David met him at the Hibbing-Chisholm airport in drizzling rain. Bob had on the round black hat he wore on the cover of *John Wesley Harding.* He and David found the house filled with relatives and neighbors. Within minutes, Bob said: "This isn't a garden party. Let's get these people out of here." Beatty explained that this was the mourning tradition. Bob insisted the family should be by themselves.

David was struck by Bob's demeanor. His older brother seemed to have quietude, firmness, and serenity befitting "a fifty-year-old man." When the two discussed the funeral, David was startled by Bob's familiarity with Jewish ritual, especially *Kaddish,* the Hebrew prayer through which the parent's soul benefits from a surviving son's piety. Early on Friday morning, David and Bob went to the Dougherty Funeral Home on First Avenue. Upon seeing his father's body, Bob, previously restrained, was deeply upset. He took the death harder than either Beatty or David, as if he were caught up by all the things he and his father had never been able to say. ("I never knew my father," Bob later told Woody Guthrie's former agent.) By the time the funeral home opened to the lines of mourners, Bob, again his controlled self, stood in one corner, taking it all in like a camera.

Two years before Abe died, Bob spewed out to me in choppy guillotine cuts his thoughts on death and suicide: "I just know that I've been at it too long. I've been at it longer than a fifty-year-old man. Hey, death to me is nothing, as long as I can die fast. Many times I've known I could have died fast. There was a time when I was afraid of dying. I'll admit to having this suicidal thing. I've been living under a suicidal hex now for the last six months. . . .

"I was actually most afraid of death in those first years around New York. When I started writing all those songs and everyone started calling me a genius—genius this and genius that. I knew it was bull, because I still hadn't written what I wanted to. I had written 'Blowin' in the Wind,' but I wasn't satisfied with that. I was never satisfied with 'Blowin' in the Wind.' I wrote that in ten minutes. 'Blowin' in the Wind' was a lucky classic song. No more, no less than 'Your Cheatin' Heart.' But it was one-dimensional. . . .

"I've really got a sickness, man. I don't write when I'm feeling groovy, you understand. I play when I'm feeling groovy. I write when I'm sick. I'm not going to push that on anybody. Man, nobody knows what is the matter with me, and I'm not about to go tell anybody. . . . If I had ever been like Woody Guthrie in his situation, I don't know what I would do. A living decay. I can't decay. I would not let myself decay. I'm against decay. That's nature's will—decay. I am against nature. I don't dig nature at all. I think nature is very unnatural. I think the truly natural things are dreams, which nature can't touch with decay. . . .

"I was so frightened of death when I was in New York. I wasn't turning out anything. Everything I turned out could be done better tomorrow. . . . I did not want to die. I would ride on airplanes not wanting to die, because I just had to get something said. Because I knew people were going to listen. . . . I don't want to see myself die. . . I don't want to hear myself dying, or taste myself or smell myself dying. . . . All this talk about equality. The only thing people really have in common is that they are all going to die."

At the synagogue service, Bob wore a gray double-breasted suit with jade cuff links, a white tie, and the traditional skull cap, a final concession to his mother. He had wanted to wear his John Wesley Harding hat, which could have passed for the black hat worn by some pious Jewish sects. Most of the mourners took the long ride to the cemetery in Duluth. Beatty, David, and Bob were silent most of the trip.

That afternoon, David took Bob for a drive around Hibbing in the rain. Bob let the town pass before his eyes like a long, silent movie flashback. He passed the hill where some boys had once put up a small sign: HIB-BING, MINNESOTA—HOMETOWN OF BOB DYLAN. It was Thomas Wolfe's Asheville and Sinclair Lewis's Sauk Centre. Bob told David the town looked like a giant funeral parlor to him. Again, David was struck by his brother's serenity. "So calm, so reserved, so clean . . . almost so saintly!" That night, Bob asked to see a few of his old friends. Bonn Rolfsen and Father Michael Hayes of the Catholic Church up Seventh Avenue came by. Echo, John Bucklen, and Monte Edwardson were gone. And so was Bobby Zimmerman. A stranger in his own house, who, he said, "no longer felt himself the same person he had been in Hibbing," spoke to his visitors gently, courteously.

Beatty was pleased that Bob could stay on until the following Tuesday. He urged her to sell the house and think about doing something different to readjust. They talked about the early years, and Bob assured her that she and Abe had been good parents. Had they acted differently, had they not resisted him at crucial points, could they have been the diving board from which he sprang? Didn't they give him the impetus to run, the cause to rebel, the materials from which to build his own special personality? The "saintly" son who came home to bury Abe was proof that he and Beatty had not failed. Beatty told Bob that all the family money was frozen until the estate was settled. Bob took out his checkbook and wrote her a five-figure check. Beatty and David were staggered. She insisted: "Bobby, I don't want to deny your children anything." "I can always do a couple of concerts," he replied.

Over the weekend, Bob slept in his father's old bedroom, and spent hours poring over his childhood memorabilia—the comics, *Illustrated Classics,* the photographs, the old recordings, the home tapes. Some people around Hibbing now found him amazingly like his father: He was some-what stern with his children, careful then with his money, reserved and conservative in manner. Could he have become what he had so long op-posed?

His wife was expecting another baby, and Bob had to be on hand. On his way to the airport, he took one final swing down Howard Street, pass-ing the window of a drugstore, where, weeks earlier, a visitor to Hibbing had been startled by the juxtaposition of two paperback books. *Don't Look Back,* drawn from the film starring Dylan, was right next to a novel called *The Runaway.*

2

THE WRONG END
OF THE MISSISSIPPI

"The old saw around Minneapolis was that Dylan was a
pathological liar. I don't think this was true. Dylan was
just a romantic. He remembered what should have
been.... He walked around here like a young
Shelley...."

—HARRY WEBER, 1966

"Dylan was his own guru. After learning what he could
from others, he taught himself."

—DAVE MORTON, 1966

"His old self, from Minneapolis, and what he became in
the East, are two different people."

—PAUL NELSON, 1968

"How does it feel
To be on your own
With no direction home
Like a complete unknown
Like a rolling stone?"

—DYLAN, 1965[1]

Dylan arrived at the University of Minnesota on Highway 61, took byways, blind alleys, and detours, and left on Highway 12.

Shortly after his abortive encounter with the Bobby Vee band in Fargo in summer 1959, Dylan ended up in a reconstructed nineteenth-century gold-mining boomtown high in the Rockies, singing in a sleazy striptease joint. Bob and his family told me he went to Denver and Central City, Colorado, before enrolling at Minnesota. Others have placed him in Colorado in summer 1960. I know he returned in early 1964, and I was with him there in March 1966.

He first made the twenty-five-mile trek from Denver to Central City by bus and thumb. It was the Wild West reincarnate—gold mines, sheriffs, buildings out of a movie set. In 1966, on a Sunday afternoon, Bob made a sentimental return, circling slowly along twisting Highway 58. Once a lifeline to Denver, for supplies going up and gold nuggets going out, this route through scrubby, eroded hilltops was just a tourist road now.

Bob sat in the front of the car, conserving his voice for the Denver concert. Looking like the *Blonde on Blonde* cover, his frizzy electric halo, which Hendrix and others soon affected, surrounded a lean face drawn with fatigue. I mentioned that some old Village friends of ours had just been divorced. "Are they any happier now?" he asked, eyes still on the road.

Within a few turns we were back in 1859: worn stone buildings, gingerbread wood houses on hillsides. Dylan said, "When I first went up here, Central City seemed so far from anything I'd ever seen or done before, it was sort of magic for me." In May 1859, nine Georgia prospectors, led by one John Gregory, struck gold here. Gregory's Diggings, as it was dubbed, was mobbed with twenty thousand people in three months. Cornish miners brought their love of music. The first local hit song was "Paddy Casey's Night Hands," about a legendary Irish miner. An opera house was built in 1878. Boosters called the town "the American Salzburg." By the time Dylan first got there, arts festivals were annual events.

We parked near the old courthouse, ambled down Eureka Street into Main. "Nothing's changed. It's almost exactly the way it was," Bob said. We passed the opera house, like a film crew sizing up a location. Some tourists ogled Dylan. A teenager yelped, "What's *he* doing here?" Up Main Street, a small nameless bar was dark. It had a large, circular window front, like an aquarium. "This was the place," Dylan said, peering into the fishbowl. He'd described The Gilded Garter to me in 1961: "I was onstage for just a few minutes with my folky songs. As the night got longer, the air got heavier, the audience got drunker and nastier, I got sicker, and finally I got fired."

We edged away from the saloon. "Oh, it only lasted a few weeks," Dylan said, "but I suppose I'll never forget it. They paid me very little, but they threw in sandwiches and drinks, and all the strippers I could watch. All the noisy drunks were thrown in free too." As we headed back to Denver, he mused, "The time has gone so fast. It almost seems like it happened to someone else."

In 1959, Bob heard from one of The Golden Chords, Monte Edwardson, that there was a lively folk-music scene around Denver. He decided to try his luck there. He plunged into the coffeehouse folk scene on his own. The Exodus Gallery Bar at 1999 Lincoln Street was the focal point for local beats, artists, and poets, and a sprinkling of button-down college kids. Denver's trendies gravitated to the Exodus for art shows, poetry readings, and folk sessions. Dylan tiptoed around for a few weeks. It seemed like the big time. There was a Kingston Trio offshoot, the Harlin Trio—three crewcut undergraduates—consistently dull and unoriginal. Other local talent included George Downing, a math teacher who sang drowsy cowboy songs. Dave Wood, a Scottish-born lad who grew up in Hawaii, was a graduate student at Boulder. He imitated Mexican singing and talking. One Exodus singer offered to share his flat with Bob for a few weeks. Walt Conley, a large, gentle, black man from Nebraska, had learned folk songs in the late 1940s from Pete Seeger and composer Earl Robinson. From Walt, Bob reportedly picked up a topical anti-KKK song called "The Klan." Dylan and Walt fell out over a girl they both were after, and over the sudden disappearance of a bunch of Walt's favorite recordings. "I was kicked out of Denver," Dylan told me without remorse. "Yeah, I was run out of Denver for robbing a cat's house."

Two Denver performers influenced Dylan. The sweetheart of the Exodus was nineteen-year-old Denverite Judy Collins. With her warm, glowing alto, the classically trained singer was beginning a long career in 1959–60. Two songs Judy was singing then ended up on Dylan's first album: "House of the Rising Sun" and "Maid of Constant Sorrow."

Judy became one of the first and best interpreters of Dylan songs. Bob also met a rollicking old gamester, the late Jesse Fuller, who often played the Exodus. Born in Jonesboro, Georgia, in 1896, Fuller fused traditional songs, blues, his own writing, rural ragtime, and just plain "good-time" sounds. He was a one-man band, working his twelve-string guitar, cymbals, harmonica, and his own curious invention, the "fotdella," a foot-operated percussion machine that struck a drum and plucked an improvised bass simultaneously. "The Lone Cat," as he called himself, came on with vitality and wit. Dylan watched the way Fuller held his harmonica and kazoo in front of his mouth in a metal neck-brace that allowed him to alternate between singing and running riffs on his mouth harp quickly. Dylan quizzed Fuller, and learned how to play the harmonica in its distinctive holder.

Bob concedes his few performances at the Exodus and other Colorado clubs were nothing memorable. Yet he was getting some experience and credits, if little money. Colorado also gave him anonymity and a chance to romanticize his background. He told his family that in Denver he had been wildly appreciated and accepted. His parents still thought, as they drove him to Minneapolis, that college would wash away this music compulsion.

"HIGHWAY 61 REVISITED"

In 1959, about twenty-five thousand students were attending the University of Minnesota, a midwestern Big Ten school with a football team, a school of animal husbandry, heavy endowments, and high academic ratings, especially in medicine and technology. The campus, nestled in a gentle bend of the Mississippi, had spread across from the east bank. By the 1960s, the main campus became the largest single college center in America, with students and faculty accounting for 10 percent of the city population. *Venture* called Minneapolis, with its 150 parks and 20 lakes, "a city as American as Scotch tape and Wheaties, as invigorating as a morning swim in Hiawatha Lake, as wholesome as a Pillsbury Bake-Off. . . . It is not a place . . . for exotic new excitements, but one where you feel back home among the comfortable, cherished national virtues—friendliness, decency, optimism, humor, enthusiasm, diligence, sanity, pride."

A cousin, a law student, belonged to Sigma Alpha Mu, and Bob lived briefly at the fraternity house. Bob's first reaction to the group, called—not so benevolently—"Sammies" because it was a Jewish fraternity, was negative. His father recalled: "Bob didn't think much of the college crowd. He considered most of them phonies, just spoiled kids with whom he didn't have much in common. Bobby quit Sigma Alpha Mu even before he was pledged." He wrote, in "My Life in a Stolen Moment":

> Later I sat in college . . . on a phony scholarship that I never had
> I sat in science class an' flunked out for refusin' to watch a rabbit die
> I got expelled from English class for using four-letter words in a paper describing the English teacher
> I also failed out of communication class for callin' up every day and sayin' I couldn't come
> I did OK in Spanish though but I knew it beforehand
> I's kept around for kicks at a fraternity house
> They let me live there an' I did until they wanted me to join
> I moved in with two girls from South Dakota in a two-room apartment for two nights
> I crossed the bridge to 14th Street an' moved in above a bookstore that also sold bad hamburgers basketball sweatshirts an' bulldog statues
> I fell hard for an actress girl who kneed me in the guts an' I ended up on the East Side a the Mississippi River with about ten friends in a condemned house underneath the Washington Avenue Bridge just south a Seven Corners
> That's pretty well my college life . . . [2]

Dylan's sardonic summary doesn't do justice to what he learned outside classrooms. Bob left the fraternity house amid bad feeling. A counselor recalled that Bob was "hard to know, kept very odd hours, and moped a lot." The people Bob liked were the few folk-oriented intellectuals who lived around Dinkytown, the University business district, and Bohemia. One of these beatniks, thinkers, rebels, artists, dropouts, and dreamers was "Spider John" Koerner, a middle-class Huck Finn intensely involved in music:

"I first met Bob in the Ten O'Clock Scholar, a Dinkytown coffeehouse that later burned down," Koerner told me. "Bob just drifted in. He and I both played the same sort of guitar things. He was writing some songs, but they were those folky spirituals that were popular, like 'Sinner Man.' He got very interested in those easy-rocking things of Odetta's. Dylan had a very sweet voice, a pretty voice, much different from what it became. I don't remember Bob's talking about making it in show business. We were more interested in immediate things, in making up songs. One thing that struck me hard was the great change in how Dylan speaks. It's almost impossible to recognize the same person. None of us was talking very hip then, except possibly Dave Morton, who was older. We weren't really into the hippie sort of thing then, it was mostly just singing and playing and drinking and going to parties and chasing women."

Campus people thought Spider John would be a star and that Dylan was definitely the lesser talent. One of Koerner's roommates was Harry Weber, a Ph.D. candidate in Latin literature and a ballad scholar:

"When I arrived in Minneapolis in 1955 with a guitar," Weber told me in 1966, "folk music was very much underground. The older people came from the Old Left. Their idea of folk music was a union song—Seeger and *The People's Song Book,* Gene Bluestein [who made a Folkways album, *Songs of the North Star State,* in 1958] was the big folk wheel on campus. The early Minnesota Folk Music Society was about eighty percent Jewish, mostly university people.

"The first songwriter I ever heard around here was Dylan. Old Dave Morton was the earliest to write songs, but I never heard them. The first song of Dylan's I heard was 'Every Time I Hear the Spirit.' Bob didn't make much of a fuss about it. It was like the Negro spiritual he based it on, except it had a rockabilly beat. A good adolescent lament. When Bob came down here in 1959, he looked pretty, fair-haired, absolutely beardless. His eyes were vaguely popping, and his cheeks a little bit too full. Dr. Dan Pugh, a psychiatrist, was fascinated by Dylan's looks. 'A very interesting endocrine system,' Dr. Pugh said.

"When Dylan arrived he looked awfully small-town. He dressed in an almost finicky way. He looked like Peck's Bad Boy suddenly grown five years. He acted very high-schoolish, very brash. He posed a lot, with his hand in his belt, his legs straddling the room. He wasn't big, of course, but he was heavy. I think he weighed at least twenty-five or thirty pounds more than after he made it. Almost from the start, there used to be inconsistencies in Bob's stories. He didn't really stay in school very long, maybe six or nine months. The last few months, he wasn't at school at all. He was living on and with different people, and had some little jobs, like bussing dishes.

"After he dropped out, I found him impossible. He could be very pretentious, very annoying. Maybe this was a bid for attention. I think that, like everybody, he wanted to be liked. He could be awfully rude and he certainly was vain. Koerner and Dylan were competing quite a bit. I was afraid Dylan wasn't going to have any voice left. He obviously knew what he was doing, but he was abusing his voice, shouting out raucous, loud songs.

"I met Dylan only about a month after he got here. He would get interested in some song or technique I knew. We were living at Forty-two Seventh Street Southeast, a horrible place, sort of a three-man slum. There always seemed to be a lot of music going on. I did not find it easy to communicate with Bob. I don't think anybody else did either. Even the girls he liked had a hard time talking to him, and he had a hard time talking to them. But it was different when it got to music!

"If you couldn't explain what was the matter with his way of singing, you could show him. He would pick it up just like that," continued Weber. "I don't think Bob read much, although he borrowed books a lot. He didn't talk about books at all, except of course Woody Guthrie's *Bound for Glory*. I did loan Bob a set of Randolph's *Folk Songs of Arkansas*. I wonder if he still has them. Dylan never cared much about the battle here over tradition. Maybe he became as good as he did because that sort of thing doesn't bother him. He uses what he wants to use. In 1959, Dylan met Cynthia Gooding. After her concert we had a party, and Bob sang to her for half an hour. Cynthia was amazed. It was quite a sight, because she was somebody then." Later, when Cynthia saw Dylan in New York at Folk City, she wrote Harry: "People listen . . . he talks and he laughs and just when they are about to catch him in a lie, he takes out his harmonica and blows them down."

Weber continued: "Dylan is a genius, that's all. He is irksome and irritating, very much the Chekhov genius. He is not more complex than most people; he is simpler. I knew when I met him that he was very talented. I was not awed by him then. I am now. Awed with his ability. I don't think he was aware of his talent when he came to Minneapolis. But, wait a minute. I take that back. He walked around like a young Shelley. Dylan used to carry a book of French symbolist poetry, but I think he is a very great listener. When he wasn't singing, he was very quiet. When he got nervous, he would sing. He wasn't a talker. He doesn't chat.

"The attitude of the folk purists toward Dylan when he started with an electric band was like saying that Verdi sold out when he composed 'Othello' because he was influenced by Wagner. The purists say art must be static. The people at *Sing Out!* magazine let down Josh White with a great wallop too, hurting him very much. You can't forgive such doctrinaire attitudes very often. Pete Seeger never let himself be caught up in that. What the purists did to Dylan is unbelievable."

THE UNIVERSITY OF DINKYTOWN

Although Dylan enrolled at the liberal arts college in September 1959, within a few months he was really at the University of Dinkytown, majoring in music with advanced seminars in coffeehouses, minoring in radical life-styles, doing seminars in scene-making, preparing for graduate work in Woody Guthrie. Bob's Minneapolis friends and foes formed a circle of exceptionally intelligent, colorful, talented, and perceptive characters. One was a student radical named Harvey Abrams, a bright, tough, articulate social worker I interviewed in spring 1966:

"I met Bob in summer 1960. He had already written a couple of beautiful songs, like 'The Klan.' Bob never really went to school, but he carried a notebook that never contained schoolwork. He was playing weekends at The Scholar, earning five dollars a night. Then, Bob Beull and I opened up a coffeehouse. We leased an old house near Oak and Washington Avenue and rebuilt it, and named it The Bastille.

"Dylan and I were pretty good friends by then. I lived in Melvin McCosh's boardinghouse, above his bookstore. Dave and Gretel Whitaker were also living there. Bob began to play at The Bastille weekends. I thought he was fantastic! He always went as Bob Dillon, not Dylan. The only time we saw it with the Dylan Thomas spelling was in your *New York Times* article [September, 1961]. At school, he was registered as Bob Zimmerman, but all of his music billings here were spelled Bob Dillon." Dylan has said he picked "Bob Dylan" at The Scholar, on the spur of the moment, apparently before Abrams hired him as "Dillon."

"In early winter 1960, he somehow traded his Gibson for a huge Gretsch Ranger, with a sound box of about four cubic feet! Dylan listened to flamenco played by Hugh Brown and by Steve Olson, who had studied with Carlos Montoya. But Dylan wouldn't do any flamenco. His music kept getting better and better. His poetry then was very simple stuff.

"Rock 'n' roll? Definitely not! If anyone had played him a Beatles or a Rolling Stones record, he would probably have broken it. Dylan was the purest of the pure. He had to get the oldest record and, if possible, the Library of Congress record, or go find the original people who knew the original song." When Harvey, Morton, and Bob were living at 714 Fifteenth Avenue Southeast, Dylan "would rush home to be there when the mailman arrived. We were rather young then, and perhaps cruel, but Hugh Brown and I had heard so much about Bob's Oklahoma poverty scene, we were really startled when we saw a card from his folks at the Royal Hawaiian Hotel. We finally figured out that his folks must have been sending him money."

Abrams reminisced: "Bob wore Levi's, loafers or boots, and a blue denim shirt. In the winter, an old tweed sports jacket and a thick scarf. Always some kind of eccentric hat or cap. Long before it was fashionable, Bob was saying that school wasn't relevant to life. I know he was writing night and day. A lot of it was pretty infantile. A lot showed complete identification with and copying of Guthrie's material. Somewhere along the line, Dylan got a tremendous burst of originality.

"Whitaker and I probably told Bob as much about politics as anyone. Dylan didn't read about politics; he really didn't seem to read at all. You see, Dylan can hear. If Bob were in a foreign country, he'd pick up the language very quickly. When he came here, Dylan didn't really know anything about politics and he wasn't at all interested. There were about fifty of us seriously interested in politics and in the Cuban Revolution. Let's say that Bob got a lot of exuberance about it from us. Bob probably doesn't deal with political dogma; he probably just identifies with the underdog, with the people. Look at 'Hollis Brown.' He feels these things on a very intuitive, emotional level, the way a primitive person might. If there were ever a great strike movement in America, Dylan could be another Mother Jones.

"For a while, people mostly went to parties to hear Dylan play. Later, nobody wanted to give a party because Dylan would come and play. Then he became the first guy to put the guitar and harmonica together, with that frame-holder around his neck. Nobody had ever seen this before. As far as I know, he was the first white performer to combine the Sonny Terry harmonica with the Woody Guthrie guitar."

When money was short, Abrams recalled, "I pawned Morton's and Dylan's guitars several times—Brown's guitar also." Then money would come in from somewhere and Abrams would claim the instruments. "We were all living a pretty irregular life, but Dylan especially. For Bob to knock on somebody's door at five-thirty in the morning was not unusual. When he was looking for some sort of action, he assumed everybody else was up. To Bob, Hibbing was just an awfully sad memory that he didn't want to talk about. He didn't want us to know anything about Hibbing. He would hide letters from there. Sometimes he had been born in Duluth, and sometimes in Oklahoma. We knew that he used to play rock 'n' roll, but he had totally disowned it by the time he was getting known here."

"WHEN THE STUDENT IS READY, THE TEACHER WILL APPEAR"

Weber and Abrams emerged as straight characters. Others were uncompromising, like the reigning Dinkytown guru, Dave Morton, who moved to the West Coast around 1961. Morton, Dinkytown's link between the mystic 1950s beats and the emerging 1960s hipsters, had considerable influence on Dylan. A gaunt six-and-one-half-footer, Morton looked like Abe Lincoln strung out in the East Village. Hair flowed from every pore;

he had forelocks, a beard and moustache, and a mop cascading nearly two feet down his back. He radiated gentle, distilled wisdom. He was one of the best professors at Dylan's peripheral university. Morton was probably the first to play folk music at the old Ten O'Clock Scholar, although he knew only four or five chords when he began.

Dylan recalled: "There was a lot of unrest . . . frustration . . . like a calm before a hurricane. . . . There were always a lot of poems recited . . . Kerouac, Ginsberg, Corso, and Ferlinghetti. . . . I got in at the tail end . . . and it was magic . . . every day was like Sunday." I caught up with Morton in Los Angeles in 1966. He had become a senior Coast hipster, painting, editing *Regent,* an avant-garde literary magazine, studying the *I Ching,* and leading a folk-rock band, The New Improved Jukes Savages. As chief Savage, Morton played guitar, piano, and kazoo. "Back at Minneapolis, I studied mathematics, but I didn't get far. Mostly, I was connected with the new All-American Gallery, at the Dinkytown firehouse building. I first met Bobby Dylan at a party there in the fall of 1959. Bob was pretty lively, funny, and nervous. His leg always bounced when he sat down. He never talked much about Hibbing, although he went up there for a day or two. The Iron Range is an international community with a funny kind of isolation. It's a strange place to grow up in. It seems to leave some special stamp on people. I was the butt of some ridicule because I let my hair grow for three or four months. Now, everyone is doing it, even Dylan."

Morton was deep into Asian and American Indian philosophy and myth, and psychedelic experiences. I asked him to reconstruct talks with Dylan in the old days. He seemed to fall into a trance: "According to Indian belief, there are three steps toward salvation. The first is love. The second is enjoyment of the senses. And the third is the dharma game, which is duty, such as to family and children, to a job, or even to society. Yes, we used to talk of that then. I had a fine experience on acid reading *Paterson* by William Carlos Williams. Acid simply opens up the museums of the mind. On acid, you go through funny places of history and myth. The entire Garden of Eden can be re-created in your mind. One experience I had was the feeling that my voice was not directly linked to my self. The words seemed to come from somewhere else, my memory or my unconscious mind." Morton paused. We realized he had accurately described a phase of Dylan's songwriting. "Some artists could always have been described as psychedelic. Seurat broke up colors into little points. On acid, I've seen colors the way Van Gogh painted them, flowing together like early Persian tapestries. Picasso's surrealism is realistic to me, and has always been, ever since I perceived it on this new level."

Dylan's response? "He always listened, well, intently. Although he didn't talk much to many people, we always managed to communicate. I'm not surprised Bob went on to achieve what he did. He seemed to be working on something none of us fully shared with him. Dylan was his own guru. . . . When the student is ready, the old saying goes, the teacher will appear. . . ."

Hugh Brown had been Morton's chum from high school in Portland, Oregon. Soft-spoken and humble, Hugh studied classics, wrote poetry, and later became a highway engineer. Brown: "I always liked Bob. At the time, I think I played guitar better than he did. We ended up living together, along with Dave and Max Uhler and several others. Living arrangements changed week to week. When we were living on Fifteenth Avenue Southeast, three blocks from Dinkytown, I would try to wake him when he had a special test, and it was always a struggle. One time he threatened to throw me down the stairs. Mostly, he played his guitar. Bob talked about taking off for New York, about going to see Guthrie. He also said he wanted to go to New York to strike it rich. At The Scholar most people liked him, even though he wasn't really very good then. He was on an Odetta kick, singing other people's songs. I don't know why Harvey Abrams says he spelled his name Dillon then, because as I recall, he spelled it Dylan here. Of course, he said a lot of things that proved to be untrue. He was trying to overcome being from Hibbing.

"When I got married, Bob gave us a wedding present of a toaster and an iron. Both the iron and toaster had been mine, but Bob wasn't concerned. He still regarded them as gifts. He was popular around Minneapolis. Most of the people who now dislike him began to do so after he became famous. There was a hate-Dylan rash for a while. I don't really understand it. He was elated about signing a record contract, but he wasn't particularly egotistical. It is difficult to be passive about someone as outrageous as Bob. He says some pretty outrageous things, in his music and in person. We all thought it was pretty funny he was going to New York to make his fame and fortune. He left owing people a lot of money, but we all owed a lot of people money. . . . When Bob was here, the first stirrings of a radical movement were beginning to affect the American college campus," continued Hugh.

"Among those trying to get a radical club off the ground here were Harvey, Whitaker, and Herschel Kaminsky, who was quite active down in Mississippi. We organized a Fair Play for Cuba Committee. Bob didn't come to any meetings, but he was around. Bob may have become interested in politics through Guthrie, rather than through the political people on campus. He certainly didn't appear to be politically sophisticated."

There was an anonymous adage around Dinkytown: "Dylan missed out on an extra bowl of chicken soup when he was a boy and spent the rest of his life wondering what and why he had missed." Hugh Brown's reaction was: "If you try to figure out anyone like Bob you will only discover that there is more and more that you simply can't figure out. We had all liked Ginsberg's poetry. I don't know how much of an influence he was on Bob at that time. There was not much use of drugs then. A few people had tried marijuana and peyote, but none of us had even heard about LSD. I had read Aldous Huxley's *The Doors of Perception* when I was eighteen. McCosh's Bookstore carried a few small literary reviews, but not very many. Nobody paid any attention to *The Village Voice* then. When the Dinkytown circle left here, most of them headed west, mainly to Los Angeles. Not many went to New York. Except Bob."

DAVE AND GRETEL

Dylan's Dinkytown circle were dissenters who couldn't accept "The System." Harvey Abrams: "The problem became not just a question of selling out on our student ideals, but a question of who wanted to buy." Among the most committed outsiders were Dave Whitaker and the former Gretel Hoffman, then his wife. By the time I caught up with Dave, he was a San Francisco dropout living hand to mouth. A gentle, somewhat defeated man in his late twenties, Dave seemed prematurely old. Whitaker: "Dylan's association with the Left had been almost totally instinctive. There was nothing in his background that led him toward the Jewish Left. Coincidentally, our university Bohemian circle also included the political Left."

Gretel had sharp memories of Bob: "Between January and March 1960, we used to get together at The Scholar every day. He was living in a horrible green room that had a bed, a chair, a desk, a refrigerator with moldy food in it, some beer. By early 1960, Bob had just about quit school. He was still very bitter about the fraternity house. I was struck by his being just a sweet guy. There was something very gentle about him, something a little bit sad too. He used to say frequently that he would be dead before he was twenty-one. . . . It was clear that he wouldn't do it, that he wasn't suicidal, but he just felt that that was the way his life was mapped out. I was never quite sure who he was or where he was from. He was quite good at telling stories about himself, such as having been a rock 'n' roll singer. Bobby was just a kid learning how to sing. I remember Bob's enjoyment when a group of Israeli musicians showed up at The Scholar. The freedom and ease of it all seemed to make him very happy. He seemed to be open to all sorts of experience.

"The key word in those days that describes Bob," Gretel continued, "was *enthusiasm* about the whole, wonderful world of songs. He was very proficient then, even though still hit or miss technically. He would sit for hours working on new songs, but not until about six months later [autumn 1960] did he really begin to distinguish between what was good and what was new. By a year later the picture of someone just trying things on for size had changed. Minneapolis was a very good place for someone to develop in music. Bob played at The Purple Onion in St. Paul, a Calypso sort of place that was just like every other restaurant in St. Paul. Toward the end of 1960, Bob was maturing, beginning to choose his material with much more care. He used to tell stories about playing piano with Bobby Vee. I really don't think anyone ever believed him and I don't think he believed people didn't believe him."

THE RECORD COLLECTOR

Two aficionados who helped put Minneapolis on the folk map then were
Paul Nelson and Jon Pankake. With strong opinions about style, the pair
started a lively, mimeographed shoestring publication, *Little Sandy Review*.
Cantankerous *Little Sandy* soon made an impression. While not anti-Left,
it put musical values ahead of social values. Sharp personal and critical arguments among Nelson, Pankake, and Dylan continued for years. *Little
Sandy* was the first publication to reveal that Bob had "invented" his new
personality and name.

Paul Nelson, who went on to become an editor of *Sing Out!* and a free-
lance writer-critic, could document his changing perspectives on Dylan's
growth: "In 1959, Bob and Koerner were playing the standard repertoire,
adequate guitarists and singers, but plenty of other kids were as good.
Dylan seemed to learn so incredibly fast. If you didn't see him for two
weeks, he made three years' progress. He heard Jack Elliott first on a Topic
recording from England. Dylan went in two weeks from songs like 'Jerry'
and 'Timber' to interpreting Guthrie. He got all the accents and a lot of
the guitar and harmonica playing. It would have taken a normal singer
two years to accomplish what Dylan did in two weeks! He always seemed
to have an unerring instinct for a great song, like 'Constant Sorrow.' What
impressed us all most was how fast Bob changed. Every few weeks, Bob
would become a different person with a different style."

Jon Pankake: "My first impression of Bob was that he was just beginning, still thinking about all his chord changes. I was not especially interested in Bob as a musician or as a person. Bob was very interested in
learning what he could about music from me. I played a Texas chain-gang
song from an Alan Lomax album for him. He said he was more interested
in learning and hearing directly from people rather than from records. He
didn't seem to want to make records, just to be a big guy on the coffeehouse circuit, attracting girls and attention."

Pankake was away from his flat for a weekend; following campus custom, he left his door unlocked. Returning, he discovered about twenty of
his records missing. "My first suspect was Dylan," Jon told me, "because
he had been expressing interest in my records. Tony Glover said he had
been surprised to see certain records at Bob's, including some English
recordings by Jack Elliott. He took other records—by Elizabeth Cotten [a
black songster], *Mountain Music—Bluegrass Style,* and so on. There was
also some Woody Guthrie stuff. He had very good taste. When I found
out that Bob had them, Tony, Paul, and I burst in on Dylan, unannounced. I got him up against the wall, and slapped him a couple of times
and let him know that I wasn't going to take this lightly. I was a pretty
good actor playing a tough guy. I even had a cigar that I didn't take out of
my teeth. He offered some of them to me immediately, and said he would

bring the rest over the next day. Bob insisted I keep his guitar for security. He told a whole bunch of stone-cold lies about some of the kids dropping the records over there. The next morning, Dylan brought the missing records back and exchanged them for his guitar. I think he apologized, but I am not sure. He didn't come around to see me any more after that. The funny thing is that I didn't feel that there was anything malicious about his stealing the records. I think he believed that he needed them more than I did. But it expressed a certain amount of contempt for me personally, because you don't steal from people you respect."

"I don't think Bob had ever begrudged me what happened," Paul added. "Apparently he was being chased by quite a few people. He had gone through a string of apartments pretty fast. If it hadn't been for that episode, I think Jon would have liked Dylan very much, but it just colored his whole attitude. We figured that about a hundred dollars' worth of records were involved. He had taken the very best of the lot. He had an unerring sense of what to take."

THE TEACHER APPEARS

Dylan also had an unerring sense of what to take when he found his own idol, spiritual father, and musical model in Woody Guthrie. Bob described him later:

> he was the last idol
> because he was the first idol
> I'd ever met
> that taught me
> face t' face
> that men are men
> shatterin' even himself
> as an idol ...
> Woody never made me fear
> and he didn't trample any hopes
> for he just carried a book of Man
> an' gave it t' me t' read awhile
> an' from it I learned my greatest lesson ...[3]

Guthrie was an Okie Walt Whitman, carrying his song of the open road down a modern highway, a farm-boy Carl Sandburg, a genuine hobo/tramp/wandering minstrel with dirt on his hands. When Dylan started to study Guthrie's book of man, he really didn't need more of Dinkytown. Dylan's conversion was a dramatic, explosive turning point, not unlike his later surrender to Jesus.

Dylan swallowed Woody's early autobiography, *Bound for Glory,* as if he had discovered the Bible. An amazing number of people are sure they said:

"Bobby, you've *got* to read Woody." Whitaker was probably the first. Gretel recalls: "After David turned Bob on to *Bound for Glory*, there was an awful lot of talk about Guthrie—what Woody was up to, what he was all about. Bob almost fell in love with Woody Guthrie. When he learned Guthrie was in hospital in New Jersey, he decided he had to go out and see him. Before Bob left, his attitude was 'I gotta get out of here. I gotta go see Woody Guthrie.' "

A few first editions of *Bound for Glory,* published by E. P. Dutton in 1943, were floating around Minneapolis. Bob borrowed Weber's copy. The last two hundred pages hadn't been cut. Bob took the book to The Scholar and proceeded to devour it like that bowl of chicken soup he'd missed. Some say he read the book at one sitting, cutting the pages with a kitchen knife. Few had seen Dylan read *anything* before.

Harvey Abrams: "The book came as a real shock. For the next two years he patterned his life after what he had read. Bob started doing everything the way Guthrie did. For many months thereafter, everything Bob sang sounded like Guthrie. He became very good at singing just like Woody. He would sit and listen to a record, then repeat it. It was phenomenal. Even his speech patterns began to change. That Oklahoma twang, which became much more extreme after he left here, came into his voice. That incredibly harsh gravel sound in his voice became more and more a part of him. It really became much more than identification. He *was* the people he identified with, especially Guthrie. I don't know how, but he memorized the whole of Woody's 'Tom Joad' in just one day or two. He could really sing that ballad beautifully. People who didn't know Bob very well were repelled or angered by the change in him, because they thought he was phony or he was making a dollar. Sometimes, we just thought that the Guthrie character and the Dylan character were really very much the same, anyway. We believed Bob was born with this nature, only it had been covered up for eighteen years by living in Hibbing in a fairly bourgeois setup. We really felt that Bob's real self was coming out from underneath."

To a few close friends, Dylan admitted that the change of summer 1960 grew out of a genuine need for a new identity: He simply wasn't pleased with his former bland, directionless self. Gretel: "He was very open about it. He explained that he was building a character." Tony Glover added: "He said it was an act, but only for about two days. He said: 'After that, it was me.' " Bob wanted to contact the ailing Woody, dying of an inherited disease, Huntington's chorea, at Greystone Hospital in New Jersey. Morton: "There were a lot of drinking parties at Whitaker's that fall. Bob would get drunk and call Guthrie on the phone. Some of us would get on the phone to say hello. Bob told Guthrie that he was coming out to see him." Inevitably, there was teasing, and once a cruel practical joke. Someone in Dinkytown phoned Dylan to say Woody had just showed up at a party. Dylan ran over, panting, flushed, and asked: "Where's Woody? Where is he?"

Who was this "hero with a thousand faces"? Woody Guthrie was the archetypal American troubadour, a singer, tale-teller, poet, prophet-singer, roustabout, organizer, union man, traveler, journalist, peach-picker, hitch-hiker, rambler, migrant worker, refugee. He was a footloose rebel, a very early dropout. He became the voice of the disinherited Okies and Arkies, blown off their land by the droughts and dust storms of the 1930s. He was the bard of the Depression, a walking, singing, cussing, drinking, father of the beats of the 1950s, the hippies of the 1960s, and some of the political activists of the 1970s. Woody was compounded of equal parts of Whit-man, Sandburg, Will Rogers, and Jimmie Rodgers. Whatever influences and traditions he embodied, Guthrie was his own man, an uncompromis-ing individualist who may have used his art to serve himself, but who also served music and literature and his own people.

The Guthrie of *Bound for Glory* and on recordings was still a young, healthy man. Woody was really too short to be a giant, too lean and deli-cate-faced to pose for heroic statues, too ungrammatical to be a poet. His voice was too flat and shaky to be a great singer. Yet, he was all of those things: a giant humanist, a heroic American culture figure, a major poet, still largely undiscovered, and a singer and composer of some of our great-est songs. Woody symbolized the strongest fibers in American folk cul-ture—empathy with the downtrodden, dislike for sham, joy in music, the independence of a man who can't be bought, and a sense of justice that forced him to speak up or sing out when he saw people being pushed around. This wispy hobo and self-educated ballad-maker sang, like Whit-man, of himself, but his self was a type, a cross section, a multitude.

This romantic model made Dylan think of taking on the whole world. Woody was Dylan's first Tambourine Man. Guthrie provided a way of looking at the world. Most of Guthrie's one thousand or so songs radiate an embracing love of people, the joys of kids' laughter, and the dignity of cooperative work:

"I hate a song that makes you think that you're not any good. I hate a song that makes you think that you are just born to lose. Bound to lose. No good to nobody. No good for nothing. Because you are either too old or too young or too fat or too slim or too ugly or too this or too that. Songs that run you down or songs that poke fun at you on account of your bad luck or your hard traveling. I am out to fight those kinds of songs to my very last breath of air and my last drop of blood. I am out to sing songs that will prove to you that this is your world and that if it has hit you pretty hard and knocked you for a dozen loops, no matter how hard it's run you down and rolled over you, no matter what color, what size you are, how you are built, I am out to sing the songs that make you take pride in yourself and in your work. And the songs I sing are made up for the most part by all sorts of people just about like you. . . ."[4]

Woody hit the road at seventeen, and the road kept hitting him back. He accumulated wives and ex-wives, a host of children, bills, and bad debts. He used to tell his second wife, Marjorie (Arlo's mother), that he was going downstairs for a pack of cigarettes, and three weeks later would drop her a postcard from the West Coast. When Dylan said he was anything but a poet or a folk singer, he was taking a leaf from *Bound for Glory:*

"Guess I'm what you'd call a migrant worker. Guess you had to think up some kind of name for me. I travel, yes, if that's what you mean in your red-tape and your scary offices. . . . You just set and call me off the whole book full of names, but let me be out on my job while you're doing the calling. That a way, we can save time and money and get more work turned out. . . . I travel, Hell, yes, I travel. . . . If I was to stop, you'd have to up and leave your job and start traveling, because there's a hell of a lot of traveling that's got to be done. . . ."[5]

Woodrow Wilson Guthrie was born in 1912 in Okemah, Oklahoma, oil-boom country. A few days after his father, a once-affluent hog rancher and land speculator, had built a six-room house, the place burned down. A little later, Woody's fourteen-year-old sister was burned to death in a kerosene fire explosion. His mother died from the degenerative nerve disease, Huntington's chorea. Then his father died in a fire, perhaps a suicide. Woody was farmed out to foster families. By seventeen, he was off for Galveston and the Gulf of Mexico. He joined the westward migrations of rural Okies, Arkies, and Texans. In California, some fruit ranchers paid these "Dust Bowl refugees" a dollar a ton for picking peaches. Woody was soon singing for them and doing a daily radio show for one dollar a day on Los Angeles's WKVD. Like Steinbeck's Tom Joad, hero of *Grapes of Wrath,* Guthrie was of the uprooted, disenfranchised, impoverished migrants.

Woody was part country, part folk singer. From his mother, he learned old ballads and traditional songs. From the radio, the people on his road, he heard country music. Woody's cousin, Jack Guthrie, was a country singer. Wood's guitar playing, and scores of the songs he adapted with new lyrics, were taken from recordings of the famous Carter family, who reigned over country music from 1927 until World War II. (The "new" Carter family, the late Mother Maybelle and her three daughters, and relations and colleagues of Johnny Cash, rose again to the counry-music pantheon in the late 1960s.)

Two men in Los Angeles stimulated Woody's political education—Will Geer, the actor, and Mike Quin, a poet and columnist for *The People's World,* the West Coast Communist paper. Quin is generally believed to have discovered Guthrie. Just like Dylan, Woody had a way of accumulating friends, acquaintances, influences, helpers, and cooperators. Cisco Houston, the rambling singer and hobo, became Woody's traveling companion. When Woody came east in 1939, he met and traveled with Pete Seeger. Pete, a Harvard dropout, was hell-bent on experience in music and in building unions. In 1940, Woody, twenty-eight, went down to the Library of Congress's Archive of Folk Culture to record his songs and life story for Alan Lomax. (Three hours of these recordings were later issued on Elektra.)

Woody also made commercial recordings, on Victor, then on Decca and Stinson, and finally with folk music entrepreneur Moses Asch on his various labels, mostly Folkways. By the time Woody hit New York, he was the darling of the Left. Twenty years later, Dylan nearly duplicated Woody's embrace by the New York folk-Left.

In 1940, Woody went west to rejoin his first wife and their three children. Seeger, Lee Hays, and the writer Millard Lampell formed the seminal folk group, The Almanac Singers, and Woody joined them in June 1941. The Almanacs maintained an early commune on Tenth Street in Greenwich Village. Pete Seeger: "We got bookings for five dollars here and occasionally ten dollars there, and by working hard just managed to keep body and soul together. On Sunday afternoons, we held open house. Thirty-five cents was charged at the door, and we and friends would sing all afternoon. We called 'em hootenannies."

In 1939, Woody was making a lavish two hundred dollars a week on the *Model Tobacco* radio series. Later, an agent booked The Almanacs into the glamorous Rainbow Room atop Rockefeller Center. In *Bound for Glory,* Woody savors how the group walked out, resisting an attempt to put them in corny hillbilly costumes.

Woody could sniff out the hypocrites in progressive or Leftist circles as well. He disdained the term *folk music* because it might possibly group him with the "silk-stocking balladeers." This Guthrie stance helps explain Dylan's frequent contradictoriness in refusing to call himself a folk or protest singer. Similarly, Dylan's denial that he was a poet echoed Woody's, "I ain't a writer. I want that understood. I'm just a little one-cylinder guitar picker."

Seeger encouraged Woody to start *Bound for Glory.* At Harvard, Pete had known Charles Olson, later a critic and poet. In 1942, Olson asked Woody to write for the little magazine *Common Ground.* Woody did a brilliant essay, "Ear Music." Suggestions poured in that Woody write about himself. He plunged into *Bound for Glory,* published at the height of World War II and rapturously received. After time in the Merchant Marines with Cisco Houston, Woody settled briefly in Coney Island, Brooklyn. In 1942, he married the former Marjorie Mazia Greenblatt. Through the late 1940s, he continued to write a flood of songs and poems, draw, and record. Like Dylan, Woody alternated between periods of intense talk and creativity and periods of silence and reflection. At his fancy publishing party at Amy Vanderbilt's, Woody didn't say a word all evening.

The late Cisco Houston told me in 1959: "Woody is the greatest folk poet we've had. He is like the biblical prophets who sang the news. Woody never cared about material things, except a good car, a fountain pen or typewriter, and a good guitar. Those of us who traveled by the side-door Pullman and the sunburned thumb always wanted cars. Anyone who knew a hard way of life would feel that Woody spoke for them. They identified with him."

Woody wrote at least one thousand songs, from the folk national anthem, "This Land Is Your Land," to the classic farewell, "So Long, It's Been Good to Know You"; from his children's songs, like "Car Car," to national paeans, like "Pastures of Plenty." He wrote very few original melodies, but built on folk and country tunes, remaking the songs completely with his own verses. He loved antihero outlaws who were really just against the evils of society.

By the end of the 1940s, Woody's health began to fail and his great voice and pen were stilled. Beginning in 1954, Huntington's chorea gave him thirteen years of hospital misery. His writings and sketches were collected by the Woody Guthrie Children's Trust Society, set up by Harold Leventhal, his agent, Seeger, and Lou Gordon, another friend. I edited an anthology, published by Macmillan in 1965, called *Born to Win*. Bob Dylan's work finally brought Woody to a large contemporary audience, and the success of Woody's son, Arlo Guthrie, reminded a new generation of what Woody had done. In "People I Owe," from *Born to Win*, Woody tried to pay back the human sources of his art. He felt he was only a reporter, taking down the people's poetry: ". . . I borrowed my life from the works of your life. I have felt your energy in me and seen mine move in you. You may have been taught to call me by the name of a poet, but I am no more of a poet than you are. I am no more of a writer of songs than you are, no better singer."[6]

GIRL OF THE NORTH COUNTRY

When journalists stumbled on Echo Helstrom, they were convinced they'd found Dylan's "Girl of the North Country." A much likelier candidate was Bonny Jean Beecher. Dylan almost said as much: "I fell hard for an actress girl who kneed me in the guts. . . ."[7] In 1966, Bonny was leading a West Coast beat actress's life in Los Angeles. Then, the only person this lost, gentle, self-effacing young woman could have been kneeing in the guts was herself. A delicate-featured blonde, Bonny had pellucid diction without drama-school affectation.

Bonny, to at least *some* degree, inspired Bob to succeed in the East. After he left for New York, he returned several times to Minneapolis. Although his affair with Bonny was over, their friendship was not. Bob kept in touch with other people, like Tony Glover, but Bonny *may* have supplied some of the motive behind Dylan's conquering beyond Dinkytown. Bonny was a sophisticate, from a well-to-do family in Edina, a comfortable Twin Cities suburb. Before she met Bob at a party in early 1960, she was a rebel, as anxious to adventure from her WASP background as Bob was to assimilate into the mainstream. Bonny was worldly; she read the right things, knew the right people.

Bonny often bought records from the shop where Paul Nelson worked. She never thought seriously about using her good voice as a vocalist; she was content to play small university-theater roles. There was instant rapport between Bob and Bonny. Bonny was getting her hands dirty as a short-order cook at an all-night hamburger joint, which suited Bob. If they weren't sandwiching in hamburger meetings, they were going to parties at the Alamo Apartments, known as the Anthill. She was a dedicated encourager, a sympathetic audience for him for a good part of 1960. Bob fell deeply in love, but for her the relationship wasn't as important. They drifted apart. When there was some triumph in New York, he'd call or write her. When I saw Bonny, she was involved with a Village hipster comic-monologuist, Hugh Romney, also known as Wavy Gravy. Romney, Tiny Tim, and Severn Darden made up the cast of Los Angeles's Phantom Theater, with Bonny hovering around as the troupe's spiritual overseer.

A one-time sorority sister of Bonny's was Cynthia Fincher, with whom Bob spent time in late 1960. They were intellectual soulmates. Cynthia was a banjo player and painter, intelligent and articulate. They played shows together at The Purple Onion. Gretel Hoffman was a special friend, before and after her marriage to Whitaker. By the time Bob saw Echo a few times in Minneapolis, she was part of the past. He was moving faster than any of his friends. The passions that long outlasted Dinkytown were his love of performing and of Woody Guthrie.

PROPHET WITH HONOR

One Dinkytown friendship, with Dave (Tony) Glover, outlasted others. In 1963, Bob described Glover as "a friend to everything I am. Dave Glover, who I really love. Dave Glover, who feels and thinks and walks and talks just like I do." Glover helped me reconstruct Dylan's early days in Dinkytown. Glover also saw Bob at Newport, Woodstock, and attended some of his New York recording sessions. Tony was tough and taciturn, yet gentle, cool as a bluesman, and passionate about his music and friends. Glover had chosen the nickname "Tony" to avoid confusion when he sang with Dave Ray as Koerner, Ray and Glover. Morton used to satirize Tony's frequent dark moods by singing "You Are My Sunshine" every time Glover appeared. His dark, laconic, James Dean–like manner made Bob feel Tony could be trusted.

Glover started cautiously, emphasizing that "Bob is not an ordinary kind of human being. There are two people, the cat I know and knew here and the one who's 'on' in public. Both of us were on the edges of the scene here, accepted, but outside because of some need or difference of our own. I guess that's the real basis of our friendship then, a feeling that there was more, something else, somewhere else. He's changed. Now [1966] he's almost an old man in many ways, patiently accepting that life *is* and nothing much can be done about it. I don't know if he's happy or unhappy. Perhaps he just *is*, period."

Glover was partly fascinated, mostly protective, wanting to be sure that Bob would be treated sympathetically. He kept a full file of tapes, events, clippings, and memorabilia. Tony was one of the first to *know* that Bob was going somewhere. He liked Bob as much when he was a prophet without honor in Minneapolis as when he triumphed. Tony met Bob in May 1960, at a party for Gretel. Tony: "I found Bob sitting in a corner with a guitar and we started to talk. He was wearing a crew cut and sneakers. He seemed to be out of place and uncomfortable. Lynn Castner was singing Woody's songs. Some people were not listening to Bob's singing and he got very abusive and said he wouldn't sing anymore. Some people there asked who he thought he was."

Glover, who became a music journalist and novelist, was perhaps the first musician friend who dared to criticize and advise Bob. Bob apparently took it well, but not without debate. For at least two and a half years, Bob maintained a running debate with Glover, Nelson, and Pankake about topical-political songs. By August 1962, when Bob returned to Minneapolis for his third visit, he was beginning to show signs of questioning topical-protest songs. Bob was pleased to put on a little show in 1962 for his Dinkytown friends. Speaking in his most nasal Guthriesque inflection, Bob said:

"I'm gonna sing you a song that isn't done . . . it isn't done at all." (He tunes his guitar.) "Hello. This is Bob Dylan from Paris. This is a song I wrote for CORE. CORE is a white organization for Negro people. I am sick of writing songs for everybody. You might as well get this on your tape-recording machine and you can play it for all your friends at *Little Sandy Review*. I've got a lot of respect for *Little Sandy Review*. . . . Jon Pankake is a bigger man than I am, I will say that. I'm gonna make up a few verses here, but the last verse is the one I wrote the whole song about. I wrote it because this here thing came into my mind. My girl, she's in Europe right now. She sailed on a boat over there. She'll be back September first, and till she's back, I'll never go home. It gets kind of bad sometimes. Sometimes it gets bad, but sometimes it doesn't. This isn't really my style," Dylan said over some chording, "this is the Pete Seeger style. You know, he's Mike Seeger's older brother."

Bob sang "Black Cross," then jumped to part of what became "Tomorrow Is a Long Time." Then he did a talking blues, which asked: "What kind of hippo is a hypocrite?" Next, a song he adapted from a traditional tune, "A Long Time Coming." "Do you like that song? I just sort of made up half the words to it. I wrote that for myself. I figure I've been writing too many songs for other people. I finally got to the point where I said to myself: 'Jesus, Dylan, you ain't written no songs about you,' and I said: 'You've got to get somebody to write a song about you.' Then I said to myself: 'You write songs. I can write songs about me as well as anybody else can.' So, I wrote about ten songs in a week about me." Bob was about to sing "Bob Dylan's Blues," but he suddenly found that he couldn't remember it. Then he sang "Corrina, Corrina" and "Deep Down Blues."

The party soon degenerated with Dylan being pestered for one song after another. He finally left, saying, "Everybody is dumping on me in Minneapolis."

In summer 1962, Bob was already restive about "songs for other people," yet was far from finished with his first "commitment" period. In 1963, the strongly radicalized Dylan paid another visit to Tony Glover, Paul Nelson, and others, and a hot debate raged. Tony recalled: "Paul was saying that Bob 'had to get more of a balance between his traditional style and his individual style.' Bob sang one of his latest songs, like 'Only a Pawn in Their Game,' and tried to show us that it was about what was happening today, even though it wasn't traditional. Paul was arguing that folk music wasn't good just because the cause was good. Dylan was basically agreeing, but he countered that you can't put something down just because a song is *about* something. He was maintaining social things were more important than music."

Dylan virtually supplied a sound track to the debate by singing his new songs, mostly social commentary. Not happy with the reaction, Dylan said: "Folk music has nothing to do with it! It's not music when you walk out on the street. You can play it on your phonograph, but it's not there when you walk out on the street." His voice trembled with impatience and frustration with the friends he had left behind.

As early as 1961, Tony had taped Bob doing R & B–type Chuck Berry songs. Tony often taped Dylan. On Bob's first return to Dinkytown, in May 1961, he was still very much influenced by Guthrie. At a summit meeting of Twin Cities musicians, Tony first heard Bob do an original song, his "Song to Woody." Bob told Tony that Joan Baez wanted to record it. Tony: "I don't know how much effect I had, but I said to Bob: 'Keep it for yourself. You can do a much better job on it than she could.' "

Bob returned to Minneapolis in December 1961, after cutting his first album. Gretel: "The first thing Bob did was show us *The New York Times* clipping. He talked with great velocity. He got out his guitar and said: 'Listen to what I have done. Listen to what's *happened* to me!' But then, when other people came over, he got almost shy. He had suddenly turned into a really good storyteller. He and David would sit and tell stories and elaborate on jokes for hours. He was delightful. I don't know just how much of Lenny Bruce Bob had seen, but Bruce was very much a household name around here. A lot of people here invented Lenny Bruce riffs." The Lenny Bruce influence was probably indirect, by way of Hugh Romney. Romney and Bruce, both disciples of the late Lord Buckley, the satirist-monologuist, had played in Minneapolis at a downtown club, Minor Key, when Dylan was still in town. Both parlayed the late-1950s impudence, black humor, verbal fictions, parables, and tales that would strongly influence Dylan.

In December 1961, "the change was enormous," Gretel said. "He was just beginning to experiment with poetry and to realize that it would be poetry." One younger chum, Bill Golfus: "Everyone was amazed that anyone from Dinkytown had actually made a record. The only person that had an inkling of what was happening was Dave Morton. We were all kids, just playing beatnik."

PROPHET WITHOUT HONOR

Dylan still hadn't gotten his due from many in Minneapolis. In 1966, the big poets on campus, John Berryman and Allen Tate, scarcely took any notice of him. By 1972, Berryman had killed himself, but Tate ignored Dylan until his own death. In May 1964 the student literary magazine, *Ivory Tower,* took cognizance. Roland Flint, an editor of *The Minnesota Review:* "The only things of Dylan I have read were on the record jackets, which included some so-called poems. He is a good popular entertainer. I enjoy his stuff. I like his performances and I enjoy his songs. No, I don't think he is a poet and I don't think he writes poetry. *The Minnesota Review* is not there to publish popular-song lyrics. That's what Dylan writes, and he is good at it. John Berryman would probably agree with me, and might even be more contemptuous. I would really like to see some things of his that you think have literary merit."

In 1961, Harry Weber, who preceded Flint, was, at thirty-three, the youngest editor of *The Minnesota Review.* Weber told me: "I don't think much of the poems on the back of Bob's albums, but his songs are fine poems. If I were still editor, I would have printed 'Tambourine Man' like a shot, printed his '115th Dream' very quickly. I would have printed 'Maggie's Farm' with great happiness, with all the repeats. Flint was a protégé and friend of Allen Tate. Tate made a special point of putting down Dylan as a poet, but I simply disagree with them. 'Hard Rain' is very much a young man's poem, but I would say that 'Rolling Stone' is a very good poem."

If most of the Minneapolis literary people dismissed Dylan as a serious writer, local journalists were even more hostile. P. M. Clepper of *The* (St. Paul) *Pioneer Press* made himself a specialist in Dylan history. In 1965, Clepper did a sour piece, which appeared in *This Week,* the Sunday supplement, on March 27, 1966:

> Dylan is a millionaire beatnik . . . piling in money like Irving Berlin. Dylan is not a hillbilly, nor ill-educated . . . he made himself up. . . . Dylan, in fact, has never in his 24 years had to go to work, not even as a minor. . . . Hibbing gave him no experience with racial class oppression that he could later exploit in songs. . . . Dylan had no Negro friends in Minnesota, so it came as a surprise when he showed up in the heart of the March on Washington in August, 1963. But there was obviously a

hunger for such sentiments out there in the great young land. . . . It was an irony . . . that Dylan was being paid fantastically well by the very society he castigated.

Another who wrote sardonically about Bob was Walter Eldot of *The Duluth News-Tribune*. Eldot told me that a lot of strange characters have come off the Iron Range, like Dylan and Gus Hall, the Communist leader. Eldot cited as prime evidence of Dylan's distortions his song "Walls of Red Wing," about the state training school for young delinquents. "There are *no* walls there," the Duluth arts specialist revealed.

Little Sandy Review revealed Dylan's Minneapolis background in late autumn 1962. Nelson did a highly complimentary analysis of the first Dylan album, but Pankake tempered his praise in an unsigned review:

> We recall Bob as a soft-spoken, rather unprepossessing youngster; he . . . was well-groomed and neat in the standard campus costume of slacks, sweater, white oxford sneakers, poplin raincoat, and dark glasses, and sang the standard coffeehouse songs . . . in a skilful, but not noteworthy manner. . . . Dylan left the university . . . that autumn, hitting the road for New Jersey and a fateful rendezvous with Woody Guthrie. That was the last we saw of Bob until May of 1961, when he returned for a brief but extremely telling appearance at a university hootenanny. The change in Bob was, to say the least, incredible. . . . Dylan's performance . . . of a selection of Guthrie and Gary Davis songs was hectic and shaky, but it contained all the elements of the now-perfected performing style that has made him the most original newcomer to folk music. Yes, folks, a star was born that night. . . .

Little Sandy admonished Dylan to "steer clear of the protesty people," and demolished the *Sing Out!* story on Dylan: "Dylan's quotes and his Guthriesque pose on the cover seemed to us to be quite ridiculous; both seemed phony, all-too-hard tries to be Woody himself. . . ." Bob first read this in my New York apartment. Rather than focusing on either the praise for his work or the revelation about his name change, he seemed most upset about the description of how he dressed and looked in his freshman year. "I *never* combed my hair, I *never* wore a tie," he told me emphatically.

Bad press in the Twin Cities continued through 1965. After a one-night stand in summer 1965, at the eight-thousand-seat Minneapolis Auditorium, the amusements columnist of *The St. Paul Evening Dispatch* pounced on Dylan for his "reprehensible" conduct:

> . . . He refused contact with anyone, horsed around during his show and generally left a sour taste in his wake. . . . Dylan is either very bitter or extremely conceited . . . he said: "Why should I see these people [in-

cluding members of his own family living in the area]? They had no time for me when I was nothing. Why should I see them now?" . . . When the audience finally started to whistle between the long-delayed selections, Dylan said: "I'm just as anxious to go home as you are. Don't you have any newspapers to read?" Headlines the next day read: "Bob Dylan, Go Home!" and "The Fall of an Idol." The show had been a sellout, but since the performance (or lack of one), sales of The Great One's records have nose-dived.

Dylan again filled the auditorium on November 5, 1965, grossing a tidy twenty-six thousand dollars for the evening. *The Minneapolis Star Tribune* reviewer said: "The real show was in the audience. Gum-chewing teenagers in costumes straight out of circus sideshows sat hypnotized. . . . Dylan looks like a scarecrow with ratted hair. . . . 'Desolation Road' [*sic*] showed real signs of humor and insight and it was the high point of the evening to sit and listen to his political barbs go over the heads of his disciples . . . it was not his kind of setting. . . . Nevertheless, the crowd loved it. Let the psychologists explain it."

A writer, who called himself only "Mann," wrote in the underground paper, *Twin City a Go-Go,* that Dylan's return visit "only confirmed his popularity and incomprehensibility." Ed Freeman was quoted in the *Go-Go:* "Dylan used to sound like a lung cancer victim singing Woody Guthrie. Now he sounds like a Rolling Stone singing Immanuel Kant." After this concert, Bob rambled around Dinkytown with associates and a local couple they picked up on the streets. They peeked into The Scholar, a few other bars, and doubled back to McCosh's Bookstore. Bob told how things used to look.

Dylan had left Minneapolis five years earlier, but his actual leave-taking is difficult to document. He had been sharing a flat with Brown and Max Uhler, then moved again into his own bleak little room. Dylan often made Guthriesque exits, setting out to hitchhike, but then someone would see him a few hours later at the bus terminal. Whitaker told me that right after one of those phone calls to Guthrie's hospital, Bob took off. Bob's final lines to Whitaker: "I'm leaving for New York! I'm going to see Woody!" Whitaker: "He just up and left. There was a driving blizzard in Minneapolis, but he set off for Chicago." Jerry Connors, one of the local scene-makers, distinctly recalls sitting in The Scholar at a table adjoining Dylan's and hearing Bob say: "I'm going to New York and I'm going to *be* somebody!" Connors says Bob left that very day. Whether he traveled along Highway 61, as he celebrated in song, doesn't much matter; Highway 61 is as much a metaphor as a highway, for it links Duluth to Minneapolis, then runs right down into blues country at the *right* end of the Mississippi.

Dinkytown chums had some warning that Dylan was going. Landlords and his parents certainly didn't. Abe and Beatty went to look for Bob at

his last known address. In a stark, little-furnished room, they found only a
few scraps of paper. They pulled open bureau drawers and searched empty
closets. He was gone, really gone, this time. They knew then that their son
was beyond their command. Dylan said: "I stood on the highway during a
blizzard snowstorm believing in the mercy of the world and headed east,
didn't have nothing but my guitar and suitcase."

According to a Village street person, Keven Krown, Dylan showed up
in Chicago just before Christmas, 1960. Krown places Dylan in Chicago
for a couple of weeks, while others maintain he spent several days in Madison, Wisconsin, before heading east. Here is Dylan's description of his
leave-taking in "My Life in a Stolen Moment":

That's pretty well my college life
After that I thumbed my way to Galveston, Texas in
*   four days tryin' to find an ol' friend whose*
*   ma met me at the screen door and said he's in*
*   the Army—*
*   By the time the kitchen door closed*
*   I was passin' California—almost in Oregon—*
*   I met a waitress in the woods who picked me up*
*   an' dropped me off in Washington someplace*
I danced my way from the Indian festivals in Gallup, New
*   Mexico*
To the Mardi Gras in New Orleans, Louisiana
With my thumb out, my eyes asleep, my hat turned up
*   an' my head turned on*
I's driftin' an' learnin' new lessons
I was making my own depression
I rode freight trains for kicks
An' got beat up for laughs
Cut grass for quarters
An' sang for dimes
Hitchhiked on 61—51—75—169—37—66—22
Gopher Road—Route 40 an' Howard Johnson Turnpike
Got jailed for suspicion of armed robbery
Got held four hours on a murder rap
Got busted for looking like I do
An' I never done none a them things . . .[8]

3

TALKING GREENWICH VILLAGE BLUES

"Know thyself."

—DELPHIC ORACLE, 6TH CENTURY B.C.

"Dig yuhself."

—DYLAN, A.D. 1961

Dylan arrived in New York in December 1960 on a cold, inhospitable day. He has told of his first attack on New York in several ways. The most entertaining version is in "Talking New York," which he wrote in May 1961 at a truck stop west of New York. It pictured a lonesome highway person lurching into town, struggling until attaining "success" at a dollar a day.

No community better represented personal and artistic freedom than Greenwich Village. Within the Village, no scenes were livelier than off-Broadway theater and the new upsurge of folk music, a revival that was part-circus and part-morality play. The folk boom arrived just as the first thrust of rock 'n' roll had run its course. From 1954 to 1958, rock, rhythm and blues, and rockabilly singers had a heyday, then appeared to lose inspiration and direction. Along with this temporary waning of early rock power came a wave of payola scandals. Many disc jockeys were found to be accepting bribes to play certain recordings. For a few years, folk seemed the pure alternative to tainted rock. Steeped in the traditions of musical dissent, of anticommercialism, or, at least, noncommercialism, folk songs then seemed the sane, musical corrective.

Almost anyone with a few dollars could set up a coffeehouse; almost anyone with a guitar and a few songs could entertain. The music business was jolted by such widespread decentralization of talent and audiences. For a time, the folk movement ran on greased wheels of anti–show-business idealism. More commercially oriented folk singers had to present themselves as idealistic; they had to dress simply and appear indifferent toward money. Some thought they could be idealistic and uncompromising, and still make a good living. "Why not be good *and* commercial?" rhetorically asked the late Lee Hays, an original member of The Weavers. Many others abhorred financial success.

Albert B. Grossman, later Dylan's manager, once remarked ruefully that some "pure" folk singers "act as if money were heroin." Grossman, who denied that there was anything addictive about the acquisition of wealth, did a lot to convince others that they could get rich with integrity. "The American public," Grossman said to me in 1959 at the first Newport Folk Festival, which he and George Wein co-produced, "is like Sleeping Beauty waiting to be kissed awake by the prince of folk music." Grossman was one of the first businessmen not only to kiss Sleeping Beauty but also to climb right into bed with her.

Dylan recaptured those early years of folk togetherness in a prose-poem written for the album jacket of the Peter, Paul and Mary *In the Wind* LP of 1963:

> Snow was piled up the stairs an onto the street
>   that first winter when I laid around New York City
> It was a different street then—
> It was a different village—
> Nobody had nothin—
> There was nothin t get—
> Instead a bein drawn for money you were drawn
>   for other people—
> Everybody used t hang around a heat pipe poundin
>   subterranean coffeehouse called the Gaslight—
> It was at that time buried beneath the middle a
>   MacDougal Street . . .
>
> Everybody that hung out at the Gaslight was close—
> Yuh had t be—
> In order t keep from going insane an in order t
>   survive—
> An it can't be denied—
> It was a hangout—
> But not like the street corner—
> Down there we weren't standin lookin out at the world
>   watchin girls—an findin out how they walk—

We was lookin at each other . . . and findin out about
*   ourselves—*
It is 'f these times that I remember most sadly—
For they're gone—
And they'll not never come again—
It is 'f these times I think about now— . . .
There was not such a thing as an audience—
There was not such a thing as performers—
Everybody did somethin—
An had somethin t say about somethin—
I remember Hugh who wore different kinda
*   clothes then but still shouted an tongue*
*   twisted flowin lines a poetry that anybody who*
*   could be struck by the sounds 'f a rock*
*   hittin a brick wall could understand—*
I remember Luke playin his banjo an singin "East
*   Virginia" with a tone as soft as the snow outside*
*   an "Mr. Garfield" with a bitin touch as hard as the*
*   stovepipe on the inside—*
An Dave singin "House a the Risin Sun" with his
*   back leaned against the bricks an words runnin*
*   out in a lonesome hungry growlin whisper that*
*   any girl with her face hid in the dark could*
*   understand—*
Paul then was a guitar player singer comedian—
But not the funny ha ha kind—
His funnyness could only be defined an described
*   by the word "hip" or "hyp"—*
A combination a Charlie Chaplin Jonathan Winters
*   an Peter Lorre— . . .*
Anyway it was one a these nites when Paul said
"Yuh gotta now hear me an Peter an Mary sing"
Mary's hair was down almost t her waist then—
An Peter's beard was only about half grown—
An the Gaslight stage was smaller
An the song they sung was younger—
But the walls shook
An everybody smiled—
An everybody felt good— . . .
An that's where the beginnin was at—
Inside them walls 'f a subterranean world—
But it's a concrete kind a beginnin'
It's concrete cause it's close—
An it's close cause it's gotta be close—
An that feeling aint t be forgotten—
Yuh carry it with yuh—

It's a feelin that's born an not bought
An it can't be taught—
An by livin with it yuh learn t see and know it
*   in other people*
T sing an speak as one yuh gotta think as one—
An yuh gotta believe as one—
An yuh gotta feel as one—
An Peter an Paul an Mary're now carryin the feelin
*   that was inside them walls up the steps t the*
*   whole outside world—*
The rooster never crowed on MacDougal Street—
There was no dew on the grass an the sun never came
*   shinin over the mountain—*
There was nothin t tell yuh it was mornin cept
*   the pins and needles feelin in yer arms an legs*
*   from stayin up all nite—*
But all 'f us find our way a knowin when it's
*   mornin—*
And once yuh know the feelin it don't change—
It can only grow—
For Peter's grown
An Paul's grown
An Mary's grown
An the times've grown[1]

11 P.M. COWBOY

That was how Dylan saw himself two years after those early months of
1961. By 1966, however, he asked me to amend the story. Then, he was
trying to portray himself as an urban cowboy, hustling and rustling
around Times Square: "I shucked everybody when I came to New York,"
Dylan said. "I played cute. I did not go down to the Village when I first
got to New York. I have a friend . . . he's a junkie now. We came to New
York together. He wrote plays. We hung out on Forty-third Street, and
hustled for two months, and did everything. I got the ride here in December 1960. I came down to the Village in February. But I was here, in New
York, in December. Hustling, with this cat. I'm not scared of people, you
dig? Sometimes we would make one hundred a night, really, from four in
the afternoon until three or four in the morning. We would make one
hundred fifty or two hundred fifty a night between us, and hang around in
bars. Cats would pick us up and chicks would pick us up. And we would
do anything you wanted, as long as it paid. It was very cutthroat. You
gotta shell out a lotta money just to hang around, so we weren't making
anything. We ended up in the Village. And I had the guitar. I didn't have
anyplace to stay, but it was easy for me. People took me in."

Was it a dangerous life around Times Square? "That's where I almost

got killed," Dylan replied, "before I came down to the Village. I didn't
plan to stay in New York. I left, anyway, in the spring, and didn't plan to
come back. I came back because I really missed it. There was no other
place that I really could go to. The first places I played in was on Forty-
fourth and Forty-third Streets, between Broadway and Eighth Avenue, in
any of those bars. I didn't come down to the Village until two months
later. Nobody knew that I had been hustling uptown."

Whatever happened during those two months around Times Square,
Dylan got off the subway in the Village in early February 1961 in a
furiously ambitious mood. He looked much as he did when he left Minneapolis—slight and spare in denim, sheepskin, and suede. Village people
virtually adopted him. He looked so much in need of love and attention
that he brought out the brother, sister, lover, or parent in many he met.
Dylan was already up to his earlobes in folk music, and soon his boots
were deep into beat poetry. Hugh Romney, the poet-comic-fantasist, was
big then on MacDougal Street. Dylan arrived with little beat vocabulary.
Six months later he was talking, japing, digging everything like Romney.
"Dig yuhself" became Dylan's shibboleth as it had been Romney's. The
beat poets were working alongside the folk-guitar pickers. Where the romanticism of Whitman, Sandburg, Guthrie, Kerouac, and Ginsberg left
off, the new romanticism of the city folk singers took over.

In the mid-1950s, the marriage of modern poetry and jazz had a brief
honeymoon in San Francisco. The union of poetry and folk music in
Greenwich Village during 1961–63 held, thanks in part to Dylan. By the
time he wrote the "11 Outlined Epitaphs" for his second album of April
1963, Dylan coupled folk and beat poetry. The epitaph about Guthrie su-
perimposes Dylan's early days in New York on Woody's arrival from the
West. The poem echoes François Villon, "ah where are those forces of yes-
teryear?"[2] and Seeger's "The Bells of Rhymney"—"the underground's
gone deeper/says the old chimney sweeper."[3] By the conclusion, Dylan is
far from echoes, leading his own parade:

> *an' so I step back t' the street*
> *an' then turn further down the road*
> *poundin' on doors . . .*
> *without ghosts by my side*
> *t' betray my childishness*
> *t' leadeth me down false trails*
> *an' maketh me drink from muddy waters*
> *yet it is I*
> *who is poundin' at your door*
> *if it is you inside*[4]

Dylan pounded his way through endless doors on MacDougal Street,
the Commons, the Gaslight, the Café Wha?, and the Folklore Center all
had doors facing MacDougal, a dark, bustling new main drag that made

Dinkytown look provincial. MacDougal Street smelled of romance, art, independence, cappuccino, and sausage sandwiches. Dylan was the sort of hungry immigrant who would walk into a MacDougal sandwich shop and ask for an antihero sandwich. He acquired people with stunning speed. No one seemed to challenge his travel stories or his friendships with obscure black singers like Big Joe Williams or Mance Lipscomb.

Dylan's trademark was a strange little black corduroy hat that he wore everywhere. It was a prop, a badge, and, incidentally, a piece of clothing. With its slightly peaked top, short visor, and cut, it resembled a Dutch boy's cap, or the caps Eastern European immigrants had worn upon entering Ellis Island. Dylan wore his hat onstage and off until well into 1962, when he gave it to singer Dave Van Ronk as a keepsake. Tripler, the elegant Madison Avenue men's shop, later sold a version. Arthur's, the Manhattan discotheque, kept a copy in a glass case, with a sign: YES, WE HAVE THE HAT ON SALE HERE. It inspired at least one song, by Tony Herbert. I asked Bob where and why he got the hat. "I got it someplace. I got it, man, to keep my head warm," he said, grinning.

Among the first to adopt Dylan was a middle-aged couple, Eve and Mac MacKenzie, of East Twenty-eighth Street, near Bellevue Hospital. The MacKenzies were earthy, generous people, who found another son in Bob. On and off for several months, Dylan called their home his. Mac MacKenzie was a hard-drinking, storytelling longshoreman. Bob recalled: "I really feel bad that I have never seen them again. Hey, I'll tell you somebody [else]. Let me put their name on you, right now! Mel and Lillian Bailey. I love those people. Every time I think of them, it hurts, because I never get to see them. Mel is a physician. Lillian, I have no idea. They are two of the loveliest . . . They took me in, and they let me come over to their house, man, and sleep there, when they had nothing but a room. They gave me everything, man. I could never repay them. I've tried, lotta times. Every time I come across the name of someone like that . . ." He grew dark and quiet.

Dylan first performed in the Village at the Commons coffeehouse. He wrote to Tony Glover about this milestone, sending a postcard of Woody Guthrie and rhapsodizing about having met Woody ("The greatest, holiest, Godliest one in the world") and Jack Elliott.

The Commons was a sprawling basement club on the west side of MacDougal, near Minetta Lane. The club has also been known as the Fat Black Pussycat and the Feenjon. When Dylan entered the coffeehouse circuit, an army of folk musicians were struggling for recognition. Folk music was tracking its country boots through Manhattan's night life, from the grimiest Village espresso joint up to midtown's Waldorf-Astoria Hotel. Concert audiences, meanwhile, were paying attention to a moody, sensitive young folk singer named Joan Baez. After her well-staged debut at the 1959 Newport Folk Festival, her recording company, Vanguard, was grooming her for bigger audiences. Joan, Pete Seeger, and The Kingston

Trio were really uptown folk singers then—professionals with recordings, managers, and concert circuits. The Village crew that Dylan joined were unknowns trying to break through. At the Thirdside, a Third Street coffeehouse, "passing the basket" was the only way to get a night's wages.

Some performers were dedicated artists, others simply used folk songs as a show-biz vehicle. At Trude Heller's Versailles, a honey-voiced starlet named Beverly Wright, decked out in gold lamé, told listeners she was "booked to sing folk in Vegas." In the Phase 2, Jimmy Gavin, a clean-shaven actor-singer, had a slick, unfolkish manner. At the Café Wha?, Len Chandler, an articulate and charming black performer, told me he had thrown over his classical background to rediscover his people's music.

On Bleecker Street, a cheerless bistro called the Cock 'n' Bull floundered financially despite such performing talent as Bob Gibson. Later, a former ad huckster and future film producer, Fred Weintraub, converted the club into the successful Bitter End. Guitarist Dick Rosmini remarked, "The coffeehouses are the cruelest school you'll ever see. But, it's a beautiful way to keep working." At the Café Raffio, probably the dingiest in the Village, singer Tom Pasle commented cynically: "I don't *have* to do this for a living. I *could* starve."

The Village Vanguard, under Max Gordon and Herbert Jacoby, had long fostered talent, as did Jacoby's Blue Angel uptown. The Weavers began at the Vanguard in 1948; the club gave Harry Belafonte his major launch. Another night spot dated back to the earliest days of folk's arrival in New York—One Sheridan Square. This basement club, situated where Washington Place and West Fourth Street come together like the legs of a man, had been Café Society Downtown. During World War II, under Barney Josephson, it had been the hangout of folk lovers. Josh White was a regular then. By 1960, Josh White was reappearing in the club, revamped and renamed by Kelsey Marechal and Martin Lorin. Other regulars included Carolyn Hester and a group of Irish folkniks, The Clancy Brothers and Tommy Makem. Since its 1958 opening, the Village Gate, run by Art D'Lugoff and his brother, Dr. Burt D'Lugoff, had been heavily identified with folk music. Among those who had New York debuts there were Leon Bibb, Theodore Bikel, The Limeliters, and Odetta. A more esoteric music setting was Page Three on Seventh Avenue South, a long, narrow room where many lesbians gathered. Page Three provided the chief forum for that curious campy performer, Tiny Tim.

For a time, the hottest scene was in a basement *boîte* called the Café Wha? The manager, Manny Roth, was always offering jobs to young musicians who drifted in. There, one night in early 1961, Dylan took his harmonica onstage to accompany the gifted white blues songwriter and singer, Fred Neil. Neil didn't attain recognition until 1969, when his song "Everybody's Talkin' " was the theme for the film *Midnight Cowboy*. Ironically, with that song Neil beat out his former harmonica player. Dylan told *Rolling Stone* in 1969, " 'There's a movie out now called "Midnight Cowboy." You know the song ... "Lay, Lady, Lay"? Well, I wrote that song for that movie. These producers wanted some music for the movie last summer. I came up with that song. By the time I came up with it, though, it was too late.' "

Dylan has said that any of several MacDougal Street coffeehouses could qualify for the dubious distinction of saying he sounded like a hillbilly. The Commons and the Café Wha? seem the likeliest candidates. (Some collectors maintain that Dylan's first recorded onstage words in New York were at the Wha?: "Just got here from the West. Name's Bob Dylan. I'd like to do a few songs. Can I?") The two folk clubs that gave Dylan his real start in New York were the Gaslight and Gerde's Folk City.

A'FOLK A'CITY

At 11 West Fourth Street, a mile east of MacDougal, just a verse or two between the old Bohemia of the West Village and the merging hippie East Village, stood a dingy six-story brownstone built in 1889, once a spray-gun factory. On the ground floor was a neighborhood saloon. The place was named Gerde's, after its prosperous nineteenth-century owner. Since 1958, the saloon had been run by Mike Porco, a gentle Calabrian with a thin moustache, thick glasses, and a thicker accent. The saloonkeeper and his brother John had emigrated from the impoverished toe of the Italian boot in 1933. Mike had landed in the Village in 1952, and was just about making ends meet at Gerde's. He had experimented a few times with some bongo players and avant-garde jazzman Cecil Taylor.

Late in 1959, two men approached Porco with a proposal that for four years converted the sleepy saloon into a thriving cabaret. Tom Prendergast, a New England businessman, and Israel G. Young, proprietor of the Folklore Center, a music shop, meeting place, and gossip mill at 110 MacDougal, had been looking for somewhere to stage folk music. They agreed to run the show at Gerde's for a cut of the admissions. Tom and Izzy decided to call the club the Fifth Peg, after the drone device on a folk banjo. In January 1960, they opened the club as "New York's center of folk music." For several months after the opening bill of Ed McCurdy and Molly Scott, ballad singers and instrumentalists trouped to the cramped stage. Musicians and fans congregated, but Izzy Young, an astigmatic visionary, didn't seem to know how to sell at a profit. He kept journals of folk minutiae and loved his role of Village mentor to young folk enthusiasts. Izzy's and Prendergast's inexperience as producers forced them to quit the Fifth Peg after three months. They had brought in quality performers, such as The Clancys, The Tarriers, Brownie McGee, and Sonny Terry, but Young and Prendergast lost money while Mike Porco, who then scarcely knew a ballad from a bologna sausage, raked in profits on drinks.

In February 1960, Mike inaugurated what he called "amateur night" at the Fifth Peg. Each Monday, eager young performers put on a free show to a packed house. I suggested Mike call the amateur free-for-all "hootenanny." After Prendergast and Young pulled out, Porco assumed management and renamed the club Gerde's Folk City. As his talent coordinator, he hired Charlie Rothschild, a young manager, later associated with Grossman. After a distinguished start with the late Cisco Houston and the Reverend Gary Davis, a famous blind "holy blues" man, Gerde's continued a policy of booking serious folk talent.

Izzy Young never recovered from his Fifth Peg defeat. One day Charlie Rothschild dropped into the Folklore Center for a chat. Without warning, Izzy punched him in the face. Despite tiffs and acrimony, Folk City prospered. Though musicians earned only union scale, they pushed to perform there. Rothschild left after a clash with Porco, and soon Mike was hiring talent himself, polling customers to determine their likes.

Mike used his "hoots" as public auditions, often listening not to the music, only to the applause. One female folk singer auditioned while Mike was cutting sandwiches in the kitchen. "You didn't even hear me sing," the woman complained. "I heard the clapping," Mike said. "We can put you in for a couple of weeks." Not the least of Porco's charms was the fact that he never mastered English. He called his new club "A'Folk A'City," and once telephoned an ad to *The Village Voice* that ran for two weeks billing Anita Sheer as a "flamingo singer" rather than a "flamenco singer." Another performer, who sang in several languages, was advertised as "a linguistical folk singer."

If Mike always watered down his English, occasionally his whiskey, and frequently his payments to musicians, he was usually receptive to new talent. "Give them a chance" was his working motto, while "the newer the cheaper" was his fiscal policy. When, in March 1961, one of his regular customers, Mel Bailey, urged Mike to give Bobby Dylan a chance, Mike showed interest. He liked Bobby, but was afraid he was too young. A Dylan "concert" for the NYU folk club on April 5 made a persuasive "credit." Mel and his wife, Lillian, a dress designer, kept up their campaign, joined by the MacKenzies. If Mike booked Bobby, Eve MacKenzie promised to telephone everyone she knew in order to whip up business. Finally, Mike had a two-week opening for Bob beginning April 11 on a bill with John Lee Hooker, a Mississippi bluesman who had been working in Detroit for years. It was Dylan's first real job in New York, and he was ecstatic.

"When Bobby came in to work the first time," Mike told me years later, "I didn't know if he had enough clothes. I got some of my children's old clothes and I gave them to this woman Camilla [Adams], because I knew she was very fond of Bobby, like a mother. I think he wanted the image then of the dungarees, but my kids didn't have any, so I think Camilla gave those dungarees to Bobby. Then I took him to the union [American Federation of Musicians, Local 802] because he had to join to play. The union secretary, Max Aarons, gave Bobby an application, and I put up the money for his initiation. Max said to Bobby: 'Mike tells me a whole lotta things about you. He told me he wants to put you in the union and thinks that you are going to be a star. What do you think?' So Bob says: 'Well, I'll try my best.' So Max says, with a smile: 'Well, if I do put you in the union and you become a star, what'll you do for me?' Bob said: 'Well, if I ever get there, I will do anything that it is possible for me to do.' Now, Max is president of the union," said Mike as if Dylan had actually helped.

Mike continued: "They asked how old he was and at the time he was only nineteen, I think. The union man says if you are not twenty-one you should bring your father in to sign the papers. Bob said his father and mother were not around. So the union man looks at me and asks: 'Well, what are we going to do?' I understood that his mother and father were in a different state, and also I had the feeling that he had run away. So I signed the papers as Bobby's guardian, the first contract he had. Bobby held on to that book with the membership like it was the Bible. On the way out, I said to him: Bobby, now you have to go for the cabaret permit. He had to have some pictures taken. We went into one of those Sixth Avenue subway photo machines. His hair was kinda messy, so I asked him if he wanted to comb his hair. Bob said: 'I don't ever comb it.' So, I gave him my comb, but he looked in the mirror and hesitated. He thought he would look better with more messy hair."

Dylan had a theory then: "The more hair you have outside your head, the less there is cluttering up the inside of your head. Crew cuts are bad, with all that hair cluttering around your brain. I let my hair grow long so's I can be wise and free to think." "I think," Mike continued, "that even then he was thinking about his image. He combed it a little bit, anyhow, for the picture, and I gave him two dollars to get the cabaret card. He came back to the place and he was as happy as if he had won the sweepstakes. 'Mike,' he said, 'I've got the card!' Was he happy! He was a good-natured kid. This is the place they all started, here. Peter Yarrow once told me: 'Mike, this is the luck place.' The people who started at my place went on to make a fortune—Bobby, Peter, Paul and Mary, José Feliciano, Simon and Garfunkel. I wish I would make one tenth of what they make."

Mike said he paid Bobby a little more than the union scale of ninety dollars a week. Plus the old clothes, sandwiches, drinks. Bob thought only about having his name on a New York bill with John Lee Hooker, one of the great bluesmen. His elation soon soured as he sang for apathetic or noisy drunks and heard the carping of jealous musicians. But his coterie of friends and fans kept growing.

Bob sensed how much more he had to learn about performing, how much harder he would have to develop his songs. Not a single recording official surfaced. He was stung that I, then *The New York Times* reviewer, had been so busy listening to Hooker and interviewing him that I never heard his own sets.

After he finished at Gerde's, Bob tried to get recorded. "I went up to Folkways," Dylan later reported. "I says: 'Howdy. I've written some songs.' They wouldn't even look at them. I had always heard that Folkways was a good place. Irwin Silber didn't even talk to me and I never got to see Moe Asch. They just about said 'Go.' And I had heard that *Sing Out!* was supposed to be helpful and friendly, bighearted and charitable. I thought it was the place. It must have been the wrong place, even though *Sing Out!* was written on the door."

Dylan couldn't understand why he seemed to interest only a handful. After another stop to see Guthrie, and a visit to a folk festival in Branford, Connecticut, in May, he visited Minnesota. Before he left, one other New York job added to his temporary despair. A young promoter who had met Bob in Chicago got him a curious job at a hotel on lower Fifth Avenue, playing for a Kiwanis Club. As Dylan described the gig later, it was Desolation Row Take 115: "A lot of different acts were on that night—dressed like clowns—when someone sang the clowns would perform. The clowns were paid, but not the performers. I couldn't even hear myself. A clown rolled up to pinch my cheek. I kicked him in the nuts and no one saw me—the rest of the clowns left me alone then."

The trip west to Dinkytown and Madison, Wisconsin, was decisive. Bob realized that New York was still the hurdle that had to be jumped. Upon his return in June, he began six months of his most intensive work, most purposeful accumulation of contacts. The latter half of 1961 changed Dylan from a provincial folknik into a music professional.

"HE WAS A FRIEND OF MINE"

For most of the summer of 1961, Dylan was all around the Village, impatient to be seen, to impress important people, to learn. He moved through New York and Boston folk circles like a sponge, sopping up everything he heard and saw, spying for his ambitious master plan.

While Folk City didn't immediately lead to jobs or a recording contract, he could more easily step onto Village stages to accompany featured singers. He became a sought-after backing harmonica player and guitarist. In mid-1961, he was a fixture at the Folk City hoots, developing amusing stage tricks. One hoot regular was Brother John Sellers, a gospel and blues singer who could always whip up an audience with his exuberant shouting and tambourine banging. Brother John clucked like a mother hen over newly hatched folk performers around him, lavishing praise on his accompanists with a star's beneficence. At a typical hoot, he would hammer out a lively number, like "Big Boat Up the River," and two musicians in dungarees, Mark Spoelstra and Dylan, backed him up with guitars and harmonicas. Brother John and The Dungarees were often the event of the evening. People got excited by the Spoelstra and Dylan sound. Bob used to jiggle up and down from the stage to the bar, then, laughing and scratching, cadge a rum and Coke from Mike. When other performers did guest sets, they'd get Bob behind them. Not many musicians played mouth harp then.

The two musicians who most attracted Bob were Dave Van Ronk and Jack Elliott, arguably the best Village folk singers. Elliott was the living, breathing reincarnation of Woody, a citybilly of whom Guthrie once remarked: "Jack Elliott sounds more like me than I do." Van Ronk was a white urban intellectual who masterfully interpreted black songs and blues. Their impact on Dylan was enormous.

Dave Van Ronk was the musical mayor of MacDougal Street, a tall, garrulous, hairy man of three-quarters, or, more accurately, three-fifths Irish descent. Topped by light-brownish hair and a leonine beard, which he smoothed down several times a minute, he resembled an unmade bed strewn with books, record jackets, pipes, empty whiskey bottles, lines from obscure poets, finger picks, and broken guitar strings. He was Bob's first New York guru. Van Ronk was a walking museum of the blues. Through an early interest in jazz he had gravitated toward black music—its jazz pole, its jug-band and ragtime center, its blues bedrock.

Van Ronk was born in Brooklyn in 1936. He dropped out of high school at fifteen. In 1949, he sang in a barbershop quartet, escaped unshaven, did jazz and scat singing, and became a professional performer around 1956. His manner was gruff and testy, disguising a warm, sensitive core. He sang in a plaintive, gravel voice that helped translate often unintelligible black blues for white city audiences. (Rolfe Cahn and artist Ric Von Schmidt in Boston, and Alexis Korner in London were also bringing folk blues to white sophisticates.) Presley had done the same years before, on a splashy, extroverted level. Van Ronk retold the blues intimately. Presley won the world, while Van Ronk (and John Hammond, Jr., Von Schmidt, Cahn, and Korner) won over only coteries. For a time, the most dedicated follower was Dylan.

Later, Dylan outgrew the friendship with Dave and his wife, Terri Thal, but still returned to see them. At times Van Ronk was cynical, because Dylan had taken so much of what he had taught him and made a fortune with it. But he was more often philosophical: "The part of Dylan that was the sponge could function on all eight cylinders. He gets what he can and then discards it. This is why Terri and I are not Bob's best friends anymore. He got whatever he could absorb here, and he moved on. He did the same thing with Joanie [Baez], but there was an element of professional opportunism there too. People from the early 1960s are very bitter about him. Although Bobby did treat most of them rather cavalierly, their reactions are largely their own fault," Dave said. "They just wanted to bask in the light of an obvious talent, to reflect a little glory on them. 'I gave him five bucks when he needed five bucks. . . . I fed him when he was hungry, and the least I expect is to see him now and then and to tell everyone that he still loves me.' Dylan just doesn't give a damn."

Van Ronk was less jarred than most watching Dylan catapult to fame. The Van Ronks had their own lives. Dylan could be relatively free with them. Dave and Terri spent a lot of time with Bob when they lived on Fifteenth Street and after their move to Waverly Place, across the street from me. Terri became his first business manager, arranging most of his bookings for about eight months. "Do you know he is a very good chess player?" Van Ronk asked me. "You know how nervous Dylan is. His knees bounce up against the table so much you think you are at a séance. The pieces keep jumping around the board. But he beats me every time. I agree that Dylan's way of secreting so much makes you want to find out more. But I am quite sure that he is secretive for personal, not commercial, reasons. I think it's because he is neurotic. We would spend hours with him and still find it difficult to communicate with him. For some reason, he has a very, very short attention span."

Van Ronk coined the saying "The folk community is acting toward Dylan like a Jewish mother" when Dylan became a star. Did he miss seeing Dylan? "Not terribly much. When I see him, it's always a pleasure. I listen to his stuff every now and then. The best of Dylan isn't in the drawing room, it's on the stage." Did he think Dylan had a right to use music as a vehicle for personal hostility? "Read *The Divine Comedy*," Dave suggested. "I think," he went on, "that 'Positively Fourth Street' is a great song. It was high time Bobby turned around and said something to Irwin Silber and all those Jewish mothers. It's Dylan's farewell address."

On topical songs, Dave continued: "He was always a very good barometer, very sensitive to mood. But when it comes to analyzing the content of moods, he simply never had the patience. He doesn't care." How can so intellectual a writer as Dylan be so anti-intellectual? "Bobby is very much a product of the beat generation," Van Ronk replied. "Dylan really does belong in a rack with Kerouac. You are not going to see any more like him. Bobby came into beat poetry just at the very tail end. He towers above all of them, except perhaps Ginsberg. But Bob was a latecomer and will have no successors, just as his namesake had no successors."

Did Dylan ever say he admired Dylan Thomas? "He assiduously avoided it," replied Dave. "I think the reasons are obvious. I did come on to Bob about François Villon. I also told him about Rimbaud and Apollinaire. I once asked Bobby: 'Have you ever heard about Rimbaud?' He said: 'Who?' I repeated: 'Rimbaud—R-I-M-B-A-U-D. He's a French poet. You really ought to read him,' I said. Bobby kind of twitched a little; he seemed to be thinking about it. He just said: 'Yeah, yeah.' I raised Rimbaud with him a couple of times after than. Much later, I was up at his place. I always look at people's books. On his shelf I discovered a book of translations of French symbolist poets that had obviously been thumbed through over a period of years! I think he probably knew Rimbaud backward and forward before I even mentioned him. I didn't mention Rimbaud to him again until I heard his 'A Hard Rain's A-Gonna Fall,' his first symbolist venture. I said to Bob: 'You know, that song of yours is heavy in symbolism, don't you?' He said: 'Huh?' "

Although a stubbornly individualistic Leftist, Van Ronk didn't sing political-topical material: "I don't think anyone was ever converted with a song. I just can't see one of Phil Ochs's songs keeping a movement moving, keeping a picket line picketing, or boosting morale for strikers or civil rights people. His songs are sort of an act of personal conscience, like burning your draft card, or burning yourself. It doesn't do a damn thing, except disassociate you and your audience from all the evils of the world. I can't be disassociated from the evils of the world." Did he regard protest songs as romantic anarchism? "No. It's populism. There is this social patri- otism running through all of them, but really less in Dylan. It makes me sick, because I'm an internationalist myself. I don't think the American people are any special repository of goodness and duty, nor are they a spe- cial repository of evil. I can't stand songs that pat Negroes on the back. I'd rather hear a song that says: 'Man, if you don't do something, you're going to be no better off than your father was.' "

There were only four songs in Dave's repertoire that Dylan performed regularly: "Dink's Song," "House of the Rising Sun," "Poor Lazarus," and "See That My Grave Is Kept Clean." Bob's debt to Dave was in style, per- ception, and interpretation. Van Ronk could scat, growl, or keen in rural South idioms. Dylan picked up some of Dave's guitar ideas, but a lot more of his special showmanship, the ability to space sound and silences into a whole that compelled attention. Within six months Van Ronk was no longer a guru but a colleague. Dylan had only one lasting idol.

MEETING WOODY

One Sunday, probably in early February 1961, Bob came face to face with Woody Guthrie, then deeply ravaged by Huntington's chorea. Woody had written eloquently in *Born to Win* of the way the illness had affected his mother. By November 1954, Guthrie was writing from Brooklyn State Hospital about his own ailment:

Huntington's Chorea
Means there's no help known
In the science of medicine
For me
And all of you Choreanites like me
Because all of my good nurses
And all of my good medicine men
And all of my good attenders
All look at me and say
By your words or by your looks

Or maybe by your whispers
There's just not no hope
Nor not no treatments known
To cure me of my dizzy [illegible]
Called Chorea
Maybe Jesus can think up a cure of some kind.[5]

By May 1956, Guthrie had been moved to the New Jersey state hospital in Greystone Park for better treatment. His condition deteriorated, but he could still have outings to the Village. On Sunday, July 26, 1959, folk musicians, headed by Ralph Rinzler, John Cohen, and Lionel Kilberg, gathered some two dozen friends and fans to greet Woody at Washington Square Park. Surrounded by young singers, Woody stretched out on a patch of grass and called out for some of his own songs and others he loved. The musicians obliged with "Reuben James" and "John Hardy" and "Pastures of Plenty." Woody indicated how much he enjoyed hearing his own music from young musicians. He was already sick beyond hope.

In summer 1960, folk singers Logan English, The Clancy Brothers and Tommy Makem, Molly Scott, and Martin Lorin held a special day for Woody at One Sheridan Square. On October 23, 1960, when his son Arlo Davy was marking his thirteenth birthday, Woody was brought to a Second Avenue dance studio. I tried to talk to Woody, but could not get through to him. At each outing we could see Woody failing. Soon he could no longer travel into Manhattan. A pair of middle-aged folk enthusiasts, Robert and Sidsel Gleason, who lived in East Orange, not far from Greystone Park, started Sunday gatherings for Woody. At one, Dylan, who frequently stayed with the Gleasons, finally met his first and last idol.

He found that the writer who said he was "bound for glory" was now a suffering shell. Guthrie's hands quivered, his shoulders shook involuntarily, and he spoke only in thin, unintelligible rasps. There was another dying man in the room. Cisco Houston, Guthrie's longtime sidekick, was making his final visit to Woody. For nearly two years Cisco had inoperable cancer, and by early 1961 he had to stop working. He went into the office of his manager, Harold Leventhal, and told him, with a chilling calm: "You're gonna lose a good client. The doctor said I have three to six months to live." Cisco completed final recordings for Vanguard and taped his hobo's autobiography. (About a month after the farewell in East Orange, having just recorded the album *I Ain't Got No Home,* Houston went to his sister's home in California, where he died on April 28 at forty-two.)

Woody sat propped up with pillows on the sofa as Cisco tried to tell him that they had both neared the end of their hard traveling. Jack Elliott tried to keep sadness from overcoming everyone. Dylan held back, the spy looking at those busy dying and those busy being born. As Elliott described it to me:

"Whenever I was around Woody in those days, Bob was there. Funny

. . . Bobby sort of hung back in the shadows, just watching everything, just listening. Bob was shy then, you know. He still is, you know. But, right off, I could see that Bob was very much influenced by everything about Woody. Bob probably felt he could get through more than I could, but I knew Woody so well that we would talk to each other without words. But it was the same with Bob. He told me he had the 'feeling' of talking with Woody that went beyond words. I knew then what he meant. Those were the days, when Bob was sort of commuting between East Orange and various New York sofas." Jack played and sang for Woody, and Bob played a tune or two. He wrote "Song to Woody" right after that first Sunday visit.

Dylan claimed he had met Woody a long time before East Orange. According to a log Izzy Young kept, Bob said he first heard Guthrie's recordings, the *Dust Bowl* album in particular, in South Dakota. "I used to see Woody," Dylan told Izzy on October 23, 1961, "whenever I had enough money. Met him once in California before I was really playing. I think Jack Elliott was with him. [Elliott, who was in Europe from 1955 to 1959, was traveling with Guthrie when Dylan was thirteen.] I was in Carmel, doing nothing. When I wrote 'Song to Woody' in February, I gave Woody the paper I wrote the song on. Woody liked my song." By February 1, 1962, Dylan was putting still another version into Izzy's chronicle: "I've been seeing Woody steady for a year now. I met him when I was thirteen. He likes my songs."

Elliott liked Bob's songs too. Jack was always a little unsure of himself, easily hurt behind his Stetson-topped, Marlboro-country cool, so he studied all the masters, young and old. Elliott spent so much of his youth aping Woody that only in his thirties did he become himself. As anthropologist John Greenway wrote on the Prestige album *Ramblin' Jack Elliott:* "It is a regrettable characteristic of newly successful folk singers to presume too much upon the limits of originality. . . . Jack's own borrowing has been so extensive that he became in himself a representative cross section of American folk song."

The quotation pertains as well to Dylan in his most derivative period. Van Ronk helped Bob explore books and city streets, while Elliott helped Bob explore the country. Elliott smelled of horses, leather, and saddle soap. He was also a link between the 1930s hoboes and the 1950s beats. Jack could translate the cowboy-western-hobo tradition so well for the city listener because he was a city boy himself.

The son of a Jewish physician, Ramblin' Jack Elliott was born Elliott Charles Adnopoz ten years before Dylan on what he described as "a fifteen-thousand-acre ranch in the middle of Flatbush," Brooklyn. At nine he was captured by the West through the singing cowboy films. Somewhere between the Flatbush corral and the West, he decided that a singing cowboy from Brooklyn needed a more American name. He called himself Buck Elliott first, then settled on Jack Elliott. Around 1947, Jack met a dude-ranch cowboy, named Todd Fletcher, who taught him some guitar. When he was about eighteen, Jack met Woody in Coney Island, and for a good five years thereafter, he was Woody's shadow.

Eight years before I met Dylan, I met Elliott when he was trying to study at Adelphi University. In the classroom he was a displaced person. Besides being hung up on horses, Jack was crazy about cars and trucks. A typical entrance for Elliott was a monologue that ran: "I'm sorry I'm late, folks, but my old Mack truck burned out about two miles away. Tried like the devil to get it started, but the plugs are shot and the battery isn't too healthy, and I figured the walk would do me some good anyway. . . ." Jack was as good a yarn spinner as a singer. His pacing, bumbling, and Will Rogers homespun cadences could make almost anything seem funny.

After he had spent from 1955 to 1959 becoming the voice of American folk song in Britain, Jack decided to come home. Izzy Young put him in a concert at the Carnegie Chapter Hall on February 18, 1961. Although Elliott was erratic and often lacked discipline, his singing was gritty, plaintive, and supple. Guthrie songs remained his bedrock. He could sing "The Ballad of Tom Joad" with an immediacy that swirled dust around the coffeehouse. He would do Woody's children's jape, "Car Car," with endless variations. He mulled over phrases as if chewing tobacco. "Here is a song I sung in every bar along Route Forty," Elliott would say while tuning up for the hobo's national anthem, Woody's "Hard Travelin'."

After a decade as Woody's disciple, Jack added blues and Hank Williams songs and was strongly influenced by Jesse Fuller's harmonica style, which had also excited Dylan. Jack virtually made Fuller's "San Francisco Bay Blues" his theme. Like Dylan, Jack played rambler until it was no longer a pose: He had so good an ear for the speech, song, and wit of the American plains that he wasn't a citybilly anymore. At the end of the 1960s, Elliott looked back:

"Although I am reputedly a close friend of Bob's, I never quite felt like I was really in touch with him. He always had something on his mind, even when we were spending a lot of time together. Because I'm very romantic about it, I like to think that I am a close friend of his. When I see him, I'm very thrilled to talk with him, just as if I were one of his fans and as if I had never really met him before.

"I know how sensitive Bobby always was, despite that wall he built around himself. I remember meeting him that day after his first record was out but it wasn't really selling. He had on baggy Levi's and he looked rather down. 'I gotta get out of this folk-song game and paint.'" Elliott mimicked Dylan. "I always get the same constant message out of Dylan. He is always sort of saying: 'Let's all just dig the world as artists. . . . Let's not measure it in pounds or ounces or money. Let's just be artists, huh!'"

Did Jack resent Bob's success? Elliott munched on that awhile. "He had a tremendous energetic drive for success that I've never had. If he was tramping on anyone's toes to get where he was going, he could have tramped on mine, but he didn't. I suppose I could have made it," said Jack. "It doesn't make me jealous, it just makes me hate myself. It's funny, you know, but for a while Bob Dylan was often known as 'the son of Jack Elliott.' Sometimes I would introduce 'Don't Think Twice' or some other song to the crowd: 'Here's a song by my son, Bob Dylan.' I suppose I taught Bobby a few of my songs. Those old VD songs by Woody that nobody wanted the young kids to know, he picked them up from me. But I also remember when Bob sang some of the grooviest hobo songs in the style of Jimmie Rodgers, like 'The Baggage Coach Ahead.' There was some of that sad spirit in Bob's song about Hibbing, you know, 'North Country Blues.' He hummed it to me once in a taxi. I just thought it was about a deserted mining town; I didn't realize till later that it was about Hibbing."

Elliott consoled himself that he could remain his own man. "Bob was always a little more uptight when Albert [Grossman] was around. Mostly, Bob's on guard toward everyone and everything. It was that way from the start. Everything Bob says, he seems to have read over before he says it."

Jack was still proud that Dylan had sat in on mouth harp for Elliott's first recording on Vanguard; playing a touch of harp on the old gospel tune, "Will the Circle Be Unbroken?" Bob used one of his recording pseudonyms, Tedham Porterhouse. One of the ironies of their relationship was that Bob didn't immediately realize that Jack was a citybilly. Around March 1961, Dylan was in the Figaro with musician-publisher Barry Kornfeld and Van Ronk. When they referred to Elliott's being a Jewish cowboy from Brooklyn, Van Ronk said, "Bobby nearly fell off his chair laughing. It seemed to strike him much funnier than it did us, because we always assumed that Jack had been a cowboy. Then, two years before Newsweek revealed Bob's own background, I knew that Bobby too was an actor. He never said anything, he just laughed till I thought he would burst."

Jack also gave Bob a model of the easygoing drifter. While Dylan knew too much slackness wasted time, he also knew that an impression of aimless drifting made people relaxed and communicative. So Bob learned to conceal his ambitions. Elliott had once meandered into a Hollywood parking lot and played his guitar there for James Dean. Dylan, who was wide-eyed at that story, would never have let such a valuable contact rest unexploited. Jack had ached for years to play the film role of Woody. He told Newsweek: "No one else can really do it. I know—I've been playing it for 10 years now." Ironically, the role Elliott had mastered offscreen was offered to Dylan in January 1968, and again in early 1975. Dylan turned it down, and the part went to David Carradine.

The novelist André Gide once remarked of another French writer, Charles Péguy, that "Péguy threw friendships into the fire to keep the oven going." Dylan's fire reached its peak along MacDougal Street. Woody and Cisco were happy to supply some heat, as were Dave and Jack.

The two younger survivors may have been scorched a bit, but they were not unhappy around Dylan's bonfire.

RAMBLIN' AND TUMBLIN'

Van Ronk, Guthrie, and Elliott were only three strong faces from a crowd. By autumn 1961, Dylan knew so many people, you'd think he'd been on the East Coast five years. When the loner turned gregarious he excelled at it, but he turned his sociability on and off. After his first album turned him into something of a public figure, he often showed signs of agoraphobia, walking far out of his way to avoid people along Sixth Avenue.

Having lined up the New York electorate, Dylan attacked the vital precinct of Boston and neighboring Cambridge, the hub of northeastern college life. This was Newport Folk Festival turf, the country where Baez started. Music dominated the less frenetic scene along the Charles River. In June 1961, Dylan got a three-day job at Cambridge's Club 47, and acquired fans and friends. Betsy Siggins, the 47's hard-driving talent coordinator, was the Boston folk clan's den mother, and she readily adopted Dylan. He befriended the bearded, uncommonly warm Eric Von Schmidt. Ric, a commercial artist, was as passionately interested in folk song as were the careerists. He was as smitten with the blues as Van Ronk, nearly as gravelly voiced but considerably less didactic. Another new Boston chum was Jim Kweskin, a bright, rakish singer who later formed his own popular jug band. Kweskin dressed like an 1890s Mississippi riverboat gambler, wore broad-rimmed black hats, and performed with wit and flair. Geno Foreman, a zany motorcycle maverick, was another Bostonian who appealed to Dylan. Carrot-topped Fritz Richmond, whose wit was as outlandish as his music-making, found rapport with Bob.

One Boston couple helped Bob land his first recording contract. Carolyn Hester and her then husband, Richard Fariña, had moved to Boston because they found it less rancorous than New York. I had introduced Fariña to Carolyn at the Village's White Horse Tavern, and after a whirlwind thirteen-day courtship, they married. They got to know each other afterward around Boston, and in Europe and North Africa. Later, when Dylan was involved with Joan Baez, he and Fariña met again after Fariña married Joan's sister, Mimi. Carolyn and Richard loved Bob's harmonica playing. In September, when Carolyn cut her first recording for Columbia, she asked Bob to join her sessions. Because Dylan showed up in the right climate, he won a recording contract.

Dylan returned to New York for more intensive electioneering. He oscillated between the Gaslight, Folk City, the Commons, the Folklore Center, the bar of the Mills Hotel, the Kettle of Fish, and the White Horse. Sometimes he joined me at McGowan's after the Horse closed. He always carved out hours for practicing, listening to records, and writing songs, but mostly he was a street person. His New York friendships multiplied. John Herald, lead singer of the bluegrass group The Greenbriar Boys, nearly inarticulate until his music transformed him into a whopping extrovert, found Bob easy to be with. John Hammond, Jr., a gifted young white blues re-creator, also became a pal. A handsome leather-jacketed boy, Hammond occasionally briefed his producer-father on promising talent.

Len Chandler and Dylan became close around this time. Len was not one bit reticent or repressed. Even when things were tough for him, and they were for years, Len had dash and bravado, and he loved a put-on as much as Dylan did. He and Len walked around a cityful of blocks for many a smoke. If Dylan's first Village cronies could be divided into the self-assured and the shy, the singer Mark Spoelstra fell into the latter group.

I first encountered Dylan at a Monday night hoot at Folk City in June 1961. Because my reaction then to his performing was so strong, I know that I either never saw him at Folk City the previous April, or that I had looked right through him. At the hoot, Bob was doing his musical shaggy-dog story, "Bear Mountain," inspired by routines that Noel (Paul) Stookey, later of Peter, Paul and Mary, was doing at the Gaslight.

Bob looked like a European street singer or tumbler. He bobbed and swayed, played with his black corduroy Huck Finn cap, made faces, winced, and joked his way through the ridiculous narrative. I walked over to Pat Clancy, the Irish folk singer, and said: "Hey, Pat, you have to catch this kid!" Pat turned from his Jameson's whiskey and joined me to watch Bob. "Well, what have we here!" Pat exclaimed, half-curious and half-joyful. When the enthusiastic audience released Bob from the stage, I told him how much I liked his work. He appreciated my appreciation. "Yeah, great! I'm glad you liked it. I've done better sets than that. Glad you liked it," he said. I told him when he had his next job to call me and I'd try to review him in *The Times*. "I sure will, I sure will," he replied. "I think you missed me when I was here last April," Dylan said, and I admitted that I sure did, I sure did.

A week or two later, my phone rang and a thin, nasal voice said: "Hi, I'm Bob Dylan. You said I should call you if I got a job. Well, I got a job. I'm at the Gaslight for a week." Several days later I arrived at the Gaslight to see the regulars listening to Van Ronk and Dylan. At his usual table in the rear was Albert B. Grossman, who appeared to be getting a great deal of satisfaction from a cup of coffee. In the early days, Albert often held court in coffeehouses. He usually smoked a king-size cigarette the way an oil sheik would hold a hookah, making a circle of his thumb and forefinger, slightly crooking his little finger, and blowing the smoke out slowly through his hand. I told Dylan the gig was too short to write up, but I introduced him to Albert, saying I thought this kid was going to be the next sensation. Grossman, as usual, said nothing. After Dylan left our table, Grossman asked what I though of Van Ronk. I was enthusiastic but I predicted that Dylan would go further. Grossman smiled, a Cheshire cat in untouched acres of field mice.

The Gaslight was then owned by a wild-looking Bohemian, John Mitchell, who had fought many legal battles against police and fire authorities who had cracked down on the MacDougal Street coffeehouses. Mitchell found Dylan especially droll. Although Dylan was frequently nostalgic about the Gaslight, he also made fun of his first job there. He once told me the Gaslight was "the Broadway of folk song, where all the stars were—Dave Van Ronk, [banjoist] Billy Faier, [balladeer] Hal Waters." His Gaslight stint ended inconclusively. Grossman said nothing. I hadn't written a word about him. Bob kept working at his music, at his western speech. Sometimes his mangled dialect made words virtually indistinguishable. He started to mumble about "ramblin' and tumblin' with his coat collar turned up high." Soon, a few of us were calling him "the rambler" and "the tumbler."

Dylan rambled and tumbled into his first New York concert appearance and radio broadcast on Saturday, July 29, 1961. The marathon was run by a new FM station, WRVR, operated by The Riverside Church. To inaugurate the station's live-music project, Izzy Young and Bob Yellin mobilized folk musicians. In those days, at a call for folk talent, youngsters like Tom Paxton and Molly Scott, and old-timers like the Reverend Gary Davis and blues singer Victoria Spivey, would rush to perform, even without pay. WRVR's twelve-hour folk parade had enough lapses of broadcasting techniques to gray an FCC commissioner's head. On the hour every hour, eager performers hit their mikes with swinging banjo necks, voices faded in and out, cues were missed. The studio audience was as restless and partisan as a high-school assembly.

There were workshops on the blues, an Eastern Mediterranean segment, and showcases for various banjo styles. No big-name stars, but the show was an impressive display of available folk-song and instrumental talent around town. Midway through the afternoon, a slight musician who sang, looked, and twanged like Woody Guthrie made his way to the microphone. Introduced as hailing from Gallup, New Mexico, Dylan, with his harmonica in a holder improvised from a metal coat hanger, was on for five quick songs, joined on some by Elliott and bluesman Danny Kalb. In *The Times,* I briefly described Dylan's style as a "curiously arresting, mumbling, country-steeped manner." Dylan's little stint stimulated his coterie into enough noise to simulate a crowd.

After he left the stage, he was introduced to a seventeen-year-old, wide-eyed, long-haired beauty named Suze Rotolo, and began two years of an ecstatic, erratic romance. Dylan's reputation was growing as another Jack Elliott or Woody Guthrie, yet recording seemed the only doorway to national recognition. In late summer, a bright pair of Village girls, Sybil Weinberger, who worked in TV production, and Suze's older sister, Carla Rotolo, then personal assistant to Alan Lomax, came up with an idea to help record Dylan and some other unknowns. They suggested a demonstration tape of half a dozen of the best Village folk singers, including Van Ronk and Elliott.

Describing the project and raving about Dylan in particular, Sybil wrote to producer John Hammond at Columbia Records. "Sybil's letter called attention to a whole group that had tremendous talent," Carla recalled. "By putting in people who had some recognition, we thought we might get some recognition for the unrecognized, like Bobby and John Wynn. But the original idea was to get Bobby something." There was no reply: Carla maintains Hammond just let the letter sit on his desk and may not even have read it. She thinks Hammond did not associate the Bobby Dylan in Sybil's letter and the boy he signed weeks later to a five-year Columbia contract.

Because of the urgings of the Dylan coterie in general, Carla in particular, and my interest in reviewing, Mike Porco booked Bob into Folk City again for two weeks: SEPTEMBER 25 THRU OCTOBER 8: GREENBRIAR BOYS, PICKING & SINGING THRU BLUEGRASS WITH THE SENSATIONAL BOB DYLAN. The Greenbriar Boys (Ralph Rinzler, Herald, and Yellin) were city bluegrass wizards. Yellin's banjo lines hopped around like confetti in the wind. Herald's vocal acrobatics keened in old-timey folk songs or in country burlesque, like "We Need a Whole Lot More of Jesus and a Lot Less Rock and Roll." Rinzler's delicate mandolin figures coursed like nervous birds nesting. All three sang and whooped it up with wit and musicianship. They were not an easy act to follow, but Dylan followed superbly.

During those two weeks, he alternated between three costumes, each seedier than the next. One outfit was a faded blue shirt, khaki trousers, a dark sleeveless pullover sweater, an incongruous foulard tie, all topped with his famous hat. Other nights he wore a chamois jacket or a tieless wool shirt. His Gibson guitar had a song-sequence sheet pasted on its upper curve, and his harmonica holder hung around his neck. He looked studiously unkempt and very slight and frail, until he began to sing. His pinched, constricted voice seemed to be fighting its way out of his throat. It was a rusty voice, suggesting Guthrie's old recordings. It was etched in gravel, like Van Ronk's. It sometimes crooned a bit, like Elliott's. Yet it was also a voice quite unlike anyone else's. You didn't think of it as something beautiful or sinuous, but as something that roiled up from the heart. He didn't sound a bit citified, but more like a farmhand folk singer. Most of the audience liked Dylan those two weeks, regarding him as a masterly ethnic singer, but many thought he was just a bad joke.

Bob started a typical set with "I'm Gonna Get You, Sally Gal," in a lively tempo. He set up a three-way conversation between his voice, guitar, and mouth harp. Suddenly you saw how he could share the stage with as brilliant a trio as The Greenbriars. "Here's a song suitable to this occasion," Dylan said, as he retuned his guitar and changed his mouth harp. He sailed into a traditional blues dirge, "This Life Is Killing Me." His technique was everywhere, the covert technique of the folk idiom. It was antipolish, anticonscious of surface form, yet all those elements lay below. He gave the impression that he had started in music yesterday, not five years earlier. But one couldn't be sure.

Between songs, Dylan droned a soliloquy, formless yet very funny. He started to tell a story about a toad. It was an open-ended shaggy-toad story that didn't start anyplace, didn't go anywhere, and didn't end anywhere, but it gave him a bit of fill-in patter while he tuned. His face was pouting and boyish. His slow delivery made him sound half-awake to optimists and half-asleep to pessimists. Next, he growled his way through "a train song," "900 Miles." To punctuate certain guitar breaks, he raised the body of his guitar to the microphone, an old country-music gambit that magnified the stringed sound.

In the background were the usual Folk City distractions. Bartenders clinked and poured as if starring in TV commercials. The cash register rang during soft passages. At the bar a few drunks were gabbing while others tried to silence them. Dylan was all concentration. "Here's a song outa my own head," he said, tuning his guitar for "Talking New York," a very old style of talking blues, in which three sparse chords support wry lyrics more spoken than sung. Dylan delivered his first protest song with a comic's timing.

Bob turned to other songs out of other people's heads. He moaned his way through "Dink's Song," long favored by Josh White and Cynthia Gooding; Dylan said he had picked it up on the Brazos River when he was down in Texas. Actually, the ballad hunter John A. Lomax had heard it in 1904 from a gin-drinking black woman who sang it as she wearily scrubbed her man's laundry. It is one of the most pathetic women's laments in American folk song. Bob did a variation on Van Ronk, with vamping guitar figures keeping the underlying pattern moving. At times his voice sounded like gravel being shoveled, at other times like a sob. He caught the original's tension, grit, and plaintiveness. "I was never a motherless child," folk singer Ed McCurdy used to say, "but I know what it feels like." Dylan was never a black laundress, but he knew what it felt like. Occasionally, Dylan threw his head back full as if he were scanning the ceiling for his next words.

From Texas, the twenty-year-old world traveler took his audience to a famous Chicago bar, Muddy Water's Place, where he said he had picked up another blues song. He shuffled to the junk-heap upright piano and played primitive chords. Then he hit Woody's road again, with "Hard Travelin'," a lurching, careening road song, sticky with hot asphalt, aching with calloused feet. Then he did another couple of songs out of his own head, including "Bear Mountain" and "Talkin' Hava Negilah Blues," his little jape of international "stylists" like Harry Belafonte and Theo Bikel.

The audience responded more to Dylan's wit than to his slow, serious, intense material. Audience reaction led him to play Chaplinesque clown. He closed with his own "Song to Woody," suspensefully built to keep attention focused on each new line.

After his set, we went back to the Folk City kitchen for his first press interview. The answers came fast, but I had a feeling that he was improvising and concealing. It went like this: "I'm twenty years old, don't turn twenty-one until May. I've been singing all my life, since I was ten. I was born in Duluth, Minnesota, or maybe it was Superior, Wisconsin, right across the line. I started traveling with a carnival at the age of thirteen. I did odd jobs and sang with the carnival. I cleaned up ponies and ran steam shovels, in Minnesota, North Dakota, and then on south. I graduated from high school. For a while, Sioux Falls, South Dakota, was a home, and so was Gallup, New Mexico. I also lived in Fargo, North Dakota, and in a place called Hibbing, Minnesota. I went to the University of Minnesota for about eight months, but I didn't like it too much. I used to play piano with Bobby Vee and The Shadows, a country rockabilly band. I came east in February 1961, and it's just as hard as any town I've seen."

When he sang "Poor Girl," he had pulled out a kitchen table knife and used the back of the blade to fret his guitar. Where did he learn that old blues bottleneck guitar? "I learned to use a butcher knife," Bob replied, "from an old guy named Wigglefoot in Gallup, New Mexico. He was a beaten-down old bluesman who wore a patch on his eye. I do a lot of material I learned from Mance Lipscomb, but not in public. Mance was a big influence. I met him in Navasota, Texas, five years ago. I've been a farmhand too. I learned 'House of the Rising Sun' from Dave Van Ronk and 'See That My Grave Is Kept Clean' from Blind Lemon Jefferson. I like the recordings of Rabbit Brown a lot too.

"Jack Elliott and Dave Van Ronk are the two best folk singers in New York. I can only sing one way . . . in the way I like to hear it. I don't have a pretty voice. I can't sing pretty, and I don't want to sing pretty." Bob dropped the names of a lot of admired musicians, a mélange of those he had heard on recordings only and those he said he'd met and worked with. He appeared to have known them all. "Yes, I like Ray Charles very much. I picked up the harmonica after hearing Walter Jacobs—you know, Little Walter—of the Muddy Waters band. But I play my own style of harmonica. I played piano for dancers in the carnival."

Had he made any recordings? "The recordings I've made haven't been released. I played with Gene Vincent in Nashville, but I don't know if they have been released. . . . As to that bottleneck guitar, when I played a coffeehouse in Detroit I used a switchblade knife to get that sound. But when I pulled out the switchblade, six people in the audience walked out. They looked afraid. Now, I just use a kitchen knife so no one will walk out." Any other musical influences? "A lot, quite a lot. Woody Guthrie, of course. I have seen quite a lot of Woody since last winter. We can talk, even though he is sick. He likes my songs a lot. I met Jesse Fuller two years ago in Denver and studied with him."

Bob went on for another set. I told Carla that it had been a good interview and that I really loved his work and manner. But, I told her, I had the strange feeling he was putting me on. He seemed to have traveled so far and known so many famous and obscure musicians. He was evasive about his past. I told Carla to tell Bob there was a difference between kidding around with a Village guy and talking for publication. Minutes after Dylan's set Carla huddled with Bobby, and then we continued the interview at a table in between songs by The Greenbriar Boys.

"Listen," Bob told me, "I'm giving it to you straight. I wouldn't tell you anything that isn't true." Did he want me to call him Bobby Dylan or Bob Dylan? He thought that one out, as if he were about to sign a contract. Half aloud, he repeated the two names to himself: "Bob Dylan, Bobby Dylan, Bob Dylan, Bobby Dylan . . . Make it Bob Dylan! That's what I'm really known as," he declared confidently. I wrote the review, which appeared in *The Times* on Friday, September 29, 1961:

A bright new face in folk music is appearing at Gerde's Folk City. Although only 20 years old, Bob Dylan is one of the most distinctive stylists to play in a Manhattan cabaret in months.

Resembling a cross between a choir boy and a beatnik, Mr. Dylan has a cherubic look and a mop of tousled hair he partly covers with a Huck Finn black corduroy cap. His clothes may need a bit of tailoring, but when he works his guitar, harmonica or piano and composes new songs faster than he can remember them, there is no doubt that he is bursting at the seems with talent. Mr. Dylan's voice is anything but pretty. He is consciously trying to recapture the rude beauty of a Southern field hand musing in melody on his back porch. All the "husk and bark" are left on his notes, and a searing intensity pervades his songs.

Mr. Dylan is both comedian and tragedian. Like a vaudeville actor on the rural circuit, he offers a variety of droll musical monologues. "Talking Bear Mountain" lampoons the overcrowding of an excursion boat. "Talking New York" satirizes his troubles in gaining recognition and "Talkin' Hava Negilah" burlesques the folk-music craze and the singer himself. In his serious vein, Mr. Dylan seems to be performing in a slow-motion film. Elasticized phrases are drawn out until you think they may snap. He rocks his head and body. He closes his eyes in reverie, seems to be groping for a word or a mood, then resolves the tension benevolently by finding the word and the mood. He may mumble the text of "House of the Rising Sun" in a scarcely understandable growl, or sob, or clearly enunciate the poetic poignancy of a Blind Lemon Jefferson blues, "One kind favor I ask of you—See that my grave is kept clean."

Mr. Dylan's highly personalized approach toward folk song is still evolving. He has been sopping up influences like a sponge. At times, the drama he aims at is off-target melodrama and his stylization threatens to topple over as a mannered excess. But if not for every taste, his music-making has the mark of originality and inspiration, all the more noteworthy for his youth. Mr. Dylan is vague about his antecedents and birthplace, but it matters less where he has been than where he is going, and that would seem to be straight up. . . .

This was followed by four laudatory paragraphs about The Greenbriar Boys. As good as they were, Dylan seemed to be the news. By chance, the entertainment section had a canyon at the top of one review page. Across three columns ran the headline: BOB DYLAN: A DISTINCTIVE STYLIST. A rough photo of Dylan with his hat, his tie, and his big guitar got three inches of space. The layout, the picture, and the headline trumpeted Dylan even louder than my story.

Reactions couldn't have varied more. A very few musicians were pleased. Elliott read the notice aloud in his best Dylanesque voice to a few drinkers at the Dugout on Bleecker Street. Van Ronk, cool but gulping hard, told me I had done "a very, very fine thing." Pat Clancy and his brother, Tom, said, "Bobby has a lot of talent. He deserves to go places." Izzy Young said he had discovered Dylan months earlier than anyone. And much of the Village music coterie reacted with jealousy, contempt, and ridicule. Eric Weissberg and Marshall Brickman, two of the ablest instrumentalists about, told me I needed a hearing aid. Logan English, a singer who had suffered inordinate difficulties getting his own career moving, was sarcastic and rueful. To a man, The Greenbriar Boys were hurt that this "kid" had eclipsed them. Bob Yellin didn't talk to me for weeks. Fred Hellerman, a songwriter and arranger, formerly of The Weavers, was openly derisive: "How on earth can you say that he is such a great this-and-that?" he asked me on a street corner. "He can't sing, and he can barely play, and he doesn't know much about music at all. I think you've gone off the deep end!" Manny Greenhill, Baez's kindly manager, said my review was "talking about Bobby in a year or two, not now." Charlie Rothschild said he saw some potential in Dylan "but he's got a long way to go." Most enthusiastic, however, were Carolyn and Richard Fariña. They were delighted because they liked Bob, personally and musically, and because he was scheduled to play on Carolyn's upcoming recording.

Dylan showed up at Folk City that Friday night pale and shaken. There was a very big turnout. As he walked in, patrons turned to each other and said: "There he is! That's the guy!" Bob looked uncertain that he could deliver, now that the order had been placed. He thanked me warmly and began his long years of telling me, "You're a very good writer, not just music, but a very good writer." Through twenty years of reviewing, I can recall no other performer who seemed more concerned about a reviewer's feelings. When he was spinning out of orbit, Dylan lashed out at me for things I wrote, but those moments were exceptions. From the start, he knew that writers are as hungry for applause as musicians.

That fourth night of his gig, Bob had an even more engrossed audience. One stranger at the bar puzzled us. He was fiftyish, moon-faced, well dressed, smiled a great deal, and offered drinks to some of the kids who knew Dylan. Bob passed the word quickly: "Fuzz!" Much later he described the man as one of the many police who "followed" him. "He was a cop," Bob said later. "I told you about that at the time. Why, cops have been following me all my life. Cops haven't been following me much after 1964, but until then they used to come from all over." No one ever found out who the wicked messenger was that night.

Later in the evening, Dylan steered me to a quiet corner and said: "I don't want you to tell anybody about this, but I saw John Hammond, Sr., this afternoon and he offered me a five-year contract with Columbia! But, please, man, keep it quiet because it won't be definite until Monday. I met him at Carolyn's session today. I shook his hand with my right hand and I gave him your review with my left hand. He offered to sign me without even hearing me sing! But don't tell anyone, not one single soul! It could get messed up by someone at the top of Columbia, but I think it is really going to happen. Five years on Columbia! How do you like that?"

Each participant in Dylan's meeting with Hammond told it differently. A synthesis indicates that Hammond acted on instinct and reputation more than any objective proof of Dylan's talent. Yet Hammond had the experience to trust his instincts. Carolyn Hester's first recording for Columbia was a step forward for the attractive young Texan singer, but proved an even bigger break for Dylan, who was just a walk-on with a mouth harp. Carolyn had arrived in New York in the late 1950s with a gorgeous voice and cascading long brown hair. She had first recorded for Coral Records, then for Tradition. Her voice's range and power were astounding. Dylan was also impressed because Carolyn had briefly known and deeply admired Buddy Holly.

At one point, Grossman had considered Carolyn for the trio he eventually named Peter, Paul and Mary. Soon after The Kingston Trio's enormous success in 1959, Grossman set out to form a pop-folk trio that would incorporate aspects of The Kingstons with one cardinal difference, a pretty girl. He openly searched for his "components" for two years. He had briefly considered Molly Scott and Logan English. Next, having long admired Bob Gibson, he thought he would use the former Chicagoan as a keystone. For some months, Grossman worked informally with Gibson, Carolyn, and Ray Boguslav, a commercial artist and highly schooled musician. But this group didn't jell either. Gibson had periodic losses of voice and was befouled with problems. Boguslav was a serious musician, but he wasn't about to chuck his art career unless there were ample guarantees. Carolyn was ready, willing, and able to be the pretty girl. But by March 1960, she began to despair. "I really have grave doubts the trio will work out," she wrote me. "We made some tapes, I wasn't terribly good, but we could do something if we worked at it. Boguslav's range is so much different than mine. We ended up with little semblance of a 'blend' or 'sound.'" The trio also lacked the dedicated toughness Albert ultimately found with Peter, Mary, and Paul.

Dylan's version was simply that he handed Hammond *The Times* review and went around the room doing his harmonica business. By the end of the session, at which Bob had not sung one note, Hammond said that he

had heard a great many good things about Dylan from his son and others
and wanted to sign him to Columbia for a "standard" contract—one LP
album—with options to do four more LPs for the next four years. Dylan
was immediately willing, not even asking contract terms. Fariña generally
substantiated this account, although he told me that he had huddled with
Hammond during the session to say that Dylan was a first-rate singer and
songwriter.

Hammond was one of the great jazz producers, Billie Holiday's discoverer, Benny Goodman's close associate in the 1930s. Hammond had
also been closely identified with Count Basie, Teddy Wilson, Benny Carter
and the kings of boogie-woogie piano, Meade "Lux" Lewis, Albert
Ammons, and Pete Johnson. Hammond was a wealthy Ivy Leaguer whose
devotion to jazz and black musicians was great. "Spirituals to Swing" concerts he organized in 1938 and 1939 at Carnegie Hall were a preview, by
thirty years, of all the elements that would cross-fertilize rock. Big John
Hammond, as he was called, to distinguish him from his son, was a tall
man of almost military dignity, with a long head and a pleasant demeanor.
Hammond's mother was a Vanderbilt and his father was a banker, so he
pursued the jazz he fell in love with at Yale without any great financial
strain, even during the Depression. In 1933, during a fling as a journalist,
Hammond had covered the famous Scottsboro case, in which nine southern blacks were accused of rape, for *The Nation* and later for *The New Republic.* He wrote jazz and blues commentaries in *Downbeat, Metronome,
Melody Maker, The Brooklyn Eagle,* and *The New York Compass.* In the mid-
1930s, he wrote for the left-wing *New Masses,* under his own name and
under the pseudonym of Henry Johnson.

Hammond had discovered the gifted, self-destructive singer Billie Holiday when she was only seventeen. John had gone up to Monette Moore's
speakeasy on West 133rd Street in Harlem to hear Monette, but was more
impressed by Billie, and worked with her, in and out of the studio,
throughout the 1930s.

Hammond has always been uneasy about Dylan's assertion that he offered to sign him without hearing him sing. After nine frustrating months
of being snubbed by the leading folk-music labels—Elektra, Folkways, and
Vanguard Records—Dylan was ironically handed his big chance on a
major label without even an audition! Hammond met him at a rehearsal at
a West Tenth Street apartment that Carolyn and Fariña were borrowing.
Hammond's recollection is fuzzy: "He had on his cap and he had just
come to New York. This was before he opened at Folk City the first time.
I liked what I heard of him there so much, I asked him to come up to the
studio. I didn't know that he did much singing, but I knew that he wrote.
I heard some of the things that he did and I signed him on the spot. He
said he didn't have a manager or parents—he was underage at the time.
We made our first album almost immediately. This was when Bob was
writing three or four songs a day and was unused to mike techniques. His

guitar playing, let us say charitably, was rudimentary, and his harmonica was barely passable, but he had a sound and a point of view and an idea. He was very disenchanted with our social system. I encouraged him to put all his hostility on tape because I figured this was the way, really, to get to the true Bob Dylan.

"So, for about the first eight months I had an absolute ball working with Bob. I had no direction on him at all because I felt Bob was a poet, somebody who could communicate with his generation. Now, Columbia was not known for doing that at the time. I thought the less a record producer interferes, the better results we'd get from Bob. I remember the first album cost something like four-hundred-and-two dollars because he was the only guy on it, no arranging costs, no musicians to pay. While he was doing his second album for us, he came up to me and asked me about Albert Grossman, who wanted to sign him. I said we'd been on the board of the Newport Festival together and I thought I could work with him. I found out later I couldn't."

Hammond was equally fuzzy about his son's role in Dylan's discovery: "My son knew Dylan before he came to New York. My son, who was playing in some coffeehouse in Minneapolis, told me right after I signed Dylan in sixty-one: 'Dad, I've just been out in Minneapolis. Did you know that Bobby's real name is Zimmerman and that he went to the University of Minnesota?' And I said: 'No, that's news to me.' But, I said, 'It doesn't matter, that's his business.' "

Carolyn's record (*Carolyn Hester,* Columbia CL 1796: stereo CS 8590, now out of print) is a pleasant folk album, made as Columbia was beginning to take the folk boom seriously. Dylan can be heard on three tracks. On "I'll Fly Away," a bright, spiritual-like song, his mouth harp comes on strongly staccato and rhythmic, takes a brief break, alternately lyrical and scuffling, and ends with a bluesy little swallowing riff. On "Swing and Turn Jubilee," Carolyn sings with square-dance hoedown joy. Bruce Langhorne, who could play florid Spanish guitar lacings one minute and barnyard fiddle the next, gives the song its dancing propulsion. Dylan's mouth harp blows hot and hard, goading the bouncy tune along. Still another side of Dylan's flavorful harmonica playing comes through on "Come Back, Baby." Bluesy and mournful, Dylan's harp work serves the accompanist's proper function—to give nearly invisible support. Hammond was pleased with Carolyn's sessions and anxious to get Dylan in the following week to sign. It was a dreadful contract, as Dylan was to discover, but it meant a chance to record, and that was all that mattered then. At first, he liked Hammond's enthusiasm, warmth, and encouragement, and was flattered to work with the man associated with so many jazz greats.

"A five-year contract with Columbia Records!" clucked Brother John Sellers at Folk City. "That boy is really something!" As the news filtered around, Dylan felt the sting of professional jealousy. He began to lose

friends as fast as he had made them. The folk world tended to knock anyone who was "making it." Harry Belafonte was considered the epitome of
the sellout because he had an organization, an orchestra, a huge cast to accompany him. Burl Ives, who had become a well-known actor, was a pariah. Even when as natural a group of traditional singers as The Clancy
Brothers and Tommy Makem got a job at the chic uptown Blue Angel,
the Village rumbled that "they had sold out ... weren't as good as they
used to be." The folk field's disdain of mass media, show business, and recognition continued well into the mid-1960s. Dylan was always caught in
the middle. Each time he changed his style, folk purists thought sinister
commercial forces were at work.

Once he began to do well, Dylan the performer was the object of an ex-
ceptional amount of instant love and instant aversion. With each new success, both his followers and detractors grew in number. Envy even
reverberated back from Minneapolis. "We couldn't quite understand why
Dylan made it and John Koerner, who was really better in those days,
didn't," Susan Gardner of Minneapolis told me in 1968. By then, she and
the early doubters had long since seen why. Dylan was doing nothing to
irritate anyone, as he later did, but he still inspired hostility and animosity.

The pressures that later nearly destroyed him began that last week in
September 1961. Could he live up to public praise? Could he ride out jealousy? All the doubts rambled and tumbled in his mind while he prepared
each Folk City set. There the only thing he could be sure about was that
people liked to laugh at his antics. The laughter, the ringing cash register,
the clinking glasses, the verbal snipers, and the curiosity seekers were all
easier to handle if he played them mostly for laughs. He moved about the
stage more. He used his hat as a prop, pulling it low, tipping it, replacing
it on his head, wiping his brow with it, swatting flies with it, dusting his
guitar with it. His monologues between songs became more ludicrous,
their timing more calculated. He developed so quickly that by the end of
his two-week stand he was a stronger, more secure performer. Even those
who hadn't liked Dylan took him more seriously by the end of the
gig. Very few people felt lukewarm about Dylan; they either loved or
hated him.

THE FIRST ALBUM

After a brief run-through session, Bob and Hammond were ready to move
into Columbia Studio A on Seventh Avenue. After all the old and limited
recording equipment he had known during the 1930s, this was nearly ef-
fortless. All Hammond needed was his singer-instrumentalist, an engineer,
and himself. Dylan brought his talent and the girl with the long brown
hair, Suze. He remained outwardly cool, putting down most of his songs
in less than five takes. A few songs came off in a remarkable two takes;
even Sinatra often does a dozen takes just to warm up. Hammond was de-

lighted to be working with a kid who knew so much about the blues. He cautioned Bob repeatedly to step back from the microphone to avoid the plosive sound of *p*'s. After the first twenty minutes, Dylan's confidence grew. At one point, Hammond left the control booth and brought back a longtime friend, Goddard Lieberson, a former studio woodwind player, then president of Columbia Records. Hammond had helped Lieberson get his first job at Columbia Records. Lieberson beamed at Dylan in the studio, and both older men voiced appreciation over the studio intercom.

Nothing impressed Dylan more, he told me the next day, than that while he was taping "Fixing to Die," an old black janitor who was cleaning up the hall stepped into the studio to listen. Bob knew then that he could get a lot more people to listen.

The first album, simply entitled *Bob Dylan*, was recorded at three sessions in November 1961, but not released until March 19, 1962. A gap between taping sessions and release is customary, but this long delay, caused by bureaucracy, annoyed Dylan very much. He felt he was moving with such momentum in late 1961 that to have the record in limbo for five months was a cruel anticlimax. By the time the album was released, he was embarrassed, regarding it as early work left in a bottom desk drawer. Dylan's letdown had set in as early as December, after the engineering and editing work were complete. Few recording artists are completely pleased with their first work. Within days of completing the album, Bob said that the liner notes were better than the contents, and that he wished he could have done this or that over again. Alternatively, he said how much he liked this or that song as he had done it. His perfectionism surfaced before the ink was dry on the contract.

Over the years, Dylan's negative reaction became typical. After putting enormous energy into writing, singing, recording, and performing, he would have a brief period of elation, followed by despair. Right after he finished each recording he thought it was the best he had done, and then the album became "just something I did." (The 1968 *John Wesley Harding* album was, he thought for a while, his finest work ever, and then, publicly at least, it was "just the sort of album that the people seemed to want at the time.")

The first album was the last will and testament of one Dylan and the herald of a new Dylan. The cover photograph of the callow boy barely matches the performance by the musical old man within. A picture of that elderly Columbia janitor leaning on his broom might have better caught the mood. Dylan's picture looks almost delicate and tentative, yet the singing and playing are packed with bold assertion. Even at this time, when he was deeply in love with Suze, Dylan was preoccupied with songs about death and sadness. Suze dedicatedly sat at the sessions in quiet admiration, yet their relationship was tempestuous. Many of the songs were clearly for Suze. The changes he made in traditional lyrics showed how strongly he wished to express himself to and about her.

If the cover photograph didn't mirror the album's contents, it did show Dylan much as he looked in those days, the hat making him appear even younger than he was. The unsmiling, pudgy face reflected a mixture of shyness and aloofness. His pseudo-western gear was standard 1961 hippie dress. The absence of a smile was also characteristic, for by then Dylan wasn't finding too much to smile about.

In spite of what Hammond said in late 1969 about the limits of Bob's guitar, harmonica, or mike technique, he was openly rapturous about the album when it was released. Dylan's guitar work was strong for a twenty-year-old's debut album. His harmonica work may not have been virtuoso, but it gave the album some of its flavor and texture. The mouth harp weaves the fabric of voice and guitar together, and it helped stimulate the resurgence of interest in blues harmonica in the early 1960s. Dylan's understanding of black blues remains the dominant impression of the album, but songs concerned with death and sadness alternate with wit and games. (Later, when Tony Glover, John Koerner, and Dave Ray were recording their excellent white blues albums for Elektra, they asked, by way of writer Paul Nelson: "Who says we can't sing good blues just because we're on the wrong end of the Mississippi?")

The album in detail:

"YOU'RE NO GOOD": A sprightly jape out of Jesse Fuller's song bag. Fuller could get up to six instruments going simultaneously as he sang. His rural ragtime made people happy. "You're No Good," typical Fuller gamesmanship, becomes, in Dylan's hands, a nonsense song of the beleaguered male running down the offending female in his life. "You're No Good" was inaccurately listed on the label of some American pressings and the British LP (CBS 62022) as "She's No Good." Programmed because of its brightness and tempo, the song scarcely proclaims a new singer of stature. Yet, the voice's spirit, drive, timbre, bite, and propulsion win attention, as does the instrumental work. At the break, Dylan builds his own one-man band. His galloping mouth harp talks to the guitar, which answers right back. Then the voice soars again, and the colloquy continues. Soon, we have a rollicking tumble of witty nonsense. The guitar work is quite clean here. As Dylan gets into the song, the broadness of his put-on comes forward, culminating in a couple of vocal riffs that suggest Elliott at his slyest. "You're No Good" is one of the album's brightest moments. This old man is comic.

"TALKING NEW YORK": Vintage Dylan, this proclaims his own writing talent, his sardonic view of the music business, and his control of humor and timing. One Woody Guthrie song served as a model from which Dylan drew his own. Another Guthrie song gave flavor, and still a third supplied a bit of philosophy on which Dylan embroidered his message. The framework Guthrie song was "Talkin' Subway," which went, in part:

I struck out for old New York
Thought I'd find me a job of work
One leg up and the other leg down
I come in through a hole in the ground.
    Holland Tunnel. Three mile tube
    Skipping through the Hudson River dew.

I blowed into New York town,
I looked up and I looked down.
Everybody I seen on the streets,
Was all a-running down in a hole in the ground.
I followed 'em. See where they's a-going.
Newsboy said they're tryin' to smoke a rat out of a hole . . .[6]

The second influential Guthrie song was "New York Town," where, also, Dylan improved structure and control. In his seventh verse, Dylan cites Woody indirectly, then makes his own summary from Guthrie's "Pretty Boy Floyd":

Now as through this world I ramble
I see lots of funny men,
Some will rob you with a six-gun
And some with a fountain pen . . .[7]

"Talking blues" is a very old form, speech delivered against simple guitar background. The narrative tells a wry story in near deadpan. Each verse ends with sardonic asides. Most talking blues since Guthrie were vehicles for folk humor. The form is like the "preaching" introductions to black gospel songs. The congregation leader flows from verbal sermonizing into song with rhythm building up. And many blues are done in a nearly spoken vocal line. Leadbelly often talked his way into a song.

The "father of talking blues" was a South Carolina singer named Chris Bouchillon, who recorded "Original Talking Blues" in the 1920s. Robert Lunn, a more commercial country singer of the 1930s and 1940s, also called himself "the original talking-blues man." Bouchillon was recorded by Frank Walker, a pioneer field recording official, who hated Bouchillon's singing, "but loved the way he talked." A musical genre was born because a man sang so poorly! Guthrie and Dylan usually used Carter family guitar style, with either a flat pick or with thumb and forefinger. A bass note is hit, followed by a downward brush across the first three or four strings, and then an upward brush. Dylan does his "Talking New York" in G with only three chords.

This critique of the music business, New York aloofness, the coffeehouse circuit, and music impressarios, was written, Bob said, "in May 1961, [when] I was hitchhiking from the Holland Tunnel, but got a bum steer and started heading toward Florida, instead of toward California, where I wanted to go. I left at seven A.M., but it was a false start. Then I left at five P.M. I started to write out the words at a truck stop on the highway. I just wrote it out on paper. I got as far as St. Louis, Minneapolis, and Madison, Wisconsin." Dylan freely cursed coffeehouses: "They wanted satin shirts and gut strings, while I played all steel strings, and you know I don't wear satin shirts," he told me. Dylan's suspicions of the music business, as early as his first recording, is another glimpse of the old man's spirit and insight.

"IN MY TIME OF DYIN' ": This old spiritual is perhaps the album's most compelling track. Dylan said that he didn't know where he first heard it and that this was the first time he ever performed it. White sang it on his *Josh at Midnight* (Elektra) in the late 1950s, but had also recorded it in 1933 under the pseudonym of the Singing Christian. Josh used the title "Jesus Gonna Make Up My Dyin' Bed" on a considerably sweeter version than Dylan's. Another recording, by Dock Reed on a 1950 Folkways album, was a disconsolate, unaccompanied version. Dylan's is much deeper and better structured than Josh White's. White conceded this in 1963 when I played Dylan for him. He smiled approvingly when he heard the track: "That boy really knows what he is doing!"

Dylan's excellent guitar work reflects his study of Robert Johnson and Rabbit Brown, highly inventive technically. By using old modal tuning, he establishes a totally new texture. His capo is set on the fourth fret, the low E string tuned down a tone to D to be an octave below the fourth string. The top E string is tuned down to an octave above the fourth string, leaving three D notes in successive octaves. This D-modal tuning omits the customary sweet progression of thirds, moving instead in fourths and fifths, providing the stark, antique flavor. Dylan used the metal cap of Suze's lipstick as his bottleneck on the small finger of his left hand. With the metal tube, the strings yielded inner resonances and a slightly ringing sound. Many old Delta bluesmen used whiskey bottle-necks to get that ringing sound. The voice is an urgent vehicle for emotional autobiography. The identification with the spiritual's death-haunted figure is amazing for a young singer. Dylan didn't sing the song in public, but it stands as one of his finest recorded performances.

"MAN OF CONSTANT SORROW": A traditional southern white mountain song permeated with trouble, this folk singer's standard was probably first recorded in the late 1920s by Emry Arthur, a Kentuckian who moved to Port Washington, Wisconsin, where he worked in a chair factory. He claims composition. In the 1930s, a Kentucky miner's wife, Sarah Gunning, wrote her own version, called "I Am a Girl of Constant Sorrow." Dylan has rewritten the version that was being sung in the early 1960s by The New Lost City Ramblers, Baez, and others. The place of origin becomes Colorado. Reflecting problems with Suze's mother, he has changed "Your friends may think I'm a stranger" to "Your mother says

I'm a stranger."[8] He returns to guitar flat-picking that is highly under-stated, in traditional mountain manner. It emerges as a shiveringly lone-some personal statement.

"FIXIN' TO DIE": Dylan learned this other face of death from an old Okeh recording by Booker T. Washington (Bukka) White, a bluesman who served time in the Mississippi State Prison Farm at Parchman. Bukka White sang it almost as a hymn, while Dylan brightens the tempo. "Fixin' to Die" opens with the sort of slide or smear that rock guitarists later used frequently. Dylan's flat-picked guitar is again in open D-modal tuning. Many of the Bukka White images are similar in mood and vein to those of the older spiritual, "In My Time of Dyin'." The title was picked up in 1965 by Joe McDonald of Country Joe and the Fish, whose "I-Feel-Like-I'm-Fixin'-to-Die Rag" was a snorting rant against the Vietnam War.

"PRETTY PEGGY-O": A rollicking broad satire. Dylan takes a Baez standard and plays a dozen games with it. During World War I, an English folk-song collector, Cecil Sharp, collected several versions in the southern Appalachians. In Scotland, the song is known as "Bonnie Lass O'Fyvie-O," and in England as "Pretty Peggy of Derby." The Baez version is called "Fennario," which Dylan pictures as some strange geographical place. Others do it as a rather light, lissome tale, while Dylan clatters into it as burlesque. He aimed, I think, to mock the preciousness of revived tradition with "long gone lieutenant"[9] and rhyming "rodeo" with the ar-chaic "fairest maid in the areo."[10]

"HIGHWAY 51": Dylan insisted then he was a country or rockabilly singer, not a folk singer. "Highway 51" may be the first folk-rock recording, even without electric instruments or rhythm. The late Tom Wilson, one of Dylan's producers, believed folk-rock began when The An-imals recorded their 1964 electric "House of the Rising Sun." Another starting point was the four electric arrangements Dylan made for his sec-ond Columbia album in 1962. Still another departure was The Byrds' 1965 recording of Dylan's "Mr. Tambourine Man." Yet here are all the ele-ments of folk-rock without electrification.

Travel images permeate American folk song and blues, signifying free-dom and change.

To the southern black, the train whistle sounded escape or nostalgia for the old life. Big Joe Williams sang of Highway 49. Robert Johnson keened about "Crossroads Blues" and "Terraplane Blues." Even Nat King Cole sang of "Highway 66." Guthrie and Pete Seeger collaborated on a "66 Highway Blues," about dead ends and fresh beginnings.

"Highway 51" is credited to Curtis Jones, a Texas bluesman born in 1906. Jones's song, recorded in the 1930s on Vocalion and Conqueror, tells about one of the routes favored by migrant southern blacks. Highway 51 runs from New Orleans up to Madison, Wisconsin. The Curtis Jones song was also recorded in 1940 by that savage, raucous Chicago bluesman, Tommy McClennan. The Everly Brothers did it as rockabilly. Dylan's text and melody differ widely from Jones's. Curiously, Dylan has dropped nearly all of Jones's references to buses and McClennan's specific references to Greyhound buses.

The simple guitar work supplies the equivalent of a full rhythm section, with interweaving stresses that suggest jazz drumming. Dylan is foreshadowing some of the exciting guitar work of Richie Havens, who used the flat-picking brushstroke so inventively. The reappearing opening guitar figure is the same used on the Everlys' "Wake Up Little Susie." Against this chugging guitar, Dylan delivers a vocally strong blues-rockabilly song. The pulse, tempo, and motion build up into several strong climaxes within two minutes, forty-nine seconds. Death is in the lyrics, but overabundant life is in the voice and guitar.

"GOSPEL PLOW": An old spiritual converted into a modern pop-folk song, done up-tempo in a major key. "Keeping the hand on the plow" was a folk saying from farmland America. The phrase often expresses strong resolve, but Dylan, in his near-yelping voice, stresses motion and drive riding over swarming guitar figures. This is the album's least successful interpretation, because he can't seem to keep his hand steady on the mood. Both sides begin with songs in which the singing is not Dylan's best. "Gospel Plow" foreshadows his later involvement with Christianity.

"BABY, LET ME FOLLOW YOU DOWN": After some delicate guitar work reminiscent of Rabbit Brown, Dylan shoulders his way into this romance song. The spoken introduction satirizes folk-music prefaces. Dylan gives tongue-in-cheek credit for the song to Ric Von Schmidt of Cambridge. In the notes, Dylan said he believed that Ric had gotten some elements from an old recording by Horace Sprott, an Alabama sharecropper whom Frederick Ramsey, Jr., had recorded for Folkways. Dylan's three-finger picking supplies gentle harplike backing. A fine colloquy between harmonica, voice, and guitar is established. The singing has a striking sensuousness. "Baby" was clearly for Suze, who regarded it for a time as "her song." Dylan later linked the song to the Reverend Gary Davis's "Baby, Let Me Lay It on You."

"HOUSE OF THE RISIN' SUN": Alan Lomax first recorded what he called a "modern Southern white song" in 1937 in Middlesborough, Kentucky. Lomax traced it to some older bawdy English songs, the melody with the classic "Little Musgrave and Lady Barnard" ("Child Ballad 81") and its American variant, "Little Mathy Groves." This lament of a woman dragged into prostitution has been recorded by Josh, Gooding, Guthrie, Seeger, and others. At this time, Carolyn Hester was singing a highly dramatic version, while Van Ronk had a roughhewn, laconic interpretation. Dylan said: "I always knew this song, but never really knew it until Dave Van Ronk sang it."

The younger singer attenuated the phrases almost to an emotional breaking point, using space and silence with as much effect as sound. Like thin pieces of Giacometti sculpture, the words are surrounded by space drawn toward the work itself. When a male folk musician sings a woman's song, he usually changes the gender, but Dylan let the lyrics stand. Picked up by The Animals, the old woman's song became Dylan's entrée into the English rock scene. The song reappeared high on the American hit charts in March 1970, in a rock single by a group called Frijid Pink.

"FREIGHT TRAIN BLUES": A relieving light moment here of an old, hillbilly, up-tempo jape. Bob ascribed it to a recording by "the king of country music," Roy Acuff, though he probably learned it from Elliott. At the sessions, Dylan kept his various mouth harps moist in a glass of water. A swarm of harmonica slides and swoops sets a jolly hillbilly mood, as Dylan yodels and chants. The vocal lines play against steady, metrical guitar. In the Acuff vein, Dylan holds one note for a long time, simulating a lonesome train whistle, typical country panache. Unfortunately, Bob didn't hit the train whistle on the head, and the note wavers in a few seconds.

"SONG TO WOODY": Dylan wrote this elegy in February 1961, reportedly at the Mills Hotel bar after the sad encounter at the Gleasons'. The folkish melody, a variant on a traditional tune Guthrie used in "1913 Massacre," sways delicately. It has a very intimate atmosphere, a sedative lullaby tone, so that we visualize him only a reach away from Woody. "Song to Woody" moves in three-quarter time with an easy waltz grace. Bob's shock at his idol's decay may have prompted the album's preoccupation with death. The song, however, dwells on the young Guthrie's rambling days. The sensuous vocalizing, against transparently simple guitar work, makes its impact through understatement.

In early autumn 1961, Dylan had performed his "Song to Woody" at a Folk City hootenanny. Joan Baez was there and asked Maynard Solomon of Vanguard to get her the song. I asked Maynard then if he wanted to record Dylan. He said he didn't, but that Joan wanted to sing his "Woody Song." Joan never got a tape or a copy, and forgot the episode until spring 1963, when she met Dylan on the West Coast.

A sad footnote to "Song to Woody" appeared in the April/May 1966 issue of *Sing Out!* Robert Ferris of Youngstown, Ohio, used Dylan's melody and structure for "Song to Woody" to write his own song about his disillusionment with Dylan, who had "gone electric." Ferris wrote: "I have written this song which can be used by anyone to show disgust for their particular fallen idol."

"SEE THAT MY GRAVE IS KEPT CLEAN": A traditional spiritual that Blind Lemon Jefferson made classic. Lemon recorded it for Paramount in October 1927. Released in February 1928, it became one of the best-known "race" recordings. When Blind Lemon learned the song, it was a folk spiritual called "Two White Horses in a Line," also known as "One Kind Favor." (Another "Two White Horses," a spiritual with different text and melody, appeared in Carl Sandburg's 1927 collection, *The American Songbag*.) Blind Lemon's and Dylan's versions are rich in traditional

Anglo-American ballad imagery—digging of a grave with a silver spade, lowering of a coffin, two white horses bearing the coffin, and so on. Bob reflects tradition while impressing his own stamp. Blind Lemon's recording is sprightly, sweet, and benevolent, while Dylan's is stark and morose.

Bob's sense of timing sustains the drama. Between September and these recording sessions, he was able to rein in some of his melodramatic excesses. Of the entire album, perhaps only "Gospel Plow" spins out of interpretative control. On such songs as "Grave," his involvement never gets beyond temperate bounds: The coffin is lowered, the epitaph decreed. Mature artists often want to live down their first work. But after five years of preparation, Dylan had made a strong start.

He taped four additional songs not included on the album. The four supplemental songs, never released by Columbia, were:

"THE HOUSE CARPENTER," a traditional southern mountain ballad, popularized by Baez and Bob Gibson.

"HE WAS A FRIEND OF MINE," which Dylan adapted from a song he learned from a Chicago street singer, Blind Arvella Gray. The Byrds later recorded it in tribute to President John F. Kennedy.

Guthrie's cheerful "RAMBLIN' BLUES," also known as "Ramblin' Round" and "Ramblin' Around."

"MAN ON THE STREET," an original based on an episode on West Fourth Street in the Village. Bob had seen a policeman jab a dead man with his club to stir him.

Hammond sent me the test pressings so that I could write the liner notes under the pseudonym of Stacey Williams. *The Times* music department had an unwritten code that members should have nothing to do with the production of recordings that they might review. But nearly every member earned supplementary income by writing liner notes, anonymously or pseudonymously. When I told Dylan about the ruse he was delighted, but continued his far larger game of concealing his Hibbing background. We agreed that if anyone should ask who Stacey Williams was, Bob would "just mumble something about some old jazz and blues guy who wrote things for Columbia Records."

To prepare his official story, Dylan came to my pad one afternoon in December 1961 and spoke volubly and quickly. He was keen to praise his sources and influences. "No one could phrase and use timing like those old blues singers," Bob said, singling out Robert Johnson and Big Joe Williams. He emphasized that although he didn't record his own versions of "See That My Grave Is Kept Clean," he generally sang: "Dig my grave/With a bloody spade/And see that my digger gets well paid."

Dylan said that he had graduated from high school in Hibbing, "way up by the Canadian border." For a spell before graduating, he went on, he lived in Sioux Falls, South Dakota, and Gallup, New Mexico. "I went to the University of Minnesota on a scholarship, but I left after six months. I didn't agree with school. I flunked out. I read a lot, but not the required readings. I read a lot of humanities, economics, Adam Smith's *Wealth of Nations,* I read Zola and Rousseau, 'cause people would recommend 'em. I stayed up all night reading the philosophy of Kant instead of *Living with the Birds* for a science course. I took a Spanish course to get an easy good mark. But the teacher started tearing me apart, even though I could talk with people in Spanish. I lived on the banks of the Mississippi River under the Washington Avenue Bridge with four other guys." Of his pilgrimage east, Bob said: "I headed for Greystone Hospital to see Woody. I talked with Woody, and it was an experience I'll never forget. Now, when I get depressed, I visit Woody in Brooklyn and then I get to feel better. I've visited Woody many, many times, but I would never want to be another Woody Guthrie."

Did he anticipate stardom? "I never thought I would shoot lightning through the sky in the entertainment field," he replied. Dylan sketched his influences: "I started to sing and play the guitar at the age of ten. Hank Williams had just died and I first liked country music—people like Jimmie Rodgers. Then I got interested in old blues, and people like Jelly Roll Morton. I remember Leadbelly and 'See See (C. C.) Rider,' but I also liked the country songs of Jack Guthrie. I really couldn't decide which I liked best, country or blues. So I suppose I ended by becoming a mixture of Hank Williams and Woody Guthrie."

What about his fascination with Charlie Chaplin? "He influences me, even in the way I sing. His films really sank in. I like to see the humor in the world. There is so little of it around. I guess I'm always conscious of the Chaplin tramp." Then what about death songs? "Well, I feel a closeness to songs like 'See That My Grave Is Kept Clean.' I'm representing myself and a whole lot of people who sing in that manner." He was anxious to be in the very best company, song-swapping with Van Ronk and Elliott. He was a great fan of old rock 'n' roll—Presley, Little Richard, and rockabilly singer Carl Perkins.

He linked his harmonica work to Jesse Fuller, "Little Walter" Jacobs, and Sonny Terry. "Now I am 'blowing out' more in my own style." What did the future look like? "I would just like to keep on singing like I am. I just want to get along. I don't think about making a million dollars." If he had money, what would he do with it? Bob smiled: "If I had money, I would buy a couple of motorcycles, a few air-conditioners, and four or five couches." We joked about the folk-record companies, Folkways, Vanguard, and Elektra, who had either ignored or rejected him. "I was around and all the folk-record people heard me. Now, I'm grateful that they didn't sign me."

He summarized his songwriting: "Either the song comes fast, or it

won't come at all." (He later said that deadline pressure made him "prolific." Some songs marinate for a long time. "I just jot down little phrases
and things I overhear." In 1985, Dylan spoke of fits and starts in writing,
with some intense periods of total work, lasting "twenty-four or thirty
hours, fourteen hours at a time." He "hears" melodies in his head, tries
them on guitar or piano. Since he cannot write musical notation, the tape
recorder is a valuable tool for him.) He mentioned films that were inspir-
ing his songs. Right after seeing *The Ox-Bow Incident,* about a western
lynching, he wrote "Ballad of the Ox-Bow Incident." He had just seen the
poignant Soviet antiwar film *Ballad of a Soldier,* and said, "I just know I'll
write a song based on that." When I tried to probe his fascination with
death, Dylan became nearly inarticulate. He said he had been seriously ill
three years earlier and had begun then to think a lot about death.

The recording, which came out in March 1962, received several very fine
reviews, but, as they say in the record business, "nothing happened." Not
until two years later did the creditable first recording begin to sell in
quantity. Around Columbia they began to call Bob Dylan "John Hammond's folly." Only a handful of people thought Dylan had much promise. Suze did, but almost from the beginning she feared Bob's dark
death-hauntedness. By November 1961, love was a four-letter word to
Dylan, and so was Suze. Bob felt the romance was doomed—enough to
make any twenty-year-old sing an old man's record and think that life
might be over.

4

POSITIVELY 161
WEST FOURTH STREET

"Bobby didn't change, he just growed."

—BIG JOE WILLIAMS

"I can't see my reflection in the waters,
I can't speak the sounds that show no pain,
I can't hear the echo of my footsteps,
Or can't remember the sound of my own name. . . ."

—DYLAN[1]

In the old joke, a stranger in New York asks, "How do you get to Carnegie Hall?" A musician replies, "Practice." Within two weeks of taping his first album, Dylan found his way to Carnegie Hall—not the main Carnegie, but its neighboring debut room, Carnegie Chapter Hall. For his first important solo concert, on Saturday, November 4, 1961, fifty-three people turned out, mostly the Village gang. Dylan performed with assurance. The audience still responded most warmly to the comic bits.

The concert was sponsored by Izzy Young of the Folklore Center. Charging two dollars a ticket, Izzy, the sweat-shirted Sol Hurok, had pulled off another of his aesthetic coups and financial flops. That Izzy later became the folkniks' noisiest Dylan detractor should not obscure his early encouragement. He chronicled interviews with musicians who drifted into his shop, talking with Dylan on October 20 and 23, 1961, and February 1, 7, 22, and March 14, 1962. Dylan offered Izzy a few insights, ample wit, and a stack of tall tales:

"My songs aren't easy to listen to.... My favorite singers are Van Ronk, Elliott, Peter Stampfel, Kweskin, and Von Schmidt. Joan Baez? Her voice goes through me. She's OK.... Played piano with Bobby Vee—would have been a millionaire if I'd stayed with him.... Have no religion. Tried a bunch of different religions. Churches are divided. Can't make up their minds, neither can I. Never saw a God; can't say till I saw one ... sort of like New York.... I like to walk around.... Like to ride motorcycles— was a racer in North and South Dakota and Minnesota.... Before I met Jesse Fuller in Denver, there was a farmhand in Sioux Falls, South Dakota, who played the Autoharp. Picked up Wilbur's way of singing—never remember his last name. . . . Cowboy styles I learned from real cowboys. Can't remember their names. Met some in Cheyenne. Cowboys nowadays go to cowboy movies and sit there and criticize, wear their hat this way or that—pick up their way of walking from the movies.... Used to see girls from the Bronx at Chicago, Antioch, with their gut-string guitars singing 'Pastures of Plenty.' No lipstick, brotherhood songs. Struck me funny, not clowns, opened up a whole new world of people. I like the New York kind of girl now, can't remember what the old kind was like.... Don't care for classical music. Don't go for any foreign music. I really like Irish music, and Scottish music too.... Colleges are the best audiences, much better than nightclubs...."

Around Christmas, Dylan did a small concert at Rutgers University in New Jersey. He went over very well, but again the comic eclipsed the musician. Throughout, he gibed at a picture of an elderly university trustee on the wall behind him: "Howdy, Mr. Rutgers, nice of you to ask me down here."

In February 1962, Bob went upstate to a small coffeehouse, the Caffé Lena, in Saratoga Springs. Arriving in the old spa center, he headed for the local pool hall. A local shark challenged him, and Bob obligingly lost the first two games, while the Saratoga stranger kept raising the stakes. In the third game, Dylan cleaned the stranger out. Terri Van Ronk had arranged the gig. Lena and Bill Spencer hadn't been easily persuaded. Lena: "You know I don't book unknowns." Terri: "I've done all sorts of favors for you ... now you do me a favor and take this guy, because he's really good. You won't regret it." Lena regretted it.

Virtually none of the Skidmore College girls were tuned in to Dylan. At one point, when the audience persisted in talking over Bob's singing, Spencer grabbed the microphone: "Maybe you don't understand what this kid is doing. Maybe you are too stupid to understand what he is saying. If you would only shut up and listen, maybe you would understand!" Bob started one of his comic monologues, putting down the audience and the owners as well. If there was anything he disdained, it was fraternities, sororities, and rude audiences. He did very little other stage work during 1962. He had played at a Toronto coffeehouse and a benefit concert at City College in Manhattan for the Congress on Racial Equality (CORE). From April 24 to May 6, he returned to Folk City, where he could always be sure of a warm reception.

Right after the Columbia taping, Harry Belafonte was looking for an "ethnic" harmonica player. Why Belafonte did not think of any of a dozen black harp players is a mystery, but somehow Dylan was asked to play on Belafonte's RCA sessions for the album *Midnight Special*. In those days, folkniks used to run Belafonte into the ground. "It's easy to criticize the big money-makers like Belafonte and The Kingston Trio," Dylan reportedly told Izzy in 1961. "The stuff Belafonte does is really like popular singing. I won't criticize him until he sings one of my songs. But then he'll make a lot of money for me."

He developed the story of the session into an offstage talking blues. "You see, this Harry Belafonte is quite a big man," Dylan told me immediately afterward. "He has a small army that fights for him. Why, his arranger just goes crazy trying to think up great new ideas. When I got there, the studio men were working out something special. The first guitar man did this, the second guitar man did that. Another guy scraped two drumsticks together, and another guy shuffled his feet. It wasn't bad. They went over and over it till they had it just right. Then, in walks Belafonte himself. He was nice and friendly, and everyone greeted him like he was God himself. Then Belafonte walked over to where these studio men had been working so hard on this little riff. 'Harry,' the arranger said, 'we've whipped up something really great for that arrangement.' 'That's nice,' Harry says, 'let's hear it.' So then," Dylan continued, giggling, "the first guitar man did this, the second guitar man did that. Another guy scraped two drumsticks together, and another guy shuffled his feet. They finished, and all eyes turned toward Belafonte. 'I don't think so,' said Harry, walking away, and the smiles on those poor guys just froze, they just froze!"

After the release of the Belafonte album, some radio jocks, like Bob Fass of WBAI, played the track, not saying: "That was Harry Belafonte singing 'Midnight Special,'" but: "That was Bob Dylan playing the harmonica." (Belafonte and others at the sessions had some laughs at Dylan's expense: To keep rhythm, Bob tapped out the time with his booted right foot, but the vibrations kept registering on the tape. An engineer slipped a pillow under Bob's thudding foot.)

Dylan's diary as an artist, from late 1961 through most of 1962, was dominated by his seeking out established performers, his songwriting, his contact with *Broadside* and the civil rights movement, and his managerial affiliations. Above all, his long, stormy love affair with Suze Rotolo affected much of what he did throughout 1962.

"THE TRUE FORTUNETELLER OF MY SOUL"[2]

Returning from Minneapolis in early summer 1961, convinced that Bonny and he had no future, Dylan pinned his hopes on Suze (pronounced Suzy) Rotolo. Her light brown hair flowed below her shoulders. Her pumpkin smile could warm a room. Her manner was shy, tentative, gentle. Her eyes and ears caught everything, although she was often curiously inarticulate. She was creative, whether sketching and drawing, planning a stage production, or helping to run the little magazine, *Streets*.

From mid-1961 through the spring of 1964, whether living with Dylan or running away from him, whether in Greenwich Village, Woodstock, or Italy, whether trying to come to emotional terms with Bob or battling with him, whether trying to get closer than he would allow or farther than he wanted, Suze was a central figure in Dylan's most important periods of growth. He probably wrote more than a dozen songs for or about her, and she inspired countless more. She was only seventeen when they met. She was a New Yorker from an urbane Italian-American family of readers, political activists, cultured and socially concerned people. Suze looked, acted, and thought just like a woman, not a little girl. Bob wrote most directly of her in an "Outlined Epitaph":

> *I think of Sue most times*
> *beautiful Sue*
> *with the lines of a swan*
> *frightened easy*
> *as a fawn in the forest . . .*
> *I think love poems*
> *as a poor lonesome invalid*
> *knowin' of my power*
> *t' destroy*
> *the good souls of the road*
> *that know no sickness*
> *except that of kindness . . .*
> *ah but Sue*
> *she knows me well*
> *perhaps too well*
> *an' is above all*
> *the true fortuneteller of my soul*
> *I think perhaps the only one . . .*[3]

Although I spent dozens of evenings with Suze and Bob, I had difficulty grasping her spirit. She seemed overshadowed by Dylan when she was with him. Although I sensed her keen artistic perception, she generally did not assert herself in those early years. I tended to take Bob's part. Dylan was a handful to live with, a challenge to an experienced woman, let alone one of eighteen. I knew only that she had a power over Bob, and, to her chagrin, I often urged her to put his needs above hers. I couldn't see then that she was right from her side too, grasping for her own identity in the whirlpool of his needs. Before the end of 1961, he was talking about marriage, sometimes flippantly, sometimes in dead earnest, planning the ceremony in detail. One winter night in the White Horse, he told Suze and me how it would go: "We'll get Reverend Gary Davis [the blind street singer-preacher] to perform the ceremony. Naw, he can just sing the ceremony. And we'll have all the singers there." He started to list guests. Suze smiled, eyes flashing flattery, but she didn't say yes and she didn't say no.

Suze's mother had other ideas. Mary Rotolo was a volatile, strong-headed, intelligent woman in her early forties, whose factory-worker husband had recently died. She was a translator for a medical journal and was planning to marry a New Jersey teacher. Suze was too young to become involved with anyone, let alone that scruffy beatnik, she felt. Mrs. Rotolo didn't approve of Bobby at all, although both her daughters, Suze and twenty-year-old Carla, thought so highly of him. "My mother was the only one at that point who disliked Dylan heartily," said Carla (whom Dylan often called "Carla-in-law"). "Yet, when Bob was sick, she put him up at her flat." Suze knew little of Bob's background. Some friends maintained that she thought he was an Italian orphan until *Newsweek* broke the story of his parents and Hibbing in 1963. Carla: "In fall 1961, my mother somehow found out that his name was Zimmerman—perhaps he told her. My mother had a way of finding out things. She felt he was taking advantage of everyone around to get ahead. She called him a sponge to his face. Suze's mother, Dylan could fight. But the fact that she saw through him, which no one else did, scared him. He respected our mother as a person, but he always hated her. He paid court to her, he did everything he could over the years to win her over, and it never worked. The ultimate thing was that 'Ballad in Plain D.' "

Years later, Bob still was protective toward Suze, still had faith in her good sense. She was his witness: "The thing Suze could tell you," Dylan told me, "is that Suze knows, more than anybody else, she knows that I played, back in 1961 and 1962, when nobody was around, all those old Elvis Presley records. She'll tell you that. Actually, I told her not to talk to anybody at all. I told her to shuck off anybody that calls. If anybody ever gives her any trouble, man, I'll fix them good. But if you want to talk to her, fine. But don't come on with her, OK? Everybody comes on with her. Don't come on with her about how I was, ask her what I did. She'll tell you. She'll tell you how many nights I stayed up and wrote songs and showed them to her and asked her: 'Is this right?' Because her father and her mother were associated with unions and she was into this equality-freedom thing long before I was. I checked the songs out with her. She would like all the songs. Suze is a very talented girl, man. But she is very frightened. . . ."

At seventeen, Suze was tortured by her mother's protectiveness and frightened by Dylan's intensity, restlessness, and darkness. It was all happening too soon and too fast. Although Suze tried repeatedly to break away, she was ineluctably drawn to Bob. Especially at the beginning, Bob and Suze seemed magic lovers closely bound in a hostile world. I was surprised at their first split-up.

In summer 1961, Mary Rotolo was living in the penthouse of One Sheridan Square, atop the old Café Society Downtown. On the fourth floor lived a folk den mother, Miki Isaacson, who ran a kibbutz for strays. Miki's large triangular living room housed folkniks Jack Elliott, Greg Levasseur, John Herald, and, soon, Dylan. Toward the end of the summer, Jean Redpath, a Scottish singer, joined the family-style commune. Nearly everyone picked or sang until three in the morning, then dropped off to sleep. Jean Redpath recalled, "I nearly blew a gasket blowing up so many of those rubber mattresses." Dylan glided into this permissive family, pleased to be sleeping under the same roof as Suze.

Suze graduated from Bryant High School in Queens, spent part of 1961 at the New School, and held part-time office jobs. She was interested in drawing, theater, design, and poetry, and worked as an usher in off-Broadway theaters, like One Sheridan Square. When she first met Dylan at Riverside Radio, "I thought he was a joke," Suze told me in 1966, through her sunburst smile. "A nice joke, but a joke. . . . I soon discovered that he wasn't a joke at all. When you got to know him separately you knew just how frighteningly sharp he was. Even in 1961. He could be sitting in a room filled with people and be absorbing rays from everyone, from everywhere." Was it difficult to live with a genius? "I guess it was hard," Suze replied. "Their heads are going all the time. But you can't treat them as being so extraordinary. You can't treat geniuses like they are precious china objects all the time. They are just human beings."

Did he communicate well? "Yes, definitely," she answered. "But he certainly can express himself better in what he writes than in what he says. Those first few months at Gerde's and at the first recording session, I was very awed. I wasn't fully aware of what was happening. When I see his pictures everywhere and see him quoted, I still think it's a joke. You see, to me, it's still old Bobby."

Suze was in Italy from May until December, 1962. "When I came back, he was really getting big. Even though he wrote me often and called me all the time in Italy, he would only talk about us, and would never talk about what he was doing." Dylan was in England when Suze returned. She was greeted instead by his songs sung by Janet Reynolds and others. Hearing "letters" written to her on a jukebox was "very strange. I was torn. It became very flattering to sit back and hear a song like 'Don't Think Twice' or 'Tomorrow Is a Long Time' on the radio. It was especially strange to hear them being sung by other people."

Suze recalled Bob at work in early 1962: "He would just say to me: 'I'm going to do some writing tonight,' and would sit down at the typewriter, or would play with his guitar. I never minded that all that much. The apartment on Fourth Street was a very small place to have someone constantly playing chords over and over again. He was very fast about his writing. He also liked to go out to write. He would sit at a table in some cheesy little luncheonette and write. He would write in his little spiral notebook while drinking coffee. He used to take that notebook with him to places like the Fat Black Pussy Cat." While Romney, Stookey, Elliott, and other floaters were often brilliant talkers, Dylan, "the spy," was nearly invisible. He hung back and listened. He'd laugh at their jokes, but more often than not he would make a note in his ten-cent notebook.

Did people ask Suze what he was really like? "Yes, often. He is mystifying. Most of it he created, and then added to it by just being himself. I think he must have enjoyed this. You get afraid to ask him things because he has a whole cloud around him. People have said that they get afraid of him. A lot of people that know him best don't ask him anything, because they don't know on what ground they will have to defend themselves if he answers." ("Outlaw Blues": "Don't ask me nothin' about nothin',/I just might tell you the the truth.")[4]

"That was why," Suze went on, "there was such a horror over what his real name was. He was always very paranoid. I remember that just thinking of going out for a walk, his knee would start to twitch. He would wonder: Who was he going to run into? I couldn't figure out what made him so frightened of crowds, of strangers." Suze maintained that Dylan was as elusive to her as she had been to him. She told me: "You probably know as much about him in New York as anyone."

In spring 1962, before she left for Italy, Suze said, "He was especially closemouthed. The thing that struck me about Bobby was his despair, that deathlike quality about him. I sensed, long after we had gone our separate ways, a lack of excitement to him. It's his feeling that says: 'Isn't everything just so blah, there is really no hope that people are always living for.' People live with hope for green trees and beautiful flowers, but Dylan seems to lack that sort of simple hope, at least he did from 1964 to 1966. This darkness wasn't new to me. It became stronger as the years passed by—or else, I was just becoming more aware of it." I told Suze how Bob had once talked to me at length about suicide, and the next day had said that if I thought he was pessimistic, then I didn't understand him at all. "He's like that," Suze agreed. "He just won't accept anybody's point of view about himself. . . . That's his way. There is something there I see in him that I just don't like. Maybe he doesn't like that quality in himself either. It's somehow all too negative, too pessimistic. But on another level he is so alive, so very much alive, it's frightening. And then there is something in him that is so very funny. That's what made me run away in the past."

Suze's sister grew more hostile to the relationship. Carla was fantastically enthusiastic about Dylan and yet often jealous of her sister. As "big sister," she always seemed to know what was best, and that didn't always mean Dylan. At first, Carla big-sistered him as well. When she was living at 129 Perry Street in autumn 1961, Bob stayed there.

Carla: "Bobby was still in his dirty period then. But he was very fussy about his clothes. His concern about his image started then. He would always ask if he looked right, jiggling with his dungarees: 'Are they tight enough? Is the shirt OK?' I would go to work in the morning and Bobby would be asleep on my living room couch. He spent most of his time listening to my records, days and nights." He studied the Folkways *Anthology of American Folk Music,* the singing of Ewan MacColl and A. L. Lloyd, Rabbit Brown's guitar, Guthrie, of course, and blues. He read voraciously. "My library was quite eclectic," Carla recalled, "and he read whatever he found. He started with our poetry books. I think he met François Villon through us. He was borrowing from anyone who had a large book collection." While still giving the public impression of being neither reader nor student, Dylan jumped headlong into the best folk-music collections, by the Lomaxes, Sharp, Child, and as much poetry as he could absorb. Bob read Suze's European and American poetry books, and bought her more, which they read together. All the time he scribbled notes. Whatever dormant energy remained from the university was unleashed in the Village.

Carla sensed that the kid she was mothering needed very little protection. "Bobby was still at my flat, and his record was in the planning stages. We were all concerned about what songs Dylan was going to do. I clearly remember talking about it. Suddenly, I realized Bobby *knew* what he was going to do and how he was going to go about it. He knew exactly where he was going and how big he was going to be.

"Bobby certainly is a classic Gemini," Carla continued. "I've known other Geminis in Italy, just like him—schizy. The classic Gemini definition really fits Bobby—split, flashes of brilliance, contradictions, and the inability to stay in one place. I was Pisces and Suze was a Scorpio. Geminis and Pisces think alike, but can't get along. Geminis are supposed to devour Scorpios, just eat them up, and that's just what happened with Bobby and Suze. I'll never forget that day when I got that feeling that he didn't need me or *anyone.* Up until then, he had just been a bumbling kid, and everybody was helping him with money, clothes, and everything. He knew what he was doing, all along. None of us had seen it, because he was so good at masking it, with the kid stuff, with the indifferent, lost attitude. Even musically, he knew every step he was taking. He used to sing 'Highway Fifty-one' very slow, drawling it like Rabbit Brown, yet when he got to the studio, he cut it fast. He had absolutely never done it with such drive and tempo before. Here was a man who instinctively knew which way to go. The only mistake he made was being caught up in the vortex of being 'the messiah.' "

Did Carla feel she had been wasting concern on him? "Not so much that as the feeling of 'What a stupid fool I've been. He's probably been laughing at me all the time.' All of us were buzzing about him like mother hens. We were all quite necessary to Bobby, but how foolish we were all in that time, when he was laughing at us, and yet he needed us just the same. He may still have been the shambling, bumbling, angelic one with the cap on, on the surface, but he wasn't that underneath, to me. It was a time to pull off the masks. The bumbling child covered over the ambition and the carefully thought-out plan. He didn't need anyone's help or advice. . . . From then on, I made no reference about his recording or how he should do it. My mother was the only one who disliked Dylan. I still liked him very much, and may have even admired him more after I saw how smart he was."

After having slept on so many sofas around the Village, Bob decided to get a sofa of his own. Early in 1962, he found a two-room apartment at 161 West Fourth Street. The building rose four flights over Bruno's spaghetti parlor. A concrete stoop rose to the flats above. Dylan rented the first floor rear for about sixty dollars a month. There was a tiny bedroom and another kitchenette/dining/living room. He had bought a small, second-hand Motorola TV, which didn't work, and he proceeded to rebuild it, covering it with a blond-wood cabinet. He built a table with space for meals, the TV in the middle, and a niche for his typewriter. The portable nearly always stood ready with a piece of yellow copy paper in it, a few lines of a song-in-progress peeking out. The apartment was decorated with dust, a hard wooden chair, instruments of all sorts, a few Mexican belts, guitar straps, and a ceramic bull. There was barely room for one person. When Suze moved in, there was scarcely room for anyone.

Within months, Suze fell under heavy pressures to go to Italy. Her mother and stepfather wanted her to study, and she wanted perspective. She decided to take a summer course at the University of Perugia, then study art at the Accademia. Through the spring, Dylan was miserable and Suze was ambivalent, wanting to stay and wanting to be on her own. She seriously considered marrying him. "Maybe you should marry him," Carla told Suze, equivocating that if the relationship were good it would be just as good after six months. At the end of May, Suze left for Italy. At the boat, both Bob and Suze were distraught. During nine months of separation, Bob spun chaotically in a great whirlpool of personal loss but artistic gain. Acutely lonely, he turned to his New York friends—the MacDougal Street hippies—me, Sybil Weinberger, Gil Turner, and, increasingly, to various southern civil rights activists.

After Suze left, Dylan suffered many anxieties about his health. He told one friend that he feared he was going blind, that a doctor had once told him he *was* going blind. Frequent phone calls to Suze, often costing one hundred dollars each, didn't bring her back any earlier. Bob turned to other Village girls, who listened to him talk about Suze. Said one: "I remember ironing his shirt and thinking that I was being such a Jewish mama. Yet, I was frightened by him. There was no real communication."

Sybil Weinberger: "He was a dirty, sloppy, way-out young man, immature, irresponsible. He had a great compassion, always for things outside of himself, like the Negro situation. Bobby was not the least caught up in the pettiness, jealousies, and professional competition around at the time. I respected him for that. But, I resented him for it, because everybody was a critic then, and everybody was busy judging and categorizing everyone trying to make it. Bobby was above and beyond all that. When we walked down the street, he saw things that absolutely nobody else saw. He was so aware of his surroundings, in every situation, it was almost like he couldn't write fast enough. He would get thoughts and reactions and he would stop on a street corner and write things down. That was frightening to me too. His reactions to things amazed me—to weather, people, cars, buildings, shapes. I always felt his comments had a great deal of objectivity. He would reach for that little spiral notebook and write about animals on the street or a newspaper headline."

Another Rotolo friend was a drawling Louisianian actor, Quinton Raines, who had been working on *Brecht on Brecht,* a musical. Suze wanted to bring Bob into her theater world; Quinton seemed the ideal bridge. An experimental meeting with Quinton, at Jack Delaney's restaurant, lasted five hours. Carla said they "tried to get Bob to see the Brecht show." (Quinton says Bob admitted that he had never seen a stage play before, a dubious contention considering Bonny Beecher appeared regularly in University of Minnesota productions.) *Brecht on Brecht* opened some doors for Dylan. Bertolt Brecht was the prolific playwright, poet, lyricist-librettist (notably with Kurt Weill in *The Threepenny Opera* and *Mahagonny*), and Marxist theoretician. A refugee from the Nazis, Brecht lived in America during the war years, returned to East Germany, and led the Berliner Ensemble until his death in 1956.

Brechtian ideas, language, and style coursed through Dylan's politicized period of 1962–63. Brecht's theme that Hitler's Germany was caused by sheepish belief in leaders was echoed in one of Dylan's cardinal tenets: "Don't follow leaders."[5] "Pirate Jenny" may have influenced "When the Ship Comes In." In the 1970s, a gifted Yugoslav-born London-based singer, Bettina Jonic, performed and recorded twenty-two works by Brecht and Dylan. Jonic saw the two writers reflecting Germany of the 1920s and America of the 1960s: "To relate Brecht with Dylan was natural. Their simplicity of style and use of language were so alike; yet they were two unique voices speaking with enormous force and directness. A black boy killed out of bigotry [Dylan] or a girl killed for sleeping with a Jew [Brecht] becomes that timeless voice speaking out against atrocity. Following this pattern leaves one with a sense of the poet's range, despair, his need to speak and hold up to life a bitter mirror."

Quinton says he tried to talk Dylan into writing a play. "Over a period of three or four months, we talked about the songs he would do for the play. Sometimes, after a long drinking session, he would get up, saying 'I feel like I'm gonna go home and write me a whole lot of songs. I feel a lot of songs coming.' And sure enough, three or four days later, he would come up with those songs he had felt coming on. But he never did produce any songs specifically for that play." Quinton noticed that Dylan "seemed to structure personal tempests to give himself the inspiration to write. He was least productive in his songwriting when things got more settled. Strange, isn't it?"

THE BALLAD OF *BROADSIDE*

One tempest that inspired Dylan was America in 1962, a time when American protest was becoming a mass movement, no longer some small splinter party of Leftist ideologues meeting in an uncrowded telephone booth.

The roots of the protesting sixties run into the loam of the fifties, when conservatism and self-interest dominated American youth. Criticizing the American way of life then was not only unfashionable, but downright dangerous. Eisenhower was in the White House and a paler shade of pale blanched the American temperament. Censorship was rampant, orthodoxy ascendant. Senator Joseph R. McCarthy, despite his outlandish sightings of a Communist under every bed, dominated national politics. The John Birch Society used its propaganda to heighten anti-Leftism. The arch-Rightist Minutemen trained at secret rifle ranges to become an armed militia against "the inevitable Communist takeover of Washington." In the 1950s, those who dissented too vociferously, or at all, could reasonably expect to be hauled before either the House of Representatives Committee on Un-American Activities, as Pete Seeger was, or the Senate Internal Security Sub-Committee, as I was.

The cold war against Leftists, dissenters, or even independent liberals in the arts had been slowly putting a glacial crust over the landscape. The investigators turned to Hollywood in the late 1940s, and managed to get nearly every Left-winger in the studios either blacklisted or otherwise barred from work. A group of noted screenwriters, The Hollywood Ten, served a year in jail for refusing to cooperate with the House Un-American Activities Committee.

In folk music, there were successive smears against the organizations People's Artists and People's Songs, outgrowths of the wartime radical folk-song movement. For a while the witch-hunt managed to silence The Weavers, who enjoyed hits in the early 1950s. Increasingly, sociological pulse-takers found postwar Americans more interested in security than sanity; more anxious to hail the status quo than to expose the status woe.

Artists, however, almost always demand free sway. One freshet of protest art started in the 1950s with the English "angry young men." Playwright John Osborne looked back in anger and wondered what victory the war had achieved, other than a chilling, purposeless conformity. In the States, dissent came from new comics like Lenny Bruce, Lord Buckley, Mort Sahl, and Dick Gregory, who found the repressive 1950s grimly laughable. Mort Sahl suggested that voters would reelect Eisenhower "to keep the White House empty for another four years."

Another form of 1950s dissent came from the beat poets and writers—Allen Ginsberg, Lawrence Ferlinghetti, Jack Kerouac, Gregory Corso, and others—who had different visions of America. The beats retreated from mainstream American life, making dropping out hip. How Dylan put the beats and Woody Guthrie on his own highway is one of the themes of this book. While Madison Avenue was the Street of American Dreams, a precious few began hiking Kerouac's open road. Keeping the flickering light of protest folk song glowing in the 1950s were Pete Seeger, People's Artists, and People's Songs, mostly through *Sing Out!* magazine. Nothing could stop lanky, country-booted Seeger's talk and songs of a better world. In the early 1960s, Guy Carawan adopted Pete's persona of a folk-singing Johnny Appleseed, and helped spur the "freedom song" movement among southern integrationists. Other Seeger devotees were Peter Yarrow, Mary Travers, and Gil Turner, from Bridgeport, Connecticut.

Gil was a good friend of Dylan's for two years, beginning in late 1961. A portly, open-faced, wholesome-looking man in his late twenties, son of a former opera singer, Gil had been a Baptist preacher. An experienced congregational singing leader, Gil left the church when he discovered Seeger's wider pastorate. Gil's attitude toward Pete resembled Dylan's attachment to Guthrie. He had a large, warm baritone, played guitar and banjo, and was a wizard chorus master. In autumn 1961, he became Folk City's emcee, and met all the singer-songwriters passing through. None struck him more forcefully than Dylan.

Several times a week, after Gerde's closed around midnight, Gil, Bob, and I walked over to the West Village to the White Horse near the docks, or to Jim and Bertha McGowan's Off-Broadway bar on Greenwich Avenue. The Horse was a storied English-style pub, a hangout of Dylan Thomas's during his declining days. Richard Burton used to come by, and in the late 1950s, The Clancy Brothers, the Irish folk singers, were regulars. Both Dylans loved the constant party atmosphere. Writer-habitués (like Mike Harrington and Jimmy Baldwin), salty longshoremen, painters, talkers, drunkards, and midnight genies kept the Horse galloping. McGowan's was quieter, but it stayed opn until four A.M. It was decorated with theater playbills and stage pictures. A framed letter from Sean O'Casey to the McGowans hung on the wall. The McGowans loved Dylan and often subsidized his sandwiches and drinks. One night there, Gil told Dylan about a new concept for a magazine, and recruited Bob into the *Broadside* experiment.

After Seeger had toured Britain in 1961, he returned excited about the

burgeoning of topical songwriting there. He wanted something comparable in the States. Seeger longed to develop younger writers to carry on the
work that he, Malvina ("Little Boxes") Reynolds, Vern Partlow, Ernie
Marrs, and others had done. Pete was joined by his old friend Sis Cun-
ningham, long in the southern labor movement, a friend of Woody's from
Oklahoma, and a member of The Almanac Singers. Her husband, Gordon
Friesen, described their idea in Volume 1 of *Broadside Songs,* published by
Oak: "How do we know that young people all over America may not be
writing topical songs right now? It's just that we're not hearing about it.
The big commercial music publishers and recording companies aren't interested in this sort of material. We may just be assuming that songs like
this aren't being written and sung. God knows, there isn't much of an
outlet for them."

At their first meeting, Pete, Sis, and Gordon launched a little mimeographed bulletin of topical songs called *Broadside,* after Elizabethan song
or news sheets, printed for rapid dissemination. Pete retained strong links
with *Sing Out!,* but *Broadside* aimed to be small. Pete and Sis found their
spark plug in Gil Turner. Besides recruiting Dylan, Gil brought the live-
liest young songwriters to the monthly meetings. Two young music journalists, Josh Dunson and Julius Lester, cut their teeth there. Much later,
self-styled Dylanologist A. J. Weberman honed his analytical ax there.
Dylan was keen on *Broadside* from the start. It printed his new songs and
made him part of a movement. He listened to song tapes from around the
country, and even tried to improve some himself. He heeded Seeger and
what Sis and Gordon could, with authority, interpret as "what Woody
would think." *Broadside* clearly stimulated Dylan's writing in 1962
and 1963. Josh Dunson described a typical, lighthearted meeting in *Broadside* 20:

"*Broadside*'s home is a small little room. . . . Gil Turner took out his 12-
stringer, borrowed a flat-pick. Sis took out the mike for the tape-recorder,
and out came a talking blues Gil just wrote about the newspaper strike
that had us all quietly laughing."

Turner's song, "The Great New York Newspaper Strike," went, in part:

So here I am sittin' in the news hungry city . . .
The publishers don't care, they ain't got no pity . . .
Can't find me a job or a place to stay; this lock-
out's took the classified away . . . Spent my last cash
money, a two dollar bill. Went to a folk music
concert at Carnegie Hall . . . There was old-timey
singers, some blues pickers, too, a cowboy and
Pete Seeger sung a song or two. It mighta been
good, it mighta been swell, but I'll be darned if
I can tell . . . Got no New York Times, Got no Bob
Shelton review . . . got no Opinion.

There's a rumor goin' around, and it's pretty
gory, So I'll pass it along and finish my story . . .
It says World War Three began last Sunday, and the
whole world was blown up by noon on Monday. Now
the earth is completely mushroom shrouded, But New
Yorkers don't know a thing about it . . . Someday this
strike'll be over . . . And that'll really be the end.
As for me, I can't wait till then—gotta have some news now.
So I'm goin' out for coffee with my friend Bob
Dylan, the only major newspaper in New York that's
not on strike.[6]

"Then," Dunson continued, "Gil took out his six-string Gibson, handed it over to Bob Dylan, saying how Bob's new song, 'Masters of War,' was one of the best Bob had ever written. I kept on thinking he had written . . . some that had real lyric poetry, like 'Blowin' in the Wind' and 'Hard Rain's Gonna Fall' which makes you think right away of [Federico García] Lorca, and I waited for the images of rain, and thunder, and lightning to come out in great spectacles. But no, this time there was a different kind of poetry, one of great anger, accusation, just saying who the masters of war are, without compromising one inch in its short sharp direct intensity . . . right after that, not waiting . . . to get two breaths, Bob came along with 'Playboys and Playgirls,' a group song Pete said 'is going to be sung by a million people in the next year.' Its tune catches whole crowds easy, and the words come right along from the feeling. . . ."[7]

In came Phil Ochs, and Happy Traum, another member of Turner's group, The New World Singers. Pete said, "You know, in the past five months I haven't heard as many good songs and as much good music as I've heard here tonight." Along with Paul Krassner's *The Realist,* and *The Village Voice, Broadside* probably pioneered the 1960s underground press. In 1970, Friesen said of those 1962 meetings: "There was no pressure from the need for commercial success. We recognized that this was unlikely in any event, with *Broadside* strong on protest songs. . . . I was willing to bet Columbia Records would never record Dylan's 'Masters of War' and 'With God on Our Side.' " Columbia became the first major record label to recognize the topical-song upheaval. Through John Hammond, Columbia signed Pete, and social-comment music began to reach a wider audience.

Dylan was only one of a half dozen regulars at *Broadside* meetings in 1962, but Pete knew that Bob was turning out topical songs of a quality unheard since Woody. Seeger was the first established performer Dylan influenced. By the end of 1962, Seeger was performing Dylan songs and singling him out as the most important new songwriter of the time. Dylan had his first song printed in *Broadside,* the lyrics to "Talkin' John Birch Paranoid Blues," in the first issue, February 1962. "Blowin' in the Wind" was on the cover of *Broadside* 6 in May 1962. For a year and a half, the first place one saw Dylan's songs, even before performance, was in *Broadside,* where Bob was listed as a contributing editor.

Among the first of the young singer-songwriters to show up was Len Chandler. Peter La Farge, Ochs, and Paxton, Canadian singer Bonnie Dobson, and Spoelstra surfaced later. When she was in town, Malvina Reynolds always came in. Said Gordon:

"We looked upon them as a school of new topical songwriters, rather than as individual stars. Bob seemed a little special, but not enough to set him above Phil or Len or the others. (Otherwise, we would have made a lot more tapes of Dylan, and got him to sing more than he did on our first album.) Bob just seemed a kid, somehow, quite nervous when he wasn't singing and playing, doing a perpetual little dance with his boot toes, even seated. He struck me as rather inarticulate while trying to talk, his sentences fading away. But there was a tremendous transformation when he started playing and singing. One was astonished to hear that kind of driving playing on guitar and powerful singing voice coming from a kid who hadn't even started growing a beard. I frankly was baffled by the discrepancy, and harbored the impression for a while that he was somehow putting us on, taking us in. I thought some of his songs were deliberate takeoffs on folk songs, hoaxes. One song especially struck me as such—'I Will Not Go Down Under the Ground.' I thought: 'Who is he trying to kid?' But you couldn't tell from his facial expression. He didn't look at you while he sang, but kept his eyes on his guitar and hands. Another song I thought was contrived to make a joke of folk song in general was the one about 'Playboys and Playgirls.' I forgot these suspicions when he wrote 'Masters òf War' and 'God on Our Side,' which seemed deeply profound statements, superior, I thought, to anything Woody had ever done."

Sis and Gordon and those gathering at their apartment in Manhattan's West Nineties were strongly political, but not the stolid sort of *Sing Out!* Left-politicos. The two publications regarded each other as siblings. *Broadside* was intimate and human, a good setting for Dylanesque jokes. Because he was under contract to Columbia, Dylan did his tracks on the first *Broadside* album under the pseudonym "Blind Boy Grunt."

Friesen, in 1970: "Bob looked upon his appearance on that record as a joyful little prank. After all, there was no money in it, the whole thing being a benefit for *Broadside....*" The record was out in spring 1963, Turner herding talent into a Folkways studio. Moe Asch advanced one hundred dollars for the first of four *Broadside* albums (a subsidiary of his main Folkways label). By the time *Broadside* was a year old, issue twenty of February 1963, "Masters of War" was on page one with illustrations by Suze, "Playboys and Playgirls" was on page two, and the issue included an early version of "Don't Think Twice." (The last, neither political nor topical, indicated *Broadside*'s flexibility.) Nearly every other 1963 issue had either a new Dylan song or some Dylanology. This continued throughout the 1960s, although Dylan had drifted away from the magazine by 1964.

Later, Dylan paid tribute to *Broadside,* but he also minimized it, reflecting his perennial ambivalence toward sources of help, which were always pitted against his disdain of "moral debts." The *Broadside* experiment was seminal. By stressing songs relevant to the real world, by underscoring "songs that said something," by encouraging young songwriters to build a new style of socially conscious musical expression, *Broadside* succeeded, out of all proportion to its modest format, its readership of a few hundred. With *Broadside*'s encouragement, Dylan flowered before he was accepted by the public, and sharpened his craft. The roots of the revolution in popular music that Dylan led lie partly in those monthly meetings and the crudely mimeographed pages of *Broadside.*

ENTER THE BEAR

Albert B. Grossman, known as "the bear," had a body and manner to match the sobriquet, and a face that suggests an owl forced into the light. A portly, prematurely gray man, he had large eyes slightly hidden by glasses that suggest Ben Franklin before *he* went electric. After Dylan went electric the third time, in 1965, Albert knotted his long hair behind his neck, like an Indian brave. "When I first met Albert, I thought he was just a street bear," Dylan told me once of the man who was his personal manager from 1962 until the relationship was legally dissolved in June 1971. After Dylan's accident, dealings between Dylan and his "Dear Landlord" were never quite the same. Grossman, who actually lived in Bearsville, just outside Woodstock, was a teddy or a grizzly, depending on your point of view.

When Dylan met Albert, he was wary. Bob knew how pivotal the right manager would be, and how many would wave pens at him. Working informally with Terri Van Ronk, Bob was still in charge, and did not have to deal with the uptown business world. Albert, however, was always around the Village, chatting with musicians, sitting like Buddha contemplating, they hoped, their futures. Bob and Albert's strange, often stormy, relationship was in some ways a true marriage of minds and temperaments, each quickly adopting the worst traits of the other. The striking difference was that Bob had appeared to be a relatively open person with considerable human compassion, while Albert had always been the chess player. At his worst, Grossman was contemptuous; at his best, he was a tasteful talent manager who worked with a minimum of commercial agentry tawdriness. At his worst, his dominant interest was money; at his best, he made money only with artists of quality.

As soon as Dylan had his Columbia contract, music-business sharks smelled blood. Bob played a waiting game. Hammond suggested Harold Leventhal, who represented Seeger, Judy Collins, The Weavers, and, best of all, Guthrie. Dylan's relationship with Leventhal never jelled. Bob started to pal around with Roy Silver, who, with Bob Gibson, an influential musician, had launched a college talent booking group, Campus Concepts. Silver—who later managed comedian Bill Cosby—was such an early Dylan freak that he later told me it cost him his first marriage: "Instead of going home at night, I was haunting Village places where I could listen to Bobby, or just hang out with him...." Silver was then working with Grossman, but he sold out to him in 1962, parting with his interest in Dylan and others for ten thousand dollars.

Paul Stookey believes that he first touted Dylan to Albert. One night at the Gaslight in 1961, Stookey either gave Bob a news clipping about a riot on a Hudson excursion boat, or just mentioned the incident. The next night, Dylan walked into the Gaslight and sang Stookey his "Talking Bear Moutain Picnic Massacre Blues." Stookey told Grossman that Dylan was a talent to watch. Albert watched. Around the time of Bob's LP release, after months of cultivating Dylan's trust, Grossman made direct overtures. Bob told me then that Albert said he was not interested in working with any artist who couldn't make at least fifty thousand dollars a year. Dylan said Albert saw him as not just a coffeehouse performer but as a concert and recording artist. Albert had built his reputation representing Odetta, whom Bob had admired since Dinkytown. The growing stature of Peter, Paul and Mary also impressed Dylan. I advised Bob to consider Grossman's bid seriously. I recalled that he had discovered Baez and staged her Newport debut in 1959.

To many, Grossman was a sinister, relentlessly nay-saying figure. "He just thinks he's God," said Tom Clancy. To others, he was a "beautiful cat," dedicated to the highest standards of performing integrity, not a hawker of talent, but a creative force. Even those whom Grossman represented vary in their opinions. And from 1960 onward, Albert changed a good deal.

When he first shuffled into the Village, he often sang sea chanteys and Bulgarian folk music in a booming bass. When he chose to be, he was a convivial talker. Grossman tended to be a sphinx. He was born on Chicago's West Side to a family that valued education and security. After graduating from Lane Technical High School, Albert got an M.S. in economic theory from the University of Chicago. He was interested in acting, politics, and music. One of his professors was Bruno Bettelheim, the child psychologist. As a trained economic theorist and a semitrained child psychologist, Albert became one of the most powerful managers in 1960s show business.

He preferred to work in the shadows and sought no limelight, but he appreciated his growing repute as a starmaker. Enduring his charges' idiosyncrasies, he was confessor and psychiatrist to them all, including Janis Joplin. His chief reward was money—tons of it, bags of it. His subsidiary reward was power, which he used judiciously at first, until he gradually became possessed by it. The performer-clients who most admire Albert describe him as a protector against the machinations of the music business. Peter Yarrow told me in 1970: "Albert is totally involved creatively. His ears are good. There would have been no Baez, no Dylan, and no Peter, Paul and Mary without Albert. He kept us insulated from the flesh-peddling aspect of show business. Next to Albert, Dylan was an amateur at cutting people down. Albert is an expert at destroying other people's sense of self. He readily admits it. Albert only attacks when others are playing a role. Albert basically doesn't trust the press. He is very shy, and cynical, because he has seen friends corrupted. He is also an idealist. Bobby was imitating everyone at one stage, and he naturally began to imitate and learn a lot of Albert's tricks. I think that Albert stimulated Bobby a great deal."

Paul Stookey answered me with a question: "If a plumber comes to your house and unplugs your drains, would you say he was helping your life, creatively? Albert was like that plumber. He would point out superfluous things we were doing or saying. When Albert says to do something, he's always right. When he says he thinks you shouldn't do something, he may not be right." Paul thought Albert was so widely misunderstood "because Albert is brutally honest and has an early-warning bullshit-detecting device that shows personal annoyance very openly."

Like Dylan, Mary Travers is a former admirer. In 1970–71, when I was seeing quite a bit of Mary in London, she clearly felt Grossman had taken advantage of her. When she discovered that Grossman had been earning more than she or Peter or Paul, she switched to Leventhal.

Managers are professional villains, doomed to represent their clients' negative sides. When Dylan wanted to say no to someone impolitic to refuse, he would often say: "I have to check that out with Albert." Albert emerged as the sourpuss saying no, and Bob appeared the amiable youngster in the older manipulator's hands. Even as saintly a star as Seeger, who would say "I hate to say no," left Leventhal to say: "Oh, no, not another benefit concert!" Albert expertly finessed management's dirty work. He seemed to enjoy saying no, just as some lawyers enjoy threatening action. Grossman the bulwark, the buffer, took the blame for everything. In 1964, when Dylan left a Tufts University audience waiting all evening for a concert, Grossman's aide, Charlie Rothschild, explained, "Someone in the office made a scheduling error." Even if Dylan had been out stoned, the Grossman office took the onus. Some suggested Grossman had engineered Dylan's going electric to make more money. Albert was probably one of the last to know about the change.

Leventhal managed to seem approachable and personable. Brian Epstein, The Beatles' manager, was impeccably polite, making me, and many another journalist, welcome at his Belgravia home. Mort Lewis, who represented Simon and Garfunkel, often hid behind the shield of "the needs and interests of the boys." Manny Greenhill, Baez's manager, would feign ignorance. Herbie Cohen, who managed the Modern Folk Quartet, Judy Henske, and Frank Zappa, would evade questions with jokes about the tough music business. Grossman said nothing. He preferred, like Dylan, to "make myself invisible." Having known Grossman for years, I see a man not blessed with the infallibility he projected. He had been rapturous over an Israeli duo, The Dudaim, who were talented but never got off the ground. Rejected by Baez, Grossman found and promoted a dark-haired soprano, Lynn Gold, who disappeared into obscurity. In the early days, Grossman was considerably more open, dropping remarks about his stars. He became increasingly tough, distant, and thick-skinned. His stars became "his people," and no one, certainly not a writer, would be welcome to ask questions about them. When I asked Grossman in 1965 what he thought Dylan had meant by something, Albert said, with a smile, "I'm just a Jewish businessman."

That Dylan and Grossman found each other was no surprise. For a while, they were amazingly similar in temperament. Although Grossman was a good dozen years older, no other performer ever so influenced him. Dylan's taste prompted Grossman's signing Paul Butterfield, John Lee Hooker, The Kweskin Jug Band, and The Band. Peter Yarrow maintained that Dylan found in Grossman the father he was looking for, and that, as their relationship deteriorated in 1965-71, Bob was symbolically destroying the father, the authority figure, to whom he was indebted. Grossman may have found a rebellious son in Dylan. Bob rarely flaunted the cracks in the family crockery, while Albert pretended there were none.

Grossman's clients tended to like his methods because they knew that the enemies Albert fought were just as cruel. He made demands that few other managers dared, put up with abuse from his artists that few others would take. From 1964 to 1966, he put up with a great deal from Dylan. Grossman feigned modesty when I told him that some people maintained Dylan would never have made it without him: "That's ridiculous! He would have made it without anyone," Albert replied.

Working closely with Grossman was a former Tommy Dorsey Band road manager, a bright, aggressive executive, Artie Mogull, who was with the publishing house of M. Witmark & Sons, of Music Publishers Holding Corporation, later Warner Bros. Music. In early summer 1962, Grossman and Silver brought Dylan to Mogull. Bob sang him nearly all his songs. Mogull wanted to sign him for Witmark, but discovered that Hammond had already arranged for Dylan to be published by Leeds/Duchess music. In a move vaguely reminiscent of the Russian sale of Alaska, Mogull got Dylan released for nothing. Dylan signed a three-year publishing contract with Witmark on July 13, 1962.

"I offered Dylan one thousand dollars to sign with Witmark," Mogull told me. "I had to fight to get that one thousand dollars, and now the songs have easily earned a million dollars and will continue to earn for years to come." Artie said he had made the one-thousand-dollar advance on his own personal note and had it deducted from his salary for ten weeks. "In his three years with Witmark, Dylan gave them two hundred thirty-seven copyrights. That was unheard of! He is amazingly prolific. Ordinarily, it would have been something to get twenty-five songs out of a writer in three years." (In his autobiography, *John Hammond on Record,* the producer said that Dylan used five hundred dollars of Artie's thousand to buy his way out of the Leeds/Duchess publishing contract.)

Mogull, the self-described "world's greatest talent scout," may have been instrumental in getting Grossman into the financial big time. For signing Peter, Paul and Mary, Warner Bros. advanced thirty thousand dollars, which Grossman parlayed into millions. Although not under Grossman's roof, Mogull was one of his key people. When MGM Records considered signing Dylan in 1967, Mogull negotiated. Although that deal never came off, luck, timing, and expertise enabled Mogull and Grossman to do an extraordinary job of plugging Dylan's songs. Through Milt Okun, they got Dylan songs recorded by three groups. Izzy Young once told me Mogull had offered him ten thousand dollars to tout Dylan songs within the folk community, an offer Izzy turned down. After autumn 1963, Dylan's songs scarcely needed pushing. Judy Collins, British star Manfred Mann, and American singer-actor Hamilton Camp—not to mention Grossman's own people, Odetta and Peter, Paul and Mary—were clamoring to record new Dylan songs. Mogull and Grossman guided these song fortunes along until 1965, when the Witmark contract ran out and Dylan and Grossman formed their own music-publishing company. Hired as its manager: Artie Mogull.

My relationship with Grossman reached its low note in late 1965 when, one night at the Limelight in the Village, I told him that some publishers had approached me about writing a Dylan book. "If you do that, I'll sue you, before the book comes out, or after it comes out, or both," Albert exploded. Mary Travers and Canadian singers Ian and Sylvia, who were also at our table, looked astonished. "Albert," I said, "some day we ought to have a talk about power and its abuse." He settled down, and when I saw him in his office a week later, he was not quite so litigious, but still huffy: "It's opportunism, it's premature, you can't report anything that hasn't been specifically stated for publication." How opportunistic was it for him, I asked, to use the press for publicity but not for documentation of what really goes on in show business? "You're being Italianate," he said. "Well," I concluded our chilly confrontation, "let's see what Bob says when he gets back from the Coast." Dylan showed immediate interest in my project, and told Albert to lay off.

As time passed, Grossman mellowed. At one point, in January 1968, he told me: "I would help if I could, but sometimes I feel I don't know *anything* about Bob Dylan." By May 1971, Grossman had his final line: "There's a girl in this office [Myra Friedman] doing a serious book about Janis Joplin, but even though Janis is dead, I had to tell Myra that I

couldn't help her. What is public is public, what is private is private."
That week, Dylan had told me: "Albert would never help you." When a
reporter misinterprets him, Grossman rages, even though a civil interview
could have prevented misinterpretation.

HAMMOND'S FOLLY

Whatever differences Bob subsequently had with his record producer, in
the early months John Hammond gave Dylan keen encouragement. Even
though the first royalty for his initial album gave Bob barely enough to
pay his electric bill, Hammond remained convinced that Dylan was a
major talent. Columbia cynics continued to call Dylan "Hammond's
Folly." Hammond arranged for Dylan to meet the head of the Music Corporation of America talent agency. Talk ensued about starring Bob as
Holden Caulfield in a film of J. D. Salinger's *Catcher in the Rye.* That
project evaporated.

Dylan's other chief advocate at Columbia was an uncommonly bright
publicist named Billy James. Even though he was handling publicity for
dozens of performers, Billy only once went out of his way to call my attention to a Columbia group, The Byrds. Journalists tended to trust Billy's
taste and integrity. He recalled:

"Hammond called me and said: 'Billy, I have a marvelous boy in the
studio right now. Do you have a moment to come up?' I knew that it was
happening . . . right there! He had such an incredible blend of influences,
and presented them with conviction. Bobby was reluctant to talk about
his past. I had encountered that often before. I was really startled to hear
of all the places he had been to. He spoke with knowledge of all those
places, not like the traveling salesman who only knows the inside of his
hotel room." Dylan asked Billy if he wanted to be his manager. "I told
him no, it isn't my line of business," said Billy.

Hammond suggested Bob get his songs published by Leeds affiliate, the
Duchess Music Corporation. Dylan told Billy later: "There were all these
little rooms and when they opened up the doors, there were these songwriters sitting there writing!" The regimentation astounded Dylan. He
told Billy he felt many around Columbia were not reacting genuinely, and
feared that if he met them on the street, they might not be so nice to him.
But Billy was different. After a hiatus, 1963–65, Bob resumed their friendship. Billy set up Dylan's first magazine interview, in 1962, with Edwin
Miller of *Seventeen:*

" '. . . There was a violent, angry emotion running through me then; I
don't know why. . . . [Hammond] asked me if I wanted to sing any of
them over again but I said no. I can't see myself singing the same song
twice in a row. . . . I don't work regularly. I don't want to make a lot of
money, really. I wander around the city a lot, I take the ferry to Staten Island or I walk down by the river. Or maybe I'll sit around all day with a

painter I know. . . . I can't go out after people. If they want what I've got, they always have to come to me with their hands out and take from me. That's the way I am.' "

Rachel Price of *FM-Stereo Guide* did a thoughtful piece in autumn 1962: " 'Some people consider me a poet, but I can't think about it. There are too many poets. . . . I just returned from a trip to the West and I had forgotten how quiet and pleasant life was there. You don't have to plan things, they just happen. Right now I'm waiting . . . waiting for my girl to come home from a trip. . . . I want to give, but on my terms. Nightclubs are not my terms. People go there to see gladiators fight, and I don't want to be part of the spectacle. . . . Teen-agers have so much stuff shot at them because they buy so much and are such easy prey. I don't want to be one more bullet in the gun aimed at them. . . .' "

Dylan was canny during early interviews. Soon, Billy simply handled arrangements, or even fought off requests for interviews.

PORTRAIT OF THE ARTIST

Throughout 1962, while Suze was in Italy, Dylan continued making friends in New York. Jimmy Richmond, who ran the Music Inn record store a few doors west along Fourth Street, knew Dylan as a regular. Bob popped in several times a week to hear new tracks. Up the street was the little grocery run by the Brignole sisters, two walk-ons from a De Sica film. Bobby was their favorite, even though he seemed to eat very little. They could always count on him for a few packs of cigarettes a day, for coffee and milk. When Bob was short of money, which was often, he would get credit, because they knew "such a nice boy" would certainly pay them back.

Then there was Harry Jackson, the rambunctious, bearded painter who adulated cowboy life. Harry, another citybilly from Chicago, had hit the road in search of a romantic life. He spent his adolescence in Wyoming, and had a genuine feel for the vanishing West. He kept that horsey ethos alive in his songs and housed his huge paintings in his cavernous loft in SoHo. Harry, an explosive maverick who did nothing by halves, was captivated. "He reminds me of some of those street musicians I see near my studio in Italy, just street waifs with a magic ability to hold your attention, to wring a few lire out of you, despite yourself." Harry told me, and everyone: "Dylan's so goddamned *real*—it's unbelievable." Harry asked Bob to sit for a portrait; maybe it could be an album cover one day. He got restless, squirming Bob down for three posing sessions. Even while concentrating on a canvas, Harry had a Stetsonful of stories about the Wyoming range. In spring 1962, Dylan told Elliott he was going to quit music and become a painter. Right after the *Newsweek* story of 1963, Dylan said he was going to quit music and paint. After his accident of 1966, he finally devoted more time to drawing.

Dylan's passion for films continued in New York, often at the Waverly Theater on Sixth Avenue, minutes from his pad. Two films had impressed him during the year, he told me. *Lonely Are the Brave* starred Kirk Douglas as the last individualist in the modern West. The hero failed, pursuing ideals being blotted out by "progress." The other film was *A Face in the Crowd,* from a Budd Schulberg story. It starred Andy Griffith as a guitar-picking "country boy" who became a celebrity, affecting advertising, TV, and, ultimately, national politics. Lonesome Rhodes was a Guthrie without a conscience, a Will Rogers with a power lust. *A Face in the Crowd* rivals *Citizen Kane* as a blistering portrait of an American parvenu undone by power. Dylan was more shaken by *A Face in the Crowd* than any film since *Rebel Without a Cause* or *The Wild One.* He could see here a country con man who used provincial charm and naïveté as a cover for manipulation. Lonesome Rhodes showed how to get to the top, but also what to avoid en route.

Dylan consolidated his friendships with musicians, learning and teaching, absorbing and sharing, influencing and being influenced. The music scene was a campus without walls. One of Dylan's favorite new friends was Paul Clayton, a gentle, lost, earnest folk singer, whose knowledge of balladry was wide. John Herald of The Greenbriar Boys became Bob's frequent companion. Herald contributed a wide grasp of folk-based country music, extrovert joy onstage, and meticulous attention to technique. Through "Gentleman Jim" Kweskin, Bob was in touch with an ease and flash, onstage and off, that was rare among Village folkniks. Long before I had really tuned in to Clayton or Kweskin, Dylan was prodding me to write them up. "It's just not fair that they're unknown," he said.

In 1962, Dylan befriended some of the leaders of the "freedom song" civil rights movement. Articulate, militant James Forman was a leader in the Student Non-Violent Coordinating Committee. Although SNICK, as it was called, was then close to the Southern Christian Leadership Council of the Reverend Martin Luther King, Jr., the student group found its own directions. Music was a prime vehicle. Two young activists, Bernice Johnson and Cordell Reagon, were leading the long desegregation campaign in Albany, Georgia. They and Forman had spent time in jail and made their way north, where folkniks became working allies and friends. Dylan took warmly to the SNICK activists, and they to him. He began to think their topical songs were more relevant than *Broadside:* "They are singing about themselves and the kind of lives they're leading." The New Yorkers embraced Bernice Johnson as a young Odetta. At eighteen, she had a gentle demeanor, yet could uncork a huge, beautiful voice. Bernice mastered the complex "Hard Rain" lyrics.

"I guess he was embarrassed at his voice then," Bernice later told me. "He seemed to think then that it was really bad. When he came up with a new song he always said that I should sing it, or Gil Turner, because we had better voices. We all thought, those of us in the movement and those of us in the Freedom Singers, that Dylan was fantastic as a songwriter and as a person." Bernice had considerable professional contact with Dylan over the next few years. As a militant, she could assess Dylan's changes. By 1964, he was going his own way, and many activists wrote him off as having "sold out" to show business. Bernice took issue: "I felt he was going through some fantastic emotional things and I didn't want to make any judgment. I knew he was displeased with his Columbia contract and he wasn't too keen to go to Europe in December 1962. I learned that his manager had the power of attorney and sent him there even though he didn't want to go. For a while, I feared that he was possibly just destroying himself. Still, I felt if he stayed alive, he would be all right. Some whites moved with us out of some special sort of love of blacks, while others were just loaded with guilt. Dylan wasn't the same. When he simply drifted away from the movement, it was the whites in SNICK who were resentful. The blacks in SNICK didn't think that, or say that. We only heard the phrase 'sellout' from the whites, not from the blacks. I've always just regarded Bob as a friend. He's never been a star to me, just a friend."

Dylan was also drawn closely to a sixty-year-old bluesman, Big Joe Williams. This Joe, not to be confused with Count Basie's singer of the same name, was born in 1903 in Oktibbeha County, Mississippi. His family had been too poor to own a radio or phonograph, but he heard music around the house. His granddad was a hymn-singing accordion player, one brother was a gospel singer, and three cousins sang spirituals and played guitar or washboard. According to Bob Koester of Delmark Records, Joe decided early on he "didn't want to plow, didn't want to chop cotton," so he made himself a primitive guitar. When Ethel Waters's minstrel show visited Joe's county, he left with the troupe. He recorded in the 1930s in Memphis for Vocalion and later on Paramount as King Solomon Hill. For a decade after 1935, he recorded prolifically for Bluebird, Columbia, and other labels. Joe recorded his most successful song, "Baby, Please Don't Go," three times; and it was also recorded by Big Bill Broonzy, Lightnin' Hopkins, and Mose Allison.

When Mike Porco considered booking Big Joe at Folk City in early 1962, Dylan hyped him: "He's the greatest old bluesman. You gotta put him in here." Mike did, for three weeks in February. Dylan showed up nearly every night, jammed with Big Joe onstage several times. For Joe, who had worked the streets, this first job in New York was exciting. It helped stimulate a revival in early blues, and Joe subsequently did LPs on several labels. The chemistry between Big Joe and Little Bob was so good that Joe invited him on his session for an LP he was scheduled to cut with Victoria Spivey, a blues doyenne, on her own Spivey label, on March 2, 1962. Bob was sure Columbia wouldn't give him permission, so he cut the session under the nom de blues of "Big Joe's Buddy." The album *Three Kings and a Queen* (Spivey LP 1004), released in October 1964, had two tracks with Dylan, "Sitting on Top of the World" and "Wichita," both by Big Joe. On "Sitting," Dylan played guitar and harmonica and did some alto-range harmonizing behind Joe's lead. The record did reasonably well.

Years later, Big Joe gave me an interview. Big Joe maintains he met Dylan in Chicago when Bob was only six! (Bob probably met Joe in Chicago in 1960 on his way east.) The matter is further obfuscated by Dylan's saying in 1962 that he had run off to Chicago when he was ten: "I saw a Negro musician playing his guitar on the street and I went up to him and began accompanying him on the spoons. I used to play the spoons when I was little." Complementing Dylan's story, Big Joe reconstructed the trip:

"I first met Bob about 1946 or 1947, in Chicago. I disremember the exact year, but he was very very young, probably no more than six. He looked the same that he looks now. I think he was just born with that talent. He used to get up on his tiptoes and was cracking wise just the way he do now. Well, I was just working on the streets of Chicago then, the way I had done since 1927. Somehow or other he knew songs I had made on records, like 'Baby, Please Don't Go' and 'Highway Forty-nine.' He met me on the North Side, around State and Grand, and we just walked down to State and Thirty-fifth Street. I was working, singing, all the way along. If we came up to some cabaret where he couldn't get in because he was too young, I would just leave him waiting outside on the curbstone. It must have taken us about three hours to make that trip. Bob was asking me all sorts of questions. He said that he was going to do this sort of thing one of these days, and I said that he would, because he had a lot of talent.

"We finally got down to that club at Thirty-fifth and State and Tampa Red was staying there with me. Well, we had one fine time back there in our room. Bob really enjoyed himself singing and playing. About six or seven years later, I saw him in Minneapolis, when he was playing with Tony Glover up there. Same Mississippi River I used to know, only the other end of it," said Joe. "Then, another time, Bob tried to look me up in Chicago, but I was working in Oakland. Bob found out my address there, and wrote me thanking me for the advice I had given him about music. What he earned, what he done, he got it honest. They ask me: 'Is he real?' And I tell them that they should let him live his own life."

In 1962, when I covered a gospel show at Randall's Island, Dylan joined me. I introduced him backstage to one of the warmest, most talented families in American music, The Staple Singers. The whole family took to Bob and were delighted, within a year, when they were all booked on a Westinghouse TV special together. Roebuck "Pop" Staples said later that Bob wrote "John Brown" for him in 1962.

The featured star at Randall's Island was Mahalia Jackson, the gospel queen. Dylan admired her music, but he was astounded that she arrived in a limousine, with aides holding up her long skirts as if she were royalty. The ostentatious show of wealth made out of people's piety rubbed Dylan the wrong way. He always saw blacks as people—good, bad, indifferent.

One lesson he learned from Mahalia was that stars should never display their wealth openly, should never turn nouveau riche, no matter how humble their origins.

Despite his depression while Suze was in Italy, Dylan kept himself prodigiously busy, but not as much as Grossman wanted. One night in the summer of 1962, Theodore Bikel, the actor-singer, threw a party at his Washington Square Village apartment. Dylan, our friend Sue Smith, and I went. Bob was more than a bit stoned. Somewhere along the way he had picked up a shiny, gray silk top hat, which ludicrously crowned his denim, suede, and boots. As Bob careened around the room in his top hat, many were appalled at this oddball. Lou Gottlieb of The Limeliters, with a background as a musicologist, was puzzled by the Dylan phenomenon, and his antics that night. Theo was gently bemused by this uninvited guest. Six months later, Theo was singing Dylan songs with passion.

Another guest at Bikel's was John Henry Faulk, the Texas-born broadcaster, a charming anecdotalist, one of the notable victims of the radio-TV blacklist. Faulk had challenged the McCarthyite faction in the performers union, AFTRA, and thereby incurred the wrath of the anti-Left vigilante blacklisting group, AWARE, Inc. Faulk was fired by CBS in 1956 and became unemployable. After years of scuffling, Faulk decided to strike back at the blacklisters. Retaining the lawyer Louis Nizer, Faulk sued AWARE for libeling him as pro-Communist. (The commentator Edward R. Murrow put up the initial $7,000 for legal fees.) Faulk won his case against the blacklisters and was awarded damages of $3.5 million, although he collected only a fraction of that amount. He was just writing his book *Fear on Trial* when Dylan met him. Dylan was fascinated by this latter-day Texas hero, friend of Alan Lomax, the folklorist.

Two important concerts in autumn 1962 advanced Dylan. On Saturday, September 22, *Sing Out!* presented its annual Hootenanny. On the bill were Seeger, The Lilly Brothers, Matt McGinn of Scotland, The Pennywhistlers, The New World Singers, and Bernice Johnson. Carnegie Hall was loaded with twenty folk singers and three thousand listeners. Dylan was not in good form. Seeger introduced Dylan as an especially important writer. Bob did only three songs, then wandered offstage disappointed with his performance.

Two weeks later, on October 5, Dylan was top-billed in a Town Hall concert with Ian and Sylvia, John Lee Hooker, Judy Collins, Lynn Gold, and instrumentalist Sandy Bull. Sponsored by the Folklore Center, the concert presented almost all Grossman clients or choices. The program was an experiment; a show of professionals coupled with amateur volunteers from the audience. "Bring your guitars and banjos," read the program for the show, scheduled to go on to various campuses. Dylan, in much better form, was among the most enthusiastically received. He did his "Talking New York," "John Birch," "Hollis Brown," and finished with "Hard Rain." Those who doubted Dylan's poetic gifts began to see what all the fuss was about.

By this time, the *Sing Out!* issue featuring Dylan was out. The cover showed Dylan dragging on a cigarette, eyes half-closed, à la Guthrie. Gil Turner's cover story called Dylan "the most prolific young songwriter in America today." Gil had him "rambling" when he was only a few months old. "Part of Dylan's magnetism is he is not the slightest bit afraid of falling flat on his face. If he gets an idea for a song or a story, he does it on the spot without worrying about whether it will come out exactly polished or right.... Reality and truth are words Dylan will use often.... They are his criteria for evaluating the world around him...."

Sing Out! voiced astonishment at Dylan's output: "Putting down songs fast ... The present record is five songs in one night. The latest is a song about blacklisting, inspired by the case of John Henry Faulk." The article included two other photographs of Dylan, the music and lyrics of "Blowin' in the Wind," "Letter to Woody," and "Ballad of Donald White," along with excerpts from other songs. *Sing Out!* never pushed a new songwriter so strongly.

FREEWHEELIN' BROADSIDE

Only three new tracks were released during 1962—his bit behind Belafonte, and a single issued at Christmas: "Mixed Up Confusion" backed with "Corrina, Corrina." To evaluate his development, the second Columbia album, *Freewheelin'*, and the first *Broadside* album have to be considered, even though not released until 1963. His first album got good reviews from *The Village Voice, Sing Out!*, and *Little Sandy Review*, but it sold less than five thousand copies in the first few months, a disappointment for a giant like Columbia, and for someone who had garnered as much good press. Bob thought of quitting music. But *Broadside*, Hammond, Grossman, and the Village clique gave him the support that record buyers didn't.

The Belafonte album, which also came out in May 1962, caused only a ripple. Dylan started to tape more tracks for Columbia. The final version of *The Freewheelin' Bob Dylan* was not released until July 1963, following nearly a year of uncongenial dealings among Hammond, Dylan, and Grossman, as well as Grossman's then partner, John Court, a former manager of the Chicago Playboy Club and one-time jazz drummer.

Nearly the first management step Grossman took was to try to get Bob out of his Columbia contract. He saw all its flaws, from percentages to its "special publishing rate," under which Dylan's compositions earned more if recorded by others than if he recorded them. Hammond's version of the hassle: "By this time, Bob had written 'Blowin' in the Wind' and Peter, Paul and Mary were convinced this was a masterpiece, as I was. He'd gone over to Warner Brothers [Witmark, later acquired by Warners]. Grossman's first idea was to combine Dylan with a Dixieland band. I didn't think this was any answer. I ordered John Court out of the studio one day. Grossman tried to take Dylan away from Columbia because his parents hadn't signed his contract also. Bobby had told me he didn't have any parents. The letter from the lawyer didn't mean anything, because Bobby by that time was twenty-one, and had been in the studio four times since he was twenty-one. I got Bobby to repudiate the letter, which got Grossman very uptight. We then decided that since Tom Wilson loved Bobby, this would be a very good marriage. . . ."

Wilson, a tall, handsome, affable man, was Columbia's first black producer. Although Hammond is listed as producer of Bob's second album, Wilson was the de facto producer of "Girl from the North Country," "Talkin' World War III Blues," "Bob Dylan's Dream," and "Masters of War." After Dylan's first single, "Mixed Up Confusion" and "Corrina," was released on December 24, 1962, it soon went out of print, but "Confusion" is historic. Had it been more widely known, "Confusion" could have stemmed confusion that Dylan was only an acoustic-guitar folk-topical performer. "Mixed Up Confusion" was recorded on November 14, 1962. When Dylan endured audience ferocity by switching to electric music in 1965, he was anxious to call attention to his first single and deleted tracks from *Freewheelin'*. They prove how early he had been into an electric sound. Here was folk-rock long before The Beatles.

"Nobody told me to go electric. No, I didn't ask anybody. I asked not a soul, believe me, I didn't ask anybody," Dylan stressed later. "Hey, I went electric on my second record. Why don't you bring that out in the book?" Dylan said. *Freewheelin*'s electric songs, including "Rocks and Gravel," were taken out to make room for his "Blowin' in the Wind," "Masters of War," and "Girl from the North Country."

The line from "Mixed Up Confusion," ". . . there's too many people/And they're all too hard to please . . ."[8] was an aside on the hassles around him. Still another hassle was the exclusion of "John Birch." Just after the Columbia Broadcasting System censor had refused to allow the song on *The Ed Sullivan Show,* Columbia Records panicked. Hammond: ". . . The CBS lawyers, not Columbia Records, decided that the reference to Hitler involved every single member of the John Birch Society, therefore it was libelous, or some crap like that. I get away with much worse material with Seeger than was ever on a Dylan album." Fewer than three hundred copies of the album went out with "John Birch" and three other deleted songs on it. These collectors' items went mostly to the Coast. The final *Freewheelin'* album appeared without "John Birch," "Rocks and Gravel," "Rambling Gambling Willie," and "Let Me Die in My Footsteps."

Freewheelin', released just after the tremendous success of Peter, Paul and Mary, did amazingly well. The cover shows Suze and Bobby shivering but reunited in a slushy Village street. By the Newport Festival of 1963, scores of young girls were adopting Suze's long hair and boots. Bob asked me to do the liner notes again, but I said that Nat Hentoff could do him more good. The album, track by track:

"BLOWIN' IN THE WIND": By release time, a major hit by Peter,

Paul and Mary. The civil rights movement was cresting, and this under-stated song summed up the passions and questions of the time. Some found it weak because it asked questions and did not answer them. Dylan's reply: "The first way to answer these questions . . . is by asking them. But lots of people have to first find the wind." Gordon Friesen suggested ellip-tical reference to the American flag, citing Emerson's "an old rag of bun-ting blowing in the wind," the national flag symbolizing unquestioning patriotism. The song, which became a civil rights anthem, also sparked unjust allegations of plagiarism, charges not fully refuted until the mid-1970s. It's also possible to link the song's central metaphor to a line in the nuclear-holocaust film *On the Beach.* Dylan says: "I wrote it in a café across the street from The Gaslight."

"GIRL FROM THE NORTH COUNTRY": Tender, yearning love lyric. In the songbook, and subsequently, the title's "from" was changed to "of." Many have pointed out the connection to the English folk song "Scarborough Fair," which singers Paul Simon and Art Garfunkel directly co-opted for a hit. Simon and Dylan probably learned the version from British singer Martin Carthy. Dylan said he had had this song in his mind for years before writing it down in late 1962. It was probably inspired by Bonny Beecher. Dylan re-recorded it in 1969 in duet with Johnny Cash. (A very affecting version is "La Fille Du Nord" by Hugues Aufray, on *Aufray Chante Dylan* [Barclay 80.280 S].)

"MASTERS OF WAR": A blistering indictment of war profiteers, it points fingers, in the vein of 1930s plays like *Idiot's Delight* or *Bury the Dead.* Later inquiries into the military-industrial complex confirm Dylan's charges. When Judy Collins recorded "War," she dropped the final venge-ful lines, but Bob said her version blunted his intent. In another powerful recording, taped by Seeger on tour, each line was interpolated by a Japa-nese translation, setting up an arresting antiphony. The eerie melody of this old modal song, believed to be an old magic song from an English mummers' play, has been handed down via Jean Ritchie's singing of "Nottamun Town." Ritchie affixed the copyright of her Geordie Music Publishing Company on "Nottamun" in 1964. Geordie made claims against Dylan for use of the melody, but he successfully maintained that his variant and his original words made a new song.

"DOWN THE HIGHWAY" and "BOB DYLAN'S BLUES": Two faces of the blues—one deep, one superficial. "Down the Highway" has a distinctive modal lay, unified by a stunning guitar figure exuding shiv-ering mournfulness. "Highway" demonstrates Dylan's remark that he saw classic blues as a form of catharsis. Suze's flight is a recurring theme. "Blues" is a sprightly Elliottesque nonsense song that pokes at Tin Pan Alley in the spoken intro, then sets up crisp dialogues between singer and mouth harp. The two blues songs juxtapose the tragic and the ludicrous. They say to me: Despair is all around, so let's laugh our way through it.

"A HARD RAIN'S A-GONNA FALL": An apocalyptic vision in a series of grotesqueries foreshadowed by the Cuban missile crisis of 1962. It opens with a paraphrase of the classic ballad "Lord Randall," but the son's reply has become as modern as push-button warfare. Lines etched in acid paint the ruins of war. A panorama of Spanish battle scenes comes to my mind, out of García Lorca's poetry, "Guernica" of Picasso, the antiwar sketches of Goya. Although the title is in modern argot, the diction of the text has a thrust of imagery that owes a debt to García Lorca and Rimbaud. Rimbaud was perhaps the first poet to create, in his late teens, a poetic cosmos whose extremes of horror and lost tenderness somehow match the hells and heavens of modern reality. Dylan said the imagery came so fast that "every line in it is actually the start of a whole song. I thought I wouldn't have enough time alive to write all those songs so I put all I could into this one." "Hard Rain" inspired Canadian poet Leonard Cohen to write songs. A landmark in topical, folk-based songwriting, here blooms the promised fruit of the 1950s poetry-jazz fusion of Ginsberg, Ferlinghetti, and Rexroth.

"DON'T THINK TWICE, IT'S ALL RIGHT": Introduces essentially the same studio band that accompanied Dylan on the "Confusion"/"Corrina" single, with the notable addition of Bruce Langhorne, Odetta's guitarist. An early commercial hit, recorded widely, it was clearly about Suze. Dylan's sardonicism contrasts with most recordings by others, who stressed the sweet and ignored the bitter. Only a few days before he finished this song I had been talking to Dylan about Suze's flight to Europe. Trying to support him, I remarked that she was still a child, a line he worked in. The melody was adapted from Paul Clayton's adaptation of a folk tune, "Scarlet Ribbons for Her Hair." Clayton and Dylan had an amicable legal tiff, settling without rancor out of court. Johnny Cash wrote his own version, "Understand Your Man." Of special interest in the notes is Dylan's strong respect for older musicians. Even when Dylan later hurled the slogans of "Times Changing," he could differentiate between the old who were busy dying and those busy being reborn.

"BOB DYLAN'S DREAM": A major work, not widely enough known. For the melody, he credited his English friend, Martin Carthy, with the traditional singing of "Lord Franklin." The song is imbued with nostalgia, world-weariness at twenty-one, a feeling of lost innocence. As his life grew increasingly complex, Dylan reflects during a return to Minnesota, how simple the answers seemed during adolescence. John Bucklen believed the song directly related to times he and Bob spent in Hibbing with Echo and John's sister. It could as easily refer to days at Minneapolis with Tony Glover or Bonny.

"OXFORD TOWN": The sort of topical statement that heated the *Broadside* mimeograph. James Meredith was the first black to risk enrollment at the University of Mississippi in Oxford. Melody and tempo are jaunty, the lyrics are not.

"TALKIN' WORLD WAR III BLUES": A Guthrie-style, dry-witted

fantasy, half of which Dylan composed in the studio. Satire slashing out at everything from doctors to Abraham Lincoln to war to the author himself. The wit is acerbic, the musical line pungent.

"CORRINA, CORRINA": Lilts beautifully with the backup band, although the folk-rock beat was muted. A slightly different track from the single. Blind Lemon had his variant of the "C. C. Rider" tradition in the song "Corrina Blues," the last verse of which resembles this one. Between Blind Lemon and Dylan stood a fine old "Corrina" recorded by Joe Turner and credited to Jay M. Williams, Bo Chatman, and Mitchell Parish. Dylan shaped it to be both tender and ruefully jealous. He cited the strong influence of bluesman Lonnie Johnson.

"HONEY, JUST ALLOW ME ONE MORE CHANCE": Lighthearted, almost inconsequential. Although Bob claimed to have learned it from a nameless Texas blues recording, his performance owes influence to Jesse Fuller, who often burlesqued sadness.

"I SHALL BE FREE": A decided anticlimax. Although the album has at least a half dozen blockbusters, two of the weakest songs are tucked in at the end, like shirttails.

The other LP that portrayed Dylan appeared in 1962: *Broadside Ballads, Vol. 1* (*Broadside* Records 301), was a modest effort, one of those one-take specials for which low-budget Folkways was known. The album illustrated what *Broadside* had been publishing in its first year. Since spring 1963, *Broadside* 301 probably has not sold ten thousand copies, yet it stands as an important documentary of the topical movement. In an introduction, Gordon Friesen sketched the trail of topical songs, from prehistory through the English broadsides to contemporary America. The Dylan student will find the album fascinating because it makes clear that Dylan was becoming *Broadside*'s darling. Side one, band one, has "Blowin' in the Wind" by The New World Singers, in a small-scale but obviously affectionate version. Quoted in the notes are Dylan's remarks from the October-November 1962 issue of *Sing Out!*:

> There ain't too much I can say about this song except that the answer is blowing in the wind. It ain't in no book or movie or TV show or discussion group. Man, it's in the wind—and it's blowing in the wind. Too many of these hip people are telling me where the answer is, but oh, I won't believe that. I still say it's in the wind and just like a restless piece of paper, it's got to come down some time. . . . But the only trouble is that no one picks up the answer when it comes down so not too many people get to see and know it . . . and then it flies away again. . . . I still say that some of the biggest criminals are those that turn their heads away when they see wrong and know it's wrong. I'm only 21 years old and I know that there's been too many wars. . . . You people over 21 should know better . . . cause after all, you're older and smarter.

The debut of Blind Boy Grunt is on side one, band three, in Dylan's "JOHN BROWN." A free adaptation of the traditional melody of "900 Miles," the song attacks the concept of war heroes. He tells of a modern-day John Brown, fighting on a foreign shore for some unknown cause. The parents were proud when he left, prouder still of the medals he earned, but distraught when he returned a blinded cripple. Although the ironies of battlefield heroism are timeworn, the story is effective. The song has been rarely performed, but Bettina Jonic does it well beside a Brechtian antiwar polemic.

"I WILL NOT GO DOWN UNDER THE GROUND": Sung by Happy Traum, then of The New World Singers, later the editor of *Sing Out!* and a renewed friend of Dylan in Woodstock from 1967 onward. From the 1950s on, through the Cuban missile crisis, sales of bomb and fallout shelters were brisk. A refusal to join the parade to the shelters, this song preaches a pride of standing to fight the threats of war. Dylan is hitting back against the hope of escape, saying we're learning to die, not learning to live. Widely misinterpreted as resignation to the war-makers, the song actually affirms that war itself must be stopped because protection against war is illusory. The last two verses, which Friesen suspected were put on, were, in fact, Guthriesque evocations of the American landscape.

"ONLY A HOBO" and "TALKIN' DEVIL": A Dylan song and a fragment, respectively, also sung by Blind Boy Grunt. "Hobo" continues Dylan's recurring fascination with the misfit outsider squeezed out of the mainstream. The two verses of "Talkin' Devil," a work in progress, present a germinal idea about the hidden devils of the earth.

There are ten other songs on the *Broadside* album, sung by others. But five of the fifteen tracks are Dylan compositions. In 1965, the public, the press, and his own impatience pushed Dylan into apparent refutation of his *Broadside* period. DYLAN DISOWNS HIS PROTEST SONGS was the headline in *The Long Island Press* of October 17, 1965. In an inept interview, Dylan called "Wind" and "God on Our Side" "ghosts," and insisted that "Desolation Row" was more important than all his earlier political-topical songs. Later, he did not need to downgrade one past approach in order to elevate a current interest. In the 1970s, his writing and performing still carried echoes of *Broadside* days. His ears could still hear:

> ... *music in the cafes at night*
> *And revolution in the air* ...[9]

5

NOT A PUPPET LAUREATE

"Dylan is the most important song-writer in the country today.... He has his finger on the pulse of America's youth...."

—PETER, PAUL AND MARY, 1963

"I feel it, but Dylan can say it. He's phenomenal.... His songs are powerful as poetry and music.... Bob is expressing what all these kids want to say.... He speaks for me...."

—JOAN BAEZ, 1963

"He is the voice of the oppressed ... the champion of the little man...."

—THE NEWPORT DAILY NEWS, 1963

"It makes me think that I'm not being heard yet above all the mumble jumble and rave praises ... there is no guidance at all except from one's own natural senses...."

—DYLAN, 1963[1]

Timing is almost as crucial to star-making as talent is. Grossman gave the impression of an unhurried, unscheduled man, yet he had a fine Swiss movement ticking in his mind. He worked out in detail his timetable for launching Dylan. Dylan was not always aware of Grossman's strategic moves, just as Grossman was not always aware of Dylan's. But in 1963, their schedules merged, like a Southern Pacific engine switching onto Sante Fe tracks.

Albert's master plan required a hit recording, strong word-of-mouth from stars, and, most of all, a major publicity break, like the Newport Folk Festival. If Newport '59 could launch Baez, he reasoned, then Newport '63 could launch Dylan.

One of Albert's deals had to proceed without Bob's knowledge, for nothing is so fragile as a young performer's ego. Applying his economic theory, Grossman bought out Roy Silver's share of their partnership using OPM—Other People's Money. The OPM principle minimizes risks and keeps one's own capital free. So, of the ten thousand dollars that Albert paid to buy out Silver and to get Dylan into his fold, one half was put up by Peter, Paul and Mary. The deal was kept quiet mostly to give Dylan the feeling that he was achieving everything on his own. The alleys of show business are strewn with the wrecks of young talent who lacked the right support at the right time. Even in late 1970, Peter and Paul remained evasive about the Dylan deal, while Mary, who had fallen out with Grossman, was candid but cautious.

From 1962 on, there were rumors that Peter, Paul and Mary had a part interest in Dylan's future, but the trio's constant denials tended to make the arrangement seem sinister. All it meant was that the trio was backing privately what they said publicly: They believed Dylan had strong potential. Dylan did not learn that they had put a little bit of their money where their beliefs were until some time after "Blowin' in the Wind" became a Peter, Paul and Mary hit. After he knew, Bob's recurring litany, for a while, was: "Albert's a genius, a real genius."

After signing Dylan to Witmark, Grossman and Mogull got to work spreading Dylan's songs. Bob had already done a prodigious job, but now the powerhouse stepped in. Artie, a hard-sell expert, got tapes, demo acetates, and lead sheets to key people. Albert, the soft-sell specialist, concentrated on Yarrow and Milt Okun, music director for Peter, Paul and Mary, The Chad Mitchell Trio, and The Brothers Four. Okun had been with Belafonte, and later became John Denver's publisher and producer.

"Albert brought me a Dylan tape of 'Blowin' in the Wind' and 'Tomorrow Is a Long Time,'" Okun told me. "He was flipping out and got me interested." Grossman may have created Peter, Paul and Mary, but Okun helped give their disparate voices musical unity. "Albert didn't specifically say that he was thinking of 'Blowin' in the Wind' for Peter, Paul and Mary. My first thought was that The Mitchell Trio would like it," Okun continued. He believed songs should not just be pretty tunes, but should *say* something. Okun brought the tape to the Mitchells, who were performing in Washington, D.C. A day later, it went into their show. Two weeks later they wanted to release "Wind" as a single.

The Mitchells were then working under the corporate flag of Belafonte, and their records were being produced by the late Bob Bollard. "Wind" started a series of battles between the Mitchells and Bollard, who said: "You just can't talk of such weighty, controversial subjects in a popular single." Bollard didn't always reflect Belafonte's thinking, yet his fiat enraged the Mitchells, who were already annoyed by Bollard's stiffness toward their then controversial number, "The Twelve Days of Christmas." The Mitchells continued to perform "Wind" as their encore to "Christmas" to consistently strong audience response. The Mitchells recorded the Dylan song on their Kapp album, *In Action,* in late 1962. It was well received, but no hit.

Meanwhile, in late 1962, at the Gate of Horn in Chicago, Grossman played Peter, Paul and Mary another Dylan tape of "Wind." Peter was enraptured; neither Paul nor Mary was quite that ecstatic. "I thought it was an OK tune," Paul recalled, "but I was something of an ostrich in those days." Soon, they worked out their own arrangement; Peter was convinced that "Wind" was the ideal sequel to their hit single of the Seeger–Lee Hays "If I Had a Hammer." The trio and Okun changed some harmonies, principally altering Dylan's main melody phrase from the tonic. In the trio's version, Peter sang the word *wind* in the dominant, giving it more urgency.

On June 18, 1963, Warner Bros. released the single. Within eight business days, "Wind" sold 320,000 copies. Mogull described it as Warner's fastest moving single ever. Two key radio taste-makers, Bill Randle and Bill Gavin, began to call it "the record of the year." Some Cleveland, Washington, and Philadelphia stations were playing it hourly. Airplay and sales in the Deep South were surprisingly strong, probably because Peter, Paul and Mary were no strangers to the charts. "Hammer" and "Puff (The Magic Dragon)" had each sold about 700,000. As "Blowin' in the Wind" went over a million, American popular hits were being redefined.

"Wind" inspired a wave of northern freedom songs. By 1962, integration was a hot topic for folk and pop singers. *Variety* did a lead story on message songs, stressing "Wind" as the trendsetter. The Chad Mitchells were then scoring, even on southern campuses, with a satiric college-segregation tune called "Alma Mater" (or "Ole Miss"). Tom Paxton sang his "Dogs of Alabama" in nightclubs. The rage for integrationist songs was so prevalent by mid-1963 that in a coffeehouse in Ogunquit, Maine, I heard a girl call out: "Sing something about segregation!"

One of the strangest currents in the wind was the rumor that Dylan had stolen the song. The day after my survey of northern freedom songs appeared in *The Times,* I got a call from a Rutgers economics instructor, Henry Levin. He insisted Dylan had bought "Wind" from a boy in Mill-

burn, New Jersey, named Lorre Wyatt. Levin alleged Wyatt had written
the song at fifteen, that Dylan had heard it around the Village and offered
to "buy" the lyrics. What was the price for this unusual deal? "Dylan
made a one-thousand-dollar contribution to CARE in exchange for the
lyrics," said the Rutgers sleuth. For that charitable act, Levin claimed,
Wyatt gave the lyrics to Witmark, the publisher, for Dylan's use. The
Rutgers man told me Wyatt's father had a lawyer seeking some of the
song's profits.

Mogull dismissed Levin's story as nonsense. That night, Dylan said angrily that if I believed that, I would believe anything. He categorically denied the whole matter, said he had never heard of Wyatt, but guessed the
rumor was motivated by jealousy over "some girl" in New Jersey. Gil
Turner maintained openly that the melody was vaguely based on the folk
spiritual "No More Auction Block for Me," but that the lyrics were
Dylan's. The rumor continued to circulate, surfacing in *Newsweek* that fall.
Meanwhile, Wyatt wrote to *Broadside* on June 5, 1963, disavowing Levin's
charge:

"Last year, I wrote a song called 'Freedom Is Blowing in the Wind,'
long before I'd ever heard Dylan's 'Blowin' in the Wind.' The lyrics are
nothing whatsoever like Bob's, and the tune also is completely different.
But the titles were similar ... some kids confused it with his, and were
very indignant when they heard that Dylan 'stole' my song, which I
hadn't bothered to copyright.... I patiently ... explained to them that
only the titles were similar—and that was all. I've finally decided to change
the title to eliminate the confusion ... to either 'Freedom Is in the Air,' or
'Freedom Is Everywhere.' I've helped convert many indignant people into
Dylan fans.... All's well now, I hope...."

Not quite. In February 1974, Wyatt wrote "The Story Behind the
'Blowin' in the Wind' Story" for *New Times,* confessing that he had lied in
maintaining that he had written anything even vaguely like Dylan's
"Wind": "Dylan held the copyright months before I'd 'written' the
song...." In the article, Wyatt admitted he had fabricated the *Broadside*
letter:

"... The coat of fakelore I stitched years ago is threadbare now—it
never fit me very well.... Now is the time to pay the piper. With many
people angry at what they view as Dylan's recent metamorphosis from
Poet-Prophet to Profit-Poet, the dust of rumors is flying again. It is important that the insidious footnote to Dylan's words which still remains in
the minds of many be erased. The only responsible way to delete that
footnote is to make the whole story in my words available.... I'm just
sorry it's taken me 11 years to say 'I'm sorry.' ..."

Because Dylan frequently developed songs out of folk tradition, he was
often branded a song thief. Seemingly unable to explain himself, he was
his own worst defender. Critics sniped that his song, "Farewell," which
Judy Collins recorded, was "only" a new set of words to the traditional

Anglo-Irish "The Leaving of Liverpool." There were likenesses of his melodies to "I Pity the Poor Immigrant" and "Ballad of Donald White" in
two traditional songs, "Come All Ye Tramps and Hawkers" and "Peter
Amberly." They could trace Dylan's "Maggie's Farm" to a traditional song
on Seeger's first solo album, *Penny's Farm*. We've seen that "Song to
Woody" derived melodically from Guthrie's "1913 Massacre," for which
Woody himself had used a folk tune. Later, a publicity release from Mercury Records said that "Quinn, the Eskimo" was "inspired" by an Irish
folk song. "Restless Farewell" resembled "The Parting Glass," and "Willie
the Gambler" was influenced by The Clancy Brothers' singing of "Bren-
nan on the Moor."

By the end of 1963, the folk scene was bitterly divided over whether
Dylan was a song cribber or a composer working in the accepted tradition
of building on skeletal remains. By late autumn 1963, when a claim was
made on the melody of "Don't Think Twice," even Grossman began to
worry. I suggested to Grossman that Dylan indicate on his albums and in
his folios some of his songs' folk sources. I hinted that there must be in-
stances where Dylan wasn't certain where he got a phrase or melodic idea.
"He knows, all right," Grossman replied dryly.

"What did I steal?" Bob asked me. "Did I steal the word *the,* the word
a, the word *so*? Everybody has to get their words from somewhere. Woody
didn't write ten original melodies, but nobody ever called him a *thief*."

Tony Herbert, a Village folk singer, composed his own verses to "Times
Changing," denouncing Dylan's style, philosophy, and success. One of
Dylan's "11 Outlined Epitaphs" was a rebuttal to the whirlpool of rumor:

Yes, I am a thief of thoughts
not, I pray, a stealer of souls
I have built an' rebuilt
upon what is waitin'
for the sand on the beaches
carves many castles
on what has been opened
before my time
a word, a tune, a story, a line
keys in the wind t' unlock my mind
an' t' grant my closet thoughts backyard air ...[2]

Many folk-based songwriters were building on tradition as Dylan was,
yet *they* weren't considered musical kleptomaniacs. Paul Simon's "Scarborough Fair" is an adaptation of the traditional English song. Simon's
"Bridge Over Troubled Water" echoes the black gospel tune "Don't
Trouble the Water," which both Aretha Franklin and Roberta Flack sang
as schoolgirls. I once told Tom Paxton that his "Daily News" had a melody just like an old Johnny Horton country tune. Paxton said he didn't

know that. John Sebastian helped himself freely to a garland of traditional jug-band tunes to stir his Lovin' Spoonful, a group named after a line by Mississippi John Hurt. Jimmy Webb's "Wichita Lineman" derives from an Irish air. Even "Yankee Doodle" was cribbed by American colonists from an English drinking song. Adaptation of old material is as old as music and poetry themselves. The folk tunes in Mozart, Bach, even Mahler, would amaze many classical snobs. Charles Seeger, Pete's ethnomusicologist father, explained the folk process:

". . . Conscious and unconscious appropriation, borrowing, adapting, plagiarizing and plain stealing . . . always have been part and parcel of the process of artistic creation. The attempt to make sense out of copyright law reaches its limit in folk song. For here is the illustration par excellence of the Law of Plagiarism. The folk song is, by definition, and, as far as we can tell, by reality, entirely a product of plagiarism. . . ."

"Blowin' in the Wind" had a dual life as a pop standard and a civil rights anthem. Within a year of the Peter, Paul and Mary hit, nearly sixty other versions were recorded by the likes of Duke Ellington, Lena Horne, Marlene Dietrich, Spike Jones, Percy Faith, Trini Lopez, Glen Campbell, and Bobby Bare. Many more sang the song than those who recorded it. As late as 1968, Stevie Wonder had a hit with "Wind." The clouds of rumor and the dust of suspicion settled a gray patina over Dylan's triumphs for another year. As he wrote hit after hit, the carping diminished. Some thought he might have done a better job of scotching the suspicions, but his metaphorical riposte in the epitaph helped to bury gossip.

As Peter, Paul and Mary toured in concerts, Peter stressed repeatedly his belief that Dylan was sui generis: "Bob Dylan is the most important songwriter in the country today. He has his finger on the pulse of America's youth." The trio was laying down a carpet for Dylan's own grand entrance.

His return to Town Hall in a solo show on Friday, April 13, 1963, was a turning point. Leventhal, who produced it, had terms with Grossman that the concert producer could scarcely lose. Forgetting the late 1961 program, Leventhal and Grossman billed Town Hall as Dylan's first solo concert, and claimed twelve hundred tickets were sold. The audience, which predated the widespread practice of "papering" an audience with free tickets to fill all unsold seats, actually numbered about nine hundred. A squabble with Suze just before he left for Town Hall didn't help Bob's concert nerves. Once onstage, he delivered a very strong program. Now he had the material and experience to be a serious performer, as well as a witty one. In the balcony, Seeger and his wife, Toshi, glowed benevolently. Two rave reviews, one in *Billboard* and mine in *The Times,* gave Grossman fuel.

Town Hall that evening may have been the last Dylan concert that reminded listeners of his influences. From then on he could be compared only to himself. That night his hobo look evoked memories of Guthrie. With his jeans and a head of hair that shouted unfamiliarity with barbers, Dylan resembled Holden Caulfield lost in the Dust Bowl. His vulnerability, his identification with his material, suggested a young Sinatra. However, Dylan broke all past songwriting and performing rules—except those of having something to say and saying it well. Not every line seemed finished and polished, yet there was a sense of structure. Dylan's assurance grew with each wave of applause. "Hollis Brown" was a vivid film clip. "Hard Rain" bit and churned with its nightmare visions. Then, comic relief. Dylan did his various ironic talking blues, but he was not playing for laughs now, though he did introduce "a 1930 ragtime tune I wrote last week." To round off the evening, he read his poem to Guthrie, which won an ovation.

Afterward, there was an impromptu party for Bob. Yarrow volunteered his mother's upper Manhattan apartment. Grossman's partner, John Court, gently shooed away the well-wishers and escorted Bob into a waiting taxi. About twenty-five people showed up. Mrs. Yarrow, a warm, volatile woman, didn't even realize that Dylan was the guest of honor. "Would you get some ice cubes for our guests, dear?" she asked him, assuming he was just another admirer of her son, the folk singer. Bob wasn't put off. After a few drinks, he asked Mrs. Yarrow: "How'd yuh like to marry me? I really mean it, you're a real groovy chick." The long-divorced Mrs. Yarrow was, for a rare moment, speechless.

Through Yarrow, Dylan first visited Woodstock, in early summer 1963. The gracious upstate New York art colony had long been Peter's retreat. His uncle owned a forty-year-old cabin, which Peter subsequently bought, three minutes from the village center, set on a couple of acres. The first summer, Bob and Suze shared the cabin. Suze was painting, Bob was writing, and the three shared household responsibilities. Since Bob's cooking was primitive, Peter and Suze prepared most meals. "Bob was never more at peace with himself than that first summer in Woodstock," Yarrow recalled. In the afternoons, they swam in the Big Deep or at a motel pool. In 1970, Yarrow reminisced:

"We spent a lot of time together, Bobby and I, but we seldom talked. I wasn't really surprised that he wasn't all that articulate then. I just liked him. He was a little scared and within himself. He was a grubber, but we all copped from each other. That summer was a little like his song 'Bob Dylan's Dream,' even though the song didn't actually pertain. . . . Our lives were not that simple. Our stars were beginning to rise, and we just couldn't ignore that. When Bobby and Suze went back to the Village, they were down. When they returned to Woodstock, their spirits inevitably rose. Albert wasn't anywhere near Woodstock then. Milt Glazer [designer of *New York* magazine] brought him up, I didn't. Now, Albert's building an empire up there—a recording studio, a restaurant, and has a hundred twenty acres of land. Actually, I stopped going up there around 1965, when the place began to be rediscovered. Now everybody goes up there. It's not the same as it was when I was a kid, or not the same when Bobby and Suze were there with me."

During summer 1963, I saw Dylan when he bounced back to the Vil-

lage from Woodstock, refreshed. New York summers made him furtive.
He told me I should come up where "we stop the clouds, turn time back
and inside out, make the sun turn on and off. It's the greatest, man, the
greatest place."

INTO THE VAST WASTELAND

Grossman booked Dylan on TV's prestigious *Ed Sullivan Show* on Sunday
night, May 12, 1963. The Sullivan show may have seemed an unscalable
Everest for a singer identified with protest, but Sullivan based his format
on popular taste. Besides, the ABC-TV *Hootenanny* show had just allowed
The Chad Mitchell Trio to sing their anti-Birch satire. The Sullivan booking became an ironic coup for Dylan. Because he was forced to walk off it,
Dylan made national news.

For the dress rehearsal, he arrived typically dressed down. Earlier in the
week, Dylan had sung his "Talkin' John Birch Society Blues" to Sullivan
and his producer, Bob Precht, who liked both the singer and the song. But
immediately after the dress rehearsal, Stowe Phelps, editor of CBS-TV program practices—fancy title for a censor—said the song could *not* be used.
He feared possible libel action because Birchites were compared to Hitler.
Sullivan and Precht were annoyed, Grossman irate, Dylan furious. Sullivan
asked Dylan if he wanted to substitute another song. Without hesitating,
Dylan whirled around and said: "If I can't sing that song, I won't sing *any*
song." He stomped out of the studio and crashed around the Village that
night in a blazing, raging temper cursing "those bastards!" "What a story
that would make," I told him. It did.

Val Adams, *The Times* radio-TV reporter, went after the higher echelons
of CBS. Did they stand behind their censor? " 'No comment.' " On Tuesday, May 14, Bob Williams of *The New York Post* gave Sullivan's views:
" 'We told CBS: 'It's your network, but . . . the decision is wrong and the
policy behind it is wrong.' " Sullivan said that President Kennedy and
Governor Rockefeller were always kidded by TV comedians. " 'But the
John Birch Society—I said I couldn't understand why they were being
given such protection.' " Harriet Van Horne raked the network in her national column: ". . . higher-echelon thinking at CBS continues rigid, narrow, and indifferent to the grave moral issues of our time. . . . The
censored song, which was to have been sung by . . . Dylan, was neither sa-
lacious nor libelous. It simply poked fun at a society of political know-
nothings whose malicious mischief has already menaced the spirit of free
inquiry in our schools, slandered our clergymen and subverted—in the
most evil fashion—the minds of many youngsters. . . ."

Dylan, in a formal letter, asked the Federal Communications Commis-
sion for a public investigation. No hearing was held, but Dylan often retold the story at subsequent concerts. Dylan did appear on a TV show
taped before the Sullivan fiasco but not broadcast until late May. The host
of this Westinghouse Broadcasting Company special, the second of two

hour-long shows tracing American history through folk songs, was John Henry Faulk, making his comeback. Also performing were The Brothers Four, Carolyn Hester, Barbara Dane, and The Staple Singers. Dylan had his first TV experience on BBC the previous December. With total cool he stood up and sang "Wind," "Paths of Victory," and "Hollis Brown" with no mannerisms and few smiles. During the last song, the cameras crept in from a distance and shot him from below, making him look very tall.

Dylan next appeared on a "freedom songs" show on WNEW-TV, New York. The producer, Arthur Barron, later did documentaries for CBS and the Johnny Cash biography, in which Dylan had a bit part. Barron hired me as a consultant on the WNEW-TV show. I telephoned Dylan and described the civil rights content of the show. He agreed at once to do it and to "tell Albert," no matter what the money was. Odetta and The Freedom Singers rounded out the bill. Barron was shaken by Dylan's rusty voice: "I just don't know if that kind of singing will make it." By the time he heard the finished tapes, Barron was converted. Grossman groused during the taping, in July 1963, because he wasn't sure Dylan and Odetta were getting the treatment they deserved. Another annoyance was that Dylan had called Joan Baez to the studio. Joan's surprising availability for TV, which she generally ignored, unsettled the producer, who had already worked out his timing. He huddled with his director. "It would be a coup to have her on, but my show sense says that it would be wrong to start shifting everything around at the last moment," the producer told me. Grossman, defending Odetta as "star" of a show that should have negated the star system, grudgingly said Joan could go on. The show went on with Joan in the audience.

While cameras and lights were being prepared, Bob and Joan huddled in a corner. Bob played her a ragtimey dance tune, while Joan did an improvised clog dance. They were having their own party, despite audience and technicians milling around. Grossman, whose peripheral vision often matched his foresight, took in the scene. "Can you imagine the offspring of a union of those two?" he asked me. The freedom-songs show was weak aesthetically, but two months after the Sullivan show censorship, Dylan was delighted to sing out on racial issues with "Wind" and "Only a Pawn."

Afterward, his TV work dropped off, despite many offers. He wanted only the right shows under optimum conditions. In early 1964, Dylan appeared on the Steve Allen show from the West Coast. Allen wrote me in 1970: "I had not heard Dylan until . . . he walked on our stage. . . . I confess Dylan's genius escaped my observation at the time. . . . It struck me then that he is somehow not ideally suited to television and that his audience will always be limited to the young. He sang so very softly and his attitude was so off-hand and unprofessional that he seemed rather more a mystery to our studio audience than as a blazing new talent. . . ."

If Steve Allen was underwhelmed, Les Crane, who ran a provocative

show on ABC-TV, was hooked. When Dylan appeared on Crane's show
on February 17, 1965, Dylan dominated the hour. His musical peak was
"It's Alright, Ma," done with extensive close-ups. He ragged Crane at
every point, about how he dressed, or what he was planning next, or the
movie in which Dylan said he was going "to play the part of his mother,"
or in other byplay with another guest, Allen Ginsberg. Crane's show was
Dylan's most sophisticated TV appearance to date. He was outrageously
uncooperative, yet effective, leaving the viewer wondering: "What makes
this man tick?"

THE HOOTENANNY CRAZE

When Mike Porco started his Monday night hootenanny, he had no idea
that by 1963 it would become a household word. The hootenanny craze
sprang from a TV series on ABC. Dylan never appeared on it, yet the
show's influence on mass taste ultimately benefited him and other performers who shunned the show.

Hootenanny is a nonsense word, like *thingamajig* or *whatsit*. In July 1940,
according to Peter Tamony, a West Coast word detective, some Seattle
Democrats launched fund-raising parties with folk songs. Someone suggested calling them hootenannies, a word remembered from youth in Indiana, and the title stuck. Two young singers at those Seattle hoots were
Seeger and Guthrie, who brought word and concept east. *Sing Out!* and the
Old Left kept the word alive. Then an ABC producer, Richard Lewine,
and his talent coordinator, Fred Weintraub, tacked it onto a TV show set
amid lively collegiate audiences. Their cardinal mistake was to blacklist
Seeger and The Weavers. Reaction ultimately made the show perhaps the
most controversial series on American TV.

A weekly audience of up to eleven million watched *Hootenanny,* and
soon the word described or promoted sweat shirts, pinball machines, bro-
gans, and vacations. ("Wonderful things happen at the Balmoral, including a 12-day hootenanny holiday.") Ford dealers held hootenanny sales. A
chain of shoe dealers pushed hootenanny boots. New Jersey's Palisades
Amusement Park had a Miss Hootenanny contest. The music business's
reflexes were predictable: hootenanny troupes blanketed the provinces,
there was a *Hootenanny Hoot* film feature, a dance step called the hoot, and
albums titled *Hootenanny for Orchestra, Hot-Rod Hootenanny,* and *Surfing
Hootenanny.* There were two dreadful magazines called *Hootenanny,* including the late, unlamented monster I edited.

The TV series and fad were anathema to old-guard folk fans who believed folk music was a bastion against commercialism. Because the show
barred Seeger, folk singers, led initially by Carolyn Hester and Judy Collins, began a performers' boycott. An embarrassed Seeger decided on a
world tour. The folk scene was cut in half, the pure opposed to appearing,
and others, needing the work, maintained that a boycott would betray the

audience to those of limited talents. Some of the series' bitterest opponents had never been invited. Others, like Peter, Paul and Mary, *were* genuinely opposed politically, but Grossman would have turned down *Hootenanny* because he knew TV exposure was bad for college concerts. *Hootenanny* gave a few fine rural performers, like Mother Maybelle Carter and Doc Watson, greater exposure. The Chad Mitchells performed their biting songs, but most quality performers shunned the show.

In 1963, America was greening almost overnight, but there was still crabgrass in the lawn. Andy Warhol said later that as the 1970s were too empty, the 1960s had been too full. The overexploited hoot craze wore itself out. Dylan and Baez, among others, spoofed it at their concerts. Some listeners got the distorted idea that folk song meant wildly clapping singalongs. While the hootenanny fad strengthened the folk elitists' argument that mass culture was a snare and a dilution, some good performances did sneak through; some obscure musicians won recognition. The TV series probably led millions of its viewers toward quality song. At least some of them began to wonder why performers like Seeger, Dylan, and Baez had not been on their home screens.

FESTIVAL FEVER

Before the Newport Folk Festival of July 1963, when folk-song fever ran to the top of the thermometer, Dylan had four festival-like settings with different audiences—eastern collegiate, West Coast public, Mississippi political, and Puerto Rican commercial. Still only a rising star, his uphill effort demanded as much self-possession as Bob could muster. Spring and summer 1963 inaugurated three merciless years of pressured performing. His increasing popularity could only impress Suze, even while each tour meant another separation. Ready to go almost anywhere, neither he nor Albert were saying no to any reasonable invitation.

On May 10, there was a folk festival at Brandeis University, outside Boston. Grossman made sure Dylan had the two best spots—before intermission and the finale. Brandeis hailed Dylan. (Grossman roared at the festival producer for "the worst sound setup I've heard at five hundred college concerts.") Afterward, Ric Von Schmidt took Dylan, Suze, and me to a very quiet party attended by Boston's hippest—the Kweskins, Geoff and Maria Muldaur, Betsy and Bob Siggins, the staff of *Boston Broadside,* the gang from the Club 47. Bob was solemnly introduced to the Charles River cognoscenti. Albert was disappointed by Bostonian cool. He reconsidered when I told him that one guest had said they had been so awed by Dylan's presence, they just didn't know what to say.

Through agent Ben Shapiro, Dylan was booked for the first Monterey Folk Festival, on May 18; the program included The Weavers and root folk singer Mance Lipscomb. Dylan was delighted to work in Steinbeck country. "I virtually had to force Dylan down the throats of the Monterey

Festival producers," Ben told me later. He got Dylan fifteen hundred dollars for Saturday night.

Audience reaction at Monterey was quizzically appreciative. Ralph Gleason of the *San Francisco Chronicle* reacted negatively. "It was an old Dylan concert," Gleason remarked later, after he had become a passionate advocate, "and I didn't dig it. The talking blues stuff was poor imitation Guthrie. He looked wrong to me and I didn't like his voice. Although I didn't like 'Hard Rain,' I became haunted by it. Jesus, it was disturbing." Gleason clobbered Dylan, but Seeger leaped to the defense, framing a complaint, also signed by actor-singer Theodore Bikel and others. Gleason reconsidered and graciously changed his mind in print. "I was deaf," Ralph wrote later. Monterey was Dylan's first real encounter with Joan Baez, who lived in nearby Carmel. Bob had met Joan briefly at a 1962 party in Boston. She already had heard his "Song to Woody," but that weekend she became more attentive to what he was writing and saying.

In early July 1963, the Student Non-violent Coordinating Committee (SNICK) had planned a voter-registration rally in Greenwood, Mississippi, a cotton center on the Yazoo River, where Highway 82 curls its way toward the Delta. Local activists had been trying to persuade blacks to register to vote. Since August 1962, the campaign had grown; SNICK was coping with jailings, threats, murders, and disappearances. There were signs that the terror was being overcome. SNICK sent word north for singers for the rally. Seeger, Bikel, and Dylan flew down, at some personal risk, to play for a few hundred black farmers. The singers' presence helped win national publicity for the local movement. (Guy Carawan, who'd been spreading songs in the South for years, was startled that Dylan could get TV and *New York Times* coverage with just one quick visit south.) Dylan was now emerging as spokesman and star, and Bikel, who told me he had paid Dylan's plane fare, treated him with deference.

"I felt Bob should get a firsthand impression of the struggle in the South," Theo said. "We flew all night, changing planes in Atlanta, waiting there two hours, then changing again. Most of the way down, Bob was writing little notes and lines on envelopes . . . he didn't really talk too much. I didn't want to pry or shake him, because I felt there was something quite tremulous and sensitive there. I suppose I felt slightly in awe of him. There was something churning inside him all the time, something quite deep. His political attitudes were less strongly formed than many of ours. It seemed a more personal thing with him to be going down into the Deep South. He moved from the universal to the personal, while most artists and writers tend to move from the personal to the universal." Arriving at the Jackson, Mississippi, airport, Dylan saw water fountains and toilets marked WHITE and COLORED. He asked Theo what he thought would happen if he decided to drink from the COLORED ONLY fountain. They arrived, still thirsty, at Greenwood, to be greeted by Jim Forman, Bernice, Cordell, and The Freedom Singers, Julian Bond, Seeger, and Chandler. For

Bob Dylan: A Distinctive Stylist

Greenbriar Boys Are Also on Bill With Bluegrass Music

By ROBERT SHELTON

A bright new face in folk music is appearing at Gerde's Folk City. Although only 20 years old, Bob Dylan is one of the most distinctive stylists to play in a Manhattan cabaret in months.

Resembling a cross between a choir boy and a beatnik, Mr. Dylan has a cherubic look and a mop of tousled hair he partly covers with a Huck Finn black corduroy cap. His clothes may need a bit of tailoring, but when he works his guitar, harmonica or piano and composes new songs faster than he can remember them, there is no doubt that he is bursting at the seams with talent.

Mr. Dylan's voice is anything but pretty. He is consciously trying to recapture the rude beauty of a Southern field hand musing in melody on his porch. All the "husk and bark" are left on his notes and a searing intensity pervades his songs.

Mr. Dylan is both comedian and tragedian. Like a vaudeville actor on the rural circuit, he offers a variety of droll musical monologues: "Talking Bear Mountain" lampoons the over-crowding of an excursion boat, "Talking New York" satirizes his troubles in gaining recognition and "Talking Havah Nagilah" burlesques the folk-music craze and the singer himself.

Slow-motion Mood

In his serious vein, Mr. Dylan seems to be performing in a slow-motion film. Elasticized phrases are drawn out until you think they may snap. He rocks his head and body, closes his

Bob Dylan

eyes in reverie seems to be groping for a word or a mood, then resolves the tension benevolently by finding the word and the mood.

He may mumble the text of "House of the Rising Sun" in a scarcely understandable growl, or sob, or clearly enunciate the

20-Year-Old Singer Is Bright New Face at Gerde's Folk City

poetic poignancy of a Blind Lemon Jefferson blues: "One kind favor I ask of you—See that my grave is kept clean."

Mr. Dylan's highly personalized approach toward folk song is still evolving. He has sopping up influences like a sponge. At times, the drama he aims at is off-target melodrama and his stylization threatens to topple over as a mannered excess.

But if not for every taste, his music-making has the mark of originality and inspiration, all the more noteworthy for his youth. Mr. Dylan is vague about his antecedents and birthplace, but it matters less where he has been than where he is going, and that would seem to be straight up.

If Mr. Dylan's pace is slow, the other half of the show at Folk City compensates for it. A whirlwind trio, the Greenbriar Boys, whips up some of the fastest, most tempestuous Bluegrass music this side of Nashville on eight cylinders and

nineteen strings. (Five strings on Bob Yellin's banjo, six on John Herald's guitar and eight on Ralph Rinzler's mandolin.)

The Greenbriar Boys were the first Bluegrass band to play regularly in a New York night club. Messrs. Yellin and Rinzler take off their executive white collars each evening to don blue collars and black string-bow ties. They join Mr. Herald, a leather-lunged tenor whose athletic, high-range country yodeling is a thing of wonder.

The fourth member of the group, a Virginia fiddler, Buddy Pendleton, appeared with them recently at the coffee-serving One Sheridan Square, but his Pentacostal Baptist upbringing forbids his working in, let alone patronizing, a saloon.

Bluegras is a heady, vibrant sort of hoedown music, the contemporary successor to the old-time country tunes of the New Lost City Ramblers. As this trio performs it, Bluegras is a springy, tightly arranged instrumental and vocal ensemble style that is frequently very funny and always fresh. The trio's large granary includes virtuoso pieces like "Rawhide," baleful ditties such as "Farewell, Amelia Earhart, First Lady of the Air" and gospel admonitions on the order of "We Need a Whole Lot More of Jesus and a Lot Less Rock 'n Roll."

The author's *New York Times* review, which ran on Friday, September 29, 1961

Bob Dylan's parents, Abe and Beatty Zimmerman

above, **Bob Dylan, Joan Baez, and Paul Stookey at the Lincoln Memorial during the March on Washington, August 28, 1963** *right,* **Richard Fariña with his then wife, Carolyn Hester, in Pamplona, Spain, June 1962**

With Joan Baez at the 1963 Newport Folk Festival *below,* "We Shall Overcome," with (left to right) Peter Yarrow, Mary Travers, Paul Stookey, Joan Baez, Bob Dylan, The Freedom Singers, Pete Seeger, and Theo Bikel

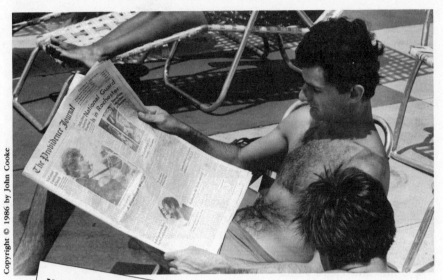

Newport 1964: playtime around the Viking Hotel pool *above*, Victor Maimudes and Tom Law study a Dylan review in The Providence Journal while *below*, Joan Baez appraises a Cavalier centerfold

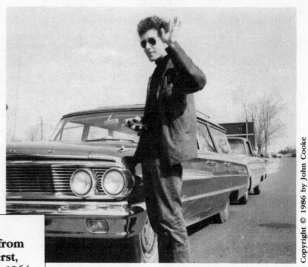

above, **On the road from Cambridge to Amherst, Massachusetts, April 1964: The Ford station wagon was Bob and Victor's first road car** *below,* **Backstage at the Brandeis Folk Festival, April 1964: With Dylan are Charlie Frizzell (left) and Doug Goldman**

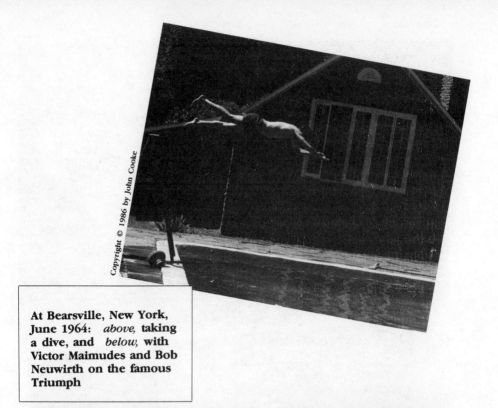

At Bearsville, New York, June 1964: *above,* **taking a dive, and** *below,* **with Victor Maimudes and Bob Neuwirth on the famous Triumph**

Copyright © 1986 by John Cooke

Copyright © 1986 by John Cooke

top, **Kenyon College, Ohio, November 1964, with Bob Neuwirth (left)** *above,* **Bob Neuwirth and his paintings, Cambridge, Massachusetts, November 1964** two and a half days they worked in the thick of the new abolition movement with dirt farmers and northern college students.

On July 6, two miles outside Greenwood, Pete, Bob, and Theo sang on the edge of a cotton patch. About three hundred people attended, mostly local blacks, with a score of young white supporters, newsmen, and four TV men from New York. The loudest response from the locals was for "We Shall Overcome," the "Marseillaise" of civil rights. Dylan's "Only a Pawn in Their Game," written only weeks earlier, about the murder of Medgar Evers, head of the National Association for the Advancement of Colored People in Mississippi, hit home base. The abstractions of Dylan's "Wind" had greater impact on the SNICK and northern activists.

"I saw Bob observing everything down there," recalled Bikel. "He was also watching the reaction to himself. He was very humble to the farmers, admitting that there wasn't such a problem where he came from. Bob said he hadn't met a colored person until he was nine years old, and he apologized that he had so little to offer." Bernice said she never felt quite so close to Bob. " 'Pawn' was the very first song that showed the poor white was as victimized by discrimination as the poor black. The Greenwood people didn't know that Pete, Theo, and Bobby were well known. They were just happy to be getting support. But they really liked Dylan down there in the cotton country."

By summer 1963, even Columbia Records began to realize Dylan's potential. In July, at the annual Columbia sales convention in Puerto Rico, Dylan was an honored guest, along with Aretha Franklin and Tony Bennett. Dylan flew to the Hotel Americana in San Juan with Albert, Suze, and Carla. Albert was busy managing; Bob and the Rotolos, who were introduced jokingly as Dylan's wife and sister-in-law, sopped up sun, swimming, food, and drink. Dylan performed only once, at a dinner, but he was expected to shake hands and banter with faceless regional distributors, sales managers, and field representatives. Except for a few private moments on the beach, he felt ill at ease.

Singing at the salesmen's dinner, Dylan was roundly applauded. Privately, promotion men, especially those from the South, rumbled about Dylan's material. "With God on Our Side" was going to be rough to sell in their market, they murmured. Still, the corporate smile beamed on Dylan. Toward the end of the week, Goddard Lieberson, president of Columbia, invited Dylan and the Rotolos to his suite. At Dylan's first recording session in 1962, sensing his interest in blues and folk roots, Lieberson had spoken to Bob about his recording field trips to the South in the 1930s. Now, aware of his guest's interest in off-Broadway, he chatted urbanely about Brecht and Lotte Lenya, and played a new Columbia set, *The Badmen,* that he expected would appeal to Bob. Dylan kept eyeing the diving boards below, muttering: "I just have to do it, just have to dive off that high board." Lieberson released them with a copy of *The Badmen.*

That evening, Lieberson invited the three to dinner. Dylan wasn't en-

thusiastic, but he met the magnate in the lobby at eight, dressed in dungarees, work shirt, boots, and tousled hair. Lieberson and Carla suggested
Bob compromise and wear a tie to get into the restaurant for the sake of a
good meal. "I will never compromise," Dylan snapped at them. "If you
can't find a place to eat where I don't have to wear a tie, I'm not interested
in going. It's your tough luck." Albert discreetly blended into the drapes.
The recording official took Carla out to dinner alone. Later, Carla told me,
Dylan decided to play blackjack at a San Juan casino. Discovering that
they wouldn't let him in tieless, he went to Albert's room to borrow a tie
to get in. Dylan then had his first of many quarrels with Carla, unleashing
a "truth attack" at her for telling him how to act. When Lieberson left
Puerto Rico, he sent the three some liquor and records, with a note: "Dear
Bobby, Suze and Carla—To be drunk only while wearing a necktie. Have a
great vacation. Love from Big Daddy."

NEWPORT—THE "FIRST" WOODSTOCK

Dylan went to the Newport Folk Festival of July 26–28, 1963, an underground conversation piece, and left a star. Newport '63 was a dress rehearsal for Woodstock Nation. The weekend's total attendance was only
forty-seven thousand, less than 10 percent of those who turned out and on
at Woodstock '69. But Newport '63 was the cocoon of an alternative culture. The seventy performers and their audience were high on the music,
high on "their" civil rights revolution. Musicians and listeners felt they
were saying something to the rest of the country about another way of
living and thinking. The hootenanny craze and the music business only
provided the vehicle for a mass expression of social purpose.

Newport '63 was a turning point for folk song as a new popular music,
and for Dylan. With his raggedy clothes, biting songs, anti–show-business
posture, identification with Negro rights and peace, and shaking off of the
outworn myths of history in "God on Our Side," Dylan became the festival's emblem. His picture was everywhere—lean, gaunt face, frail shoulders
covered in a faded khaki army shirt with wilted epaulets, blanched blue
jeans. Most of the weekend he walked around with a long leather bullwhip
wrapped tightly around one shoulder. Reporters dogged his steps. It all
looked as spontaneous as the group spirit of the festival. Yet Albert and
Dylan had done considerable planning; Albert had insisted on the honored
closing spot for Dylan at the first major concert. The pair also had timing
on their side: Newport Nation was hungry for a new leader and Dylan was
elected by acclamation.

The Newport folk festivals had begun back in 1959 as an offshoot of the
parent jazz festivals. George Wein, the portly, amiable promoter, manager,
and piano player, had fostered the jazz events during the 1950s. In 1959,
Wein had started working with Grossman on a companion folk fete,
which initially ran into opposition from the city fathers. During the 1960

jazz festival, riots broke out, causing a few years' hiatus for all Newport festivals. Late in 1962, Wein, Seeger, and Bikel formed the nonprofit Festival Foundation, a seven-man board of musician-directors to choose talent and help Wein direct the festival. The star system was soft-pedaled, native folk singers billed alongside established names. Everyone got the same fee—fifty dollars plus food, lodging, and expenses. As the first ticket sales for the 1963 festival began to soar, I walked around crowded Freebody Park with Grossman. He was no longer in the leadership of the festival, and had also split up his management partnership with Wein. "Isn't this turnout amazing?" I asked. Albert agreed: "It will mean more leisure for me. Naturally, I'm pleased." He added, "Although it's too bad that Wein had to do this the way he did, with all this board of directors stuff."

Despite the board's disavowal of the star system, Seeger and other big names still dominated. The first step out of the incubator on Friday afternoon at the Newport Casino Tennis Club was quiet enough. About one hundred youngsters sat, barefooted or in sneakers, as Bikel told a panel discussion that the swelling interest in folk music was more than a fad. It represented a rebellion against canned recreation and a return to do-it-yourself culture, he continued. Seeger said TV and its power had to be watched so that it "makes a place in the mass media for minority tastes. . . . We all know folk music has mushroomed, and now we're beginning to worry about the fallout."

A few singers commented melodically. Baez was among the first. Her silken voice was joined by Bob's raspy, raw-edged voice. As the pair went through "With God on Our Side," listeners craned to see the stranger singing with Joan. In the weeks since Monterey, Joan had learned many Dylan songs. Around this time she spoke to Nat Hentoff in *HiFi/Stereo Review:*

> "The majority of those "protest" songs are stupid. They're without beauty. By contrast, Bob Dylan's songs . . . are powerful as poetry and . . . as music . . . Bob is expressing what all these kids want to say. And I love his singing! Oh, my God, the boy can sing! He can be so terribly moving. I've never heard anyone like him. When he starts singing . . . 'Hard Rain,' I cry and have to leave the room."

That was the first time Joan and Bob sang together publicly. For the next two years, and intermittently until 1984, they appeared dozens of times on each other's programs. According to Ralph Gleason: "Much as I dig Joanie, she never sang as well by herself as she did with Dylan. And she never sang as well with him as she did in the dressing room with him . . . she can't swing, and he can. He can make her swing as much as she can swing . . . when he has her locked eye to eye with him, those performances are celestial. . . . Whatever they might say, they both had acts, and they both are hams. Onstage, they both had to look at the audience instead of each other."

For the major opening concert at Newport that Friday night, July 26, more than thirteen thousand people turned out, as many as at the entire 1959 Festival. Newport police rated it the city's biggest single crowd. The folk stepchild had outgrown its jazz parent. According to *The Newport Daily News,* Peter, Paul and Mary did best on "Wind," after Yarrow's standard homily to Dylan. The audience didn't want to let the trio off the stage.

Of Dylan's solo set in the second half, *The Newport News* said: ". . . He is the voice of the oppressed in America and the champion of the little man." Dylan sang "Dream," "God on Our Side," "John Birch," and "Hard Rain." The audience was hushed, then applauded generously. After his set, Dylan, for once without the leather bullwhip, relaxed backstage on the grass with me and my girlfriend Shelden Ogilvy. He signed a few autographs, fenced with some reporters about interviews, snapped at another newsman: "I don't have time to give you my time, man. Can't you see I'm talking to my friends?" Generally, he was amiable. "We've got a little surprise for you at the end of the show," Dylan teased me. Peter, Paul and Mary returned and sang "Wind" again, then brought on Dylan, Joan, The Freedom Singers, Seeger, and Bikel for a grand finale of "We Shall Overcome." Dylan stood between Joan and Bernice, his guitar and harmonica hanging from his neck. The eleven singers clasped hands, a chorus for Negro freedom.

Dylan made two more stage appearances during the weekend. A workshop hosted by Seeger, on topical songs and new songwriters, drew the largest crowd, about five hundred, of the eight workshops. *The Providence Journal:* "It was obvious that many had been waiting to hear the short, slight young man's bitter songs. He did not disappoint them." The audience joined him on "Playboys and Playgirls." Sunday night, at Baez's main appearance, she announced: "Here's another Bobby song," as she returned. "This is a song about a love affair that has lasted too long," she said before singing "Don't Think Twice." In the audience, Suze Rotolo turned pale and got up to walk out. Ric Von Schmidt went with her, trying to comfort her after this public gibe.

Joan then brought Dylan, unscheduled, onto the stage, to join her in "God on Our Side." Grossman was all smiles. At the first Newport Folk Festival, Ewan MacColl and Peggy Seeger had, without scheduling it, brought on Guy Carawan for a number, which annoyed Grossman. But now, the shoe was on the other client, and he couldn't have been happier. The program ended again with a mass grouping onstage for "This Land Is Your Land." It lacked the impact of Friday night's finale. The concept of a festival run by musicians had worked, and the civil rights commitment gave the event purpose and drive. Everyone seemed to agree that Dylan was the "find" of the festival. The weekly news magazines duly noted that

Baez, the reigning queen of folk music, had named Dylan the crown prince. Dylan's apprenticeship was over. He left Newport a star.

DIAMONDS AND RUST

Right after Newport, Baez had ten solo concerts in the East, her most rigorous schedule to date. In the past, Flatt and Scruggs or The Greenbriars had shared her stages. Everything pointed to Dylan as her next tour guest. Albert worked out details with Joan's manager, Manny Greenhill: Bob would do about half a dozen songs at each gig, and would earn slightly more than Joan! Joan, unfazed, didn't make an issue about the pie slicing. She was always keen on some cause or other, some musician, some new style or songwriter, and all that enthusiasm converged now on Dylan. There was some noblesse oblige at work on her part. This waif, she seemed to feel, needed looking after. For his part, Bob promised to bring Joan on his future shows.

A series of gigs blossomed into a close personal relationship, an erratic friendship, a stormy on-again, off-again love affair. Bob's and Joan's fans were fascinated and mystified by their motivations. Rasped Dave Van Ronk: "I think the relationship was purely opportunistic on both sides, at the beginning anyway. In 1963, he really needed Joanie and really wanted to make it. Joan was burned and Dylan wasn't. She was expecting a new bright light to save the pacifist movement, and Bobby wasn't having any of that."

I first met Joan at a post–Newport '59 party at my apartment, and remember her as being a shy, vulnerable kid. She gained confidence, becoming an Amazonian standard-bearer. I cannot ignore her talent, but in measuring her interaction with Dylan, I look from what I assume is Bob's point of view. In later years, Joan mellowed considerably, and was able to look back on Dylan with genuine, open love, even as she teased, mocked, and mimicked him. I am certain their need for each other was far from mere professional opportunism. Both responded then to heroes and heroines. To Joan, Dylan could be both idol and protégé, and she could, she thought, teach him the ropes. At first, basking in her reflected light was flattering for Bob, but it also meant a chance to reach many more listeners. Somewhere along the line, they fell in love.

Right after Newport, Joan visited Woodstock. Dylan came back to the Village happier than I'd seen him in months. He'd found a woman with an established identity and was clearly infatuated. Although Suze was still smarting from that introduction to "Don't Think Twice," she may not have realized how serious a rival she now had, and may not have even cared much. "I knew what was happening all along," Suze told me later. That summer, Dylan somehow managed to juggle two women.

On August 17, the Baez-Dylan tour was due at the Forest Hills stadium in Queens, their sixth concert since Newport. The morning of the concert, Dylan called me to join him for breakfast at the Gallery Delicatessen ("Give us this day our deli bread") on Christopher Street. Bob was no longer playing it cool. "She promised to set up a special room in her house in Carmel with a piano for me," Bob told me. "Imagine me having my own piano out on the Coast!" He sounded like a struggling painter who had just found a beautiful patroness to buy him oils. Dylan had periodically come up to my apartment to listen to records, talk, and play the piano, despite the sound of my primitive old upright. Now he had the prospect of a piano of his own.

At Forest Hills, Joan introduced Dylan as an unbilled "surprise" guest. Nearly half her program was songs by or with Dylan. "Bobby Dylan says what a lot of people my age feel but cannot say," Joan told nearly fifteen thousand listeners. She taunted the TV *Hootenanny:* "I will appear ... if they will let Pete Seeger on that program." Dylan's presence seemed to relax Joan; she became Papa Haydn introducing Beethoven to a salon—although Haydn never appreciated Beethoven's unfashionable composing. She was obviously getting a lot from having Dylan on her side. At the previous five concerts, audiences reportedly had been restrained toward Dylan; there'd even been complaints. By the time the pair arrived in Queens, Dylan won as much applause as Joan.

After the concert, Bob and Joan were returning to the Riverside Drive apartment of Clark Foreman, whom Joan called her "deputy father in New York." Clark, then chief of the Emergency Civil Liberties Committee, was a former official in Roosevelt's New Deal administration, a leader in civil-liberties battles of the McCarthy era. He had also invited other guests— John Henry Faulk, photographer Dick Rohan, me, and Shelden Ogilvy. When Joan and Bob were late, we became concerned. There had been such a crush of admirers around their dressing room and later their car, that they had been locked in for nearly an hour. This had never happened to Dylan before, although Joan was used to it. When they finally arrived, Bob looked pale and shaken, despite the evening's success. People clucked and fussed, mothered and fathered him. He listened to it all, but it was clear that he really didn't want all the advice. Joan was hugging and kissing him, but whenever the photographer tried to capture an intimate shot, she shooed him off. "Remember our agreement," Joan chided him, and he meekly lowered his camera.

Foreman and Faulk were Dutch uncles, telling Dylan to stand up to all audiences and crowds, whether sympathetic, smothering, or hostile. The two civil-liberties veterans hurled advice and directions. They played Dylan a recording of a speech by Nedrick Young, the late screenwriter, about the social responsibility of writers. If this had been down in the Village, Bob probably would have gone storming out onto the streets, into the coffeehouses, down to where the sound of music, the taste of wine, or the scent of grass would spell freedom. That night, he couldn't escape.

In mid-1963, everybody was fussing again over "Bobby," almost like two years earlier. He didn't want to be treated like a *kid* anymore. Joan probably made her major mistake here: She had three years' headstart; she thought she knew the answers. Then, she was also an unformed, frightened young woman. The simplest way to build herself up was to take the role of the more experienced performer. Although he seemed to encourage her looking after him, Bob eventually resented it. This contradiction constantly put him at loggerheads with others, except for those rare few who could deal with him on totally equal grounds. Yet before he outgrew his patron, he seemed to need Joan. At the gathering, Dylan was nearly swallowed by the Old Left. He had not yet defined where he was himself. Seeger was leaving that month for his year-long world trip, and Bob had duly paid his respects at a Carnegie Hall reception after Pete's farewell concert.

Dylan's own natural senses told him to accept Joan's invitation to stay with her in Carmel that autumn. He probably still loved Suze, but she had decided to move out of Fourth Street that summer. It was a break, but not yet the end. Bob still thought he could balance things with Joan and with Suze. I had visited Joan, her sister Mimi, her brother-in-law Dick Fariña, and her mother Joan in Carmel only a few weeks before Dylan arrived. On her mother's TV, we watched a report on the August 28 march on Washington. That day, Martin Luther King, Jr., enunciated his eloquent dream. Dylan, Joan, Odetta, Peter, Paul and Mary, Belafonte, Mahalia, and two hundred thousand peaceful marchers had lifted their voices to support that dream.

Joan was waiting for her new home to be built in Carmel Valley, and was living in a modest, modern, wood-beamed cottage, nestled in a secluded brush-covered ravine less than a mile from the Pacific. Glass walls brought the countryside right into the spacious living room, dotted with modern sculpture, benches, and casual chairs. I had a preview of the serenity that Dylan was to find there, a repose that put New York tensions a million miles behind. Carmel and the Big Sur was a land of craggy coastlines and wind-twisted cypresses—Robinson Jeffers country. There, that hermit poet had found his setting, the detached hills like those where ancient Chinese poets wrote. At Joan's place, in autumn 1963, as Dylan had his first sojourn in peaceful country, he wrote his first withdrawal song, "Lay Down Your Weary Tune." "What good are fans?" Dylan asked me just before he headed west. "You can't eat applause for breakfast. You can't sleep with it," he said, after three months of stardom, ready for the simpler country life.

Carmel was the Bakersfield he had dreamed of. Not far north was Steinbeck's Cannery Row in Monterey, and the lettuce fields of Salinas. The district became Dylan's "East of Eden," perhaps even beyond his "Gates of Eden." He set up his typewriter and worked hard each morning at his writing. He could turn day into day again and night into night. Down from Joan's cottage was a deserted beach cove, which they could reach in

ten minutes in her sports car or in half an hour's walk. There he loved to
swim and ponder the Pacific. He had the first intimations of the peace he
would find again four years later with another dark-haired woman in the
countryside. (Dylan wrote "Lay Down Your Weary Tune" at Joan's cottage. The melody "haunted" him from an old Scots ballad recording he
heard there.)

"I tried to get Bobby to look after his health," Joan told me later. "I
tried to get him to cut down on his smoking and to brush his teeth and all
of that," she said. When pressed in 1966 as to what Dylan really meant to
her, she grew dark and thoughtful. Maybe she still wasn't ready to evaluate
what had happened. Choosing words carefully, she said, with a touch of
acidity:

"He is a complicated, problematic, difficult person. I see Bobby with a
slightly damaged diamond in his head ... a slightly chipped diamond in
his head. More fragile than the average person. When I was sitting and
watching him play, how easily he could be blown apart by a comment or
by something passing! But you never know that he feels these things, because he's very good at covering all that up. For some reason, in my opinion, he wants to relieve himself of all responsibility. Any responsibility,
about anybody, it seems to me. To barely get by with what people have to
offer. If you don't really care about yourself, then you don't have to care
about anybody else. He is terribly, terribly bright, with a funny magnet
inside him that makes you drawn to him. I mean, I love Bobby, and I
would do anything for him, ever. Whatever went wrong between us, I
really don't know. I don't know how Bobby feels about me. It obviously
can't matter."

When I said no one but he knew what he felt, and that Bob had said
little about her aside from matters professional, Joan replied: "Wow, he
really keeps it in there, doesn't he? Well, actions scream, and so do his
songs. It's just fantastic that he won't admit it. I'm not pompous enough
to say that anything was written because of me. But it sure is hard to think
otherwise when I hear some of the lyrics, and then I wonder." I looked
down at Joan's Egyptian ring. "Is that a little gift from a pharaoh in
Cairo?" Joan laughed: "Yes, it's the funniest thing. The fact of the matter
is that ... well ... that's supposed to be a secret. Anyway, it's in the
song. . . . I have only the feeling that I wish that Bobby would be all right.
I feel he is killing himself. . . . I feel Bobby could have tremendous power
for social good, but he could also have tremendous power to take a lot of
people down in the hole that he's in, to coin a phrase. . . . I've already
asked him too many things. Even questions about his songs seemed to be
imposing on something that he just didn't want to be bothered with. The
split between us came on a professional level, but it made things clear in
my head about what I wanted to do. At one point in our little scene,"
Joan continued, "when we were still doing concerts together . . . although
I was enjoying those concerts, I froze up and said to him: 'Bobby, you'd be
doing it as rock 'n' roll king, but I'd be doing it as peace queen.' And he

was not even rock 'n' roll king then yet, but I just had the feeling he would be soon."

Joan's path was so clearly commitment that nothing would swerve her. Dylan and his songs had helped her find that path, but she wouldn't follow him on any detour. She had to criticize him for leaving the one true way: "There is nothing wrong with social criticism," she said, "except, where we end up is that he criticizes society and I criticize it, but he ends up saying there is not a goddamned thing you can do about it, so screw it. And I say just the opposite. I am afraid the message that comes through from Dylan in 1965 and 1966 is: Let's all go home and smoke pot, because there's nothing else to do . . . we might as well go down smoking. That's where our ways part." Even though we were discussing Dylan and his world view when he was not actively committed politically, Joan thought that, beneath it all, Dylan was still concerned:

"I do think he was really as involved with civil rights, peace, and all the things he appeared to be involved with much more than he would ever like to say." Why, then, did he change in 1964? Was he forced into changing? "No," Joan shot back, "I don't think he wants the responsibility for anybody, including himself. I just think that Bobby would prefer to be exempt. Period. Exempt from everything that matters. I think he is often trying to say that *nothing* matters. Bobby and I are just direct opposites. It took me a long time to figure it out. I feel that everything has to matter, however difficult it may be. I don't think you can kid yourself into thinking that nothing does matter. Bobby is very, very bright. He can put up a good argument about that."

Joan was often self-righteously critical about Bob's life-style, or death-style, of 1965–66: "Life is what you make it. The way he lives is enough of a bad show. I love the way I live, which is not that bad." Didn't all poets tend to destroy themselves? "I can't answer that," Joan said, but her guru, pacifist educator Ira Sandperl, jumped in: "There are a lot of real poets who have not destroyed themselves. There is Wallace Stevens and e. e. cummings. I don't think that the poet is always self-destructive."

Joan believed pop stars needn't be gobbled up by the pressures of fame. Because she had made her own peace then, spiritually and psychoanalytically, she felt that any star could do the same. "I am giving up concerts for the rest of 1966," she continued.

During the long, uneven, public, and private affair between Bob and Joan, not even they always knew what was happening to them. Dylan seemed flattered by her interest. He had found so little order or calm with Suze, that Joan offered the promise of at least a brief escape from the chaos that "accepted" him. Whatever prior experience Joan had, Bob knew a lot more about music than she did. In an article for *Mademoiselle,* Richard Fariña recalled that in January 1963, before knowing her, Dylan had criticized Joan for lack of contemporary substance in her song choice. "It ain't nothin' just to walk around an' sing," Dylan told Fariña. "Take Joanie, man, she's still singin' about Mary Hamilton. I mean, where's that at?

She's walked around on picket lines, she's got all kinds of feeling, so why ain't she steppin' out?"

By the end of 1967, Joan had served a total of sixty days in jail for antiwar protests, and was soon to marry a draft-resistance leader about to spend years in jail. By then, Dylan was looking at things both more mundane and more transcendental. Turning the tables, Joan was then condemning him for lack of social commitment, although she came to understand that his commitment was expressing itself along other lines. He undoubtedly learned from Baez. He made some of his most candid comments in the long prose-poem on the jacket of *Joan Baez in Concert, Part 2,* released by Vanguard in March 1964. In a fine piece of page writing, he mixed childhood memories with Joan's, showing how he learned a new concept of beauty from her. Previously, he had been able to say what Joan meant to him in songs only, a dozen classic songs.

Dylan's attitude toward Joan changed sharply by the end of 1963. I doubt that, as Baez has said, it was ever a question of his thinking about marriage and her rejecting the idea. Perhaps there was just too much self-doubt, ego, and narcissism under one roof in Carmel. When passionate love ended, professional admiration survived. At times, that too became strained. Years later, Dylan sounded a bit patronizing:

"I feel bad for her because she has nobody to ask, she has nobody to turn to that's going to be straight with her. Ira Sandperl may be straight with her about her school, but when she is going to make a record, I mean, how can he be straight with her? She has nobody, and I've found my people. She just hasn't got that much in common with the street vagabonds who play insane instruments. She's not that kind of person. Her family is a very gentle kind of family. Joan's very fragile. I lived with her. When I first got there, I lived with her in Carmel. I loved the place.... Hey, you know, I'll tell you who I dig in her family ... Joan's mother. Man, Joan's mother is just groovy. She really is a very knowing person. She sees everything. Her sister Pauline is groovy.... You know, Bob, about Joan, I could never really *talk* to Joan," Dylan said. "I clammed up. Like we made the concert tours, but I wouldn't talk to her.

"Now, me and Joan had this thing. It wasn't a thing at first. It was just that she was getting a kick outa having me come up onstage—baggy elephant me—and sing my songs, which nobody had ever heard before. And her audiences, which are just like pieces of wheat, anyway, when they heard my songs, they were just flabbergasted. Joan brought me up, man. She recorded my songs and she was as important on that level as Peter, Paul and Mary. They are the only ones in the folk-song field I would give my songs to...."

At one point, Dylan said that he didn't feel Baez merited much mention in any book about him. As unbelievable as that is, when Joan's book *Daybreak* was submitted, there was no reference to Dylan. I asked her editor, Ed Doctorow of Dial Press, who later wrote *Ragtime,* about that. In early

1968, he told her that she just couldn't write a whole book about herself leaving Dylan out completely. Joan added a brief passage, entitled "The Dada King." It didn't mention Dylan by name, and was very ambivalent about his wicked charm. Although harshly describing him onstage as "a huge transparent bubble of ego," the passage ended with loving benevolence: "Listen, God, look closely after him. He's more fragile than most people and, besides, I love him. I also keep the cards that read 'Have Mercy on his soul . . .' "[3]

Of course, Joan had a lot more to say about Dylan than that, and she said it down the years in many eloquent ways. In a stunning, two-disk Vanguard album of his songs, *Any Day Now,* which she recorded in Nashville with some musicians Dylan had used a year earlier on *John Wesley Harding,* her interpretations were deep and affecting; her involvement with the songs and their composer was obvious. When the album was released in January 1969, she told a *New York Times* reporter:

"I had always wanted to do an album of Dylan songs." (She had told him so in summer 1963.) "Whether or not he decides to join forces with the human race, he's a genius. Something of Bobby will survive in history. . . . When someone is that much of a mystic and genius, you have to get an insight from listening to anything he's written. . . . I just can't sing his nasty, hateful, ugly songs; I can appreciate the honesty of them, and melodically they're good, but I can't sing them. . . . I was also spoiled by Dylan. When we were closest, I loved all the songs he was turning out. . . . I took all his songs—about a hundred of them—spread them out on the floor, put the ones I thought I'd like on the music stand, and just started singing."

At that time, Joan hadn't spoken to Dylan for perhaps two years. Her all-Dylan album, *Any Day Now,* was a letter to an old lover, telling him that she still loved him and his writing, even though that love worked better for her at a distance. From neither Dylan nor Baez, and certainly no observer or friend, can there be a final word on their relationship. One serious rupture came in England in spring 1965, and lasted years, even after *Any Day Now.*

There have been other serious breaks, some of which lasted for years. Yet they somehow managed to pick up the threads, well into the 1980s. Joan told me at meetings in London in 1980 and 1982 of her contact with Dylan. She told the world about it in her finest song, "Diamonds and Rust," on her 1975 album of that name. Joan seemed to have, if not a love-hate relationship with him, then the very strong ambivalence that would touch the borderlines of love and hate.

She went along with the filming of *Renaldo and Clara,* even though she was rather embarrassed at how she looked in the film. Whenever Joan talked to me about him, she would do the full-scale mimicry of his gestures, slang, smoking, phrasing. It was funny, and yet somehow sad, as if it were the only way she could get mastery over this impossible, elusive man.

More important is how their work and outlooks were affected by each other. Again, it is not easy to sort out, although the songs of Dylan I attach to Joan are discussed often in this book. When Joan said to me in 1966: "He can say it, but I can't write, but I wish I could," she was forecasting a future direction for herself. That "Diamonds and Rust" is her finest song, and that she continues to perform it so widely and so well, speaks more than any random comment she might have made in praise or criticism of him.

I felt her song of 1971, "To Bobby," was naïve and childlike; she was almost pleading for him to play the savior of the lost lambs, a role he had long ago discarded. After the Rolling Thunder tour, Joan's tempo of songwriting quickened. On the *Gulf Winds* album, "Sweeter for Me," "Oh, Brother," and "Time Is Passing Us By" are all clearly, I think, directed to or influenced by Dylan. Joan could also say things in a song she could never bring herself to say about Dylan to friends.

Love relationships are problematic enough, let alone those in the public gaze. Joan changed down the years, admitting even in song how self-righteous she had been back in the 1960s. Finally, she could admit to her mistakes and a posture toward him that was too judgmental, too early, too unrelenting for too long. For either of them to pretend that their twenty-year relationship was not important was just window dressing, for the public and for their own pride systems. They haunted each other down the years much as they haunted their fans.

Originally, way back in 1963–64, they may have grown apart because no roof could contain two such bubbles of ego. Two lead singers can't always harmonize. Back then, they were still too preoccupied with defining themselves as individuals to have found a consistency as a couple. It's probably easier to idolize someone at a distance.

"I AM MY WORDS"

Dylan's illusions about stardom, if any, began to dissipate within three months of Newport. His disillusionment showed in his shifting attitude toward the press. Dylan's news-making instincts were both natural and self-taught. He did not get much advice on press relations from Grossman, who did not hire a full-time press aide until 1968, after he had been a manager for nearly a decade. Until then, Grossman's press relations were handled by his partner, John Court, Charlie Rothschild, record companies, or the artists themselves. The Monterey Festival taught Dylan how wounding the printed word could be. First came Gleason's criticism; then *Time*, on May 31, 1963, was truculent:

> ... who can believe him? ... Hard-lick guitar, whooping harmonica, skinny little voice. Beardless chin ... porcelain pussy-cat eyes ... he looks 14, and his accent belongs to a jive Nebraskan, or maybe a Brooklyn Hillbilly. He is a dime-store philosopher, a drugstore cowboy,

a men's room conversationalist ... something faintly ridiculous about such a citybilly, yet Dylan is the newest hero of an art that has made a fetish out of authenticity.... At its very best, his voice sounds as if it were drifting over the walls of a tuberculosis sanitarium—but that's part of the charm ... something unique to say, and he says it in ... the best songs of their style since Woody Guthrie's. ...

After Newport, smart-aleck comments subsided; the folk press was uniformly elegiac. New York *Broadside* continued its hosannas, *Boston Broadside* featured Dylan and Joan on one cover, and within two months used Bob alone on another. Rhapsodic praise came in the October-November *Sing Out!*, when it hailed the work of "Bob Dylan, touching the nerve centers of our own time with the measureless flights of the poet who speaks for his generation." On September 12, 1963, Sidney Fields of the *Daily Mirror* reported Dylan's comment: " 'But I didn't want to see the atomic bathrooms and electronic bedrooms and souped-up can-openers; I wanted to watch and feel the people and the dust and ditches and the fields and fences.' " He elaborated: " 'Because Dickens and Dostoyevsky and Woody Guthrie were telling their stories much better than I ever could.' Dylan says, 'I decided to stick to my own mind....' "

Dylan was both more direct and more fanciful in a New York *Daily News* spread on October 20, 1963, headed MUSIC WITH A MESSAGE: TODAY'S ANGRY YOUNG MEN DON'T MAKE SPEECHES—THEY BUY GUITARS AND BECOME FOLK SINGERS. Wrote Michael Iachetta:

"Why are we in the midst of a folk music boom?" asked Dylan.... "Because the times cry for the truth ... and people want to hear the truth and that's just what they're hearin' in good folk music today.... When I listen to people talk, all I hear is what they're not tellin' me....

"There's mystery, magic, truth, and the Bible in great folk music. I can't hope to touch that. But I'm goin' to try."

Dylan, still building his rootless runaway character, let the press magnify the image. Dylan never said he was misquoted by the *National Guardian* on August 22, 1963, but he chafed at this article, which categorized him as a spokesman for the Old Left:

... Dylan utilizes the most trenchant weapons at his command—a poetic imagination and contempt for injustice—to denounce those who want to run it for him, whether they hide behind a KKK hood or a stockmarket ticker....

"I don't think when I write," he said. "I just react and put it down on paper. I'm serious about everything I write. For instance, I get mad when I see friends of mine sitting in Southern jails, getting their heads beat in. What comes out in my music is to call for action....

"You should'a seen what he did to the town I was raised in—seen

how he left it. He sucked up my town. It's too late now for the people—they're lost. When will it be too late for him? The same guy who
sucked up my town wants to bomb Cuba, but he don't want to do it
himself—send the kids. He made all this money, but what does he do to
earn it? Take away his money and he'd die. Punch him in the gut
enough times and he'd die. He's a criminal, a crook, a murderer."

The *National Guardian* extracted his capsule comments on major issues:

Capitalism? "Well, I object to somebody riding around in a Cadillac
when somebody else is lying in the gutter." Socialism? "I'd like to visit
Russia some day; see what it's like, maybe meet a Russian girl." United
States? "Ain't nobody can say anything honest in the United States.
Every place you look is cluttered with phoneys and lies." Politics? "No,
I'm not gonna vote because there's nobody to vote for; nobody that
looks like me, the way I feel. . . . I'd like to see a government made up
of people like Bertrand Russell, Jim Forman, Marlon Brando and people
like that."
    . . . In Mississippi, he says, "there's a feeling in the air. More people
are willing to say: 'To hell with my security, I want my rights.' I want
to help them if I can. They really dig my music down there, too."

The *National Guardian* piece exasperated Dylan. Publications beyond
his command were now tailoring his image. Dylan felt he was being
pushed, as Guthrie had been, into being a troubadour of the Old Left, a
puppet laureate who would respond on call with a song for each cause. He
tried with a song for each cause. He tried to pull back from the messianic
role followers were thrusting at him, asking him to speak not only for the
young folkniks but for all youth. Suze empathized with Bob's struggle for
ideological independence. What Baez later oversimplified as Dylan's "retreat from responsibility" was considerably more complex. Dylan did not
want his every word carved in stone, even though he sometimes seemed to
walk around with a mallet and chisel in his hip pocket. I asked Suze why
Bob appeared to be souring on the Left:
    "I don't think he really soured on it, I think he always saw things per-
sonally. The Left opened a door to him, but he just saw more little boxes
behind the door, factions that wanted something else from him. I remember just how he felt when he read that *National Guardian* story. It all came
out as 'Our Spokesman.' Even then, he didn't want that. Everybody does
that when they write something—they turn it around to fit for them.
Dylan wasn't Joe Hill then, or ever, and he did not want to be Joe Hill,
then or ever. That kind of stuff turned him off."
    Carla Rotolo: "The Irwin Silbers of *Sing Out!* were smashing him up
against the wall. *Sing Out!* had found in Dylan a prophet for its cause.
Bobby was twenty-two then. How, in God's name, could he have the an-

swers? But the messiah-makers told him that he 'had' the answers, and soon they began to believe that he really did. That was the turning point for Dylan. He became the hard, all-knowing, bitter kid. During August and September, 1963, he was really frightened, and Suze saw it and understood it. Part frightened, and part laughing at the messiah-makers and at himself."

At summer's end, Suze left West Fourth Street again. She needed to be alone. Meanwhile, Dylan had a major solo concert at Carnegie Hall, and suffered a trauma with the press. Billy James and John Kurland of Columbia publicity had approached *Newsweek* about a cover story. A *Newsweek* researcher, Andrea Svedberg, was impressed with the Baez-Dylan Forest Hills concert. Then Svedberg telephoned Billy in annoyance, saying she was having trouble reaching Dylan or Grossman. Billy: "She said that they were very interested in determining certain things about Dylan's past. I tried to tell her that Bobby didn't like to talk about such things. I told her to let it lay."

The story, on November 4, 1963, turned into a hatchet job that threw Dylan into a depression, ruptured his contact with his family, interrupted his relationship with Billy James for almost two years, drove Grossman further into distrust of the press, embarrassed *Newsweek,* and led, directly or indirectly, to both Svedberg and Dick Schaap, who wrote the story, leaving the magazine. Dylan turned from an accessible subject into a cagey game-player who toyed with interview questions, who developed the outrageous "anti-interview," saying shocking, even deleterious things, things he often didn't believe. He became dubious that even the emerging underground press could understand him.

The *Newsweek* story appeared, under the headline "I AM MY WORDS." The adjectives were abrasive: "unscrubbed face ... bewildered-hair ... skinny frame ... hip talk, punctuated with obscenities. His singing voice scratches and shouts so jarringly that his success, at first, seems incredible ... his knack for stirring audiences is unmistakable. ..." Attributed to the words of his two hundred songs: "simple words that pounce upon the obvious. ..." Admitting that "Dylan is practically a religion," the article challenged his believability:

He has suffered; he has been hung up, man, without bread, without a chick, with twisted wires growing inside him ... his audiences share his pain, and seem jealous because they grew up in conventional homes and ... schools. The ironic thing is that Bob Dylan, too, grew up in a conventional home, and went to conventional schools. He shrouds his past in contradictions, but he is the elder son of a Hibbing, Minn., appliance dealer named Abe Zimmerman. ...

"Dig it, man": Dylan admits he was born in Duluth and raised in Hibbing, but ... he denied that Bob Dylan was ever Bobby Zimmerman. "Dig my draft card, man," he said. "Bob Dylan." (He changed his name legally on August 9, 1962.) His parents? "I don't know my parents," he said. "They don't know me. I've lost contact with them for years." A few blocks away, in one of New York's motor inns, Mr. and Mrs. Abe Zimmerman . . . were looking forward to seeing their son sing at Carnegie Hall. Bobby had paid their way east and had sent them tickets, they had told friends in Minnesota. "He was home a few days in August," said David Zimmerman, Bobby's 17-year-old brother.

"We were kind of close. We're both kind of ambitious. When we set out to do something, we usually get it done. He set out to become what he is." "My past is so complicated, you wouldn't believe it, man," said Dylan. "Bobby is hard to understand," said David Zimmerman.

The Image: Why Dylan—he picked the name in admiration for Dylan Thomas—should bother to deny his past is a mystery. Perhaps he feels it would spoil the image he works so hard to cultivate. . . . There is even a rumor circulating that Dylan did not write "Blowin' in the Wind," that it was written by a Millburn (N.J.) High student named Lorre Wyatt, who sold it to the singer. Dylan says he is writing a book that will explain everything. But, he insists, the explanations are irrelevant. "I am my words," he says. . . .

The article was illustrated with a photo of Dylan recording, above the caption "Bob Dylan: What's in a name?" The imputation that he had stolen "Blowin' in the Wind" was the coup de grâce. He lashed out at Billy James for having suggested the piece. He sniped at his parents for talking to Eldot, not only for *Newsweek* but also for the equally irritating piece in *The Duluth News-Tribune* of October 11, 1963. Finally, Dylan blamed Grossman, who had unsuccessfully tried to bargain an interview in exchange for final approval.

On October 29, 1963, I wrote to *Newsweek* editor Osborn Elliott. In my letter, which was never published, I accused *Newsweek* of departing from its own high journalistic standards in running a "hatchet job" that more fittingly belonged to *Confidential*. I called Andrea Svedberg's interview with me rankly incompetent. "Although I was willing to supply two years' anecdotes about Mr. Dylan's rise to national popularity, she was primarily concerned with his alleged 'song-snatching.' The common practice of folk-song composers in building new works on known or traditional melodies was a fact of obviously little interest to your writers," I complained. The article suggested vindictive repayment for difficulties in obtaining an interview: "Is the non-conventional artist fair game for vilification when he does not bow to the majesty of the press?" I sent copies to fifteen writers, editors, and music-world leaders. About two weeks later, Joan Wharton of *Newsweek* wrote to me: "We regret that you disapproved of our story on Bob Dylan, but we thought our readers would be interested in a detailed account of the popular young singer who so quickly became an established leader of the folk-music movement. Clearly, the final judgment of the value of any performer rests with the public, and we appreciate your forthright opinions; however, we stand by the professionalism and integrity of our reporting. It was good of you to get in touch with us; we hope we have clarified the points you raised. . . ."

Nothing was revealed. Grossman's lawyers indicated that there was a seven-year statute on limitations of libel regarding the rumor about "Wind." Grossman later began to realize the drawbacks in his surly attitude toward the press. In 1968, Grossman invited *Newsweek*'s music editor, Hubert Saal, to Woodstock to interview Dylan. After the death of Janis Joplin, Albert even said a few words to *Newsweek*.

I spoke to Dylan within an hour of his reading the *Newsweek* article. I was doing a story for *Hootenanny*. Bob was nearly screaming: "You want to interview me . . . all right, you can interview me, but I'm sticking to my friends from here on in. Just wait till you read that piece in *Newsweek*. No, I won't read it to you. Read it for yourself and then you'll know why Joan told me not to even talk to *Time* and *Newsweek*. *Time* [cover story of November 23, 1962] screwed up Joan's head for a year, and now it's my turn. I've got over five thousand pages written of all sorts of things . . . poems and plays and a novel. . . . I just want to be known for what I do. . . . That girl over at *Newsweek* has plenty to be scared of, I'll tell you. What about those two girls who were just killed? They worked on *Newsweek,* didn't they?" (Two *Newsweek* editorial assistants, Janice Wylie and Emily Hoffert, had been murdered on August 28, 1963, the day Dylan had been at the march on Washington.)

I once asked Joan why, if the *Time* story had so disturbed her, she had never tried to rebut it. She replied: "Talking about *Time* magazine, the things that upset you are the things that they say about you that are true, or partly true. They said that I had bare feet, stringy hair, and rode about in an open car. They put it in a terrible way, but those things are true, so why bother to rebut it?" (She later wrote and recorded a song flaying *Time.*)

Dylan decided not to rebut *Newsweek* directly. After a concert in Boston, he went underground for three weeks, spending time with the Van Ronks and Barry Kornfeld. Grossman bought Bob a few books by Martin Buber, the Jewish philosopher, as a peace offering. During his retreat, Dylan read Buber, mused sullenly, wrote like a flood tide. He often faced the press again, but his words often formed curious conundrums. Dylan and *The Chicago Daily News* in November 1965:

Q: Will you sing any of the so-called folk-rock music?
A: No, it's not folk rock, it's just instruments. . . . I call it the mathematical sound, sort of Indian music. I can't really explain it. . . . I was playing rock 'n' roll when I was 13 or 14 and 15, but I had to quit when I was 16 or 17 because I just couldn't make it that way. . . .

Q: Why did you give up the folk sound?

A: I've been on too many other streets to just do that . . . the real folk never see 42nd Street; they've never ridden an airplane. . . .

Q: You talk as if you are terribly separated from people.

A: I'm not disconnected for anything because of a force, just habit. It's just the way I am. . . . I don't know, I have no idea that it's easier to be disconnected than to be connected. I've got a huge hallelujah for all the people who're connected. . . . I've been connected so many times. Things haven't worked out right, so rather than break myself up, I just don't get connected. . . .

Q: Do you avoid close relationships with people?

A: I have relationships with people. People like me, also disconnected; there are a lot of disconnected people. I don't feel alienated or disconnected or afraid. I don't feel there's any kind of organization of disconnected people. I just can't go along with any kind of organization. Some day I might find myself all alone in a subway car, stranded when the lights go out, with 40 people, and I'll have to get to know them. Then I'll just do what has to be.[4]

Even the hippest reporters had to cope with Dylan's ironies. On March 25, 1965, Jack Goddard of *The Village Voice* wrote from Woodstock:

Dylan . . . had consented to answer all those deep, meaningful, searching questions he's been bombarded with . . . for years. The following . . . took place between Dylan and the large numbers of newsmen on hand: Q.: Who did you write songs like before [Woody Guthrie]? A.: Ever hear of Gene Vincent? Buddy Holly? Q.: Then you had a rock and roll band in high school? A.: I had a banana band in high school. Q.: So then you heard of Guthrie and he changed your life? A.: Then I heard of Josh White . . . Q.: Then you heard of Guthrie . . . A.: Then I heard about those riots in San Francisco . . . Q.: The HUAC riots? A.: An' I missed out on meeting James Dean so I decided to meet Woody Guthrie. Q.: Was he your greatest influence? A.: . . . for a spell the idea of him affected me quite much. Q.: What about Brecht? Read much of him? A.: No. But I've read him. Q.: Rimbaud? A.: I've read his little tiny book, 'Evil Flowers.' Q.: You're thinking of Baudelaire. A.: Yes. I've read his tiny little book, too.

   Q.: How about Hank Williams? Do you consider him an influence? A.: Hey, look, I consider Hank Williams, Captain Marvel, Marlon Brando, The Tennessee Stud, Clark Kent, Walter Cronkite, and J. Carroll Naish all influences. . . . Q.: Tell us about your movie. A.: It's gonna be in black and white. Q.: Will it be in the Andy Warhol style? A.: Who's Andy Warhol? Listen, my movie will be . . . in the style of the early Puerto Rican films. Q.: Who's writing it? A.: Allen Ginsberg. I'm going to rewrite it. Q.: Who will you play in the film? A.: The Hero. Q.: Who is that going to be? A.: My mother . . . Q.: Bob, do you have any philosophy about life and death? About death? A.: How do I know, I haven't died yet. Hey you're insulting me all to shit ... Q.: What goes on between you and Joan Baez that doesn't meet the eye? A.: She's my fortune-teller. Q.: Bobby, we know you changed your name. Come on now, what's your real name? A.: Philip Ochs. I'm gonna change it back again when I see it pays.

... Q.: Bob, what about the situation of American poets. Kenneth Rexroth has estimated that since 1900 about 30 American poets have committed suicide. A.: 30 poets! What about American housewives, mailmen, street cleaners, miners? Jesus Christ, what's so special about 30 people that are called poets? I've known some very good people that have committed suicide. One didn't do nothing but work in a gas station all his life. Nobody referred to him as a poet, but if you're gonna call people like Robert Frost a poet, then I got to say this gas station boy was a poet, too.

Q.: Bob, we understand you're writing a book. A.: Yeah, it's a funny book. I think it's coming out by spring. Q.: What's it about? A.: Angels. Q.: ... don't you have any important philosophy for the world? A.: I don't drink hard liquor, if that's what you mean. Q.: No. The world in general. You and the world? A.: Are you kidding? The world don't need me. Christ, I'm only five feet ten. The world could get along fine without me. Don'tcha know, everybody dies. It don't matter how important you think you are. Look at Shakespeare, Napoleon. Edgar Allan Poe, for that matter. They're all dead, right? Q.: Well, Bob, in your opinion, then, is there one man who can save the world? A.: Al Aronowitz.[5]

Each reporter who got a "rare" interview hoped he or she alone would persuade the sphinx to take the sand out his mouth. Stuart Crump of *The Brown* (University) *Daily Herald*, left an interview saying, "The result can resemble a farce as much as an interview." Wrote Crump:

When I handed him a copy of his third record album and [asked for his] autograph, he drew a beard and mustache on his own picture, and then signed it. ... I asked him to define the blues. He said: "The blues is a pair of pants without any pockets. Do you like that?" ... he continued, "The blues is a pair of torn pants without anything in the pockets." He added, "Blues is a color. That's all." "What do you consider is your place in American folk music?" "I'm not a folk singer any more than anybody is." As he climbed into the car he hollered out, much to the delight of some three or four dozen fans: "Folk singers are Communists."

"What do you think will happen to you as you grow older ... and the upcoming generations (our children) find their own leaders?" Dylan replied ... a little more seriously, "I dig the new generation. ... Soon the new generation will rebel against me just like I rebelled against the older generation. ... There's nothing so stable as change. I think those are the words. . . . I try to think about my own life. Important things, like my head. I worry about my head. Not the commercialization of folk music! . . .

"Folk-singers don't eat enough mushrooms. I think that unless they get on the mushrooms, they're all going to go to waste. They're all going to turn into Harry Belafontes." "Anything else?" "Also frog legs!"

Dylan was quite impartial about whose journalistic leg he pulled. When *McCall's* asked him what sort of beauty he revered in women, he replied: " 'Dirt on women is very attractive. It triggers the animal emotions. I want dirty long hair hanging all over the place. I hate shaven legs or arms. I hate cleaning and astringent lotions, because those antiseptic smells revolt me. . . .' " Dylan's refuge in sarcasm, irony, and verbal ploys sent coded subliminal messages to the initiate. He revealed while concealing in diplomats' mumbo jumbo, poets' veils, Aesop's fables, jokes within jokes. " 'I am my words,' " he told *Newsweek,* but they didn't believe him. " 'There is nothing so stable as change,' " he told a college editor. Was anybody listening?

JUST A VOICE SINGING

During mid-1963's offstage turmoil, Dylan gave solo concerts at Carnegie Hall, Philadelphia's Town Hall, and Boston's Jordan Hall. He carried off all three like a pro. In Boston on November 2, after *Newsweek,* he showed some signs of being rattled.

The Carnegie concert was singular in that "teenyboppers" surfaced. Previously, folk audiences dressed and acted differently than pop audiences. The first Beatles single hit, "Please, Please Me," was a success in Britain in February 1963. Beatlemania erupted by October, just about the time the first wave of Dylanmania hit America. The Carnegie audience was younger, more exuberant and unruly than Kingston Trio fans had been. This wasn't a folk-campfire crowd. Dylan churned up his listeners. The folk Old Guard was caught off guard by this entertainer and haranguer. He moved through about twenty songs: "Hattie Carroll," "Oxford Town," "Hero Blues," and, of course, "Talkin' John Birch" ("Here's a song they wouldn't let me sing on TV"). He had arrived as a moralist. Dylan spoke more than he had since Gerde's. He used stage center to lambast Fabian, soap commercials on TV, *Hootenanny,* censorship in general. In a caustic remark, which few could fathom, he hit out at that rumor-mongering Rutgers teacher who, he said, didn't even know what the phrase "blowin' in the wind" meant.

Dylan still had not conquered all critics. In *Variety,* Leonard L. Levinson conceded that "Dylan was the voice of the future. . . . But . . . the future holds nothing but complaints of the past and the present. . . . Nowhere . . .

one word of hope or remedy. . . . Dylan's numbers vied with each other in lugubriousity. . . ." *Variety* was put off by a style of "writing and delivery . . . deliberately iggerunt [*sic*]. While several of his lyrics are well-thought-out and effective, more are filled with sloppy rhymes, lack of basic literary discipline and an apparent willingness to settle for the first idea and form that entered the writer's head."

Not everyone in the audience was stirred either. A sixteen-year-old from Westport, Connecticut, Anne Lyons, wrote me that she had left after a half hour. Also, paraphrasing "Hard Rain," she wrote: "I saw wealthy girls trying to look depraved; I saw boys with ascetic faces and boys with no faces. I saw people who looked like sheep and who acted like sheep. I saw tangles and tangles of hair. I was extremely glad that I was escorted by a boy with a tie and jacket on. Identification with that feculent [*sic*] group was not desirable to me. . . ."

Leventhal gave a party later at his West Ninety-sixth Street home for Dylan and friends, including a contingent of Suze's chums, then strong Castro supporters, and Ronnie Gilbert, a member of The Weavers since 1948. Ronnie told me: "Such passion! I've never heard such singing or such songs! It's more than just the topical movement, it's that Dylan is absolutely classic. He's in a class all by himself." The star was being toasted all around. Bob came over to me: "Well, man, you didn't think I could do it, did you?" I assured him I had thought he could do it, but he pushed right on: "Well, I did it, I did it!"

Two days later came the *Newsweek* article. His triumph soured. Somehow, amid all that intense work and limelight, Dylan began to lose his sense of whimsy, his youthfulness. Within a month, the assassination of President John F. Kennedy on November 22 plunged America into a troubled depression. Although some of Dylan's Castroite friends took the assassination with detachment, Dylan was stunned. To criticize a society where bullets could strike down even the mightiest and wealthiest reformers seemed pointless. When the cover of *Esquire's* 1965 college issue showed a composite drawing of four student heroes—Kennedy, Malcolm X, Che Guevara, and Dylan—we thought Bob might one day join the other three in violent death. It squared with his adolescent death-hauntedness. Men of larger vision than Buddy Holly, Hank Williams, and James Dean were dying. It seemed that the God-like men were the ones to be crucified on earth. Meanwhile, the climate of opinion wanted to elevate Dylan to the role of messiah, who could lead American youth to salvation.

The concept of Dylan as messianic figure stretches far. In November 1970, this letter ran in *Melody Maker*, the British pop weekly, under the headline DYLAN IS THE NEW CHRIST, with a picture captioned "Dylan: Messiah":

Bob Dylan (and not, as previously reported, Jesus of Nazareth) is the living Messiah to today's young people. . . . You can learn more about life from Dylan than from 10 Jesuses. . . . Quote from Dylan: "Being noticed can be a burden. Jesus got himself crucified because he got himself noticed. So I disappear a lot."—Ken Payne

Clark Foreman's Emergency Civil Liberties Committee yearly held a fund-raising dinner marking Bill of Rights Day, and honored with its Tom Paine Award some public figure who epitomized the good fight for freedom and equality. In 1962, the ECLC gave the award to Lord Bertrand Russell. In 1968, the recipient was Dr. Benjamin Spock. The choice for the 1963 Tom Paine was Dylan, who felt undeserving because he had "only" written a few songs.

On December 13, 1963, Dylan began to drink too early. He saw the other dignitaries on the dais: Corliss Lamont, writer-educator, heir of the Lamont fortune; toastmaster John Henry Faulk; James Baldwin, the author, dressed in neat suit and tie. Bob looked at the faces and gray or balding heads of about fifteen hundred Old Left burghers in new middle-class security and mellowed radicalism. Presented with the Tom Paine award, Dylan started to speak. He hadn't prepared a speech. His almost disembodied voice began a Dylan truth attack:

I haven't got any guitar, I can talk though. I want to thank you for the Tom Paine Award on behalf of everybody that went down to Cuba. First of all because they're all young and it's took me a long time to get young and now I consider myself young. And I'm proud of it. I'm proud that I'm young. And I only wish that all you people who are sitting out here today or tonight weren't here and I could see all kinds of faces with hair on their head and everything like that, everything leading to youngness, celebrating the anniversary when we overthrew the House Un-American Activities just yesterday—because you people should be at the beach. You should be . . . swimming and . . . just relaxing in the time you have to relax. [Laughter] It is not an old people's world. It has nothing to do with old people. Old people when their hair grows out, *they* should go out. [Laughter] And I look down to see the people that are governing me and making my rules—and they haven't got any hair on their head—I get very uptight about it. [Laughter] And they talk about Negroes, and they talk about black and white. And they talk about colors of red and blue and yellow. Man, then I just don't see any colors at all when I look out. . . . I've never seen one history book that tells how anybody feels. . . .

And it don't help me one little bit to look back. I wish sometimes I could have come in here in the 1930s like my first idol—used to have an idol, Woody Guthrie, who came in the 1930s. [Applause] But it has sure changed in the time Woody's been here and the time I've been here. It's not that easy anymore. People seem to have more fears. . . .

There's no black and white, left and right to me anymore; there's only up and down and down is very close to the ground. And I'm try-ing to go up without thinking of anything trivial such as politics. They has got nothing to do with it. I'm thinking about the general people and when they get hurt. Now I want to accept this ... Tom Paine Award, from the Emergency Civil Liberties Committee. I want to ac-cept it in my name, but I'm not really accepting it in my name and I'm not accepting it in any kind of group's name, any Negro group or any other kind of group. ... I was on the March on Washington up on the platform and I looked around at all the Negroes there and I didn't see any Negroes that looked like none of my friends. My friends don't wear *suits*. My friends don't have to wear any kind of thing to prove that they're respectable Negroes. My friends are my friends, and they're kind, gentle people if they're my friends. And I'm not going to try to push nothing over. [Applause] So, I accept this award in behalf of Phillip Luce [an ardent New Leftist who later turned on his radical friends], who led the group to Cuba which all people should go down to Cuba. I don't see why anybody can't go to Cuba. I don't see what's going to hurt by going anyplace. I don't [see] what's going to hurt anybody's eyes to see anything. On the other hand, Phillip is a friend of mine who went to Cuba. I'll stand up and to get uncompromisable about it, which I have to be to be honest, I just got to be, as I got to admit that the man who shot President Kennedy, Lee Oswald, I don't know ex-actly where—what he thought he was doing, but I got to admit hon-estly that I, too—I saw some of myself in him. I don't think it would have gone—I don't think it could go that far. But I got to stand up and say I saw things that he felt in me—not to go that far and shoot. [Boos and hisses] You can boo, but booing's got nothing to do with it. It's a—I just, ah—I've got to tell you, man, it's Bill of Rights is free speech and [Someone says to Dylan: "Time's about up"] I just want to admit that I accept this Tom Paine Award in behalf of James Forman of the Students Non-Violent Coordinating Committee and the people on be-half of who went to Cuba. [Boos mixed with applause][6]

The audience buzzed. Had this kid really been saying that Oswald de-served sympathy, three weeks after the assassination? Had he called them outdated, bald men ready for the junk pile of history? As the fund raising proceeded, Foreman realized the enormity of his gaff. Contributions were grudging and pale. The outraged men weren't going to support an organi-zation that would let that kid speak with such disrespect. Geno Foreman, Clark Foreman's son who died three years later in an accident, told me that the collection was three thousand dollars short of expectations, although his father later told Dylan the sum was six thousand.

As the repercussions broadened, Dylan realized the ECLC hadn't gotten his message at all. Bob had staged his own Bay of Pigs. Like Kennedy going to consult Eisenhower, Bob went to talk with music promotor

Harold Leventhal. Harold, in his fifties, bald and Old Left, told Dylan those old-timers, who now looked so prosperous and well fed, had been fighting most of their lives. Harold recounted the McCarthy era, when many of these people had been blacklisted, had scuffled for a living, yet had remained socially conscious. Dylan listened, then went to his typewriter. He sent the Emergency Civil Liberties Committee an open letter, which made the rounds of the group's leadership in mimeographed form. Dylan described his moodiness and how futile it was for anyone to try to say what Dylan meant, something he couldn't even do himself. He was only a songwriter, not a public speaker.

He probably just should have said "thank you," Dylan wrote, but he felt more was expected from him. So, as if walking a plank or running in front of a car, he screamed a last song and jumped. He talked of Lee Oswald and that he was so tired of hearing that we all share the blame for every crime. He qualified his remarks about free travel and how he was sick of having everything interpreted for him by the mass media. He wanted to learn about things for himself.

Dylan wrote of his home country and that, despite the rumors, he was proud of his background and the bloodstreams in his roots. And how New York really made him feel reborn. He qualified his spoken remarks about old people and how much what they had done in the thirties through the fifties had affected what he was doing in the sixties. Repeatedly, he underlined the fact that this was clarification, not apology. Dylan offered to return the beautiful award with Tom Paine's smile on it. Dylan said he didn't know much about Tom Paine, but he would like to sing for him. Yes, he was proud of the award, but he'd give it back if he had to. He hadn't known that the purpose of the dinner was donations, and that his speech had cost the organizers money. He felt he owed the committee a moral debt. He offered to pay the bill, and said that, once again, he'd return to the road.

Writing, Dylan continued, for him is motivated by a wish to keep from going mad, a thought too alarming for him to think about. Yes, it's a frightening world, he ended. He sent his love to those whom he knew at the committee. It's so hard to hate, so fatiguing and not even worth the trouble. He likened life to an open window, through which he had then to jump back through. He called the letter "A Message."

The episode should have been resolved there. But about six months later, in 1964, Nat Hentoff, profiling Dylan for *The New Yorker,* heard Bob describe the episode yet another way. When I later asked Bob if he felt accurately quoted, Bob said: "Basically that was what I said about the whole Tom Paine business." As Hentoff took notes, Dylan described the episode to an actor acquaintance from The Living Theater:

I'm not part of no Movement. If I was, I wouldn't be able to do anything else but be in "the Movement." I just can't have people sit around and make rules for me. I do a lot of things no Movement would

allow. . . . I just can't make it with any organization. I fell into a trap
. . . when I agreed to accept the Tom Paine Award. . . . At the Americana Hotel! In the Grand Ballroom! As soon as I got there, I felt up
tight . . . the people with me couldn't get in. They looked even funkier
than I did. . . . I really got up tight. I began to drink. I . . . saw a bunch
of people who had nothing to do with my kind of politics. I looked
down and I got scared. They were supposed to be on my side, but I
didn't feel any connection with them. Here were these people who'd
been all involved with the left in the Thirties, and now they were supporting civil-rights drives. That's groovy, but they also had minks and
jewels, and it was like they were giving their money out of guilt. I got
up to leave, and they followed me and caught me. They told me I had
to accept the award. When I got up to make my speech, I couldn't say
anything by that time but what was passing through my mind. They'd
been talking about Kennedy being killed, and Bill Moore and Medgar
Evers and the Buddhist monks in Vietnam being killed. I had to say
something about Lee Oswald. I told them I'd read a lot of his feelings
in the papers, and I knew he was up tight. Said I'd been up tight, too,
so I'd got a lot of his feelings. I saw a lot of myself in Oswald, I said,
and I saw in him a lot of the times we're all living in. And, you know,
they started booing. They looked at me like I was an animal. They actually thought I was saying it was a good thing Kennedy had been
killed. That's how far out they are. I was talking about Oswald. And
then I started talking about friends of mine in Harlem—some of them
junkies, all of them poor. And I said they need freedom as much as anybody else, and what's anybody doing for them? The chairman was kicking my leg under the table and I told him, "Get out of here." . . . I was
supposed to be . . . a nice cat. I was supposed to say, "I appreciate your
award and I'm a great singer and I'm a great believer in liberals, and you
buy my records and I'll support your cause!" But I didn't, so I wasn't
accepted that night. That's the cause of a lot of those chains I was talking about—people wanting to be alone . . . what is it to be alone? I've
been alone sometimes in front of three thousand people. I was alone
that night. . . . You know, they were talking about Freedom Fighters
that night. I've been in Mississippi, man. I know those people on another level besides civil-rights campaigns. I know them as friends. Like
Jim Forman, one of the heads of S.N.C.C. I'll stand on his side any
time. But those people that night were actually getting me to look at
colored people as colored people. I tell you, I'm never going to have
anything to do with any political organization again in my life. I might
help a friend if he was campaigning for office. But I'm not going to be
part of any organization. Those people at that dinner were the same as
everybody else. They're doing their time. They're chained to what
they're doing. The only thing is, they're trying to put morals and great
deeds on their chains, but basically they don't want to jeopardize their
positions. They got their jobs to keep. Ther's nothing there for me,

and there's nothing there for the kind of people I hang around with. The only thing I'm sorry about is that I guess I hurt the collection at the dinner. I didn't know they were going to try to collect money after my speech. I guess I lost them a lot of money. Well, I offered to pay them whatever it was they figured they'd lost because of the way I talked. I told them I didn't care how much it was. I hate debts, especially moral debts. They're worse than money debts." [7]

Right after *The New Yorker* piece ran, Clark Foreman went into battle over the "unpaid debt." He wrote to Dylan on November 2, 1964:

Dear Bobby: Your profile in *The New Yorker* has caused several of our friends ... to ask what bill I did send you. My answer has been that I was waiting to see if we couldn't make out without taking you up on your generous offer. Now I see we can't. As far as I can figure it, the damage to our collection resulting from the fact that many of our potential givers felt that you had insulted them, amounts to $6,000. If you are able to help us with that amount I think that any moral or financial debt will be squared. . . .

A week later, Foreman wrote *The New Yorker*:

Your profile of Bob Dylan was very much in error in that part which dealt with ... our Bill of Rights Dinner. It is not credible that he said the things which he is quoted as having said. They were so patently false that no amount of Beaujolais would have produced them. Aside from a moment of silent tribute to the recently assassinated President, there was no discussion of the subjects which are alleged to have caused Dylan to speak of Oswald. Neither the remarks of the toastmaster ... nor the ... only speaker ahead of Dylan, Mrs. Cyrus Eaton, could possibly have made him, as the profile alleges, race conscious ... it is hardly likely that Dylan would have been more sensitive to any such remarks than the final speaker, James Baldwin.

Hentoff riposted to Foreman:

The fact is that I quoted Mr. Dylan exactly. And when I read him that passage on the phone to make sure that I had indeed been accurate, he had no change to suggest. . . .

On November 20, Foreman wrote Hentoff again:

... the remarks you attribute to Dylan about the other speakers are equally not credible, as you had the reason to know not only from the issue of Rights, which I sent you, but also from Dylan's own poem of explanation, which you seem to have ignored altogether. It would seem to me that you did it unconscionably, for by so doing you damaged not only Dylan and The New Yorker, but also the Emergency Civil Liberties Committee.

Meanwhile, on November 9, 1962, Grossman made a friendly call to Foreman conveying Dylan's wish to give a benefit concert for the ECLC. The date of February 5, 1965, was set, and a contract signed, but soon John Court called to say Grossman was in Mexico and the February 5 date had to be scrapped because Dylan would be in Europe. According to Court, another date would be offered in the early spring. As spring arrived without a concert date, Foreman began to dun Dylan again. Writing Dylan on December 13, 1965, two years after the original brouhaha, Foreman quoted from the Dylan message: "Please send me my bill, etc. . . . for money means very little t me. . . ." "Since then," Foreman snapped, "words, words, words—no concert, no cash. . . . As you can see from the enclosed statement we are trying to save the boys who don't want to fight in Vietnam. Money now is our greatest need."

The file wasn't closed until May 15, 1968, when Edith Tiger of the ECLC wrote Grossman to say that Foreman was leaving civil-liberties work and that a farewell party was being planned, "a sort of cultural festival and buffet lunch at Lamont's place in Ossining. . . . I am sure that you would want to inform Bobby Dylan about this occasion. His association with Dr. Foreman has been a close and valuable one. Therefore, I feel that he would like to be present to thank this man for his great contribution to society and all of us." Penciled on the carbon copy of this final letter: "Did not receive an answer."

The episode was gradually forgotten, along with the night in August 1963 when Dylan had sat restively in Foreman's apartment, listening to Foreman's and Faulk's homilies. As Joan hovered around lovingly, the two old battlers had told Dylan never to fear to speak his mind; never, never to shrink from telling any audience anywhere just what he thought. Four months after Bob had longed to escape the advice and control of the Old Left, he made his escape. Yet his "message" proved that he was incapable of being just an unruly taunter. He had learned what he once advised me: "You don't have to put something down to leave it." He was wrestling with a major dichotomy: In spite of his gift of words and vision, he had to admit that the only way he could truly communicate was with his typewriter and his guitar.

ALL KINDS OF ME

Late fall and winter of 1963 found Dylan at low ebb at the end of a year, just when he deserved to be enjoying his success. Partly it was the letdown many stars experience right after they have made it. Until new goals replace old ones, there's an anticlimax. He was also burdened by the general malaise after the assassination. Dylan knew that nearly every day in the South, obscure black people were being shot, beaten, intimidated, harassed. His despair was deepened by increasing loneliness: Suze had moved out and their relationship had become miserable. Suze became suicidal. All his "famiousity," as he called it, didn't spell happiness. He sat alone in his dingy West Fourth Street hole, pouring out his songs and his back pages.

Suze first moved in with Carla, on Perry Street; then she found a place at 106 Avenue B. Bob stayed there often, but it wasn't the same. Frictions between Bob and Suze were exacerbated by Carla and Mary Rotolo. Carla suggested that she and Bob shift apartments, but he still wanted to keep his own place. He brought Suze gifts, like expensive art books. Some nights they sat staring at TV, saying virtually nothing. Carla told me that as Dylan grew famous, Suze grew vegetablelike. She was still fighting for her own identity, sampling art schools and various jobs.

Around Christmas, 1963, everyone tried to bury that dying year. On Christmas Eve, there was a dinner at Mrs. Rotolo's in New Jersey. Among the guests was Virginia Eggleston, one of the few at the Paine Award dinner who had actually approved of Dylan's unorthodox speech. On Christmas night, twenty people turned out for a party at the Avenue B apartment. Bob was very outgoing and friendly; Carla recalled that "he seemed to be at peace with himself Christmas Day, and I was his 'sister-in-law' again." The guests sang rock 'n' roll and had a cool Yule. Still, Dylan was planning an extended trip to California. The Rotolos were beginning to get a lot of telephone calls for Dylan from young girl fans, some very offensive. Anonymity for anyone close to Dylan was disappearing.

One night after Christmas, Bob dropped in to see me. I was struggling with another issue of the short-lived magazine *Hootenanny*, which I was editing with Lynn Musgrave, former editor of *Boston Broadside*. Dylan had written two article-poems for *Hootenanny*, yet he was wondering more vocally than I what the magazine stood for. "I don't mind handing you a brick, or a tile if you're building something," he said to me. "But what are you building? A wall? A house? I can't just throw bricks into the air and hope that someone will catch them and build something with them. I want to know where the bricks go." Since the Kennedy assassination, the folk movement's idealism was waning. What good did words do?

Dylan looked at an array of Christmas cards on my mantelpiece and TV. He remarked that the majority of the "season's greetings" were not from friends, but from publicity and promotion departments of recording companies. He said he knew I would have liked more cards from friends. Bob's eye caught a strange little portrait of thin-faced Phil Spector, the pop songwriter and producer. Spector's head was surrounded with long hair, and a black gremlin figure sat menacingly on his shoulder. Dylan doubled up with laughter. "Oh, no," he said, "not that for Christmas!" Spector's outrageous image struck Dylan. Within two years, Dylan had befriended Spector, wore shades and hair at least as long as Spector's, and had approved the hawklike cut-out photograph of himself that Columbia used to promote his folk-rock albums. But at Christmas, 1963, Dylan gave no sign he would drift back into the pop world, with all its seeming absurdities.

On New Year's Eve, a ritual that closed 1963 more than it opened 1964, Dylan was at a small party at the Van Ronks'. A year earlier Bob had been at a big, impersonal party at my place. Now, he wanted to be with very few people. Suze looked subdued, Bob haggard. I had been party-hopping, and the Van Ronks' was my final stop. Dylan and half a dozen friends in their twenties sat as if at a wake. Bob had started 1963 filled with hope and ambition, and had closed a year with fame and achievement, but he seemed a lot less happy. Even Van Ronk's ribald jokes were not producing smiles. I went across the street to bed, and I thought of how very old and tired those kids seemed. If something didn't change, I felt Dylan would be dead before 1964 was out.

In autumn 1963, Bob had written a remarkable open letter to his friends at *Broadside*. It was the last time—for that period—that he was prepared to publish anything so personal. Dylan could speak honestly to Sis and Gordon Friesen, who always thought in human terms, not slogans. The Old Left, Gordon wrote to me in late 1970, "never did understand how to treat artists. I remembered Woody showing me a letter from his section organizer in the Village ordering him to appear to answer charges for 'lack of discipline.' It seems he had failed to show up at a certain corner to sell *Daily Workers* as he had pledged to do. Shit! They couldn't comprehend that Woody's role was to write songs, not to sell their paper. I could name other artists who were subjected to this short-sightedness. Novelists, like Richard Wright in Chicago after he published 'Native Son,' and photographers and essayists . . . it was the same old tune when they alienated Bob Dylan at the very first encounter." Sis and Gordon published Dylan's letter in *Broadside* in January 1964. It was a remnant of the old Dylan, but hinted that the new Dylan was to be an even more solitary and tortured artist than he had been before the world took notice of him.

This was a soul-baring letter to friends. Through it one could see Dylan was the artist overwhelmed by fame, yet terribly lonely. He sensed the conflict over giving his autographs, he liked and hated it. He found himself living a contradiction. Dylan felt that fears had to be faced up to and feelings admitted. He admitted to feeling guilty. How remarkable that everyone needs to be secure and protected. He asked why God must be so fearful. He flailed the managers and agents, the buyers and sellers. He talked of the *Hootenanny* TV show, and of the heroes of the campaign against those who need the work, not the stars who don't.

He described his filthy flat and how he must move out of it amid falling plaster and rotting floorboards. But he could find a certain beauty in it, especially hearing Pete Seeger on his record player singing "Guantana-

mera." He called Pete a saint he loved more than he could show. And love
leads to Suze, who had left, and he wished he could love everyone as he did
her. He would be Christ-like if he were to love everyone as he loved Sue.
He laughed at that idea.

It is here that Dylan made his prayer for the acceptance of his many
selves:

> *away away be gone all you demons*
> *an' just let me be me*
> *human me*
> *ruthless me*
> *wild me*
> *gentle me*
> *all kinds of me*[8]

Dylan made a few comments about the progress of *Broadside*, and of the
writers Paul Wolfe and Phil Ochs. His "novel" *Tarantula* was stalled,
without a plot, just fragmented scenes on little scraps of paper. A few
words in praise of Brecht and playwriting. He saw that the greatest virtue
of drama over songs is that he can only talk about his own feelings in
songs but he can talk of the feelings of many in a play.

He bid a restless farewell to *Broadside*. But not without some old angers
at *Newsweek* and the jealous gossipmongers. The nightmares he faced and
his hates and angers suffused into his own hope for himself: "An I shall
wake in the mornin an try t start/lovin again." [9]

6

ROLL OVER, GUTENBERG

"It is very important to get poetry out of the hands of
the professors and ... the squares.... If we can get poetry out into the life of the country, it can be creative.... Homer, or the guy who recited 'Beowulf,' was
show business. We simply want to make poetry a part
of show business."

—KENNETH REXROTH, 1957[1]

"The poets today are talking to themselves.... The
competition from the mass media is too much.... Poetry used to have an audience.... Gutenberg had a
good idea with printing, but it ran away from him and
ruined it for the poets!"

—LAWRENCE FERLINGHETTI, 1957[2]

"The jazz and poetry guys of the 1950's ... woke up 10
years later and here is this squirrelly little kid who has
done the things they wanted to do ... to get poetry
into the streets, to the people and on the jukeboxes...."

—RALPH J. GLEASON, 1966

"Great paintings shouldn't be in museums. Museums
are cemeteries. Paintings should be on the walls of restaurants, in dime stores, in gas stations, in men's
rooms. . . . Music is the only thing that's in tune with
what's happening. It's not in book form, it's not on the
stage. . . . It's not the bomb that has to go, man, it's the
museums."

—DYLAN, 1965

In 1963 and 1964, Dylan was developing as a mass-media poet, regardless
of his denial that he was a poet. By using the mass media in his special
way, he was developing a new genre. The San Francisco beat poets had
tried to wed spoken poetry with jazz—an experiment that scarcely got out
of the basement. The French *chansonniers,* like Jacques Brel, had long
known that song was an ideal vehicle for poetry, as had history's nameless
bards, scops, goliards, troubadours, minstrels, jongleurs, broadside balladeers, and buskers.

During 1963, I played editor to Dylan because I felt that he could handle any sort of writing job. He knew I'd run things exactly as he'd written
them, retain his eccentric orthography, and wouldn't tell him what to say.
The first assignment I gave him was a piece for the 1963 Newport Folk
Festival program, which I edited under the pseudonym Stacey Williams.
He chose to write an open letter to Dave (Tony) Glover, his old Minneapolis sidekick. Dylan handed me the piece typed single-spaced on tired yellow sheets, written in a cross between Guthrie's folk talk and his own
invented punk-tuation. Roughly one hundred fifty lines of free verse recollected the good old days and the friend "who knew me before I hit or
got hit by New York City." [3]

The Minneapolis group stood resolutely for the old music, mostly blues,
and were alarmed by Dylan's drift into political slogans and protest and
topical writing. Dylan recalled the old songs he and Glover used to sing,
which came out of a time when, in Woody's view, there were only two
roads to choose—"The American way or the Fascist way" [4] and only two
sides to every question. Time changed that, he wrote, "An them two simple sides that was so easy t tell apart bashed an boomed an exploded so
hard an heavy that t'day all 'ts left and made for us is this one big rockin
rollin COMPLICATED CIRCLE—" [5] After describing the blights on society—John Birchers waving flags and carrying shotguns, killer dogs and
sprays, instant food and fads—Dylan wrote: "I don know who the people
were man that let it get this way but they got what they wanted out a
their lives an left me and you facin a scared raped world—" [6] This pre-echo
of "Desolation Row" and "Idiot Wind" indicted what "they" had done to
America: "They robbed the Constitution of the land an stuck in the cen-

sors of the mind—/They bought up everythin at the auction an left us with a garbage market a fools an fears an frustratin phoniness—" [7]

So Dylan couldn't then sing traditional songs anymore, but rather "Masters of War," "Seven Curses," "Hollis Brown," and others. Yet, he emphasized he was not rejecting apolitical folk songs, for they "showed me the way . . . that songs can say somethin human—" [8] Although he later claimed that he wrote protest songs specifically to please the New York folk-song movement, this letter was obviously sincere. He was then in the bloodstream of the topical-song movement. Some weeks later, I asked Bob if he'd received a reply from Glover. He grinned. "Not yet, man, but I hope he got my message."

In late summer 1963, I assumed the editorship of a folk-song magazine, *Hootenanny,* that slid into merciful oblivion after four issues, along with the craze that spawned it. I asked Dylan to do a bimonthly column, called "Blowin' in the Wind," for which he could choose any form, length, or subject. I offered him the princely sum of seventy-five dollars a column, which annoyed Grossman but seemed to amuse Dylan. "It's not the bread," Dylan told me, "it's the idea of it I like."

His first column appeared in early autumn 1963, in *Hootenanny'*s first issue. Knowing that I was planning a magazine considerably broader than *Sing Out!,* Dylan appealed to folk fans to avoid hairsplitting debates about the music. "It just ain't healthy t let the music run yer life like that—/Yer life's gotta run the music. . . . Just get up in the mornin and go—/Just open yer eyes an walk—" [9] Then he hailed the natural beauties of the open country, from Monterey eastward. New York was stressful and ugly, but also full of curiously beautiful energy and variety. The neo-Guthrie tone of the piece was obvious, underlining the need to throw oneself into experience, life, and music, and to learn from them. Don't let the categorizers, analyzers, or rule-makers "boundary it all up," [10] he wrote.

Dylan's second *Hootenanny* column castigated two unnamed pop-folk singers (Ira and Inman). He described their slick, pandering, bowing-and-scraping black music for whites. The singers' patter, which patronized Negroes, appalled Dylan. As he listened his mind wandered back to black militants and artists he admired: Ivan Donaldson, Jim Forman, John Lewis, Mrs. McGee, Bernice Johnson and The Freedom Singers, Miles Davis, Mavis Staples, Paul Robeson, Diana Sands, James Baldwin. Then, Dylan wrote of "the poor petty thief who gets nailed for/robbin' a jewelry store an' all he wanted t do was/pawn a watch so his wife an kids could get better—" [11] The stage lights dimmed again, as the Uncle Tom act proceeded "an I asked the mirror in my mind . . ./'What's this word, criminal, anyway?'/'Who's the biggest criminal?'/'Who distorts the most about the world?'/'Who covers up the most about the way things really are?' " [12] If he had his way, Dylan would stand the despised singers against the wall, frisk them, handcuff them, "an hang a sign around their/heads so innocent people wouldn't get too near . . . 'BUSTED' " [13]

This was a prelude to many songs he wrote challenging false laws. Aside from his individualistic spelling, punctuation, and syntax, this essay was notable for another stylistic experiment. He succeeded in making the singing style of the duo actually resonate on the page. As they sang "Black Is the Color of My True Love's Hair," Dylan attenuated the first word, across three lines of type with thirty letter *a*'s and eight *k*'s.

By the end of 1963, Dylan told me that he had so much work, he couldn't continue the *Hootenanny* column. I think he was being polite, for he also challenged me with a barrage of questions. What was the use of this magazine? What difference did it make if he wrote a column or not? My replies didn't convince him, or myself either. After one more issue, *Hootenanny* folded, because of bad management and lack of focus—it had attempted to reach everyone interested in folk music. The folk audience was already too fragmented to accept any single magazine. At least, I'd had the opportunity to encourage Dylan to write for the page. I had the feeling he could handle *anything* with words. Although Dylan seemed to enjoy journalism, he was already working on *Tarantula*, and was feverishly writing songs and a few surprises for his next album. He knew that the record album had the greatest power to reach people.

TURNTABLE LITERATURE

When the album *The Times They Are A-Changin'* was released in February 1964, Columbia finally recognized that it had a star in Dylan. He virtually had complete control over the album, which Tom Wilson produced. The jacket notes were a bold departure for a pop LP. Continued on a printed insert, "11 Outlined Epitaphs" constituted Dylan's first published poetry. The cover photograph, by Barry Feinstein, then Mary Travers's husband, showed a ferociously intense and tortured Dylan exuding sullen anger. A strong sense of apocalypse dominates the album. Dylan's development of the topical song had far outstripped even his own previous efforts. "Hattie Carroll," "Only a Pawn," and "Hollis Brown" had been triggered by news items, but Dylan, brimming with confidence, was imbuing his more complex "stories" with larger vision and greater universality.

"THE TIMES THEY ARE A-CHANGIN' ": A summation of the sixties mood. No cautious questioning now, but a prophetic voice trumpeting a changing order. The song was widely recorded and translated into Serbian, French, Hebrew, and other languages. The imagery is primal, homespun: a flood tide, fate's spinning wheel, a blocked doorway, the storm of battle, a changing road. While this could be played over film clips of Prague, Paris, Chicago, and Berkeley, it is also a timeless dialogue between those restrained by old ways and those daring something new.

At first the lyrics' biblical roll seems to reflect black gospel song. The title line suggests the warning in Revelation 1:3: ". . . for the time is near."

There is an echo from Mark 10:31: "But many that are first will be last, and the last first." In Dylan's lines: "For the loser now/Will be later to win ..." and "And the first one now/Will later be last ..." [14]

As biblical flood waters rise and Armageddon approaches: "There's a battle outside/And it is ragin'," [15] we are warned about "future shock"—change will be too rapid to assimilate. Although it became a youth anthem, "Times Changin' " does not criticize the old as much as entrenched, rigid thinking, "to separate aliveness from deadness," as he later said. In the midst of a stern challenge, Dylan offers parents, writers, critics, and even politicians a chance to join the changing tide: "Please heed the call"; "Please get out of the new [road]/If you can't lend your hand." [16] The hortatory performance, seemingly sung through clenched teeth, matches the lyrics' bold cadences and messianic tone. Dylan calls it "definitely a song with a purpose ... influenced by Scottish ballads."

"BALLAD OF HOLLIS BROWN": A neo-folk ballad that draws heavily on traditional elements, with a melody that suggests the modal sadness of such songs as "Pretty Polly," "Poor Boy," or "Poor Man." A strong musical vehicle for a harrowing narrative of rural poverty and disaster. There is a prevailing sense of loneliness—"If there's anyone that knows/Is there anyone that cares?" [17] —and a buildup of domestic hopelessness, chronicled by rats in the flour, a dead horse, blackened grass, a dry well. As in Shakespeare's *Macbeth,* the murder weapon, a shotgun, takes on a power of its own, drawing us toward the lines: "Seven shots ring out/Like the ocean's pounding roar." [18] During the death tableau, seven new people are born in the distance. Is this a sign of hope, or a suggestion that seven more may face a similar fate? "Hollis Brown" deserves wider recognition for its drama, economy, and persuasive storytelling, high tragedy in 11 verses.

"WITH GOD ON OUR SIDE": One of Dylan's most cutting mythbreakers. It preceded widespread challenges to education, curriculum, and textbooks. The title line appears in Robert Southey ("The laws are with us and God's on our side") and in Shaw's *Saint Joan.* Ironically, this song led one fan's mother to relent: "At least he believes in God." This track is not Dylan's best performance of the song, which he often sang with Baez. It is very pointedly cast in a folk matrix, with the naïve, humble lad describing his background and schooling, which entrenched the myth of God's approval for ungodly wars. After shifting God's approbation from our side to even Judas Iscariot's side, the final verse hammers home the narrator's new morality: "If God's on our side/He'll stop the next war." [19] Dominic Behan, brother of Brendan, chided Dylan publicly for lifting Dominic's melody to his Irish rebel song, "The Patriot Game." Actually, Dominic himself had borrowed the melody from the once-popular tune "The Merry Month of May." "God on Our Side" can be contrasted startlingly with his later, evangelical songs on *Slow Train Coming.*

"ONE TOO MANY MORNINGS": One of two songs on the album

linked to the loss of Suze. As dull Manhattan dawn creeps in, a weary
Dylan trudges back to the Village from Suze's. Sedative harmonica suggests a bluesman solacing his "restless hungry feeling." [20] No anger, no
judgment on the lovers' troubles: "You're right from your side,/I'm right
from mine." [21] Nothing burdened this young romantic more than the fra-
gility of love.

"NORTH COUNTRY BLUES": Ready to look back at Hibbing,
Dylan distanced himself in the persona of a miner's wife to tell this "tale."
Even though he calls it a "blues," the song resembles a nineteenth-century
western ballad. Dylan's explanation for the Iron Range mine closings is
economic realism: "That it's much cheaper down/In the South American
towns/Where the miners work almost for nothing." [22]

"ONLY A PAWN IN THEIR GAME": More social realism in how
divide and conquer in southern racialism kept the poor white as sup-
pressed as the black: "But the poor white man's used in the hands of them
all like a tool." [23] In early summer 1963, the slaying of Medgar Evers,
leader of the Mississippi NAACP, shocked the nation. The *Broadside* circle
responded quickly with songs from Turner and Ochs, among others.
Dylan's was the strongest, using the murder of one black to probe root
causes, power alliances, and confusion of victim with victimizer.

"BOOTS OF SPANISH LEATHER": Another lament of love, longing,
and loss, in a dialogue between parting lovers. Archaic language and diction conjure up visions of galleons and exotic lands. While probably
sparked by Suze's stay in Italy, the song broadened into a universal plaint.
Christopher Ricks has called this Dylan's finest love song.

"WHEN THE SHIP COMES IN": One of Dylan's prophecies, optimistic and vengeful in heralding the day when evil will be purged. The
allusions have the powerful roll of gospel, evoking both Old Testament
figures, like Pharaoh and Goliath, and the spirit of the Revelation of St.
John the Divine. The ship is a universal salvation symbol. Gabrielle
Goodchild: "Throughout myth and literature, we find water as the symbol
of the unconscious, spirituality, and death, and the ship as the tiny ego of
man making its lonely or triumphant voyage across dangerous deeps."
Carolyn Bliss in her master's thesis closely parallels Revelation 7:1, where
"no wind might blow on earth or sea or against any tree" to Dylan's
opening: "Oh the time will come up/When the winds will stop/And the
breeze will cease to be breathin'." [24] The line "the whole wide world is
watchin' " [25] was chanted by protesters during the 1968 Democratic National Convention in Chicago.

"THE LONESOME DEATH OF HATTIE CARROLL": A news item
inspired this ballad about racist justice. On February 8, 1963, a Baltimore
socialite struck Mrs. Carroll with a lightweight cane. She was a mother of
eleven and suffered from arteriosclerosis. She collapsed and died the next
day of a massive cerebral hemorrhage. Her attacker, whose father was active in Maryland politics, was convicted of manslaughter and assault, and
escaped with a light sentence. Dylan converted this drama into a song

with, he told me, a structure from François Villon. Dylan took poetic license with some facts, but not with the theme of class justice. He never specifically states that Hattie Carroll is black, but we sense she is throughout the song. Ricks has lectured widely on this "national song of faith misplaced in the law," praising its fierceness without an angry tone. He cited Dylan's "exact control of each word," the use of feminine endings for Hattie Carroll's lines, the craft behind what at first seems clumsy: "With rich wealthy parents who provide and protect him." [26] Five years later, the episode and song inspired C. Lester Franklin's play *A Scaffold for Marionettes,* advertised in Baltimore as "a sensational and shocking exposé of the bigotry and prejudice that runs rampant in our city." (On *Biograph* Dylan drops the Villon reference and says: "The set pattern to the song, I think, is based on Brecht, The Ship, The Black Freighter.")

"RESTLESS FAREWELL": Remorse and self-examination dominate the album's final song, based on the melody of "The Parting Glass," an Irish drinking song. Dylan often ended albums with new departures. At this point, he was unnerved by the *Newsweek* exposé and the weary, misunderstood artist says farewell. "Time" is crucial, contrasting with its use in the album title. The singer realizes that his times are also changing: "Oh a false clock tries to tick out my time/To disgrace, distract, and bother me." [27]

During a drinking reverie, the narrator reviews the money he's spent, the friends he's squandered, the bottles he's killed, the girls he's touched, the foes he's fought, the thoughts that have tortured him, the gossip that's surrounded him. He concluded confidently that "I'll make my stand/And remain as I am/And bid farewell and not give a damn." [28] He sang me the unfinished version of this song and asked me if I thought it would be understood. I said that I thought so, but that the only person he ever had to please was really himself.

"11 OUTLINED EPITAPHS"

Dylan augmented these songs with eleven prose-poems, published on the back of the album and on an insert. In this subjective poem cycle he spoke more freely of himself. The epitaphs, published in *Lyrics, 1962–1985,* remind me of the Dylan Thomas line: "Poems are statements on the way to the grave." Tom Lask, poetry editor of *The New York Times,* once tore into Dylan-as-poet for these lines from epitaph eight:

(*if it rhymes, it rhymes*
if it don't, it don't
if it comes, it comes
if it won't it won't) [29]

The excerpt actually can hold its own beside this jazz-infused section from T. S. Eliot's "Sweeney Agonistes."

I gotta use words when I talk to you
But if you understand or if you don't
That's nothing to me and nothing to you
We all gotta do what we gotta do ... [30]

In the epitaphs, for all their unevenness and sometimes apparent auto-
matism, the writer occasionally has flashes of brilliance and insight as he
steps out without his guitar and harmonica. These poems can be read as
autobiographical notes. They appear casual, yet fine balance, control, and
contour can be discerned. There are recurring references to the road, and of
the writer running. The poems move from early evening to deep into the
night and on to dawn. The word *epitaph* has dual connotations here: a
commemoration of something in Dylan's life that has already died, and, in
epitaphs eight, ten, and eleven, the glorification of what he holds most sacred, what he might one day choose as his own epitaph. Throughout, his
identity evolves from adolescent to man as he says his own "restless farewell" to the past. Because the epitaphs are "outlined," they can be filled in
further. There are formulations he later developed into songs, notably
"Love Minus Zero/No Limit" and "Hurricane." Pervading the poem cycle
is a high sense of color and rhythm, and the strong current of change.

EPITAPH 1: To surrender to the sanctuary of his own imagination, he
must "slam the shutters of my eyes." [31] Voices say " 'he's a crazy man/he
never opens up his eyes.' " [32] The narrator describes his sundown confusions, his loss of direction and ideology. Then, a flash of enlightenment
comes: "the shot has shook/me up ... for I've never/heard that sound before." [33] Was it the shot that killed Kennedy, or Medgar Evers, or the shot
of recognition that to find his own world he must withdraw?

EPITAPH 2: A more mature look at his childhood milieu than "Stolen
Moment." Duluth "holds no memories," but Hibbing "has left me with
my legacy visions." [34] He describes the death of old north Hibbing and the
movement to the new town. The pervasive decay, the cold wind blowing
"as though/the rains of wartime had/left the land bombed-out an' shattered." [35] He's still running: "but my road has seen many changes/for I've
served my time as a refugee ..." [36] He envisions he'll return with
"changed eyes." There's a Whitmanesque ring to how he'll talk to the
old and the young. At this point he can almost see himself coming to
terms with his adolescent rebellion, to stop and embrace and even to
love the town, "—for I learned by now/never t' expect/what it cannot
give me." [37]

EPITAPH 3: Dylan considers some of the romantic myths that inspired
him, like Guthrie's arrival in New York. No union movement was there
to greet Dylan. He toys with Villon ("ah where are those forces of yester-
year?") [38] then parallels Idris Davies's and Pete Seeger's "Bells of Rhymney," putting the swarming lyrics by the Welsh miner into an American
setting. He's trying to find his own welcome into New York: He's not

lost, nor is he a stranger, "but rather someone/who just doesn't live here." [39] His conclusion puns on a legendary bluesman and Psalm 23 as he declares himself free of past guides on his solitary quest:

never pretendin' t' be knowin'
what's worth seekin'
but at least
without ghosts by my side
t' betray my childishness
t' leadeth me down false trails
an' maketh me drink from muddy waters
yes it is I
who is poundin' at your door
if it is you inside
who hears the noise[40]

Columbia Records ran full-page ads for the album using the last four lines.

EPITAPH 4: A death poem against organized politics; there is no party or movement he sees that can answer his demands. ("Jim" is probably James Forman of SNCC.) This is also an epitaph for the "brainwashed dream" [41] of both ideology and education. He "ran for my life" [42] to his highway, his open road, "not carin' no more/what people knew about things/but rather how they felt about things." [43]

EPITAPH 5: A visit to the home of writer Al Aronowitz and his wife, Anne, turns into an exchange of vexsome questions and elusive answers. Asked how he can be happy singing such depressing songs, he responds:

"Lenny Bruce says there're no dirty
words . . . just dirty minds an' I say there're
no depressed words just depressed minds" [44]

This epitaph ambiguously describes poetry as " 'anything that ain't got no end' " [45] and his songs onstage as " 'nothin' but the unwindin' of/my happiness.' " [46]

EPITAPH 6: On idols and the dangers of idolatry. From his first and last idol, Guthrie, he learned "that men are men." [47]

EPITAPH 7: Stop fighting foreign demons, Dylan writes, until we can get the rats out of Harlem kitchens: "ain't there no closer villains/than the baby-eatin' Russians/rats eat babies too." [48] This epitaph also contains a widely quoted gibe at political labels:

there is no right wing
or left wing . . .
there is only up wing
an' down wing[49]

EPITAPH 8: He defends himself against gossip that he was a plagiarist. He explains the folk process of building on the old to "grant my closet thoughts backyard air." [50] Acknowledging the myriad influences that play on him, he writes:

> *for all songs lead back t' the sea*
> *an' at one time, there was*
> *no singin' tongue t' imitate it*[51]

There is no one free of guilt, Dylan writes, and, yet, "the world is but a courtroom." [52] He warns that the defendants are busy cleaning up that courtroom and the prosecutors will soon be swept away—echoes of the "Hattie Carroll" theme of false justice.

EPITAPH 9: There is another courtroom, of trial-by-press: a defiant riposte to *Newsweek, Little Sandy Review, Sing Out!,* and other publications that have hectored him: "No I shall not cooperate with reporters' whims." [53] He will not participate in such an exposure, he writes, for "I 'expose' myself/every time I step out/on the stage." [54]

EPITAPH 10: The final two poems leave enemies, causes, and politics behind, and celebrate life, love, and song. The epitaphs follow Dylan's habitual emotional pendulum: expunging anger before expressing love. The tenth epitaph is a nocturne—Dylan flies from "the dungeons of my constant night" [55] toward the dawn. Admitting his destructiveness, he has only tender thoughts for Suze. Other friends appear: Eric (Ric) Von Schmidt, Geno Foreman, the Van Ronks. Then he hails music, and his own speeding muse:

> *for I am runnin' in a fair race*
> *with no racetrack but the night*
> *an' no competition but the dawn*[56]

EPITAPH 11: Elegiac language now as he forecasts constant change in the climate. As desire drives him onward, he names a few of his inspirations, a long list that leaps from William Blake to Johnny Cash to Seeger. The lyricism reminds me of Joyce's farewell to Ireland in *Portrait of the Artist As a Young Man* where Stephen girds himself with silence, cunning, and exile. Dylan places himself in a continuum of lonely singers:

> *an' mine shall be a strong loneliness*
> *dissolvin' deep*
> *t' the depths of my freedom*
> *an' that, then, shall*
> *remain my song*[57]

The *Times Changing* album and the epitaphs drew mixed reviews. *Little Sandy Review* called these "45 minutes of gloom ... by far his weakest album, musically." The "822 lines of free-association blank verse" were dismissed as "spiritual masochism." *High Fidelity* cautioned that "Dylan will not entertain you. That's not his line. But he will sear your soul." *HiFi/Stereo Review* rated Dylan as equal to Guthrie, but feared he might "become only a mannered apologist for his own wounded self-esteem." An obscure Village folknik named Tony Herbert wrote a parody of "With God on Our Side," suggesting there was money in protest. But the album and the poems also won praise and broadened Dylan's reputation. The harsh crucible of public opinion be damned, he was growing beyond anyone's command, choosing his own lonely road to travel. For a man who'd just outlined his epitaphs, Dylan had plenty of life left.

ANOTHER SIDE

After an appearance in London in May 1964, Dylan made a lightning trip to Paris and then Greece, where, with his road manager, Victor Maimudes, he visited the small village of Vermilya. After returning in June, he recorded in only two nights a total of eleven songs, and wrote more poems for the jacket. (Columbia had originally scheduled a *Bob Dylan in Concert* album, for release in early summer 1964. This album would have been largely based on Dylan's October 26, 1963, Carnegie Hall concert, along with one song and his "Last Thoughts on Woody Guthrie" poem from his April 12, 1963, Town Hall concert. But this album was canceled, and in August 1964, *Another Side of Bob Dylan* was released.)

Many critics received *Another Side* coolly. The folk-Left saw him drifting into "too much subjectivity." Other critics carped for aesthetic reasons. Probably the snidest review was a parody doggerel in *High Fidelity*: "... but bob/he got two problems/small ones/the language he write in/aint english/the measure he beats out/aint song/n this kind of/inverted intellectuality/just bores/the hell/out of me." *Another Side* was indeed taped hastily and the singing was not Dylan's subtlest. But the album does capture weariness, cynicism, and road ennui. It enunciates new self-reliant directions. It brings back Dylan's mocking wit, notably absent on *Times Changing*. Dylan reluctantly accepted Tom Wilson's album title.

"ALL I REALLY WANT TO DO": A jape about a "simple" man trying to relate to a complex, defensive, and Freudian-oriented woman. Rich in outlandish catalogs, internal and external rhymes, Dylan laughs at his own jokes as he sings, yodels, and plays games. A lampoon of "boy meets girl" in the era of psychoanalysis and shifting values in social-sexual relationships.

"BLACK CROW BLUES": Dylan's grasp of country blues idioms has always been strong. This original blues simmers with the sorrow, fatigue, and longing that might emanate from a Delta farm. A gently swinging performance, in which an out-of-tune, honky-tonk piano adds authenticity.

"SPANISH HARLEM INCIDENT": The parade of women and muse figures in Dylan's love songs is long. Any friend might have served as a model for this song of surrender to a gypsy fortune-teller. Dylan has often disdained the emptiness of the middle-class, collegiate, intellectual women, claiming that black earth-mothers, the Arethas of *Tarantula,* put him in touch with deeper realities. Sung with passionate projection, his voice breaks, almost in Mexican *ranchero* style, on the word *homeless.*

"CHIMES OF FREEDOM": In language, sweep, universality, and compassion, one of his most profound song-poems. This is among my half-dozen favorite Dylan works, a triumph of word-color and metaphor encompassing humanity. Dylan's affinity with the underdog has rarely attained such noble expression. He hears "the chimes of freedom flashing" [58] for a legion of the abused. This is perhaps Dylan's most political song and his greatest love song, for he is extending his love and identification: ". . . for the aching ones whose wounds cannot be nursed/For the countless confused, accused, misused, strung-out ones an' worse . . ." [59]

The song is set in a dramatic storm, a "wild cathedral evening," [60] developing his favorite metaphor of tempest: "Through the mad mystic hammering of the wild ripping hail/The sky cracked its poems in naked wonder." [61]

Jack McDonough sees this as part of an album that is making a modern excursion into "a Romantic, Blakean childhood . . . 'Chimes of Freedom' is an emotional protest against emotional deprivation." The song is laden with extravagant and often violent imagery known as synesthesia, the supervividness found in Poe, Hart Crane, and notably in Rimbaud's "Sonnet of the Vowels," in which colors emerge from common vowels. In her paper "Bob Dylan and French Symbolist Poetry," Belle D. Levinson found in "Hard Rain" and "Chimes of Freedom" "a Dylan whose style as well as theme is close to Rimbaud's." I find "Chimes of Freedom" a landmark lyric in which Dylan has progressed from "Hard Rain" toward his full poetic powers.

"I SHALL BE FREE NO. 10": An abrupt shift toward whimsy and Dada nonsense. Gabrielle Goodchild sees this transition as comic relief with a dramatic purpose: "After the visions that his own suffering, and the world's disorder, brought Lear in the storm, we are grateful for the Fool's apparent nonsense." This title, which last appeared, unnumbered, on *Freewheelin',* jokes at Cassius Clay, at the lunar race with Russia, at himself: "Now they asked me to read a poem/At the sorority sister's home/I got knocked down and my head was swimmin'/I wound up with the Dean of Women/Yippee! I'm a poet, and I know it,/Hope I don't blow it." [62]

"TO RAMONA": A gentle lecture mixed with sexual longing that urges the woman to fight for her own identity. Although the song could be addressed to an amalgam of Dylan's women friends, it may be meant for one active in the southern civil rights movement, pondering her un-ease in New York: "The flowers of the city/Though breathlike, get death-like at times." [63] Yet, as in the blues, the narrator addresses a lover while counseling himself to avoid conformity: "From fixtures and forces and friends,/Your sorrow does stem,/That hype you and type you,/Making you feel/That you must be exactly like them." [64] The narrator is humbler as he offers comfort: "Everything passes,/Everything changes." [65] One day he may need the comfort and direction the woman is seeking. In his paper on Blake and Dylan, Eugene Stelzig wrote that Dylan's attempt to define freedom goes beyond mundane "politics" into "the politics of experience." Dylan had already told Nat Hentoff in *The New Yorker:* " 'What's wrong goes much deeper than the bomb. What's wrong is how few people are free.' " In the line "The pangs of your sadness/Shall pass as your senses will rise," [66] Bill King pointed out the King James Bible associations of "to pass," which crop up again in "Poor Immigrant." King found that for Dylan, *sense* had a dual meaning: "That sense derives from sense ... that the truth is in what we feel, not in what we think."

"MOTORPSYCHO NIGHTMARE": Side two begins with intima-tions of folk-rock to come on the next three albums. The rhythm section can almost be imagined from the rat-a-tat of double-entendre lyrics that re-shape the old bawdy tale of the farmer's daughter and the traveling sales-man. Dylan converts a *Psycho*-like scenario into Middle American panic at the thought of Fidel Castro, and his beard. This sly, charming story of a hipster confronting a reactionary, whose first weapon is *Reader's Digest,* is well-sustained satire.

"MY BACK PAGES": A mournful melody reminiscent of "Hattie Car-roll" declares independence from cant, doctrine, and easy answers. As early as the Newport letter, Dylan realized that he could no longer accept from "corpse evangelists" [67] the message that "life is black and white." [68] He even turns upon himself for becoming his own enemy "In the instant that I preach." [69] The refrain is an internal dialogue between what he once ac-cepted and now doubts:

Ah, but I was so much older then,
I'm younger than that now. [70]

From Blakean "Experience," Dylan has moved back toward "Inno-cence," which will keep him forever young. This song of self-discovery re-turns to a child's openness. According to Jack McDonough, "One of Dylan's most important poetic achievements has been this transposition of the worlds of Wordsworth and Blake into post-war America." Two themes dominating Dylan's whole work are the struggle of life versus death and the possibility of renewal through adoption of a younger view-point.

Three love songs complete the album—"I Don't Believe You," "Ballad in Plain D," and "It Ain't Me, Babe." Despite their wide range in mood, they are unified by Dylan's total departure from trivialized, insipid love ideals that had so long characterized Tin Pan Alley. In *Writings and Drawings,* Dylan gave "I DON'T BELIEVE YOU" the alternate title "She Acts Like We Never Have Met." In a lament that is usually a woman's, he describes the intoxication of a night of love followed by the throbbing headache of his partner's emotional abandonment and detachment. He sings of love's illusions contrasting with reality: "It's all new t' me,/Like some mystery,/It could even be like a myth." [71] The jaunty melody is a crosscurrent to the sardonic words. Dylan laughs in verse three, perhaps because he'd reversed the last five lines as published with verse four.

"BALLAD IN PLAIN D" is one of Dylan's most directly biographical songs, brimming with regret. "Plain D," a key indication, could easily stand for death, desperation, or desolation. In mid-March 1964, there was a harrowing row at Suze and Carla's apartment on Avenue B. As Suze got hysterical, Dylan and Carla scuffled on the floor. Two friends, Paul Clayton and Barry Kornfeld, were dragged in. The crisis effectively ended Bob and Suze's romance. There was no contact between them for some months. They did not reestablish a friendship for several years. Although Suze understood why Bob wrote the song, in 1968 she told me: "That song just went too far. There are some things you just can't do, no matter how much power you have." Carla told me that she was only trying to protect her sister: "I was no parasite. I always worked, I always contributed to the food and rent." She said Dylan ultimately apologized to her for the song. But Dylan stuck to his position, telling me: "I think the song pretty well summarized the situation." Dylan, who generally spouted slang in conversation then, used totally different diction here: "unknown consciousness," "silhouetted anger to manufactured peace," "the tombstones of damage." [72] The final verse, Dylan's view of "the politics of love" likens the losing lover to a prisoner who has no wish to be free:

> *Ah, my friends from the prison, they ask unto me,*
> *"How good, how good does it feel to be free?"*
> *And I answer them most mysteriously,*
> *"Are birds free from the chains of the skyway?"* [73]

The album closes with the well-known "IT AIN'T ME, BABE," a catalog of love's burdens. Stelzig sees this song and "Don't Think Twice" as reflections of the "Female Will" that Blake attacked in his proverb from "Eternity": "He who binds to himself a joy/Does the winged life destroy," although Dylan has just declared that even winged birds aren't free. If, as Bill King maintains, "Dylan used the love song to speak metaphorically about human relationships in general," this song, a rejection of the mythology of true love, could also represent Dylan's rejection of the audience's demands.

"SOME OTHER KINDS OF SONGS" . . . POEMS

The jacket notes for *Another Side* were titled "Some Other Kinds of Songs
. . . Poems by Bob Dylan." As his songs extended page poetry, his page poetry extended his music. Columbia Records printed five of the poems in a
cramped, telephone-directory-sized typeface. *Writings and Drawings* offers a
more readable text and the full cycle of eleven poems, the same number as
the epitaphs. "Some Other Kinds of Songs" further documents Dylan's
experimentation with verbal music and his often elusive world view. The
style is impressionistic and surreal.

POEM 1: This monometrical, highly rhythmic episode bounces in the
jaunty tempo of a skip-rope or hopscotch rhyme. (This form of street poetry has been collected by the Opies, by Tony Schwartz, and sung by
Dominic Behan, and by Ewan MacColl on their Topic/Folkways album,
The Singing Streets.) The central figure of Dylan's first poem is "baby
black," apparently a young Harlem girl, who has been forced into a cruel
life to survive: "baby black/hits back/robs, pawns/lives by trade." [74] We
recognize the hustler of the first *Hootenanny* column. "Baby black" is also
related to "Spanish Harlem Incident": "you ask of order/she'd hock/the
world/for a dollar an' a quarter . . . i'm givin' you/myself t' pawn." [75]

POEM 2: Dedicated to the gentle French singer Françoise Hardy, a
tender evocation of Dylan's Paris visit in spring 1964. Snapshot visions of
Paris in the spring counterpoint a top-level political meeting.

POEM 3: A chess game opens with a dialogue in which a compulsive
winner wants to make the loser "crawl." Another section foreshadows The
Rolling Stones' 1969 song, "Mother's Little Helper," describing "common
housewives strung out/fully on drugstore dope, legally/sold t' help clean
the kitchen." [76] The third episode alludes to a Ping-Pong game Dylan
played in California with the late novelist Henry Miller. Dylan gibes at a
lady reporter who "wants me/t' say what she wants me t' say. she/wants
me t' say what she/can understand." [77] The final section is a dark scene of
"eviction. infection gangrene an'/atom bombs. both ends exist only/be-
cause there is someone who wants/profit." [78] After elliptical references to
Jesus, the section comes back to the natural world of insects, snakes, ants,
turtles, lizards, and eventually to the chess player: "an' everything still
crawls." [79]

POEM 4: From chess imagery to a card game, with that serviceable old
trump, the jack of diamonds, taken from traditional blues. This poem cries
to be read aloud, thumping along rhythmically, bright with rhymes and
lightning pictures. Dylan roamed the Paris night streets with an American
actor, Ben Carruthers, who adapted some "Poem 4" lines for a song un-
authorized by Dylan, "Jack O' Diamonds." In 1965, Carruthers and a British group, The Deep, recorded the song; it was also recorded by Fairport
Convention. Odetta's "Jack" had been an early influence.

POEM 5: A highlight of the cycle, fragmentary glimpses of self-examination played out against the black spiritual "Joshua Fit the Battle of Jeri-
cho." There is a compelling scene of a man on the Brooklyn Bridge poised
to jump to his doom: "i could tell at a glance/he was uselessly lonely." [80]
In the watching mob, Dylan feels shame that he *wanted* to see the man
jump. He identifies both with the mob and the jumper. He ponders the
hollowness of the modern world's lonely crowd, then shifts to New Orleans mobs at Mardi Gras. A foretaste of *Tarantula:* "intellectual spi-
ders/weave down sixth avenue." [81] He rambles along Fourteenth Street,
meeting someone who wants to draw him down to his own level, despair.
He knows he must fight self-destructiveness or others' destructiveness.
Compassionately, he views the movie-going, escapist mob: "slaves are of
no special color/an' the links of chains/fall into no special order." [82] His
guitar sets an old Greek woman dancing and laughing. He ruminates on
lost love and vows: "for the rest of my life/i will never chase a livin'
soul/into the prison grasp/of my own self-love." [83] So he tells Joshua to
go fight his battle while the narrator retreats to Walden-like woods, believing, as an existentialist and romantic, that self-awareness can best be
gained in isolation. Dylan slyly tells Joshua he will join him in battle next
time, and that Joshua may even have his battling celebrated in song.

POEM 6: A brief declaration of envy and past hate toward a rival for
Suze's affections, Enzo. It echoes "My Back Pages" in its effort to fight
jealousy.

POEM 7: Six-line enigma about a man called Charlie who slept on a
Michelangelo cherub's face.

POEM 8: Saga of a girl hitchhiker who gets a lift and makes small talk
with the driver. That Kerouac road feeling carries dangers with its free-
doms.

POEM 9: The wistful tale of poor, empty Johnny, whose parents took
care of him, no matter what he did. But they couldn't buy him into college, so they said, "here son have a [cadillac] car good boy" [84] instead. He
crashed it.

POEM 10: Could be titled "There Are No Politics." A dialogue between a cynic and a person whose life seems organized and structured, but
who is one of the hollow men: "holy hollowness too/yes hollow holi-
ness." [85] A fine section returns to Dylan's fascination with riddles and
truth:

> *you ask me questions*
> *an' i say that every question*
> *if it's a truthful question*
> *can be answered by askin' it* [86]

POEM 11: In the cycle's final poem, "high treachery sails" [87] amid bells
and wedding songs that echo "Bells of Rhymney." Although larkish in
tone, it closes with a shivering blast of shattered illusions:

inside of the altar
outside of the theater
mystery fails
when treachery prevails
the forgotten rosary
nails
itself t' a cross
of sand
an' rich men
stare t' their
private own-ed murals
all is lost Cinderella
all is lost [88]

For all their obscurities, "other kinds of songs" show metaphoric daring, control of nuance, flowing rhythms. Dylan's self-probing concludes that more questions must be raised to find meaning. His seemingly random arrangements make his words into fortune-telling cards that reveal his emerging inner self. These poems were written in a period of personal loss and reorientation. Dylan has arrived at a major insight: The question can be the answer. Ahead lies the frenzied vision of his three great albums of 1965 and 1966, and the larger questions they posed.

LITERATURE TURNS TABLES

To put a tombstone over all narrow definitions of literature, can't we now reverse Dylan's definition of his poems as "some other kinds of songs" and call his songs "some other kinds of poems"? After these two albums of 1964, the acceptance of Dylan as a literary voice grew. Still, two decades later, there is a widespread reluctance in the glacierlike literary establishment to accept any sort of song lyric as any kind of literature.

Ironically, this attitude fails to acknowledge the roots of poetry and literature as an oral art. In nearly every culture, song was the oldest vehicle for poetry. Lying at the roots of poetry and music is the unifying element of rhythm. Oral literature has recounted tales, legends, myths, epics, and romances; accompanied work and worship; venerated heroes, heroines, gods, and goddesses. Oral literature has taught moral precepts, and, since prehistory, it has also entertained.

Before Gutenberg, poetry was a social art: Only gradually did it then become a private art. Poetry was once a popular form, long before it became patrician or elitist. Dylan's central achievement was to help make poetry popular again, or, at least, to have been one of the few to attempt to make it popular. A great deal of page poetry benefits by being read aloud. Shakespeare and Blake are filled with song, whether for the speaker's voice or the singer's.

s certainly nothing unique in fighting for the acceptance of qual-
lyrics as oral literature. Folklorists have been waging that battle
g time. A group of Shakespeare scholars at Harvard championed
ic Scots-English ballads. Biblical scholars contend that much of
the Old Testament was sung before it was ever committed to writing.
Blues scholars, like Paul Oliver, Charles Keil, and Samuel Charters, and
ballad collectors, like the Lomaxes and others, have drawn portraits of a
· people or a community from blues, folk songs, and ballads. The well of
folk song and folk poetry has watered the roots of such composers as Bach,
Mahler, and Bartók, and such poets as Yeats and Sandburg.

For the moment, we have to avoid the measuring of quality. Those who
refuse to recognize any trace of oral literature in popular music will always
head for the jugular vein of the ephemeral, banal, and vapid. But who
among us could deny the poetic gifts of Chuck Berry, Smokey Robinson,
Hank Williams, or Robert Johnson? Biblical prophets and psalmists
chanted their heirloom wisdom. Hellenic mythology and literature?
Homer was a busker, and the mythic Orpheus and Dionysus were foun-
tainheads of music and poetry. Medieval Welsh poets? Robert Graves's
"The White Goddess" details the attainments of court poets and bards.
The tellers of the great Germanic and Scandinavian epics entered that tradition as they chanted, mouth to ear, the oral/aural history of their tribes.

My favorite example of historical literary singers is the goliards, the
singer-poets whose heyday was about 1160, just eight hundred years before
Dylan got to his Village. The goliards composed Latin lyrics, using styles
and forms drawn, subversively, from Church litany, in order to celebrate
pagan joys of the tavern and the flesh. They were rebels who used burlesque and parody to hound corrupt clergy, to satirize errant monks. Most
goliards were threadbare drifters, dropouts and runaways who often hit the
open road from university to university, begging, stealing, cadging, singing. (Goliard songs passed into classical music when Carl Orff used them
in his masterpiece, *Carmina Burana.*)

What of the most storied of the mythic Greek singing poets, Orpheus,
whose legend has been told repeatedly in opera and drama? His love for
Eurydice sent him to Hades on a rescue mission. Losing her on his return
ascent, he was a doomed man, refusing to know women thereafter. The
women of Thrace tore Orpheus to pieces, as a crowd of rock teenyboppers
would a rock star, if they could. Only the head of Orpheus was saved,
taken to the Isle of Lesbos where it became a famed oracle, figurehead of
the religious cult of Orphics.

I'm not arguing that Dylan is a reborn Orpheus, a neo-goliard, or a res-
urrected François Villon. Yet, the vagabond-poet-rebel inhabits our consciousness. The folk movement knew what it had in Woody Guthrie.
When beat poets of the 1950s took their poems into the San Francisco jazz
haunt, the Cellar, Ferlinghetti, Rexroth, and, later, Ginsberg knew that
poetry and music were natural bedfellows. Dylan made himself internationally known and imitated as a neo-troubadour. The mass media ac-

cepted Dylan's prototype faster than the academics did. In 1965, John Ciardi, poetry editor of *Saturday Review,* granted that his nephew thought Dylan was a poet: "But like all Dylan fans I have met, he knows nothing about poetry. Neither does Bob Dylan." Four years later, Ciardi still challenged the aesthetics of "rock poetry": "Is it poetry? How would it look written out? Animal sounds could be put to the same beat. . . . I think the critics have flipped their categories." Which, of course, is the point exactly.

At the other pole stood Kenneth Rexroth, writer, poet, and translator, who'd often appeared in *Saturday Review.* In 1957, he had been a prime mover in the Cellar jazz-and-poetry scene, and, in the 1930s, had experimented with jazz-poetry fusions in Chicago. Rexroth told me in 1966:

"Dylan is the first of his kind in America. There have been singers in that tradition in France and Germany since Charlemagne, but Dylan developed in a vacuum. The importance of Dylan is that he is being imitated right and left. It is a very important phenomenon that in the new-leisure society of barefoot boys and girls, poetry is dissolving into the community. All of this is creating an extremely broad base for poetry. It is diffusing out. In classical China, all civil servants had to write a couplet of poetry to qualify. It led to a heaven built upon the highest poetry." In *Holiday* magazine, March 1966, Rexroth's summation of the prospects for poetry concluded: "Probably the most important event in recent poetry is Bob Dylan . . . he is the American beginning of a tradition as old as civilization in France, and some of his stuff is surprisingly good read over in hypercritical cold blood. This Dylan breakthrough is another great hope for poetry."

In December 1965, *Books* magazine called Dylan the American Yevtushenko and polled writers on Dylan and poetry. Poet Sandra Hochman: "I think it's wonderful that poets are becoming bards again. Since all poetry has to do with song, he is making a real contribution to our idea of what poetry can be." Novelist John Clellon Holmes: "Dylan reminds me of an American Brecht, the Brecht whose poems were meant to be sung. There is the same cold humor, the same ironic warmth, the same violent and splintered imagery, the same urgent idiomatic involvement in the way things actually are. . . . Dylan has returned poetry to song. . . ." Samuel Bogorad of the University of Vermont told *Books:* "Anyone who calls Dylan 'the greatest poet in the U.S. today has rocks in his head . . . having once heard him on a record, I can testify that he can't even sing! Dylan is for the birds—and the bird-brained!" Hart Leavitt of Phillips Academy: "His poetry sounds like a very self-conscious imitation of Kerouac. . . ."

In September 1963, *The New York Times* (Sunday) *Magazine* dismissed my proposal of a serious appraisal of Dylan as poet, philosopher, and moralist. They wanted him portrayed only as an entertainer. By December 1965, the magazine ran a major piece on Dylan, headlined PUBLIC WRITER NO. 1? The subtitle ran: WHO NEEDS SAUL BELLOW? There are those who say that *the* literary voice of our time—and a poet of high degree—is . . . Bob Dylan." The writer, Thomas Meehan, said that since the death of Faulkner and Hemingway, an informal survey of students majoring in

English at three leading Ivy League colleges "revealed" that "their favorite contemporary American writer" was Dylan. A Brown University student: "We don't give a damn about Herzog's angst or Mailer's private fantasies. We're concerned with things like the threat of the nuclear war, the civil-rights movement and the spreading blight of dishonesty, conformism and hypocrisy in the United States . . . and Dylan is the only American writer dealing with these subjects in a way that makes any sense to us. As modern poetry, we feel that his songs have a high literary quality . . . any one of his songs, like 'Hard Rain,' is more interesting to us . . . than an entire volume of . . . verse by someone like Robert Lowell." Meehan wrote that some of Dylan's social protest echoed Odets and Maxwell Anderson of the 1930s, and compared some lines from "It's Alright, Ma" to a "hillbilly W. H. Auden—specifically the earlier Auden of such poems as 'September 1, 1939.' " The article found that a number of leading American literary crit-ics profess "never even to have heard of Dylan."

In *Esquire* in May 1972, literary critic Frank Kermode and poet Stephen Spender pondered Dylan's poetics. *Esquire* added: "Finally, we called up Dylan, after months of fruitless trying, and asked the Wordsworth of the microgroove himself. 'Well, how do *you* see me?' he responded. 'Well, as a kind of human metaphor at the end of a corporate funnel,' we answered. 'Well, that ain't bad,' he said, and hung up." Spender put Dylan into the context of folk traditions and past periods of stress when youth was em-battled. He found Dylan "highly skilled. . . . It is difficult to judge the lyrics as 'poems' because they don't really have to be poetry. They just have to produce their simple effects of feeling, color and mild wit."

Kermode, much more rhapsodic, had even contemplated a book on Dylan's poetics. He stressed the importance of *hearing* the songs: "He is a virtuoso executant, and since he writes the words with virtuoso perfor-mance in mind, they can't, on the page, be more than . . . reminders, hints or shadows." Much good poetry, such as Greek tragedy and the medieval ballad, began in a similar way, Kermode wrote. "Certainly," he continued, Dylan's "long-established preference for mystery . . . a sort of emptiness in his texts, a passivity about meaning, is no doubt a deep temperamental trait." Kermode was intrigued that while Shakespeare and Beethoven are traditionally "allowed four periods," Dylan, by 1972, had already used up three. He found Dylan's rapid stylistic changes a response to "necessary public participation." Kermode concluded that Dylan's greatest strength is his mysteriousness: "The listener provides the only mystery . . . not just opacity, a geometry of innocence which they [the listeners] can flesh out. His poems have to be open, empty, inviting collusion. To write thus is to practice a very modern art, though, as Dylan is well aware, it is an art with a complicated past."

In *The Village Voice* of January 26, 1967, Jack Newfield's page-one piece hailed Dylan as "the Brecht of the jukebox." He complained that "almost nobody over 30 in the literary and intellectual establishments even pays attention to his electronic . . . nightmare visions of America." Calling Dylan "the clown juggler of fact and fantasy, the bastard child of Chaplin, Céline and Hart Crane," Newfield concluded: "And he is a poet. If Whitman were alive today, he, too, would be playing an electric guitar." In Britain, as early as April 16, 1965, *The Guardian* had assessed Dylan as "Homer in Denim," finding his "loose framework of assonant and consonant rhyme, using shifting eight to twelve syllable iambic rhythms, which adjust themselves as naturally to speech as to song put him in a league with the youthfully committed Pound, Auden and MacNeice." *The Guardian* was astonished at the size of Dylan's audiences for a writer working in "the same tradition, in essentials, as Homer."

I have periodically conducted my own survey about Dylan as a poet. British novelist Anthony Burgess replied: "The trouble is that, though I've heard him, I've never seen any of his lyrics set down on paper. I know that verse being oral/aural, this ought to be a good thing, but I like to look at words, sometimes. I know that his skill as a composer of 'folk' lyrics is considerable, though I'm dubious as to whether folk art exists as more than a pastiche form among the sophisticated. I would say that he has achieved a very high standard in a very limited genre—first-class pop-art, some might say. But that he can't compare as a poet with, say, people like Philip Larkin or even Adrian Mitchell. I'm not disparaging, but prais-ing. I'd like him to tackle a volume of verse, separable from song, and then make my judgment."

By August 1968, Rod McKuen, a singer-songwriter, had sold a million copies of his three volumes of very slight verse, and had become the best-selling "poet" in America. In trade papers, record companies were pushing songs by Jerry Jeff Walker and Laura Nyro with full-page ads running texts of their lyrics. Columbia University professor F. W. Dupee saw growing acceptance of pop poetics among academicians. "After all," he told me, "Homer was chanted and so were the Scandinavian epics. I think that in general the movement is great. They can arrive at standards later."

During the middle to late sixties, the pop audience and the pop critics, rather than major literary taste-makers, were discovering this outpouring of new poetics. As Dylan, a poet of the electronic age, entered millions of homes, poetry became once again a democratic, social art. The shoe-shop clerk and the Ph.D. candidate—even though they may have had little to say to each other at the record shop—were both buying Dylan, Beatles, Fugs, and Byrds albums. Enthusiasts felt pop had joined film as the first real contemporary "mass art." A sober report on young poets in *Newsweek* (March 3, 1969) saw an incredible flowering, offering not only survival but also success. *Newsweek:* "One common ground for young poets, white and black, is rock. 'My poems are involved with the spoken voice and with melody,' insists Tom Clark, 27. 'My listening to rock—its spirit and gai-ety—is bound to affect what I write.' The extraordinary popularity, and talent of the rock poets—Cohen, The Beatles, Jim Morrison and Dylan (sometimes called 'the major poet of his generation')—has prompted some word-poets to incorporate rock lyrics in their work."

A bloodless cultural revolution was taking place, led by "rock intellectuals." No longer, we then believed, could the dance hall, the discotheque, or the record collection be dismissed as mindless teenybopper blare. We saw the shows at the East Village's Dom and the Balloon Farm, the Fillmore in San Francisco, Murray the K's Long Island airplane hangar as our arts festivals. The senses were assaulted with the insistent beat, light play, strobes, film clips, kinetic murals, all against that heavy sound. Through it all, the lyrics were repeated until they became part of us. Perhaps we were naïve, like Richard Neville in *Playpower* and Charles Reich in *The Greening of America*. If it was naïveté, then it was also sheer idealism, the belief that youth culture could change society. Viewed from the cool, cynical 1980s, we need to accept that deep change is not that simple to effect. We didn't necessarily think that the Gutenberg era was over or that books and the theater were dead; we thought their vitality and energy had passed over into popular music.

Pop pacemakers did not disdain books; they wrote them. John Lennon wrote two Edward Lear-like books, *In His Own Write* and *Spaniards in the Works*. Leonard Cohen closed his poetry readings with guitar in hand. Cohen told me that Dylan had inspired him to sing his own poems. "Dylan is not just a great poet, he's a great man," Cohen told me. Paul Simon's work reflected this new wave, and he was soon singing about alienation and vacuums. Jim Morrison of The Doors wrote astonishing lyrics. Ginsberg taught Indian chants to The Byrds. Richard Fariña moved from page writing to singing and composing with his wife, Mimi Baez. Five experimental New York poets, led by Ed Sanders, taught themselves music and formed The Fugs. Phil Ochs adorned one of his album jackets with poems by Mao, and told me: "I want to be the first Left-wing star."

The young person of the sixties was more adult. In their songs, Randy Newman and James Taylor, like memoir writers, plumbed lonely episodes of their adolescences. The Beatles sang about the hollowness of the lonely crowd, and about tortured existences like Eleanor Rigby's. Pap records still made hits, but we were convinced in the sixties that a sort of Pop Millennium had arrived. Fariña wrote that Dylan Thomas might have played a portable instrument, although he knew that Thomas's verbal music and resonant projection formed another stream bringing poetry back to the ear. Fariña wrote in 1965: "One could argue . . . that if verse is never very far from song, that more people are listening to poetry at the moment than have in the history of mankind."

THE GREENING OF THE CAMPUS

Such a burst of 1960s rhetoric may ring hollow by the 1980s. The intervening years have seen growth in the literary and sociological study of popular music. During this period, the scrutiny of popular culture as a multi-disciplinary field has mushroomed. As many as six thousand courses in popular culture have been offered in American colleges. Bob Dylan's work is stage center in a great many of them.

A survey of one hundred fifty heads of English departments at major colleges and universities was undertaken in 1977 by Professor Louis Cantor, a historian, of Purdue-Indiana University at Fort Wayne. He estimated that more than one hundred courses had by then been taught on Dylan's poetics alone. Cantor reported that "Dylan's roots have, at last, been firmly planted in the groves of academe. It's not unusual to find Dylan being taught in literature survey courses along with Blake and Eliot. Dylan is apparently winning out in the academic controversy over his legitimacy as a poet."

For several years now, I've had a lively interchange with academics in several countries regarding their literary analyses of Dylan's lyrics. I've read several dozen dissertations and papers linking aspects of his visionary Romantic song-poetry to that of Yeats, Eliot, the Cabala, Whitman, biblical prophets and apostles, the French symbolists, Blake, Kafka, and the beats.

Perhaps the most prestigious Dylan commentator is Christopher Ricks, professor of English at Christ's College, Cambridge University. His books include *Milton's Grand Style, Tennyson,* and *Keats and Embarrassment.* He also co-edited *The State of the Language.* He has lectured internationally on Dylan's poetics. Ricks calls Dylan: "A great amuser, a great entertainer, who belongs with the artists who've looked for the widest popular constituency, like Dickens and Shakespeare." Ricks believes that, since the deaths of John Berryman and Robert Lowell, Dylan has become "the best American *user* of words."Although "reluctant to call him a poet," because "he's got more than words to use," Ricks praises his "great, brilliant" work as a rhymester. Says the professor: "I'm not so besotted with Dylan's genius not to know that not all of his work is perfect. He's only as good as Shakespeare, who had a lot wrong, too!"

The first big conclave of Dylan literary scholars occurred in December 1975, at the annual meeting of the Modern Language Association in San Francisco. A popular literature seminar on Dylan was organized by Professor Patrick D. Morrow of Auburn University in Alabama. Some faculty folkniks played and sang the songs, and three papers were read: Belle D. Levinson's "The Deranged Seer: The Poetry of Rimbaud and Dylan," Emily Toth's "The Women in Bob Dylan," and W. T. Lhamon's "Dylan and the Cultural Context." Richard Goodall organized conventions called Dylan Revisited in Manchester, England, in 1979 and 1980. Films, tapes, and videos were used, and there were serious panels and trivial quizzes. To balance the fevers of collectors, talks were given by such literary scholars as Ricks and Lhamon, and musicologist Wilfrid Mellers.

During the 1970s, literature Ph.D.'s were granted to Bill King by the University of North Carolina and to Betsy Bowden by the University of California at Berkeley for their Dylan dissertations. Other doctoral literary dissertations were in progress in the early 1980s in West Germany, Belgium, Britain, as well as in America. Probably half a dozen master's degrees have been earned by American students studying Dylan. Of those I've seen, I was especially impressed by the work of Jack McDonough, formerly of Chapel Hill, North Carolina, and Carolyn Jane Bliss, of the University of Utah.

Not all of the scholarship is rooted to the campus. The erudition of such collector-analysts as Stephen Pickering, John Bauldie, Paul Cable, and Jacques Van Son is legendary among Dylan students. Various academic and literary magazines have published studies on Dylan, and the *Journal of Popular Culture* and *Journal of Popular Music* have devoted a good deal of space to his work.

A valuable essay on Dylan and Blake has been written by Eugene Stelzig of the English department at the State University of New York at Geneseo. "Once I started to look at Dylan's songpoetry critically," Stelzig wrote me, "it was obvious that he is one of the major contemporary voices rooted in the whole Romantic tradition of the artist as a seer/prophet." When he and a music department colleague offered a Dylan course, they found that the one hundred fifty students who turned out proved too many to handle—and also that quite a few came to be entertained, not to study! In other survey courses, Stelzig placed "Desolation Row" between *Faust* and *The Flowers of Evil*, while "Tambourine Man," as an example of "the Romantic escape artist," was analyzed between *Peer Gynt* and *The Great Gatsby*.

A widely published literature professor, David R. Pichaske, of Bradley University, compiled an offbeat anthology, *Beowulf to Beatles: Approaches to Poetry*. Ten complete Dylan song texts are printed alongside works by Ben Jonson, Auden, Frost, and others. In a seminar at Dartmouth, Louis A. Renza had the students "discuss the songs as if they were poems, or treat albums as if they were somehow unitary texts . . . keeping alive the issue of a strictly 'literary' interpretation. . . . The students are often surprised at the poetic quality of his lyrics and his insistent meta-poetic turns."

A literature professor at Florida State University at Tallahassee, W. T. Lhamon, Jr., has written brilliantly about Dylan in *The New Republic* and *Bennington Review*. In his trailblazing essay, "Poplore and Dylan," Lhamon maintains that poplore has succeeded folklore in contemporary America. "Pop," he wrote, "helps a few people make money. Poplore helps the rest of us live. Investing pop images with mythic resonance, poplore locates patterns of usefulness in the bewildering panoply of instant images that the electronic media and other distribution nets of consumer culture throw before contemporary audiences. . . . A society that has no available folk—but still needs lore—produces poplore. . . . *Dylan's embrace of rock altered the course of American culture* [my italics]. This return to the on-going rhythms of popular culture has always been the hallmark of a new cultural era's beginning. Such a return occurred when literature, via the novel, turned in the 18th-century from the life of the aristocracy to the life of the middle class."

The Popular Culture Association of the South has heard several papers on Dylan, from such scholars as Dr. Kenneth J. Cook, Greg Keeler of Montana State University, and, from Tulsa University, Bob Graalman and Lynn DeVore. Professor Suzanne H. MacRae of the University of Arkansas has included Dylan's work in several humanities courses, "and I've even compared him to some writers in the medieval satiric tradition." Her essay, "Bob Dylan Is the Weatherman," written long before *Slow Train Coming,* is strong on the rebirth theme. At the University of Texas at Arlington, Jerome L. Rodnitzky, associate professor of history, encourages graduate students to work with popular music in research courses. His book, *Minstrels of the Dawn: The Folk-Protest Singer As a Cultural Hero,* contains a thirty-five-page chapter on Dylan, entitled "Beyond Left and Right."

Dylan literary studies have even weathered the waters out to Pelican Island, off Galveston, to the Texas A & M University's Moody College of Marine Sciences and Maritime Resources. There, Dr. Thomas S. Johnson, a lecturer in the humanities, holds that "Dylan's work is certainly hearty enough to bear the close examination of any open-minded humanist." Johnson wrote me of his concern that academic studies of a figure like Dylan run the risk of "didacticism—of overwhelming the reader's or listener's ability to respond directly, personally to the lyric, itself." At North Texas State University, Dr. James Baird has taught courses on the lyrics, using the albums and *Tarantula* as study materials. Baird says: "We're trying to broaden the traditional range of English and provide a new frame of reference. Most students don't realize that Dylan has read a lot, and his songs reflect that reading." Steven Tucker, doing a history doctorate at Tulane, reported to me that "Dylan is alive and well in the academic world." At Rutgers, Kevin Hayes has taught a course on "three revolutionary visionary writers—Blake, Ginsberg and Dylan."

As Dylan studies spread throughout the academic world, as the sixties accrete an ever-deepening luster of great times past, it's impossible to predict where it will all end. There's always the danger of the academic world's analyzing popular-culture artifacts in a fashion inimical to its original vitality and street validity. When they were University of Wisconsin undergraduates in 1968, Betsy Bowden and Andy Mirer satirized this potential academic overkill in a spoof "six-week exam," which called for "a clear-headed grasp of the facts, not for vague generalizations. Use your time wisely." Among their mocking questions were: "Analyze two of the following: a. Courtly-love conventions in 'She Belongs to Me'; b. Fertility goddess and/or Fisher King imagery in 'Maggie's Farm'; c. The tradition of the Gothic novel in 'Love Minus Zero.' Compare and contrast style and thematic import of 'Gates of Eden' and Milton's *Paradise Lost.* Relate 'Bringing It All Back Home' to the whole of Western literature. Be specific." We can only hope with these two students that the greening of the campus with more attention toward popular culture, in general, and Dylan studies, in particular, doesn't sprout too much crabgrass.

GUTENBERG ROLLS BACK

Despite the McLuhanite predictions, the book hasn't died yet. Even in the study of oral/aural literature, the printed word is not completely irreplaceable by the phonograph recording. Ideally, the published song lyric will resonate off the page for those familiar with the recorded song. Dylan's first book, *Tarantula*, also proves, conversely, that some page writing can best be fully appreciated when it is read aloud, reminding us of Gerard Manley Hopkins's suggestion: "Read it with the ear."

Dylan's first collection of song lyrics, aside from the album song folios, emerged in *Writings and Drawings by Bob Dylan*, published in April 1973 by Alfred A. Knopf. Robert Gottlieb, Knopf's president and editor-in-chief, wrote me that it "delighted" him to work on it. "I have a lifelong passion for pop music, and a great admiration for Dylan in particular. The book had a very smooth passage, once we had found a design or tone that Bob liked; everyone worked well with everyone else." *Writings and Drawings* appeared in a pink paper-on-board edition of 319 pages. Within two months, Cape published a British edition. Late in 1973, Shobun Sha, Ltd., published the book in Japan. The autumn of 1975 saw its release in France, by Editions Robert Laffont-Seghiers, and in Spain, by Aguillera and Castilla. The German edition came out in October 1975, from Zweitausendeins Vernads Dienst.

The work is set out in chronological order, in 11 sections ranging from the first album through *New Morning*. There are a total of 187 song lyrics, 17 drawings, 5 pages of manuscript text, and 26 poems, including the "11 Outlined Epitaphs" and the 11 "Some Other Kinds of Songs." There are the lyrics of songs that have been officially recorded as well as some yet to be heard. Of special interest, two years before their official release, were *The Basement Tapes* lyrics.

Dylan's folkish line drawings remind us of his debt to Guthrie, who also illustrated many of his own songs and other writings. A dedicatory note rolls with Woody's open-plains cadences. Guthrie and Robert Johnson, the great Delta bluesman, are lauded for having "sparked it off." Those wanting an insight into Dylan's battle for just the right word and phrase will be drawn to the four endpapers of songs in progress and a full-page reproduction of an early draft of "Subterranean Homesick Blues." Although *Writings and Drawings* has gone through many reprintings and continues to sell well, it was not received by the establishment or literary press as a poetry volume of significance. Ralph Gleason devoted a column to it, citing its value "for anyone who is interested in the cultural history of America, for those interested in the most important contemporary

poets. . . . Napoleon in rags cannot be dismissed merely as a fad or as a topical songwriter. He is a poet."

The British edition got ample notice in *The Times* and *Observer,* but the
reviews were dismissive on the question: "Is it poetry?" Snorted Robert
Nye in *The Times:* ". . . as a poet he is strictly for the birds. He emerges
from this book as a canny-hearted, miserable fellow, with an uncontrolla-
ble gift for imperfect rhymes and a positive genius for repetition." Clive
James, himself a one-time lyricist for songwriter Pete Atkin, wrote in *The
Observer,* ". . . The frustration of reading this book lies in the realization
that no stanza will ever be as good as its best line and no song will ever be
as good as its best stanza."

In November 1976, Knopf published *The Songs of Bob Dylan from 1966
Through 1975.* This spiral-bound, boxed, 383-page handsome book includes piano arrangements and guitar tablatures along with the text of
lyrics, from "I Want You" and other *Blonde on Blonde* works through *Desire,* ending with "Sara." The arrangements were mostly by Ronnie Ball,
except for twenty-six songs arranged by Milt Okun. This opulent collection, priced at $19.95, was not designed as a poetry collection, but that
didn't stop the faithful from treating it as such.

In autumn 1985, Dylan wrapped up a significant part of his writing and
recording with the publication of *Lyrics, 1962–1985* by Bob Dylan. It was,
in fact, a revised edition of *Writings and Drawings* with 120 new writings,
Lyrics adding 210 pages. Although there will never be an exact count of
songs, and the overlapping question of which are songs without words
and which are words without music, a safe working number for Dylan's
works now becomes around five hundred.

Lyrics carries on with completion of the *New Morning* period through
Empire Burlesque. One remarkable addition is a page poem, "Alternatives
to College." Very much in the vein of *Highway 61 Revisited* and *Tarantula,*
it carries a 1985 copyright date. Gone are the dedications of *Writings and
Drawings* and its endpapers of manuscripts in progress. Not gone is the
mystification, the pain and anger, and the magical word flow. From the biographical point of view, not previously discussed songs among the new
material most worth scrutiny are "Abandoned Love," "Coming from the
Heart (The Road Is Long)," "Trouble in Mind," and "Caribbean Wind."
Lyrics, 1982–1985 is laconically dedicated "For Narette," who replaces all
others for the moment, or so the writer would have us believe.

TARANTULA

While Dylan students can grapple with one of his ambiguous phrases in a
song lyric, his "novel," *Tarantula,* has curiously not deeply engaged many
of them. The literary world barely paid it any credence at all. *Tarantula* is
an enigma wrapped in a question mark. Some of it is automatic writing,
most of it is highly musical, and all of it offers more when read aloud.

Dylan held the book back at the time of the crucial motorcycle accident of 1966, having reservations about how it was being built up and promoted by Macmillan. He also had doubts about how book reviewers would deal with it. With Macmillan already touting him as a "young James Joyce," the publication of the book would put him in that literary coliseum in front of lions he chose not to face.

I asked my first personal editor on this book, Gabrielle Goodchild, to undertake an analysis and discussion of *Tarantula*. She found the book "a circus of dreams ... concerned with night-time truths and half-truths." Linking the bite of the poisonous tarantula to the dancing mania called tarantism, she found "it is as a mad 'dance' and as 'music' that the book succeeds." Although the Left was vexed with Dylan for not having made more overt comments on the Vietnam War, we find a great deal of that war in the book. Goodchild holds it is a surrealist sort of "war" going on "beyond our control and yet poisoning our lives."

From Dylan's phrase "combined in a stolen mirror," she reads the book as a two-way mirror "that looks out one way to the actual world of supermarkets and malnutrition" and the other way into the artist's mind. He is searching for order while accepting chaos. Goodchild places *Tarantula* in the "Highway 61 Revisited" frame "in dramatic stance, personae, sound patterns" and rhythm. She finds him using "language of concurrence, coincidence and contradiction." From the standpoint of revealing Dylan, his veneration of a junkyard angel, Aretha, is important, especially in the light of his later association with many women gospel singers. Aretha is "a symbol of innocent physicality whose 'nakedness is a piercing thing.' She's also spiritual renewal in the hollow desert of modern existence."

Goodchild maintains that *Tarantula* "works best where the combination is funny ... where the 'wit' is effective, language is pressurized into producing a new and purposeful energy, a lateral connection, time-warp, a new world: extra-sense. It repeatedly falls flat, becoming only obscure: nonsense." Many reviewers invoked Joyce, one even calling the book "Finnegans Wake of the Pepsi generation." Goodchild says it is more useful to place the book in the context of the beat writers, notably William Burroughs, with a debt to Jack Kerouac for spontaneity. "On the road, but ten years on, and light years into inner depths, and into a different sense of guilt and involvement, a greater inner awareness of a greater inner and outer violence. A lot had happened in the 10 years between *On the Road* and *Tarantula*."

Goodchild found the influence of Kenneth Patchen's *The Journal of Albion Moonlight* most relevant, even though it dates from 1941. (I was clued on that one night by George Plimpton, at a Village party after he had received the original galleys of *Tarantula*. Patchen was also a favored writer of Tony Glover.) "The similarity between the two books is more than that of sound, surface and jokes, for both are dramas in which the writer struggles to get a response from us and is often frustrated. Both are halls of mirrors, where illusion is the only reality," Goodchild writes. With Patchen reaching back to Blake and Dylan reaching back to Rimbaud, Goodchild wonders: "Why is this dream-world so violent? It is because there's a war going on: for Patchen, in 1941, Hitler's war, and for Dylan, in 1965, Vietnam."

The novel, she wrote, reflects Dylan's "hilarious love of the wisdom and idiocy of words ... it carries us, in great waves until we are deposited, dizzy, danced out, with only dim memories of the stoned laughter and manic violence.... Dylan presents his 'world' in the very process of its being created and discovered, its outlines sometimes only half formed before the mirror cracks, the image fades, the scene fragments and disperses, its contents all jumbled up and reassembled into another picture." If *Tarantula* has a subject, Goodchild wrote, it is about chaos, and the artistic struggle to find artistic form for expressing it.

"After the accident," Goodchild wrote, "it became less and less possible for him to rewrite the book. By 1968, he was repudiating the project" to *Newsweek* and *Sing Out!* And in 1969, he was saying he'd thrown it together like a collage of scraps of paper. But Goodchild believes "this was partly smokescreen," for it had been "a serious, deliberate, perhaps desperate endeavour." Citing Stephen Pickering's essay, "The Two Tarantulas: A Textual Comparison," she wrote, "We see how rigorously Dylan had edited the earlier manuscript, *Tarantula Meets Rex Paste,* which ended with an epilogue from Rimbaud's *Les Poétes de Sept Ans.*" She believes that "certainly the book wrote him as much as he wrote it.... We make better sense of the electric prose, originally to have been called *Off the Record* or *Side One,* if we hear behind it the melodies from *Another Side* to *Blonde on Blonde.* The novel only really works where we can hear it with the emphatic rhythms of Dylan's 1965 voice, the way he sang, *in italics ...*"

Of the many characters who appear in *Tarantula,* Goodchild finds only two are dominant: "Aretha, a soulful Mama, Muse and helper ... a symbol of innocent physicality who is also spiritual renewal in the hollow desert of modern existence. Her element is Music.... The other figure is the narrator, both entirely Dylan ... and everything he is not.... There is one other main player in this pitchfork drama—the reader. We are challenged and hectored; occasionally, courted.... If the book can partly be seen as a Courtly Love Poem, an Adoration by the kneeling yet fearless lover to the unattainable beloved he has created, she of the 'religious thighs,' then we make up the court in which the madman-jester performs and is judged."

But the book is alive with other characters, Goodchild writes, "crammed together at *Desolation Row* carnivals, society parties and with funny psychedelic soubriquets, characters from TV and film, nursery rhymes and comics, art and philosophy and literature, the Bible, legend, history, politics, the folk songbook, the book of the blues, jazz, pop music, show business, and the news." Finding some relationship to Kerouac, she also links *Tarantula* to the New Journalist and his celebration of violence, paranoia, and artificial stimulants. Dylan inspired some of the Novel Reporters and shares with them the decision to produce under pressure, using language with a Shakespearean disregard for Latinate grammar, with nouns as adjectives and capitals as exclamation marks, taking from the mud of the immediate moment, garlic or sapphires, hurling it all together inside of the frozen traffic."

For all the effort it demands, Goodchild urges readers not to fear it, or listeners not to try it. "Travelling back along Highway 61 in a different Buick is worth the undertaking even if you never actually make it to Edge City.... Beware the Spider's Web, the Lady Tarantula, and Beware America. Beware the dream and beware the reality! But, above all, 'live before you board your *Titanic*.' We all know it sails at dawn."

Tarantula is difficult reading. It is howlingly funny, at times very violent, but it is original, inventive, and challenging. I suggest you give *Tarantula* a go. Try reading it aloud. Play "Highway 61" a few times before you plunge in. Good luck, and have a nice trip. Gutenberg would roll over in his grave!

7

SEVERAL SEASONS IN HELL

"I've walked and I've crawled on six crooked high-
ways. . . ." [1]

—DYLAN, 1963

"To be in hell is to drift . . . to be in heaven is to
steer. . . ."

—GEORGE BERNARD SHAW, *DON JUAN IN HELL*

"I accept chaos. I am not sure whether it accepts
me . . ." [2]

—DYLAN, 1965

"You certainly look like an intense young man . . ."

—CARL SANDBURG TO DYLAN, 1964

Before we join our antihero on a mad, careening, chaotic road show that
began on February 3, 1964—and scarcely paused for breath for two and a
half years—let's retrace our steps a bit. While all that stage/page/electric
poetry we looked at in the last chapter was pumping out, the narrative of
Dylan's outer life picks up at the end of 1963: Kennedy dead, the romance
with Suze dying, the Tom Paine award more pain than gain, Dylan's sum-

mary of the dying year in his letter to *Broadside*. In 1964, when he decided
to try rediscovering America, he was not yet twenty-three.

The journey that began in February 1964 went from New York to California with a half dozen detours to see embattled miners in Kentucky, a
father-poet, Mardi Gras, and southern civil rights fighters. Only four concerts were scheduled. Dylan carried no compass, just "road-maps of the
soul." [3] After years of steering toward goals, Orpheus was descending for
several seasons in hell. He rolled like thunder across America's landscape,
right through Whitman's "Open Road," Guthrie's *Hard Travellin'*,
Kerouac's *On the Road,* Hopper and Fonda's *Easy Rider,* and Kesey's *Acid
Test*. Dylan's compulsion was to keep in physical and spiritual motion.

He chose his companions carefully; the alchemy of four men in a car was
not easy to balance. Later, Dylan told me: "I'm lucky. Not because I make
a lot of bread, but because I can be around groovy people. I don't fear anything and nobody around me has to fear anything. That's where it's at:
bread, freedom, and no fear." Doing most of the driving and keeping business affairs straight was Victor Maimudes. Tall, taciturn, suggesting Clint
Eastwood crossed with Vittorio Gassman, Victor had penetrating dark
eyes, turbulent hair, and an uncanny ability to keep his mouth shut.

Pete Karman, longtime friend of the Rotolos, came along for kicks. The
previous year he had visited Cuba. He had been a reporter on the *Daily
Mirror,* and later became a travel-magazine editor. He never wrote about
the Dylan trip, just talked of its madness and his disillusionment. "I used
to call Dylan 'the punk.' I used to ask: "How're you doing, punk?' I was
twenty and he was only nineteen." By the time of the trip, Pete wasn't
calling him the punk anymore. Dylan later told me: "We had to kick Pete
out and send him home on a plane."

The final member of the supporting cast was Paul Clayton, an intro-
spective singer and folklorist, with a Jesus-like beard and gentleness. A
scholar and romantic, Clayton wanted to live his old ballads. With some
twenty albums to his credit, he was once called "the most recorded young
folk singer in America," but he was scarcely known. Despite his two degrees and encyclopedic knowledge of folklore, Clayton remained unpretentious, self-effacing, and dedicated to his art and his friends, of whom he
had no greater than Dylan. Pete Karman said that during this trip, Clayton seemed to be traveling under some undefined personal burden. Paul
had been going out with Carla, and at times he and Dylan and the sisters
had become so involved with each other that the problems of all the relationships were geometrically enlarged. According to Pete, Paul got stoned
more often than anyone on the trip. (Succumbing to professional frustra-
tions and a dependency on drugs, Clayton was found dead in his bathtub,
of electrocution, on April 6, 1967.)

The trip began unceremoniously. Victor loaded up with traveler's
checks. Pete arrived at Grossman's at ten A.M., but due to farewells and
rounding up clothes for striking miners in Hazard, Kentucky, they didn't

leave until dusk. The blue Ford station wagon was cluttered with suitcases, instruments, and old clothing. Once the clothes had been delivered, Dylan often perched in the rear of that mobile writer's garret to scribble out some lyrics or a chord progression. Between talk and games, the foursome frequently fell into long silences. One could almost feel the palpable solitude into which Dylan withdrew, a shell that created space around him. He wrote at least two important songs on the trip: "Chimes of Freedom" and "Ballad in Plain D."

The first night's goal was Clayton's gracious old university town, Charlottesville, Virginia. A year and a half earlier, Clayton had taken Bob into Charlottesville's Gaslight, praising him to folkniks like Bill Clifton and Mike Seeger. Clifton recalled "a good, late evening with Bob, just picking and singing." Although Clayton had a rough country cabin outside town, the four stayed with Paul's friend, Steve Wilson. Buying two dozen copies of *Times Changing* to hand out along the way, Dylan was recognized by students and sales people.

They left Charlottesville next morning, for eastern Kentucky coal country. Near Abingdon, Virginia, they picked up a young coal miner, Robert Swann, wearing a miner's lighted helmet, his face smudged with coal dust. Dylan gave the miner *Freewheelin'*, and the hitchhiker seemed impressed. Swann was their introduction to Harlan County and the men of the other underground. They crossed Harlan County and looked for the strike leader, Hamish Sinclair, secretary of the National Committee for Miners. Sinclair, who had sung at benefits in New York, linked the pickets and their supporters. He greeted Dylan's group warmly; they unloaded the clothing. Hamish was up to his ears bailing people out of jail, seeing to strikers' welfare, organizing legal moves. In January 1963, miner Berman Gibson told *The Reporter:*

" 'Well, God Almighty, it ain't right! Man out here braggin' he made $60,000 in 60 days, and the men that made it for him takin' home four to six dollars a day! . . . The man that makes it for him down in the mines can't feed his kids, can't put shoes on 'em. Now we got nothin' against an operator making a profit . . . want him to. But when he does it working a man 60 hours paying him 16 dollars, then we got something to say!' "

Dylan wanted to contribute more than clothes—a benefit concert, perhaps. Sinclair was too preoccupied, and sent them to visit a picket leader, Jason Combes. Dylan's crew left earlier than expected. They headed southeast. First night, a motel in Pineville, Kentucky. Then, Asheville, North Carolina, birthplace of novelist Thomas Wolfe, who wrote *You Can't Go Home Again*. Asheville was still segregated, although during store hours, the white shops welcomed black customers. The group went bowling in a black bowling alley, shot pool, and went to a nudie movie. In the film, Dylan recognized a girl who'd been a Gaslight waitress in the Village, folk singer Jimmy Gavin, and another musician who had worked with Pete at *The Mirror*.

On to Hendersonville, near Flat Rock, North Carolina. They couldn't
find the home of Carl Sandburg, the writer, but were directed to the home
of a Sandburg who raised goats. Same man. Sandburg was a towering figure to his visitors. There was much that Dylan had in common with the
eighty-six-year-old poet, biographer of Lincoln, collector and singer of folk
songs. Sandburg was born of immigrants in the Midwest. Much as the
young Sandburg had revered Whitman, Dylan now revered Sandburg.
The old writer had been, in critic Harvey Breit's words: "milk-wagon
driver in Illinois, wheat harvester in Kansas, dish-washer in Colorado, coal
shoveler in Omaha, soldier in Puerto Rico . . . hobo, newspaper man, novelist, historian, biographer, balladeer, goat farmer . . ." In 1919, in a letter
to French novelist and pacifist Romain Rolland, Sandburg had written
words that might have come from Woody: "I am an I.W.W., but I don't
carry a red card. I am an anarchist, but not a member of the organization. . . . I belong to everything and nothing. . . . I would say I am with all
rebels everywhere all the time as against all people who are satisfied."

When the travelers' station wagon pulled into Sandburg's 240-acre
Connemara Farm, on the porch was a buxom grandmother figure out of
Norman Rockwell, Mrs. Lillian Sandburg. She didn't seem startled by the
hairy foursome. According to Pete, Dylan announced: "I am a poet. My
name is Robert Dylan, and I would like to see Mr. Sandburg." She disappeared into the house while they looked over the serene, sloping pasture,
where goats grazed, into a heavy wood backed by Sugarloaf Mountain. To
the rear, large pine trees ran thickly from Little and Big Glassy Mountains
down to the house. It had been built one hundred years earlier by Christopher Memminger, Confederate Treasury Secretary. The Sandburgs and
their daughters lived there from 1945 until his death in July 1967.

They waited impatiently. Was he sleeping in his attic room, or talking
to other visitors? Was he writing? (Sandburg once advised a writer friend:
"Watch your time and your sleep. You're a writer. Let 'em steal as little as
possible from your writing time.") Finally, the poet appeared, a genial,
slow-moving man. His gray hair tumbled over his left ear, his face was
stubbled. He obviously didn't care about shaving daily either. He wore an
old plaid wool shirt, baggy trousers, and a green eye shade over shell-
rimmed glasses. Sandburg's penetrating eyes assessed his visitors carefully
in their dungarees, jackets, cowboy boots. Instinctively, his pale blue eyes
locked with Dylan's bright blue eyes. (Pete later told me: "Sandburg
looked at the rest of us, but he just wasn't as interested as he was in Dylan.
There was an immediate, unspoken communication between them.")
Sandburg: "You look like you are ready for anything. I would like to ask
you about forty good questions. Your group looks able to prepare for any
emergency." Dylan handed the old writer *Times Changing* and Clayton
stepped forward with one of his albums. Sandburg said he didn't know
Dylan's work at all, but he was interested in poetry and folk singing and
regarded them as kindred arts. The visitors praised Sandburg for his pio-

neer song-collecting, indicating familiarity with his *American Songbag* (280 songs and ballads first published in 1927).

For about twenty minutes, the five chatted on the porch. Dylan had wanted this great writer to "open up" and take them into his study to see his books, his piles of manuscripts. Sandburg repeated that he'd listen to the two albums, and Dylan reiterated that he too was a poet. Every time the word *poet* was mentioned, Sandburg seemed to prick up his ears. The old poet excused himself, saying that he simply had to work on some manuscripts and letters. Pete recalls: "We had a definite feeling of disappointment, mainly because Sandburg had never heard of Bobby. As I recall, during the rest of the trip Sandburg was never mentioned again. Dylan sank into one of his quiet funks."

From Flat Rock into South Carolina, where fireworks were sold legally. They filled the car with rockets, whizbangs, and cherry bombs. Then, Athens, Georgia—another university center. The pinball wizards headed for a pool hall, and they played the tables and machines. Along the streets, students right and left recognized Dylan; some sidled up for an autograph. Another record-shop flurry of recognition. Next day, they looked around progressive Atlanta. That evening, Dylan's concert at nearby Emory University. The student audience knew nearly every song by its opening phrase. Afterward, a party, to which local *éminences grises* of folk music and southern radicalism were invited. Grainy, gritty Ernie Marrs, a chip off Woody's quarry, looked over "this Dylan kid" with curiosity. Fresh from some picket line or sit-in were Bernice Johnson and Cordell Reagon. Next day, Dylan visited them in Atlanta.

Westward through the Deep South black belt toward Mississippi: WHITE ONLY signs, garish billboards, and indolent miasma. They couldn't believe they were still in the United States. The South hadn't really changed all that much. Dylan scanned the roadside. He scribbled a few notes on small scraps of paper and heard "Chimes of Freedom" ringing. Crossing into Mississippi, a fork on their road. Should they join SNICK at Tougaloo College, as half-promised, or drift southward toward Mardi Gras in New Orleans? Excitement and curiosity pointed them toward New Orleans. They stopped overnight at Meridian, Mississippi, the birthplace of Jimmie Rodgers, the "singing brakeman" who became the father of country music. Did anyone need to remind them what a fabled music city New Orleans was? The lures of colorful Crescent City and its yearly carnival of abandon sent them skittering toward the Gulf.

Many had made the pilgrimage before to the fountainhead of jazz, home of the Creole street cry, focus of the swamp music from the Cajun bayous, a town where the heat of the blues was stoked up. There had been a great cavalcade of sounds through New Orleans: brass-band music to and from the cemeteries, pianists toying with the cakewalk and ragtime in Storyville's red-light houses. New Orleans was the town of jazz giants Buddy Bolden, George Lewis, Louis Armstrong. Here Mahalia Jackson learned to sing. In the streets, clogs and buck-and-wings, shufflers and juba dancers, had competed for pennies. Here was the town of street violinists and alley fiddlers, the town that took an old-world folk ballad like "Derbyshire Ram" and turned it into that jazz classic, "Didn't He Ramble." Everything about New Orleans's musical past spelled freedom, a hell-bent stew of styles, where nobody told a jazzman he couldn't play this or that; he played whatever he wanted, borrowed and embellished what he pleased. New Orleans was the Jerusalem of all musical faiths, where the work song mated with the spiritual to give birth to the blues, where the blues moved from country to city, where anything that could be banged, hit, struck, or malleted, blown through or blown at, became an instrument. The chimney sweep and the hawker of wild berries had sung through these streets. All that was vibrant and classic in American popular music was at home in this languorous, easy-talking city. New Orleans was a carnival any time of the year, but especially at Mardi Gras.

Each year, just before the gloomy onset of Lent, New Orleans blows its collective cool in a multimillion-dollar festival that lures world visitors. Mardi Gras (literally, "Fat Tuesday") had passed from pagan to Christian to commercial. Now it was partly a come-on for nightclubs, souvenir shops, and hotels. Still, the most crowded part of the festival took place on the streets, for free. WELCOME TO CRESCENT CITY, SIGN UP FOR THE MARCH OF KING ZULU, or THIS WAY FOR KING REX PARADE read the banners. Masked and costumed marchers, dancing bands, and marching societies lined the pavements. It was *Black Orpheus* and *Easy Rider* on one reel, with Mephisto as stage manager and Dionysus tending bar.

The only room they could find cost fifty dollars. They started to explore the whirling streets. Pete, out on his own, made a few foolish moves. Somewhere along Bourbon Street he met a stripper with a New York accent who'd known Hugh Romney. She was looking for grass, and Pete said he might know where to get some. He gave her the motel number, but supposedly didn't tell her whom he was traveling with. Back at the motel, everyone turned in early. At three A.M., the stripper called Pete. Pete tried to explain his indiscretion to his half-awake companions, and was swamped with instant paranoia. They threw him out. When he blearily returned the next morning, he found the others ready to take on Mardi Gras at full tilt. They set out to explore the town and find the stripper who knew Hugh Romney.

By tradition, Mardi Gras street revelry surrounds the parades, and everyone carries his own bottle. Another tradition of segregationist New Orleans soon became apparent. The four positioned themselves at a crowded corner where the view was good. Although the time was just after breakfast, each carried a bottle of wine and took huge gulps. A costumed Negro dancer passed, carrying candlelit flambeaux aloft. The torchbearer stopped in front of Dylan's group. Having danced for two miles he was exhausted and thirsty. He saw Dylan holding a wine bottle and pointed at it word-

SEVERAL SEASONS IN HELL 245

lessly; Bob handed him his bottle and the dancer took a generous gulp. The crowd around Dylan became uneasy. A kindly faced little old lady whined: "You mean that you would give a nigger a drink out of your very own bottle?" Dylan didn't reply. Several sailors moved forward menacingly. Pete said: "This is it, boys. We're all going to be murdered!" Dylan told his fellows: "Disappear into the crowd." When they reassembled, Dylan mused: "It's not the same country."

Although Mardi Gras madness made many lasting impressions on Dylan that appear in songs from "Desolation Row" to "Visions of Johanna," he only made passing specific references to it in his writings. On the liner notes of *Another Side,* he mentioned the carnival fleetingly, in the fifth poem, referring obscurely to a "white Southern poet," Joe B. Stuart. Although he had misspelled Stewart's name, Dylan remembered an instant New Orleans friendship. Joe B. Stewart remembered Dylan and set down his recollections in 1967. He was a high-school English teacher from Mobile, with a shining young face, a sharp ear, and warm eyes. Joe took an immediate liking to Dylan and vice versa. By the time he chanced to meet Dylan, Joe and his friends had been up for five days and nights: "It had been sweet and I was open for anything," he wrote. "Standing in the second bar of La Casa . . . I would not have been surprised if Walt Disney had come through the door. I looked at his little pale face, which was set in a serious scowl with eyes darting back and forth . . . waiting to see if he would be recognized." Joe simply said: "Hi, Bob." Dylan's response was to keep moving.

In New Orleans, 1964 was also the year of the folk singer. Around the corner from La Casa, a contingent of folkniks sang in a bar in exchange for free beer and tips. Young white folknik pilgrims congregated on the street, strumming, singing, and trying to look like Dylan. At one corner stood an old black woman, large-boned and intense, dressed in white, who preached about hell and salvation and then sang gospel songs and spirituals, keeping time with her tambourine.

Stewart: ". . . Back down near La Casa, I again passed Dylan and his 'buddies.' . . . They were moving along, quiet, serious, and not drunk. . . . I said hello once again, but, just as before, he kept right on going. . . ." Stewart and a friend, Jim Furhmann, moved on through the chaos. Somewhere, they picked up a young girl from across the river. She was with them when Joe saw Dylan for the third time. Bob ran up and said: "Man, I'm so sorry I didn't speak to you before. . . ." Then, looking at their Louisiana girl, Wendy, Dylan said: "Look at those watery blue eyes!" Wendy to Dylan: "You sure do have long hair." He replied: "Yes, and I'm gonna let my hair grow to the streets and write my poems from the top of these buildings."

Jim and Wendy departed, and Dylan opened up to the Alabama teacher. Dylan wanted more wine, so back to the weaving, lurching La Casa, throbbing with Spanish music. Some of Joe's friends were there. Norman

Boyles, working on a Ph.D. at Tulane, debated the values of formal education with Dylan. The graduate student defended education as a road
map. The music rose and the drunken shouting increased. Dylan produced
the address of a private party. As the five stood at the corner of Iberville
near Canal and watched another flambeaux carrier, the Comus Parade, the
last and best, was stretching out along the road. The five passed the bottle
and jumped for the beads and doubloons that the paraders were throwing.
Stewart: "We were all caught up in the magic and there was no holding
back on anyone's part."

As the Comus ended, they moved to Wanda's Seven Seas, as noisy as the
streets. Dylan tried to get into every conversation, moving from group to
group, asking questions and interjecting comments. Exhausted, he and the
others tumbled out onto Bourbon Street, where a kid was standing against
a wall, playing his guitar and singing "Don't Think Twice." Dylan: "You
sing that very well. Let's hear one more." The boy started to sing and
Dylan and others joined in. The folk singer stammered: "You! . . . I mean
. . . it couldn't be. . . . No, it's impossible!" Dylan repeated: "You sing that
real well," and they moved on leaving one confused folk singer.

Dylan approached a worn-out black man and invited him to join them
for a drink. They headed to Cosimo's. As the five whites and one black approached, the bartender came running to meet them at the door. "Joe,
don't come in here," the bartender pleaded. "Get him out. We don't want
any trouble." An argument, then a compromise: Joe would buy a beer for
their black friend but bring it out for him to drink on the street. Joe suggested another bar where there would be less trouble—Baby Green's, run
by blacks. The black man said, "If I can't go into one of your places, you
can come to one of mine." All six were blasting down Burgundy, but the
minute they got to Baby Green's, Dylan got into an argument. "Why,
man? Why?" Dylan kept shouting at the black bartender. The bartender
said, "We don't want any trouble. The cops'll come and put us all in jail.
Go on, son. Somewhere your mother is on her knees praying for you."
The others persuaded Bob to stop challenging segregation. They headed
into the French Quarter and the Seven Seas bar, where Victor and Joe
played Ping-Pong and chess. The others followed Dylan to the Morning
Call coffee bar nearby, then joined up again.

Joe had a friend in the *vieux carré,* and as they headed that way, Joe felt
an urge to run. Dylan ran after him, a drunken chase leading nowhere,
until Dylan tripped on a curb and sprawled out on the pavement. They
carried Bob to a friend's apartment. A married woman named Susan had
endured drunks dropping in on her all week and was fed up. Joe shouted
back that Bob Dylan was with him. Susan opened the door.

They delivered a giggling Dylan with a sprained ankle. Sitting in a
rocking chair he poured himself a jelly glass of wine and rocked rhythmically back and forth, sometimes hitting a table filled with fragile objects.
He and his hostess, Susan, did most of the talking. Dylan described his

entire journey as a series of encounters with famous writers. Sandburg "came out on his porch and he said to me: 'You certainly are an intense young man.'" As he watched, Stewart thought: "This guy won't last long, he'll either burn himself out or get himself killed in some stupid accident, the way James Dean did." Joe had seen Dylan running out in front of cars without looking. Victor had told Joe over their chess game that on the highway Dylan wouldn't let him stop the car; he just "wanted to go on and on." The dialogue between Dylan and Susan touched on names of southern writers. Dylan dismissed Tennessee Williams as a "guilty cat, man." Faulkner headed Dylan's list of writers to meet.

Dylan wanted to walk the streets again, and they headed for the Gin Mill. As the group walked along toward Canal, Stewart quoted from a poem. "Who wrote that, Hank Williams?" Dylan asked. "Naw," Joe replied, "I did." Dylan said: "Man, I wish I had had some crazy schoolteachers like you." He complained that his formal education had been predictable, dull. Joe asked him when he was due to go into service. Dylan: "I tried to join, but they wouldn't take me." The growing group of wanderers returned to La Casa; they spent a few minutes at each of the saloon's bars in search of some new excitement. Someone suggested a lively Greek bar. By now, they'd picked up yet another teacher. Dylan: "Schoolteachers! Schoolteachers! I'm surrounded by schoolteachers!" He told Joe that he liked college students and was very interested in what they are thinking, but ..." As they teetered toward the Greek bar, a bunch of roughnecks screeched up beside them in a car. They jumped out: "All right, Dylan, are you coming with us, or not?" Bob backed off and murmured coolly: "I don't have anything to say. Victor speaks for me." Victor, drawing up to his full height, told the hoodish crew to get lost. As fast as they had appeared, they disappeared. "Well, all right, man, have it your way," one shouted from the car, and they were gone in the night.

The Athenian Room, nearly three A.M.: Upstairs, a drunken sailor was dancing with a drag queen. The transvestite swooped the sailor over half-backward, kissed him, and pinched his bottom provocatively. At a nearby table, the drag queen's friends roared. The drinking, walking, and excitement were wearing out everyone except Dylan, who kept pummeling the teachers: "Will you teach my poems to your students? If you do, I'll come to your class." Stewart and his friends bid Dylan good-bye. Dylan tried to delay them: "Why do you have to go, man?" Joe replied that he had to get up at eight. "You're a brave cat," Dylan said, "to teach high school, a brave cat." Dylan said they had to get on the road for Denver. Joe Stewart, just an album-cover note in Dylan's life, left at three-thirty A.M. The Mardi Gras was over; the penitents' Lent was beginning. The last time Joe saw Dylan, he was standing by the jukebox, all wound up, with a lot left unsaid. He seemed a little sad and lonely, as he waited for dawn.

Back on the road again. Only two days before the Denver concert. They had to put in an appearance in Tougaloo, and zoomed in and out. Time enough only to greet civil rights people, like Dorie Larner, Robert Moses, and Tom Hayden, who pulled together an audience. Dylan sang for about an hour. After well-wishing, Victor made apologies for Dylan and hustled his group into the station wagon. They stopped to study road maps again. Jackson to Denver in two days! Dylan suggested they go by way of Dallas.

It was only three months after the Kennedy assassination, and the papers had been filled with reconstructions. As the freeway swung near Dallas, everyone was keyed up. They asked several people for the street on which Kennedy was shot, but no one seemed to know it by name. Even asking for the Texas School Book depository failed to bring a response. Finally, they asked: "How do we get to the place where the president was shot?" The first man replied: "Do you mean that son-of-a-bitch Kennedy? Well, you go up two blocks this way, and turn a block right." At Dealey Plaza, they appraised the theory that Oswald acted alone. Then, they took the station wagon along Kennedy's path, everyone but the driver looking back toward the depository from which the shots supposedly came. Pete recalled: "Everybody, including Bobby, started acting like a detective. We looked at that distant row of windows and we all pretty much decided that if someone had shot Kennedy from that window, he would have to have been a fantastic marksman."

On to Denver, via Forth Worth, through the Panhandle, toward Wichita Falls. Somewhere near the Texas–New Mexico border, they stopped at a little chili joint. A waitress, no more than nineteen, asked, "Where you all from?" She'd never met anyone from New York. When somebody said Bob was a singer, she flipped. They gave her an album. She kept looking from the picture to Bob's face with total disbelief. A few hours later, another Texan roadside joint, near Claude. Sarcastically, they inquired: "What's been happening here, lately?" "Ain't nothing happened here lately, but about a year ago we had a big fuss when Paul Newman and all them Hollywood people came in to shoot that movie *Hud,* right here." The swaggering, thumb-in-belt arrogance of *Hud* was one Dylan echoed in dozens of pictures taken by Barry Feinstein. They learned what they could about the filming.

In southern Colorado, Dylan spotted Ludlow on the map. Paul gave them some background about the site of a vicious 1914 antiunion massacre that inspired many ballads, notably Guthrie's "Ludlow Massacre." John Greenway, labor historian, had called the incident "the most wanton atrocity in the history of American unionism." Some southern Colorado mining areas then were so strongly ruled by coal operators that they constituted a government unto themselves. On September 23, 1913, the impoverished Ludlow miners struck. When the state militia illegally imprisoned a union leader, Mother Jones, one thousand women and children protested. Adjutant General Chase organized a company to meet this demonstration, but en route the general toppled off his horse. The demonstrators laughed and he ordered his mounted troops to charge, inflicting saber wounds on four women and a boy. The actual massacre occurred in April 1914, when the strike was in its eighth month. The miners, who had been evicted from their company-owned homes, were living in tent colonies. Chase, although relieved from command of the militia, organized two National Guard companies of roughnecks. On April 20, after an accidental shooting, two hundred so-called Guardsmen riddled the tents with bullets from a ring of machine guns. All day long they fired; that night, they set fire to the tents. Many miners survived by hiding in trenches, but after a fourteen-hour battle, more than one hundred members of miners' families were wounded and more than thirty were dead. Dylan and friends stood before a memorial plaque put up by the United Mine Workers of America. The young man who had never paid much attention to history at school was getting his lessons on the road.

Denver: Dylan washed, shaved, and changed from dirty old clothes to clean old clothes. The concert producer, Hal Neustadt, was pleased with the performance at the Denver Civic Auditorium. Later, Bob's group made the rounds of the local coffee shops and folk hangouts, looking for Judy Collins. She was out of town, so Dylan took his companions up into the mountains to see Central City, his first return to the reconstructed boomtown since 1959. It was snow-clogged and ghostlier than ever. They went into the only open shop, a drugstore, to pick up some historical postcards.

Heading to San Francisco, they had to go over the Rockies in one of the winter's worst snowstorms. Loveland Pass: Their tire chains broke under the effort. They spent a night in Grand Junction, Colorado, where the temperature was down to zero, yet they could run from the hotel and plunge into a naturally heated spring pool. Victor took the wheel from Pete. Before them was a long funeral procession of thirty cars twisting up a mountain road. Victor passed the funeral at more than seventy miles an hour. A police car led the procession. A chase began. "We panicked," said Pete. They hid all the smoking materials fast. Victor talked to the cop fast, really fast: "We're part of a singing group, have to be in Reno in a couple of hours or we miss out on a job." He showed the car's registration, and the cop, seeing the name of some unknown corporation, Ashes and Sand, decided to relent, and let them go.

The four roared with relief, but Dylan told Paul and Pete to share the driving. They arrived in Reno at eight A.M. and tried the gambling tables, but lost. Pete quickly ran through his last thirty-two dollars and was then totally dependent on Dylan. Bob lost about a hundred dollars at blackjack. As they were leaving, Bob stopped in front of a slot machine and put in his remaining quarters. Suddenly the machine lit up like Times Square. Quarters came out in a flood. Pete reflected on winners and losers.

Somewhere near Reno, at a desert space—as in the film *Zabriskie Point*—they set up the fireworks from South Carolina. They giggled like kids at the magnificent bursting rockets and flares. When they got to the

Sierras, they had one more boyish fling. Sitting in the swaying chairs of a ski lift, they climbed the side of a mountain—another freedom game. This was their farewell to spacious landscape. As they hurtled toward San Francisco, the roads were busier, and there were signs of farming and commerce. The trip was nearly at an end.

Dylan had a concert at Berkeley on February 24, 1964. Anyone with as free-floating a temperament as his would be at home on the West Coast. There was Berkeley's radical tradition, San Francisco's openness to new ideas, and the whole ambience of California, where people put no ties around their necks and few around their thinking. The leading West Coast critic had swung firmly into Dylan's corner. Ralph Gleason gave Dylan's concert at the Berkeley Community Theater a strong advance story and review. Opinion-makers, like Malvina Reynolds, spread the *Broadside* gospel around local territory. Gleason, who reported that no concert in recent memory had stirred so much advance interest, was beginning to see Dylan as a standard-bearer for the developing counterculture. Even to the Bay Area, where beats, Bohemians, outsiders, and rebels were no strangers, Dylan's arrival meant something special. Wrote Gleason:

"To the generations who were raised on solid Judeo-Christian principles, on the rock of moral values of our fathers, on the idea that cleanliness is next to godliness, the deliberate sloppiness, the disdain for what we have thought of as perfect by Dylan's generation is shocking. But we are wrong. Look where our generation has gotten us . . . a hard core of reality connects the music of Dylan, the best of jazz, of contemporary poetry, painting, all the arts, in fact, with the social revolution that has resulted in CORE and SNCC, Dick Gregory, James Baldwin and the rest."

Fariña was at the Berkeley concert, taking notes for a *Mademoiselle* story. His report augured his own motorcycle doom and Dylan's deliverance: "There was no sensation of his having performed somewhere the previous night or of a schedule that would take him away once the inevitable post-concert party was over. There was, instead, the familiar comparison with James Dean, at times explicit, at times unspoken, an impulsive awareness of his physical perishability. Catch him now, was the idea. Next week he might be mangled on a motorcycle."

After the Berkeley concert, the station wagon headed toward Joan's place in Carmel. Karman was, by this time, completely on the outs: "I'm not going on with this trip. If I do, I'll be going crazy," he said. The others were happy to see him replaced by Bob Neuwirth, the vagabond madcap artist/moviemaker/country singer who later succeeded Victor as Dylan's road manager. They arrived at Joan's with gifts of nuts and fruit. Joan's mother whipped up a beef stew. "The only overt reference to Dylan's music came," Fariña chronicled, "when Joan said she might want to record an entire album of his songs and he told her 'sure thing.' " The next day, Bob and Joan each headed toward southern California. Joan drove her Jaguar XKE while Dylan and the others continued on in the station wagon. Fariña: "Dylan stayed at the Thunderbird Motel in Hollywood, drifting out to parties and local folk nightclubs between engagements; Joan stayed with family friends in Redlands, lying in the sun, going to bed early. She sang at her old high school one afternoon and was moved to tears by the standing ovation. When she did an encore, her mention of Dylan's name brought cheers. That same night, he returned the compliment to a devoted audience in Riverside. . . ."

Dylan was reluctant to return to New York. It meant more turmoil with Suze. The affair finally ended in March 1964. The same month, at Folk City, Dylan had an encounter typical of New York's instant paranoia and rivalries. An unusual duo, Simon and Garfunkel, was making its debut. As Tom and Jerry, the pair had enjoyed an earlier pop life, and had even had a chart hit with "Hey Schoolgirl." Looking for a comeback formula, Simon had floated from London's East End to the Village. He took a leaf from Dylan's book, but simultaneously spread resentment toward Dylan. In early 1964, Simon's co-publisher was Barry Kornfeld. They decided that Simon should bury his pop past and reemerge as a folk singer. One night, Carla introduced Dylan to Simon, assuming they'd have a lot in common, at least their friendship for English singer Martin Carthy. Simon and Dylan chatted, but the harmonies weren't sweet. A few nights later, Dylan and I were at Folk City as Simon and Garfunkel came on. Simon cast a hostile look Dylan's way. Onstage, Simon and Garfunkel began to sing ethereal choirboy harmonies that sounded out of place at Gerde's, home of weather-beaten ethnic songs. At the bar, Bob and I, who had been doing quite a bit of drinking, had an advanced case of giggles over nothing. We weren't laughing at the performance, but Simon was furious. Afterward, Simon acted as though there were a Dylan cabal against him, while Dylan tended to ignore Simon. Dylan had deprecated the work of other singers, but usually to their faces. Once, at the Limelight, he reduced Judy Henske to tears for her castration of the blues. Although Garfunkel never joined the one-way vendetta, Simon seemed determined to elevate himself at Dylan's expense. On their first album, Simon and Garfunkel recorded "Times Changing," but by the second album, Simon was not only emulating Dylan's alienation, protest, and brotherhood, but also directly satirizing Dylan. Simon's "Simple Desultory Philippic" was a vicious burlesque. Its harmonica playing and shouts for "Albert" left little doubt about its target.

At a Simon and Garfunkel session in autumn 1966, I heard Simon snap at Billie Wallington, a Columbia publicist, "for having ignored us for years!" He poked at Dylan in the English pop press. As late as May 1968, Simon told *Seventeen:* " '. . . I don't believe that the kind of obscurity Bob Dylan practices is good. I think it is more of a hoax. . . .' " He went on to lump Dylan with rock groups, like The Animals, The Kinks, Herman's Hermits, and called them musicians whose " 'stuff is a hoax or pap or a copy of something somebody else should be doing.' " Dylan's mystique haunted Simon. Even after he and Garfunkel broke through, Dylan's shadow pursued Simon. He tried dropping out for a while, and absolutely nothing happened. Then he wrote "The Boxer," with obvious allusions to Dylan. Dylan eventually replied by recording "The Boxer." Until Simon no longer needed to emulate anyone, he was probably Dylan's most skillful imitator. Certainly Simon's talent is great, and he's sold a lot more records than Dylan. But he was obsessed by the man he thought had once laughed at him.

Bob had little to laugh about through most of 1964. Despite depressions, he kept growing professionally and artistically. The bust-up with Suze, the confusions with Joan, the anchorless feeling of being alone in front of thousands of people, all colored his life in dark shades. That year, he was often one very stoned rolling stone, apparently out of control, racing at his "own chosen speed." [4] He was kept from spinning right off the road, I believe, by the demands, urgency, and discipline of his writing.

STREETS OF LONDON

May 1964: Off to England again. Dylan had had mixed feelings about England dating from his first trips there—December 1962 and January 1963. In 1962, he had been scheduled to star in a BBC play. Very much the bewildered young man from the provinces, he reported to London's Mayfair Hotel:

"The Mayfair had these hooded little guards outside looking you over. They looked like George Washington all dressed up. They come and take your baggage into the hotel. Then you get inside the door and somebody else comes to meet you there and you tip the guard from outside for having taken your baggage inside. Then when your baggage goes from inside to the elevator, someone else hits you for a tip to take your baggage to the elevator. Then you tip him and then the elevator chap puts your baggage in and you have to tip him when you get out of the elevator. Then someone else takes the baggage out of the elevator and he opens the door to your room and puts your baggage by the end of the bed. Man, you end up tipping about ten guys. . . ." After running this changing of the guard, Dylan looked around his room and decided he really didn't belong there. "This is the end, man," he said to himself. "I completely flipped!" He checked out, went looking for Philip Saville, producer of his play, and asked him if he would find some "groovy" people for him to stay with. Of his sojourn in London, Dylan said: "I knew then what it is like to be a Negro."

He drifted into a well-known London folk club, the Troubadour, and there met Anthea Joseph, who regularly looked after strays. (She later became an official in artists relations for EMI and CBS Records.) Anthea: "I was on the door and these boots came marching down the stairs, large,

brown leather boots. I thought to myself: 'Oh, my God, here comes another one of those children from Southend.' There are a lot of dreadful
children from there, some dressed like Jack Elliott, while some wore Dylanesque gear. As those boots came down the stairs and were connected to
legs and a body above them, I said to myself: 'I know that young man!'
Then I recognized the face at the other end of the boots. 'It can't be Bob
Dylan! He's not supposed to be here!' It came up to me and said: 'Are you
Anthea? I'm Bob Dylan, can I come in?' 'Of course,' I said, 'providing
that you sing for me; then you won't have to pay to get in.' I found him
completely charming, great fun. Although he didn't talk a lot, he seemed
to be enjoying himself enormously inside. He never stopped watching
people, never stopped laughing. That was the day he had walked out of
the Mayfair and he asked me if I knew where he could stay that night. I
was amazed that no one had arranged a room for this waif. He went off
with somebody he met at the Troubadour after singing there. Generally,
people were terribly impressed by his singing; they thought he was marvelous."

Anthea took Dylan to the Singers' Club at the Prospect of Whitby pub,
Gray's Inn Road. "Peggy Seeger just had to ask him to sing because too
many people knew who he was. She really didn't want to. They are funny
people, Ewan MacColl and Peggy. After Bob sang 'Hollis Brown,' the audience almost fell apart, because they had never come up against anything
so forceful in their lives. Hearing that terrifying chorus going through it
every time, I, for one, felt the need for a good, strong drink. Peggy and
Ewan just sat there in stony silence. Peggy went up to him and said:
'Thank you, very much,' and that was all. I was shocked. Not one word of
praise from her, and Ewan didn't even bother to say anything. We left
straightaway. Bob didn't want to stay. And he was the one who would
sing for hours if the atmosphere was right. . . ."

On his first trip, Bob befriended Martin and Dorothy Carthy. Carthy's
catholic approach toward modernized tradition put Bob at ease. Recalled
Carthy: "I had read about him in *Sing Out!* Naturally, I asked him to sing.
When the King and Queen audience heard his guest set, they fairly went
mad. Strange, though, that after he left the club, that same audience
started to put him down and said his appearance there 'was all a big mistake.' "

Dylan went to Britain originally for the BBC play, which had a role for
"an anarchic young student who wrote songs." Having signed this unknown for the then-large fee of five hundred pounds, Saville discovered
he'd also hired a would-be playwright. "We found he had trouble delivering the lines Evan Jones had written for him. Bob wanted to write his
own lines," Saville told me in 1971. "At rehearsals, when he did show up,"
Saville recounted, "there was no problem with his saying his lines, but he
was such an individualist that he wanted to write the play, or at least his
part, over completely. Mutually, we realized that he just couldn't play it as

written. We decided to make the central character into two people."
David Warner, a rising Shakespearean actor, who later starred in the film
Morgan, took the speaking role originally meant for Dylan. Bob and
Warner got on famously. Staying at Saville's Hampstead home a few
nights—one way Saville could guarantee his appearance at rehearsals—
Dylan began to run through his song repertoire. The producer, quite impressed, decided to have Dylan sing "Blowin' in the Wind" behind the
opening and closing credits. (Saville also recalled that Dylan was working
on "Tambourine Man.")

The bright young talents around the Establishment got wind he was in
town and staged an impromptu concert. The Establishment had grown
out of the revue *Beyond the Fringe,* and had produced such wits as David
Frost, Peter Cook, Dudley Moore, and Jonathan Miller. At the Establishment, Dylan's antiestablishment songs "went down a bomb," as they say
in Soho about a triumph.

Several technical hitches developed in the play, and Saville told Grossman there would be a delay of several weeks. Albert said Bob had a commitment, and wrung another fee and round-trip airline ticket out of the
BBC. "This became undoubtedly the most expensive money ever paid for
a singer to do the opening and closing music for a play and to deliver only
one spoken line," Saville told me. (The line: "Well, I don't know, I'll
have to go home and think about it.") Nevertheless, Saville felt proud to
introduce Dylan and "Blowin' in the Wind" to Britain. He was charmed
with Dylan's "almost Buddhist inner concentration, and his little naïvetés
about sophisticated London." The extra time in London allowed Dylan to
meet two old friends from Boston, Von Schmidt and Fariña, who were
cutting an album on the Folklore label. They easily persuaded Dylan, as
Blind Boy Grunt, to fill in with his traveling mouth harp on "You Can't
Always Tell," "Xmas Island," "Cocaine," and "Glory, Glory." The sessions were at Dobell's Jazz Record Shop, January 14 and 15, 1963.

England became a rich source of anecdotes. He told me about various
surreal parties, with fat Americans, an adolescent English girl who looked
French, and a crippled old lady who took ten minutes to hobble from the
door to the middle of a room. At another party, while the piercing English
winter was penetrating his bones, everyone else walked about in short-
sleeved shirts. At a party of "England's top hippies," Bob positioned himself so close to the gas fire, his trousers nearly caught fire. They danced to
Everly Brothers records. "The English could do the twist by moving only
one leg!" He sang for them, but their looks matched the room's chill.
When Odetta was ready to go to Rome, he flew there with her for a few
days. Suze had already returned to New York. Upon his first return from
Britain I asked him how he liked London: "Man," he said, "you gotta see
Rome. Rome is wonderful!" In Italy, Bob wrote "It Ain't Me, Babe,"
"Girl from the North Country," and "maybe" wrote "Boots of Spanish
Leather."

Fifteen months later, in May 1964, Dylan returned to England. The Carthys had written several times, but Bob only wrote them one long letter, in spring 1963, which showed how strongly he was thinking about the topical-song debate, the demands on his time, and his loving memories of them. A booking at Royal Festival Hall, May 17, 1964, perked him up. Anthea couldn't buy a ticket, so he insisted she come backstage. "You gotta come to this one, because the Rolling Stones are coming," he said. The modern lines of Festival Hall on the Thames South Bank contrasted with the storied profiles of Big Ben and Parliament across the river. A queue several thousand yards long stretched all the way to County Hall. The twenty-seven hundred seats had long since been sold out. Anthea: "In those days, we all had long hair, wore jeans, and the boys with their long hair were carrying bedrolls, with their chicks walking exactly two steps behind with the guitar. Here the birds always carried the guitar. There were no returned tickets. Bob's first question was: 'Are the Rolling Stones here?' I said: 'If you want to see rolling stones, put your head out the door.' He said: 'My God, I've never seen anything like it!' His admirers had hitchhiked from absolutely everywhere."

The concert was successful. Bob misplaced his capo and asked if his listeners had one. There was a general surge forward: "Have mine," "Please take mine." Dylan smilingly accepted one: "Don't forget that I have it, or you won't get it back." *The Times* said Dylan's drawing power put him in a class of "sheer personal magnetism," shared only by Callas, Segovia, and Count Basie. The *London Daily Sketch* headline: NO VOICE—BUT SOME SINGER. The singer who only a little more than a year earlier had found England so cool, heard cheers from an audience of intellectuals and beats who thronged around the stage door like pubescent fans. Publicist Kenneth Pitt: "I worried about his safety, because he is such a slight person. I remember almost giving him a bear hug as we worked our way through the crowd to a waiting taxi. The fans started to bang on the side of the car. Finally, we got away, but at one point the kids seemed determined to stop the car and pull Bob out. Dylan kept saying: 'Hey, man, get me out of here.' . . . I realized what a wonderful thing had happened. I think the people in this crowd just wanted to touch him. This was not wild fan hysteria. They seemed to have a genuine love for the man and wanted to express it."

Dylan then taped a half-hour show for the BBC-TV *Tonight* show and also recorded for BBC-radio's *Saturday Club* and the TV *Hallelujah Club*. He left behind the makings of an articulate audience that, in 1965, would project him to superstardom. The English singer-songwriter, Sidney Carter, told me:

"A large part of the young songwriters in Britain are inspired by Dylan. Dylan Thomas had more influence on Bob Dylan than Woody Guthrie did, with an image of the bard who went forth as a kind of romantic prophet, doomed to an early death. One was mistakenly brought up to think that such romantic bards usually are doomed, that they live in garrets or caves. Shakespeare did very well commercially. Tennyson became a lord. But one's image of a poet is someone, preferably under twenty-five, revolutionary, good-looking, and doing something to excess, whether women, or drugs, or wine. It strikes the imagination very powerfully. There are many intimations of death in Dylan's writing, but what attracted me has been, rather, the affirmation of life. It's like the blues, in which one is struck by the hopeful things that push through the gloom. There is plenty of life and guts in Dylan, as there was in Dylan Thomas. Joan Baez reminds me of that classic painting by Delacroix of the 'Woman at the Barricades.' This is what is happening to folk music, and I am not knocking it. This romantic picture is as much with us in the 1960s as it was in the 1830s. There was trouble in Greece, and Byron the poet had to go right out there, the way your folk singers have had to go to the South. Fight for right and die young doing it.... The word *poet* means different things to different people. Strange, you can talk about a commercial artist, but you can't talk about a commercial poet. A poet has to be something holy as well as to have genius. As difficult a role as this must be for Dylan, he definitely fits into that romantic concept of a poet, the listener to inner voices that are driving him. What the poets have been trying to do for a long time ... to get through to a large public, the folk singers have done behind their backs. There is no doubt that in the folksong clubs of Britain they are singing poetry.... It is also a matter of image. He's like the footballer or the bullfighter, only his weapons are words and harmonies. It's a new kind of hero-image for youth, and it's also a way to become rich and famous. You can fail your grammar school and still make a million. It's like the bullfighter in Spain or Mexico, like a Negro boxer rising out of the slums with power, grace, and strength."

Sometimes a boxer without grace. Karl Dallas, the veteran folk-song reporter and critic, ran into Dylan during his 1964 visit. Dylan: "Are you for me or against me?" Dallas: "Frankly, I don't know you." After that, Dallas said, "I was given the polite bum's rush." One veteran of the British folk scene, Rory McEwen, recalled the night he asked Bob out to dinner and "about thirty people" showed up with him. He was as repelled by Bob as he was attracted: "I disliked his arrogance. He runs through so much experience because of his pressured existence. He can walk into a room and give the impression that he knows just a little bit more about the world than anyone in that room. He probably does, but it rankles a little that he should act as if he does. Perhaps Dylan is the first of the real twentieth-century technocrats. He turns all the knobs. But after his breakout in Britain, he was on the horns of a dilemma, because acceptance can be as great a problem to him as rejection."

After Festival Hall, Dylan darted off for a few days in Paris, and then traveled with Victor to Greece for a short holiday. In the town of Vernilya, outside Athens, Dylan did a great deal of writing for *Another Side*. He was beginning to feel some calm. He wanted to stay on in Greece, but had too many commitments, and he returned to New York and to Woodstock. Each time Dylan left England, he vowed never to return. (This was before his triumph of 1978, when he totally reversed his opinion.) Earlier, though, he found most people cold, the folk community narrow, and the aggressive British press particularly difficult. But each year he returned. His return in 1965 was to change his attitude toward Britain dramatically.

NEWPORT '64 REVISITED

Newport '63 had been so Dylan-centered that, not surprisingly, he found the 1964 festival an anticlimax. He had had time to consider the burdens of leadership and to decide that overtly political songs were only part of his work. No longer was he "writing songs for everybody else, but writing songs now for myself." As Dylan had grabbed the spotlight in 1963, he virtually shunned it in 1964. He was prepared, like Seeger before him, to step back from stage center and feel wonder at the numbers who were working the same vein. Phil Ochs was coming on strongly as the chief political banner-waver. For the Newport program book, Phil wrote that there'd been such an upsurge of topical song "that I wouldn't be surprised to see an album called 'Elvis Presley Sings Songs of the Spanish Civil War' or The Beatles with 'The Best of the Chinese-Indian Border Dispute Songs.' "

In the year between the festivals, topical songwriting had established itself. Ochs was becoming a campus darling; Paxton, the careful craftsman, was not far behind. Len Chandler was a rising figure; and Buffy Sainte-Marie was emerging as the most adroit woman writer, while Malvina Reynolds was still the doyenne. Seeger remained the leader, although he was still away on a world tour. Other rising topical songwriters included Billy Edd Wheeler, Pat Sky, Fred Hellerman, Peter LaFarge and Tim Hardin, Jim Friedman, Julius Lester, Shel Silverstein, Bob Gibson. Two newer talents had difficulties in establishing their own identities: Eric Andersen and David Cohen (also known as David Blue) began almost as replicas of Dylan. Although both were concerned about human folly and errant institutions, neither trod on Dylan's early political path. Their writing was more subjective and personal. Still in the background was thirteen-year-old Janis Ian, soon to cause a stir with "Society's Child."

Dylan performed publicly three times at Newport '64. On Friday afternoon at the topical-song workshop, he sang "It Ain't Me, Babe" and "Tambourine Man." No one seemed to mind that Dylan's two new songs were topical only to the singer. At that night's evening concert, which broke all previous Newport attendance records, Baez closed by bringing Dylan on for a duet of "It Ain't Me, Babe." The audience hankered for political inspiration and Joan obliged, leading "We Shall Overcome."

Dylan's solo appearance was Sunday night. There was unintended irony when Ronnie Gilbert introduced Dylan as "a young man who grew out of a need." He started with "All I Really Want to Do." Many were glad to hear his wit surface again in a new "anti–love song." The rest of his set was not very well received; the longer he stayed on, the sloppier his performance became. "To Ramona" was so lackluster that I wrote a tentative question in my notebook: "Has the American Yevtushenko turned into the American Edgar Guest?" He sang "Tambourine Man," but so haltingly, between clenched teeth, that the floating imagery sagged. As he tuned between numbers, Dylan sometimes staggered onstage. Being stoned had rarely prevented his giving winning performances, but he was clearly out of control. He finished with "Chimes of Freedom," and then for an encore, called Joan on for a duet of "God on Our Side."

The desultory performance surprised many, but not two friends backstage. Before he had gone on, Bob had been chatting with Tony Glover and Betsy Siggins of Cambridge. Tony had noticed that Bob was extremely uptight about facing the capacity audience of more than fifteen thousand. Dylan said to Tony: "I don't care. I'll just do my music. I don't care." Tony, teasing, suggested Dylan turn his back on the audience to avoid hostility. For a moment during his performance, Dylan actually did so. Dylan got his round of applause, but there was uneasiness. John Hammond, Sr., scolded: "He ought to be spanked for putting on that sort of a show." "He's too great a talent, Bobby is, to throw away a performance like that," Pat Clancy clucked. As I headed toward the press tent, I conveyed the general disappointment to Charlie Rothschild, who was suggesting that I had just seen a great Dylan performance.

The evening emphasized something Bob already knew well: A performer must be always on his mettle. Critical ears won't accept mediocrity from masters. At Newport, perhaps no one felt let down more keenly than those who had earlier heaped praise on Dylan. Dylan's friends, old and new, also disappointed by the contents of *Another Side,* began to give him pep talks in person or in print. In the November 1964 issue of *Sing Out!,* editor Irwin Silber wrote "An Open Letter to Bob Dylan," which summarized past veneration but expressed worry: "... I saw at Newport how you had somehow lost contact with people ... the paraphernalia of fame were getting in your way.... I thought ... of Jimmy Dean ... and I cried a little ... for that awful potential of self-destruction ... in a sense we are all responsible for what's been happening to you.... The American Success Machinery chews up geniuses ... one a day and still hungers for more...."

The letter cheered Dylan as much as a week's holiday in Hibbing would have. Everything he did seemed to displease someone. Minneapolis people hit him for carrying picket signs; then he was stoned for selling out. Now the preachy folksters were sermonizing him. Was there no way an artist could listen to himself, could write, perform, act, dress like himself? All kinds of himself? Not when he is public property. Many waited for the

November release of *Another Side* to confirm that Dylan was "going apolitical." In December, a *Broadside* writer, Paul Wolfe, who Dylan had praised, treated Newport '64 as the point when Ochs emerged the political-song champion and Dylan "renounced" protest. The "new" Dylan, Wolfe found, has "defected . . . into higher forms of art." Pitting Dylan vs. Ochs, the writer weighed "meaning vs. innocuousness, sincerity vs. utter disregard for the tastes of the audience, idealistic principle vs. self-conscious egotism." Wolfe deemed "Tambourine Man" "a failure," and lambasted "Chimes of Freedom" for raising "bewilderment to the highest degree." The Dylan he sketched was a Lonesome Rhodes—a trickster, hypocrite, and manipulator of his audience.

Ochs leaped to Dylan's defense: "It is as if the entire folk community was a huge biology class and Bob was a rare, prize frog. Professor Silber and Student Wolfe appear to be quite annoyed that the frog keeps hopping in all different directions while they're trying to dissect him. . . . Who does Dylan think he is anyway? When I grow used to an artist's style, I damn well expect him not to disappoint me by switching it radically. My time is too precious to waste trying to change a pattern of my thought. . . . " Ochs's sarcasm here was followed by straight anger: "To cater to an audience's taste is not to respect them, and if the audience doesn't understand that, they don't deserve respect."

A key word in Silber's letter was "entourage," meaning that Dylan was now surrounded by pay-rolled sycophants. Dylan always had an ability to encircle himself, even though he was constantly centrifugally shedding those at the outer perimeter. Back at the May 1963 Brandeis Folk Festival, Dylan had seemed a maharaja in denim held aloft by an elephant pack of supporters. In spring 1964, *Life* magazine showed Dylan in his surliest mood with Geno Foreman and Albert Maher. Maher, a Harvard Square radical who had visited Cuba in 1963, traveled in 1964 on some Dylan concert tours out of his own romantic radicalism and admiration for the singer. Maher was the son of John F. "Big John" Maher, a millionaire Houston industrialist. The son's radicalization began at fifteen, when he read Castro, then accelerated in 1961 after the Bay of Pigs. In early 1964, Dylan hung out with Maher sporadically. Some months after Bob and Suze split up, she and Maher began a long relationship.

A closer member of the Dylan entourage was Paul Clayton, whom folk moralists found difficult to criticize. Of the Dylan of 1963–64, Paul said: "He gave the appearance of expecting success, but he found himself before a public he wasn't ready to face. Once he had the public, he was frightened to death, mostly of all the questions people asked him. I remember a concert at Brown University. After the concert, Victor, Neuwirth, and I formed a cordon around him. Reporters ran after him with tape recorders, asking if he thought he was a folk singer! That's the sort of confrontation he feared. He may pour forth for half an hour without a stop, and is almost apologetic about his opinions. He never gives concrete evidence, but lets you draw a conclusion. He almost always lets you challenge yourself to make a choice, but he doesn't make you want to reach it. He uses all the hip slang, all the grunts and the *hey, man*'s as a shield when he's unsure of himself. But he doesn't do that when he writes. He can always edit his writing, but not his speech, and so he doesn't completely trust himself verbally. He always gets reticent in front of a lot of people. There are about twenty people he feels safe with, and only about five or six of those whom he can spend much time with. Even with people around, he spends a lot of time with himself."

Around the Village, what *Eye* later titled "The Dylan Gang," was a half dozen folk singers whom he felt to be kindred spirits—Elliott, Andersen, Van Ronk, Blue, Ochs, Tim Hardin, and a very few others. These Villagers felt compelled to explain and defend Dylan when he did not do so himself. Ochs remained the most articulate, even after the many times Dylan put him down. Summarizing Dylan's impact on his Village entourage, Michael Thomas wrote in *Eye,* August 1968: "Dylan made everybody aware of themselves, while he became aware of himself, and because he could hear the tambourine man, he was a prophet. He touched his contemporaries at the core of their ambitions. Some, like Ochs and Paxton and Tim Hardin, felt his energy and were energized; some, like Andersen and Blue, and others, like Richard Fariña, the destructive hero of his own life, and Paul Simon, the last great sophomore, were stricken by Dylan, but he was not to blame. . . ."

After Newport '64, there was another round of controversy. If Dylan worked in blues, he was a white man stealing black music. If he developed Woody's talking blues, he was an imitator. If he adapted Anglo-Irish folk songs, he was a thief. If he wrote topical-protest songs, traditionalists thought he was a traitor, yet if he turned subjective, he was a self-involved existentialist. Watching the melee, Gleason concluded: "The one unforgivable sin in the American money culture is to break through to the top rungs of success while, at the same time, spurning the power apparatus. Do that and the demons that lurk beneath the surface come up and attack you."

Dylan's defenders came from all corners. In March 1964, Johnny Cash, the country singer then known only vaguely to the folk crowd, had leaped into *Broadside* with the demand: "SHUT UP! . . . AND LET HIM SING!" At Newport '64, Cash did a stunning performance. The festival, in its finest hour, brought in an established Nashville star who also spoke folk. Cash was the real thing—off an Ozarks farm, tough as rawhide and tender as raw flesh. Son of a railroad man, product of a Depression childhood, part Cherokee Indian, Cash was also a sophisticated man who would walk the line in several music worlds. Right after his performance on Friday night, Cash was hustled off to Baez's room at the Viking Motor Inn, where he and Dylan taped some songs for her. Cash, whose craggy, granite-hewn exterior made him look tough all the way through, was deeply touched by his acceptance. He had been a big country star and then his emotions and hard living had nearly done him in. He was beginning that long march toward stardom again, and he was filled with fears, mostly of his own turbulent self-destructiveness. To find Newport so warm made him feel even taller than he was. It touched him to find that the two young stars of the folk world, Baez and Dylan, cared enough about him to spend the whole night taping him. To show his appreciation, he gave Dylan one of his own guitars. The next morning, Baez talked proudly of the evening: Her protégé had sustained another victory.

Sensitive ears at Newport may have heard another modest giant, Muddy Waters, from Chicago, who showed that the blues had many faces and foreshadowed Dylan's going electric in 1965. Muddy was a farmhand and sharecropper, much like Cash; only Muddy had been a Mississippi black, which meant he was poorer and just a little more desperate. At thirteen, Muddy, born McKinley Morganfield, had been blowing his mouth harp at Saturday night fish fries for fifty cents a night and all the fish and liquor he could hold. In 1941, Alan Lomax had recorded Morganfield's country blues for the Library of Congress. Muddy got the idea that his salvation lay in music up north. As Cash had gone to Memphis, Muddy "came up to Chicago on a train. Alone. With a suitcase, one suit of clothes, and a guitar." In the city after the war, Muddy Waters's country blues grew tough, projective, and electric. In 1954, Muddy recorded a strong rhythm and blues song. "Rollin' Stone," which provided Mick Jagger with a group name, Jann Wenner with a magazine title, and Dylan with a song title and a name for his cat in Woodstock. "Rollin' Stone" gathered no dust.

The historic moments at Newport '64 tended to pass people by. Only when Dylan later appeared with rock backing, and, still later, went to Nashville, did all the pieces fit together. It was all brought back home at Newport '64, when Dylan went beyond topical songs, Cash sang of country troubles, and Muddy Waters brought on his band to show that music, if it is alive, is always in motion.

HAMLET OF WOODSTOCK

In summer and fall of 1964, Dylan had more time to spend in Woodstock. The barren pad on West Fourth Street was too empty. He was anxious to move his few possessions. If he had to stay in New York, he could always stay at Albert's big apartment on Gramercy Park West or at the Chelsea Hotel. Woodstock was then an unpressured and uncrowded hamlet, and he had devoted friends there. He had a special room with a private entrance at Albert's large house in nearby Bearsville, and a place to hang out, the Café Espresso at 59 Tinker Street, in Woodstock.

The Espresso was a bit of pastoral Greenwich Village. It had a well-worn brown look; the lighting was soft and indirect, the tables far enough apart for conversation. There was a large open fireplace, and tables outdoors with a view of main-street amblers. Chessboards and checkered tablecloths gave the Espresso a Gallic atmosphere. The place was owned by French-born Bernard Paturel, whose easy manner helped give the café and Dylan's Woodstock their informality. Bernard had moved to Woodstock in 1961 after serving his time at such lustrous New York restaurants as Le Veau d'Or and Lutèce. The old Woodstock reminded him of the French art colony in St. Paul-de-Vence, in the hills above the Côte d'Azur. Hearing that the Café Espresso was up for sale, Bernard and his wife, Mary Lou, bought the place on credit. "We pasted it together and kept it going for five years." For live entertainment, folk music seemed right. There had long been a folk colony around Woodstock. Sam Eskin, an early ballad collector, was a veteran resident, and Billy Faier, banjoist-singer, had been a town mascot since the late 1950s. Bernard called on Billy and a French folk singer, Sonia Malkine, to help him get singers. The first group Bernard booked was a duo, Dan the The Deacon. Among others who worked there were Paxton (who performed for three days for fifty dollars and food), John Wynn, Ed McCurdy, The Reverend Gary Davis, and Happy Traum.

Those were days when Woodstock was a refuge, not yet a zoo or a "nation." Dylan often practiced on the streets, sitting on a fence here, a bench there. Bernard soon saw Bob back in his club with Joan again. Bob had been drinking a bit and his genial host politely escorted him upstairs to a large white room in the Paturels' apartment, where Bob slept off his binge. Dylan took an immediate liking to the room. It was quiet and secret, and yet so close to the club downstairs that it fought off loneliness. "He kind of moved in with us and held a symbolic key to the room," Bernard told me. "No rent involved, just a mutual understanding that he could stay there whenever he pleased."

After his hectic trips in winter and spring of 1964, Bob returned to Woodstock. He was getting ready to record *Another Side,* and the refuge he found with Bernard and Mary Lou was duly acknowledged in "Some Other Kind of Songs." In Bearsville, Albert was always surrounding himself with people: his wife Sally, filmmakers Jones and Howard Alk, Peter Yarrow, John Court, visiting singers like Judy Collins, Odetta, and Ian and Sylvia. Among the amenities at Albert's was a swimming pool that Bob favored. He kept a motorcycle in Albert's garage so that he could roar around the back roads. Sometimes Bob liked the "in-crowd" excitement around Albert's, but he often needed to be alone. Although Albert's was only three miles from the Espresso, Bob frequently hid away in Bernard's room. He spent hours downstairs playing chess with Victor or Bernard, or drove with Bernard to Kingston, to a musty old poolroom over a Chinese restaurant.

In front of Albert's Bearsville house, a sign warned: IF YOU HAVE NOT TELEPHONED, YOU ARE TRESPASSING. Albert had three listed Woodstock phone numbers; Dylan had none. Dylan's own guest list was highly selective. Clayton used to come often in early 1964, but he was gradually ostracized. After Newport, Johnny Cash visited. Daniel Kramer went to Woodstock in 1964 and began several months' intermittent service as Dylan's court photographer. Later, Kramer was summarily dropped, and Jerry Schatzberg took over until *he* fell out of favor. Kramer found Dylan a restless subject, insistent about poses. Kramer wanted to capture Dylan writing music or playing the guitar, but Dylan objected because he only wrote along. Kramer did take some wonderful shots of Dylan walking up country roads, sitting in the Espresso, rocking on the porch of Albert's house, standing high in the branches of a tree. When Bob saw the tree picture, he said that he should try singing from a tree branch at his next concert. One of Kramer's best shots was a smiling Bob on a porch swing, like the swing in front of Echo's shack in Hibbing.

During Dylan's time in Woodstock in 1964–65, he turned out many songs. Amid Woodstock's greenery, gentle hills, and quiet lanes, he worked on the sharp, declarative, tension-filled music of his next albums. If we accept Wordsworth's commonplace about poetry, then Dylan recollected his emotions in Woodstock's tranquillity. Concerts and recording sessions were always beckoning, so that he only could catch his breath in Woodstock. Had he remained in New York, he might have really lost his emotional equilibrium. From Woodstock, he traveled to two major concerts in 1964.

On August 8, 1964, Joan sang at the Forest Hills Music Festival to an outdoor audience of fifteen thousand. Her singing was typically smooth and orderly. In the second half, Joan slipped out of her shoes onstage, then brought Dylan on. I have never heard him in such poor shape. Dylan seemed to be struggling on one wing, never quite able to leave the ground. His voice was harsh, badly projected. Joan's cool only heightened Dylan's disorder. I had to write some stinging words about Dylan. Later, Joan and her manager told me that after Dylan read *The Times* review he went on a rampage, swearing at me, vowing vengeance.

I had another chance to hear Dylan, on October 31, 1964, at New York's Philharmonic Hall, at what is often called the Halloween Concert. Dylan gave one of his greatest concerts. For the first time in nearly six months, he was back at the tiller steering, not drifting. He dusted off "Times Changing," "John Birch," "Hard Rain," "Hattie Carroll," "Davey Moore," "Dream," "God on Our Side." He sang "It Ain't Me, Babe" in well-rehearsed tandem with Joan. The luminous wanderings of "Tambourine Man" began to shine through. "Gates of Eden" was stunning. Dylan did "It's Alright, Ma," and the stinging lines hit hard. I ended my review: "After half a year of detours, Dylan seems to have returned his enormous musical and literary gifts to a forward course. His developing control of those gifts and his ability to shape a meaningful program added up to a frequently spellbinding evening by the brilliant singing poet laureate of young America."

After the concert, Dylan gave a party at a banquet hall off Second Avenue. I arrived with friends. Joan and Bob, linked arm and arm, greeted me warmly; Dylan had apparently forgotten my harsh review in August. He knew he had just triumphed.

He had quite a few things to say to all his detractors via the Philharmonic Hall program book. "Advice for Geraldine on Her Miscellaneous Birthday" included such sardonic rules that tried to bind him:

> *stay in line. stay in step, people*
> *are afraid of someone who is not*
> *in step with them. it makes them*
> *look foolish t' themselves for*
> *being in step. it might even*
> *cross their mind that they themselves*
> *are in the wrong step. . . .*
> *when asked t' define yourself exactly,*
> *say you are an exact mathematician.*
> *do not say or do anything that*
> *he who standing in front of you*
> *watching cannot understand, he will*
> *feel you know something he*
> *doesn't. . . .*[5]

Typical of many of his "middle-period" finger-pointing songs, like "Positively Fourth Street," "Advice for Geraldine," may have sounded like a paranoid talking blues, but it was an artist's declaration of independence. Dylan hated authority figures, including arbiters of taste who wrote for *Sing Out!, Broadside, Billboard,* or *The Times.* No one was sure just whom he meant, and many were positive that he meant them. Dylan simply did not want to conform. Dylan's "truth attacks" were outbursts he rarely examined to weigh the damage he might inflict. He still felt the message serviceable enough to reprint in the Carnegie Hall program book on October 1, 1965, when he appeared with The Hawks (later The Band).

Dylan preferred to battle his critics obliquely. Face to face, he was as polite as possible. Shortly after his weak performance at Forest Hills, I spent an evening with him in the Village. He made no reference to my negative review. Although slightly reserved, he had a bit of information and another bit of free advice. The information, stated in roundabout terms, was that he was about to gross his first million. He was clearly startled, even though he knew that he would be lucky to see 20 percent of the total, after paying his team and taxes. He asked what I was writing, and I told him about various projects, some for pleasure, some just for bread. Charlie Rothschild had told him that under a pseudonym I had written the liner notes on Linda Mason's mediocre album of Dylan songs. Bitingly, Bob said that if I ever got that hard up for money again I should ask him for some. He was strongly reminding me that my protégé no longer needed protection.

The next day he returned to Woodstock, away from professional judges and old Village friends who reminded him of a past he was quickly outgrowing. In the next few months he made new, influential friends, including several young musicians who called themselves The Byrds and The Beatles.

8

ORPHEUS PLUGS IN

"If they can't understand my songs, they're missing
something. If they can't understand pornographic ashtrays, green clocks, wet chairs, purple lamps, hostile
statues, charcoal ... then they're missing something,
too. ... It's all music, no more, no less."

—DYLAN, 1965

"Dylan was the single most important force in maturing our popular music."

—JOHN PEEL, 1970

"Can there be no songs as violent as the age? ... Maybe
Dylan didn't put it in the best way. Maybe he was rude.
But he shook us. And that is why we have poets and
artists."

—JIM ROONEY, 1965

"Nobody told me to go electric. ... No, I didn't ask
anybody. I asked not a soul, believe me."

—DYLAN, 1966

As the "roads scholar" through time and space, Dylan had never really abandoned his high-school rock 'n' roll, his schoolboy radio music. In late 1964, The Beatles were only one of many new rock groups proliferating. The monophony, if not the monotony, of the self-accompanied folk singer yielded to multitracked panoplies of sound. The mock-rock era of Fabian, Frankie Avalon, and Bobby Vee was history. Because Bobby Vee hadn't signed Dylan in 1959, he had been free to find folk songs, where he could draw from areas unexplored previously by rock musicians.

Yet, by 1964, in Woodstock's stillness, Dylan heard drum rolls, cymbals, thumping Fender basses, and squirming metallic lines sliding from electric guitars. He didn't discard his old solo singing with acoustic guitar and mouth harp. He only wanted to put those words into a different context. But public and critical reactions to Dylan's 1965 albums, *Bringing It All Back Home* and *Highway 61 Revisited*, couldn't have been more extreme. He was traitor-opportunist to some, genius-messiah to others.

Dylan had not been surreptitiously manipulated. He alone decided to leap back into rock, taking with him folk song's storytelling and comment. The controversy over Dylan's adding a beat and subtracting topical sloganeering detracted attention from a significant development: Dylan was creating a new *kind* of expression, more sophisticated than that of his previous three years. Dylan's creation of "folk-rock" was a turning point in popular culture. Before Dylan's new work, most rock musicians, including The Beatles, had been using insipid, frivolous lyrics. While many folk slowpokes took time to assimilate Dylan's new approach, his large new pop pastorate tuned in quickly.

Despite widespread reviews of Dylan's 1965 albums, most critics dwelled on obvious points: *Back Home* and *Highway 61* changed pop lyrics by successfully amalgamating oral literature, folk tradition, and rock experimentation. Where was Dylan headed in 1965? I think his road maps pointed toward three aesthetic and philosophical concepts: exploration of the grotesque and the absurd in art; existentialism; dreams and hallucinations as mirrors of consciousness.

THE GROTESQUE: There are plenty of grotesques among Dylan's new dramatis personae: "Einstein disguised as Robin Hood," [1] and "Napoleon in rags" [2] fall into a venerable tradition. Mister Jones, Doctor Filth, Savage Rose, and the Phantom of the Opera are second cousins to the medieval gargoyles on Notre Dame, stepchildren of types in Rimbaud and Apollinaire, neighbors of the vermin in Kafka's *Metamorphosis*. Dylan's rogues' gallery is distantly related to tortured figures in the paintings of Goya, Velázquez, Bosch, and Callot. Dylan used his "shaping power of imagination"—the ability to create his own poetic otherworld, into whose dramas we enter half-fearfully. From life's cruel parade, Dylan enlarged, distorted, shaped, and misshaped a host of unsettling demons, spirits, devils, and

malignant muses. Rilke saw his angels, Blake met his prophets Isaiah and
Ezekiel, Dylan painted freaks and geeks.

We don't have to spend a season in hell to meet grotesques in everyday
life. Turn your radio on. Sing a song of Adolf Eichmann and Lieutenant
Calley. The black laughter of the grotesque has long echoed in the arts.
The grotesque tends to grip humanity when belief in a natural, protective,
traditional order of life has broken down. Then people are delivered into
the control of demons, caricatures, and spirits, which surge up from the
underworld, the chaotic subconscious.

By 1964, Dylan saw that slogans could change nothing. Had "Blowin'
in the Wind" improved life for American blacks? Wasn't it like a church
hymn—buoying the spirit and affirming the goal? But could it really effect
change? What happens then to the social prophet who has passionately
preached solutions only to find them ignored? Perhaps the prophet-singer
fears he is really unheard. Perhaps he turns inward, becomes a seer whose
slogans have changed into strange riddles. Darkness and satiric humor fill
the vacuum of unresolved crises, seem the best way to deal with an insane
world. The following definition of the grotesque could apply to surrealist
painting, the monologues of Lenny Bruce, the howls of Allen Ginsberg
and Ferlinghetti, and many of Dylan's song-poems.

In *The Grotesque in Art and Literature,* Wolfgang Kayser wrote:

> Suddenness and surprise are essential elements of the grotesque ... we
> are ... terrified because it is our world which ceases to be reliable....
> The grotesque instills fear of life rather than fear of death ... the
> progressive dissolution, which has occurred since the ornamental art of
> the Renaissance; ... the loss of identity, the disorder of "natural" size
> and shape, the suspension of the category of objects, the destruction of
> personality, and the fragmentation of the historical order. Apocalyptic
> beasts emerge ... demons intrude upon us.... What intrudes remains
> incomprehensible, inexplicable and impersonal.... We are unable to
> orient ourselves in the alienated world, because it is absurd.... As an
> artistic genre, tragedy opens precisely within the sphere of the meaning-
> less and the absurd the possibility of a deeper meaning ... the creator of
> grotesques, however, must not and cannot suggest a meaning. [Tracing
> the use of the grotesque from romanticism through surrealism, we
> come upon] an unimpassioned view of life on earth as a meaningless
> puppet play or a caricatural marionette theater ... laughter originates
> on the comic and caricatural fringe of the grotesque. Filled with bitter-
> ness, it takes on characteristics of the mocking, cynical and ultimately
> satanic laughter.... The grotesque is a play with the absurd. It may
> begin in a carefree manner.... But it must also carry the player away,
> deprive him of his freedom, and make him afraid of the ghosts which he
> so frivolously invoked.... In spite of all the helplessness and horror in-
> spired by the dark forces ... the truly artistic portrayal effects a secret

liberation. . . . The darkness has been sighted, the ominous powers discovered, the incomprehensible forces challenged . . . a final interpretation of the grotesque: an attempt to invoke and subdue the demonic
aspects of the world. . . .[3]

In finding artistic structures that could contain the absurd chaos he saw,
Dylan somehow gained control over his world, his material, and attained a
form of liberation.

EXISTENTIALISM: He now avoided political, social, or moral philoso-
phizing. In his *Broadside* days and nights, he provided shallow social analysis—discrimination is bad, poverty is unjust, war is evil, peace and
brotherhood are where it's at, man. In 1964, earlier than most radicals,
Dylan could no longer find picket-sign philosophy serviceable. Following
Sartre, Camus, and others, he traveled to a street existentialism that came
less from ordered thinking than from emotional reaction. Dylan didn't
discard earlier insights or orientations; he didn't spout Sartre or Heidegger.
But if we take existentialism out of the seminar and onto the highway, we
can find compass points throughout Dylan's 1965–66 work. Here is one
working definition of existentialism:

> The point of departure is human consciousness and mental processes . . .
> the concept that a man has an essential self is shown to be an illu-
> sion. . . . A man's self is nothing except what he has become; at any
> given moment, it is the sum of the life he has shaped until then. The
> "nothing" he begins with is thus the source of man's freedom. . . .
> Man's mind cannot discern any meaning for this existence in the uni-
> verse; when he abandons his illusions, he finds himself horrified by the
> absurdity of the human condition. . . . Thus man must create a human
> morality in the absence of any known predetermined absolute values.
> *Honesty with oneself is perhaps the major value common to existentialist think-
> ing; all existentialist writings describe the emotional anguish of trying to
> achieve it.* . . . The man of good faith judges a potential action by esti-
> mating the result if everyone, not just himself, were to perform it. Yet
> despite the difficulty of choice, he does not withdraw from life, but is
> *engagé,* actively engaged in the business of living with himself and with
> other men. . . .

After citing the mystic Martin Buber as one writer in this tradition, this
passage by Camus then makes a distinction:

> "Man of the absurd" resembles Sartre's "man of good faith" in that
> both acknowledge man's lonely condition in the face of the silence of
> the universe; both reject despair and commit themselves to the anguish
> and responsibility of loving as best one can; and both consider the exer-

cise of one's own freedom inseparable from the opportunity for all men to exercise theirs, which is contingent on their freedom from poverty, political oppression, and other avoidable external limitations. . . .[4]

Dylan was also engaged in an anguished search for honesty amid an awareness of death and despair, to which one does not succumb. Out on the streets, he was weighing his anguish and his responsibility, pitting his loneliness against that of the lonely crowd, filling his absurd rock life with absurdist inventions of his imagination. To him, they were all "real people."

THE DREAM-HALLUCINATION AS MIRROR OF REALITY: The priest-seer-artist dreams of a reality that lies outside ordinary time and space yet mirrors the everyday world. They see more intensely and clearly, and may also, by giving their vision structure, help us to perceive and understand things we may have only fleetingly glimpsed. For surrealist artists, dreams, imaginings, even hallucinations, natural or chemical, have helped broaden and deepen the scope of art. To these artists, life is sur-real, life is sur-earnest. This is the aesthetic of surrealism. The folk aesthetic maintains that all men and women are potential artists. The artist-in-every-man and the "holy" artist co-exist and overlap. The artist, as dreamer-in-chief, lends structure, shape, and color to the visions he will, at some point, share with his audience. The best art is a flame warming our own imaginations, a campfire that irradiates some universal human experiences.

Especially since the late 1950s, when use of marijuana became more widespread, pot-induced dreams have made many feel they are artists and visionaries. Dope smokers grunting to each other "Beautiful, man!" are experiencing something beyond their abilities to articulate. A Blake or Coleridge, a Rimbaud or Baudelaire, found the words, sounds, and colors that give existence and substance to that "other world."

Innumerable Dylan followers have assured me it is *impossible* to understand much of Dylan's 1965–66 work without dropping acid. "Acid music," the three middle-period albums used to be called. The listener does not have to shop at the same drugstore as the artist. One does not need the same quantities of gin and fizz Fitzgerald required to savor *The Great Gatsby* or *Tender Is the Night*. Dylan certainly asks for his listener's intense concentration and ability to let go and follow him. At first, literal-minded folkniks were simply not prepared to let go. While they were still following heroes of the Spanish Civil War, Dylan had followed his Tambourine Man into decadent, alienated, surrealist, existential sensation and vision.

Bringing It All Back Home is not a series of intentionally "difficult" song-poems. The album title is a fine colloquial phrase which Dylan tattooed onto our language. It reminds Beatles' and Stones' fans, who vaguely thought rock was a British invention, that it all started in

America. The phrase also means a homecoming for Dylan's own beloved rhythmic music. Trenchant protest returns, not for any sect, but for all of us. The dishonesties Dylan sees leveled at American youth are cataloged to be fought, to be ridiculed. And the love songs are bringing Dylan back home to consider himself, his search for identity, his comprehension of what constitutes Eden and hell. About this time, he said: "Chaos is a close friend of mine. . . . Truth is chaos. Maybe beauty is chaos." Yet in portraying chaos, of society or of soul, he converts his "close friend" into artistic order.

Daniel Kramer's cover photograph, shot through an edge-softened lens, is an essay in symbols. Dylan fondles his cat—named Rolling Stone. Behind him, albums by Von Schmidt, Lenya, Robert Johnson, The Impressions. Far behind him stands his own last album. The attractive brunette is Sally Grossman, Albert's wife. Elsewhere, a fallout shelter sign, a copy of *Time,* a nineteenth-century portrait. Just left of center on the mantelpiece is Dylan's *The Clown,* a glass collage he made for Bernard Paturel from some bits of colored glass Bernard was about to discard. On the back of the album, other photographs offer glimpses of the singer's life: Joan goofs with a Dylan mouth harp; Peter Yarrow scratches his head at the gendarmes while Dylan seemingly boards the Orient Express; a sedate Allen Ginsberg appears in top hat and tie; Dylan works at a studio keyboard; filmmaker Barbara Rubin gives the master a head massage; wearing the top hat and a broad grin out of *Alice in Wonderland,* Dylan meets some fans. Many regard *Back Home* as a high point of his recording career. Although several tracks have rock backing, an after-echo of the electric band resonates through the second, mainly acoustic, side.

"SUBTERRANEAN HOMESICK BLUES": The first indication that Dylan was going electric again was this song, released as a single early in 1965. It rose to number thirty-nine on the charts. It shows heavy musical influence from that impudent rhythm and blues fantasist, Chuck Berry. From Berry, Dylan borrowed simple, basic ensemble blues-chord structure, use of the voice as a prominent instrument, sarcastic lyrics, bright mood, and tripping tempo. "Subterranean" grew out of "Motorpsycho Nightmare" and the "Baby Black" poem of *Another Side.* The lyric structure, with short, punchy phrases, owes much to skip-rope rhymes. Blues and R & B often use this traditional form, known to every kid who ever played on an American street. Guthrie and "Paul Campbell" (a Pete Seeger pseudonym) used this device in "Taking It Easy":

> Mom was in the kitchen, preparing to eat,
> Sis was in the pantry looking for some yeast,
> Pa was in the cellar mixing up the hops,
> And Brother's at the window, he's watching for the cops.[5]

Dylan's rapid-fire rhymes appear sheer fun, but black absurdity shadows this inspired nonsense. The militant Weatherman faction of the Students for Democratic Society took its name from: "You don't need a weather man/To know which way the wind blows." [6] "Don't follow leaders" [7] is another basic antiauthoritarian tenet. Dylan takes another swipe at formal education: "Twenty years of schoolin'/And they put you on the day shift ..." [8]

"Subterranean" lyrics resemble fast-forward images of cops, government men, and district attorneys in a silent-movie slapstick chase, followed by a "Baby Black" life story—a sad, meaningless life, always one jump ahead of failure—told in a few deft strokes. Gleason: "Dylan hit on the mindless drive to blame the young, the new, and the different, and on the true hypocrisy of the American dream."

"SHE BELONGS TO ME": Dylan may have invented the anti–love song. In the past, pop had dealt almost exclusively with sophomoric love. Dylan considerably matured the form, without hesitating to hit back at women who hurt, disappointed, or confused his narrators. Irony was always his best weapon. If this song, in quite symmetrical blues form with orderly rhyme scheme and line length, is not partly about Baez, then there must be some unknown woman artist to whom Dylan gave an Egyptian ring. "She never stumbles/She's got no place to fall" [9] is echoed in verse three from a traditional folk blues, "I'm a Stranger Here." Dylan's first verse contains the seed of his later film title *Don't Look Back,* itself the title of a John Lee Hooker blues. The song's bitter words are couched in a gentle, warm melody and the phrasing is relaxed; the loping, swaying tempo has waltzlike grace. Engineering brought Dylan's presence physically closer. Electric guitar and mouth-harp embroidery sweeten this bitter song.

"MAGGIE'S FARM": During 1961, Dylan used to sing "Hard Times in the Country," a rural protest song about the tough life of a tenant farmer with an exploitative landlord. I traced that song to "Penny's Farm," which Pete Seeger recorded in 1950 on Folkways. Seeger's George Penny was as mean a landlord as ever drew breath. After living with "Hard Times" on "Penny's Farm," Dylan gradually remade their words and melody completely into "Maggie's Farm." Dylan learned early that traditional protest material doesn't limit itself to heavy-handed, somber songs, but can wrap social comment in many guises. As in "Subterranean," the laughter is satanic, the social criticism stern. This "antiwork song" contains a strong condemnation of all meaningless labor. Dylan sounds a declaration of independence against conformity. His voice projects with cornet-clarion hardness, over a band swinging on a simple R & B structure. We may laugh at the plight of the narrator, until we realize that we're all working on somebody's farm. In Britain, the song had a strong revival after 1978 as a gibe at Maggie Thatcher's Conservative government. The title was adapted for a cartoon series in *Time Out,* later in *City Limits.*

"LOVE MINUS ZERO/NO LIMIT": Although increasingly sardonic

in his anti–love songs, Dylan still dreamed of a faithful woman, wise enough to avoid all the entrapping games of neurotic, competitive love. The title, borrowed from gambling parlance, suggests all love's a wager.

> *My love she speaks like silence,*
> *Without ideals or violence,*
> *She doesn't have to say she's faithful,*
> *Yet she's true, like ice, like fire. . . .*[10]

Here Dylan exercises new poetic sinews. Christopher Ricks has delighted in the linking of ideals with violence. Jack McDonough linked Dylan and Boris Pasternak's fascination with the "two godmothers of silence and mystery." He found another Dylan preoccupation, ". . . self-awareness through isolation, a theme both romantic and existential. . . ." Bill King's thesis on Dylan pointed out that he raises the problem of isolation for the American writer, citing the line: "there's no success like failure/And that failure's no success at all." [11] The musical flow of "Love Minus Zero" is so sedative that even the ominous images of cloaks and daggers and a bridge trembling at midnight do not mar the tranquillity that the love object exudes.

"OUTLAW BLUES": Lots of primitive R & B beat here, and a chord structure from the suburbs of Berry's "Memphis." In the traditional R & B context, Dylan satirizes some blues writing. Drawn again to the image of stumbling, he slides over pathos and lands in a goony lagoon. Verse two, badman mythology: Jesse James was shot by his so-called friend, Robert Ford, while hanging a picture. Verse four, another R & B takeoff: Instead of some mojo-voodoo symbol, Dylan has a black tooth and dark shades. He ends the verse with a couplet that epitomizes his attitude toward the press: "Don't ask me nothin' about nothin',/I just might tell you the truth." [12] The song rocks nicely and allows one vocal break at the end of each verse. (Paul Williams used *Outlaw Blues* as the title for a book about rock; it also became the name of a 1977 film on country music that starred Peter Fonda.)

"ON THE ROAD AGAIN": Enter the grotesque, a foretaste of things to come. Daddy in a Napoleon mask, milkman in a derby, contentious mailmen and butlers, frogs inside socks—just a quiet day on a phantasmagoric farm. A bright, simple rock structure against which flash some effective harmonica breaks. But musically, the track, with thrusting beat and opposing riff overriding everything, is as untidy as a lot of early rock.

"BOB DYLAN'S 115th DREAM": Skipping blithely over 113 dreams since his first dream-song, Dylan decided to give us his "115th." In a studio session, there's often a great deal of tension. Tension's brother, laughter, often sits nearby. When the band missed its entrance cue on the first take, the laughter was so natural and contagious that Dylan and producer Tom Wilson decided to leave it in. Dylan loved the tall tale and shaggy-dog story as a vehicle for free-floating satire and odd snippets of instant wit. This time, the grotesque dream concerns the discovery of America. The famed hunter of Moby Dick is disguised as "Captain Arab," and the whale of chaos he found is America. Again, the choppy, comic jump cuts of film: Keystone Kops chasing. The trotting tempo and fluid meter keep this film galloping along at high velocity, one scene superimposed upon the next. Before Dylan's dreams turned dark, he still found life ludicrous rather than horrific. His ear was always looking for the rhyme that would work, unsettle, and amuse.

The impudence that began *Back Home* scarcely prepares us for the second side's poetic flights. The four songs here rank among Dylan's most durable classics. If given a time limit to illustrate his gifts, I would still play the twenty-three minutes of side two. Even the tracks' lengths set trends; Dylan broke the pop convention that the album track should be limited to the length of a three-minute single. He inaugurated what was known by the late 1960s as the "heavy" album track.

"MR. TAMBOURINE MAN": A great lyric poem about the artist's search for transcendence. Dylan's concern again is with feeling—its nature and whether to surrender to it or control it with humor or toughness. Originally better known in Judy Collins's and The Byrds' versions, Dylan brings us closer to the song's elusive core. In 1968, Dylan told *Sing Out!:* " 'There was one thing I tried to do which wasn't a good idea for me. I tried to write another "Mr. Tambourine Man." It's the only song I tried to write "another one." But after enough going at it, it just began bothering me, so I dropped it. I don't do that anymore.' "

In *The* (New York) *Sunday News* of November 11, 1973, Al Aronowitz recounted that Dylan wrote the song at Al's house in Berkeley Heights, New Jersey: "Bob must have stayed up past dawn, rapping away at the keys in his cigarette fog. He had just broken up with . . . Suze. . . . For him, it was a long step farther into loneliness. . . . I found a wastebasket full of crumpled false starts. I took it out the side door to empty it into the trash can when a whispering emotion caught me. . . . I took the crumpled sheets, smoothed them out, read the crazy leaping lines, smiled to myself at the leaps that never landed and then put the sheets into a file folder. I still have them somewhere. . . ."

"Tambourine" is bold in definition, yet resonates with ambiguity. Dylan asks what experience, path, new door can bring us to happiness and fulfillment. The most widely accepted decodification is that Dylan was talking about drugs. (Richard Goldstein was planning to title his first book, about drugs on campus, *Mr. Tambourine Man.* Grossman's partner, John Court, requested, or demanded, that the publisher change the title.) The drug-metaphor case is easy to build: transcendence, freedom, escape, and direct references, in verse two, to a trip and stripped senses, and in verse four, to "the smoke rings of my mind." [13]

The song reaches toward a more universal experience than drugs.

of himself, or describing the plight of his listener? Besides several mis-spelled or poorly transcribed words, the folio and *The Bob Dylan Song Book* omitted verses four and five, forty-five lines. Note his later changes in *Writings and Drawings.*

"It's Alright, Ma" disputes that Dylan had become socially unconscious. He moved his protest here to a higher level, to polemize the human con-dition. In a remarkable verse, Dylan previews the sexual revolution that didn't erupt until years later. He lashes out at the "Old lady judges" [26] he knew so well in Hibbing. The fierce defense of security, he knows, is no insurance against death. His targets have widened to include advertising, propaganda, obscenity, false gods, and goals. Despite his anger, he accepts lies and malaise as part of life, tempering an outraged snort into sadness. Implicitly, he sees that the flaws of life are beyond good and evil. This is almost a spoken poem, like Ginsberg's "Howl." In fact, an excellent me-lodic, rhythmic base provides hammer strokes for nailing down a steel spike. Repetition of certain phrases heightens dramatic impact, builds ten-sion.

"IT'S ALL OVER NOW, BABY BLUE": Farewell on several levels; an adieu to any of his women, a farewell to the Left, or to his own youthful illusions. It's also Dylan's conversation with himself; he is the orphan tell-ing himself: "Forget the dead you've left, they will not follow you." [27] This is no epitaph, for one can "Strike another match, go start anew." [28] Consider verse two: "Take what you have gathered from coincidence" [29] in the light of Carl Jung's foreword to the *I Ching.* There, Jung expounded his theory of synchronicity, which "takes the coincidence of events in space and time as meaning something more than mere chance, namely a peculiar interdependence of objective events among themselves as well as with the subjective (psychic) states of the observer." [30] "Baby Blue" was Dylan's finest song about pain . . . before *Blood on the Tracks.* The vocaliz-ing captures harsh experience softened into tender resignation. *On Bio-graph* Dylan makes an association with Gene Vincent's "Baby Blue."

The liner notes begin with *Tarantula*-like nervous thought-fragments, name lists, and wild juxtapositions. The second section is riddled with aphorisms: a farewell to perfectionism, annoyance at White House Philis-tinism, acceptance of chaos, a description of fear, and his discovery that "experience teaches that silence terrifies people the most. . . ." [31] For all his gnomic games, he was ready now to declare "a poem is a naked person . . . some people say that I am a poet. . . ." [32] He's almost ready to declare him-self a poet, but not quite.

HIGHWAY 61 REVISITED

Highway 61 Revisited was released in August 1965. There was no gap in Dylan's momentum, for "Like a Rolling Stone" had been released as a sin-gle in June. Although it was a great success, heading the charts for weeks, Dylan split with his second producer, Tom Wilson. For a time, he found an ideal match in the shy, soft-spoken Nashville cat, Bob Johnston. Johnston had been an independent producer for two years before joining Columbia in early 1965. Two years later, he became director of Columbia's Country and Western A & R, and produced Cash, Simon and Garfunkel, Louis Armstrong, The Byrds, Aretha, Patti Page, Flatt and Scruggs, Seeger, Leonard Cohen. Although he wrote several dozen hits, many of which were recorded by Presley, Johnston thought the record producer should help while allowing a maximum amount of freedom. "Dylan's king, and I'll not tell Dylan what I think of his material unless he asks me," Johnston once said.

Dylan, according to Johnston, developed a very good studio atmosphere: "If it gets to the point where it doesn't feel right, we split and come back next afternoon or evening. Dylan has got his songs worked out definitely. No matter who he's working with." Of studio musicians in New York or Nashville: "They know they are playing with one of the greatest artists in the world, so Dylan takes advantage of it. Dylan's not a follower, he's a leader and he's always changed. When Dylan recorded a country song, the rest of the world followed. Change is one of the things that keeps him where he is and what he is. If he just wanted somebody to push a button he'd get himself an engineer," Johnston said. He described a typical session:

"Bob will suddenly ring me up and say that he's got a whole new batch of songs together, which he'd like to record. The studios are usually well booked, but it's quite easy for me to get another group, no matter how big, to vacate the studios. Everyone has so much respect for Dylan. The studio session men may be guys Bob has heard and wants to use. . . . With Dylan, almost everything is done live, with a minimum of overdubbing. This way we can get things done in just a couple of takes. I can work a week on the mixing, and if it's wrong as far as he's concerned, I would do it again. The sequencing lies with him. He's the boss, but we work together. Dylan is a perfectionist. He won't settle for second best. Dylan is so intense, he is quite unlike any other artist I've worked with. I don't really 'produce' his albums, but just do my best to make him smile when he leaves the studio."

Highway 61 generally has a cleaner ensemble sound than *Back Home,* giving more definition to individual instruments and the overriding voice. Another Kramer photograph covers *Highway 61.* Although Dylan poses indoors, his motorcycle T-shirt and colored silk shirt put him on the road again. On the back, three studio shots catch Dylan in the session.

"LIKE A ROLLING STONE": In 1976, *New Musical Express* called it "the top rock single of all time." It develops suspense right through its six minutes. At first, the narrator seems vindictive, as if he enjoys watching an overprotected person forced out into a cruel world. Dylan had little sympathy with those who hadn't fought easy comforts. Yet this and subsequent versions reveal a sad resignation that softens the tone of "I told you so." One night, I got Dylan to talk about this song:

"Why does everybody say of something like 'Like a Rolling Stone,' 'That Dylan . . . is that all he can do, put down people?' I've never put down anybody in a song, man. It's their idea. 'Like a Rolling Stone,' man, was very vomitific in its structure. . . . It seemed like twenty pages, but it was really six. I wrote it in six pages. You know how you get sometimes. And I did it on a piano. And when I made the record, I called the people who made the record with me, and I told them how to play on it, and if they didn't want to play it like that, well, they couldn't play with me. . . . When I wrote 'all you got to do is find a school and learn to get juiced in it,' I wasn't making this song about school. That's their idea. Their definition of school is much different than mine. My language is different than theirs. I mean REALLY TOTALLY DIFFERENT! The finest school, I mean, might just be out in the swamps. 'School' here can be anything. This song is definitely not about school."

He was probably using "school" as a symbol of a way of life. He sees horror enveloping anyone who suddenly makes a break after being closely attached to any form of life. For some, the experience is liberating; to others, it brings panic and helplessness. The "schoolgirl" he seems to be chastising here is probably anyone afraid to step out of his or her cocoon and into life's mainstream without guidance, parents, structure, or crutches. The words seem crueler on the page than they sound in performance. A song that seems to hail the dropout life for those who can take it segues into compassion for those who have dropped out of bourgeois surroundings. "Rolling Stone" is about the loss of innocence and the harshness of experience. Myths, props, and old beliefs fall away to reveal a very taxing reality.

Musically, the song jells beautifully; there is little feeling of prestudio rehearsal, just of a group that takes off on a splendid progression of chords. Dylan says the song was recorded in one take. The organ work—Al Kooper's strongly cohesive legato tones, the lighter filigree of runs and configurations—is brilliant. Thanks to Mike Bloomfield's guitar, even clichés are flavorful and skillfully timed. The drums swing brightly, while Dylan's voice urgently seems to anticipate the beat. The basic chord sequence is curiously familiar, suggesting "La Bamba," "Guantanamera," "Twist and Shout." Yet the massive, full sound moves away into a very complex structure. In *Backstage Passes,* Al Kooper tells how he improvised what is now a famous instrumental part to the delight of Dylan and all hands. Twenty years later, Dylan recalled recording it in a single day. Sara and he lived in a Woodstock cabin and he wrote it there. "It just came, you know," he said.

"TOMBSTONE BLUES": Chuck Berry-ful thrust in this up-tempo romp. The basic chord sequence in the verse is C, C7, F, and back to C, while in the middle eight bars, F and C chords alternate. This is a song of the grotesque, but we're more amused than frightened by the incongruities. The cast is large: children in bed, city fathers, Paul Revere's horse, Belle Starr, Jezebel, Jack the Ripper, John the Baptist, the list goes on. Allusions to Vietnam are apparent throughout, especially in the title and in verses three and four, where I see Lyndon Johnson as King of the Philistines. Another skip-rope-like rhyme in the refrain mixes insouciance with complaint.

Highly episodic; one well-planned absurdity suggests another, whether biblical, historical, or musical. Ma Rainey, the blues singer, and Beethoven are superseded by brass-band tuba players rehearsing a military march. One impudent image reminds us that Dylan's control of language was absolute: "The geometry of innocence flesh on the bone/Causes Galileo's math book to get thrown." [33] "Tombstone" trots along effortlessly. The slide-guitar breaks are primitive, but so well timed they seem inspired. In one break, the foot pedal changes the texture of an elongated guitar figure. The song goes out on a finger tremor, wobbling on a string for yet another texture. Recorded on July 19, 1965 on the same day as "Positively Fourth Street" and "It Takes a Train to Cry." A cop's talk about death was an influence on his lyrics. Dylan calls "Jet Pilot," released for the first time on *Biograph,* the original version of "Tombstone."

"IT TAKES A LOT TO LAUGH, IT TAKES A TRAIN TO CRY": Wry title for a traditional blues form, rooted in an old shuffle sound from Kansas City or St. Louis of the 1940s. Bobby Gregg's lazy-slap drumming sets the draggy tempo with an ever-so-slight emphasis on the offbeat. No room here for technical flourishes, which would have robbed the song of its old-timey feeling. The unusual harmonica fabric adds to the rough-hewn texture. The singing is straightforward blues, with sustained holds on *sea* and *boss* that add a little dramatic push to an otherwise low-key blues.

"FROM A BUICK 6": The title reminds us of how Chuck Berry raced automobiles through his lyrics, as a symbol of freedom, status, escape, and sexuality. The feel of this blues in C is quite antique, predating Berry; the principal guitar figure sounds like electrified riffs out of Robert Johnson, Charlie Patton, or Big Joe Williams. Aside from some incidental spoofing, the lyrics are traditional couplets. An earthy tribute to another funky earth-mother.

"THE BALLAD OF A THIN MAN": "Mister Jones," one of Dylan's greatest archetypes, is a Philistine, an observer who does not see, a person who does not reach for the right questions. He piously pays his social dues through self-serving tax deductions, pays to watch freak shows but doesn't like the entertainment, is superficially educated and well bred but not very smart about the things that count. I once tried to corner Dylan about Mr. Jones:

"Mr. Jones is . . . like a very weak, ah, well-to-do person. Not well-to-do in the terms of bread or shelter, but well-to-do, knowing he can always go home. Friends will put Mr. Jones up, not because they like him, but because they must, out of the mores in which they live. Mr. Jones has his own environment and his own people. Mr. Jones's loneliness can easily be covered up to the point where he can't recognize that he is alone. Mr. Jones is suddenly locked in a room . . . he stumbled into a room. God knows, we all do that! It's not so incredibly absurd and it's not so imaginative to have Mr. Jones in a room with three walls and a midget and a geek and a naked man. Plus a voice . . . a voice coming in his dream. I am just a voice speaking. Any time I'm singing about people and if the songs are dreamed, it's like my voice is coming out of their dream. . . . Mr. Jones is powerful, because it is very concise and very emotional, do you dig?"

We all know many Mr. Joneses who just don't seem to be aware of what is happening. Who, specifically, might Mr. Jones have been to Dylan? A *Time* reporter named Jeffrey Jones wrote in *Rolling Stone* in 1975 that it must have been him. I would nominate Pete Seeger, thrown for a complete loss by Dylan's electric music; Tom Wilson, not understanding Dylan's concepts about recording; another *Time* reporter, Horace Judson, whom Dylan scourged in the film *Don't Look Back;* Howard Alk, husband of Jones Alk, both members of the film crew. Mr. Jones is undoubtedly a composite. To Dylan's free-flowing accusations, many people pleaded guilty. Other theories bandied about: Mr. Jones was LeRoi Jones, militant black writer; Mr. Jones is patois for the heroin-user; Jones is a masculinization of Joan; Mr. Jones is the farmer in Orwell's *Animal Farm*. When I was slow in getting Dylan's rock message, some people thought I was Mr. Jones, but I hadn't been a thin man in years. Musically, the song is almost stately, with fine organ work again lending cohesion. Novelist Joseph Heller reportedly took his title *Something Happened* from this song.

"QUEEN JANE APPROXIMATELY": A puckish title wide open to interpretation. Some believe Dylan is still on an anti-Baez kick here, with *Jane* barely disguising *Joan*. There is a classic early-sixteenth-century English-Scottish ballad (Child Ballad 170) written not long after Jane Seymour gave birth to Prince Edward, called "The Death of Queen Jane." How does Mick Jagger's Queen Jane relate to Dylan's? Since "Mary Jane" is Aesopian for marijuana, some think the song alludes to drugs. The lyrics stingingly attack a formalized, dutiful family life, filled with joyless, meaningless, ritualistic proprieties. Musically, a bit lackluster. The band sounds muddy; the electric guitar, if not out of tune, is certainly out of phase. A minor work that says very little to me, other than an undercurrent of rueful feeling.

"HIGHWAY 61 REVISITED": Because U.S. Highway 61 passes from Duluth through Minneapolis before heading down through Wisconsin toward the blues country of Mississippi, it is a particularly useful highway for Dylan to hitch back on. Highway 61 links America's most alienated group, southern blacks, with the singer, alienated at his end of the road. This bright blues shuffle is augmented by a police-car whistle. The band trots along, paced by the drumming, flavored with bottleneck guitar and fine piano that is almost too subdued. The verse begins with a takeoff on biblical lore reminiscent of Lord Buckley or Bill Cosby rather than "holy blues." If God were chatting with Abe close to the northern end of the highway, the son would be Dylan himself. The "killing" would have struck him down just as he was setting off on the road. The song's ludicrousness grows with mention of Georgia Sam, poor Howard (a folk figure), Mack the Finger, Louie the King, and the bluesy mumbo jumbo of mystical magic about seventh sons. Finally, a jab at a concert promoter who, when asked to promote another world war, says he'll try. There's a disturbing undercurrent of probability.

"JUST LIKE TOM THUMB'S BLUES": Before arriving at "Desolation Row," the singer visits a border-town skid row. In seamy Juarez, our anti-hero stumbles amid sickness, despair, whores, and saints. "When you're lost in the rain in Juarez/And it's Eastertime too" [34] establishes a smoldering nightmare under Malcolm Lowry's volcano. The mournful music supports the ugly scene. The jangly piano adds a honky-tonk edge. A man's "going down slow," pulled by gravity, negativity, drink, illness, remorse, memories, until the surprising final couplet: He has found the means of returning to New York, an intimation that things might go better there. Beautiful scene painting, with edges purposefully scumbled out of focus. Was Rue Morgue an avenue, or a nightmare alley where echoes of Poe suggest murder and suicide?

A Halifax academic, David M. Monaghan, has written that the song suggests T. S. Eliot's " 'The Love Song of J. Alfred Prufrock,' Eliot's near-definitive modern alienated man." Monaghan finds Dylan "calling on modern man to seek the spiritual values that are to be found by looking in the past." What is nursery rhyme Tom Thumb doing here? The 1870 poem of Rimbaud, "My Bohemian Life (Fantasy)": ". . . I went off, my fists in my torn pockets; . . . My only pair of trousers had a big hole. Tom Thumb in a daze, I sowed rhymes/As I went along. My inn was at the Big Dipper . . . rhyming in the midst of fantastic shadows, Like lyres I plucked the elastics/Of my wounded shoes, one foot near my heart!" [35]

"DESOLATION ROW": In a near-sequel to "Hard Rain," Dylan describes your neighborhood after that rain. Both thunder with prophecy: Unless we renounce materialism, this will be our future. Dylan articulates the rock visions of contemporary apocalypse. "Desolation Row" belongs beside Eliot's "The Waste Land" and Ginsberg's "Howl" as one of the strongest expressions of apocalypse. Eugene Stelzig maintains, however, that "Eliot's disillusionment is resigned; Dylan's is charged with rebellion. . . ." The scenery is a dreamed mental landscape. Dylan's description combines the grotesque, the existential, and the dream powerfully. "Desolation Row" is a grotesque Mardi Gras where heroes and villains of our mytho-history range side by side. They are laughable, but our smiles freeze. The writer who questioned society for two years now sees answers, but doesn't like what he sees. Everything is cockeyed, topsy-turvy; all is lost; all is ludicrous; the only truth lies along Desolation Row. As bizarre as his cast is, they are real people. To maintain their veil of secrecy, the faces have been rearranged and the names changed—shades of Cubism. There is no point in inspecting the traveling papers of Cinderella, the Good Samaritan, Ophelia, Einstein, Doctor Filth. Follow the gargoyles as they head down Desolation Row. Along the way, we encounter Dylan's condemnation of the modern assembly line: mad human robots out of Chaplin's *Modern Times*. Then, almost as an aside, Dylan makes a shambles of simpleminded political commitment. What difference which side you're on if you're sailing on the Titanic? Irony and sarcasm are streetlamps along "Desolation Row," keeping away total, despairing darkness. Gallows humor for a mass hanging.

The slow musical matrix heightens the song's biblical roll. Repetition, like Old Testament cantillating, underscores the warning. A masterful, romantic guitar above and behind the vocal line softens the repetition somewhat, but is repeated until it provides only underlining, not relief. This image of the world is far removed from marches toward social progress. One of the curses of poetic vision is seeing too clearly the difference between how things are and how they ought to be.

"... I JUST MIGHT TELL YOU THE TRUTH..."

Dylan made press interviews a performance. Fans cherished several that were particularly outrageous. If the reporter was knowledgeable and sympathetic, Dylan generally revealed more. If he didn't like the questions, he would give oblique or absurd responses.

Dylan knew that by limiting interviews he could ultimately guarantee himself more space. He also knew how elusiveness intrigues. Locked eye to eye with an interviewer, he could still parry adroitly. Like his music, statements that appeared unguarded or spontaneous were often thought out in advance. He knew how a line sounded, how it would look in print. In late summer 1965, Nora Ephron and Susan Edmiston of the *New York Post* got a fair amount from him, but also hit stone walls: "Q: Some American folk singers—Carolyn Hester, for example—say that what you're now doing, the new sound, 'folk-rock,' is liberating them. Dylan: Did Carolyn say that? You tell her she can call around and see me anytime now that she's liberated. . . . Q: Who is 'Mister Jones' . . . ? Dylan: He's a real person. You know him. . . . I saw him come into the room one night and he looked like a camel. He proceeded to put his eyes in his pocket. . . . It's all there, it's a true story. . . . Q: Who is Queen Jane? Dylan: Queen Jane is a man. . . ."

When I interviewed Dylan for *Cavalier* in winter 1965, I was struck by his control: " 'All I do is write songs and sing them. I can't dig a ditch. I can't splice an electric wire. I'm no carpenter. . . . I'm in the show business

now. I'm not in the folk-music business. That's where it's at. So is Roscoe
Holcomb, Jean Ritchie, Little Orphan Annie, Dick Tracy, all the way up
to President Johnson. . . ." Dylan was beginning to look wizened, but he
remained sharply acute. " 'Don't tell me anything I say is off the record. A
performer is *always* on the record, all the time.' " When I asked about
Silber's critical "Open Letter" in *Sing Out!*, Dylan sidestepped: " 'His letter
was all right. If it makes him feel better, that's O.K. People write me letters all the time.' " Was he interested in lowering the drinking age or le-
galizing pot? " 'You name it, I'll legalize it. I'm not making any rules for
anyone,' " he said, as he finished his salad and started eating mine. Was he
looking after his health? " 'If I died tomorrow, the world would go right
on. Kennedy died. Edgar Allan Poe died. The world goes right on. Marx
died. Winston Churchill died. . . . Johnson'll die, too. Time doesn't
stop.' "

At press conferences, he was so often misunderstood, his annoyance
would show. From his December 3, 1965, press conference for San Francisco's KQED-TV: "Q: Do you think of yourself primarily as a singer or a
poet? D: Oh, I think of myself more as a song-and-dance man. . . . Q: Josh
Dunson . . . implies that you have sold out to commercial interests . . . D:
. . . I sincerely don't feel guilty. Q: If you were going to sell out to a commercial interest, which one would you choose? D: Ladies garments . . . Q:
What's your new album about? D: . . . all kinds of different things—rats,
balloons . . . Q: How would you define folk music? D: As a constitutional
replay of mass production. Q: Who is 'Mister Jones'? D: Mr. Jones? I'm
not going to tell you his first name. I'd get sued. Q: What does [Mister
Jones] do for a living? D: He's a pinboy. He also wears suspenders. Q:
What are your own personal hopes for the future and what do you hope to
change in the world? D: . . . I don't have any hopes for the future and I
just hope to have enough boots to be able to change them. . . . Q: Why do
you think you're so popular? D: I don't know. I'm not a reporter. I'm not
a newsman. . . . I'm not even a philosopher, so I have no idea. . . ."

At a Los Angeles press conference a few weeks later, Dylan was close to
overt anger. "Q: I wonder if you could tell me, among folk singers, how
many could be characterized as protest singers today? D: I don't understand. Could you ask the question again? A: How many people who labor
in the same musical vineyards in which you toil, how many are protest
singers? That is, how many use their music to protest about the social state
in which we are today? D: How many? One hundred thirty-six. [Laugh-
ter] It's either one hundred thirty-six or one hundred thirty-two. Q: What
does the word *protest* mean to you? D: It means singing when you really
don't want to sing. It means singing against your wishes to sing. Q: Do
you sing protest songs? D: No. Q: What do you sing? D: I sing all love
songs. Q: Is it true that you changed your name? If so, what was your
other name? D: . . . Kunezevitch. I changed it to avoid obvious relatives
who would come up to me in different parts of the country and want

tickets for concerts and stuff like that. Kunezevitch, yeah. Q: Was that your first or last name? D: That was my first name. [Laughter and applause] I don't really want to tell you what my last name was.

"Q: Bob, why is there such a widespread use of drugs among singers today? [Laughter] D: I don't know. Are you a singer? . . . Q: Do you take drugs yourself? D: I don't even know what a drug is. I have never even seen a drug. I would not know what one looked like if I saw one. Q: Bob, what sort of technique do you use when you write a song, or don't you call it any sort of technique? D: Well, I just sit down and the next thing I know, it's there. . . . Q: Why are you putting us, and the rest of the world, on so? D: I'm just trying to answer your questions as good as you can ask them. Q: I am sure you must have been asked a thousand times—what are you trying to say in your music? I don't understand *one* of the songs. D: Well, you shouldn't feel offended or anything. I am not trying to say anything to you. If you don't get it, you don't have to really think about it, 'cause it's not addressed to you. Q: Are you trying to say something when you write? Or are you just entertaining? D: I'm just an entertainer. That's all. Q: Do you really feel that it's important for you to write and sing? D: [Menacingly] Now, you are gonna make me mad now. Q: Or do you just want to do it because you're successful? Do you really feel the things that you write? D: What is there to feel? Name me some things. Q: We are talking about standard emotions—pain, remorse, love . . . D: I have none of those feelings. Q: What sort of feelings do you have when you write a song? D: I don't have to explain my feelings! I am not on trial here!

"Q: You sound and look very tired, very ill. Is this your normal state? D: I take that as an insult. I don't like to hear that kind of thing. . . . Q: What's the reason for your visit to California? D: Oh, I'm here looking for some donkeys. I am making a movie about Jesus. Q: Where are you making it? D: Back east. Q: Did your parents give you any special advice when you last saw them? Did they say 'good-bye' or 'good luck' or anything like that? D: No, do your parents do that to you? Q: As a little boy, did you want to write songs and be a singer? D: No, I wanted to be a movie usher. It's been my lifelong ambition to be a movie usher, and I have failed, as far as I am concerned.

"Q: Why do you think that kids are listening to you now? D: I really don't know. I just heard something a couple of days ago that amazed me . . . outside a concert we played at San José, there was this fifteen-year-old girl . . . being interviewed as to why she was there . . . she knew all the poets, like William Blake, and she knew his works and she was hip to all kinds of different things which people are usually not acquainted with at that age. So, maybe, it's just a new kind of person, a new kind of fifteen-year-old. I do know that today there's more freedom in the mind of twenty-two-year-old college students. I know that, that's true. Q: What's the attitude today among young people? D: Oh, God! I don't know any of these people. Q: What do you spend your money on? You seem to lead a very simple, uncomplicated life. You don't seem to be interested in motor cars, girls, yachts . . . ? D: Well, that's the way it goes. [Laughter]"

In March 1965, Bob was in Woodstock in a jaunty mood; Maura Davis pretended to be from a high-school paper. *Cavalier* ran the interview opposite a photograph of Dylan in a bright yellow and brown plaid wool tie. Some highlights: "Q: Mr. Dye-lan, I'm from the New Buffalo Consolidated High School, and . . . all the students want to know . . . what's the most important thing in the world to you? D: Oh, my God! Do they really want to know that? . . . I'd say this tie I'm wearing right now. . . . Q: Why . . . that tie? D: Well, President Johnson used to wear a tie like this—before he got to be President. . . . It's a sign of the common man, and I'm a common man. So I wear a tie like this just to . . . just to get involved. Q: Do you wear that tie when you're writing your songs? D: When I write? No, I usually wear this . . . after I finish something very good. To make myself feel good, I put on the tie, and then I feel much better about it—and usually I have a hit. . . ."

An intrepid Los Angeles reporter asked Dylan in September 1965 what the most important thing in his life was: "Well, I've got a monkey-wrench collection and I'm very interested in that." Why did he hold such sway with teenagers? "I have no recollection of ever having been a teenager myself. I can't say why they like me. It's a different world." Then Dylan turned irascible: "The protest thing is old. And how valid is it anyway? Is it going to stop anything? Is anybody going to listen? People think this helps. . . . But songs aren't gonna save the world. . . ."

That month, Dylan flew to Toronto for rehearsals with The Hawks. Robert Fuller, book columnist of *The Toronto Star,* later wrote that seeing Dylan "is just a little more difficult than arranging a private chat with the Pope." In Toronto a few months later, Margaret Steen interviewed the pop pope and did a substantial story about Dylan's electric music under the headline: NOT *YOU,* BOB DYLAN! SURELY NOT! IT CAN'T BE THAT THE FOLK-SINGING IDOL OF THE YOUNG HAS GONE COMMERCIAL. THE STAR WHO IS NEVER—WELL, ALMOST NEVER—INTERVIEWED TELLS A *STAR WEEKLY* WRITER HOW IT REALLY IS. Had Dylan really "sold out"? He replied:

"It's easy for people to classify it as rock 'n' roll, to put it down. Rock 'n' roll is a straight 12-bar blues progression. My new songs aren't. I used to play rock 'n' roll a long time ago, before I even started playing old-fashioned folk, 10 years ago when I was a kid, for God's sake . . . the music industry is totally different. . . . Rock 'n' roll singers now . . . make the old people look sick. . . . Tin Pan Alley! I know that scene. Fat guys chewing cigars and carrying around gold records, and selling songs, selling talent, selling an image. I never hung out there. . . . The singers 10 years ago were kids, but the old guys ran things; now the people actually in control are younger—the managers, the record company bosses, kids, in their 20's. . . . Why, man, just with the experiences I've experienced already, I could never step outside this room again and still write songs until the end of time. . . . No. I'm not disillusioned. I'm just not illusioned, either. The civil rights and protest songs, I wrote when nobody else was writing them. Now, everyone is. But I've found out some things. The groups promoting these things, the movement, would try to get me involved with them, be their singing spokesman—and inside these groups, with all their president–vice-president–secretary stuff, it's politics. Inside their own pettinesses they're as bad as the hate groups. I won't even have a fan club because it'd have to have a president, it'd be a group. They think the more people you have behind something the more influence it has. Maybe so, but the more it gets watered down, too. I'm not a believer in doing things by numbers. I believe that the best things get done by individuals. . . ."

In the first draft of Nat Hentoff's famous *Playboy* interview, too much editing angered Dylan and led him, in a second session, to sarcastic heights. He told me: "I read the proofs and I said: 'Where in the fuck did you get these words?' Hentoff told me that the man from *Playboy* wrote in things to make it sound a little better. . . . And they were downright fucking, silly-ass, you know, geech-like phrases. Peacock phrases. Just dumb bullshit, assinine things that . . . anybody that has ever met me and heard me talk knows I would not say. I said: 'You're not getting this article, man.' I called the lawyers right away, and Albert. And the lawyers sent *Playboy* a letter and they got frightened. So they called back and I said: 'Could I have the article rewritten . . . ?' I answered the questions. I did it very bad, man. I should have done it much better." Hentoff, and most readers, felt he'd done it brilliantly. Hentoff, in an interview in the fanzine *Zimmerman Blues* (issue 6), told Brian Stibal that he thought *Playboy* editors "put some words in his mouth. They fooled around with it." Hentoff said that he played straight man as Dylan improvised the outlandish interview that eventually ran:

"*Playboy:* . . . Why have you stopped composing and singing protest songs? D: . . . message songs, as everybody knows, are a drag . . . what I'm going to do is rent Town Hall and put about 30 Western Union boys on the bill. I mean, then there'll really be some messages. . . . *Playboy:* You told an interviewer last year, 'I've done everything I've ever wanted to do.' If that's true, what do you have to look forward to? D: Salvation. Just plain salvation. *Playboy:* Anything else? D: Praying. I'd also like to start a cookbook magazine. And I've always wanted to be a boxing referee. *Playboy:* Did you ever have the standard boyhood dream of growing up to be President? D: No. When I was a boy, Harry Truman was President; who'd want to be Harry Truman? *Playboy:* Well, let's suppose that you were the President. What would you accomplish during your first thousand days? D: . . . the first thing I'd do is probably move the White House. Instead of being in Texas, it'd be on the East Side in New York. McGeorge Bundy would definitely have to change his name, and General McNamara would be forced to wear a coonskin cap and shades. I would immediately rewrite 'The Star-Spangled Banner,' and little school children, instead of memorizing 'America the Beautiful' would have to memorize 'Desolation Row.' And I would immediately call for a showdown with Mao Tze-Tung; I would fight him personally—and I'd get somebody to film it. . . ."[37]

In an elegiac March 1966 cover story for *Ramparts*, Ralph Gleason got Dylan to discuss his "complex" songs: " 'These songs aren't complicated to me at all. It's all very clear and simple to me. . . . There's nothing hard to figure out for me. I wouldn't write anything I can't really see. They're all about real people. I'm sure you've seen all the people in my songs at one time or another.' " Dylan still respected the complexity and subtlety of folk songs: " '. . . based on myth and the Bible and plague and famine and all kinds of things like that which are just nuthin' but mystery and you can see it in all the songs—roses growin' right up out of people's hearts and naked cats in bed with, you know, spears growing right out of their back and seven years of this and eight years of that and it's all really something that nobody can really touch. . . .' " Dylan tried to explain his changes: " '. . . I just went through that other thing of writing songs until I couldn't write like it anymore. It was just too easy and it wasn't really right . . .' But now I just write a song like I *know* that it's just going to be all right and I don't really know exactly what it's all about, but I do know the minute and the layers of what it's all about. "Rolling Stone" is the best song I wrote. I wrote "Rolling Stone" after England. I boiled it down, but it's all there. I had to quit after England. I had to stop and when I was writing it I knew I had to sing it with a band. I always sing when I write, even prose, and I heard it like that.' "

BREAK-OUT IN BRITAIN

Dylan's trip to England in spring 1965 was a turning point. Although he played to only fifty thousand people in eight concerts, the April-June tour changed him from a folk star into an international pop superstar. At this time, most pop excitement emanated from England and Dylan's shock waves flashed back to America. The first clue: In March, seven thousand tickets for his May 10 Albert Hall concert sold out within two hours.

If a single external factor triggered Dylan's British breakthrough, it was The Beatles' public endorsement. When Dylan had played New Haven and Santa Monica in March 1965, there were local reviews, not the lionization he was to receive in the British national press. In a small country, excitement was like steam in a kettle. The pop and national press had a carnival.

Dylanmania was probably triggered by Ray Coleman's article in *Melody Maker* on January 9, 1965, headlined: BEATLES SAY—DYLAN SHOWS THE WAY. The story, with photos of Lennon, Harrison, and Dylan, was reproduced on the sleeve of the Columbia single of "Subterranean," backed with "She Belongs to Me." Coleman, later editor of *Disc and Music Echo*, and then *Melody Maker*, wrote me:

"1965 was the year Dylan conquered Britain, the year 'Wind' and 'Times Changing' became favorites of the university students and the pop screamers. Dylan emerged from the relative obscurity of the folk world to the wider, more dangerous world of pop idol. For Dylan, it was fraught with trouble. I was among the hundreds who met Dylan at London Airport ... he was bemused by it all. In seven major cities, Dylan faced an uncanny audience. Half was converted, half was the pop cult.... Dylan made absolutely no concession to hit-parade status . . . he commanded utter silence at his concerts. Even the noisy pop fans were stunned into silence by his words, the honesty of his performances. Bob consistently showed an endearing modesty. He wandered on stage with no sign of the 'big star' atmosphere we had come to expect from pop immortals. At Leicester's sensationally successful concert, a cross-section of the audience agreed his performances were more electrifying, more important than his recordings. They clutched copies of 'Back Home.' A student said: 'What made it for us was that he sang the words of his songs as if they had meaning. You see so many artists who perform like zombies, as if they're there for the money and that's all.' "

The buildup began long before his arrival on Monday, April 26. The March 19 *London Evening News* and next morning's *Daily Sketch* announced that his Albert Hall tickets were selling "like gold dust." The *Daily Mirror* did an advance story from the States. The pop weeklies ran background stories. Additional blessings from Manfred Mann and The Animals helped build anticipation. As Dylan's plane came into the London airport, two hundred fans waited in the rain, some wearing replicas of "the hat" or antibomb badges. The fans began to give him Beatles treatment, pulling at his hair and tugging at his clothes, virtually carrying him into the airport conference room. Police helped him through the mob; Dylan, looking somewhat shaken, said: "It's never been like this before! It was OK—they didn't hurt me. They just gave me a haircut. I'm ready to get drunk now." Dylan looked to see how the rest of his party—Baez, the Grossmans, and the film crew of *Don't Look Back*—was faring. Dylan carried an outsize light bulb, a prankish Diogenes lamp. Asked, "What is your message?" Dylan replied: "Keep a good head and always carry a light bulb."

Mike Hurst, who taped a ten-minute interview for BBC, told me later: "He was a living myth before he got here. Many in the press were waiting to break the myth. At first, he was very vague. When I got down to his music, he really started to talk. He was almost interviewing *me* then." (A cartoon in *The Sunday Citizen* pictured Dylan in a prison cell. Caption: "Three jails have held him—on suspicion of murder—on suspicion of armed robbery—and for just looking like he does....")

"Hair that would set the teeth of a comb on edge.... A loud shirt that would dim the neon lights of Leicester Square," went one description. "He looks like an undernourished cockatoo," wrote another. "Mr. Dylan managed to exasperate practically everybody.... He wafted a red rose beneath his nose and could be heard ... to say: 'Stiff, cold and mortistic,' " wrote Maureen Cleave of *The Evening Standard.* (Cleave complained: "What do I do with him, how do you make him talk? He just says yes or no and rocks and sways as if he is masturbating himself.")

Dylan had considerably more to say to her: " 'I don't want to give the impression of being a star, because I don't think of myself as one.... I've ... seen all these crazes come and go, and I don't think I'm more than a craze. In a coupla years time, I shall be right back where I started—an unknown.... All I'm really interested in is singing to people who want to listen to me.... I seem to be more popular here than I am at home ... the only difference success has brought is that I now feel I must make my records even better.... I am bored with the atom bomb. I am bored with our Government. I do wish somebody in our Government had a beard, just to be different.' "

A *Daily Mail* reporter was offered Dylan's heavy green glasses. Dylan: "See the world as Bob Dylan sees it.... I'm alone up here. I was over here three years back and on the streets. In two years, I'll be gone and you'll be talking to someone else.' " Why was he staying at the Savoy, a hotel where even minor clerks wear swallow-tailed jackets? Dylan snapped: " 'I can't live in a shack!' " Grossman hustled *The Daily Mail* man into another room, saying: "We're not here to sell rubber dolls, you know. We're not here to perform for newsmen. Reporters get annoyed at artists for their own stupidity. Pop music has aimed below the waist for so long. It's time it did something to the mind. Bob is one of the most important figures, not just in pop, you know, but in American life." Baez sat singing "Sally, Go Round the Roses." For the *Mirror,* Bob and Joan posed together on the balcony. One reporter wanted to know why Dylan sounded like a man of seventy-five who was always cross. Dylan: " 'I hate injustice, that's why I sing about racial discrimination and freedom, and I preach for people to be able to do the things they want. On some of my earlier records, I sounded cross because I was poor. Lived on less than two cents a day in those times. Now I'm cross because I'm rich.... I'm not spreading disillusionment by singing the truth.... I guess listening to me is like reading a newspaper. I wanna be entertaining as well as truthful.' "

Singer Martin Carthy told me: "All the times we went to visit him, only half a minute of the time could we actually contact him. The Savoy rooms were always filled with people. Bob became very, very detached; he had so many people to cope with. The more famous he became, the more he tended just to sit in his hotel."

Dylan clashed with Laurie Henshaw of *Disc Weekly* after the tour. *Disc:* "Q: You must obviously make a lot of money nowadays.... D: I spend it all. I have six Cadillacs. I have four houses. I have a plantation in Georgia. I'm also now working on some kind of rocket.... Q: Do you have personal things—cameras, watches and that sort of thing? D: No, I buy cars. I have lots of cars. The Cadillacs . . . a few Oldsmobiles. . . . Listen. I really couldn't care less what your paper writes about me. . . . The people that listen to me don't need your paper. . . . Q: Why be so hostile? D: Because you're hostile to me. You're using me. I'm an object to you. I went through this before. . . . There's nothing personal, I've nothing against you at all. I just don't want to be bothered with your paper, that's all . . . Why don't you just say my name is Kessenovitch . . . and I . . . come from Acapulco, Mexico. That my father was an escaped thief from South Africa. O.K.? Q: Are your tastes in clothes changing at all? D: I like to wear drapes, umbrellas, hats. Q: When did you start making records? D: I started making recordings in 1947. . . . A race record. I made it down South. Actually, the first record I made was in 1935. John Hammond came and recorded me. Discovered me in 1935, sitting on a farm."

New Musical Express had the temerity to send Dylan one of its "Life-Lines" questionnaires. His answers: " 'First important public appearance: Closet at O'Henry's Square Shop. Other disc in best-sellers: "I Lost My Love In San Francisco, But She Appeared Again in Honduras and We Took a Trip to Hong Kong and Stayed Awhile in Reno But Lost Her Again in Oklahoma." Latest Release: "The Queens are Coming." Albums: Yes. Personal Manager: Dog Jones. Musical Director: Big Dog. . . . Favorite food: Turkish Marvin (a form of eggplant coming from Nebraska). Favorite clothes: Nose-guards. Favorite bands/instrumentalists: Corky the Kid (Sombreros). Favorite Composers: Brown Bumpkin and Sidney Ciggy. Favorite groups: The Fab Clocks. Miscellaneous likes: Trucks with no wheels. French telephones, anything with a stewed prune in the middle. Miscellaneous dislikes: Hairy firemen, toe-nails, glass Mober forks, birds with ears. Most thrilling experience: Getting my birthday cake stomped on by Norman Mailer. Taste in music: Sort of peanut butter. Personal ambition: To be a waitress. Professional ambition: To be a stewardess.' "

A reporter for *The Jewish Chronicle* asked him: "Are you Jewish?" He replied: " 'No, I am not, but some of my best friends are.' " Dylan assuaged the *Chronicle:* " 'You'd better interview Tito Burns, the agent for the tour, because I know he is Jewish.' "

Burns was delighted with the tour. He felt three elements had helped make Dylan in Britain: his initial appeal to the folk audience, the tour, and the fact that CBS Records, Columbia's English affiliate, had begun pushing his records. Dylan's seven concerts sold out in an hour or so. Burns: "We got threatening phone calls and letters from people who had not had a chance to buy tickets. I asked Albert to get me off the hook. I said I wouldn't get lynched, but he and Bob would be. I got Albert Hall for a second concert, May 9. Those tickets sold out in about an hour and a quarter, and still thousands of people were turned away. I went up to Sheffield. I have never seen Dylan work before and I went in, for a few numbers. I stayed there two hours, because it got to me. I'm not an intellectual, and I only understood about half of it, but the magic still got to me.... In 1964, I don't think he took in a lot of money at Festival Hall. In 1965, he took the maximum. In his coming concert tour, in spring 1966, when he could double the price of the tickets, he is refusing to do that. They said to me, leave the prices exactly the same, of a one-pound top for tickets....

"The Beatles and The Stones were at Albert Hall and we had to get them boxes way back. They came in just after the show commenced and got out just before it stopped. Everyone was there! Marianne Faithfull rang up for eight tickets. Her mother is a baroness, you know. Just about every star was there ... Robert Morley.... We held back about one hundred fifty house seats because we knew what would happen. The names that were coming through ... the Earl of Harewood ... fantastic!"

The first concert, Sheffield, April 30: "We approached Sheffield in a fleet of Austin Princesses, looking like royalty," Fred Perry, the English road manager, told me. The Sheffield City Hall auditorium was circular; an overflow audience sat onstage. Perry: "I have done thirty English tours, but never saw anything like this! The audience acted as if they were going into a church. In their minds, Dylan was a legend, and you could see the awe on their faces."

New Musical Express reported such reverent silence in Sheffield Hall that Dylan, peering out into the darkness, said: "It's mighty quiet. Where are you all?" Concluded *NME:* "Dylan couldn't do a thing wrong." *The Guardian:* "The audience ... radiated a religious fervor ... the second coming of Bob Dylan, their singing Messiah.... The times, they are a-changing ... when a poet and not a pop singer fills a hall. For this ultimately is what Dylan is.... With his voice, the lyrics are astonishing; without it, in print, they are poetry...."

Dylan brought it all back home May 1 to Liverpool, The Beatles' hometown. "If there would be any adverse reaction to Dylan, it would be in Liverpool," Perry said. "They just walked in quietly to the Odeon and sat down as if they were in church." The Adelphi Hotel was a Liverpudlian Savoy, requiring ties in its restaurant. In walked Dylan with a black turtleneck sweater, with his tie around his waist. "It hung there like a sporran on a Scot's kilt," said Perry. The management was caught off guard; he had to be served. The next morning, several hundred fans gathered at the hotel. According to *Disc Weekly,* Liverpool listeners were quite "unlike the laughing, smiling, chatting people at other concerts, everyone was quiet and solemn. They had been entertained and were now meditating on the songs."

In Leicester, *The Daily Worker* reported the singer's "magnetism... power to hold an audience captive, his perfect timing...." The Leicester concert manager called the response "the biggest thing since the Beatles." About three hundred girls of the audience of three thousand tried to mob Dylan in his car; he mockingly brandished a shillelagh at them. By Leicester, *Melody Maker* was calling Dylan "the most important folk singer of today," and proclaiming: "Dylan fever is sweeping the country." After two days rest, Dylan played Birmingham Town Hall. Some paid five pounds for a ticket priced at less than a pound. *Birmingham Post:* ". . . This boy has the poet's power to open our eyes and to make us think of our little world anew. . . ."

Before the Newcastle Town Hall concert, May 6, the local High Sheriff's Lady, all fox furs and teenage sons, burst into the dressing room. After starting to give her welcoming speech to two roadies, she finally found Dylan and gushed, in faultless uppah-class tones: "And these are my three boys . . . they think you're so marvelous they've left all their exam papers . . . they've left everything to come and listen to you. . . . I think the songs are very wonderful . . . and you write them yourself too, don't you, sometimes? . . . I think you're really a good example for the youth. . . ." As she chirped good-byes, she said to her escort loud enough for all to hear: "Why, he's chahming." Robin Hood had conquered a High Sheriff's Lady. Newcastle, despite a microphone that died for six minutes, leaving the star joking with his audience, was another success. May 7, Manchester Free Trade Hall: similar program and response. Perry agonized that they only had forty minutes to catch their plane. He told the troupe: "Don't bring in someone who's hitchhiked from Glasgow who wants a lock of his hair."

The two Albert Hall gigs resembled the provinces. The *Daily Mirror:* "It was the quietest 'jean-age' audience I have seen. . . . He held the fans enraptured." *Melody Maker*'s Max Jones: "Like a mysterious troubadour who'd lost his horse," Dylan had quietly taken over "with his weirdly compelling songs." Maurice Rosenbaum, in *The Daily Telegraph and Morning Post:* "There are better singers, better guitarists, better harmonica players and better poets. But there is no other 23-year-old who does all these things with even a semblance of the power, the originality, or the fire . . . this haystack-headed young American has achieved in an age of more and more pictures, and less and less text, of emotional noises rather than meanings, an astounding popular victory for the word."

Dylan still had to tape a BBC-TV show, do some recording, continue to star in *Don't Look Back,* meet fellow musicians, and sit for his portrait and for yet another long *Melody Maker* interview: " 'It's hard for me to accept the silent audiences. I think a lot more about what I'm singing and saying when they're so quiet. . . . I was kinda inhibited. . . . People don't grow up the same way, you know? . . . in England they are more ready, the young people. . . . Over there, you could get killed for having long hair, if you're in the wrong part of the country. . . . You could actually get killed for saying something out of place. . . . I think England's more open-minded. . . . My songs are just me talking to myself. . . . I have no responsibility to anybody except myself. If people like me—fine. If they don't, then maybe I'll do something else. Songs are just pictures of what I'm seeing—glimpses of things—life, maybe. . . . You know, every one of my songs could be written better. This used to bother me, but it doesn't anymore. There's nothing perfect anywhere, so I should not expect myself to be perfect. . . .' "

The tour gave Bob occasion to see old friends and to make new ones, including the Manfred Mann band, notably Paul Jones. During Dylan's tour, Mann had a recording of "God on Our Side" on the English charts. "Dylan's influence on the English pop scene was absolutely enormous," Jones told me later. "You can even look at The Beatles and see how much they were influenced." Dylan had been on good terms with The Animals, notably Eric Burdon, lead singer, and Alan Price, singer, pianist, and organist. In 1964, The Animals had made Dylan's version of "House of the Rising Sun" a British chart hit. Early in 1965, when The Animals were on an American tour, Dylan had corralled them, along with The Supremes, who were appearing at Harlem's Apollo Theatre, down to the surprised Village folkniks at the Kettle of Fish. In *The Sound of the City,* a history of pop music, Charlie Gillett said the first Animals record was a version of Dylan's version of "Baby, Let Me Follow You Down."

Dylan fostered his links to the Beatles. Lennon visited Dylan late one night at the Savoy. He thought those who criticized Dylan for staying at such a plush hotel were fools. Lennon asked: "What's wrong with staying at the Savoy? Does starving in a garret make his points any more valid? They say that to be ethnic as a *FOLKER* you must also be poor and act the part. Absolute rubbish! Especially when you consider that the people he's sometimes having a go at—politicians especially—are probably twice as well off, anyway. If you've got a lot to say, like Dylan has, and if you want to make it heard, you've just got to elevate yourself and make yourself famous so people will listen. Earning a fortune's nothing to do with that side of it, but if he happens to do that as well, good luck to him." As soon as John discovered Dylan couldn't be served at the Savoy, he invited Dylan to his house in Weybridge, Surrey, for dinner one evening. Lennon: "We played a few records and talked. He's an interesting bloke with some good ideas. We swapped addresses and said we'd exchange ideas for songs, but it never happened. He said he sent me things, but he got the address wrong and it never arrived. Maybe that's why we get on well—we're both pretty disorganized blokes." Between Dylan's visits to Britain in 1965 and 1966, he told me about his visit with Lennon: "I dug his situation where he lived. It was a twenty-two-room house. Do you know what I did when I got back from England, man? I bought me a thirty-one-room house, can you imagine that? Mine! I bought one just as soon as I got back from England. And it turned into a *nightmare!*" (In the *Biograph* notes, Dylan said he and John tried writing a song together on a tape recorder.)

Reporters tried to stoke up a rivalry between Dylan and Donovan, the monomial minstrel from Glasgow, whose first recording, "Catch the Wind," was, to put it kindly, derivative. Once clued in to Donovan, Bob joked about him at several concerts. Dylan once changed his lyrics of

"Talkin' World War III Blues" to "I turned on my record player—it was Donovan." Bob had listened attentively to "Catch the Wind," and reportedly said: "It's a great record. I didn't care for those de-de-de-de parts, but I did like the way he said the word *uncertainty*. You know, there's this guy in the States who sounds exactly like him. He's got an imitator, I'm telling you. . . ." When a reporter asked if he had been influenced by Donovan, Bob asked: "Who is this Donovan? I'd never even heard of him until yesterday! Let's put him on the wall and talk to him." At the Savoy, Donovan played several songs for his master. Donovan's manager barred journalists: "We don't want any stunt—the disciple meeting the messiah." When some Sheffield University students pressed Dylan to agree that "Catch the Wind" was patterned after the melody of "Chimes of Freedom," Dylan brushed them aside: "Oh, I don't care what he takes from me. Frankly, I don't care what other singers do to my songs. They can't hurt me any."

For CBS Records, Dylan's tour came at an ideal time. The first CBS single, "Times Changing," released in March 1965, did very well. "Subterranean," released during the tour, sold even better, thanks to its electric beat and The Beatles' endorsement. "Maggie's Farm" came out as a single as the tour ended. CBS Records manager of merchandising promotion, Stan West, told me later: "During 1965, from March through December, Dylan's recordings sold substantially more than anyone in our entire catalog." West credited pirate offshore radio ships that were flourishing in 1965, carrying advertising and challenging the BBC state-owned radio monopoly. "Subterranean" and "Rolling Stone" were especially strong on pirate radio, which also broke The Byrds' "Tambourine Man."

Encouraged by Dylan's breakout in Britain—four LPs on the Top Twenty with *Back Home* the number one album—Columbia Records began to push Hammond's Folly heavily back home. In June, Columbia announced a major Dylan American promotion campaign: "The slogan that Dylan is 'Bringing It All Back Home' is the primary theme of the campaign." Columbia cooked up another slogan, "No One Sings Dylan Like Dylan," an eight-inch-die-cut cardboard Dylan doll, a deluxe press kit, and national advertising.

On May 12, Bob went to Levy's Recording Studios on New Bond Street for a brief session that became a bootleg tape. Tom Wilson greeted James Craig of *Record Mirror:* "We're going to try a little experimental stuff tonight," he said, waving toward a piano and two organs. "Some new material Bobby wants to get on tape. Maybe we'll get an album out of it, maybe not." In walked Albert and Sally, folk singers Nadia Catouse and Sidney Carter, Eric Clapton, Paul Jones, John McVie, Hughie Flint, bluesman John Mayall, and three female backup singers. Dylan cut "If You Gotta Go," for a promotional message to a CBS sales committee, and, reportedly, "Help." While mikes were tested, Dylan said in a southern accent: "Hello there, folks. Great to be here in Miami and I sure wish I could really be with all you folks now, but I'm kinda tied up. Anyway, God bless y'all and thanks for buyin' ma records."

Baez was curiously absent from the stage. She was at the airport, the Savoy press conferences, and on several legs of the provincial tour. En route to the Midlands and Liverpool, Joan rode in a separate car. She did not appear on Dylan's TV shows. I later asked Bob why she was along. Dylan: "She came on with me, man, and I didn't owe her nothing. As far as I'm concerned, I paid her back. I told her while we were in the States— that she couldn't sing with me. I told her that before we left. And she came on like a little kitten. . . . She's done everything I've done, man. She liked to watch and see what I do. . . . There is no place for her in my music. . . . She don't fit into my music. Hey, I can fit into her music, but she doesn't fit into my music, my show. It would have been dumb. It wouldn't have added to me, and it would have been misleading to the audience." Joan had never appeared in Britain, and was keen to establish herself there. It was only natural that she would have expected reciprocity in getting some time on his concert tour. She didn't, and was visibly shaken; Baez's "farewell kiss" is her exit cue from *Don't Look Back*. Joan later said: "I thought he would do what I had done with him, would introduce me. . . . I was very, very hurt. I was miserable." She felt she should have left after the first concert, but, as is typical of the Diamond and Rust twins, she felt an inner compulsion to stay.

After a quick holiday in Portugal, which Dylan later referred to in his song "Sara," he returned to England the last week in May to tape the BBC-TV show. The taping was delayed two weeks because Dylan came down with a stomach virus and spent several days in St. Mary's Hospital in Paddington. According to Richard Fariña, Joan, who had been traveling independently since Dylan's Liverpool concert, arrived at the hospital room to visit him. His wife, Sara, appeared at the door and said Dylan didn't want to see anybody. Joan, dazed and hurt, left. On June 8, Dylan showed up at the TV studio looking pale and tired, and finished taping two half-hour segments on June 24.

Despite the breadth of his British triumph, the folk old guard was still ready to pounce. To the purists, led by Ewan MacColl and Peggy Seeger, success spelled compromise. In September 1965, in a *Melody Maker* interview, MacColl predicted: " 'We're going to get lots of copies of Dylan— one foot in folk and one foot in pop. . . . Dylan is to me the perfect symbol of the anti-artist in our society. He is against everything—the last resort of someone who doesn't really want to change the world. . . . I think his poetry is punk. It's derivative and terribly old hat. . . . Dylan songs accept the world as it is.' " Such dissenting voices aside, Dylan had captured both the mass and the leadership of British taste. On May 15, 1965, a seventeen-year-old lad from Chilham, Kent, stole a Dylan album cover from a chemist's shop in Canterbury. "Yes, I admit it," the fan told the judge. "I knew there wasn't even a record in there, but Bob Dylan is the greatest."

DON'T LOOK BACK

During the 1965 English tour, hand-held cameras were focused on Dylan for about twenty hours, as he improvised dialogue and starred in his first feature-length film. The film title, *Don't Look Back,* suggests an arch twist on *Look Back in Anger,* the 1950s play by John Osborne. The title also recalls the biblical story of Lot's wife. Released in 1967, the film earned as many raves as negative reviews. Until 1975, it played in isolated art and college theaters, portraying the urgency and confusion of Dylan on tour, onstage, backstage, at ease and ill at ease, in flight from fans, tilting with reporters. It was rereleased in 1982, and got feature treatment at the ICA in London.

Dylan's reactions to the film shifted. After he'd seen the unedited footage, he told me: "It's a documentary kind of thing. It's going to be just a piece of film, no matter what it turns out to be. . . . [Donn] Pennebaker [the filmmaker] is the best. . . ." Later, Dylan was at loggerheads with Pennebaker and Grossman about the film's portrait of a man too restless to sit for portraits. After some years during which he was apparently embarrassed by the film, he changed his mind again. By 1971, Dylan told me: "In the last couple of years, I've come to like the film a lot more than I used to." Did he mean the man who said "don't look back" was ready to look back at a portion of his life? "No, I meant don't look back *over your shoulder,"* Dylan joked.

Don't Look Back includes a half dozen stage performances, a few songs offstage by Dylan, Baez, and Donovan, arguments, interviews, plenty of *cinéma vérité* confusion-cum-realism. As the film begins in a London alleyway, "Subterranean Homesick Blues," the only electric music of the film, is playing. Dylan, large in the foreground with Allen Ginsberg at the edge of the frame, holds posterlike cards of the lyrics, and throws down each card in sync with his singing. A dressing-room scene follows, then the London airport crowd, excerpts of the press conference there. Then, the Savoy conference. Dylan closeted with Neuwirth and Alan Price discussing the "Donovan" question. The film, continuing its staccato tempo, cuts to a radio interview: "How did it all begin for you?" We see Dylan singing at the civil rights rally in Greenwood, Mississippi. The first concert sequence: "Times Changing" in Sheffield. A *Guardian* writer phones in his review. Backstage, students try to get Dylan to reveal "his philosophy." Grossman being surly with a Savoy official. Backstage in Liverpool with girl fans. After the Leicester performance, Dylan talks with rock musicians. Next, a Beatles-like escape from fans.

An affecting scene follows: Dylan and British singer Marianne Faithfull watch Joan sing some Hank Williams, some Dylan, and the classic dirge "Long Black Veil." In *cinéma vérité* at its best, Dylan and Neuwirth chat about country singer Bill Anderson. Next, Dylan between Joan and John

Mayall in a Birmingham-bound car, with Grossman and Burns negotiating a TV fee, playing the old agents' game of illusory counteroffers. Jump cuts and quick shots: concerts, parties, talk sessions, more car conversations, more performances. Dominating the conclusion are two scenes of Dylan facing two interviewers, a science student, and Horace Judson, then the arts reporter for *Time*'s London bureau. An embattled Dylan confoundingly refuses to sum up his thinking, taunting his interviewers like a matador. Dylan, while seeming a lout, is fighting for his individuality: Expect him to communicate through his work, but don't expect him to explain himself.

Don't Look Back was produced by Grossman and John Court, and Leacock Pennebaker, Inc., the firm Pennebaker formed with Richard Leacock, another cameraman. Concerts were recorded by Bob Van Dyke. Jones and Howard Alk and Neuwirth alternated recording, lighting, filming, and editing. Donn Pennebaker designed power stations and ran an electronics company. After making some documentaries for the YWCA and the Boy Scouts, he worked on small films, *New York, New York, Daybreak Express,* a documentary on John F. Kennedy, and Norman Mailer's *Maidstone.* After *Don't Look Back,* Pennebaker went on to film *Monterey Pop* and the 1969 Toronto Pop Festival.

Don't Look Back has a peculiar life because Dylan is an extraordinary person," Pennebaker said in 1971. "A lot of people still can't stand the idea that this 'degenerate long-hair hippie' could be somebody important, but he keeps a peculiar sort of balance. People want to know about him and they're never going to. . . . His whole interest is his charisma, the mystery. . . . With a music film, your first concern is the actual performance. . . . You must use a hand-held camera—that's fundamental. You cannot become part of a piece of music unless you are free to move that camera in any direction at any time. The idea of the film was from his wife, Sara. She worked with me for about one year as liaison between us and Time-Life. One day, February or March, 1965, Albert came in: 'Would you like to do something with Bob?' Of course, I said I would. Albert put up an initial three thousand or four thousand dollars and then we approached Bob Altshuler [vice-president of press and public affairs, CBS Records Group] with the idea of supplying some footage for Columbia. We offered him half the film for only five thousand dollars, but Columbia turned it down. I wanted to make the film without loading any burden onto Bob. . . . I shot about twenty-five thousand feet, at about two and one half reels a day. I was really hoarding film. I'd shoot a line of a song here, another line there. When we got down to the editing for two or three weeks in the winter of 1965–66, I found that we had wasted very little film. . . .

"There were a lot of big hassles with Albert. I wanted to go to the quality art theaters. I felt the film, like Dylan, should be hard to see. Doing it in theaters calls for a lot of money. Some big Hollywood producers Albert brought in didn't know what to make of the film. We got the Art Theater Guild, with forty houses, interested in distributing. At first, we never called it a documentary. We regarded it as an entertainment film. We opened it in San Francisco, [in May 1967] because we were frankly afraid we would be killed in a big New York release. After four months outside New York, at all forty houses of the Guild, we brought the film to the Thirty-fourth Street East and it was a hit with critics and audience.

"Dylan's great strength is in the questions he leaves unanswered. It never occurred to me to supply *information* in the film. Dylan asked me if I could take out the fight in the hotel room. . . . He didn't want it to indicate that was the way he lived. I understood, but thought there were more important considerations. 'You are what you think you are.' What a marvelous thing to say! It's the fundamental existentialist concept. And Dylan's doing it, not like Norman Mailer, writing about it; that's what the film's about, so it couldn't be left out.

"When Bob first saw the film, in North Hollywood, he was shocked and said we needed a lot of changes. The second time he saw it, with a writing pad in his hand, he came out saying 'no changes.' These guys (Kennedy, Mailer, Dylan) don't say lines. They would never put up with the ceremony of a written script. The central problem is that the person shooting must do the editing." The film's cost, including editing, music rights, and the blowup from 16mm to 35mm, came to about $40,000, Pennebaker told me. The film's box-office gross was more than a million dollars, one third of which was the producer's gross. Leacock and Pennebaker were splitting about $100,000 with Dylan.

Critical reaction to *Don't Look Back* centered on Dylan, not the film. Gleason: ". . . really about the problem of the artist in communicating with his audience and . . . the problem of the Old World in communicating with the New Youth and vice versa. . . . Dylan can be shown snarling, swearing, singing, smiling, shining, and sulking and still be the genius he is, and this honesty in portrayal makes the film very valuable. . . ."

Joe Morgenstern of *Newsweek:* "Pennebaker's camera is as much an intruder into Dylan's life as any of the other intruders it records. . . . The honest truth it shows is a singing genius who does not know where his songs come from, and who is brave enough and wise enough not to let it bother him too much. . . ." *Life*'s reviewer found the film engrossing, but complained: ". . . the picture is incomplete. What we do not see, or feel, is what is going on inside Dylan. Things happen to, and around him, and he reacts. . . . Dylan is skilled at guarding his personal life and feelings from the public and he does not let down for the movie."

Richard Goldstein, in *The New York Times,* called Dylan "Shakespeare and Judy Garland to my generation. We trust what he tells us. But his flagrant mysterioso—even if it is sincere—evokes hungry demands for at least a penetrating glimpse of the oracle-star. . . . Pennebaker's camera is almost too willing to play cinematic straight man. Without a program, you can hardly tell the vaudeville from the vérité.... [The film] poses the same problem ... New Journalism presents.... With realism heightened by novelistic technique, how do you tell fact from formula?" Citing Grossman's role as producer, Goldstein called the film "at best a commissioned portrait. It's an artistic job, but still a bit flattering around the edges."

Some ads, and the Ballantine paperback of the film, carried such blasts as: "The worst film I've ever seen. Repetitious, boring, as organized as a small boy's room." *Kansas City Star:* "Should be buried ... a cheap, in part, a dirty movie, if it is a movie at all ... certainly not for moviegoers who bathe and/or shave. It is 'underground' and should be buried at once. Burn a rag, as was once said of filth." "Phew!"—Cleveland *Plain Dealer.* "Boring, off-color home movie of the neighborhood's biggest brat blowing his nose for 90 minutes."—Atlanta *Journal.*

Dylan joined Pennebaker during the 1966 tour for the rarely shown *Eat the Document,* made for ABC-TV. Although he often received scripts, he didn't find one that "seemed right to me," for a film encore, until a part was written in for him in Sam Peckinpah's *Pat Garrett and Billy the Kid.* Two of Dylan's frequent film courtiers were Harold Leventhal, manager of Alan Arkin, and Arlo Guthrie, star of *Alice's Restaurant,* of which Leventhal was associate producer. In 1969, Leventhal arranged an Arkin-Dylan meeting, but, according to Leventhal, "Bob didn't communicate." By early 1971, Leventhal said that if Dylan wanted to star in almost any film, Leventhal "could pick up the phone and get two million dollars" to produce it. By 1975, Leventhal showed Dylan, among others, the final script of *Bound for Glory,* a film biography of Woody Guthrie. Leventhal said he was relieved that Dylan didn't want to play Woody's role.

For a while, Dylan appeared to be sidling into films by way of Marlon Brando. After meeting Brando in September 1965, Dylan told me: "I hung out with Marlon Brando so much, in California and also when he came here. We talked here about four or five hours. He came to a concert and he called me in New York. Marlon Brando's a friend of mine, I actually consider him a friend of mine.... I love him. Somehow, Brando pulled through all the bullshit he had from the press and the public." As early as 1964, Brando was considering a script, *Fargo,* which had a role for Brando's younger brother. Agent Ben Shapiro thought Brando and Dylan should meet. In September 1965, Ben arranged a party after Dylan's Hollywood Bowl concert, just a modest affair with about three hundred guests—like Burgess Meredith, Dennis Hopper, John Barrymore, Jr., Jean-Pierre Aumont, James Coburn—"a cross section of Hollywood society," but it didn't result in a film.

The year 1967 saw the premiere of a ninety-five-minute documentary, *Festival,* produced and directed by Murray Lerner from miles of footage of Newport folk festivals from 1963 to 1966. Dylan, one of fifty performers, sang "Tambourine Man" and "Maggie's Farm." Peter, Paul and Mary sang "Times Changing." Dylan's flirtations with stage and film often caused speculation. Leonard Lyons's column in 1965: "Dylan probably will star on Broadway next season." Not another word of that project, or of Dylan starring in *Catcher in the Rye*. In 1963–64, Dylan was touted as a likely co-star in a Les Pine script, *Daffy*, with Hayley Mills. In June 1965, Allen Ginsberg told the London *Daily Mail* he was writing a film for Dylan: " 'It will be shot all over the world, including Russia, we hope.' " Dylan often joked about a film he was either writing with or for Ginsberg. In 1966, Dylan reportedly held talks with Paul Sills, a Chicago writer-comedian, about a Hollywood film. By 1970, reports circulated that Dylan was writing the music for a Broadway version of *A Face in the Crowd*, but he later denied it.

Dylan had long wanted to direct a film biography of Woody Guthrie, but in 1975, Harold Leventhal told Bob he could not be considered because Hal Ashby had just been signed. Bob almost immediately uncorked the Rolling Thunder Revue, his national tour, for which many stars joined him, and assembled his own crew to film it. From that venture resulted Dylan's most venturesome, but troubled, film effort, *Renaldo and Clara*. As usual, Dylan wanted to run his own show. For his earlier pivotal drama at Newport '65, Dylan had not needed a film crew or camera, just an electric guitar and an outlet into which he could plug his amplifiers.

"BRING BACK COUSIN EMMY!"

At the Newport Festival in July 1965, Dylan played three songs with a rock backing and unleashed a storm of derision. From the start, Newport '65 did not augur well. Baez sported her newest protégé, Donovan, on her arm. At an afternoon workshop, Alan Lomax, folk purist, and Albert Grossman clashed openly, over the way Lomax had introduced Grossman's soon-to-be clients, The Paul Butterfield Blues Band. Hosting the "Bluesville Workshop," Lomax, never a skilled diplomat, waxed elegiac over the panel's black bluesman. He challenged the Butterfield Band in words to this effect: "Let's see if these Chicago boys know what the blues are all about." After the Butterfield Band had played to an ovation, Grossman belabored Lomax for his patronizing introduction. Invective began to fly, and shortly the giant of folklore and the titan of folk business were wrestling on the ground. Onlookers separated the mastodons. While the scuffle had been personal, it had some theoretical roots. Lomax's concept of rock as black man's music was only resented in some folk circles.

Typically, Dylan told no more people than necessary about his plans for Sunday night. He relished the dramatic departure. He couldn't envision a backfire. Since January, his two electric singles and an album had done fabulously well. At the festival, the Butterfield Band and The Chambers Brothers this year, and Muddy Waters the year before, had shown that amplified-electric instrumentation and heavy rhythm were not taboo. It was, to Dylan, "all music, no more, no less."

In the 1965 Newport program book, I had appealed for tolerance toward folk-related popular and country music: "The middle-class collegiate audience of folk music is only a part of the music scene. The tastes, interests and social attitudes of the high-school student or drop-out, the working-class kid, must also be appreciated." I was by no means preaching to the converted, for all too many folk fans, while twisting their radio dials to The Beatles, other English rock groups, and R & B, felt their traditional music embodied the only "healthy" elements, the only "honest" verities.

To compound Dylan's difficulties, Seeger announced that the Sunday night final program was a message from today's folk musicians to a newborn baby about the world we live in. Unfortunately, this theme did not correspond to Dylan's conception of his performance. Dylan's Sunday segment was sandwiched between Cousin Emmy and the Sea Island singers, two very traditional acts. Cousin Emmy's high spot was "Turkey in the Straw." Dylan had to do his bit at the appointed spot, without a sound check for his pick-up band.

At the festival, Al Kooper, whose session work had already impressed Dylan, was strolling about when Albert said Bob was looking for him. Dylan told Kooper he wanted to bring the "Rolling Stone" sound onstage. Three members of the Butterfield Band were recruited: guitarist Mike Bloomfield, drummer Sam Lay, and bassist Jerome Arnold. At a party in Newport, Dylan completed his band with pianist Barry Goldberg. In a Newport mansion, Dylan rehearsed this instant group until dawn. They kept their plan secret until they walked onstage, Dylan, in a matador-outlaw orange shirt and black leather, carrying an electric guitar. From the moment the group swung into a rocking electric version of "Maggie's Farm," the Newport audience registered hostility. As the group finished "Farm," there was some reserved applause and a flurry of boos. Someone shouted: "Bring back Cousin Emmy!" The microphones and speakers were all out of balance, and the sound was poor and lopsided. For even the most ardent fan of the new music, the performance was unpersuasive. As Dylan led his band into "Rolling Stone," the audience grew shriller: "Play folk music! . . . Sell out! . . . This is a folk festival! . . . Get rid of that band!" Dylan began "It Takes a Train to Cry," and the applause diminished as the heckling increased. Dylan and the group disappeared offstage, and there was a long, clumsy silence. Peter Yarrow urged Bob to return and gave him his acoustic guitar. As Bob returned on the stage alone, he discovered he didn't have the right harmonica. "What are you doing to me?" Dylan demanded of Yarrow. To shouts for "Tambourine Man," Dylan said: "OK, I'll do that one for you." The older song had a palliative effect and won strong applause. Then Dylan did "It's All Over Now, Baby Blue," singing adieu to Newport, good-bye to the folk-purist audience.

Backstage, there had been almost as much excitement as out front. At the first sound of the amplified instruments, Pete Seeger had turned a bright purple and begun kicking his feet and flailing his arms. (A festival official said later: "I had never seen any trace of violence in Pete, except at that moment. He was *furious* with Dylan!") Reportedly, one festival board member—probably Seeger—was so upset that he threatened to pull out the entire electrical wiring system. Cooler heads cautioned that plunging the audience into the dark might cause a real riot.

At a party later that night, The Chambers Brothers played rock for dancing, and a discotheque ambience descended on Newport. I asked George Wein, the festival's technical producer, why he didn't like folk-rock. He countered: "You've been brainwashed by the recording industry." Off in a corner, a sullen Dylan sat on the lap of Betsy Siggins, of Cambridge's Club 47. He looked stunned, shaken, and disappointed.

(The outbursts at Newport that Sunday night, July 25, 1965, brought to mind another startling event in music history. At the premiere of Stravinsky's "The Rite of Spring," on May 29, 1913, at the Théâtre des Champs-Élysées, the Paris audience was torn in two by Stravinsky's pioneering score and Nijinsky's choreography. When the curtains parted on the ballet troupe, a storm broke loose. Stravinsky stomped backstage. Carl Van Vechten wrote later that many outraged listeners thought the Stravinsky work "was a blasphemous attempt to destroy music as an art." There was so much racket, the orchestra played unheard. Catcalls, boos, and hissing interrupted music and dancing. People in the gallery called out for a doctor, two doctors, even a dentist! Backstage, pandemonium. Diaghilev, the famous choreographer, thought the only way to curb the noise was to turn off the lights. He kept ordering the electricians to turn the house lights on, then off. On a chair in the wings, Nijinsky stood, with Stravinsky behind him, "beating out the rhythms with his fists and shouting numbers to the dancers like a coxswain." At the end, orchestra, dancers, leaders of the production, and audience, were completely exhausted.)

As cast and audience left Newport '65, a definite break in community brotherhood had occurred. Dylan had served another declaration of aesthetic independence. Later, in *Sing Out!,* Jim Rooney, a gentle Boston musician, wrote: "It was disturbing to the Old Guard ... Bob is no longer a Neo-Woody Guthrie.... The highway he travels now is unfamiliar to those who bummed around ... during the Depression. He travels by plane ... the mountains and valleys he knows are those of the mind—a mind extremely aware of the violence of the inner and outer world. 'The people' so loved by Pete Seeger are 'the mob' so hated by Dylan.... They seemed to understand that night for the first time what Dylan has been trying to say for over a year—that he is not theirs or anyone else's and they didn't like what they heard and booed.... Can there be no songs as violent as the age? Must a folk song be of mountains, valleys, and love between my brother and my sister all over this land? Do we allow for despair only in the blues? ... The only one in the entire festival who questioned our position was Bob Dylan. Maybe he didn't put it in the best way. Maybe he was rude. But he shook us. And that is why we have poets and artists."

I saw Dylan twice in New York the week after the festival. He still seemed stunned and distressed that he had sparked such animosity. He was shaken that people had yelled "Get rid of that electric guitar!" But he refused to enter squabbles. Of his introducing electric music at Newport and the years of controversy that ensued, Dylan said, over and over again, "It was honest. It was honest."

9

INSIDE THE COLISEUM

"If you live under the magnifying glass of public curiosity, just as your every honest act seems heroic to some, so your every weakness seems criminal to others. Even your honest acts come into question. . . . Readers are too despotic. Once in love with a poet for something, they expect it to appear again and again, forever. They interpret any change in a poet's character, and consequently in his poetry, not as a normal development, but as a retreat from principle. . . .

—YEVTUSHENKO[1]

"The poet skims off the best of life and puts it in his work. That is why his work is beautiful and his life bad."

—TOLSTOY

"God, I'm glad I'm not me."

—DYLAN, READING A NEWSPAPER
ACCOUNT OF HIMSELF, 1965

The booing didn't stop at Newport, but continued sporadically at Dylan's American concerts until October 1965, and resumed during his world tour until late spring 1966. In July 1965, Dylan began a year of personal stress. He was lionized now by the pop world as he was being rejected by many folkniks who had once deified him. Dylan was imitated, castigated, emulated, berated, upbraided, and celebrated. All he really wanted to do was write and sing. "Oh, the hours/I've spent inside the Coliseum,/Dodging lions and wastin' time . . ."[2]

Dylan sustained himself with little sleep and food and with what he once called "a lot of medicine." As public pressures devoured him, he privately planned to marry. Debate about his going electric raged on. Singer-actor Theodore Bikel said of the Newport debacle: "Dylan made a tactical mistake. He should have started with acoustic music, then gone into electric. He didn't bother to reach out. He didn't talk to the audience. A lesser person would have given up performing after such a reception."

Dylan remained silent about the Newport noise until his August 28, 1965, concert at the Forest Hills Music Festival in Queens. Charlie Rothschild telephoned *The New York Times* to offer an interview. From my notes: "I'm not really bothered by Newport, because I know in my own mind what I'm doing. If anyone has imagination, he'll know what I'm doing. If they can't understand my songs, they're missing something. . . . I'll have some electricity at Forest Hills. At Newport, whoever was in charge of the sound didn't know what was happening. This time I'll have . . . a couple or three or four new songs. Time goes by very fast up there on stage. I have to think of what not to do, rather than what to do. I get very bored. I can't sing 'With God on Our Side' for 15 years."

That summer, only Dylan, Sinatra, and Streisand had sold out the fifteen thousand seats at Forest Hills, grossing seventy-five thousand dollars for one evening. At Dylan's concert, after a warm-up group, Murray the K (Kaufman), the pop disc jockey, canted: "It's not rock, it's not folk, it's a new thing called Dylan. . . . Dylan is definitely what's happening." The fans waited, while Grossman, backstage, blew his top. Who let Murray the K up there? I'll sue you all, roared Grossman.

Dylan began an acoustic set with "She Belongs to Me," followed by "Ramona," "Gates of Eden," and "Love Minus Zero." The reception was respectful, the applause generous. Dylan was in control. "Desolation Row" had a stunning debut, the audience hanging on every grotesque image. Then, "Baby Blue" and "Tambourine Man." After intermission, Dylan returned with Robbie Robertson on electric guitar, Al Kooper on electric piano and organ, Harvey Brooks on electric bass, and Levon Helm on drums. The band and high-voltage singing raised a crackling intensity. At the end of each number, there were boos and shouts of "We want the old Dylan!" After "Maggie's Farm," someone shouted: "Traitor!" Others yelled: "Where's Ringo?" and "Play folk music!" In a confused jangle of music and audience discord, someone yelled: "Scum bag!" Dylan remarked: "Ah, come on now." Some "listeners" threw fruit, and some young rockers were evicted. One prankster got onstage and knocked Al Kooper off his chair. Dylan told the band to keep playing the intro to "Thin Man." After a five-minute intro, the palliative worked. The muted backing for "It Ain't Me, Babe" elicited very few catcalls. By the time Dylan did "Rolling Stone," already a hit single, the audience mostly sang along! Critics who held that Newport '65 had been the wrong way to introduce the new music were wrong. At Forest Hills, the sound was right, the programming intelligent, the presentation persuasive. The problem lay with the audience.

The Village Voice gave Forest Hills a front-page headline: MODS, ROCKERS FIGHT OVER NEW THING CALLED "DYLAN." *Variety:* "Dylan has apparently evolved too fast for some of his young followers, who are ready for radical change in practically everything else." My story in *The Times* before the concert (headlined POP SINGERS AND SONG WRITERS RACING DOWN BOB DYLAN'S ROAD) and an enthusiastic review (DYLAN CONQUERS UNRULY AUDIENCE) elicited more letters—pro and con—than anything I had written in seven years.

The booing was virtually over in the East. When Dylan played Carnegie Hall on October 1, he heard cheers for the new music. In the interim, he had spent three buoying weeks in Los Angeles. "I was almost disappointed that there was no trouble at the L.A. concert," he told me. At sold-out Carnegie, Dylan's backup was Levon & The Hawks. After "Rolling Stone," dozens rushed the stage screaming "More!" "I didn't know you felt that way," Dylan said drily. Before an encore, he mumbled: "I didn't think you would like it." One commentator likened the concert to a "Defend Bob Dylan Rally."

FOLK INTO ROCK

Folk-rock became a runaway music-business trend and a clattering controversy. This outgrowth of Dylan's fusion of symbolic poetry and folk music had a major impact on the pop market. Having rejected political leadership, Dylan had assumed musical leadership. As we've seen, he had potential folk-rock sound on his first album, four electric tracks for his second album, and a single with a band as early as 1962. Even on his bandless fourth album, one heard implicit folk-rock beat. As for protest folk-rock, Dylan also set the style. Sonny and Cher and P. F. Sloan, who wrote "Eve of Destruction," were following Dylan of two years earlier. As a craze, folk-rock ran its course by the end of 1965, but dozens of styles that grew out of folk-rock are still flourishing.

Folk-rock roots lay deep in the sociology, messages, protest and social commentary of blues and country music. Jazz had also been an expression of rebellion. In the 1950s, folk-rockery was to be heard in Chuck Berry and the rockabilly stories of Johnny Cash, in Eddie Cochran's "Summertime

Blues," in songs by Phil Spector, Leiber and Stoller, Mann and Weil. Trini
Lopez rocked "The Hammer Song" and "Lemon Tree" in 1963 and 1964.
There had been poetry in pop ballads by the Gershwins, Rodgers and Hart,
Cole Porter. Musical theater had long delivered messages.

In 1963, American protest had centered on civil rights; in Britain, it was
reflected in Ban the Bomb marches. In autumn 1964, massive student
demonstrations at the University of California at Berkeley ushered in the
new dissent. The Free Speech Movement foreshadowed student uprisings
in Paris and Prague in 1968, Athens and Bangkok in 1973. American collegians were questioning not only the form and substance of their education but also the bias of its teachers and textbooks and the relevance of
studies to daily life. Students were also protesting the support the military-industrial complex was giving university research. Some "masters of
war" were wearing mortar boards and gowns. In such a climate, the new
music could only thrive.

Off campus, an even greater social malaise was developing in American
involvement in the Indo-Chinese war. Lyndon Johnson was leading
America deeper into what Pete Seeger's song called "The Big Muddy," ordering mass troop shipments, stepping up the draft. Peace campaigns affected more people than civil rights did. A rage for protest and comment
made folk-rock considerably more than a simple merger of styles. In *The
Making of a Counter Culture,* Theodore Roszak wrote that "one is apt to
find out more about ... youth ... by paying attention to posters ... and
dance—and especially to the pop music, which now knits together the
whole 13 to 30 age group." Earlier, Dylan had been regarded as the voice
of his generation, although he spoke for only a radical fringe. Now, in
front of folk-rock's greater audience, he represented his constituency.

The Byrds, who in 1965 cut "Mr. Tambourine Man," one of the decade's most successful singles, assisted Dylan's entry into rock, and later
into country music. The Byrds, whose early publicity was handled by Billy
James, frequently recorded Dylan songs; as they grew more popular, they
took Dylan with them.

The chief Byrd, twelve-string guitarist Jim (later Roger) McGuinn, had
played with The Chad Mitchell Trio, The Limeliters, and Bobby Darin.
McGuinn saw that in 1964, folk music "was getting very commercial and
plastic packaged in Cellophane.... I wanted to get into something else."
In summer 1964, McGuinn met Gene Clark at the Troubadour in Los
Angeles, and they formed a group. David Crosby then joined them, and
they rehearsed as Jet Set. Jet Set's first album, *Preflyte,* which included a
weak "Mr. Tambourine Man," wasn't a direct hit. Manager Jim Dickson
asked Chris Hillman to join. Drummer Mike Clarke rounded out the
group. McGuinn: "I saw this gap, with Dylan and The Beatles leaning toward each other in concept. That's where we aimed." And that's where
they hit. To avoid sounding effeminate, they eschewed "The Birds." By
1968, Brian Epstein, the Beatles' manager, was touting a new group, The

Cyrcle. He told me the y spelling had a winning mystique. The Byrds cut a single for Elektra as The Beefeaters, but the single failed and Elektra dropped them. In January 1965, signed to Columbia, The Byrds rerecorded "Tambourine Man."

How The Byrds got "Tambourine Man" is unclear. Most likely Dickson obtained a copy before Dylan made an official acetate, probably as an outtake from Dylan's fourth album, with Jack Elliott also singing. Hillman claimed Dickson "picked the song; we didn't really like it or even understand it at the time, but he drove it down our throats until we realized what it was." McGuinn saw Dylan in L.A. "and we showed him our arrangement of 'Tambourine.' " Dylan said: "Wow, man, you can dance to that!" McGuinn described Dylan as "astounded." "We sang him some of his other stuff and he didn't even recognize them. We got pretty chummy for a while, but he was the guru and we were the students. He didn't start influencing me until I started singing his material. But then he started doing to his own music what he had done with his earlier stuff—so we couldn't really do any more of his music because he was doing it himself. I got the feeling that he was guilty about making all the bread."

One of the ironies of the second recording of "Tambourine Man" was that, instrumentally, McGuinn was the only Byrd on the recording. The others couldn't make the session, so the famous bass introduction was by Larry Knechtel, with Hal Blaine on drums and Leon Russell on second guitar. The Byrds put crucial vocal harmonies in later. There were three other Dylan songs on their first Columbia album. The "Tambourine" single was released in March 1965, while The Byrds were at Ciro's in Los Angeles. Everyone who was anyone, including Dylan, showed up. SRO at Ciro's marked a new American hip scene. Hollywood danced again! "Tambourine" topped American charts in three months. In June, The Byrds released another single, "All I Really Want to Do," but in the States, a Sonny and Cher cover version eclipsed it. McGuinn said what most disappointed him "was Dylan coming up to me and saying, 'They beat you, man'—and he lost faith in me. He was shattered . . . his material had been bastardized; there we were, the defenders and protectors of his music, and we'd let Sonny and Cher get away with it!" In July, The Byrds became the first American group to top the British charts since The Beatles breakout. They made a lightning British tour, but Britain would not easily yield to an American group, and the tour flopped.

The Byrds returned to Columbia's studios. They tried "Baby Blue" and "Times Changing," and decided neither was right. Finally, they did Seeger's "Turn! Turn! Turn!" In five weeks, it became number one. McGuinn once described The Byrds as "an electronic magazine." When they moved from folk-rock into acid-rock, raga-rock, and country-rock, they often chose Dylan songs as vehicles. In 1971, McGuinn told Penny Valentine of Sounds: " 'Dylan's always been a step or two ahead of me. . . . I think what I did to lose his favor was "Ballad of Easy Rider." When I wrote that track for the film he had something to do with it, and so his name came up on the original screen credits. He called me up very angrily and he said: "Take that off. I told you not to give me any credit. I do things like that for people every day. I just gave you a line—that's all." Which actually was true, we hadn't really got deeply involved together over that song.' " By 1973, Crosby and Hillman and others had joined influential 1970s rock bands. McGuinn, the original Byrd, was recording solo sessions on the West Coast when Dylan dropped in to wish him well. To seal the renewed friendship, Dylan played harmonica behind the lead track, "I'm So Restless," on the album *Roger McGuinn.* By 1975, McGuinn featured in Dylan's Rolling Thunder Revue.

Back in 1965, Dylan was soon appropriated by the music business as the trend of the year, "the biggest thing" since The Beatles. *Variety,* September 8, 1965: "Bob Dylan a One-Man Music Biz in Creation of Rock-Folk Genre?" At that point, eight Dylan songs, half of them his own recordings, were in the Top Forty. *Variety* caught the sense of music-business stampeding: "This week, Dino, Desi and Billy are rush-releasing 'Chimes of Freedom,' Sonny and Cher have etched 'Blowin' In the Wind' and Cher is to include three Dylan tunes in her next album. . . . David Rose will incorporate two Dylan ditties in his next album . . . and The Liverpool Five . . . was also doing a Dylan tune." *Variety* concluded: "You need a computer to keep track."

A hit of mid-1965 embodying folk-rock protest was "Eve of Destruction," by P. F. Sloan, recorded by Barry McGuire, formerly of The New Christy Minstrels. "Eve" cataloged social inequities and warned that if change were not imminent, a nuclear holocaust was. Still, "Eve," not Dylan's "Subterranean," swam right to the Top Forty radio mainstream. Released July 26, its easy beat and puerile discontent won heavy airplay in August. Then the censorship began in earnest. A number of Top Forty stations and the ABC radio network blacklisted "Eve." Sociologist R. Serge Denisoff, in *The Journal of Popular Music,* found the song's march-like qualities similar to "Spanish Civil War songs and, indeed, to Nazi hymns." Perhaps because the indictments of "Eve" were so broad, Denisoff found that only 14 percent among a sampling of college undergraduates understood the theme, and only 45 percent understood part of the message. "Eve" was opposed by Right and Left. *Sing Out!* called the popularization of protest a confusing sop. A third-rate group, The Spokesmen, recorded an "answer" song, "Dawn of Correction," which saw nothing but beauty and optimism.

Dozens of Dylan-inspired folk-rock hits came out during summer 1965. "It Ain't Me, Babe" provided a chart entry for The Turtles. Both Sonny and Cher tried to sing like Dylan and aped his general style. Their "I Got You, Babe" was an instant hit. After they were asked to leave a restaurant because of their wild clothes, they ground out a quasi-protest folk-rock tune, "Laugh at Me," that was soon selling five thousand records a day!

Janis Ian, a fifteen-year-old *Broadside* alumna, wrote "Society's Child," commenting on interracial dating. Shunned by major labels, finally recorded on Verve/Folkways, it was systematically banned from radio. Other folk-protest songs returned in folk-rock garb: Buffy Sainte-Marie's "Universal Soldier," Ochs's "There but for Fortune," and several Donovan tunes. Only when Simon and Garfunkel overdubbed their acoustic "Sounds of Silence" with a rhythmic beat did they emerge from obscurity in their second career. Some pop composers who had been striving to put substance into rock lyrics also surfaced. Barry Mann and Cynthia Weil's "We Gotta Get Out of This Place," which protested black ghetto life, was recorded by Eric Burdon and The Animals.

In September, Dylan told *Newsweek:* " 'I've never written a political song. Songs can't save the world. I've gone through all that.' " Pressed about his "enemies," Dylan replied: " 'They can crush you. They can kill you and lay you out on 42nd Street and put the hoses on you and flush you in the sewers. They can put you on a subway out to Coney Island and bury you on a Ferris Wheel. Who cares?' "

In her *New York Post* folk-rock survey on September 26, Nora Ephron: "He loves to read [letters] which call him: 'sellout, fink, fascist, Red.' " Dylan: " 'I probably will record with strings some time. It's just a different color. . . . I've never written anything hard to understand, not in my head anyway and nothing as far out as some of the old songs. They were out of sight. They say, 'Keep things simple.' Folk music is the only music where it *isn't* simple! It's weird, man, full of legend, myth, Bible and ghosts. . . .' And chaos? 'Yeah, chaos, watermelons, clocks, everything. . . .' " Sometimes Dylan got more credit than he wanted for fathering folk-rock. A *Life* survey was headed: "The Children of Bobby Dylan." Dylan hardly desired playing daddy to P. F. Sloan and Barry McGuire. The folk-rock craze stirred older singers. Bobby Vinton recorded "What Color Is a Man," Bobby Darin taped "Me and Mr. Hohner." Even Frankie Laine got the message. Not all singers espoused the sentiments of the new material. Glen Campbell recorded "Universal Soldier." Replying to right-wing static about this antiwar song, Campbell said, as reported in *Variety,* that those who burn their draft cards ought to "be hanged."

Shortly, such folk singers as Ochs, Andersen, Blue, Hamilton Camp, and Judy Collins added electric backing. In Britain, Donovan was exploring contemporary folk-rock permutations. The Manfred Mann group played "God on Our Side" on a British TV show, *Ready, Steady, Go.* By September 1965, British charts listed McGuire's "Eve" and Donovan's "Universal Soldier." By October, at least a dozen protest songs were on the British charts. The Hollies' "Too Many People" talked of overpopulation and ended with an H-bomb explosion. Jonathan King's "It's Good News Week," written for the group Hedgehoppers Anonymous, had a ridiculous lyric about bombs dropping. By December, British protest was no longer chic. Paul McCartney told *Melody Maker:* " 'Well, the songs are getting a bit silly, aren't they? . . . Protest songs make me concentrate too much on the lyric, which I don't like.' "

Folk-rock has been repeatedly misconstrued as entirely protest. "Turn! Turn! Turn!," Seeger's musical setting for a bit of Ecclesiastes, was certainly not a protest song. Murray the K preferred to call folk-rock attitude music. Although the folk-rock protest boom waned in early 1966, folk-rock attitude music has persisted. Before 1965, many assumed that pop and rock were supposed to be about trivia, to be not only nonintellectual but even anti-intellectual. This surface judgment belied a true understanding of popular music as social expression. Folk-rock, after its fad phase cooled, effected a major improvement of popular music.

HERESY TOWARD WHAT DOGMA?

As Dylan and folk-rock succeeded, orthodox folk fans shunned him as a heretic, an apostate. The prime architects of folk doctrine were academic folklorists and collectors who believed that "folklore ain't nothing but history born out of wedlock." The folklorists saw music (and legend, tale, art, and design) passed on orally as a great body of popular knowledge, craft, and art—a richness reared in poverty. These scholars could understandably decry the shallowness of mass culture, and the depredations that resulted whenever mass culture tried to adapt or "refine" folk materials. Most folklorists simply couldn't envision the potential benefits of folk elements in popular, commercial culture. Hard-core folk fanatics wanted music unamplified, without ballyhoo, framing, or staging.

These views were most flamboyantly advanced by Alan Lomax, no mean popularizer himself. In notes for a Carnegie Hall program Lomax produced in 1959, he stressed traditional artists, but was keenly aware of new developments in bluegrass and gospel. Although bluegrass modernized old-time string-band music, it won Lomax's approval. Black music, he felt, could withstand *any* permutations. But he drew the line at white rock and urban folk interpreters. By virtue of his forceful personality and his vast knowledge, Lomax spread his views widely.

In Britain, the two leading folk-song theorists were A. L. (Bert) Lloyd and Ewan MacColl, both articulate singing scholars. To MacColl, popularization meant linking folk music with the proletariat. He scorned middle-class, urban singer-songwriters, even though he was one. Since 1950, when the folk audience was small, *Sing Out!*, under editor Irwin Silber, had laid down the "correct line" on folk song. Trumpeted by these men, the folk aesthetic denounced show business and mass culture, and advocated that Leftist, humanist views always be reflected in folk song. Deviation from belief in "art as a weapon in the social and class struggle" meant a sellout to commercial forces. Small wonder that Dylan's freewheeling exploration was apostasy.

Silber's "Open Letter to Bob Dylan," published in *Sing Out!* in November 1964, was particularly sharp: "I saw at Newport how you had some-how lost contact with people . . . some of the paraphernalia of fame were getting in your way." Dylan was outraged that Silber was telling him in public how to write and behave. Why didn't Silber telephone or write a personal letter? Silber was just using him to sell his magazine. Dylan told Grossman that his songs were no longer available for publication in *Sing Out!* Aside from "Advice for Geraldine," he gave no direct reply. In September 1965, singer Ewan MacColl scourged Dylan again in *Sing Out!:* ". . . our traditional songs and ballads are the creations of extraordinarily talented artists, working inside disciplines formulated over . . . time . . . the present crop of contemporary American songs has been made by writers who are either unaware or incapable of working inside the disciplines, or are at pains to destroy them. 'But what of Bobby Dylan?' scream the out-raged teenagers of all ages . . . a youth of mediocre talent. Only a com-pletely non-critical audience, nourished on the watery pap of pop music, could have fallen for such tenth-rate drivel. 'But the poetry?' What poetry? The cultivated illiteracy of his topical songs or the embarrassing fourth-grade schoolboy attempts at free verse? The latter reminds me of elderly female schoolteachers clad in Greek tunics rolling hoops across lawns at weekend theater school. . . ."

Izzy Young's *Sing Out!* column for November 1965: "Dylan . . . has set-tled for a liaison with the music trade's Top-Forty Hit Parade . . . the charts require him to write rock-and-roll and he does. . . . Next year, he'll be writing rhythm and blues songs . . . the Polish polka will make it, and then he'll write them, too. . . ." Animosity reached its high-water mark in the *Sing Out!* of January 1966. Tom Paxton lashed out in a column headed "Folk Rot": ". . . it isn't folk, and if Dylan hadn't led, fed and bred it, no one would ever have dreamed of confusing it with folk music." Josh Dunson complained: "There is more protest and guts in one minute of good 'race music' than in two hours of folk-rock. . . ."

Although I had misgivings about performers like Barry McGuire and The Turtles, I took on the doctrinaires. In *The Sunday New York Times* on January 30, 1966, I swung a two-paragraph right hook at *Sing Out!* It un-leashed such a personalized and vitriolic storm that some people asked *The Times* to remove me! I was accused of nefarious dealings with big-business music interests. I had accused *Sing Out!* of disturbing narrow-mindedness and opposition to an avant-garde. It reminded me "of Soviet cultural organs denouncing Yevtushenko for heresies, prodding him back to the pastures of orthodoxy." Silber riposted testily, and my editors offered fees to Nat Hentoff and Paul Nelson, former managing editor of *Sing Out!,* to enter the debate. Hentoff and Nelson joined me in an affirmative view of folk-rock; Silber was on the run.

Dylan avoided the scuffle as much as he could, occasionally claiming he gave the matter little thought. But he was hurt, and he seemed curiously unable to "explain himself." His bitterness was tempered by satisfaction over his new audience. In *Broadside,* Gordon Friesen hoped the disputants would not destroy each other with vitriol. Ed Badeaux, the new managing editor of *Sing Out!,* wrote that Silber's views were personal, and that not all the editorial board agreed with him. Seeger somehow managed to stay above the scuffle. The battle lines remained relatively firm for years. After the folk-rock fad waned, and Dylan had surprised everyone with *John Wesley Harding,* the Old Guard ultimately relented. In Britain, in spite of initially rigorous objection to folk-rock, musical developments were even more imaginative. English, Scots, and Irish groups like The Incredible String Band, Steeleye Span, Fairport Convention, Albion Country Band, the JSD Band, and Gryphon, infused traditional materials with modern ideas. Eventually, in 1968, Silber rendered an eloquent *mea culpa* in the American Leftist weekly, *The Guardian:*

> Many of us who did not fully understand the dynamics of the political changes ... in America ... felt deserted by a poet who—we had come to believe—cared. And Dylan did desert—not us, but an outmoded style of values which had become unequal to the task of reclaiming America. "This land is *not* your land," Dylan told us in 1965. But some of us raised on the songs of Guthrie and Seeger ... inheritors of a superficial "Marxism" based on diluted Leninism and rationalized Stalinism were not ready to accept the revolutionary implications of Dylan's statements. Because if we accepted them ... we would have to act on them! So long as the diagnosis was chicken pox or mumps, we could think of applying some new medicine for our social ills. But the poets were telling us that it was cancer....
>
> Well, we learned. And for some of us older heads, the learning process was painful, involving, as it did, a reappraisal of so many basic assumptions.... Dylan is our poet—not our leader. Poets touch us where we want to be touched.... And if he fails to touch, the failure may be ours, not his. Is Dylan political, anti-political, apolitical, unpolitical? The question is sillier than it sounds. If they listen to and play Dylan's songs in Fayerweather Hall during "liberation week" and in Lincoln Park during "free elections week," then someone is communicating where it counts. The question remains: Why has Dylan remained the emotional essentialization of the S.D.S. generation?

Tom Paxton also admitted he'd been too harsh. To my knowledge, Izzy Young never recanted. MacColl chose not to write about Dylan again.

THE BAND

Since Hibbing, Dylan had dreamed of having his own band. As early as the studio-combo sessions for his second album, Dylan was thinking about sidemen. From 1961 to 1964, he loved to jam. Forming the right band

took time and work. Dylan gave thought to working with Paul Butterfield and his brilliant guitarist, Mike Bloomfield, but finally found his men
in summer 1965, in a Canadian-based group, The Hawks, later briefly
known as The Crackers, and, ultimately, The Band. Dylan's involvement
with The Band became what *Time* called "the most decisive moment in
rock history." It developed into one of the most enduring relationships
between a pop star and a supporting group. Their rapport began with musical ideas. The Band, steeped in blues, country, R & B, the old rock 'n'
roll, and the new rock, gave Dylan special camaraderie. The group had
been on the road—surviving, if not thriving—even longer than Bob. They
had a maturity Dylan sorely needed in a trying year.

The comradeship apparently did not entail great sacrifices. If Dylan
waxed outrageous, The Band could take it in its stride. When they joined
Dylan on his world tour of 1965–66, he continued to perform at least half
of his programs solo. But by the tour's end, The Band had become a
strongly stylistic entity, not just a backing group. They retained their own
identities in a field where stars without their backing groups, or the con-
verse, can be lost. The Band found that artistic and commercial success
unleashed creativity they scarcely knew they possessed.

For Robbie Robertson, Levon Helm, Rick Danko, Richard Manuel, and
Garth Hudson, the transition from years working out of Toronto with the
raunchy Ronnie Hawkins to Dylan was a quantum leap. As The Hawks,
they'd endured a grind only young musicians could romanticize: one-night
stands, discos, raffish honky-tonks, Saturday nights in stale-smelling gym-
nasiums, pounding out hard-beat music of minimal subtlety to raucous
crowds. When The Hawks left Hawkins in 1965, they were essentially
bluesmen. Dylan's world tour promised to be an enviable assignment, but
folkniks still roared at Dylan's going electric, and his five wicked messen-
gers were vilified for the electric shrieking and heavy-metal rock thrust.

Not until The Band's first album, *Music from Big Pink* (1968), did the
public really hear a totally individualistic group. The album ran counter to
the voguish, psychedelic acid-rock wave. The Band's music was played at
humane volumes with an understated, almost diffident stagecraft. *Big Pink*
took rock into serene pathways, filled with country breezes and a sort of
devotional religious timbre. There was something so rooted in our subconscious past as to evoke a church in a peaceful valley. *Big Pink* followed
Dylan's *John Wesley Harding,* and the two albums were on nearly every list
of the best 1968 albums. The two albums' sedative influence on pop was
almost immediate. Dylan found solace, healing, and rebirth in the country. The Band followed him, geographically and aesthetically, into the
same curative pastures of plenty.

John Hammond, Jr., reportedly "discovered" The Hawks at a Toronto
gig in 1964. Hammond asked three Hawks to back him for his spring 1965
taping of his Vanguard album *So Many Roads.* Listed as sidemen were
Jaime R. Robertson on guitar, Mark Levon Helm on drums, and Eric

Hudson on Hammond organ, along with C. D. Musselwhite, Bloomfield, and Jimmy Lewis. Hammond's enthusiasm about The Hawks spread. Mary Martin, Grossman's executive secretary, had heard The Hawks on visits home to Toronto and was ecstatic, possibly earlier than Hammond.

"Easy enough" to get together, Dylan once said, not mentioning the hours of jamming and rehearsing, discussions, exploring, and soul-searching to determine if The Hawks spoke Dylanese and if Dylan spoke Hawk-talk. Robbie Robertson could only vaguely describe those important early meetings: ". . . Let's just say that he didn't call us and we didn't call him . . . that's all I can remember. . . . We'd had one of his albums . . . and we all liked it, but it didn't snap us like that, you know. And we had no idea he was as strong as we later found out he was. . . . We were a scrounge road group when we met him. He taught us about flying in airplanes, about meeting important people. . . ." Earlier, Robertson had said: "I think we were playing in Atlantic City. . . . I didn't really know who he was or that he was that famous. I didn't think we could play with each other, at all. Then we jammed together and a lot of things happened. We've had a great effect on each other." Helm remembered a phone call to Somers Point, New Jersey, where The Hawks were playing. "You wanna play Hollywood Bowl?" Dylan asked. Helm said they had never heard of Dylan, and proceeded to inquire who else was going to be on the show. "Just us," Dylan said to the astonished Helm.

Dylan became especially close to Robertson. The two stood face-to-face onstage, weaving sound patterns like strands of friendship. Dylan's most often quoted paean to Robbie was an absurdist metaphor: "He's the only mathematical guitar genius I've ever run into who does not offend my intestinal nervousness with his rear-guard sound." Meaning, presumably, that Robbie was as strong on technique as he was on a gut sound. Robbie was also North Country, from Toronto. Both fought boyish isolation with radio from the Southeast. Both led loner, dream-filled youths, and both were interested in composing and writing. They shared an interest in older musicians. At fifteen, Robbie joined Ronnie Hawkins as a roadie. The Hawks' Fred Carter schooled Robbie on bass, then on rhythm guitar. About 1960, Robertson became lead guitarist.

They were shortly joined by Levon Helm, a high-school dropout from West Helena, Arkansas, which Hawkins also called home. Until he was twelve, Helm had sweated his summers picking cotton. He formed a high-school band, The Jungle Bush Beaters: "The way to get off that stinking tractor and out of that one-hundred-five-degree heat was to get on that guitar." He soon turned to the drums and won the top prize in a county fair, accompanied by his sister on washtub bass.

The Hawks' organist was Garth Hudson, son of a World War I pilot turned farm inspector. He studied music at the University of Western Ontario, rebuilt pump organs around his house, then fingered and pedaled his way through Bach, playing organ at an uncle's funeral parlor. At twelve,

Hudson played accordion in a country band, and later formed his own rock group in Detroit.

Rick Danko, bass-guitarist, came from Canada's tobacco belt. The son of a woodcutter, Rick lived in a house without electricity until he was ten. Before his teens, he played regularly with a local rock 'n' roll band. His worldly musical education came from Grand Ole Opry broadcasts from Nashville. Having learned mandolin at five, Danko was the first Hawk to decide on a music life. As a toddler, he had sat in with his three brothers at weekly home music sessions.

Richard Manuel, pianist from Stratford, Ontario, also relied on Nashville radio for early influences. When Helm opted out of part of the first world tour with Dylan, Sandy Konikoff took over on drums on the American leg of the tour. Overseas, Mickey Jones, former drummer with Johnny Rivers, filled in. Bobby Gregg also played drums on some Hawks-Dylan dates during Helm's absence.

Onstage, The Band, a no-nonsense ensemble, kept theatrics to a minimum. Garth would rock like a jolly bear, Danko would puff out his cheeks, or Robbie would stroll about restlessly as if pursuing ideas. Four could alternate lead singing, while Hudson often sang along on ensembles. The Band, who can command seventeen instruments, used its technical skills to play music, not to whip up applause. They sought excitements in subtleties and nuances, curves and circles rather than jagged edges. On guitar, Robertson is a perfectionist technician, while Dylan remains primarily an expressionist who generally uses instrumental technique as a vehicle, not an end. Vocally, Robbie soon joined the legions who felt the strong pull of Dylan's hydra-headed singing—the urgent, pained involvement, the hand-on-the-shoulder intimacy, the eccentric accentuation, the chilling directness.

After Robertson and Helm appeared with Dylan at Forest Hills in 1965, Bob signed the group for the world tour. After the tour, The Band followed Dylan's retreat to the country. They took a house called Big Pink, outside Saugerties, near Woodstock, to concentrate on their own new directions. The Band soon aped Dylan's petulance to the press. In 1968, Robbie was delegated to halt the puerile publicity campaign Capitol Records planned to launch for The Band's first album, *Music from Big Pink*. Capitol wanted to unleash a clattering "Big Pink Think Campaign," with a contest to name Dylan's album-cover drawing, a watercolor in primitive folk-art style of five musicians at play.

Dylan singled out Robertson to play on *Blonde on Blonde*. The first public indication of later recording collaboration was in 1967, on the bootlegged *Basement Tapes* of Dylan and The Band playing in Woodstock. The Band backed Dylan at the two-performance "Tribute to Woody Guthrie" on January 20, 1968, at Carnegie Hall. Dylan made a surprise appearance with The Band on July 14, 1969, at the Mississippi River Festival in Edwardsville, Illinois. Introduced as Elmer Johnson, Dylan sang three numbers, including the old hill tune, "In the Pines." He returned with The Band to do an encore of Buddy Holly's "Slippin' and Slidin'." A few weeks later, on August 31, 1969, Dylan and The Band appeared at the Isle of Wight Festival, where they suffered from the festival's vast, impersonal setting and general mismanagement. On New Year's Eve, 1971, Dylan popped up, again unannounced, at an ambitious Band concert at Manhattan's Academy of Music. With supplementary horns, The Band was recording their double *Rock of Ages* album. The most notable, sustained, and prominent evidence of the collaboration between Dylan and The Band was their tour in 1974 and the simultaneous release of *Planet Waves,* the collaborators' first commercially released album. Out of the tour came the double-LP set *Before the Flood.* Dylan appeared November 25, 1976, at "The Last Waltz," The Band's farewell public concert at Winterland, San Francisco.

Among the many Dylan songs The Band recorded, the group gave four their official debut to the American public: "I Shall Be Released," "Tears of Rage," "This Wheel's on Fire," from *Big Pink,* and "When I Paint My Masterpiece," from The Band's 1971 *Cahoots* album. "Released" first surfaced on *Big Pink* and was later recorded by Dylan and Happy Traum in October 1971 for *Greatest Hits, Volume II.* "Released" has the religious yearning of the *John Wesley Harding* album. Vague mysticism surrounds a recurring Dylan subject: the physical or spiritual prisoner contemplating imprisonment and deliverance. Lyrics have a biblical flow and serenity that swell toward each verse's line about ultimate release. Dylan may be speaking of his jail of isolation, or his earlier imprisonment in entangling relationships. On *The Basement Tapes,* "Released" links *Blonde* and *John Wesley Harding.* By the time The Band recorded "Released," they had arrived at a spacy effect in which the keyboards suggest eerie disorientation.

"Tears of Rage" is cut from similar cloth. Music was by Richard Manuel. "Rage," a parent's desperate plea for a child's love, inhabits the same landscape as King Lear. It was written while Dylan himself was learning about fatherhood. "Rage" can also be read as an allusion to King Lear, or even to Steinbeck's *East of Eden,* a retelling of the biblical Cain and Abel story.

"This Wheel's on Fire," also on *Basement,* surfaced on an English recording by Julie Driscoll and Brian Auger. The Band did it on *Big Pink* and *Rock of Ages.* Danko wrote the music. The title comes from the biblical prophet Ezekiel's vision, recounted in the black spiritual "Ezekiel Saw the Wheel." The image of man's life as a wheel of fortune appears in Chaucer and other medieval literature. Shakespeare described King Lear in decline as ". . . bound/Upon a wheel of fire . . ." Dylan's shadowy narrator is a returning traveler who develops a vague personal tale into a grim portent of the future—fire and explosion as the mysterious wheel rolls onward. A motorcycle wheel causing a personal explosion? In *Writings and Drawings,* Dylan's jaunty sketches convert this dark wheel into a plaything. "Wheel" contains some of Dylan's most opaque writing, yet the song builds firmly in a series of tension-and-release peaks. Sometimes the words' sonorities become more important than their literal sense.

A song that leaves much clearer marks is "When I Paint My Masterpiece," performed often during the Rolling Thunder Revue. The Band recorded it on the superlative track of *Cahoots,* their fourth album. The accordion effect here is electronic, played on an organ supplement, the clavinette. On the page, the words seem somber. This recording (and Dylan's own version in the track produced by Leon Russell) hones the edge of the ironic wit that lies dormant on the page. In "Masterpiece," the narrator relates the monuments of an old culture to himself, product of a young culture. Michael Gray, in his book *Song and Dance Man: The Art of Bob Dylan,* has made a cogent case for the "Masterpiece" narrator as an extension of Dick Diver in F. Scott Fitzgerald's *Tender Is the Night.* Gray finds "fragmentary pictures" from the novel, notably the Roman episode when Diver's affair with Rosemary collapses, and he watches Rome and its mystique disintegrate. Gray links the footprints and the Spanish Stairs directly to the novel. While Diver is in Rome, "he comes to admit to himself that he is never actually going to write the masterpiece that he's been aiming at. So Dylan's title line has this fascinating double-edge: 'when' may mean 'never.' "

This song is the last in *Writings and Drawings,* perhaps as a parting preamble. The narrator lets fly an impassive wisecrack, so that we do not mistake this for melodrama. Dylan's visit to Rome in early 1963 brought him back to the Village with renewed hope. One night he told Gil Turner and me that if he made any money he would fly us both over to Italy. "We'll drink red wine, night and day, until we explode," Dylan said. The Coliseum motif is a metaphor for the gladiatorial public arena of the star's life. After the delicious rhyme of "gondola" and "Coca-Cola," the narrator is off to Belgium. "Newspapermen eating candy/Had to be held down by big police"[3] is a finger-pointing couplet in his hostile fashion. The song is memorable for its easy mix of the direct statement and the elusive.

Given the close relationship between Dylan and The Band, it is strange that so much time passed between 1965 and the two albums of 1974. The collaborators may have agreed that detachment allowed air for more ideas to circulate with other musicians behind Dylan at sessions. There was some recording collaboration in 1965: The Band supplied backing on the single "Can *You* Please Crawl Out Your Window?" Before their work on *The Basement Tapes* and Tour '74, Dylan and The Band enjoyed their best chemistry during the world tour of 1965–66.

BLONDE ON BLONDE

The world tour spelled heavy pressure: three, sometimes four concerts a week; listeners hungering for a new album; acolytes awaiting new direction; businessmen demanding more product, more profit. From autumn through spring, as he careened around the States, Dylan continued to write new songs. During a concert break, he scribbled an idea in his dressing room. While The Band slept on the tour's chartered Lockheed Lodestar, Dylan worked past the midnight hours on a new melody. In the back of a car, while others made small talk, Dylan saw visions beyond the passing landscape. In smoky motel rooms, he squeezed out a riff, a phrase from his guitar. "Sometimes I'll be able to hear the melody and everything right in my head," he said in 1985.

Although *Blonde on Blonde* was not released until May 1966, its material had been evolving for more than a year. He seemed to thrive artistically under the deadline, giving first-rate performances and assembling the remarkable contents of his first double album. But every day the strain became increasingly obvious. He was chronically tired, boiling with anxiety under a surface he strove to keep cool. When I told John Court I was starting a book about Dylan, Court replied sardonically: "You better hurry."

Blonde is a particularly high achievement, a hallmark collection that completes his first major rock cycle, which began with *Back Home*. No Dylan recording until then required as much studio time. Preliminary work began before Christmas, 1965, and ran on, intermittently, through the winter. Sessions began in Columbia's New York studios, where one eleven-hour taping yielded nothing. Not until the whole operation moved to Nashville in February 1966 did things jell. Nashville studios, "the Mayo Clinic of pop," have long proved therapeutic. Even Perry Como, Rosemary Clooney, and Burl Ives had restored their jangled nerves by working there. Tennessee's capital is less abrasive, and quality sidemen can be corralled quickly. On the *Blonde* sessions were Wayne Moss, Charlie McCoy, Kenneth Buttrey, Hargus Robbins, Jerry Kennedy, Joe South, Al Kooper, Bill Aikins, Henry Strzeleci, and Robbie Robertson. Dylan went to Nashville for relief, but also because his producer, Bob Johnston, was based there.

Al Kooper said Johnston's faith in Nashville sidemen convinced Dylan to go south. At one point, Johnston wanted to do "Rainy Day Women" in Salvation Army style, but he needed a brass player instantly. At four-thirty A.M., McCoy made a phone call. Half an hour later, Kooper swears, a trombone player marched in, sat through three takes, and went home in an hour with the hit recorded. Although Kooper was nearly beaten up by some local toughs, he reported great vibrations in Nashville. (Emptying studio ashtrays was a young janitor named Kris Kristofferson.) As usual, Dylan did a great deal of writing and rewriting in the studio, developing his songs from roughed-out versions he had brought with him. For "Johanna" and "Sad-Eyed Lady," Dylan hunched over his piano in his hotel room for up to five hours. Occasionally Kooper would come in, strum some chords to Dylan's work in progress, then teach the rest of the crew the changes.

There is a distinctive "sound" to the album, which Dylan later tried to
·re-create in *Street-Legal*. He described it as "that thin, that wild mercury
sound." *Blonde* begins with a joke and ends with a hymn; in between, wit
alternates with a dominant theme of entrapment—by circumstance, love,
society, illusions, and unrealized hopes. "We sit here stranded, though
we're all doin' our best to deny it"[4] describes the singer's position. "We
see this empty cage now corrode"[5] offers some hope. Dylan is "stuck" inside Mobile, inside roles. He perhaps best summarizes his effort to remain
strong and cool, despite his weariness, in "Pledging My Time":

> *I got a poison headache,*
> *But I feel all right.*
> *I'm pledging my time to you,*
> *Hopin' you'll come through, too. . . .*[6]

More amazing weariness, yet more resolve to keep cool and to pledge
time and effort. Ferlinghetti's characterization of Dylan's work as "higher
than surreal" certainly fits *Blonde*. Through the shadow and smoke we feel
his doomsday imprisonment, as he pledges his will to go on living, loving,
and singing. Still that battle against lifelessness.

There's a remarkable marriage here of a funky, bluesy, rock expressionism, and Rimbaud-like visions of discontinuity, chaos, emptiness, loss,
being "stuck." ". . . the room is so stuffy,/ I can hardly breathe,"[7] he sings.
Words sometimes have exact meanings, but also a musical value beyond
cognition. As Fowlie wrote of Rimbaud, we can think of Dylan here "bent
upon subordinating words to their sounds and colors."

"RAINY DAY WOMEN #12 & 35": This song, which charted at
number two, satirizes the 1960s generation gap. Dylan at his most truculent—toying with the title, the raggle-taggle ensemble singing, the giggling, the manic instrumentation, and a variety of implied games about
liquor or dope. "Rainy Day Women" is an outburst of sheer joy. His
drollness triggered a drug-song controversy so feverish that Dylan announced: "I never have and never will write a 'drug song.' " "Rainy Day
Women" was banned by American and British radio stations. *Time,* July 1,
1966: "In the shifting, multi-level jargon of teenagers, to 'get stoned' does
not mean to get drunk, but to get high on drugs . . . a 'rainy-day woman,'
as any junkie [*sic!*] knows, is a marijuana cigarette."

When former Vice-President Spiro Agnew attacked rock drug songs
that were leading American youth toward the heroin needle, he included
Valerie Simpson and Nicholas Ashford's "Let's Go Get Stoned," which
Ray Charles performed widely. "That's really silly, isn't it," Valerie Simpson said. "It was written so long ago, it was obviously about gin, not
dope." Phil Spector was with Dylan in a Los Angeles hangout, the Fred C.
Dobbs Coffee Shop, when they heard the Ray Charles "Stoned" on a juke-

box. Both of them, Spector told me later, "were surprised to hear a song that free, that explicit." A few months later, Dylan recorded "Rainy Day Women." The sound is comparable to a jazzy old street procession, à la Bunk Johnson. The lugubrious slide trombone and oompah drums evoke New Orleans. The shouting, laughter, and giggling all convey abandon, being high—or stoned—on music, life, chaos, watermelons. There is also a bitter undercurrent; that year, crowds were figuratively stoning Bob.

"PLEDGING MY TIME": A slow blues, strong and pulsing, with heavy Chicago influence. Mouth-harp swipes and extended harp breaks after the third and fifth verses build atmosphere. The lyric resembles improvised blues, with sophistication creeping in. Continuity of mood vanquishes disorder in phrasing. In the light of Dylan's subsequent motorcycle accident, the last verse seems prophetic. How does one get "lucky" with an accident?

"VISIONS OF JOHANNA": A major work in which five long verses and a coda structure nightmares, hallucinations, trances. The instrumental introduction draws us into a seven-and-a-half-minute work. The mournful mouth harp plaintively breaks the silence; chugging drums and stealthy organ insinuate themselves. The organ maintains the haunting feeling. The singing is superb, so purposefully phrased, so weary with ryhthmic emphases as portentous as heartbeats. Electric guitar fills in, underlining and deepening. The skittering images hurl off like fragmentary chips from a mind floating downstream, neither time nor structure holding forces in check. The nonsequential visions are like a swiveling camera recording a fractured consciousness. The atmosphere is almost unbearably fetid and sad until verse four, where the rapidly piled-up rhymes of "freeze," "sneeze," "Jeeze," and "knees"[8] lighten the mood. We are back again among the grotesques: peddlers, countesses, all-night girls, lost little boy, Mona Lisa.

Bill King's doctoral thesis, "The Artist in the Marketplace," calls "Johanna" Dylan's most haunting and complex love song and his "finest poem." He finds that the writer "constantly seeks to transcend the physical world, to reach the ideal where the visions of Johanna become real. That can never be, and yet life without the quest is worthless: this is the paradox at the heart of 'Visions,' the same paradox that Keats explored in his 'Ode on a Grecian Urn.' " In the final two ambiguous lines of the song, King is tantalized by the Keatsian ambiguity of the skeleton-key image, "suggesting both death and the key which opens every door."

"ONE OF US MUST KNOW (SOONER OR LATER)": A startling change, from the shadowiness of "Johanna" to the almost mundane literalness of this colloquy. This brisk rouser ticks away in 4/4 like Big Ben on amphetamines. On one level, it's the story of a man talking to a girl about the difficulties of intimacy. He also may have been talking to the folk world, a lover that turned on him. The music has bite and drive: Piano block chords set the pace.

"I WANT YOU": Once rumored the album title, Dylan only knows why he dropped it. He could quite readily turn out a chart hit; this reached number twenty. A study in contrasts: The hook that ends the four verses sounds nearly inane, with the short, easily remembered cadences that make a hit. They are counterbalanced by the felicitous metaphors that pepper the main verses. The presence of that guilt-ridden undertaker and the boozed-up politician add the implied sense of frustration. (Bill King also found a "rebuttal of the 'true love' myth," a song about "wanting and never getting.")

"MEMPHIS BLUES AGAIN": In blues and country songs, there is recurring lamentation about places left behind. Whatever flights of mad imagery the song takes, the full title, and its mordant message of disruption, make a jackhammer finish to each of the nine verses. The singing is blues shouting, moaning, drawling. Band support enhances the drive that makes a giant lyric speed. What a cast: the ragman, Shakespeare as a dandy, and a bunch of "neon madmen." If "Desolation Row" has become Main Street, the "Memphis Blues" has become the national condition of a mobile, lonely, and lost society.

"LEOPARD-SKIN PILL-BOX HAT": A sustained joke about mindless excess. The hat could mean any trend in fashion or speech, popular or high culture. Bitingly, Dylan shows how tastes are subject to external manipulation.

"JUST LIKE A WOMAN": Despite this work's enduring melodic appeal, its view of women is controversial. Marion Meade wrote in *The New York Times* on March 14, 1971, that "there's no more complete catalogue of sexist slurs" than this song where Dylan "defines women's natural traits as greed, hypocrisy, whining and hysteria." The title is a male platitude that justifiably angers women. I think Dylan is ironically toying with that platitude.

Bill King has called this Dylan's "finest poem on the failure of human relationships because of illusion created by social myth." Dylan may be implicitly criticizing sexist men as much as the woman, or women, who fail them. Roberta Flack has recorded a vastly different version, in which she converts the song into a compassionate lament for women's victimization and depth of feeling. She achieves this through an interpretative shift, but also changes the lyrics' viewpoint. Perhaps she was trying to write an "answer song" based on the original. Reexamine "Woman" in the light of the imagery of *Blood on the Tracks,* where rain, pain, and thirst are also recurring allusions, but in a context of remorseful self-criticism. Were his later, gentler performances of "Woman" an attempt to say it had been misinterpreted? One memorable line softens the harsh edges: "I was hungry and it was your world."[9] For those who find sexist slurs, I recommend Flack's recording, as either reinterpretation or rejoinder. The song is on the soundtrack of the film *Coming Home.*

"MOST LIKELY YOU GO YOUR WAY(AND I'LL GO MINE)":

Bright-tempoed blues riff with a walloping forward motion, structured on one insistent pattern above, an almost martial drum figure below. Dylan gave the song fresh life during Tour '74, then as the lead track on *Flood*. "Most Likely" became one of his most infectious stompers. The lyrics, for all their mundaneness, build with economy a dialogue of lovers parting.

"TEMPORARY LIKE ACHILLES": This smoky, slow-drag blues is barrelhouse New Orleans, with brothel piano and Tennessee Williams summertime sloth. The singing is classic blues, croaking and rough, with ax-chop emphasis, especially in the last line of each verse. Achilles is standing guard for the woman whom the narrator is losing. Why name her bodyguard after the vulnerable Greek hero? Why is he "temporary"? A whole poem could grow from one throwaway line: "I'm helpless, like a rich man's child."[10]

"ABSOLUTELY SWEET MARIE": Up-tempo blues shuffle, pure Memphis. Some effective little stage props: a ruined balcony, a yellow railroad, a man beating his trumpet, a riverboat captain. The narrator has done time, but he is also bitter about the time he's done for Marie. Old blues here, even though touches, like the Persian drunkard, are strictly Dylan. The six white horses echo Blind Lemon Jefferson. One phrase, often quoted as a rationale against oppressive class law: "But to live outside the law, you must be honest."[11] "Marie" is catchy and bright, sparked off by a great organ proclamation. The interlude after the first and third choruses extends the hard riffing. The Band's ensemble sound is tight, over insistent drumming. A pungent harmonica break comes after the fourth chorus.

"FOURTH TIME AROUND": John Lennon thought this was a take-off on The Beatles' "Norwegian Wood." Dylan had played it for them in London. Lennon, who later admitted he was very paranoid, said he didn't like it. Later, he described it as "great." Dylan's voice is the tired, old bluesman. The guitar figure repeats a rippling, romantic Mexican cadence. I asked about the Latin influence. Dylan replied: "I was hip to Tex-Mex music and to *cangacero* music [a Mexican pop-folk sound somewhat deeper than *ranchero* and mariachi music] all my life. I was in Mexico in my youth. 'Baby Blue' and 'Tom Thumb's Blues' is all back to that." The lyric is runaway fantasy, almost incongruous against the soft musical flow.

"OBVIOUSLY FIVE BELIEVERS": Perhaps the best R & B song on the album, pure honky-tonk. Riding high is the mouth harp of Charlie McCoy. This rattletrap blues chugs along with vintage R & B *honey*'s and *mama*'s coming right off the street. More developed images, as in verses three and five, are also traditional. "Black dog," like black snake, is a sexual image, a blues trademark.

"SAD-EYED LADY OF THE LOWLANDS": Before taping this, Dylan told me he regarded this as "the best song I ever wrote." In the last side of *Blonde*, folk tradition meets modern poetry. The title line, echoed in the five verses, has an antique flavor, since Scots-English balladry often refers to lowlands. Paul Nelson called this haunting portrait of a woman: "celebration of woman as work of art, religious figure, and object of eternal majesty and wonder."

The otherworldly woman suffers from the incursions of the material world. She is spiritual, yet corporeal; mystic, yet human; noble, yet pathetic. Her travails seem beyond endurance, yet she radiates an inner strength, an ability to be reborn. This is Dylan at his most romantic. "Bob never wrote a song about any one person," Bob Neuwirth once told me. "They are about a lot of people, and sometimes not about any people at all." One can savor "Sad-Eyed Lady" without knowing its model. Yet this is virtually a wedding song for the former Sara Shirley H. Lowndes, who was married to Dylan in a private civil ceremony on November 22, 1965. Only a few close associates, including Grossman and one of Dylan's lawyers, Saul (Pete) Pryor, attended the ceremony, which was generally kept quiet until a *Melody Maker* report on December 25. Nora Ephron broke the story in the *New York Post* on February 9, 1966: HUSH! BOB DYLAN IS WED. (The couple were divorced on June 28, 1977.)

While determined to keep Sara from fans' fishbowl stares, Dylan revealed her through many songs. Dylan zealously guarded the privacy of his wife and their five children, yet Sara was often a prominent image in his work. While Lennon and McCartney made public rituals out of their respective marriages to Yoko Ono and Linda Eastman, Dylan kept his family life and artistic processes covert. Until he wrote "Sara" in 1975, he would talk only in metaphors about the "madonna-like woman," whose sagacity, calmness, and warmth changed his life. Until "Sara," he never dedicated songs to her, never talked explicitly of her, relying on his songs only to proclaim his love or pain.

There are specifics in "Sad-Eyed Lady" that reveal Sara. She had dark hair, well-sculptured features, a short, graceful body. And she did have sad eyes. Sara had been married to Victor Lownes, the Chicago and London executive of the *Playboy* magazine empire, and has a daughter, Maria, by that marriage. Dylan's greatest praise of Sara was that "she is a very private person. . . . She doesn't have to be on the scene, any scene, to be happy." He admired her inner resources, her quietude and philosophic calm, her ability to be herself, with or without him. The song tells us of a woman mystic and mysterious, half-child, half-woman, deep, detached, compassionate, frightened, scarred by her past, but full of life. In Woodstock, Sara was quietly respected. Her manner, while never cold or rude, seemed to say: "No trespassing, please."

Lynn Musgrave, a music journalist who lived in Woodstock, told me: "Johnny Herald and I were walking and Bob came along driving his blue station wagon. Sara was in the front seat with Bob and her little girl. Neuwirth was in back. Sara's little girl turned to me and asked: 'Where do you live?' I said I couldn't show her because we had already passed the house. Then she asked, pointing at Johnny, 'Do you live with him?' I said

yes, and Sara turned around with glee in her eye, just rolling glee. I think
Sara is very clearly described in the song as 'the junkyard angel.'[12] She is
not Mother Earth in the heavy way, but she just rolls with nature. She has
a low center of gravity, if not quite indestructible, then something close to
it. That is what it must take to sit up there in Woodstock, being married
to Dylan and never going out much. I don't think she complains much,
either. . . . I got the impression of her being strong. That line, 'she speaks
like silence'[13] . . . that's Sara."

Bob and Sara's first major New York appearance together was at the
Guthrie tribute at Carnegie Hall in January 1968. Sara, mostly on her own,
moved about rather shyly, gravitating toward people she knew from
Woodstock. She appeared demure, yet slightly ill at ease in a throng fascinated by her husband. I chatted briefly with her, and noted the deep large
eyes, the glowing complexion, the air of quiet detachment. Friends of Sara
considered her then as extremely warm and devoted toward a select few.
Her ability to suppress her own ego was described as graceful and reassuring to Bob. She had a Romany spirit, seeming to be wise beyond her years,
knowledgeable about magic and folklore and traditional wisdom.

Dylan evidently felt he'd still revealed too much about his sad-eyed lady,
for when Richard Goldstein cited the lyric in his 1968 book, *The Poetry of
Rock,* he was denied permission to quote the third verse. However, the
verse, which had appeared in the album folio, was later published in *Writings and Drawings.* Goldstein: " 'Sad-Eyed Lady' is one of Dylan's least self-
conscious songs . . . the most moving love song in rock. Even its foibles
conspire to convey the paradoxical reality of its heroine; this sad-eyed lady
who can be so nonchalantly strong, and so predictably weak; so innocent,
yet so corrupted. . . . His sad-eyed lady is everyone's girl, and everyone's
girl is what the love song is all about. . . ."

The successive similes seem thoroughly successful at draping a subject
in a richly brocaded tapestry of language. Dylan has brought high metaphoric development and literary allusion into rock. The sad-eyed lady, like
Shakespeare's dark lady, is an elusive source of inspiration and wonder.
Sara and Bob for a time built a new life together, perhaps using "skele-
ton keys" to open another door. Until 1973, they stood as a most solidly
loving couple. In Dylan's songs after "Sad-Eyed Lady," a highly romanticized view of an ideal woman recurs. For a while, Sara fleshed that
image.

Blonde closed a period that, until 1974, has often been regarded as
Dylan's most fluent, poetic, and experimental. He and others were turning
rock into a new art form of vast horizons. Dylan's art stimulated a coterie
of new commentators. One was Paul Williams, who launched a mimeographed, rough-and-ready bulletin called *Crawdaddy,* and collected some of
his best pieces in a book with a Dylan title, *Outlaw Blues. Rolling Stone* and
pop coverage in *The Village Voice* and other alternative periodicals re-

flected new acceptance of rock. Some fan magazines turned literary or sociological. Ellen Willis, who in 1968 became *The New Yorker*'s rock critic, wrote about Dylan with great insight. The *East Village Other* quoted the poet Frank O'Hara on "Sad-Eyed Lady": "... such sweet Rimbaud lyricism...." Dylan also reminded O'Hara of young Auden, "in the sense of being a public poet. Even if the work was in the form of song, it was essentially presented as poem."

Goldstein, then regarded as America's hippest rock critic, wrote in *The Village Voice* in September 1966, that *Blonde* was neither mysterious nor forbidding and was Dylan's "least esoteric work.... The songs are all about women." In his folio preface of *Blonde,* Paul Nelson called the album a "circus-book of styles that would challenge a Picasso." The title suggested to him "both the singularity and the duality we expect from Dylan's music of illusion and delusion—with the tramp as explorer and the clown as happy victim...."[14] Jon Landau, in *Crawdaddy,* found his singing "one of the most brilliant rock performances ever recorded." Steven Goldberg's *Saturday Review* cover story (May 30, 1970) saw in "Johanna" and "Memphis Blues" Dylan's "imminent discovery that the mystical experience must give way to a life infused with mysticism and compassion lest even the mystical experience be perverted into an excuse for evasion."

At the time of *Blonde*'s release, the older pop critics were reorienting their sights and the new rock critics were realizing that literature, art, and rock were all converging. Some performers, like Leonard Cohen and Richard Fariña, were flexing their muscles as singing *writers*. A few weeks before his death, I interviewed Fariña: "What bugs me most about the contemporary music scene is that people demand change within a four- or five-year period. I suppose we're all expected to move as quickly as he does." Why did people find Dylan so enigmatic? Fariña: "Paradoxically, because he's the real thing. What he says and what he does are the same thing. His expression is precisely what he is. Probably because he is so blank, so open. Although he has been hit a lot for affectation, he tries a lot of things. It's very human.... I find him not ready or willing to talk about a lot most people are willing to talk about.... The only thing I know for sure about him is that he is fragile. But I don't believe that I understand what is going through his mind.... The particular magic that Dylan has over, say, twenty million people, is the paradox and the inaccessibility of him. In his music, people are struck by something and yet they don't really seem to know what it is. That's always been the case with the most acute and exalted poetry. There are lines of Shakespeare like this, in which you don't have to know who plays what to be struck by the magic of words. Then the insight of the listener is followed by intense perplexity. We hear something that we finally realize is saying something we think ourselves and then we want to know more about the writer who can tell us something about ourselves. Joan, on the other hand, reinterprets what others have written in a way that makes us listen. Joan is a mother who gives birth to a new meaning in a song for us, and Bobby is the father, the one who does the fertilizing. While Hemingway has brought us the physical hero, whose presence and appearance are so exciting, Dylan has brought us the 'head hero,' whose brain attracts and compels our interest. . . . But he is complicated! Everything he does and writes is complicated. How can you possibly be walking around upright on this earth and possibly be simple?"

"HARD TRAVELING" INTO FUTURE SHOCK

Launching a tour after Newport and Forest Hills took nerve, but Dylan wanted to "show the audience what we're doing these days." He described his mood then: "There doesn't seem to be any tomorrow. Every time I wake up, no matter in what position, it's always been today." But many in the heavily politicized audience wanted slogans, not the new beat. The times were changing: On October 15, 1965, one hundred thousand persons gathered in Washington to demonstrate against the Vietnam War. Half were students. In Ann Arbor, Michigan, thirty-eight were arrested for a draft-board sit-in. Fifty University of Wisconsin students at Madison marched on Truax Air Force Base and tried unsuccessfully to arrest the commander as "an accessory to mass murder and genocide." At November 1965 anti–Vietnam War teach-ins, buttons and posters articulated youth outrage: MAKE LOVE, NOT WAR!, POWER TO THE PEOPLE!, YOU CAN'T TRUST ANYBODY OVER 30.

Dylan had spent three years supplying marching songs for the campus protest against war, hypocrisy, and discrimination, but now he was changing the tempo, saying he wasn't "a schoolteacher, a shepherd, a soul-saver." He was interested in "salvation," something considerably more basic.

A minority of Dylan's audience could accept a salvational message, but only in a folkish vein. Most listeners came to him with empty baskets labeled "political power and direction," "some kind of salvation," "stone me." They were yearning for an experience comparable to pop in the visual arts—the museum, the comic book, TV, fashion. In these areas, *pop* stressed fun, rebellion, silliness, the hip-kicks pleasure principle of a restless, experimental society. Pop art was an offshoot of post–World War I Dadaism. Susan Sontag, in her famous essay "Notes on Camp," found pop the "triumph of the epicine style . . . love of the unnatural; of artifice and exaggeration." Trivia was camp; old movies were pop nostalgia. Andy Warhol, who became a Dylan freak, regarded pop as a way "to see beauty in all things." Warhol opened his own Village rock club, the Plastic Inevitable, and sponsored a punk-rock band, The Velvet Underground.

To heavily politicized youth, most rock ("the new numbness," Dave

Van Ronk called it) represented escape to a palmier time before Vietnam. Dylan's *Blonde on Blonde* visions were very much in the new pop mood. Although most pop—shoddy Carnaby Street clothes, comic books—was disposable, Warhol's canvases became classics, and Dylan's art endured. But Dylan did not have an easy time setting out on his 1965–66 world tour in this jumbled ambience. Dylan later described to me his state of mind: "I was touring for a couple of years. That's a fast pace . . . we were doing a whole show, no other acts. It's pretty straining to do a show like that . . . a lot of really unhealthy situations rise up. . . . I was just going out there performing these songs. Everyone else was having a good time. . . . I did it enough to know that there must be something else to do. . . . It wasn't my own choice. I was more or less being pushed into it—pushed in and carried out. . . ."

The first concert was at Hollywood Bowl, on Friday, September 3, 1965. An earlier press conference became an hour-long cat-and-mouse game. Charles Champlin of the *Los Angeles Times* found Dylan "as cryptic, elusive and biting *a capella* and in recitation as he is in full song." To a Mr. Jones reporter who asked why he wasn't "as accessible as Frankie Laine," Dylan said: "I should hope not. I'm not a preacher or a traveling salesman. I do what I do. There was a time I cared if anyone understood. Not anymore. . . ." Later on, he explained: "I'm hard. I don't have to look to anyone to tell me I'm good. I know I'm honest. When I do something for the wrong reason, I'm embarrassed to be around people." Dylan was so caustic in Los Angeles that Billy James doubted such interviews should continue.

The autumn 1965 itinerary: Austin, Sept. 23; Dallas, Sept. 24; Carnegie Hall, Oct. 1; Newark, Oct. 2; Atlanta, Oct. 9; Worcester, Oct. 22; Detroit, Oct. 24; Boston, Oct. 29 and 31; and Hartford, Oct. 30. Concerts resumed Nov. 12 in Cleveland; Nov. 14 and 15 in Toronto; Nov. 19 in Columbus; and Nov. 21 in Syracuse. Dylan and company played Nov. 26 and 27 at the Arie Crown Theatre in Chicago, and Nov. 28 in Washington, D.C. They swooped down on California beginning Dec. 3.

Moving Dylan and The Hawks on the thirteen-seat, twin-engine Lockheed Lodestar took generalship. Bobby Neuwirth and Victor Maimudes alternated as road manager. When Neuwirth was aboard, Victor or Bill Avis served as Hawks roadie. Two movers and truck drivers loaded eight crates of equipment and raced all night to the next stop, where they set up the thirty-thousand-dollar amplification system.

Sporadically, *Variety* totted up the tour's receipts. Dylan's October 29 sold-out Boston concert grossed $12,000. *Variety* called Dylan "one of the hottest phenomena of show business today." In 1965, he played to 10,000 people, a fraction of his future audiences. In Toronto, *Variety* reported, Dylan "grossed a whopping $17,278 on November 14 and 15, at Massey Hall. Dylan took away 70% of the gross." The Syracuse report was less than euphoric: On November 21, 3,486 out of 6,600 seats grossed $12,500, and there was a hassle with the local musicians union, which demanded at least 15 musicians onstage.

In early autumn, trouble began that continued for the remainder of the tour: Most of the halls had inadequate sound balances. Sports-arena acoustics were a far cry from those of theaters and concert halls. After each concert, Dylan asked, "How did it sound? I don't mean the song, but how did it actually sound where you were?" From Newport to Albert Hall, concerts were plagued by distorted amplification. With better acoustics, the audience might have been faster converted to folk-rock.

On Sunday, December 12, the *New York Herald Tribune* ran a major feature about the tour, supplemented by a six-page spread, billed as Daniel Kramer's "photographic portfolio." (Actually, Dylan's pal, Al Aronowitz, wrote the text and Dylan rewrote it.) This piece caught the tour's haphazardness: musicians maundering in droves, dudes and groupies coming and going. In what sounded like Grossman's Gramercy Park pad, Dylan is playing a Temptations disk while Robertson strums an Autoharp. Brian Jones of The Rolling Stones rolls up in a Rolls. All tumble over to a bar, where Dylan says: "You can write on the walls here . . . and nobody calls you a poet." Enter a muscular woman, sailors, the chauffeur, Neuwirth. A sailor leaps on their table. The merry pranksters go to an underground cinema, with no film, "but instead a group of green painted musicians . . . presenting a spontaneous ritual which had taken them three months to prepare." On to a pinball arcade, a fortune-teller's, a disco, and a cathedral. Finally back to "the borrowed pad," where Dylan muses: "I think . . . Brando should play W. C. Fields . . . Warren Beatty should play . . . Johnny Weissmuller. . . . I plan to play the life story of Victor Mature. . . ."

This episode from Dylan's life was not all fantasy. Shortly before Christmas, 1965, I witnessed an evening almost as absurd. Paul and Betty Stookey gave a black-tie party at their lovely old brick house on Bedford Street in the Village. Scruffies were transformed into dudes. Grossman looked like a penguin headwaiter at an iceberg Bar Mitzvah. Grossman's lieutenant, Charlie Rothschild, fell asleep in the bathtub, while a chamber trio on the minstrel's gallery sawed away at the greatest hits of Boccherini, Corelli, and Vivaldi.

As the party loped toward finale, in marched a mob of uninvited street people. Heading the invading force was a very stoned Dylan in jeans and suede. Betty Stookey looked aghast as her careful planning evaporated. She stood beside me while Tommy Flanders of The Blues Project systematically assailed the party, the guests, the chamber trio. "Meet your hostess," I said, waving at Betty, and they glowered at each other. Dylan launched a heavy discussion with Albert, circling him so that the manager had to pan 360 degrees to listen to his client.

At almost three A.M., Dylan assembled Dave (Blue) Cohen, Phil Ochs, my date, Liz Newman, and me to depart for the next stop. We piled into

Bob's rented limousine, chauffeured by a middle-aged uniformed driver named Morris, who looked as relaxed as a charioteer in *Ben Hur*. Dylan directed him to an all-night club, the Clique, at 158 East Forty-ninth Street. The hangout fell silent as Dylan led us to a table. Strangers came by with questions, menus to be autographed, regards from some second cousin's brother-in-law in Kansas City who thought *he* was Mister Jones. A former Village friend of Bob's, Kathy Perry, bounced up, but Dylan was so tired he dismissed her as if she were a groupie. Bob said he'd read my letter about my tackling his biography and it sounded like a good idea to him. "As long as it's in context," he repeated, over and over. He asked piercing questions: "What sort of contract do you have? Do you have control over your words? Will they chop it up and change it all around? Will they write in things against the truth?" I reassured him. "I'll help you out on it," Dylan said. He said he'd call me later in the week to go into details. A tired Dylan sat with his "entourage," and told me how much he hated that idea: "I resent it very much when I read in magazines that people say: 'Dylan was here with his hangers-on! I never had, in my whole life, any hangers-on. That's a very ugly word, *entourage.* It puts down everyone who works for me and it puts you down for ... having *friends.*"

Dave (Blue) Cohen was a comparatively new friend, who later took some acting honors in *Renaldo and Clara.* Just as Dylan was elevating Cohen, he was downgrading Phil Ochs, even though Ochs had revered Dylan for years. Two months earlier, Dylan had played his single "Crawl out Your Window" for Cohen and Ochs. Dave loved it, but Phil said he didn't think it would be a hit. That night, Dylan stopped his limousine and made Ochs crawl out the door, saying: "You're not a folk singer, you're just a journalist." Undaunted, Ochs was back, risking more abuse. Dave hung back, while Dylan attacked Phil's political-topical songwriting: "It's all wrong, you know. That isn't where it's at anymore. It's way beyond that now." Dylan's familiarity with Ochs's works surprised us. Ochs drank in the abuse, and while Dylan was away from the table, I asked Ochs how he could take all this. Ochs said: "After all, man, if Dylan tells you something, you *gotta* listen." Dave split early, perhaps fearing he might be next on the carpet. Dylan returned to the table and continued the ax-chops. "Why don't you just become a stand-up comic?" he asked Phil. Dylan wasn't amusing; he looked ghostly pale, and was reluctant to go home to the Chelsea Hotel. As Liz and I hailed a taxi to the Village, Liz said: "My God, he looks like he's dying."

Dylan's old friends had only the vaguest idea of what he'd been doing on tour during the previous weeks. He'd pass a remark about what a drag Austin was, or how great the Coast was, but only hinted at his daily tensions. Sitting in the Village, we had no idea what Texas had been like to him. Austin had concert ushers from the American Legion, who paraded smartly in their little soldiers' caps. Shades of "Masters of War"! The press

332   NO DIRECTION HOME

conference before the Austin concert attracted some reporters playing district attorney:

"Q: What do you consider yourself? How would you classify yourself? D: Well, I like to think of myself in terms of a trapeze artist. . . . Q: You said before that you sang because you had to. Why do you sing now? D: Because I have to. Q: Your voice . . . here is gentle . . . in some of your records, there's a harsh twang. D: I just got up. Q: Are you trying to accomplish anything? . . . to change the world or anything? . . . Are you trying to push idealism to the people? D: Well, what do you think my ideas are? Q: I don't exactly know. Are you singing just to be singing? D: No . . . there's a much deeper reason for it than that. . . . Q: Who are your favorite performers? I don't mean folk. I mean general. D: Rasputin . . . Charles de Gaulle . . . The Staple Singers . . . Q: What is your belief in a God? Are you a Christian? D: Well, first of all, God is a woman, we all know that. Well, you take it from there. . . ."

In the San Francisco KQED-TV interview on December 3, Philistine questions elicited verbal slingshots: "Q: What poets do you dig? D: Rimbaud . . . W. C. Fields . . . the trapeze family . . . in the circus . . . Smokey Robinson . . . Allen Ginsberg . . . Charlie Rich . . . Q: What do you think of people who analyze your songs? D: I welcome them . . . with open arms. Q: For those of us well over thirty, could you label yourself and perhaps tell us what your role is? D: . . . I'd sort of label myself a 'well under thirty.' And my role is . . . to just stay here as long as I can. . . . Q: Have you ever played a dance? . . . D: No. It's not that kind of music. Q: It is. D: Well, what can I say? You must know more about the music than I do. How long have you been playing it?"

In the winter of 1965–66, Ralph Gleason agreed that Dylan looked close to death: "I was very worried about him. . . . I figured he was in mortal pain. I wanted to ask him what was killing him. I was astounded he was still working, because I figured he would have had a breakdown. I thought he was having some severe abdominal pains, or a brain tumor. . . ." The audience at Dylan's northern California series, sold out by mid-November, had no clue of Dylan's condition. Shows were set for December 3 and 4 at the Berkeley Community Theater, the following Saturday at the San Francisco Masonic Auditorium, and the next night at the San Jose Civic Auditorium. Another Masonic concert was added on Sunday, December 5.

An agent, Mary Ann Pollar, worked with Grossman on these bookings, and also arranged three parties. Gleason ran the KQED-TV press conference and attended all the California events. Gleason had a lot to offer me:

". . . One night . . . we walked . . . up and down Broadway in San Francisco, with Dylan complaining he couldn't go anywhere on the streets. We arranged to meet later. Where did we meet, at his direction? At Mike's Pool Hall, right in the center of the San Francisco night life, on Broadway near Enrico's. In the pool hall! I think it's absolutely beautiful! He insisted on sitting in the window! In full view of the street! In ten minutes there was a crowd there and he had to leave. He looked very tired and very hard." At the first Berkeley concert, Gleason recalled, "in the front row were Larry Ferlinghetti, Ginsberg, Ken Kesey, and two Hell's Angels. The following week, there must have been a dozen Hell's Angels. Allen is very big with the Angels. In a way, he thinks he invented them." What turned the beat poets on to Dylan? "Larry [Ferlinghetti] turned him on to Allen or Allen got a letter from Bob after reading [Ginsberg's poem] 'Kaddish.' Dylan keeps talking about Rimbaud, and not Ginsberg, even though Bob gives the appearance of having memorized everything that Ginsberg ever wrote. Michael McClure [poet/playright, author of *The Beard*] was sitting in Dylan's dressing room at the Masonic. McClure was cross-examining him on how you write a hit song and get to be a millionaire.

"The San Francisco poets freaked out when they saw this Dylan thing happening. I thought Larry was a tragic figure that weekend, a shaken and embittered man. You know, 'What is that stringy kid doing up there with his electric guitar?' I mean, 'I am a major poet, and this kid has thirty-five hundred kids in this hall.' And Larry has been mumbling to himself ever since. The rest of them just flocked around. This is the first time the poets ever showed up. Allen made Dylan and The Beatles respectable. Dylan and Allen had long talks about 'Desolation Row.' There's Dylan sitting in the corner, and on the floor, like some ancient tribe of hill people about to go on an assaulting raid, is this mob of bearded Hell's Angels with all that leather and medals dripping off them. Obviously, Dylan couldn't talk to them. He just kept repeating: 'Good seats? Got good seats?' When Dylan's cigarette and leg start going, they're a thermometer of his tensions.

"He is a power figure, surrounded by satellites—Grossman, Neuwirth. The only person he can really believe is Robbie." Why did Ralph frequently compare Dylan to Miles Davis? "Both are little bantam roosters, seriously proud. Distrustful, on the surface, of the whole world. Really aching to trust somebody. Sentimental, and filled with all sorts of good instincts, which they won't, for an instant, admit they have. If you ask Miles or Dylan a question, that's certainly not the way to get an answer. The only way I can have a rational relationship with Miles is to leave him alone. It's like winning the confidence of a scared puppy that has been mistreated. Patience is the only thing. You've got to demonstrate that you are not like all those other people that have been bugging him . . . you are never proven. You are always on trial. You can always blow it."

On dope and musicians, Gleason said, "Dylan is the sort of glowing, charismatic character that if you spent six months with a team of doctors spending every waking minute with him and you wrote that he does NOT use heroin, nobody would believe it. I keep running into people all the time who tell me they were with Dylan when he had his first fix. He would have had to have had his first fix over a period of seventeen years to account for all those people."

By the time of the Berkeley concerts, the single of "Positively Fourth Street" had charted at number seven. Gleason could report in the *San Francisco Chronicle:* "Dylan's band went over like the discovery of gold. . . . Dozens of university professors were scattered in the audience, some looking rather shattered by the experience . . . the audience lingered. . . . They simply didn't want to go home. Something most certainly *IS* happening here. . . ." Four paintings by Neuwirth hung above the Berkeley stage, an early attempt to heighten rock visually. Gleason thought each painting was "an abstraction of Dylan's own image, or so it seemed to me after two glasses of milk and a Hershey bar."

If the senior journalist was tripping on milk and chocolate, many in the audiences were into pharmaceuticals. Some of the concerts were conventions of heads, hints of future Woodstocks. The only way to get answers from Dylan about dope was never to ask questions. Usually, he spoke elliptically, or not at all. Although Dylan had been the first person to turn me on with pot, I confessed no knowledge and considerable fear about other chemicals. Dylan conveyed the feeling that he knew what he was doing, that he had everything under control, legally and medically.

During visits to Los Angeles in autumn 1965, Dylan befriended producer and songwriter Phil Spector. According to Gleason, "In a certain sense, Dylan appealed directly to Spector for help. There are so many parallels in their careers. The type of help that Bob was looking for was: 'Tell me how to live.' " Seeing Spector was no easy matter. He was in the throes of producing one of his most famous singles, "River Deep, Mountain High." At his Sunset Strip offices, I waited nearly an hour, then nudged Spector's secretary for the third time. She disappeared within, and I heard a frantic, high-pitched shout from behind the imperial doors: "Tell the son of a bitch that I'm not here!" The secretary emerged looking pale. I spared her a lie; "I get the idea." I grumbled to Billy James, some phone calls were made, and I was told to show up two days later at the Gold Star Studio. In the studio, Spector was a wizard with a dozen ears, presiding over eighteen musicians. In her booth with headphones, singer Tina Turner waited for cues. She and the band were into their third week of work on the single. After every phrase, everyone turned to Spector for reaction. Spector was a perfectionist who elicited relaxed performances by joking. Three pianos and three rhythm guitars helped build his "wall of sound." A run-through sounded superb, but Spector stopped and asked one of the acoustic guitarists if his instrument was in tune. The guitarist, to everyone's amazement, found one string slightly off-center. After the session, the wiry little producer, with a feline grin, puckish eyes, and a hipper-than-thou manner, said:

"I could give you one of my put-on interviews, you know, pulling your leg like I usually do, like The Beatles and Dylan are doing these days. But you look straight to me, so why bother?" He drove me to his home tucked away behind a Hollywood Hills driveway and heavy iron gate. Intermittently, for the next six hours, he talked on about Dylan and the pop life. His opulent mansion evidently housed a tremendously lonely young man. (Dylan had just told a California press conference: "It's always lonely where I am.") Spector told me how hurt he had been when The Righteous Brothers, after years of his careful grooming, had left him. Spector: "Songwriting IS poetry, but the only poet around is Bob Dylan. The Beatles should play Dylan's records five hours a day and learn what he's doing. Dylan doesn't compete, he doesn't care. It's very easy to talk a poem, but very difficult to sing a poem. . . . Dylan is a reporter, a philosopher. A unique talent, the most piercing and the most aware insight at work today. His genius lies in his insight into the truth and the phony. . . . If he were *only* in the hands of someone who really knew how to record him." Would *he* like to produce Dylan sessions? Spector's eyes gleamed assent. "There are avenues untouched. I knew that he was going to go through periods like this, when everything was getting him down. The whole image of Dylan was created by others. He became a Beatle, but he really wasn't. They gave him a role, he didn't take the role, he just sort of worked inside it. . . .

"Dylan doesn't owe anyone anything. . . . What he was writing three years ago, he was living. . . . They poisoned Socrates. What happened to Jesus the last time he went out in public? Two or three years ago, they said Dylan was a social-protest singer. Now, he becomes a possession. Dylan's going through things I went through a couple of years ago. He is nervous and he is suffering. The most amazing thing, I think, was when Dylan and Baez were doing 'With God on Our Side.' The hardcore American is one of those midwestern coal miners, the flag-wavers. With that song, he challenged everything they believed in. I am surprised there aren't more outraged pickets outside every one of his concerts. He sang an atheistic song in a country that has 'In God We Trust' on every penny."

During the evening, lush young Hollywood girls showed up, looked around, giggled, watched Spector for a sign. A bust of Wagner glowered on the piano. There was a telephone in every richly furnished room, none bearing numbers. Spector played a master tape at screeching level. He found someone to drive his limousine out to a club out on La Collina Road to watch Ike and Tina Turner. Energy flow! You wondered how Tina could return to Spector's studio the next day. He dropped me off at a friend's apartment. Spector sat in the backseat of his limousine, enveloped in soft luxury and unabated loneliness.

One evening, in December 1965, Dylan, Neuwirth, and Suze Rotolo sat at the back of the Kettle of Fish with filmmaker Barbara Rubin. Suze and Bob were having a pleasant reunion as old friends. Dylan was ranting on about the "literary establishment": "Those cats at the Poetry Center want me to go up on their stage now. Where were they all a few years ago? Now, they are just getting on the bandwagon, but I couldn't care less." Lurking at the bar was a gentle man in a black leather jacket, Andy Warhol. He shyly waved at Dylan, who waved back but made no effort to draw Warhol to his table. Next in line was Jan Cremer, a Dutch professional hipster, who had dedicated his modest book *I, Jan Cremer,* to Dylan. Cremer approached, but Neuwirth fended off the Dutch intruder.

A black-leather motorcycle type—a Hell's Angel in spirit if not membership—approached Bob with photographs. I assumed he was showing pictures of his girlfriend or baby. Dylan remarked approvingly of each picture, and when I asked to see, Bob handed over a pile of snapshots of the guy's motorcycle. Dylan's conversation was hardly sequential. He raved about Michael McClure: "I gave him an Autoharp and told him he ought to sing his poems." Then Dylan sang the praises of Ginsberg. "Read 'Kaddish,' man, if you want to read something really great." He had seen the anthology of Woody Guthrie writing, *Born to Win,* which I had edited. "I like it, all right," Dylan said, "but that was for a particular time and place." I told Bob that Mary Travers thought Dylan was turning into "another Norman Mailer." "I never read Norman Mailer," Dylan snapped. (Mailer had once said: "If Dylan's a poet, I'm a basketball player." Later, in 1975, he told *Rolling Stone:* " 'Dylan may prove to be our greatest lyric poet of this period. Like many another lyric poet, he can't necessarily read his own lyrics. . . .' ") Had Dylan liked Judy Collins's single of his "I'll Keep It with Mine"? He did, but when I asked if it referred to Sara and her child, Dylan chafed: "You don't know where it's at!" Neuwirth leaped in to say: "That song was for Nico, man. Just for Nico!" Dylan calmed down. (Nico was the star of the Velvet Underground band. There should be no surmise that Dylan and she had ever been involved.)

Soon he was back on the road again. February 5, at the Westchester County Center, White Plains. February 6, Rochester Auditorium. Then, a sweep through Memphis, Richmond, and Norfolk. The Westchester County show, which 5,000 attended, drew typically mixed reactions. *The Eastchester High School Eaglet* said Dylan resembled "a sad marionette . . . he looked half asleep or half dead. . . ." On February 10, Dylan appeared in Memphis. I asked Granville Allison, Jr., of *The Memphis Commercial-Appeal,* to send me a report: "The crowd was so young, so well-behaved . . . there were 2,995 in the Ellis Auditorium Amphitheater, which seats 5,778. A crucial basketball game undoubtedly held down the crowd. There weren't 100 people in the audience who were over 25. . . . Although Memphis, with 600,000 population, is 35% Negro, I saw no Negro kids, and there's no segregation in Memphis public facilities. . . . The sound system was awful. Not one word in 10 was intelligible, but it didn't seem to bother the crowd. . . ."

Richmond, Norfolk, New Haven, Ottawa . . . Montreal on February 20, two concerts at Philadelphia's Academy of Music, then West Hempstead on Long Island, February 26. *Newsday* found Dylan "in a tight form-fitting brown-checked suit inspired by Liverpool out of W. C. Fields. . . . Be¿- fore an audience of 5,100, nearly all teenagers, nobody seemed . . . sur- prised that the social critic for the disenchanted had run out of things to say. . . . These days, Dylan has little to protest against, except, perhaps his tailor."

I joined the tour at the two Philadelphia concerts on February 24 and 25. An usher warned one amateur photographer away from the stage po- litely: "The artist doesn't like the flashing while he's performing." The man sneered: "What's an artist for?" The performances were absorbing. I polled some listeners. Three students from the Camden Catholic High School said their favorite poets were Dylan Thomas and Ferlinghetti. A Susquehanna University undergraduate praised "Dylan's special weirdness. I believe in his freedom of choice . . . that is what he says to me, and I don't care whether he says it alone or with electricity. . . ." By the arrival at Miami Beach, on March 3, Sam Hood of the Gaslight was arranging the Convention Hall concert. *The Miami Daily Sun* interviewed a girl: " 'I think Dylan is the Tennessee Williams of song-writing . . . I said that.' " Another girl: " 'My sister thinks he is the Messiah. . . . I think he is a great poet.' " A surprise guest at the Miami concert was Anthony Quinn, the actor who had portrayed an eskimo in a recent film. No one needed to ask what brought "The Mighty Quinn" out of his igloo.

RETURN TO MIDDLE AMERICA

When I joined Dylan on tour in St. Louis in March 1966, he was wearing his "rabbit suit," a mod black and brown houndstooth check, which he said had been made for him by Robbie's tailor in Toronto. He was im- pressed by "some of the mail that comes in. It's amazing! I couldn't ever hope to read it all, let alone to answer it all. From people all over, talking about my songs and records. And talking about their problems and their heads and how they're stuck somewhere and want to get out." One St. Louis University undergraduate told me: "If I were Dylan, I'd drop out of sight for a few years. Like to an island in the Pacific. There has been so much stupid criticism of him, he ought to go away and make people ap- preciate him more."

On to Lincoln, Nebraska, March 12, 1966. Plumb dead center in the Great Plains, Dylan was on Middle America's home ground. Population 120,000, 98 percent white. Flour mills, creameries, meat packing, insurance companies, grain and cattle markets, brick and tile works. Site of Nebraska State University, with about 20,000 students. The big news, aside from basketball: President Johnson said spending on Vietnam was running below estimates. In Laredo, Timothy Leary got a thirty-year sentence for transporting marijuana. No Dylan news, but the manager of the Per- shing Memorial Auditorium was still delighted: "It's really amazing, how much press that boy gets. None here in Lincoln, mind you, but a lot nationally."

By now, Dylan had enforced rules: no picture taking, no tape recorders in the hall. Bootlegging had begun. The audience filed in for the electric set. Dylan plugged in his black-and-white, solid-body electric guitar, chatted with Robbie, turned his back to the audience. The listeners stared motionless. Dylan turned his toes in like a pigeon. His longish hair fell down to his collar. As he led the band behind him into the song, he spread his legs far apart in a near split. Another standing ovation. At the hotel, I found a note from Victor to call Dylan in his room. I was asked down immediately. Two dozen kids were in the corridor outside. Robbie and Dylan were stretched out on twin beds, other Band members lounging about. Dylan: "Bob, you're older, maybe they'll listen to you. Tell those kids I can't see them. Tell them I'm really tired." I tell the kids and half leave; the others hang about. Dylan on my book: "I'll go along, if it's a respectful book. I resent it when they try to treat me like a kid. I resent being placed in some little pigeonhole as some sort of 'rock-star millionaire freak.' "

Dylan seemed eager to use the minutes until the plane was ready to depart, and we turned to literature: "Rimbaud? I can't read him now. Rather read what I want these days. 'Kaddish' is the best thing yet. Everything else is a shuck. I never dug Pound or Eliot. I dig Shakespeare. A raving queen and a cosmic amphetamine brain." On his new music: "There was never any change. No instrument will change love, death, in any soul. Unless some radioactive society . . . unless they eat their hearts out . . . then it might. Look at the South. It's groovy. Blacks are taking over the town. But how groovy is it? Power, that's all it is. Rich blacks will take over . . . the kids are just a start. . . . If I was black, I don't know if I'd want to go to school with whites. It's bullshit. All is death, I'm afraid. I don't want to see myself die. I'd just as soon dive a car off a cliff than do something I don't believe in. Got to beat the pressure. . . . My music is my music. Licked them all after the last album. Nobody can do it. . . . A lot can run the parallel. Buddy Holly was a poet. Way ahead of his time. Read his story. I played with Buddy Holly in North Dakota, South Dakota, ballrooms, youth dances. . . .

"Folk music was such a shuck. I never recorded a folk song. My idea of a folk song is Jeannie Robertson or Dock Boggs. Call it historical-traditional music. . . . I saw Chuck Berry at St. Louis Airport. . . . You can listen to Buddy Holly when you're all alone, but Chuck Berry? You have to be out on the highway. . . . I want to write songs now. Until *Bringing It All Back Home* songwriting was a sideline. I was still a performer. Then I knew I had to write songs. . . . Get some of those literary people, some of those poetry people to sit down with my records . . . that would be good."

Victor said the plane was ready. Two cars heading for the Lincoln airport waited in front of the hotel. Half of us went down the stairs while Dylan and the rest took the elevator. In the lobby, fifty fans clustered. We rushed for the cars, so quickly the fans said: "There he is. . . . There he goes!" We took off like bank robbers. Victor smiled as wheels screeched from the curb. "That wasn't too bad," Dylan said. "Sometimes you can't even get to the car." We headed for the airport at Lincoln.

10

ONE FOOT ON
THE HIGHWAY ...

"I have a death thing. . . . I have a suicidal thing, I
know. . . . If the songs are dreamed, it's like my voice is
coming out of their dream."

—DYLAN, 1966

"Judas!"

—HECKLER AT ALBERT HALL, 1966

"Bob Dylan, go home."

—PARIS JOUR, 1966

In the dark, Lincoln Municipal Airport blended into the surrounding
farmland. It was just past the break of midnight on a Saturday in mid-
March 1966. As Dylan, The Band, two roadies, and I arrived, runway
lights flashed on, tower controllers stirred, and mechanics busied themselves around Dylan's private plane, the two-engine Lockheed Lodestar jet.

Denver was next, then back to New York, then up to the Pacific
Northwest, Hawaii, Australia, Scandinavia, Ireland, England, France, then
back home. This was the beginning of the end of one of Dylan's many
careers. As he walked into the lunch-canteen room, a mechanic in white

overalls peered into the night. "It must get lonely out here," Bob said. Both looked at the field. "It does," the mechanic replied, "but it's a job. I just take the hours they give me." "I know how that feels, I really do," Dylan said, as they stared across prairie land.

He had just evaded fifty fans at his hotel, but a half dozen clustered around the plane. He scribbled his autograph a few times. A shy youth, about seventeen, approached. "Mr. Dylan," he said, nervously, "I'm interested in poetry too." "Yeah, is that so?" Dylan replied. "Yes, sir," the boy answered. "I was wondering if you could spare a few minutes, sometime, to read some poems I've written." "Sure," Bob responded. The young man handed Dylan a large envelope that bulged like a football. "Are all these poems?" Dylan asked. "Yes ... I've been writing more since I began to study your songs." "Well," Dylan said, "thank you. I'll try to read some tonight. Is your address on the envelope? I'll let you know what I think of them." The boy glowed: "That's wonderful. I hope you like them."

Inside the plane, The Band members were dozing off, a pile of slumping bodies. Road managers Bill Avis and Victor Maimudes checked everyone's seat belt. Dylan and I sat face to face. On one knee rested a packet of proofs of his book, *Tarantula*. On his other knee was the fan's envelope. I fussed with my tape recorder, cursing the engine noise. His eyes were nearly slits, but he told me he wouldn't have slept even if I hadn't been there. He just had too much to do.

"It takes a lot of medicine to keep up this pace," Dylan said. "It's very hard, man. A concert tour like this has almost killed me. It's been like this since October. . . . It really drove me out of my mind. . . . I'm really going to cut down. Next year, the concert tour is only going to last a month . . . or two. I'm only doing it like this because I want everyone to know what we're doing." Dylan sent a cloud of cigarette smoke over his head, tugged his shirt collar, and continued: "It's just absurd for people to sit around being offended by their own meaninglessness, so that they have to force everything else to come into the hole with them, and die trying. That's the hang-up here. But I'm not involved with that anymore. I've told you that many times. I don't know if you think I'm kidding, or if you think it's a front. I really just don't *care*—honestly just don't *care*—what people say about me. I don't care what people think about me. I don't care what people know about me.

"Playing on the stage is a kick for me, now. It wasn't before, because I knew what I was doing then was just too empty. . . . It was just dead ambassadors who would come and see me and clap and say: 'Oh, groovy, I would like to meet him and have a cocktail. Perhaps I'll bring my son, Joseph, with me.' And the first thing you know you've got about five or six little boys and girls hanging around with Coke bottles and ginger-ale bottles ... and you're confronted by some ambassador who's got his hand in your pocket trying to shake your spine and give you compliments. I won't

342   NO DIRECTION HOME

let *anybody* backstage anymore. Even to give me a compliment. I just don't care. . . ."

His eyes cleared: "You can't ask me about how I sleep. You can't ask me about how I make it, and you cannot ask me what I think I am doing here. Other than that, we'll just get along fine. You just ask me anything and I will shoot right back. . . . Now, we have one thing straight about the book. I'm going to tell Albert we have come to an understanding about the book. I'll give you as much time as I can. I'll come very quickly to the point in all the things that I want done, but you can easily go back on me. . . . But I won't forgive you for doing that, man. It's not going to be a biography, because I'm not dead yet. It's going to be a timeless thing, right?

"Nobody knows about me. What do people really know? That my father's name is Zimmerman and my mother's family is middle class? I'm not about to go around telling people that this is false. . . . I'm not covering up anything I did before. I'm not going back on anything, any statement or anything I've ever done. . . . I've given up trying to tell anybody that they are wrong in their thinking about anything, about the world, or me, or whatever. . . . Now, you are not going to say 'authorized by Bob Dylan.' I'll write that on the cover. I'll write four sentences on the cover and sign my name, to something like: 'Bob Shelton wrote me up in *The New York Times* five years ago. And he's a nice guy and I like him. And he wrote this book and for that, it is not'—just to make sure it sells in Nebraska and Wyoming— 'it's not chintzy.' " Dylan laughed.

"There is nothing anybody can expose about me. Everybody thinks that there is such an exposé, on millions of little tiny things, like name change. It doesn't really matter to me. Obviously, there are people who like to read that shit. And people might say 'Oh, I don't believe it,' or 'That doesn't matter to me.' But it tickled them, you know." Twisting restlessly, Dylan was getting angry at the hungers of his audience. He seemed to want to *explain* himself. He tried a new beginning: "I think of all that I do as my *writing.* It cheapens it to call it anything else but writing. But there is not a person on the earth who takes it less seriously than I do. I know that it's not going to help me into heaven one little bit. It's not going to keep me out of the fiery furnace. It's not going to extend my life any and it's not going to make me happy."

What did he think would make him happy? I asked. "I'm happy, you know," he said. "I'm happy to just be able to come across things. I don't need to be happy. Happiness is a kind of cheap word. Let's face it, I'm not the kind of cat that's going to cut off an ear if I can't do something. I would commit suicide. I would shoot myself in the brain if things got bad. I would jump from a window. . . . You know, I can think about death openly. It's nothing to fear. It's nothing sacred. I've seen so many people die." I asked: Is life sacred? "Life's not sacred either," Dylan replied. "Look at all the spirits that actually control the atmosphere, which are not living and yet which attract you, as ideas, or like games with the solar system. Or look at the farce of politics, economy, and war."

Another variation on an old theme: inner despair battling outer hope. "It's become so easy for me to do everything, you have no idea, man, everything at my command. I can make money now doing absolutely anything. But I don't want that kind of money. I'm not a millionaire now, in terms of everything I have. But it is really close. . . . This next year, I'm going to be a millionaire, but that means nothing. To be a millionaire means that next year you can lose it all. You must realize that I have not copped out on one thing. I mean, I love what I do. I also make money off it. . . . Hey, I sing honest stuff, man, and it's consistent. It's *all* I do. I don't give a damn what anybody says. Nobody can criticize what I do that's going to have any effect on me. I never really read what people say about me. I'm just not interested.

"When I first really knew that I had money that I couldn't see, I looked around to see what a few of my agents were doing with it. First of all, I like chauffeurs. When I came back from England last time, I didn't buy a chauffeur, but I sure rented one. I make no bones about it . . . I *need* the money to *employ* people. It all works hand in hand. If I had no money, I could walk *invisible*. But it costs me money now to be able to walk invisible. That's the *only* reason I need the money. I don't need the money to buy clothes or nothing. . . ." Again his anger mounted. "I'm sick of giving creeps money off my soul. When I lose my teeth tomorrow, they are not going to buy me a new pair of teeth. I don't like little short people who smoke Tiparillo cigarettes and have their pockets turned inside out all the time and wear glasses and who once wanted to be Groucho Marx making all the money off me. And there are a lot of them. . . . All in the music business.

"Oh, if it's not the promoter cheating you, it's the box office cheating you. Somebody is always giving you a hard time. . . . Even the record company figures won't be right. Nobody's going to be straight with you because nobody wants the information out. Do you know that up to a certain point I made more money on a song I wrote if it were on an album by Carolyn Hester, or anybody, than if I did it myself. That's the contract they gave me. Horrible! Horrible! . . .

"I'm not going to be accepted, but I would like to be accepted . . . by *The Hogtown Dispatch* literary crowd, who wear violets in their crotch and make sure that they get on all the movie and TV reviews and also write about the ladies' auxiliary meetings and the PTA gatherings, you know, all in the same column. I would like to be accepted by them people. But I don't think I'm ever going to be. Whereas The Beatles have been." Did he want The Beatles' sort of acceptance? "No, no, no . . . I'm not saying that. I'm just saying The Beatles have arrived, right? In all music forms, whether Stravinsky or Leopold Jake the Second, who plays in the Five Spot, The Black Muslim Twins, or whatever. The Beatles are accepted, and you've got to accept them for what they do. They play songs like 'Michelle' and 'Yesterday.' A lot of smoothness there."

When I told him Joan Baez planned to record "Yesterday" on her next album, Bob responded: "Yeah, it's the thing to do, to tell all the teenyboppers, 'I dig The Beatles,' and you sing a song like 'Yesterday' or 'Michelle.' Hey, God knows, it's such a cop-out, man, both of those songs. If you go into the Library of Congress, you can find a lot better than that. There are millions of songs like 'Michelle' and 'Yesterday' written in Tin Pan Alley." There aren't millions of songs like *his* being written by anyone, I suggested. "I don't know if I fully appreciate that because it's going to get to the point where nobody else is going to be able to sing my songs but me. Like, I'm going to drive myself right out of business. I'll have to put out ten thousand records a year, for God's sake, because nobody will record the songs I write." Did he influence young people because he broke the rules? "It's not a question of breaking the rules, don't you understand? I don't break the rules, because I don't see any rules to break. As far as I'm concerned, there aren't any rules. . . ."

Like Lenny Bruce, he was riffing, in and out of communication, like a jazzman going in and out of a melody line. It was word music, chin music, symbol music. "My thing is with colors. It's not black and white. It's always been with colors, whether with clothes or anything. Color. Now, with something like that driving you, sometimes it gets very fiery red, you understand? And at times it gets very jet black.

"You just have to make it. When I say 'make it,' I don't mean being a popular folk-rock star. Making it means finding your line. Everybody's line is there, someplace. People think they just have to go through living hell on earth, but I don't really believe that attitude. The only people who believe . . . that life is a tragedy, are the people who are simple, closed-minded, who have to make excuses for themselves. Despite everybody who has been born and has died, the world has just gone on. I mean, look at Napoleon—but we went right on. Look at Harpo Marx—the world went around, it didn't stop for a second. It's sad but true. John Kennedy, right?"

Isn't the difference in what people did when they were here on earth? "Don't you see they did *nothing*? Has anybody done anything? Name anybody you think has done something." Shaw, I said. "George Bernard Shaw," Dylan slowly repeated. "Who has he helped?" "He helped a lot of people to use their heads," I replied, adding: "You've helped a lot of people to use their heads and their ears." "Well," Dylan rejoined, "I don't think I have, that's all. It's funny people think I have. I'm certainly not the one to go around saying that that is what I do. . . . At one time I did read a lot of the stuff that was written about me, maybe three or four years ago. Now, I don't even read anything anymore. So I have no idea what people say about me. I really don't. I do know that a lot of people really like me. I know that. . . ."

**Bob Dylan in Sheridan
Square Park, January
1965**

above, Sometime in early 1965, with Joan Baez, her mother, Joan Baez, Sr., and sister Mimi Fariña   *right,* Lathered up and ready for a close shave, Holiday House Inn, New Haven, Connecticut, March 1965 *above,* **Bob Dylan in London, the *Don't Look Back* tour, 1965** *right,* **Albert Grossman at the office of Leacock-Pennebaker, New York City, May 1967**

Broadside #93

BOB DYLAN: WHAT HIS SONGS REALLY SAY

Photo: DIANA DAVIES

IN THIS ISSUE: Bob Dylan's songs interpreted by Alan Weberman, who finds in them the radical militant continuing to protest The Establishment.

ALSO: Songs by ARLO GUTHRIE, BRUCE PHILLIPS, PABLO NERUDA, JAN DAVIDSON.

50¢

JULY/AUGUST 1968

Broadside No. 93

right, **Bob Dylan at the Isle of Wight Festival, 1969** *below,* **Bob Dylan as Alias in** *Pat Garrett and Billy the Kid*

Blackbushe *below,* **Bob Dylan with Robbie Robertson,** *The Last Waltz,* **1976**

**Bob Dylan at Earl's Court,
London, 1981**

The European tour: a
press conference in
Hamburg, May 31, 1984,
with (left to right) Carlos
Santana, Joan Baez, and
Bob Dylan

Eight miles high, over the Great Plains, he joggled *Tarantula* on one knee and the Nebraska boy's poems on the other, an unconscious seesaw. Did he think *Tarantula* was going to be accepted by the literary establishment, by serious poets? "... I think a poet is anybody who wouldn't call himself a poet. Anybody who could possibly call himself a poet just cannot be a poet.... When people start calling me a poet, I say: 'Oh, groovy, how groovy to be called a poet!' But it didn't do me any good, I'll tell you that. It didn't make me any happier.

"Hey, I would love to say that I am a poet. I would really like to think of myself as a poet, but I just can't because of all the slobs who are called poets." Who was a poet, then? Allen Ginsberg? "He's a poet," Dylan fired back. "To be a poet does not necessarily mean that you have to write words on paper. One of those truck drivers at the motel is a poet. He talks like a poet. I mean what else does a poet have to do? Poets—" his voice trailed off inchoately, ideas running too fast for his tongue. "People like Robert Frost poetry about trees and branches, but that isn't what I mean.... Allen Ginsberg is the only writer I know. The rest of the writers I don't have that much respect for. If they really want to do it, they're going to have to *sing* it.... I wouldn't call myself a poet for any more reason than I would call myself a protest singer. All that would do would put me in a category with a whole lot of people who would just bother me. To tell anybody I'm a poet would just be fooling people. That would put me in a class, man, with people like Carl Sandburg, T. S. Eliot, Stephen Spender, and Rupert Brooke. Hey, name them—Edna St. Vincent Millay and Robert Louis Stevenson and Edgar Allan Poe and Robert Lowell.

"I know two saintly people," Bob continued. "I know just two holy people. Allen Ginsberg is one. The other, for lack of a better term I just want to call 'this person named Sara.' What I mean by 'holy' is crossing all the boundaries of time and usefulness.... William Burroughs is a poet. I like all his old books and Jean Genet's old books. Genet's scholastical lectures are just a waste of time, they are just boring. But if we are talking now in terms of writers I think can be called poets, then Allen must be the best. I mean Allen's 'Kaddish,' not 'Howl.' Allen doesn't have to sing 'Kaddish,' man. You understand what I mean? He just has to lay it down. He's the only poet that I know of. He's the only person I respect who writes, that just totally writes. He don't have to do nothing, man. Allen Ginsberg, he's just holy." How is Sara holy? "I don't want to put her in this book. I want to keep her out of this. I don't want to call her 'a girl.' I know it's very corny, but the only thing I can think of is, more or less, 'madonna-like.' "

I was beginning to think he'd forgotten my tape recorder, when he asked: "Are you getting it all? How much tape do you have left? Is it still running?" He plunged on: "Love and sex are things that really hang everybody up. When things aren't going right and you're really nobody, if you don't get laid in one way or another, you get mean, you know. You get cruel. Now, why in the world sex should force this is beyond me. I truthfully can tell you that male and female are not here to have sex, you know, that's not the purpose. I don't believe that that's God's will, that females have been created so that they can be a counterpart of man's urge. There are too many other things that people just won't let themselves be involved in. Sex and love have nothing to do with female and male. It is just whatever two souls happen to be. It could be male and female, and it might not be male and female. It might be female and female or it might be male and male. You can try to pretend that it doesn't happen, and you can make fun of it and be snide, but that's not really the rightful thing. I know, I know."

His verbal floodstream seemed driven by pressure built up during years of talking guardedly for publication. Inevitably, music displaced all other topics, even though he had remarked to me before we got on the plane that "music is only twenty percent of what I am." "I want you to have explanations of my songs in your book," Dylan said. "Things nobody else will ever have." "Such as," I broke in, "who Mr. Jones is to you?" "Well," Bob parried, "I'm not going to tell you that way. I'm going to tell you about the stuff that *I* want to tell you about. . . . I could tell you who Mr. Jones is in my life, but, like, everybody has got their Mr. Jones, so I can't really say that he is the same for everyone." Nothing struck me so strongly as this passage in his two-in-the-morning monologue: "Mr. Jones's loneliness can easily be covered up to the point where he can't recognize that he is alone . . . suddenly locked in a room . . . it's not so incredibly absurd, and it's not so imaginative, to have Mr. Jones in a room with three walls with a midget and a geech and a naked man. Plus a voice, a voice coming in his dream. I'm just a voice speaking. Anytime I'm singing about people, and if the songs are dreamed, it's like my voice is coming out of their dream. . . ."

He was speeding along, now attacking some false myths: "I hung around college, but it's a cop-out from life, from experience. A lot of people started out to be lawyers, but I venture to say that one hundred percent of the really groovy lawyers haven't gotten through school the way they ought to. They've always been freaks in their school, and have always had a hard time making it . . . so many lawyers just take people for what they're worth. They all made deals and all are very criminal . . . but doctors, lawyers, all these kinds of people—they're just in it for money . . . and for resentment. They put in their time and they're going to get it back. I agree with them that way. But I'm sure it could be done in other ways, and it's not. . . . I've known people who've been really loaded down with burdens and who have been in the right to collect, and who have been so innocent, that when they got lawyers to get them what they deserve . . . Do you follow me? The parties they are suing make deals with their lawyers. Like, it happens all the time, man. How anybody could have respect for lawyers baffles me! I have lawyers working for me I never see. I don't see my lawyers. Anytime they see the chance, they jump on it. ...."

Did he want to talk about Joan Baez? Would he shed any light on his attitudes *then* toward one of the most intriguing show-business liaisons of the times, or would he bite my head off? "Me and Joan?" Bob asked. "I'll tell you. I hope you do explain it, if you can do this book straight. She brought me up.... I rode on her, but I don't think I owe her anything.... I want you to print that, because I am not joking. I feel sorry for her, knowing that I don't have to feel sorry for her, or anybody to feel sorry for her.... I feel bad for her because she has nobody to turn to that's going to be straight with her.... She hasn't got that much in common with the street vagabonds who play insane instruments. She's not that kind of person. Her family is a very gentle kind of family. She's very fragile and very sick and I lived with her and I loved the place.... Can you write this in your book? If you can't, man, it's a waste of time. I mean, is your book going to be a mature book, or is this all just a waste of time?" I reassured him.

Dylan's strangely defiant mood seemed to stress his most unappealing, antiheroic side, daring me, it seemed, to take at face value all his negative thinking or self-destructive patterns. I think that he wanted it understood that behind all the applause, there was a lot of pain. He talked of when we had knocked around the Village together. "After Suze moved out of the house ... I got very, very strung out for a while. I mean, really, very strung out." But, he told me, he'd survived. "I can do anything, knowing in front that it's not going to catch me and pull me ... 'cause I've been through it once already. I've been through people. A lot of times you get strung out with people. They are just like junk.... The same thing, no more, no less. They kill you the same way.... They rot you the same way...." I suggested it reminded me of the line in Sartre's *No Exit:* "Hell is other people." Dylan joked: "Whatever it is, man. I don't know Sartre. He's cross-eyed, that's all I know about him. Anybody cross-eyed can't be all bad...." Then he seemed to hit bottom: "I have a death thing, I know. I have a suicidal thing, I know...."

Later, I asked if he wanted to leave all this despair on the record. He said: "I haven't explained those things I said against myself.... A lot of people *think* that I shoot heroin. But that's *baby talk*.... I do a lot of things. Hey, I'm not going to sit here and lie to you ... and make you wonder about all the things I do. I do a lot of things, man, which help me.... And I'm smart enough to know that I don't depend on them for my existence, you know, and that's all. Man, that's where it lays, like that...."

I'd been thinking then of how one night at the Gaslight Dylan had advised me "to just write about something that is really important to you." At that time, I couldn't envision that it would be about the man who'd given me the advice. Dylan continued: "I can't be hurt, man, if the book is honest. No kidding, I can't be hurt. Hey, I'm trusting you. . . ." We were bitter then because the folk world was so hostile toward his electric merging of folk and rock. "Nobody told me to go electric," Bob said emphatically. "No, I didn't even ask anybody. I asked not a soul, believe me. . . . Hey, I went electric on my second record. Why don't you bring that out in the book?" Dylan reminded me that the *Freewheelin'* album, released in May 1963, had been meant to include "four electric songs. The only reason they cut out the electric ones was because I didn't write them. . . . Columbia still has them. I don't know if they would play them for you, because I know they are trying to retouch them."

Before The Beatles were known in America and before the folk-rock craze of 1965, Dylan had tried to show he was not a performer to pigeonhole. "I hate all the labels people have put on me . . . because they are labels. It's just that they are ugly, and I know, in my heart, that it's not me. . . . I have not *arrived* at where I am at now, I have just *returned* to where I am now, knowing it's the only way. What I am doing now is what I must do before I move on."

Dylan dug his heels in about the music world and his early attraction toward folk music: "I hate to say this, because I don't want it to be taken the wrong way, but I latched on, when I got to New York City, because I saw a huge audience was there. People I *knew* I was not taking advantage of. I knew I wasn't going to stay there. I knew it wasn't my thing. Many times I spoiled it. Many times I went against it. Anytime they tried to think I was like them, I knew I wasn't like them. I just told them whatever happened to be in my mind at the time. I didn't have any respect for any of the organizations. In New York City, they are all organizations. I had respect for the people.

"Woody [Guthrie] turned me on romantically. . . . Woody used his own time, in a way nobody else did. He was just a little bit better . . . just a little smarter, because he was from the country. . . . I met Woody and I talked with him. I dug him. I would dig him, I imagine, if he were around today. . . ." He cited some reservations about Guthrie's style, and I asked if Woody's work seemed too simple for him. "No, not simple at all! The fundamental objection is that I can see *why* he wrote what he wrote. I can see him sitting down and writing what he wrote, in a very calm kindofa way. I am *not* putting him down. I'm not copping out on my attraction to him and his influence on me. His influence on me was never in inflection or in voice. What drew me to him was that hearing his voice I could tell he was very lonesome, very alone, and very lost out in his time. That's why I dug him."

Dylan stressed that at the height of his involvement in the folk world, he still loved rock 'n' roll. "Suze Rotolo could tell you, because Suze knows more than anybody else that I played, back in 1961 and 1962, when nobody was around, all those Elvis Presley records. She'll tell you how many nights I stayed up and wrote songs and showed them to her and

asked her: 'Is this right?' Because I knew her father and mother were associated with unions and she was into this equality-freedom thing long before I was. I checked the songs out with her. . . . Suze is a very talented
girl, man, but she is very frightened. . . ."

We talked about *Sing Out!,* the folk-song magazine. In defense of
Dylan's changes, I had wrangled with them. He cautioned me against my
wasting time with polemics. Dylan: "Don't you understand? If you're
smart, you just gotta keep going, you're just not going to stand still. Everyone else is going to die. I don't mean *die.* I mean, they are going to
decay and go crazy. If I could help them, I would love to see them
straightened out. But I know in my heart that it is impossible to
straighten all these people out, because they are all so nine-to-five, and so
involved with that life that it is impossible. I don't want nothing to do
with it. *Sing Out!* has a big organization . . . they know they control a lot.
They have a very big hand in a lot of money. They have an Establishment.
The only person in that organization I respect . . . is Moe Asch, who is old
and hip. He's the only one who knows that he's not a clown, that the
whole world is not a circus. He knows. The rest of the people there don't
know it. They have power . . . fake, phony power. . . . They're dumb,
man. . . . They're clods. I never signed their petitions. If you're out of it,
groovy! But I'm telling you, man, get out of it. It's not that you have to
put them down to leave it."

He eyed the boy's poems, knowing he wouldn't read them that night. I
told him how touching it was when he told that airport mechanic how
lonely it got out there. "Well, I loved him, man," Dylan replied. "He's a
poor cat. What's he doing out there in Nebraska? I just wanted to know.
Hey, it's lonesome everyplace. The people that can't live with it, that can't
accept it . . . They are just going to blow up the world . . . and make things
bad for everybody, only because they feel so out of place. . . . Everybody
has that in common—they are all going to die.

"I quit after England, and it was just done. I could quit again." Already,
he told me, he'd withdrawn for a while from Woodstock. Dylan: "I
moved out a long time ago. Before the summer [of 1965] ended, I moved
into New York City. I couldn't make it up there anymore because it
wasn't private anymore. It will *never, ever* happen again. I'm *never* going to
tell anybody where I live again. . . . People want to tear me apart, man.
Hey, I don't take people up to the country now, because the country is a
very alone place. And if you don't dig being alone, if you haven't got
something to do, you're just going to take the bus back. I can be alone . . .
as long as I have to be alone. I don't have anything to say to anybody. But
it's hard for other people like that."

Dylan's search for the place to be "alone" has kept a lot of real-estate
agents and moving men busy. He asked me: "Do you know what I did
when I got back from England, man? I bought me a thirty-one-room
house . . . can you imagine that? . . . It turned into a nightmare, because,

first of all, I wrote *Highway 61 Revisited* there and I don't believe in writing some total other thing in the same place twice. It's just a hang-up, a voodoo kind of thing. I just can't do it. When I need someplace to make something new, I can't go back there because ... Have you ever smelled birth? Well, I just can't stand the smell of birth. It just lingers, so I just lived there and tried to go on, but couldn't. And so the house is up for sale now, and I've moved back into Albert's."

We talked a bit about The Beatles, whom he had first met at New York's Delmonico Hotel during their 1964 tour. He told me, however, that he felt, at that point, much closer to Marlon Brando than he did to any of The Beatles. "I wish you could meet Brando," Bob said. "There's nobody like Brando.... Nobody has treated him right, in the press...."

I'd seen a lot of cracks developing in Dylan's relationship with his manager. Dylan: "There are some things Albert and I naturally agree on, and some things that I have to tell him to agree on. He's only come across once on his side. The rest of the time, I don't want him telling me shit...." I suggested that people should realize a manager is a star's employee, not his employer, but Dylan flared. Like the man who grumbles about his wife but won't let anyone else criticize her, Dylan leaped to Grossman's defense: "... It's not that Albert works for me.... People who put Albert down ought to be ... I mean, critic people.... First of all, did you know? Sara told me this, and it's true—that in hell there is a special place for critics? Did you ever know that? That was before Dante's time. Before the *Inferno* and before the Black Plague. And when you think about it, it is very weird. Obviously, now, you see the ragman walking around a couple of thousand years B.C. did not like to be confronted with a bunch of mouths. That's still where it's at...."

I'd grown accustomed to Dylan's wide swings in mood. After one encounter this trip, in which he expressed deep and pervasive pessimism, I tried to counter his depression. A few days later, he scorned me: "I am *not* pessimistic," he told me. "If I am pessimistic, I am not even going to talk, I'm just going to go in the corner. One thing I have never done and will never do is force my moods on other people. Why should I sit around and talk to somebody for hours and then ... have them think that I am pessimistic? That's an insult! I'll tell you what the drag is, what hangs everybody up is that I'm not *stopping*. They call me dead. It is very silly for them to call me dead, and they know it. There was a time, last year, when it just went overboard. Everybody recorded my songs and it would have been very easy for me, at that time, to have written up another huge batch. Everyone would have done them. They would have just lapped them up," he said.

Dylan's ambivalence has confounded everyone who has ever been close to him. It sometimes confuses him. As late as 1976, he would say his Gemini personality "forces me to extremes. I'm never really balanced in the middle. I go from one side to the other without staying in either place very long. I'm happy, sad, up, down, in, out, up in the sky, and down in the depths of the earth. . . ." Ten years earlier, as we rode on this plane, he was swinging widely. When I said I'd like to interview Phil Spector, Dylan said, "Sure, sure, go see him." Then he told me how Spector had annoyed him, but "tell him that when I think about him, I really love him. . . ." More ambivalence about the press, critics, taste-makers, and opinion-molders: "Hey, magazines, critics, *Newsweek, Time, Look, Life* . . . all of it is very meaningless. It doesn't seem to me to change anybody's mind. When people *like* something, other people go around trying to figure out why people like these things. I mean, when they really like something, they like it. They just get involved in something, that's all. It happens to them. *Like* and *dislike* are just unreal words."

Sic transit the Fourth Estate, in the estimation of one who has used the press with much artfulness. I tried to move to his enthusiasm for black musicians. "Ask Aretha Franklin about me, man," Dylan said. "Or talk to The Staple Singers. Why don't you talk to Mavis Staples? I'd be interested in what she says. And to Purvis and Roebuck Staples too. Remember that night when Mahalia Jackson came out from the dugout with her goddamn maids, who lifted up her dresses and opened up her doors? She sure has class!

"A lot of people think that the modern spade musicians are getting a raw deal. A lot of them are, because there are real genius people playing in dives. But an awful lot of the records you hear are all copies. They too are imitating who they think they should imitate. . . . That don't mean you have to give them a million dollars and a house in the suburbs and a golf course. That's what we're talking about here. We're not talking about equality . . . or enough food to eat. . . ."

Why had he become so hopeless about the civil rights movement? "I'm not pessimistic about it," Bob replied. "No, no, I don't want to be misunderstood about Negro rights. But I don't know what a Negro is. What's a Negro? A black person? How black? What's a Negro? A person living in a two-room shack with twelve kids? A lot of white people live in a two-room shack with twelve kids. Does this make them Negro? What's a Negro? Someone with African blood? A lot of white people have African blood. What's a Negro? An Ethiopian kind of thing? That's not a Negro, that's an ancient, religious, pajama-riding freak! I've got nothing against Negro rights. I never did."

Dylan reminisced about some black friends from his early days in New York: about Mel and Lillian Bailey, who had treated him like a son and a brother, about Jim Forman, former leader of the Student Non-Violent Coordinating Committee. He spoke nostalgically about some other young blacks from Albany, Georgia, like Bernice Johnson and Cordell Reagon. "I love Cordell. He's a madman. He's the only faithful madman, the only madman—let me put it this way—that can wipe you out with pure strength who I could trust to go anywhere with. I never get to see so many people.

That's why I would like you to say things about a lot of people that I loved. Say that I said good things about them. Hey, I've turned down everybody, Bob. I'm giving you all this. I'm trusting you to go along with me. Hey, I've never been wrong. I'll tell you something about this book. If I tell you something, I'm not trying to horn in. I don't want any of your bread."

Knowing how mercurial Dylan was, I began to explore how he changes his mind about people, his own music, his past work. I said: "You have always been wildly enthusiastic about the recording you have just finished, and then you turn around a few months later and say it was nothing. At least, you always did that in the past." "No, no," Dylan flashed. "I like the last record. Hey, I made *Bringing It All Back Home* and I love that record. I made *Highway 61 Revisited* and I love that record. I love the *Blonde on Blonde* album. What I was trying to do on my fourth album—on *Another Side of Bob Dylan*—well, I was just too out of it, man, to come across with what I was trying to do. It was all done too fast. All done in one session. I liked the idea of it. No, I don't like the first album. You know, though, I've done some stuff on that first record that still stands up. Like my harmonica playing. Like in 'Man of Constant Sorrow,' the arrangement of that I like. 'In My Time of Dying' still stands up. But as a whole, it's not consistent."

Wasn't he really his own worst critic? "Of course I am my own worst critic! Those aren't my words, those are your words. A lot of the stuff I've done, man, the last three things I've done on records, is beyond criticism. I'm not saying that because I think I'm any kind of god. I'm just saying that because I just know. I've been at it too long. . . . I wanted to call that album *Highway 61 Revisited*. Nobody understood it. I had to go up the fucking ladder until finally the word came down and said: 'Let him call it what he wants to call it.' I have to fight for songs on the albums. I put them on there because I know it is right. And sure enough, it turns out to be right."

Dylan had been repeatedly irked by problems of sound amplification, especially in sports arenas, despite the setup that audio engineer Richard Alderson had assembled. "It turns out that we have wasted a lot of time . . . no matter how groovy and good it is, if it can't be heard, then it doesn't do anybody any good." Dylan asked me my reactions to the amplification at the various concerts I'd heard. He said he wanted, at the end of this tour, to bring the show into Carnegie Hall. I jokingly suggested that for optimum acoustics he try the Metropolitan Opera House. Dylan laughed, then asked, seriously: "How many people does it hold?"

I asked him about "My Life in a Stolen Moment." Dylan wove a web of ambivalence: "I don't disavow it. It is just not *me*. Somebody else wrote that. But I am not the person of five years ago. It's almost as if I were him," he said, pointing at one of the sleeping Band members. I asked him: "Can I say that when I quote things you wrote or said in the past, then?"

Dylan replied: "Sure. All right, but put it in context. It was done out of
. . . It was bled from my hand and from my arm. . . ." "By who?" I asked.
"By my brain," Dylan replied. "I remember all of it. I remember the drafts.
I remember the words. I used to write them, thinking they might some
day be novels. I remember why I did them. I remember all the shucks and
all the cons. All the cute, funny things. Like, man, I am so lucky now. . . .
I wouldn't be lucky if I couldn't produce. That's what I thought the last
six months. Oh, I was really down. I mean, in ten recording sessions, man,
we didn't get one song," he said, referring to *Blonde on Blonde*. What
slowed things down? "It was the band. But you see, I didn't know that. I
didn't want to think that. If I go back to Nashville, man . . . and everybody down there can't make it, I'm going to take a plane until something
else happens. I don't have the right to blame anybody else. It's not that I
blame myself, man, it is just that I was down. I was down. . . ."

I chanced a Hollywood-star interview question—just what does he do
with his money? "Tell them," Dylan said, making his first and last full financial disclosure, "tell them to check their pockets." We laughed. What
did he see in his future? "I can't talk of the future," Dylan said slowly. "I
can only talk a little more about it than I used to be able to talk about it,
but, still, I can't talk about it all that much. I know there's a movie. I'm
going to make a movie, and it's going to be groovy, you know. Then,
there's this book for Macmillan," Dylan said, tapping one of the envelopes. "It's already been fucking publicized and written about, and everybody's expected it and that kind of stuff," he went on, eyeing the
Tarantula envelope warily. "Every time I look in the paper there is something about this book. And I gave away the title, which I shouldn't have
done. So, I'm thinking of changing it now. You know, I just don't like
the obvious. Obvious things are a step backward. Nobody should step
backward because nobody knows what's behind them. The only direction
you can see is in front of you, not in back of you. . . ."

The plane's vibrations had been diminishing, even though it hadn't
been descending sharply. We'd forgotten that at Denver the ground
comes up to meet a plane arriving from the East. The Band stirred. They
were surprised he was still wide awake, still talking. Bob gave directions to
Victor and Bill about deplaning. He asked Robbie Robertson if he was up
to a few hours' work when they got to the motel, and Robbie nodded. As
the plane touched down, Dylan kept talking. He looked at the package of
poems and said he'd have to read them some other time. His eyes went
back and forth between the two envelopes on his lap as he said: "I know
how that boy feels. I know what it's like being a boy in a small town,
somewhere, trying to become a writer."

We arrived in Denver at nearly three A.M. I thought that Dylan was
finished for the night. "Give us about ten minutes, Bob," Dylan said, "and
then come down to the room." Robbie and Dylan were again sprawled
out on twin beds, each holding acoustic guitars, starting an hour's jam-

ming. I drank some coffee and tried to bring myself to life to tape them at work. It was all new material; I couldn't put a title on anything. When Dylan came to "Sad-Eyed Lady," he said: "This is the best song I've ever written. Wait till you hear the whole thing." Robbie's face was gray with fatigue. I assumed that tomorrow would be a long sleep-in. Dylan said: "Let's go out to Central City tomorrow morning. You'll like it. Meet me here at about eleven."

Next morning Bob called Grossman in New York. "I've got five new songs to tape," Dylan told the telephone. "Uh-huh, uh-huh ... Sinatra wants it? What about Otis Redding? I'd rather he do it. . . ." After the Central City outing, we returned to the Denver motel for more interview taping. I asked him how he could get any work done on such a rough tour. "It's very hard, man. It's killed me, ever since September. I never really had it like that before. I don't know how long until somebody will just clamp down, you know what I mean?"

We talked about people who had been important to him along the way. "Suze, I will be kind to her the rest of my life. Suze, anytime she wants anything, she could always come to me." But he had no patience with some others: "Just con people—they shouldn't be associated with me, because they are just going to get hung up by idiots that know they have known me."

In Denver, Dylan gave another concert for three thousand people. The amplification at the Denver Municipal Auditorium was a jangled echo. After the concert, I returned to Dylan's crowded motel room, where he started to describe Lennon and McCartney beating a retreat from his Albert Hall concert a year earlier. Dylan mimicked The Beatles running downstairs, halting for breath at landings, looking to see if they were pursued, then running down another flight. It was good pantomime. The Hawks roared. Some fans began calling up and friends dropped in. Bob was expansive, but couldn't conceal his fatigue. He saw me to the door.

"Now, Bob, I'm trusting you to be honest with your story," Dylan said. There was the old graciousness coming out, through all the fatigue and stoned haze. "See if you can't make it to El Paso, or to England. It'll be different there. It'll be better there. Say hello to Ralph." Ralph? Oh, yes! I had told him several days ago that I was going to see Ralph Gleason in San Francisco. I couldn't believe that with all he had on his mind he could remember something that I said *I* was going to do. He returned to the room and started telling everyone that it was getting late and he had some things to do. The party was over, for that night.

THEN, MIDDLE AUSTRALIA

Grossman should have guessed that Australia, even more middlebrow and muddled than Middle America, would spell trouble for Dylan. But The Kingstons and Peter, Paul and Mary had sold there; why not Dylan? After spring concerts in Seattle, Tacoma, Vancouver, and Honolulu, Dylan and The Band arrived in Sydney on April 12 for a fifteen-day tour. The *Melbourne News Weekly* greeted them: "Manly boys and sweet girls are OUT, now. . . . Young men who look like girls soon begin to think like girls; young girls who look like men eventually try to play the role of men . . . whenever this happens, civilization falls apart, and a more primitive virile race takes over. . . ."

There was not much advance notice that Australian civilization was about to fall apart. Pretour publicity was minimal, and disc jockeys were not spinning Dylan. He flew from city to city, meeting reporters who were mostly hostile, inane, callous, or uninformed. He gave them his best truculence. Newspaper stories seemed more like counterattacks than reports. After each concert and mixed reviews, the troupe pushed onward. At the arrival of Flight 305 in Sydney, about fifty fans joined the press. He signed a few autographs as "The Phantom," then his ringleted hair and dark shades provoked this: "Q: Why have you started playing rock 'n' roll? D: Is that what they call it? Q: Are you a professional beatnik? D: Well, I was in the Brigade once . . . we used t' get paid . . . but it didn't pay enough, so I became a singer. Q: Why don't you see your family? D: I wouldn't know where t' find them. Q: Why do you wear those outlandish clothes? D: I look very normal where I live." *The Sydney Sun* described the encounter: ". . . pygmy-sized, pallid-faced . . . the expression of a man being wheeled out of the operating theater still partly under an anaesthetic . . . 45 minutes of nonsensical spluttering, ho-hum mumbling and vague gabbing. . . ." *The Australian*'s headline was: DYLAN'S MANY HATS COME TO TOWN, and *The Sydney Daily Mirror* flailed Dylan's "insincerity." Throughout Dylan's tour, the Australian press indicated he didn't deserve publicity, but they grudgingly gave it to him. The most balanced and sympathetic reporting was in *The Sydney Morning Herald* by Craig McGregor, who later helped me with research.

After the first Sydney concert on April 13, *The Sun* shone in two directions, the first day headlining: SYDNEY'S WACKIEST CONCERT, and the second day calling the concert "a rare blend of integrity, artistry and intellectualism." On April 15, the troupe flew north to Brisbane. *The Telegraph* fanfared: NO FANFARE TO GREET FOLKSINGER, a curious piece of nonnews. To the Brisbane press, Dylan conceded that his songs had a message, but couldn't say what it was for fear of offending people. The two-hour Brisbane concert had amplification problems, although some witnesses said the sheer volume of sound was "colossal." No particular animosity during the electric set. The next day, *The Bulletin* did a cover story with two pages of inaccurate, speculative appraisal. *The Brisbane Courier* headline: ADVICE TO DYLAN: STAY DYLAN. Caption in *The Adelaide Mail:* "Folksy Millionaire." *The Perth News* went to lengths: "10-inch long hair, half-inch long fingernails and a very long bank account. And a long list of Australian fans were shocked when he said . . . he was not disturbed about

color discrimination nor young people dying in war. . . ." No such list
could be compiled. Dylan's main Australian support came from Sydney
artists and writers, including the founders of the underground magazine
OZ, Richard Neville and Martin Sharp. Among folk fans, controversy ran
high, but *The Australian*'s folk critic, Edgar Waters, wrote sympathetically, "Dylan remains the most effective voice for the feelings of the most
intelligent and sensitive people of his generation. The ugly sound and the
hysterical tone are essential for what he has to say. . . ."

For his final Sydney stadium concert, the sound system was better and
the audience more appreciative. Dylan was beginning to feel somewhat
more at home. The following morning, Sunday, as *The Sun-Herald* headlined: DYLAN NOT HERE TO WIN HEARTS, the troupe flew to Melbourne for
two concerts. They were greeted by about four hundred fans and/or curiosity seekers and the press: "Q: What is your greatest ambition? D: To be
a meatcutter. Q: Can you enlarge on that? D: Large pieces of meat. Q: Do
you think it's a good thing or a bad thing that youngsters try to copy you?
D: It's a thing. Q: What do you think of Australia? D: Since I was a little
boy, I've wanted to come to Australia. I once knew someone who knew
somebody whose grandfather was supposed to have heard of Australia.
This gave me a tremendous curiosity to find out whether this fellow really
did have a grandfather. Q: You also came for the money, I take it? D: I
take it. Q: How do you present your show? D: With my clothes on. That's
the only part of my act that I haven't got under control yet. Q: Is it true
that you don't care about color discrimination or war any longer? D: I'm
just a storyteller. Q: Don't you really care? D: I can't really tell you how I
care. I just can't. They never ask me these questions in America. They tried
to make a clown of me for three years and now I won't give interviews. I
have been writing myself—for fifteen years. I know how reporters have to
eat, but I won't let them use me. Sure, I have a feeling about war, about
Vietnam. My thoughts lie in the futility of war, not the morality of it. . . ."

At the two concerts in Melbourne, audiences were puzzled rather than
annoyed by the rock segments. A *Melbourne Age* reporter showed some
understanding: ". . . Dylan rocked backwards and forwards as if feeling
faint from the onslaught . . . for a few he wove long answers of fairy-tale
fancy—nonsensical but sharply amusing. . . if anybody had been tempted
to lose his patience, it was Dylan. . . . Dylan tries without conceit to explain that he's a 'watcher,' embroiled in nothing. . . . But the publicity
people these days demand nonconformists who are conforming nonconformists. . . ."

Early on April 21, Dylan went off to Adelaide, where he was greeted by
a reception committee of eight. He asked: "Where are all the cowboys,
huh?" before driving off to another hotel, another press conference. From
one of the most cramped stages he'd ever appeared on, he remarked sarcastically: "This is one of the nicest stages I've ever been on." During the
electric segment, a few people walked out. *The Adelaide Advertiser* said he

"captivated his audience," but described him as "sounding ... like Peter Lorre, looking like ... Harpo Marx and walking like a marionette...." The next day, he flew two thousand miles westward to Perth. On arrival, a barefoot Dylan said: "I had a choppy flight across your desert." About one hundred people met him. Another press conference found him in good, bitter form:

"Q: When do you write your songs? D: I never write on Fridays, or on Tuesday nights. It's an old Mexican tradition. Q: Why do you write? D: People get thirsty, they drink. People get hungry, they eat. When I get hungry, I write.... Q: What do you think of the Vietnam War? D: Nothing. It's Australia's war. Q: But Americans are there. D: They're just helping the Australians. Q: Some people call you a genius; do you agree? D: People who call me a genius don't have any grandparents. Q: You say you don't want to be thought an oddball. Why do you wear clothes like that, and long hair? D: My clothes are traditional. Q: Is it true you don't wash your hair or clean your teeth? D: It's a lie. I have four sets of teeth. ... Q: How much money have you made out of your songs? D: Seventy-five billion dollars. Q: How have you found your Australian tour? D: It's the differentest I've done."

After a concert at Perth's Capitol Theater on April 23, Bob went to a party briefly, then returned to his hotel to find a young actress, Rosemary Gerrette. Her mother was *The Canberra Times*'s features editor, and although Rosemary knew virtually nothing about Dylan, she wanted an interview. She befriended him over the next few days. Evidently deeply affected by the encounter, she retold it for years afterward. She contacted me in 1977. When I said she'd already been heard from, albeit as an anonymous actress, in several pages in the Anthony Scaduto book, she replied: "I deserve more than that." Her account, in *The Canberra Times* of May 7, was of a typical late-night songwriting session. Dylan read to her from *Tarantula* and told her: " 'People don't value their obscurity. They don't know what it's like to have it taken away....' " She heard a lot of literature talk and observed Baudelaire, Durrell, Australian poetry, and a Norman Mailer work strewn around the room. Dylan and crew left Perth on a twenty-seven-hour flight to Stockholm. Ripples in the Australian press continued for some weeks. "Rainy Day Women" was duly released, and duly banned.

CRUSADE IN EUROPE

Heavy with fatigue and jet lag, Bob and The Hawks arrived in Stockholm for a one-nighter on April 29. Scandinavian audiences were surprised by the presence of "The Group," which some saw as a sellout. In Stockholm, Dylan did a five-minute radio interview, which has since been bootlegged, and a press conference. Dylan had some questions for the Copenhagen press: "How far is the nearest cow?" and "Where's Hamlet's castle?"

Dylan's May 5 concert in Dublin's Adelphi Theater was a critical disaster. By now the show was truncated to ninety-five minutes, with fifty minutes for the acoustic set and the last three quarters of an hour electric. *Disc and Music Echo* said an "appreciative and orderly" audience erupted during the second half. Shouts of "traitor," "throw out the backing group," "stuffed golliwog," and "lower the mike" broke out. The Anglo-Irish form of derision, the slow handclap, resounded. Even the music press was taken aback. *Melody Maker:* "It was unbelievable to see a hip-swinging Dylan trying to look and sound like Mick Jagger . . . for most, it was the night of the big let-down." My correspondent, Ray Coleman, summarized Dylan's return to Britain: "If the 1965 tour was an unequivocal success, his return must be reckoned as taking the British public back to square one. There was widespread bitterness about his abandonment of the acoustic guitar. The Beatles turned out for his Albert Hall concert and pronounced Bob 'Great, just great.' Afterward, George Harrison defended Dylan's right to use a band: 'The people . . . who walked out . . . must have been idiots and they couldn't have known the real Dylan. . . . It was all still pure Dylan, and he has to find out his own directions. If he felt he wanted electrification, that's the way he had to do it. . . . Who's laying down rules?' When the jeering was going on," Coleman continued, "The Beatles, sitting in a box behind me in Albert Hall, shouted 'Leave him alone—SHUT UP!' to the moaners."

By the time Dylan arrived in London, his camera crew, many of whom had worked on *Don't Look Back* the previous year, were shooting again. They shot a 1-hour, 16-mm color film that was originally scheduled for the ABC-TV series *Stage 67*. The film, *Eat the Document,* has rarely been shown publicly. It was screened twice on February 9, 1971, at the Academy of Music in Manhattan, and from November 30 through December 13, 1972, at the Whitney Museum of American Art. By then the film ran 54 minutes, after Dylan's and Howard Alk's editing. The museum's publicity described it as an "anti-document . . . an adventuresome . . . challenge to all the preconceived notions we have of a star and his public image. . . ." Jonas Mekas wrote in *The Village Voice:* "About the richest . . . the best, of all films on rock . . . we can feel his attitude . . . a combination of expectation, exuberance, and great joy of living. . . ."

Vincent Canby in *The New York Times* (December 1, 1972) was skeptical about this portrait of "the poet of paranoia." Canby credited Alk for having shot much of the film with Pennebaker, and also for making, with Dylan, the new cut after ABC-TV had rejected the version for not telling: "What city are we in? What's happening?" From Alk's program notes: ". . . the editors looked . . . for . . . conversations unheld, events untranspired. Some real music, some not. Murder, villainy, travel, slavery and lust. We hope a real movie. Perhaps even a comedy. . . ."

During the shooting, Donn Pennebaker was again nominally in charge, but he later told me that *Eat the Document* had "become Dylan's film. He took over. He was quite dragged by the performances, but I thought the songs were extraordinary. The original title was *Dylan By Pennebaker,* but Dylan changed it to *The Document,* from a line by Al Aronowitz. This time, Dylan got much more involved in the actual filmmaking. My new high-speed film really caught the psychedelic aura of drugs and rock on-stage. Whatever Bob's reservations, I think it was a major jump forward from *Don't Look Back.*"

A twenty-minute press conference in London brought out some hostility, but the reporter from *Disc and Music Echo* understood his quizzical style: "He is rude . . . to people . . . he considers ask stupid questions. He is uncooperative. . . . But is also a very sympathetic man with a vast sense of humor . . . this man . . . was asked . . . ridiculous questions . . . no wonder he lost his patience. . . ." Another *Disc* writer, Jonathan King, said Dylan treated the press like "a faceless crowd of starving vultures . . . downright bad manners. . . ."

The first English concert, May 10 in Bristol's Colston Hall. Walkouts among the capacity audience, no encores, and uniformly bad reviews. *The Gloucester Citizen:* ". . . The majority who stuck it out remained icily indifferent to their idol's sacrifice of lyric and melody to the god of big beat. . . ." Letters to *The Bristol Evening Post:* ". . . the outstanding poet who had meant so much in my life, has now ruined himself. . . ." Another: "I have just attended a funeral. . . . They buried . . . Dylan . . . in a grave of guitars . . . and deafening drums. . . . My only consolation, Woody Guthrie wasn't there to witness it."

The Welsh audience of twenty-five hundred at Cardiff's Capitol Theater, May 11, showed more respect. While ironing out amplification problems, one of the English roadies evicted all press and even theater staff: "One would not expect to be allowed to see Marlene Dietrich before she was completely ready." *Stage and Television Today* remarked that the Cardiff audience "seem to have accepted the new image . . . with remarkably little pain."

In Birmingham on May 12, twenty-five hundred at the Odeon waited for the show to start forty-five minutes late. The pre-Cardiff pattern returned: respect for the acoustic solo section and hostility toward the rock segment. There were huffy walkouts, cries of "Folk phony," "Traitor," "Give us the real Dylan," "Yank, go home," and "We want folk." *The Birmingham Mail and Dispatch:* DYLAN, THE LEGEND, DISAPPOINTS. *Melody Maker:* ". . . Birmingham flatly rejected . . . all-electric folk. . . . Between numbers, he turned his back to the audience for long periods . . . giving the hecklers plenty of opportunity." From Shakespeare's turf, *The Stratford-upon-Avon Herald* saw this as image destruction: ". . . hero of our time, a sort of demigod we had all gone along to worship . . . tried to smash his halo. . . . I'm with you, Bob . . . all the way. . . ."

Then to The Beatles' turf, the Liverpool Odeon, on May 14. No advance publicity and precious little notice he had been there. When one heckler shouted: "Where's the poet in you?" and "What's happened to your conscience?" Dylan retorted: "There's a guy up there looking for a saint." After a successful first half in Leicester on May 15, jeers of "Get them off" greeted The Hawks, along with whistling and walkouts. *The Cambridge Times:* "... to say his audience didn't appreciate this 'kick in the teeth' would be ... an understatement." In *The Illustrated Leicester Chronicle,* David Sandison, later press chief for Island, EMI, and CBS Records: "... Dylan has a great band to support him ... probably one of the greatest young poets alive ... doing what ... Ginsberg and Corso have been doing in free verse.... Dylan is producing poetry.... Perhaps those who spoiled ... the concert will also mature ... and realize ... their prejudice is almost as great as the prejudices Dylan used to campaign against...."

Probably a crank, not a folklore purist, telephoned the Sheffield Gaumont on May 16, warning of "a big bang." The fire brigade and bomb squad searched fruitlessly while two thousand people remained unaware in the theater. By the Manchester gig, the rude part of the press and audience appeared to be a conformist, Neanderthal mob. Why they continued to hoot is difficult to fathom. They certainly knew what to expect, yet they seemed to delight in taking folk-rock as a personal affront. The Manchester Free Trade Hall concert on May 17—another station of the cross. Dylan apologized that the sound was too loud, but this didn't quell the hostility.

Although there were hecklers and walkouts among the three thousand at the Glasgow Odeon on May 19, those who liked the new music shouted down those who didn't. Someone yelled: "We want Dylan." Bob replied: "Dylan got sick backstage. I'm here to take his place." While the antis were yelling: "Traitor!" and "Belt up!," the pros were shouting: "Get your ears washed!" Edinburgh, Friday, May 20, the ABC Theater, another divided audience. Dylan found a broken reed in his mouth harp, but Andrew Young of Haystack Cottage handed up his own. Dylan finished the song, got a new harmonica backstage, and returned the borrowed harp along with one of his own. *The Scottish Daily Express:* "... booed off the stage again last night.... Some of the audience took out mouth-organs and tried to play down his singing...." When Dylan played the Newcastle Odeon on May 21, "One Too Many Mornings" elicited shouts of "Show us what you can do" and "Take some lessons from The Animals!" But when he began "Rolling Stone," listeners greeted it warmly.

Dylan's Paris Olympia concert was on May 24, his twenty-fifth birthday. Two thousand seats costing up to sixty francs (about twelve dollars) sold out a month in advance. Some tickets went to French performers Johnny Halliday, Charles Trenet, Françoise Hardy, Hugues Aufray, and Antoine. Nowhere did the press gallivant as in France. The day Dylan arrived, some ten thousand young people were attending a festival at Oullins organized by the French labor unions. Aufray, whose Barclay recording of Dylan songs had made him the leading Gallic interpreter, announced the arrival, "at this moment," at Le Bourget airport, of "my friend" Dylan. Remarked the Lyons paper *Le Progrès:* "The applause doubled in intensity. The star,

one sensed, was Dylan, not Aufray." Other references compared Dylan to
Rimbaud, Proust, James Dean, François Villon, and Homer. The French
"hipoisie" had an especial affinity for Dylan because of their chansonniers,
poet-singers like Jacques Brel, Gilbert Becaud, and Georges Brassens. Even
Halliday, then the twenty-three-year-old Gallic rock star, felt Dylan was *un
ami.* He spent one night taking him around Paris, and gave him a Turkish
water pipe for his birthday. Paris has more astrologers than psychothera-
pists, and the French press relished the coincidence that Halliday, Antoine,
and Dylan were all Geminis.

The French also liked Dylan for his allegiance to peace, for his fondness
for Beaujolais and Bardot, and for his poetics. Philippe Labro in *Elle,* May
6: "He ... sings of the America of back streets, dirty little bars, back-room
pool-players ... air filled with smoke, heavy and sweaty ... snatches of
speech ... nothing actually happens, but it is from this that the greatest
books (Steinbeck, Caldwell, Faulkner) and the greatest films (Rossen,
especially) have come. ... Dylan is an authentic poet, a writer. He is, in
this milieu, the only true writer. ..."

One newspaper inaccurately reported he had sold eighteen million
recordings and his annual income was more than a million dollars. Parisian
journalists also noted that at the Olympia, Dylan would command as
much as Maria Callas—"more," opined *Paris Jour,* "than a worker earns in
10 years." The press was also truculent about Dylan's staying at the
George V Hotel, where he was ushered into a luxurious suite bedizened
with Spanish master paintings and Louis XV furniture. "What's this?"
Dylan reportedly said to the maître d'hôtel. "You should have known I
don't dig Louis the Fifteenth. If you don't get me a decent suite in the
next five minutes, I'll take the airplane right back to America." Monsieur
was shown into another luxurious suite sans Louis XV but with a carpet
whose color monsieur didn't like. He relented, "Well, if we have to camp,
let's camp." The press conference at the George V on May 23 was a predictable debacle. One reporter asked what Dylan thought about the Allied
invasion in World War II! Dylan was offhand and petulant. Some photographs show him holding a large wooden puppet, named Monsieur Finian.
Asked what song he would choose to conclude the conference, Dylan said:
"Hello, Dolly."

In Paris, an old friend surfaced—Mike Porco of Gerde's Folk City. Returning from his native Calabria, Mike went to considerable lengths to see
"Bobby." Heading toward the George V, Mike ran into Grossman, who
said, "Dylan isn't seeing anyone. He is tired. I don't think it can be arranged." Mike persisted and got into Bob's suite, where he got a gracious
welcome. "Bobby couldn't do enough for me ... just the opposite of what
Grossman had made me feel. ... He introduced me to everyone, and said I
was like his father, like his uncle, like his pal. It really made me feel good.
It was funny, remembering what he'd looked like here, to see him in that
hotel in Paris."

The concert was anticlimactic. The audience tended to be unruly, but

Bob wasn't passive to heckling. Someone had draped the stage with a large American flag. Many shouted: "Happy birthday." When he took time to tune his guitar (some said fourteen minutes), jeers were silenced by Dylan saying: "I'm doing this for you. I couldn't care less. I wouldn't behave like that if I came to see you." *The Paris Trib,* reporting that Dylan's nervous strain had weakened his performance, concluded that "this strange figure, with his beautiful handling of an unruly audience and his haunting 'Desolation Row' . . . leaves an impression that will linger."

The Olympia crowd seemed to like the electric set; the band thawed out a rather tense audience. Still, most reviews were vitriolic. *Le Figaro,* under the headline THE FALL OF AN IDOL, suggested that the audience had heard Dylan's double, an ill-looking puppet "unable to overcome his narcotism." *Arts Paris* lambasted Dylan for abandoning music-hall tradition, and concluded that derision, violence, and mental breakdown were themes too serious for songs. *Le Havre Libre* unequivocally called the concert a failure. *Paris Jour* took umbrage at Dylan's remarks during tuning breaks, such as "Hasn't anyone got a newspaper to read?" and "Don't worry, I'm just as eager to finish and leave as you are."

A few critics were sympathetic. *L'Événement* said he was misunderstood. *L'Humanité* wrote that "they found his 'Dylano-American' difficult and consequently did not understand what he was singing about." In fact, Dylan had asked his audience if they understood English, and many in the audience had said yes. Rouen's *Liberté Dimanche* acclaimed Dylan because he had "re-established poetry for the masses. He is in some way, The Homer of the 20th Century." A Paris paper, *The Detective,* proferred a clue: "The secret of his success is his indifference. He is irritating, and therefore he interests people." *Paris Jour*'s headline writer was most explicit: BOB DYLAN, GO HOME. After returning to London's Albert Hall, he did.

The Victorian pile that is Royal Albert Hall, despite its notorious acoustics, its antediluvian pomp and impersonality, is Britain's Carnegie Hall. There, on May 26 and 27, Dylan's first world tour ended with two contentious concerts that followed the provincial pattern: rapt attention for his solo acoustic work and anger during his electric set. According to Ray Coleman, "Hundreds walked out during his final show. There is no doubt Dylan was angry with the people who walked out. He was visibly hurt and their walkout seemed to inject even more determination into him to carry on with the electrified group. I thought the group was a shame, because on that night it was such a shambles of noise. We just couldn't hear his words." Dylan probably talked most to the Albert Hall audiences. To hecklers demanding protest songs, he said: "Oh, come on, these are all protest songs." *The Daily Telegraph* wrote that this remark "checked a dangerous situation, but after that, whole rows sat with scarcely a sign of applause. . . . He is beginning to show the signs of a man who does not care whether he communicates or not."

Dylan students there, including those who appreciated folk-rock, said the sound was dreadful. Yet the famous Albert Hall bootleg has long been regarded as technically brilliant. Rock critic Dave Marsh called it: ". . . The most supremely elegant piece of rock 'n' roll music I've ever heard . . . royal music." The other startling aspect was his remarkable speech from the stage. Coleman wrote me that Dylan exploded to his listeners: "Aw, it's the same stuff as always—can't you HEAR?" Evidently completely fed up at the heckling and the growing storm over "Rainy Day Women," Dylan stormed back. The "Rainy Day" single was being blacklisted by American radio. Home Secretary Roy Jenkins had received an appeal from one Birmingham city councillor to ban it in Britain along with The Byrds' "Eight Miles High."

According to *Melody Maker,* Dylan lashed back during the acoustic set: " 'I'm not going to play any more concerts in England. So I'd just like to say this next song is what your English musical papers would call a "drug song." I never have and never will write a "drug song." I don't know how to. It's not a "drug song," it's just vulgar. I like all my old songs. It's just that things change all the time. Everybody knows that. I never said they were "rubbish." That's not in my vocabulary. I wouldn't use the word "rubbish" if it was lying on the stage and I could pick it up. This music you are going to hear . . . if anyone has any suggestions on how it can be played better, or how the words can be improved . . . We've been playing this music since we were 10 years old. Folk music was just an interruption, which was very useful. If you don't like it, that's fine. This is not English music you are listening to. You really haven't heard American music before. I want now to say what you're hearing is just songs. You're not hearing anything else but words and sounds. You can take it or leave it. If there's something you disagree with, that's great. I'm sick of people asking: "What does it mean?" It means nothing.' "

The *Melody Maker* reporter heard shouts that included " 'Woody Guthrie would turn over in his grave' " and " 'Rubbish!' " But the majority wanted to hear Dylan and shouted down the hecklers. Dylan continued with "Desolation Row," "Baby Blue," and then the final electric set. Finishing with "Rolling Stone," he fairly yelled the line about having to get used to it. Summarized Coleman: "The crowd who stayed, the loyal ones, cheered. He had conquered again, all right, despite the outbursts. But still we were left asking: 'Where is he going? Does anyone know? Does he?' "

A COMPLICATED TWIST OF FATE

Dylan and The Hawks limped back to America in June, dispirited, exhausted, and angry, only to find that Grossman had scheduled sixty-four concerts in the States for the immediate future. Dylan could say "don't look forward" as well as "don't look back." Late Friday night, July 29, I received a telephone call from Hibbing. Dylan's father sounded distraught: "They just called me from the radio station here. They said they had a news bulletin that Bob's been badly hurt in a motorcycle accident. Do you know anything about it?" I said this was the first I had heard of it. "The Grossman office won't help me one bit on this," said Abe. "And I can't get through to Sara. Would you please see if you can find out something—anything—and call us back, collect? Bob's mother is very worried—and so am I!' " Four months earlier, a similar phone call had informed me of Fariña's death in a motorcycle accident. I rang *The Times* for more information.

11

LISTENING TO THE SILENCE

"That man is very far from being an artist ... who does not know longing for the innocent, the simple ... for a little friendship, devotion, familiar human happiness— the gnawing, surreptitious hankering ... for the bliss of the commonplace."

—THOMAS MANN, "TONIO KRÖGER"

"The condition of alienation, of being asleep, of being unconscious, of being out of one's mind, is the condition of the normal man."

—R. D. LAING

"The poet seeks refuge in muteness."

—GEORGE STEINER, "SILENCE AND THE POET"[1]

"... by leaving things out, he allows us the grand privilege of creating along with him. His song becomes our song because we live in those spaces. If we listen, if we work at it, we fill up the mystery, we expand and inhabit the work of art. It is the most democratic form of creation...."

—PETE HAMILL, 1974[2]

"By silence, [the artist] frees himself from servile bondage to the world, which appears as patron, client, consumer, antagonist, arbiter, and distorter of his work. . . . Once he has surpassed his peers . . . his pride has only one place left to go . . . the craving for silence is to be . . . superior to everyone else. It suggests that the artist has had the wit to ask more questions than other people, and that he possesses stronger nerves and higher standards of excellence. . . ."

—SUSAN SONTAG, "THE AESTHETICS OF SILENCE"

Details about Dylan's motorcycle accident on July 29, 1966, were not easy to ascertain. It was widely reported that Dylan nearly lost his life. It seems more likely that his mishap *saved* his life.

Ellen Willis in *Cheetah:* "Gruesome rumors circulated: Dylan was dead . . . badly disfigured . . . paralyzed . . . insane . . . the new rumor was the accident had been a cover for retreat. . . . Not since Rimbaud said 'I is another' had an artist been so obsessed with escaping identity. . . . Dylan as an identifiable *persona* has been disappearing into his songs, which is what he wants. This terrifies his audiences. . . ." A Tokyo music journalist published a hospital-bedside "interview," which Dylan emphatically told me never happened. *The Chicago Tribune* in 1967: "A traditional gesture of the prophet is the retreat and the re-emergence . . . with a new message. A good deal of what will or won't be in pop music hangs on Dylan's re-emergence and his message."

Grossman, who had set up more than sixty concerts for 1966–67, was shopping around for a good recording contract. Dylan emphasized the serious aftereffects of the accident. Albert said that although Dylan had broken his neck, he would need only a couple of months before resuming work. Even this got garbled. Dylan's brother told me: "Bob never said he broke his neck. Albert broke *his* neck." So, I speculated in print that the accident's effects had been exaggerated. Immediately, David came down from Woodstock insisting: "There *was* an accident. There definitely *was* an accident." Hubert Saal, music editor of *Newsweek,* interviewed Dylan in early 1968 and concluded: "Dylan's current reluctance to give concerts has nothing to do with the accident, from which he appears fully recovered. 'I have more responsibilities now,' he says."

Dylan told me only: "It happened one morning after I'd been up for three days. I hit an oil slick. The damp weather still affects the wound." He was riding along Striebel Road, not far from his Woodstock home, taking the bike into the garage for repairs, when the back wheel locked and he went hurtling over the handlebars. After the fall, he was rushed in a friend's car to Middletown Hospital with reported broken vertebrae of the neck, a possible concussion, and head and facial bruises. A major concert at the Yale Bowl, scheduled eight days later, was canceled. Dylan only knows just how severely he was hurt and at what point in his convalescence he discovered that he wanted to think, reorganize his life, spend time with his family, and listen to the silence. The accident began seven and a half years of withdrawal to a more tranquil existence.

The music-business machine doesn't like "undisciplined" performers who fall off motorbikes. Grossman is reported to have said after the accident: "How could he do this to me?" His aide, Charlie Rothschild, asked me: "Do you know how much work was involved in setting up sixty concerts?" (When I told Dylan about Grossman's remark, Bob laughed: "That shows you where he was at, worrying about those concerts!")

Allen Ginsberg visited Dylan in late September, bringing some Emily Dickinson and Bertolt Brecht books, and said he didn't think Dylan was seriously hurt. By January 1967, Dylan's editor at Macmillan, Robert Markel, was saying: "Dylan is making a slow recovery from a bad accident. He couldn't use his eyes for a period of time and it made it difficult for him to work. But he's alive and well." Donn Pennebaker, the filmmaker, told *Melody Maker:* "I know he wasn't as sick as he made out. This provided the basis of an excuse for delaying delivery of that TV show, which is what he wanted to do. But I know he was at a doctor's. I went to see him a number of times and he was in a brace. . . . I knew he'd been hurt in other ways, so in either event, what he was doing was recovering.' "

A *World Journal Tribune* reporter got as far as the rambling Cape Cod house behind Albert's, where Sara, presumably, turned him away: " 'We are afraid of all kinds of nuts coming around and bothering him. . . . It gets very lonely here. Very few friends have come up and we never go into town.' " In January 1967, a *New York Post* reporter was chased off the property by two watchdogs, and Sara, who said he was trespassing, called the local deputy. The first reporter who did get through was Michael Iachetta of the New York *Daily News.* Dylan told Iachetta, in May 1967, that he'd been " 'seein' only a few close friends, readin' little 'bout the outside world, porin' over books by people you never heard of, thinkin' about where I'm goin' and why am I runnin' and am I mixed up too much, and what am I knowin' and what am I givin' and what am I takin'. And mainly what I've been doin' is workin' on gettin' better and makin' better music, which is what my life is all about.' " The *News* story described him as "emotionally and physically scarred." Yet Ralph Gleason quoted Grossman as saying that Dylan was putting on the *News* reporter and "is well, absolutely unscarred, and is planning possible concerts this fall."

During Dylan's retreat in Woodstock and New York City until the end of 1973, his creative work flourished. He immersed himself in the family life so often denied the pop star. Apparently in retreat behind a cloud of mystery, he was continually sending out messages to friends in random interviews and in songs. A handful reveal Dylan's changing world view. "Too Much of Nothing," with its Lear-like stress on nothingness, and its "waters of oblivion" line echoing the English poet Ernest Dowson, indicted the vacuous rock scene from which he was detaching himself. "I Shall Be Released" was clearly a search for personal salvation. "The Drifter's Escape" was a transparent parable about a person, trapped by a role, who awaits a sentence of doom before a hostile crowd, when he is almost magically delivered from the courtroom. The song's "bolt of lightning" could be Dylan's accident. In "Watching the River Flow," a man changes from participant to observer. "Sign on the Window" and "If Dogs Run Free" are the apotheosis of personal contentment in a love relationship. The audience, not aware of what he and The Band had endured around the world, couldn't understand his need for privacy, and felt rejected. Dylan was repeatedly compelled to justify his withdrawal.

To *Newsweek,* Dylan said: " 'I stared at the ceiling for a few months. But since I've often sat around staring at ceilings, it didn't bother me much. I haven't been in retreat. I'm a country boy myself, and you have to be let alone to really accomplish anything.' " In *The Chicago Tribune* on April 28, 1968, Dylan already seemed to be thinking about the 1974–75 Rolling Thunder Revue: " 'If I'm going to be out there it's got to be something that moves, that takes everyone along.' " The rumors still accreted, including one that Dylan feared he would be assassinated. By 1969, Dylan could tell *The London Evening Standard* that the accident " 'in many ways . . . was good for me. It really slowed me down . . . touring had been such a pace to keep up. And I was getting in a rut.' "

Robbie Robertson told *The Saturday Evening Post:* " 'We did it until we couldn't do it anymore. . . . We were so exhausted that everyone said this was a time to rest. We stopped listening to music for a year.' " As late as spring 1975, Dylan was explaining to Mary Travers on her radio series that "we needed to dry out." Dylan was saying that there must be another way of life for the pop star, in which *he* is in control, not *they.* He had to find ways of working to his own advantage, with the recording industry, his book publisher, the TV network. He had to come to terms with his one-time friend, longtime manager, part-time neighbor, and sometime landlord, Albert Grossman.

Dylan's Columbia recording contract had run out. Grossman had asked the new Columbia chief, Clive Davis, for an enormous guaranty for a long-term contract. When Davis asked why the figure was so high, Grossman reportedly said: "Because it is there." In 1966, when Davis took over, Columbia was in some trouble. Davis, an aggressive young corporate lawyer, had risen as a protégé of Goddard Lieberson. Before Davis left in 1973, he had changed the record division's pretax profits from five million dollars a year to fifty million. In 1966, Davis was a master at pressuring his employees and artists. He wanted to keep Dylan under contract, but did not want to get involved in the high-money sweepstakes Grossman was playing with MGM and Capitol, among others. Davis felt he held the trump card because he knew that Dylan's influence then ran considerably ahead of his actual sales.

By Christmas, 1966, MGM was announcing that Dylan had been signed. According to contract provisions, Dylan owed Columbia another fourteen tracks, or one album. In the *New York Post,* Nora Ephron revealed that a flaw in Dylan's contract would allow Columbia to dump an enormous amount of past royalties on him in one year, delivering about 90 percent of his profits for that year to the tax people. In April 1967, Columbia halted all Dylan's sales. This suspension was settled almost immediately, with Dylan committing himself to supplying the fourteen songs. Davis told Allan Klein, the controversial manager involved in a proxy fight at MGM, that Dylan's sales were not quite what MGM thought. Although MGM had Dylan's signature, MGM hadn't countersigned.

Meanwhile, Grossman and Dylan were having second thoughts about MGM. Grossman went back to Davis offering Dylan for double his former royalty. Davis wrote in his 1974 autobiography, *Clive: Inside the Record Business:* "I thought it was a perfect solution, and I grabbed it. The royalties were twice anything we'd ever paid before, but it was worth it to keep Dylan." On August 21, 1967, Columbia proudly announced it had re-signed Dylan to an exclusive, long-term contract. Soon Bob was back in the studio, recording *John Wesley Harding.*

Dylan's two previous Columbia contracts had scarcely inspired his confidence. Davis had presuaded Dylan not to challenge his first contract because he had signed as a minor. Davis had also informed Dylan that his John Birch song was potentially libelous. But as Columbia's chief operating officer, Davis got on better with Dylan. Davis maintains that at a meeting between the two Guthrie memorial concerts in January 1968, the pair established a working rapport. Dylan started to send Davis tapes from studio sessions. Davis recalls that just before each album came out, Dylan would surface. As Dylan started to handle his own business and drift away from Grossman, Davis "had the feeling that he needed someone to bring him ideas, goad him a bit, make suggestions, offer help if he needed it. This is not easy to do with Dylan, of course, and I had to tread very softly." Dylan told me that there was recurring friction at Columbia: "Whatever I want to do, somebody is against it. I work with whatever A & R man I want and have nothing whatsoever to do with Clive Davis."

After the "Lay, Lady, Lay" hit from *Nashville Skyline,* which became Dylan's best-selling album to date, reaching 1.2 million copies, Davis's litany ran that Dylan could double each album's sales with a hit single. Dylan refused to release a single from *New Morning,* which sold only half of what *Nashville* did. "Sometimes . . . he was as mercurial and unpredictable as the legends said. He would be gentle, polite, and cooperative—or indecisive, suspicious, and quite impatient . . . in the studio, he was an efficiency expert's dream . . . things happened fast . . . most songs in one take.

Simon and Garfunkel might take up to eighteen months to record an album. . . . Dylan came into the studio, played his songs . . . and that was it. He took an extremely casual, almost lax attitude toward the recording process. . . . To him, the song was the thing and everything else was secondary."[3] After the taping, Dylan would become an absolute hawk about album design, title, timing. Then, after an album release, he would drift back into his silence.

When Dylan's Columbia contract expired in 1972, another period of uncertainty began. Bob, wary of any long-term commitment, also had some deep differences of opinion with Columbia. When the film *Pat Garrett and Billy the Kid,* in which Dylan shone in a cameo role, was negatively reviewed in *The New York Times,* Davis and others suggested Dylan hold back his sound-track album. He released it, and film and album ultimately did very well.

Dylan's contract renewal also came at a time when Davis was deeply embattled at Columbia. Still, his was probably the strongest voice in the company for letting Dylan do things his way. Davis said a new contract was drawn up, allowing for the *Pat Garrett* album plus two more, at "a guaranty of about four hundred thousand dollars per album." After Davis left the company, Columbia backed out of the agreement. By this point, Dylan had already planned Tour '74 and was getting close to David Geffen of Elektra/Asylum Records, a part of the WEA empire, Columbia's chief rival. But Dylan gave Geffen only one album, *Planet Waves.* In the light of millions of requests for tour tickets, Dylan was understandably miffed that Geffen could sell only about seven hundred thousand copies of the album.

Meanwhile, Davis remained in touch with Dylan. At the end of 1973, at Columbia's annual sales meeting, Lieberson, back at the company's helm, announced: "I don't doubt that there were times when record companies exploited artists, but it had come to the point where the artists were exploiting the record companies." Nevertheless, Dylan had Lieberson and Geffen bidding up the royalty for the live double album, *Before the Flood,* until Dylan finally released it with Asylum. Then, Davis maintained, Columbia wanted Dylan back, "seemingly at any cost. They had come to understand their loss. . . . Columbia will spare nothing to bring Dylan back into the fold. They finally understand that they need Dylan and have no choice but to lure him with an outstanding royalty, not only on new albums, but also on his extensive catalogue. It's been an expensive lesson, indeed."[4]

The post-accident period also saw problems between Dylan and ABC-TV over the two-hour special for its *Stage 67* series, the film that later surfaced as *Eat the Document.* It was shot in England during Dylan's 1966 world tour. In April 1967, an ABC spokesman said the show had been canceled because of a disagreement over the format. For a $100,000 advance, ABC had received footage in November 1966 that the network described as "totally unsatisfactory." ABC was contemplating legal action. In the 1968 *Sing Out!* interview, Dylan told John Cohen: " 'The film had been cut just to nothing . . . we were hoping to discover something . . . we tried to construct a stage and an environment . . . the program folded and by the time we handed it in, they had already a state-wide search begun to confiscate the film. . . . So we were a little pressured here and there . . . it's hard to do a tour, and in the after hours to make a movie. . . .' "[5]

The accident also delayed publication of *Tarantula*. He'd been appalled by Macmillan's prepublication publicity, and he still had reservations about the work. Dylan told *Sing Out!:* " 'I learned not to do a book like that . . . where the contract comes in before the book is written, so you have to fulfill the contract . . . there was no difficulty in writing it at all, it just wasn't a book, it was just a nuisance. It didn't have that certain quality which now I think a book should have. It didn't have any structure at all, it was just one flow. It flowed for 90 pages . . . they were short little lines, nothing within a big framework. I couldn't even conceive of doing anything in a big framework at that time.' "[6]

Dylan's relationship with his manager was in delicate shape. In November 1965, they had organized a music-publishing company, Bob Dylan Words and Music, to follow his three-year contract with Witmark/Music Publishers Holding Corporation. Artie Mogull managed this enterprise, for a time. Grossman and Dylan were otherwise tightly linked, but by early 1968, Dylan wanted to be free. During the Guthrie memorial concerts in January 1968, Albert and Bob scarcely spoke to each other.

At the Isle of Wight, Grossman's partner, Bert Block, handled arrangements. By November 1969, Block sold out his interest to Grossman, after a three-year association. (Block joined Jerry Perenchio's Chartwell Artists, and was soon representing Kris Kristofferson.) In late 1970, Woodstock buzzed with reports of the falling-out of its two glamorous residents. Taxi drivers and motel owners talked of an unverified "huge settlement" that ran to more than a million dollars. Bernard Paturel, owner of Woodstock's Café Espresso and friend to both, asked me later: "The poet and the stern businessman—how long could it last?" In spring 1971, Charlie Rothschild told me that Naomi Saltzman, an executive secretary at Grossman's, had played "an important role in Dylan's split with Albert." She denied this to me. Dylan subsequently hired Mrs. Saltzman as his music publisher. In May 1971, Dylan was expressing relief that his contract with Grossman was finally settled, and that he'd be free by June. "I finally had to sue him. Because Albert wanted it quiet, he settled out of court. He had me signed up for ten years . . . can you believe that? For part of my records, for part of my everything. He only had me for twenty percent. There were others who had to give him fifty percent." Albert's Woodstock empire—his recording studio and his restaurant, The Bear—was expanding. Although Dylan's three years in Woodstock after the accident may have looked idyllic, Dylan told me afterward: "Woodstock was a daily excursion to nothingness." He said he'd moved back to the Village in late 1969 because his Woodstock home "had become a joke. There were tours, people up there were trying to pick up a piece of the earth, a piece of the lawn, or the shrubs." Another paradise lost; still no direction home.

"THE TOWN THAT FATHERED A NATION"

Woodstock, one hundred miles up the Hudson from Manhattan, in New York's Ulster County, at the eastern fringe of the Catskills, numbers six thousand residents year-round. It swells to perhaps four times that number in the summer. For more than eighty years, Woodstock has been a magnet for those seeking creativity in the clean air. Originally an arts-and-crafts colony and a rural theatrical center, it is inhabited by descendants of Dutch settlers, successive waves of artists, craftspeople, dancers, musicians, urban dropouts and rebels looking for a green alternative to Greenwich Village, executives from IBM, some wealthy people, and trendy accountants who like artsy neighbors. In the early 1960s, Peter Yarrow seduced several people up to Woodstock Valley. Soon the place had a new pop-music mystique pasted atop its old art frame. Nearly everyone agrees it used to be a lot better.

Dylan moved to Woodstock in 1965, but by 1969 he no longer had any privacy. His sanctuary had turned into a zoo. For a recluse who really likes and needs people, the secret of where he lived was difficult to keep. Although famous artists had been migrating to Woodstock since the early 1900s, none drew as many pilgrims. The writers Tagore and Thomas Mann had at one time lived in Woodstock, as had actors Lee Marvin and Edward G. Robinson, the painter Kuniyoshi, scholars, and art collectors. Among Dylan's neighbors were composer Aaron Copland, painter Anton Refregier, writer Mason Hoffenberg. Woodstock's center is an alfresco Greenwich Village—book and antique shops, health-food stores, boutiques, head shops, galleries, restaurants, real-estate agents. Richard Goldstein called Woodstock Valley "the great green hope for the urban blues"—the beautiful reservoir, the Big Deep swimming hole, Overlook Mountain and Echo Lake, the waterfall at Haines Falls.

In 1902, the heir to a Yorkshire textile fortune, Ralph Radcliffe Whitehead, set up an arts colony in Woodstock to embody a wholesome return to nature, a refuge against the Industrial Revolution. Whitehead had been influenced by British philosopher John Ruskin's alternatives to industrial society. Whitehead, with Hervey White, a writer and social worker, and Bolton Brown, an art professor, spent years combing America. Brown had climbed Overlook Mountain above Woodstock and saw there "an earthly paradise." Whitehead disliked the Catskills because they were "full of Jews," but his two aides and the scenery persuaded him. Since the 1870s, the Valley had been friendly toward circus and theater folk.

Whitehead bought up seven farms, about twelve hundred acres, below Mead's Mountain, and began constructing thirty buildings. He dubbed his colony Byrdcliffe, and spent half a million dollars to set up workshops, homes, and schools. In June 1903, craftspeople, students, and teachers poured in. Byrdcliffe colonists, in corduroy and denim, romanticized rural life.

The patrician Whitehead was no democrat; he liked to be called the Dictator of Byrdcliffe. The colony could not support itself making furniture and color prints. After the first summer, students recoiling from Whitehead's authoritarianism dropped out; the staff was divided. Brown, fired by the "Master," bought thirty acres in Woodstock's Rock City district. White led a secession from Byrdcliffe in 1904 and founded the Maverick Colony on a farm three miles southeast, in Hurley.

By 1906, the Art Students League Summer School moved to Woodstock, into a former Woodstock livery stable and undertaker's shop. The art students shook up the town. Beards and berets were in, then out. For a time, shaved heads and paint-smirched trousers were student uniforms. These first Woodstock hippies reveled in penury, slept out of doors with whom they chose. The separate colonies began to divide the town three ways. The students called Whitehead's Byrdcliffe "Boredstiffe." The League became a leading landscape school, attracting two hundred students by 1912. The Maverick let its cabins to musicians, writers, and Clarence Darrow and Thorstein Veblen.

Eventually, the Maverick and Byrdcliffe colonies began to join forces. In August 1915, at Woodstock's first festival, all three colonies joined in White's money-raising jamboree—campfire suppers, eccentric costumes, chamber music in a natural quarry amphitheater. After ten years of aloofness, Whitehead began to treat White civilly. The Woodstock art colony matured in the 1920s. Although the Art Students League School closed from 1923 to 1946, several private art schools filled the gap. The Maverick Concerts thrived, as did White's restaurant, The Intelligencia. By 1924, the Maverick Theater was built, and later Woodstock had as many as six rural theater productions at the same time. Edward G. Robinson, Eva Le Gallienne, and Maria Ouspenskaya became linked with Woodstock. An art association and a chamber of commerce found much basis for cooperation. The old prejudice against Jews diminished, but not without some Ku Klux Klan activity in the district. With Whitehead's death in 1929 and the Depression, a new phase began. In the 1940s, Leadbelly and Pete Seeger used to visit; Sam Eskin was the local folk-song authority. By White's death in 1944, neither the Maverick nor Byrdcliffe dominated; Woodstock was one community.

After the war, industry marched up the Hudson, engineers and administrators from Kingston bought Woodstock homes. Although Whitehead had imported the "simple" life of folk music, dance, and peace—Whitehead's son, Peter, kept Byrdcliffe alive, barely—the town now resisted the influx of young 1960s rebels and seekers. Now, the city fathers rallied to defend moral and land values with antihippie harassment. There were arrests for drug possession or trespassing, for skinny-dipping in local swim-

ming holes. The spring before the 1969 Woodstock Festival, locals looted
and burned a "Karma meditation center" on the state forest preserve in
Woodstock. Finally, the town banned the 1969 Woodstock Festival and
tried unsuccessfully to force the happening in Bethel to drop Woodstock's
name.

Dylan's friend/chauffeur/bodyguard Bernard Paturel on Woodstock:
"There's a magic here ... an emanation. Lots of musicians, artisans, and
writers. A gifted person would feel these vibrations, and get support from
people like that living there. There is something in the air. You can visit
someone who might have the same spirit, the same attitude. But all this
could be lost with oversaturation. Many people are coming up here who
having nothing to *give,* they're only here to *get.* Some are trying to just
bring the city up to the country." Public and private Woodstock are different entities. What you see in the restaurants, boutiques, or in music
clubs like Sled Hill, are only surface matters. The "scene" in Woodstock is
behind shrubbed driveways and closed doors. The pilgrims rarely got that
far. At the time of the Woodstock Festival, living in and around Woodstock were Dylan, The Band, Van Morrison, Frank Zappa and the Mothers
of Invention, Tim Hardin, and a fluid roster of Grossman's musicians,
aides, and roadies.

After staying at Peter Yarrow's rough Woodstock shack in 1963, Dylan
used to steal up there often. He started to use Bernard Paturel's upstairs
hideaway at the Espresso, even if he was staying at Albert's estate in adja-
cent Bearsville, where there were too many people too often. By 1970, Albert's house, the old stone Striebel place, was said to be worth three times
the forty-five thousand dollars Grossman had paid for it. Albert put in a
sauna and a greenhouse. Fariña used to visit Albert's: "It's very pretty, very
quiet. A nice place to work, sort of like a farm ... especially nice during
the days because everybody was doing something separate.... Albert and
the others were very generous, very open." Albert built his Bearsville Studios in Woodstock. For a while, the music business tried to popularize
"the Woodstock Sound," but the phrase never caught on.

After using a room at Albert's, Dylan moved into a studio behind Albert's house. By mid-1965, Bob was ensconced in his own house at Byrdcliffe, the seventy-five-year-old Webster place. Ben Webster had been an
architect and influential stage director. His house was of dark-brown cedar
wood, built on four acres along the hillside. It was big and ranchlike, but
far from luxurious. There was a swimming pool formed from a natural
quarry.

But too many people knew about Byrdcliffe. In spring 1969, Dylan
moved his family to the south side of Woodstock Valley to the old Walter
Weyl place. Weyl, a political economist and a founder of *The New Republic,* is believed to have been the first Jew to whom Whitehead had rented a
house at Byrdcliffe. Dylan followed Weyl's footsteps from Byrdcliffe to the
lonely farm on Ohayo Mountain, up above the Maverick. The Weyl place
promised privacy with more than one hundred acres of farmland. Here

Dylan sat out the excitements of 1968, including the Newport Folk Festival and the 1969 Woodstock Festival.

During three years at Woodstock, Bernard Paturel "changed fuses, drove the Cadillac or the baby-blue Mustang, tried to keep Bob's privacy. When I told Bobby, after the accident, that I might work for IBM, he said: 'I'll give you a job.' I named my own salary, but it was always a question of my saying to him: 'Tell me to do something.' My boss didn't, but his wife did. A lot of the people who came up here, the pilgrims, all said they were Bob's friends. One Australian came every day, and finally Bob talked to him. He left happy. Some people on bad trips would show up . . . strangers . . . and that was a problem. Then there was some crazy guy who said he was an ex-convict who called up and said he was going to kill Bob. The police stayed there for a while."

Friends drifted up or lived nearby: Ginsberg, in bare feet and white robes, Gregory Corso, Happy Traum, and filmmakers Howard and Jones Alk. Bernard: "Until Sara, I thought it was just a question of time until he died. But later, I had never met such a dedicated family man. There's so many sides to Bob Dylan, he's round." In the hospitable Woodstock atmosphere, the family man also pursued his painting. His proud father told me in 1967 that Bob was churning out canvas after canvas. "There's a guitar in every one," Abe said. Bernard left Dylan's employ in spring 1969, working briefly at The Bear restaurant. Then, his wife opened a little pizza parlor out on Route 212, near the Swim O'Links, on April 10, 1970. They called it Country Pie, a slice from *Nashville Skyline*.

In late 1969, when Dylan moved back to the Village, into a house on MacDougal Street, he found a privacy that Woodstock could no longer give him. He told me, "The Village is depressing. We're just passing through." People passing through Woodstock, before and after Dylan lived there, could find the superficialities of an artsy, green-swaddled town. But Dylan's Woodstock really couldn't be photographed or filmed. It could, however, be taped in a basement.

THE BASEMENT TAPES

Anyone concerned about Dylan's personal or artistic health in 1967 could have looked at the bed chart provided by *The Basement Tapes* and seen a patient who had *not* vegetated or run out of inspiration. For nearly eight years, all but one of his *Basement* songs circulated illegally, as publishing demo tapes or as a bootleg. In July 1975, the Dylan tapes, in modified versions, plus six previously unknown songs by The Band, came up out of the basement and were officially released as a two-LP set, *The Basement Tapes*.

Comment ran to superlatives at the variety, vitality, richness, and evergreen pertinence of these sixteen songs. John Rockwell in *The New York Times:* "The greatest album in the history of American popular music." Robert Christgau in *The Village Voice:* "We don't have to feel ashamed because this is the best album of 1975. It would have been the best album of 1967, too." *The Washington Post:* "He may perplex, irritate and disappoint, but Dylan has to rank as the single greatest artist modern American pop music has produced." The material was taped on a home recorder in the basement of The Band's house, Big Pink, in West Saugerties, New York, near Woodstock. The tapes' roughness pleased many, even though The Beatles had recently released their studio extravaganza, *Sergeant Pepper.* Jon Landau of *Rolling Stone* had just panned *Blood on the Tracks* for the lack of polished studio production. Lo and behold, then Landau backtracked and overdubbed his opinion of Dylan's spontaneous approach to recording.

Dylan's sixteen tracks were originally meant to be demos. In his liner notes, Greil Marcus dates the sessions from June to October, 1967. The cellar compositions take a pivotal position between *Blonde* and *John Wesley Harding.* Without the transitional evidence of *The Basement Tapes,* the leap made between the two other albums could be exaggerated. Differences between the original tapings and the official release were numerous. (Roger Ford wrote in a letter to *Melody Maker* of August 9, 1975: "Five songs are not represented . . . on the LP: 'Quinn,' 'Released,' 'I'm Not There,' 'Rocks Off' and 'Sign On the Cross.' . . . 14 cuts from the demo are not included on the LP . . . 'Apple Suckling Tree' on the LP is . . . complete. . . . Four of the tracks have been substantially remixed. . . . 'Nowhere' has a lead guitar [not] audible on the demo, while 'Mrs. Henry,' 'Odds and Ends' and 'Wheel's On Fire' all have piano brought right forward. . . .")

The LP carries an overwhelming impression of the joy of jamming, right along with flawed ensembles, roughhewn singing, unkempt instrumentalism, disbalances, distortions, basement scuffling. The bizarre cover echoes *Tarantula*—a dwarf, a sword-swallower, a weight lifter, an Eskimo, a gypsy, a clown, a fat lady, a nun, a belly dancer, and a ballet dancer. Song characters Tiny Montgomery, Mrs. Henry, and other eccentrics also are reminiscent of *Tarantula.* In the sixteen songs, Dylan has moved away from the death-heavy atmosphere, the trapped chaos of *Blonde,* into a communal feeling, somewhere between a barroom rumpus and a gospel choir. (Note how many punchy choruses the six sing.) The meditativeness of *John Wesley Harding* is forecast. Soon after these sessions, The Band recorded *Big Pink* and Dylan recorded twelve other songs for *Harding.*

Dylan's *Basement* songs fall into two principal categories. The first is songs tinctured with the search for salvation, including: "I Shall Be Released" (from the demo, not on the album), "Too Much of Nothing," "This Wheel's on Fire," "Tears of Rage," "Goin' to Acapulco," "Nothing Was Delivered," and, possibly, "Long-Distance Operator." The second category is songs of joy, signaling some form of deliverance and including most of the remaining titles. "Million Dollar Bash," the single from the album, certainly embodies this feeling. "You Ain't Goin' Nowhere" would easily fit in with the last two gentle love songs on *Harding.*

Dylan had his community at last; he was not alone. Yet the continuing lonely quest is underscored by "Tears of Rage," "This Wheel's on Fire," "Nothing Was Delivered," "Too Much of Nothing," and "I Shall Be Released." The germinal seed may well be Shakespeare's *King Lear*. ("Thou art a soul in bliss; but I am bound/Upon a wheel of fire . . .") Throughout these songs, as throughout *Lear*, "nothing" and "nowhere" perplex and nag. ("Nothing will come of nothing" [Act I, Scene 1].) In the 1968 *Sing Out!* interview, Dylan gave an oblique clue to his interest in *Lear:* " '. . . I think it was Benjamin Franklin. He said (I'm not quoting it right) something like "For a man to be—(something or other)—at ease, he must not tell all he knows, nor say all he sees." Whoever said that certainly I don't think was trying to cover up anything. . . .' " A couplet from *King Lear* runs: "Have more than thou showest,/Speak less than thou knowest." The "nothing" echoes the artist's dilemma: death versus life, vacuum versus harvest, isolation versus people, silence versus sound, the void versus the life-impulse.

The Basement Tapes could have been titled *Roots*. What a massive catalog of chanteys, old blues, early rock, and truck-driver, hoedown, gospel, and folk songs! Consider how much "Odds and Ends" owes to Fats Domino. Or "Orange Juice Blues" to early 1950s R & B. There is parody and toying with clichés. Put "Lo and Behold" next to a truck-driver song—say, Dave Dudley singing "Six Days on the Road." Put "Clothes Line Saga" out to dry with the old jug-band songs. Note the raggy gospel feel of "Apple Suckling Tree," and envision the old black preacher shaking his tambourine. Beneath the nonsense of "Yea! Heavy and a Bottle of Bread" emerges that very deep American escape mechanism: Let's get the hell out of here and try these. Chuck Berry is back in "Long-Distance Operator," which recalls his "Memphis, Tennessee" and the twin technologies of teenage sexual liberation, the automobile, and the telephone.

The old agonies of *Blonde* have not disappeared. "Acapulco" proposes a romp in that posh Mexican resort, but the heavy spirit is down in Juarez again. "Open the Door, Homer" derives its title from the Jack McVea/Don Howell 1947 novelty hit of the Dusty Fletcher/John Mason vaudeville routine. Despite its light source, agony tempers the joy, contrasting not only Dylan's conflicts but also his ability to grow despite holding opposing ideas and impulses in his mind. The Band rarely sounded brighter, and more spontaneous and involved, than on *The Basement Tapes*. Here, The Band and Dylan were relaxed and joyous, breaking the country silence.

THE BOOTLEG ERA

When Dylan told me he was being forced, as early as winter 1966, to ban tape recorders at concerts because people were "stealing" his songs, I thought he was being paranoid. His fears were justified—a virtual subindustry had developed in the trafficking of illegal tapes from Dylan's private

sessions and public performances. Soon bootleggers began to sell tapes of
The Stones, The Beatles, and others. By June 1974, *Newsweek* reported:
"More than one-fourth of the tapes sold in the U.S. are pirated, depriving
recording companies and artists of up to $200 million yearly in sales and
royalties."

The industry's defenses were virtually nil until 1972, when recordings
were brought under the protection of federal copyright laws. But this leg-
islation was not retroactive. It would be impossible to guess the number of
Dylan bootlegs sold, but it must be in the millions. One Toronto record
shop sold four hundred copies of *The Great White Wonder* for $10.95
within five days. In November 1969, the source was hit by a restraining
order from Columbia Records and Dylan's Dwarf Music. In his affidavit,
Dylan said 9 of the 26 songs were taped "by me about 18 months ago at a
friend's house, 16 cuts were taken from a tape recorded by me in December, 1961, in Minneapolis" and other material was filched from a TV show.
OZ magazine reported the album was being hawked around London at five
and a half pounds, "like dope. There's the same restrained air of paranoia,
the absurd metaphorical telephone calls." *OZ* wrote, "none of this material
was ever intended for release . . . and there lies half the appeal. . . . Here's
Mr. Dylan with his pants down. Dylan exposed. Dylan vulnerable." Dylan
has a rant against bootleggers on his *Biograph* notes.

Bootleg producers and buyers often defended themselves as romantic
battlers against big business. One producer said his "bootleg commune"
was dedicated "to bringing music directly to the people without having to
go through the bureaucracy of the music industry." A California bootleg
collective, Rubber Dubber, had a production staff of fifty and hundreds of
sales staff. A twenty-six-year-old Los Angeles bootlegger, "Uncle Wiggly,"
worked his way through business school selling pirate disks, and told *Time*
in 1971; " 'Many of our salesmen would otherwise be pushing drugs. We
give a lot of money to the free clinic and to the peace coalition. I don't
think there's anything illegal about this.' " Uncle Wiggly's only business
problem was that if he didn't take orders and deliver his bootlegs within
one day, someone else would copy the tape and bootleg it.

The first Dylan bootleg—as opposed to private "collector" tapes—seems
to have stemmed from the final concert of his world tour, at Island Garden
in June 1966. A tape went to a Long Island bootlegger, who sold nearly
sixty thousand copies at up to seven dollars each. Later, he dispatched
someone to the Isle of Wight, but the courier stole the tape recorder and
his money. A leading English disc jockey, John Peel, wrote in *Disc and
Music Echo* that while he couldn't play bootlegs on his radio show, he
would love to: "Neither The Stones nor Dylan are likely to be driven to
the wall by necessity. . . . Artists have a right, presumably, to decide what
we hear and what we don't hear . . . but even this argument . . . is somewhat unsound. Artists such as these are part of the fabric of our very lives.
'Satisfaction,' 'Desolation Row' and 'Rubber Soul' are more part of my

education than the years spent crouching low in dismal classrooms. . . .
Records should, then, perhaps, reflect life as accurately as possible rather
than being clever and often very well done studio tricks."

If *Great White Wonder* could have sold 350,000 copies in America at up
to twelve dollars, with some serious people defending the idea, here lies a
major conflict. All told, there have been more than 160 albums of Dylan
bootlegs, several of them double-LP albums, many appearing and reappearing under different names. As late as 1986, a subindustry in Dylan
bootlegs still exists. One intrepid English provincial dealer advertised in a
pop paper his extensive lists of "rare Dylan material." He printed his catalog, a list of recordings that filled twenty-four pages, as his sixth version,
and added at the end: "Also, 17 tapes of concerts from the North American tour of 1974, of which I am now preparing lists."

Under the pseudonym of Tony White, Michael Gray, author of *Song
and Dance Man: The Art of Bob Dylan,* had done a major bootleg report for
the November 1972 issue of *Let It Rock.* Gray's piece elicited more mail
than any other the British monthly had published. Gray's analysis, expanded for this book, in part:

> Bootlegging is illegal, and Dylan, more than any other contemporary
> artist, has suffered. Bootlegging goes against the artist's wishes and in-
> vades his privacy. Yet pitched against this are the claims of scholarship
> and art. The critic and his analysis are of some value, while the artist is
> neither entitled to dictate how his work is to be evaluated nor expected
> to be its best judge.
>
> It was once reasonable and inevitable that after an artist's death, out
> would come the early drafts, the practice sketches, the sheafs of jottings,
> the manuscripts from the bottom drawer. In Dylan's case, it is perhaps
> no bad thing that the bottom drawer has already been opened. Bootleg
> tapes have allowed greater scope for studying Dylan's work as much as
> they have allowed others to exploit that work commercially. . . .
>
> The spectacle of Dylan's recording company protesting about boot-
> legs violating their artist's integrity is especially absurd. It was Colum-
> bia that issued, in what many saw as a calculatedly malevolent move, an
> album called "Dylan" compiled from some of the worst recordings they
> could find in their vaults. . . . [Gray credited Dylan's elusive practices
> for feeding the hungers of bootleg buyers. There is also] the quantity of
> recordings Dylan has made and not released. The ratio must be at least
> 10 to 1. The upshot is a mass of non-released recordings that can be
> found in innumerable collections of bootleg tapes and discs.

Gray went on to list some thirty-three groups of private and public recordings, personal and broadcast interviews, concerts and recording outtakes.
While Gray argued that bootlegs could give us a deeper picture of Dylan's
artistic development, I remain ambivalent. The artist should have the right

388   NO DIRECTION HOME

to say what part of his work he wants to present to the public, and at the time and place he chooses. It is not for *us* to "nationalize" Dylan's work by expropriation. We may not be living in a perfect democracy, but to turn all of Dylan's tapes into public property is not the way a democratic audience functions. Yet I can join Gray in his suggestion that Dylan do with some of his other unreleased material now existing only as bootlegs what he did with *The Basement Tapes* and *Biograph*—release them officially. Gray concluded that the following albums should be legitimized:

1. *Dylan—The Very Early Years: My Back Pages.*
   Let Me Die in My Footsteps, Rocks and Gravel, Talking John Birch Society Blues, Talkin' Bear Mountain Picnic Massacre Blues, Quit Your Low-Down Ways, Lonesome Whistle Blues, Hava Nagilah Blues, I've Bin a Moonshiner, Poem to Woody/Last Thoughts on Woody Guthrie (live), The Walls of Red Wing (live), Stealin', Black Cross.
2. *Dylan Love Songs.*
   Corrina, Corrina (1962 version), I'll Keep It with Mine; Baby, I'm in the Mood for You; Mama You Bin on My Mind, Spanish Harlem Incident (live 1963 Halloween version), Visions of Johanna (live Dublin, 1966), One Too Many Mornings (live BBC version, 1965), To Ramona (Isle of Wight), Love Minus Zero/No Limit (alternative 1965 studio take), Except You (live, 1974 tour), You're a Big Girl Now (original New York version, 1974).
3. *Dylan Live With The Band, Royal Albert Hall, 1966.*
   Exactly as on the bootleg album, complete with electrifying confrontation atmosphere between the hostile audience and the determined artist refusing to subscribe to the showbiz maxim of "give the audience what it wants."
4. *Dylan: From Desolation Row to the Basement.*
   Maggie's Farm (live, Newport, 1965), Barbed Wire Fence (studio, 1965), I Wanna Be Your Man (studio, 1965), She's Your Lover Now (studio, 1965), Mr. Tambourine Man (live at the Dublin Adelphi, 1966), I'm Not There, I Shall Be Released, Too Much of Nothing (other version), Down in the Flood, The Mighty Quinn (the last four, all further 1967 basement tapes).
5. *A Decade of Dylan—1963 to 1974.*
   Swan on the River (BBC-TV play recording, 1963), Ramblin' Round (live Town Hall, 1963), Who Killed Davey Moore? (same), Only a Pawn in Their Game (WNEW-TV recording, 1963), Lay Down Your Weary Tune (1964), Wild Mountain Thyme (Isle of Wight), One Too Many Mornings (with Johnny Cash, 1969), It Ain't Me Babe (Isle of Wight), Sign on the Cross (1971), Tangled Up in Blue (New York version, 1974), Idiot Wind (New York version, 1974).[7]

JOHN WESLEY HARDING

In January 1968, the release of this major album, which Dylan once called "the first biblical rock album," created several new myths about Dylan and desecrated several music-business myths. In the wake of the frenzied trilogy of 1965–66, the *Harding* album brings to my mind one of Blake's "Proverbs of Hell": "The road of excess leads to the palace of wisdom." We've seen Dylan's excess of piled-up images, of wild living, of spontaneous action. Now Dylan changes to a new compassion, a sense of musical, physical, spiritual, and religious calm. The elliptical tale on the album cover is a contemporary Christ parable in ironic reverse: The Three Kings come to get, not to give. This album ushered in a period in which Dylan's life and work would reject past excesses and embrace moderation.

Although Dylan did not tour to promote the album, it reportedly sold 250,000 copies in its first week. Not until April was it certified as his fifth gold album, which then meant a retail sale of a million dollars, at that time about 250,000 albums. (Later, with the rise in cost of albums, platinum certification came to mean the sale of a million units.) Buyers were looking for "the word" and "the way," and many were shocked at how he enunciated them. The man who once said he accepted chaos was now saying: "I believe there should be an order to everything. . . ."

The surface order belies the songs' underlying complexities. In his Woodstock study, Dylan had a huge Bible opened on a raised wooden bookstand, and the songs of Hank Williams near at hand. He had assembled the cast of Colin Wilson's *The Outsider*—the outlaw, outcast, loser, victim, the oppressed, lonely, and alienated. From these elements he sketched a series of studies in allegory, psalm, parable, symbol, metaphor, and moral tale. Biblical allusion, style, and syntax mixed with commonplace language and folklore run throughout the album. As Gwendolyn Bays wrote in *The Orphic Vision:* "The true seer must be able to decipher myth, and legend," especially ancient ones, "since early peoples concealed their most profound truths under the guise of a simple story."[8] Dylan's simplest album may be his most complex. Think only of what Paul Williams called "the claustrophobia" of "All Along the Watchtower" and its haunting line, "There must be some way out of here."[9]

Bill King saw Dylan producing "the new myth of the moderate man, the basis for a new personal and artistic identity. The internal process of this rebirth is the subject." He found the old outlaw-loving, outsider-identifying Dylan locked here in debate between his new and old selves. David Pichaske sees the first side "filled with a very Judaic, even Christian sense of guilt and the need for atonement" and the second side focusing on that atonement and achieving, in the final two love songs, "an actual state of grace." Eugene Stelzig saw Dylan reemerging with "an altered, restored and even more potent vision . . . deeply religious and moral . . . not only a soul-searching self-portrait and confession . . . but also a visionary probing of the abiding spiritual realities of salvation and damnation."

Now that he'd caught his breath and balance, Dylan revealed a little about his songs and techniques. In February 1968, *Newsweek:* " 'I was always with the traditional song. I just used electricity to wrap it up in. Probably I wasn't ready yet to make it simple. . . . A song is moral just by being a song. We're all moralists. . . . I only look at them musically . . . as things to sing. It's the music that the words are sung to that's important. I write the songs because I need something to sing. It's the difference between the words on paper and the song. The song disappears into the air, the paper stays. They have little in common. A great poet, like Wallace Stevens, doesn't necessarily make a great singer. But a great singer always—like Billie Holiday—makes a great poet. I could have sung each of them better. I'm not exactly dissatisfied but I'm just not about to brag about the performance. . . . I've always tried to get simple. I haven't always succeeded. But here I took more care in the writing. In "Blonde on Blonde" I wrote out a song, we'd do it, they'd go back to their game and I'd write out another song. . . . I used to think that myself and my songs were the same thing. But I don't believe that anymore. There's myself and there's my song, which I hope is everybody's song.' "

John Cohen of *Sing Out!* said he gave Dylan a copy of Kafka's *Parables and Paradoxes* because these stories "really get to the heart of the matter, and yet you can never really decipher them." In the *Sing Out!* of October 1968, Dylan said: " '. . . the only parables that I know are the Biblical parables. I've seen others, Khalil Gibran, perhaps . . . you certainly wouldn't find it in the Bible—this type of soul. Now Mr. Kafka comes off a little closer to that. Gibran, the words are all mighty but the strength is turned into that of a contrary direction. There used to be this disk jockey, Rosko. . . . Sometimes . . . Rosko would be reciting this poetry of Khalil Gibran. It was a radiant feeling, coming across it on the radio. His voice was that of the inner voice in the night. . . . I have always read the Bible, though not necessarily the parables.' " Cohen: "I don't think you're the kind who goes to the hotel, where the Gideons leave a Bible, and you pick it up." Dylan replied: " 'Well, you never know.' "[10] (Rosko, long a disc jockey on WNEW-FM, was a devotee of the Lebanese poet whose most renowned work was *The Prophet.* Gibran, a religious mystic, gained wide popularity among Western collegians. Rosko's album *Music and Gibran* (Verve/Forecast FTS-3044) consists of readings backed by Middle Eastern music. The "shadow" of Gibran on Dylan seems less discernible on *Harding* than in some earlier works, such as "Hard Rain.")

There was disagreement over *Harding's* political content. Steven Goldberg said in *The Saturday Review:* "J.W.H. appeared at a time when the indescribable revulsion toward Lyndon Johnson was at its zenith. . . . Dylan's declaration that he was not about to argue or to move contrasted with the student rage that was asserting itself." Jon Landau found political awareness in *Harding,* however veiled. He wrote in *Crawdaddy:* "Dylan manifests a profound awareness of the war and how it is affecting all of us." In *The Village Voice,* Richard Goldstein wrote: " 'J.W.H.' . . . not only eludes, but dares interpretation. . . . Dylan's major theme is human vulnerability. . . . Dylan confronts a cliché the way a butcher eyes a chicken. His new songs abound with slaughtered platitudes. . . . Dylan is his own motif. So listen for the outlaw-confessor in 'J.W.H.' Under the suede smile, he is still naked." Stephen Pickering applied his readings in mysticism and Jewish literature, and saw the mystical experience as the core of the album. Pickering found Dylan's Jewish background "extends and pervades everything he has ever written."

The album's sparse music startled everyone: In a period of wild musical explorations, Dylan had turned to folk-country simplicity of melodic line and laconic backing. It was almost the progression from Symbolism into Imagism—from a rich overload of symbol buildup to unembellished essentials, from "too much of nothing" to just a bit of something else, from a modernist carnival of the elusive and the intuitive to a classic sort of simple line, terse stories meant always to be "listening to the silences," the meanings between the words. His dramatic change of music styles flew in the face of The Beatles' mid-1967 *Sgt. Pepper,* a daring foray into studio techniques. Dylan's spare, effective background was supplied by only three Nashville session men—Pete Drake, pedal-steel guitarist; Charlie McCoy, bassist, and Kenny Buttrey, drummer. Here was Dylan whispering in a climate of shout and scream. He had pulled the plug on electric music.

The album's cover previews mystification. Pictured with Dylan are a Woodstock workman and two Indian Baul singers of Bengal, traditional singers Grossman recorded for Elektra. Some fans saw "hidden" Beatles pictures in the trees. One *Melody Maker* reader spoofed: If you hold the album cover "right-way-up, then turn it in a clockwise direction, the record falls out." I first heard about *Harding* from Milt Okun, a messenger once associated with Grossman and Mogull, but later with Dylan. Milt was pleased Dylan had gone "full-circle" back to songs that were "fully comprehensible, almost complete folk . . . sometimes reminding me of Ewan MacColl."

The "Three Kings" liner note is, to some, *Tarantula*-like nonsense. Pichaske read it as "a short story in the Kafka-Böll-Borchert tradition which draws on both the Bible and Brecht." The "Three Kings" can be a Christ parable, or Dylan-as-Frank proclaiming himself, frankly, as the moderate man.

"JOHN WESLEY HARDING": Gentle irony, with the protagonist holding guns in "every" hand. At the time, the whole youth culture was shaken by the Warren Beatty–Arthur Penn film, *Bonnie and Clyde.* Rather than tell the story of John Wesley Hardin, the song, in Bill King's phrase, "condenses into poetic form the mythic outline of the outlaw hero." Hardin, born in Texas in 1853, started young as a gambler-gunman. In 1877, he got twenty-five years for killing a sheriff. In prison, he studied law until pardoned in 1894, then started to practice in El Paso. A year later he was killed by a local constable. (When Okun asked Dylan to name his "favorite" traditional folk song for the book *Something to Sing About,* Dylan characteristically chose a badman song, "John Hardy.") When the record was released, I twitted Dylan in print about his adding a gratuitous *g* to Hardin's name, for repaying his orthographic debt after all his singin', ramblin', and walkin'.

"Harding" is a badman ballad about an essentially good man, an unembroidered fable. In a consciously rough, ethnic folk voice, he kept the story brief. The fully armed outlaw-saint, his lady beside him, "He was never known/To make a foolish move."[11] Harding disappears, just as Dylan did at this period. The song has an open-range roll, the feel of caked mud on the boots.

"AS I WENT OUT ONE MORNING": The Anglo-American songbook is heavy with beginnings like this archaic opening line. (Bill King links this to the Appalachian song "Lolly Toodum.") Tom Paine shines as a metaphor for freethinking. He was, of course, the revolutionary writer for whom that 1963 civil liberties award was named. Dylan hints that Paine, who once proclaimed that his own mind was his church, would have been appalled to see libertarian ideas enchained by dogma. A traditional form is used here to move the story along, and to comment on the clash of contemporary values. The girl enchained is actually a dual reversal: Traditionally, fair damsels are the enslaved, not the enslaver.

"I DREAMED I SAW ST. AUGUSTINE": The first two lines paraphrase "Joe Hill," the Earl Robinson–Alfred Hayes union hymn to the singing Wobbly organizer who became a martyr. A folk saint is eclipsed by a Catholic saint, but Dylan gently disdains both houses. Preconceptions and ideology are dead; he hungers here for salvation, for answers. His isolation from a comforting faith is deeply felt. Augustine was not martyred, but died a bishop, an honored church father. His *Confessions* and *City of God* are visionary chronicles of his early wastrel life, subsequent conversion, and search for grace. Stelzig sees the narrator "among those who put the Biblical prophet of resurrection out to death. The realization . . . of his complicity and guilt is conveyed with a poignancy . . . new in Dylan's poetry. He wakes up alone, terrified—he bows his head and cries." Carolyn Bliss—the singer awaking from his vision of himself as a saint and cries "for the futile self-sacrifice of sainthood, which precludes full understanding and insists on service to the unattainable. All that was a dream and Dylan is awake now." Bliss thinks Dylan is saying: "Go with my compassion and companionship, but not with my guidance. Go through your own darkness; go find your own light." Dylan examines martyrdom and why people hunger for martyrs. But there remains much mystery in these three verses. What is "the glass" he touches before crying? A window, a telescope, or a mirror? He seems to identify simultaneously with the sinner-turned-saint and the lost souls beyond redemption by Leftist or Catholic saints.

"ALL ALONG THE WATCHTOWER": Perhaps the album's high point. After a menacing guitar introduction, intense singing and mood mix colloquial speech with archaic setting and personae. Emptiness is peopled with the joker, a wise fool out of *King Lear*. And the dialogue with the thief supports the theory that both are Dylan's contradictory spirits in dialogue. Gabrielle Goodchild: "The watchtower seems related to the fortified city as a recurring image for the moral state of man or the body politic. Here the moral order seems to be threatened by the duality Dylan sees within himself of clown and holy pickpocket."

Are the mysterious pair inside or outside humankind's fortified city, trapped or exiled? "The question is the answer." Is it worse to be locked in or locked out? In "George Jackson," Dylan said that some of us are prisoners and some are guards, but there's little difference. Jack McDonough linked the song to Isaiah, Chapter 21, foretelling the fall of Babylon. Pickering linked Isaiah also to "Messenger" and "Immigrant." At this time, Dylan must have felt that businessmen were drinking his earnings and that critics and listeners were trampling his soil. Dylan had great praise for the Jimi Hendrix recording, and strong memories of the man.

"THE BALLAD OF FRANKIE LEE AND JUDAS PRIEST": The gloom, if not the doubt, is relieved by a comic tall tale in frontier-ballad style. Echoes of Mark Twain, Bret Harte, and Robert Service. This fable offers a story as light, or a message as heavy, as the listener chooses. Frank on the liner notes and Frankie Lee might both be Dylan. Judas, the tempter with the bankroll, then becomes the music business, or success. Having exhausted himself with the alleged pleasures of the brothel of fame, which the tempter called home, Frankie is dying of thirst in a moral desert. " 'Nothing is revealed,' "[12] except stay where you want, do what you want, and don't let people tempt you with money and false claims of success. Dylan pulls off a dozen jokes here—on frontier balladry, on western types, on Bible story.

"DRIFTER'S ESCAPE": Another tale of an outsider, threatened but not defeated by society. Excellent singing with anguished intonation, careful phrasing. The song recalls Hank Williams, the drifter being a victim of the music life nicknamed Luke the Drifter, whose lonesome chants have a similarly beseeching tone. Dylan's retreat couldn't blot out the outrage he'd heard the previous three years. The drifter is the Kafkaesque victim, offense unknown. Enter God with a bolt of lightning, making the persecutors cry while the drifter escapes. The lightning could well be that motorcycle. Dylan's hatred of mob behavior was deep. After seeing the film *The Ox-Bow Incident,* he worked on a ballad about a lynching of an innocent. There are prototypes of the scansion, rhythm, and meter of this song in the Old Testament.

"DEAR LANDLORD": One of Dylan's trumps has been matching a

textual phrase with a musical phrase, as in this title. The vocalizing maintains a tone of invocation; a personal plea becomes a prayer. I see this as very personal: Grossman once owned Dylan's Woodstock cottage, Dylan owed "rent" then to Columbia Records, Macmillan, and ABC-TV. Jack McDonough links the catalog of sins of the hobo and the landlord and the immigrant to Proverbs 6:16.

"I AM A LONESOME HOBO": Another view of an outsider. The last four lines moralize heavily: Avoid jealousy, accept no one else's code of behavior, and keep your judgments to yourself. A sort of vagrant Polonius preaching his credo. "Hobo" has a peculiar unity with the earlier "Drifter"; the drifter is now a few miles from the courthouse, recalling his "crimes" before walking off alone.

"I PITY THE POOR IMMIGRANT": Compassionate and doom-laden, this lyric confounds me. Dylan may be having a tortured colloquy with himself, a love-hate debate between his own (everyone's) good side and the acquisitive, opportunist, insatiable element. Alain Rémond has suggested an attempt to balance fate and liberty. Rémond saw us all as immigrants or exiles from "The Gates of Eden." Dylan was now outside New York City, city of immigrants, but sending down messages of how sick the city seemed to him. The singing is outstanding, to one of the most beautiful melodies in Anglo-Scots tradition. He must have remembered Bonnie Dobson's singing of the Canadian "Peter Amberley," which borrows from "Come All Ye Tramps and Hawkers." The immigrant's dreadful deeds are set against such caressing cadences that the harshness of the crimes recede. Perhaps the final line, "When his gladness comes to pass,"[13] with its biblical serenity, offers hope of grace.

"THE WICKED MESSENGER": Biblical allusion enriches this quizzical fable, right down to its archaic diction. Eli is Hebrew for "God is high." The biblical Eli was a high priest and judge of Israel, teacher of young Samuel. The lyric's concept is ancient and often revived. According to Proverbs 13:17: "A wicked messenger falleth into mischief/But a faithful ambassador *is* health." In Sophocles' *Antigone,* "None love the messenger who brings bad news." Shakespeare, in *King Henry IV, Part II,* put it: "The first bringer of unwelcome news/Hath but a losing office." Dylan may be talking of the poet's duty to tell the truth. The musical line is one of the album's most inventive, a bluesy, harsh, descending contour.

"DOWN ALONG THE COVE": At first, this and the final song seemed misplaced. Later, I saw emotional, rational, and musical sense of order in their positioning. If this album is about one man's search for salvation or answers, or one man's autobiography of change, then such appealing love songs provide balance and symmetry. Now the messenger brings good news. Salvation through love—of a person, an ideal, or a religious faith—can be complex, or as simple as a woman's smile. This tune really swings, lightly, like a dance.

"I'LL BE YOUR BABY TONIGHT": Dylan toys again with the clichés of commonplace love. The contrast suggests forget philosophy and ideology and settle for simple pleasures, simple verities of "moon" and "spoon." The album that he begins with a badman cowboy ballad, ponders the immutable and the intangible until he decides to savor the comforts of love. Hank Williams used to sing about mockingbirds too, and he was far from the simple man his verses suggested. "Cove" and "Baby Tonight" not only close out one period of Dylan's work and life, but point ahead to new vistas along the Nashville skyline.

A SONG FOR WOODY

Finally, Woody Guthrie's wasting decay, trembling, and pain ended. On October 3, 1967, he died, after fifteen years of illness. Woody's longtime agent, Harold Leventhal, briefed the press on Woody's turbulent career. The obituaries startled many who thought Woody had died in the 1940s. The fragmented folk movement seemed to close ranks at the death of its elder statesman. Leventhal told me: "A lot of people got in touch to say how sorry they were, but only one singer actually suggested that we *do* something—Bob Dylan." A benefit concert seemed the appropriate tribute to a ballad-maker. The proceeds could help fight Huntington's chorea, or start a library in Woody's hometown of Okemah.

With Dylan pledging his time, the concert was easily arranged. Millard Lampell, screenwriter and former Almanac Singer, wrote and directed the production. Two Hollywood actors who had known Woody, the late Will Geer and Robert Ryan, were narrators. Singers? You almost had to fight them off. In December, an unobtrusive notice in New York papers announced twin concerts at Carnegie Hall on January 20, 1968. Listed were Dylan, Judy Collins, Jack Elliott, Arlo Guthrie, Richie Havens, Odetta, Tom Paxton, and Pete Seeger. Nearly six thousand seats sold out within hours.

Dylan's return threatened to upstage the concerts' purpose. He made some severe proscriptions: no pictures, tape recorders, or mob scenes. Still, audience and press were keyed up not to mourn the death of Guthrie so much as to celebrate the return of Dylan. At the first concert, in the afternoon, Dylan sidled on from stage left, and was not immediately recognized. He wore a Jesus beard and moustache, and was dressed in a conservative gray suit with a light-blue dress shirt open at the neck. He looked very serene. As the audience began to recognize him, a series of whoops and shouts began an effusive day.

"Nothing so perpetuates a legend as the disappearance of its subject," Richard Goldstein wrote in *Vogue*. Even though Dylan was at the microphone briefly, the day was his. The entire company started with an instrumental ensemble, then sailed into "Bound for Glory." Ryan began to read Lampell's script: "He had a little sign pasted on his guitar that said: THIS MACHINE KILLS FASCISTS. He believed in stepping up and speaking out what he was for and what he was against. His whole hard-traveling life was a one-man demonstration. He was against poverty and hunger, bigotry and bargain-basement justice, con artists, jackleg preachers, and crooked politicians. . . . He was for the outsider and the outcast, the radical and the rebel. He was for the drifter and the stray. . . ."

The heroic celebration of the Guthrie legend began. The singers interpreted his songs, taking over where Lampell's narration or Woody's words left off. The transition from singing prose to singing lyrics was easy, for there was melody to both. Some of Marjorie Guthrie's dance students performed to one song, and slides of the Pacific Northwest accompanied the federal bard's scratchy old voice singing "Talking Dust Bowl." In a period of harsh politics, acid music, pop art, and assassinations, Woody's words sounded like scripture: "I'm one walker that's stood way up and looked way down across aplenty of pretty sights in all their veiled and nakedest season. Thumbing it. Hitching it. Walking and talking it. Chalking it. Marking it. Sighting it and hearing it. Seeing and feeling and breathing and smelling it in, sucking down me, rubbing it all in the pores of my skin, and the wind between my eyes knocking honey in my comb. . . ."

The lights went out for ten seconds after Ryan finished, and there was some shuffling at stage right. The lights rose and a country jamboree ensued. Dylan and The Band jolted out one of Woody's best dam songs, "Grand Coulee Dam." Real hillbilly, strong, shouting, crackling with tumult, Dylan picking his acoustic guitar one minute, then raising it up high to the mike, or raising his right arm to "conduct" The Band with decisive ax chops. Listeners were either on their feet cheering or were smiling. A *Rolling Stone* reporter beside me was laughing out loud. With the first song still roaring away, the audience settled down. Seeger sat, chin on fist, like "The Thinker." Odetta smiled broadly, like another spotlight onstage. Dylan and The Band sailed into "Mrs. Roosevelt." Bob shifted keys like a racing driver shifting gears. The organ and the drums filled out the pattern. Who says folk music can't be done with a beat? Who says Guthrie can't be sung by a rockabilly band?

After the applause subsided, Dylan steered his drifters into "I Ain't Got No Home." It was startling to hear Woody's songs done this way. Seeger, apparently recovered from his electric shock, was drumming the back of his guitar. Dylan's voice soared over the ensemble. How unlike *John Wesley Harding*! Now his singing had become astringent. Vocal harmonies with The Band brought it all back home down in contemporary country. At intermission, everyone was chattering about Dylan. Only thirteen minutes onstage, and he'd upstaged everyone but Woody Guthrie.

Security was tight. Leventhal threatened disruption of the program if cameras were used. Just before the evening intermission, someone snapped a flashbulb, and out ran Leventhal and a uniformed guard to oust the miscreant. After the concert, Lampell was furious. He asked me, rhetorically: "What has all this policing stuff got to do with Woody?" As I went backstage before the first concert, David Gahr, the official photographer at the show, whispered heatedly: "He's here!" In one of the dressing rooms, Dylan was sitting near Robbie and Jack Elliott. Everyone looked nervous except Rambling Jack, who was cracking wise. I greeted Bob, and he stood up to shake my hand, a rare concession to manners. We were talking about the weather and the outlook for spring crops when Grossman handed Bob a piece of paper, which Dylan read, then laughed at. He'd had a good rest, I thought.

Not everyone had been pleased by Dylan's segment of the Guthrie tribute. Some folkniks thought the show was "too Hollywood," overly star-oriented. But more important, many listeners who were drawn by Dylan had been introduced to Guthrie. As the show continued, Dylan was back in perspective as a Guthrie disciple paying homage. Geer and Ryan rolled on with Woody's prose-poems: ". . . I just happen to believe in my soul that the rough people in this world are the best singers, the hard-hit people, the hard-hitting people. . . ." More songs about the little people, the union people, the good old American earth. Judy Collins sang "Roll on, Columbia." Seeger and Havens harmonized "Jackhammer John." Paxton told the story of "The Biggest Thing Man Has Ever Done," then Judy joined Seeger on "Union Maid." Seeger led a three-thousand-voice sing-along on "Reuben James." Arlo had his finest moment with "Jesus Christ," his dad's sardonic song that asked whether Jesus, if preaching today, would be crucified again. Odetta and Havens teamed up on the rarely performed "I've Got to Know."

At both performances, the sing-alongs exuded a revival-meeting spirit. People needed some affirmation, as the war droned on into the Tet offensive, civil rights became embattled, politics remained as shabby as ever. The faithful tried to find some hope in Guthrie's words that we were "born to win." Everyone sailed into "Bound for Glory." Dylan took his verse, momentarily forgot the lyric, smiled, recaught the line, and everyone joyfully sang on. Finally, the folk national anthem, "This Land Is Your Land." A few cried; most clapped, stamped, jumped to their feet, or shouted themselves hoarse. Gone for the moment was fractionalized, suspicious, partisan, self-seeking individualism. We were all together around the campfire of brotherhood and sisterhood, turning on to the fantasy of hope for a real democracy. Marjorie was up onstage now, and Odetta grabbed her hands and danced around with her. Elliott did some fancy steps in his clunky cowboy boots. Old Will Geer sang loud, if not clear. The standing ovation went on for perhaps ten minutes. Pete finally soothed us out of the hall, saying we ought to take our songs back to our factories, our communities, our homes. Our factories? Oh, well, who's going to quibble over a bit of blue-collar rhetoric?

Between concerts, Dylan and The Band relaxed at the nearby Sheraton-Plaza Hotel. Robbie had told me at the afternoon intermission to "just wait for tonight," and he was right, for the excitement of their segment was even greater. After the second show, a party for about one hundred members of the cast and friends was held at Robert Ryan's spacious apartment in the Dakota, the Central Park West building where John Lennon lived and died. Leventhal was subdued, explaining later that he had finally been hit by Woody's death that day. About midnight, Bob came in with Sara, Happy Traum, and a few friends. Bob was wearing his Ben Franklin glasses, looking relaxed but drawn inward. Conversation almost stopped when he entered. He began to make the rounds of old friends and acquaintances, including Alan Lomax. Allen Ginsberg spent a considerable time slumped in a chair in meditation.

I chatted with Dylan about the concert. He called almost everything "great, just great." Hesitantly, we drifted on to my recent *Times* review of *John Wesley Harding*. I indicated how frequently I'd listened to the album, getting something different each time. "Well, you'd better listen to it another few times," Bob said. Faced with some of his old preaccident cut and thrust, I almost felt more at ease. But we'd had that sort of artist-critic parrying before, so we quickly veered off into small talk. I noticed that he wasn't shunning small talk, and had almost become quite good at it.

The Times gave me nearly a column in which to rhapsodize. *The New Yorker* devoted nearly a page of its lead "Talk of the Town" item to a sympathetic report. *The Village Voice* snagged a good photograph of Dylan onstage for page one. The Associated Press stressed the Dylan comeback over the Guthrie tribute. Certainly there was enough in the Guthrie story, writings and songs, to have launched a national touring company. Eventually, another version of the Carnegie Hall tribute was mounted at the Hollywood Bowl, on September 12, 1970. The cast added Baez, Country Joe McDonald, and Earl Robinson. Sharing the narration with Will Geer was actor Peter Fonda. About eighteen thousand people turned out to see the Dust Bowl moved to the Hollywood Bowl. Two recordings of the twin shows, only pale reflections of the events, were released in April 1972; Volume One by Columbia and Volume Two by Warner Bros. Proceeds went to the Huntington's chorea fund and toward a Guthrie library.

Many hoped that the film of *Bound for Glory*, released in autumn 1976, might enhance Guthrie's standing. Leventhal had been trying to launch such a film for at least ten years. Shortly after Woody's death, he commissioned a script from the late Nedrick Young. Four scripts later, a screenplay by Robert Getchell was accepted. Leventhal co-produced for United Artists along with Robert Blumofe. Hal Ashby directed. The search for the "right" star was long and involved. Leventhal told *The Village Voice* on October 13, 1975: " 'I wanted a short actor. We talked to Dustin Hoffman . . . Jack Nicholson . . . Robert De Niro. . . . Arlo wanted to play the part. . . . Bob Dylan was considered. We sent him a script, although I was sure I didn't want him, and he called up a week later and said he loved the script but he would never want to play the role. Thank God, I thought. Then a week later, he called back and said he wanted to direct the movie. We had to turn him down, of course.' " Chosen for the role was

David Carradine, best known for his part in the *Kung Fu* TV series. A script devoid of Woody's word-magic got lackluster reviews. Poor attendance left the seven-million-dollar production in the red. Dylan and Pete Seeger have achieved more than the film did in bringing Guthrie forward into American life and letters.

THE SKYLINE OF NASHVILLE

Where would the late 1960s take rock? By 1969, everybody had to get stoned and make it to Woodstock, cut a psychedelic album, prove they were disturbed by Vietnam by freaking out. Then, a quiet young countryman made his way down to Nashville's Music Row, picked up a few sidemen, went into a studio, and, in a few days cut an album of gently crooned country love songs in a voice he'd never used before. While most of his fans were still stalking Desolation Row, Dylan turned the corner into Redemption Street.

"Nashville Skyline" proclaimed, in April 1969, a man reformed, subdued, and very much in love. The widespread first reaction was: "How can he let us down like this? Pouring out all that syrupy love while we're marching off stoned to *his* Woodstock? It's a sellout!" One more sudden experiment unsettled and disoriented. Many reviews stressed what was *not* on the album: no protest, no bitterness, no druggy symbolism, no hipness. How could he do this to us?

Variety called Dylan's voice "shockingly transformed." *Time:* "Dylan is definitely doing something that can be called singing. Somewhere, somehow, he has managed to add an octave to his range." Geoffrey Cannon in *The Guardian:* "The new country music, inspired always by Dylan's example, will be played more and more this year, in every American city. It will create some space and calm in the murderously fevered streets." Christgau in *The Village Voice:* "After eight years as psychic wanderer, Dylan is transmuted into man-about-the-house—friendly, stable, secure and promising not to vomit it back in our face next year." Many thought he'd lost his cutting edge because he had turned soft and plump. Artists create better work when they are suffering, and they should, indeed, suffer for their audiences and their art. Ed Ochs in *Billboard,* July 12, 1969: "Dylan, the satisfied man, speaks in clichés and blushes as if every day were Valentine's day. . . . So goodbye, Bob Dylan, I'm glad you're happy though you meant more to me when you were . . . confused like everybody else. . . ."

The unconfused Dylan sat for a *Newsweek* interview published on April 14, 1969: " 'These are the type of songs that I always felt like writing. The songs reflect more of the inner me than the songs of the past. They're more to my base than, say, "John Wesley Harding." There I felt everyone expected me to be a poet so that's what I tried to be. But the smallest line in this new album means more to me than some of the songs on any of the previous albums I've made.' "

I had always found Dylan more aware of the country currents than most other city folk singers. In December 1961, when I returned from my first visit to Nashville to begin work on my book, *The Country Music Story,* Bob asked who I'd seen and heard. He often alluded to Hank Snow, Hank Thompson, Bill Anderson, Dolly Parton. In September 1968, he stole in from Woodstock to catch Johnny Cash at Carnegie Hall. He repeatedly told associates that he regarded country music as the coming thing, long before he cut *Skyline* on his fourth set of working visits to Nashville.

Dylan's first Nashville session after *John Wesley Harding* was in Columbia's Studio A on September 24, 1968. *Skyline* was taped from February 13 through 17, 1969. Session men included Charlie Daniels, Dobro steel-guitar player, Johnny Cash, and a passel of Nashville sidemen. Six weeks after its release, the album reached number one. Although pure country, it did not score on country charts. I wondered why Glen Campbell and Johnny Cash appeared on pop *and* country charts, Aretha Franklin on as many as five charts, but Dylan on only one. Clive Davis explained: "We do know that 'Skyline' sold very well in the country-record market. What the trade papers don't know is how to allocate these sales to its acceptance as a country album, a rock album or both." Lee Zhito, editor of *Billboard,* wrote me: "There is no 'silent resistance' within the country field toward Dylan. The answer lies in the repertoire. When non-country artists choose to invade this field they invariably do so well-armed with established country song material. . . . The country fan simply did not feel at home with this repertoire, and bypassed the album. . . ." Michael Clare, managing editor of *Record Retailer,* London: ". . . I, too, often wonder how they compile their charts. . . . Unless an artist publicly states he is a country singer nobody else will do so." When I asked Dylan, he simply said: "The only people who get on country charts are those who are out at the crossroads singing every week."

He could have had no more influential "sponsor" in country music than Johnny Cash. On the last evening of the sessions, February 17–18, Big John ambled into the studio and the two jammed. They put down twelve to fifteen tracks together, including "I Walk the Line," "Big River," "Careless Love," "One Too Many Mornings," and "Understand Your Man." The only public results were the duet on *Skyline,* a brief segment of Dylan in a theatrical-TV film on Cash, and Dylan's appearance on the premiere of Cash's TV series.

The Cash-Dylan friendship actually dated back five years. By the time of the TV taping, Cash was showing some signs of irritation at being upstaged. "We're just friends. I got lots of friends," Cash said then. Reviewing the friendship in 1975, Cash said: "I became aware of Bob Dylan when the *Freewheelin'* album came out in 1963. I thought he was one of the best country singers I had ever heard. I always felt a lot in common with him. I knew a lot about him before we had ever met. I knew he had heard and listened to country music. I was in Las Vegas in 1963 and wrote him a letter telling him how much I liked his work. We developed a correspondence." Before they had met, Cash was ready to be Dylan's partisan, inside Columbia Records and within the topical-song movement. (In a letter printed in New York *Broadside* Number 41, March 10, 1964, Cash entered the Dylan controversy on Bob's side.)

At Newport 1965, Cash gave Dylan one of his guitars. In 1968, Cash retold the episode: "I had brought a couple of guitars with me, and he liked that one handmade in Chicago in the early thirties. So I gave him that old guitar of mine. I've given away a lot of guitars. We first met at Columbia Records. We just became friends like any two songwriters might, you know? Mutual admiration, I think. I was a guest of his in Woodstock four or five years ago. I saw him in England a couple of years back. Then in Nashville about a year ago when he came to record."

In autumn 1968, I interviewed John in New York for a documentary film: "I think the pop and the new breed as they come along, every year, will borrow from country music. I have a great respect for people like The Byrds and The Lovin' Spoonful. They do country that I could dig. . . . But I don't think it can be a consistent thing with anybody except . . . real country artists. . . . You have to have grass roots. If I don't sound like I know what I'm singing about, the people know it. . . . They know whether or not I'm sincere. . . . I don't say you have to live in poverty in the South to be a country singer. But it helps. Every successful country singer I know has a humble background, beginning, and the colored blues have been a part of their musical heritage. Every one of them, bar none. Elvis will tell you himself that where he got his style is from the colored blues singers."

The Dylan-Cash relationship reached its apogee in 1969 with their opening track of *Skyline* and Dylan's appearance on the Cash TV show on Saturday, June 7. Dylan's bit was minimal. He appeared restrained and youthful beside his host's towering hulk. Alone, he sang "I Threw It All Away," "Living the Blues," and then joined Cash in "Girl from the North Country." Dylan was introduced only by name, said nothing, shook Cash's hand after the duet, and then gave his first, tentative smile. Red O'Donnell of *The Nashville Banner* wrote me: "He preferred to appear on the bare, austere stage. Dylan said: 'I never want to work in front of scenery that looks better than I do.' I interviewed him during the taping at the Grand Ole Opry House, and he spoke in a whisper. 'I have a difficulty in talking to people. But I'll put something down on paper and perhaps it will tell something about me.'" O'Donnell sent me what he called Dylan's "Ten Commandments" or "Credo": " 'I love children. I love animals. I am loyal to my friends. I have a sense of humor. I have a generally happy outlook. I try to be on time for appointments. I have a good relationship with my wife. I take criticism well. I strive to do good work. . . . I try to find some good in everybody.' " Whether O'Donnell knew he was being put on or not, he pressed Dylan: " 'I wish I could explain why I'm shy. I can't really analyze my emotions to any great extent. As for my appeal, who

knows? I'm not the reporter's perfect interviewee. But perhaps my formula
for writing will be of interest. I want to help anybody who wants to write
a story about me. . . .' " O'Donnell asked why he had turned down so
much television and was doing the Cash show. Dylan: " 'Because it is a
good show. There are so few good TV shows around these days.' "

Reporters tried to breach the heavy security at the TV taping. A *Look*
team was unceremoniously thrown out. June Carter Cash tried to demys-
tify things by saying that John and Bob spent a lot of their time together
in silence. Executive producer Bill Carruthers explained to Carol Botwin
of *This Week* magazine: " 'Bob wouldn't do this unless John had asked
him to. I can't tell you how uptight he is . . . some kid got through and
forced himself on Bob, and . . . the police had to throw the kid out. . . .
Bob felt badly about it. Bob was the center of attraction, and he hates it—
just hates it. I can only tell you that the string is very taut at the moment
regarding Dylan even doing the show. . . . But he's sticking it out because
of Johnny. He said to me yesterday, "Please, no photographers, because I
look bad." Well, he doesn't. Bob looks healthy and suntanned and wants
to wear a suit and a tie on the show. . . . He's such a deep little guy you can
tell the moment he's upset because there's a little twitch in his eye or
lip.' "

Doug Kershaw, the country fiddler, said he had spent the previous evening in a motel writing songs with Dylan: "The man is so very human.
You fail to realize that he's afraid. Deathly afraid." Joni Mitchell, another
guest on the show: "Sometimes the most frightening thing is when everyone loves you too much. . . . Dylan's such a sensitive guy. . . . He used to
be better off when he was younger and an angry young man . . . he would
scream at you and diminish you if he thought your questions were stupid
or unartistic. Now, he knows he can't be an angry young kid anymore. He
can't growl. Instead, he stays silent and explodes inside. Instead of taking
it out on you, he takes it out internally."

Cash tended to deny the "magic": "That's something everybody else
sees, but I don't. We've done it dozens of times just foolin' around. But
everybody here said 'North Country' was the most magnetic, powerful
thing they ever heard. Just raving about electricity, magnetism. And all I
did was sit there hitting G chords. . . ." June Cash suggested that Dylan
wasn't scared on the show, just shy. "The Dylans are very good friends of
ours. John wants Bob to be comfortable. When they are with us, we just
try to keep everybody away because we respect his privacy, but never know
quite what he's thinking." *The Johnny Cash Show* went out on ABC-TV
and reached millions. It was an instant success, guaranteeing a regular run
budgeted at $150,000 per week, starting in January 1970.

The Dylan-Cash rapport went far beyond music. Cash never tried to
conceal that, in spite of his success, he virtually went to pieces from 1961
until 1968. Cash's redemptive marriage to June Carter brought him a new
mastery over his turbulent personality. He and Dylan were walking a simi-

lar comeback line in this period. Each drew quiet security from watching the other find stability. Dylan agreed to a brief appearance in a TV-and-theatrical film documentary, *Johnny Cash, The Man, His World, His Music,* produced by Arthur and Evelyn Barron. Dylan had met Arthur Barron back in July 1963, when he produced a small "freedom songs" special for WNDT-TV in New York. Dylan taped seven songs, but approved release of only the duet of "One Too Many Mornings." After a TV premiere on National Educational Television, sixteen minutes were added and the film was distributed worldwide in theaters starting in October 1969.

Nashville Skyline publicly reflects the private rapport that then existed between Cash and Dylan. In Cash's verse paean on the album jacket, he was saying, in effect, to his vast country audience: "Here's a good pal who knows what country music's all about. Forget what you've heard about him as a protester, hippie, or freak, and just listen to the man sing about love." For the first time on an official release, Dylan repeated a song, and did his first instrumental, "Nashville Skyline Rag"; this was also his first use of electronic echo. Most startling was his brand-new voice. In the highly sarcastic 1969 *Rolling Stone* interview, Dylan "explained": " 'When I stopped smoking, my voice changed . . . so drastically, I couldn't believe it myself. That's true. I tell you, you stop smoking those cigarettes [Laughter] . . . and you'll be able to sing like Caruso. . . .' "

No Caruso—but there are some Buddy Holly echoes, some of Roy Orbison's purling tones, some of the Elvis of "Loving You." Mostly, there is a lot of open intonation, without nasality, without an angry whine. It was "another key, another door" for Dylan as a pure country singer. This is not Merle Haggard grit, nor Hank Williams pain. Rather, the open-throated, melodic float of Jimmie Rodgers before illness constrained his voice. Bland and serene, optimistic as the "howdy neighbor" picture on the cover. *Skyline* is certainly without pretense. It begins a trend that continued until 1974—a retreat from "significance." Except the significance of an old truism: "Love is all there is/It makes the world go 'round."[14] It is a reactive album, saying again that for him, the "moderate man," his happiness in retreat has been the rediscovery of some basics about life and love.

The opening duet with Cash on "Girl from the North Country" is a rare moment. Rough at the edges, with flawed entrances, harmonies, lyrics. Yet it exudes palpable rapport. As they go out trading phrases, they do have that boozy, early-morning camaraderie. Old-timey sounds of instrumental jamming follow on the "Rag," with sidemen Kenny Buttrey, Charles McCoy, Pete Drake, Norman Blake, Charlie Daniels, and Bob Wilson swapping ideas with Dylan as if he were from the Tennessee hills. The "shave and a haircut" ending underscores the country idiom. A spoken line made "To Be Alone with You" memorable. Dylan asked Johnston if the tape had started, and while the song may have been forgotten, his question, "Is it rolling, Bob?" soon entered fans' patois. Dylan has some fun with the clichés of country and country-music whimsy on

"Peggy Day." "Lay, Lady, Lay" became the major single hit from this collection, rising to number seven. "One More Night" is reminiscent of
Presley's first single, "Blue Moon of Kentucky," an old Bill Monroe tune.
Here, the cowboy and frontier ethos is strong, the individual lonely in his
physical and emotional environment.

In the instrumental work of "Tell Me That It Isn't True," there are the
slightest musical echoes of the breaks on "Desolation Row." Sheer fun
and a child's sense of play dominate "Country Pie." Some reviewers focused on "Ain't runnin' any race"[15] as Dylan's new "statement." Little
Jack Horner has replaced Tom Thumb. The album closes with "Tonight
I'll Be Staying Here with You," a reflection of the same commitment to a
love object that marked "You Ain't Goin' Nowhere" and the last two
songs on *Harding*.

The influence of *Nashville Skyline* was unimaginable. At the end of the
1960s, pop and rock were looking for new directions, and strong elements
of country had always existed in Anglo-American pop. Still, Dylan provided the strap that began to link pop closer to country, with *Skyline* as the
buckle. A good part of the pop and rock of the 1970s explored country
music. Soon Nashville studios were crowded with pop, rock, and folk performers who had earlier disdained country as corn. Baez started to record
there with *Any Day Now*. Ringo Starr followed a year and a half after
Dylan. For his mentor/producer, the former Beatle chose Pete Drake, who
had worked on two Dylan Nashville albums. In early 1970, Paul Hemp-
hill, author of *The Nashville Sound*, told *The Village Voice* of a massive
change: " 'Folks called the outsiders "them weirdos with the funny
glasses," but when they found out those boys could really play and . . . produce, they gave them . . . respect. One of the more important people was
. . . Dylan. . . . When John began to play with Dylan, folks asked why he
did it. . . . Folks forgot about politics and listened to the way he played.' "

Within months of *Skyline*, a new flock of Byrds were taping *Sweetheart of
the Rodeo*. In the next few years came hip country artists and rock musicians gone country—Poco, The Flying Burrito Brothers, The Nitty Gritty
Dirt Band, Tracy Nelson, Captain Hook and The Medicine Show, Kris
Kristofferson, Chip Taylor, Kinky Friedman, Commander Cody. The
country influence was firmly rooted by a major 1970s group, Crosby, Stills,
Nash and Young. Dylan himself remained interested in both the
recording environment of Nashville and such country performers as Ronee
Blakley, featured on Dylan's 1975 tour, and Emmylou Harris, who came
forward dramatically on *Desire*. The brilliance and the bias of Robert Alt-
man's film *Nashville* reflected the old and new country music that met in
Dylan's *Skyline* sessions.

The influence of *Nashville Skyline* dwarfed the album itself. Dylan had
helped trigger a major shift in taste and style, and was privately amazed at
the effect the album had on other musicians. As for the audience, by the
time they got to Woodstock, its most celebrated resident had become almost an honorary citizen of Nashville.

WOODSTOCK EAST, THE ISLE OF WIGHT FESTIVAL

Ending a remarkable decade in pop music, 1969 was the year when several giants of rock resurfaced and the international audience showed what an elephantine monster it had become. During the summer of 1969, Elvis Presley, unseen on stage since the 1950s, sang for a live audience in Las Vegas. John Lennon resumed concerts that year, while The Rolling Stones gave the first free concert in London's Hyde Park. The sage of Woodstock, who had been pondering a stage return for some time, got an offer he chose not to refuse—one gig in late August at the Isle of Wight Music Festival. During the Woodstock Festival, held partly in Dylan's honor on his own doorstep, he was appearing three thousand miles eastward at Europe's Woodstock. Even in absentia, Dylan cast a long shadow. Greil Marcus in *Rolling Stone*, September 20, 1969: "... willingly or not, Bob Dylan was the presence hovering over this three-day jamboree ... he is the elder of this urban tribe ... the tribally tom-tommed message of WOODSTOCK, Dylan's refuge, WOODSTOCK, Dylan's turf, WOODSTOCK, Dylan's bringing it all back home, was as much responsible for moving this massive surge of humanity onto a 600-acre farm as any advertisements, promotion, publicity ..."

If Dylan wouldn't work on Max Yasgur's farm in Bethel, New York, some 450,000 others would. The spontaneous combustion of Woodstock was, in the words of *Time:* "... the moment when the special culture of U.S. youth ... displayed its strength ... it may well rank as one of the significant political and sociological events of the age." Woodstock inspired more hyperbole: Ginsberg called it "a major planetary event." Yippie Abbie Hoffman saw it as "the birth of the Woodstock Nation and the death of the American dinosaur." Local police, farmers, and carpenters' wives were astounded at the numbers and their gentleness. A *New York Times* editorial asked of this pilgrimage of "lemmings": "What kind of culture ... can produce so colossal a mess?" The next day, the same editorial page saw it as just "a phenomenon of innocence."

Two weeks later, like a muted European echo, came the antiphonal response from the second Isle of Wight Music Festival. From all over Europe, perhaps as many as two hundred thousand young flocked. Among them were most of The Beatles and Stones, Jane Fonda and Roger Vadim, the Paris cast of *Hair,* and a huge press corps. There were hints that a mellowed Dylan was going to be quite chatty with the press. At his Woodstock home, he told Ray Connolly of *The London Evening Standard:* " 'I don't ... live such a secluded life.... I'm just living a normal happy life like any other guy. I'm very anxious to get back on the stage.... I hope to be able to sing just about whatever the people want to hear.... The accident ... still bothers me a bit. My bones ache in the cold weather, or when it gets too humid. But in many ways it was good for me. It really slowed me down. Touring had been such a pace to keep up. And I was getting in a rut.' " Connolly was surprised: "The apparent bonhomie of the man is indeed a shock. . . ."

In another interview, Dylan went on: "Sara and I grew up as kids together in Minnesota. Then some years back we met again in a New York restaurant where Sara was working as a waitress. We fell in love—although it was not love at first sight, and five years ago we were married in New York State. We didn't advertise the fact as we feel our personal lives are what they mean. Otherwise, we would have gone to Hollywood to live and become members of the show-biz set, which we hope we never will be." Dylan spoke of accepting George Harrison's invitation to record at Apple Studios in London, and of planning a major tour with The Band, "although it won't be like the old days when we fell from exhaustion." He said he was looking for a film with a *heavy* story line. "I wouldn't mind working with someone like Alfred Hitchcock. He wouldn't do anything thin. . . ."

Two brothers, Ray and Ron Foulk, then twenty-three and twenty-four, had lured Dylan to the Isle of Wight. "We realized we couldn't attract him with money, so we decided to sell him the island," Ray said. A third brother, Bill, twenty-two, made a color film of Wight's beauty spots, the festival site, and the house they'd rent for Dylan. With Bert Block negotiating, Dylan accepted a contract that caused pop-press dismay, although he had turned down offers four times larger. The most reliable figures I could obtain were that the festival offered him £21,000 and 50 percent of the net, plus £6,000 for expenses. The Band got £8,000, and Richie Havens was paid £3,300.

The Dylan family boarded the *Queen Elizabeth 2* in New York on August 13. During a small farewell party, Jesse, then four, suddenly lost consciousness. The ship's doctor reportedly wouldn't accept responsibility for Jesse's ability to make the voyage, and Bob rushed his son to a New York hospital for observation. The boy soon revived, his condition "not serious." A few days later, the Dylans flew into Heathrow, and were soon ensconced in a sixteenth-century farmhouse, Forelands Farm, near Bembridge. It had a swimming pool, and a barn for rehearsals. Gates and guards kept the public at bay. *The London Daily Sketch*'s Chris White got past them long enough to ask Dylan what attracted him to the Isle of Wight. Tennyson had lived there, Bob replied, and he'd always wanted to visit. " 'Basically, we are just having a holiday.' " Of his English fans: " 'They are the most loyal fans I have and that was one of the reasons to . . . come to England to make my comeback. It's not the money I'm interested in, I just want to play music.' "

Bob gave a twenty-minute press conference. Some reporters seemed to want to provoke an old cat-and-mouse session, so they asked him about drugs and his marriage, whether he was becoming square, why he was there. He stuck to Tennyson. His longest comment: "My job is to play music. I'm just going to take it easy. You've got to take it easy if you're going to do your job well." No anger or defiance. Some reporters were annoyed that their bombshells had been defused. They looked to the festival site for more exciting copy. They found plenty there, with an army crossing The Solent by ferry and Hovercraft in what one paper called "a second Dunkirk." Headlines also called it D-DAY, THE ISLE OF DYLAN, and, inevitably, playing with The Beatles' title, TICKET TO RYDE, to describe where the boats landed. Every British national paper had a front-page story, many with enormous photo spreads of the crowds.

The festival began Friday, with Nice and The Bonzo Dog Band. Saturday was dominated by The Who and Joe Cocker. There were reliable performances by The Grease Band and The Pretty Things. American folk influences, and some Dylan songs, surfaced in sets by Julie Felix and Havens. The evening roster included The Edgar Broughton Band, Marsha Hunt, Family, and Bloodwyn Pig. Electric programming Sunday included the Liverpool Scene in mixed pop and poetry; The Third Ear Band and the Indo-Jazz Fusions added other colors. Poet Christopher Logue and journalist Anthony Haden-Guest read contemporary poetry, not Tennyson. One surprise was the impact of Tom Paxton. His folk-topical songs had an audience reaction that *Melody Maker* called "amazing." More folk styles followed with Pentangle.

Dylan arrived at 7:23 P.M., due to go on at 7:30. Later there was widespread anger at Dylan's late entrance and brief performance. I have never been able to determine the cause of the delay. He later told me he didn't know what it was about either, but felt the festival was run very poorly. Karl Dallas in his *Acoustic Music* magazine said the delay was conditioned by Bert Block's demand that Dylan and The Band be paid before performing. The press seats had to accommodate perhaps some five hundred reporters, VIPs, friends of the high and mighty, when probably not half that number of seats were available. I avoided that mob scene and went to the back of the crowd. To get a good spot I had to climb over hillocks of empty beer cans, around piles of rubbish, over prone, stoned bodies. One tent encampment of fans was signposted DESOLATION ROW. From my location, the figures onstage looked like ants. About 9:30, compere Rikki Farr announced that Grossman's party could come forward to their seats. Every few minutes there was a call for an ambulance, for someone on a bad trip or suffering from exhaustion. Intermission started at 8:00, but The Band did not come on until 10:00. It was a terribly restless two hours, during which Farr voiced exasperation over the mike. Only The Stones' record "You Can't Always Get What You Want" sounded like the truth.

The Band suffered from the same problems that vexed Dylan's appearance—bad sound, impersonality, too distant. From my post, perhaps a quarter of a mile away, The Band was very slow to kindle. A bit of their punch came through on "Brazos" and "Don't Ya Tell Henry." By 10:35, while they were doing "I Shall Be Released," many in the audience were shouting for Dylan. By 10:50, as they played "The Weight," they'd adjusted to their surroundings, but their set ended shortly. After interminable mike testing, Dylan walked on with The Band. Standing ovation, flashbulbs and flashlights, Roman candles. Dylan was in white, tieless, with a pastel-colored shirt. He slid into "She Belongs to Me" in a soft jazz-crooner voice that sounded unfamiliar, even after *Nashville Skyline*. Dylan's longest comment to a roaring crowd was: "It's ... ah ... great to be here. It sure is." During "I Threw It All Away" with acoustic guitar, he didn't appear nervous so much as formal. He played "Maggie's Farm" in a bluesy vein, with strong Band harmonies. Especially for English listeners, he played "Will You Go, Lassie, Go" (or "Wild Mountain Thyme"), taking some florid vocal lines unaccompanied. "It Ain't Me, Babe" and "To Ramona" were rather introverted, but the audience seemed to catch his mood and reached toward him. By "Tambourine Man," they were in his hands. He then sang "St. Augustine," "Lay, Lady, Lay," and "Highway 61." The audience, more appreciative than ecstatic, seemed to be waiting for fireworks. Then came "One Too Many Mornings," with a nod to the Manfred Mann recording, "Immigrant," the predictable excitement with "Rolling Stone," a country lullaby on "Baby Tonight," and a bit more extroversion on "Quinn" and "Rainy Day Women." Evidently, he remembered the 1966 "Rainy Day" ruckus in England. He split just before midnight, returning for encores, and repeating "Rainy Day" for the final encore. The crowd thought it was only the beginning. Dylan briskly said, "Thank you," and departed. Rikki Farr bleated: "I'm sorry! Dylan has gone! He came and he did what he had to do!"

Ever since Dylan had told Don Short of *The Daily Mirror* that he *might* do three hours, the pop press and the festival organizers had been teasing ticket buyers into expecting something transcendent. The August 30 *Melody Maker* front-page headline ran DYLAN, STONES, GEORGE HARRISON, BLIND FAITH—SUPERSESSION AT ISLE OF WIGHT, adding in smaller type below, "If Bob Approves." *Record Mirror* had forecast "The Biggest Jam Session in History." Hype led to letdown. Everywhere I saw tired, disappointed kids slogging back toward the ferries. "Dylan, RIP," said one Midlands lad. The Associated Press reported: "There was near pandemonium as outraged fans asked: 'Has he gone? Where is he?' Security guards with dogs raced ... to prevent any trouble ... no incidents and the crowd soon began to filter away." *The Daily Mail* reported bonfires and chants of: "We want Dylan—music, music, music!" *The Daily Mirror:* "100,000 pop fans threatened to riot." *The Sun* said that as many as thirty fires were ablaze, fed by wooden fences, programs, and cardboard boxes.

Dylan left England in a very disappointed mood. *The Sketch* quoted him: " 'I don't ever want to perform in England again.' " But *The Daily Mirror* quoted Dylan: " 'The concert was great—and I am coming back again next year.' " Levon Helm of The Band told *The Sketch:* " 'Bob tried everything he knew to reach the audience, but it didn't come off.' " On Tuesday, September 2, Dylan went to Heathrow Airport in a Mercedes driven by George Harrison. *The Express* quoted Dylan: " 'I was shattered by stories that the kids were angry because I was three hours late. I was there at 5:30 as promised. I don't know why we were so long before going on. Ask the producers. . . . The fans were terrific.' " The Beatles offered strong support. Harrison: " 'The concert was marvelous. Bob did not walk off . . . half-way through his act. He gave a brilliant performance.'" Lennon: " 'He gave a reasonable, albeit slightly flat, performance, but everyone was expecting Godot, a Jesus, to appear.' "

By the time Dylan got to Kennedy Airport, he said he had no wish to return to England. "They make too much of singers over there." He called the Isle of Wight a warm-up for future American tours. During Dylan's first major appearance in a year and a half, he found himself in a situation he could not fully control. In retrospect, I think the festival had a great deal to do with his holding off further live appearances until early 1974. When he did return, he wasn't doing low-key introverted work, but reaching out boldly for an audience that demanded much greater excitement.

The Isle of Wight was the beginning of a low period for Dylan professionally; many were ready to repeat that he was finished. Yet the *Melody Maker* International Pop Poll of September 20, 1969, listed Dylan as the top international male singer and *Nashville Skyline* as the top LP. But other members of the audience virtually turned Dylan into a political prisoner, telling him what and how to perform, how to spend his money, how to write his songs. One "fan" was even telling Dylan where to dump his garbage.

12

RUNNING FREE

"Einstein suffered the fate of many other revolutionaries who boldly take the first steps on a new road but shrink from the next steps. Others may come along to pick up the journey because the road seems too sinister to its discoverer."

—WERNER HEISENBERG

"So, in every individual the two trends, one toward personal happiness and the other toward unity with the rest of humanity, must contend with each other."

—FREUD, *CIVILIZATION AND ITS DISCONTENTS*

"Pain sure brings out the best in people, doesn't it?"

—DYLAN, 1971

"It's the price of fame, I guess," Dylan told me at the height of The Scavenger's campaign against him. "We loaded up our garbage with as much dog shit as we could—mousetraps, everything—but he still keeps going through my garbage!" The Scavenger was, in the words of Jerry Rubin, John Lennon, Yoko Ono, and John Peel, "leading a public campaign of lies and malicious slander against Dylan. . . ." They wrote to *The Village Voice* in December 1971: "The press is all over him trying to get information or gossip about Dylan . . . he is a self-proclaimed authority on Dylan's music . . . [he] is to Dylan as Manson is to The Beatles—and uses what he interprets from Dylan's music to try and kill Dylan and build his own fame. . . ."

The Scavenger was a would-be anarchist star, a wheeler-dealer of the freaked-out New Left, a garbage groupie, a self-promoting, speedy-talking hustler named Alan Jules Weberman. He proclaimed himself "the world's greatest authority on Dylan," "the father of Dylanology." Actually, he accused Dylan of countless crimes, harassing and vilifying him for three years. For a while, some accepted his accusations that Dylan was "a pig," a junkie, a supercapitalist backing napalm-makers and reactionaries. From 1968 through 1971, during one of the cruelest assaults ever made on the privacy of an artist, Weberman led delegations to Dylan's home in the Village, telephoned him at weird hours, taped conversations with him, then distributed these tapes and transcripts around the world. I talked to The Scavenger twice on the phone. His voice was raspy and agitated, his language abusive. I decided not to interview him.

Weberman began by publishing in *Broadside,* sounding like a Dylan student looking for hidden allusions. He found political content in Dylan songs where others couldn't, even seeing attacks on The System in "Sad-Eyed Lady"! *Broadside*'s Gordon Friesen saw A.J., as he was familiarly known, as a freakish, benign analyst of Dylan's work. Then, The Scavenger started to read *himself* into Dylan songs. He cloaked himself in Yippie rhetoric, attacking "pig" Dylan for having earned money. The Scavenger may have turned when Dylan refused to let his lyrics be quoted in a book Weberman had written. Weberman then accused Dylan of commercial rip-offs and bad personal habits. In the 1969 *Rolling Stone* interview, Dylan put down The Scavenger hard, suggesting he find other writers to misread. This only made Weberman more virulent. He began to play Dylan's records backward, finding hidden "clues." Increasingly, The Scavenger's fulminations were relayed through the Underground Press Syndicate and published uncritically.

The Scavenger formed the Dylan Liberation Front and then the Rock Liberation Front, of which he was the self-styled Minister of Defense. He researched Dylan's finances, finding royalty-check vouchers from Columbia, unearthing Dylan's alleged real-estate investments. Estimating that Dylan had earned more than twelve million dollars, he called him "the singing real-estate broker." Weberman said his evidence of Dylan's use of hard drugs "comes mainly from his poetry." The Scavenger had FREE BOB DYLAN buttons made up. The day before Dylan's thirtieth birthday, May 24, 1971, he organized a "block party" in front of Dylan's home and sounded a call to arms: "If you want to get more info on the Dylan Liberation Front and rock lyrics in general, or if you want to tell me to go fuck myself and let Dylan 'do his thing,' you can write to me, Post Office Box 340, Canal Street Station, New York City, 10013."

By 1971, The Scavenger seemed to feel that Dylan had somewhat re-

deemed himself with the "George Jackson" single and his appearance at
the concert for Bangladesh; thereafter, Weberman's attacks diminished.
Weberman claimed that Dylan's "political acts" were the results of *his*
campaign! By the end of 1971, other Rock Liberation Fronters admonished The Scavenger publicly. The Scavenger turned to other pursuits,
claiming to have made nine hundred dollars on a magazine story about
garbage. I decided not to visit The Scavenger's "Dylan Archives" on
Bleecker Street. I told him I was considering giving my own archives to
some university library where they would be available to other Dylan students. "Man, man," Weberman rasped, "What I've got is mine."

WHICH SIDE IS HE ON?

Others, less extreme than Weberman, repeatedly felt betrayed by Dylan
after 1966, for his rock star indulgences. When Dylan dropped out, he re-
linquished millions of dollars from concerts and their stimulus to record
sales. He turned down TV and film offers that would have swelled his income. In retreat, Dylan refused more money than many pop stars made in
a career.

One of The Scavenger's charges disturbed the most: "Dylan supports
the racist and counterrevolutionary organization, the Jewish Defense
League . . . a militant organization whose aim is to attack anyone they believed to be anti-Jewish. . . ." Even Weberman admitted that the JDL
stated that Dylan had never given this group any money. Still, the allega-
tion stuck. Many political sophisticates found Dylan's interest in Zionist
militancy hard to take. After the 1967 war, leftists of all backgrounds challenged Israel as an imperialist-maintained military government. Many Jews
were alarmed by Israeli denial of Palestinian rights. I saw Bob just before
his trip to Israel in May 1971, which he went to great pains to keep private. He only hinted at an interest in the JDL. He also talked of Jewish
writers he was reading, of attending a Hasidic wedding. He certainly
didn't appear to be endorsing Zionism. Because Stephen Pickering is a specialist in Jewish culture and Dylan's work, I asked his opinion in December 1975:

"Dylan visited Israel in the summers of 1969 and 1970, in May 1971,
and shortly after the filming of *Pat Garrett*. After the 1970 visit, Israel Eichenstein . . . contacted Dylan, asking for his attendance at the Israel
Birthday Be-In in Central Park. Dylan declined: 'I would attract too many
people who have nothing to do with the cause of our people. I know,
man, I identify.' Dylan and Eichenstein grew close, and it was Eichenstein
who . . . persuaded Dylan that the JDL lacked an important Jewish ingre-
dient: compassion. . . . In May 1971, the Israeli newspaper *Yediot Achronot*
published a brief interview/profile. Dylan mentioned the earlier visits, that
he had friends in Israel. . . . On May 22, 1971, Dylan and Sara walked
through Old Jerusalem, and visited the Mount Zion Yeshiva, a famous

Cabalistic training center. They sat in the ancient courtyard for the day. . . .
Several American students were introduced to Dylan by Rabbi Yoso Rosenzweig, who asked Dylan why he shied away from a personal, direct,
unmistakable declaration. 'There is no problem,' Dylan replied. 'I'm a Jew.
It touches my poetry, my life, in ways I can't describe. Why should I declare something that should be so obvious?' Two days later a UPI photographer took two photographs at the Wall of a tourist, then realized it was
Dylan.

"Dylan's brief relationship with the Jewish Defense League has been
blown out of proportion. Rabbi Meir Kahane first met Dylan when Kahane was on a WABC-FM debate with Abbie Hoffman and Paul Krassner.
Kahane asked Dylan for a donation to the JDL Soviet Jewry Fund. What
happened is a matter of some disagreement. Kahane claims, as of 1974,
that Dylan *didn't* give a contribution. . . .

"In 1972, Dylan *investigated* the possibility of emigrating to Israel. . . .
According to kibbutz Neve Eitan member Ari Davidow, 'The kibbutz had
been taken aback by two things: Dylan could bring in dope-smoking
groupies sponging off kibbutz hospitality,' and Dylan's five children didn't
fit into the kibbutz age bracket. The kibbutz secretary procrastinated, then
decided Dylan deserved just as much a chance as anyone else. He sent him
an application blank in September 1972, 'but we never heard from him
again.' . . . Dylan's identification with the idealism of Israel remains unabated, despite profound upheavals in his personal life. . . . My friend, Roberta Richards, who visited Dylan on January 10, 1974, at his Toronto
Hotel, told me: 'He noticed my Star of David and he showed me the me-
zuzah he wears. It's silver, and he got it in Israel.' Rabbi Shlomo Carlebach
has tried to get Dylan to consider his obligations as a Jew. . . . Carlebach
believes something serious has happened to Dylan since the 1974 tour. . . .
Dylan told of plans to purchase an apartment in Jerusalem. Since then he
has shown signs of being under a serious strain. . . . Dylan, on January 3,
1974, agreed with me—that his Israel visits have had a profound effect
upon him. . . . On the liner notes of *Planet Waves,* the reference to Hebrew
letters is an age-old custom for one to bring prayer/petitions to the Wall,
with which to pose operable axioms."

In the September 11, 1976, *TV Guide* interview, Dylan said: " 'There
was no great significance to that visit. . . . I'm interested in what and who
a Jew is. I'm interested in the fact that Jews are Semites, like Babylonians,
Hittites, Arabs, Syrians, Ethiopians. But a Jew is different because a lot of
people hate Jews. There's something going on here that's hard to explain.' "

Jonathan Braun, president of the New York Union of Jewish Students,
wrote in *The Jewish Digest* of September 1971, "The Bob Dylan Rumor
Machine." Braun found that "by and large, the stories turn out to be fabri-
cations of . . . clearly overzealous, young Jewish nationalists. . . ." Braun
quoted Theo Bikel: " 'Dylan has told me that Israel appears to be one of

the few places left in this world where life has any meaning.' " Braun con-cluded: "The possibility that Dylan may be examining his Jewish heritage is actually quite plausible. Dylan, after all, is Jewish; and at a time when increasing numbers of . . . young Americans are experiencing an intense rebirth of ethnic consciousness, it is more than likely that he would find himself taking a fresh look at his past."

The 1971 El Al flight list alerted the Israeli press to Dylan's arrival on a mid-May Sunday. He brushed unwelcome reporters away. CBS Records in Israel advertised in *The Jerusalem Post,* wishing him happy birthday and asking him to get in touch with them! But Catherine Rosenheim of *The Jerusalem Post Magazine* tracked him down on Herzliyya Beach. As Dylan surfaced from the waves, the intrepid reporter waited onshore: "It was all remarkably easy. . . . Perhaps he was just in a holiday mood." The swim-mer told *The Post* he'd been " 'All over the place—we've been here a long time.' " (Actually, eight days.) Dylan told her he was collecting material for his journal, to be published " 'some time' " along with some songs. Dylan: " 'Actually, that's the main reason why we're here incognito—it's impossible to work with dozens of people milling around you all the time. . . . I didn't think my records were officially released here and so didn't want any publicity.' " Would he write any songs about Israel? " 'No, but he had written one about Yugoslavia,' he said with a smile." How had he spent his thirtieth birthday? " 'We went to see a Gregory Peck movie—I'm quite a fan of his.' " *The Post:* "Rumors about changing his name were, he said, 'pure journalese and not a word of truth.' "

Many Jews believe that the only way a Jew can avoid alienation in a hostile world is to assert his Jewish identity. To some Jewish nationalists this becomes tantamount to embracing Zionism. But many Jews are not oriented toward Israel. As a young man, Dylan had wanted to be part of the American experience. Jewish friends, from Allen Ginsberg to Dylan's music publisher, Naomi Saltzman, and her husband, might have suggested Dylan could find some peace by identifying with Jewish culture. Dylan wanted to take a look at Israel, without being crowded or pledged to pub-lic commitment. Although Ginsberg heard Hebrew cantillation on *Desire,* I hear flamenco and soul. So much depends on the beholder!

WATCHING THE RIVER

The controversy over Dylan's politics, or absence of them, continued for years. If he didn't speak, his songs did. Ironically, the violent Weathermen appropriated a line from "Subterranean Homesick Blues." Conversely, in June 1972, at a Madison Square Garden benefit for Democratic presiden-tial candidate George McGovern, Peter, Paul and Mary sang "When the Ship Comes In," "Times Changing," and "Blowin' in the Wind." From 1969 on, there had been pressure on him to resume writing protest music. When he released "George Jackson" in 1971, *Rolling Stone* remarked that the song immediately "divided speculators into two camps, those who see it as the poet's return to social relevance and those who feel that it's a cheap way for Dylan to get a lot of people off his back." Robert Christgau hit back in *The Village Voice* on December 17, 1971: "This is ugly nonsense, of course, because the song is neither . . . the protest Dylan and the anti-protest Dylan are both part of the persona now. . . . Dylan has never lacked social relevance. . . . Dylan responded with real human sympathy to a hideous assassination. . . ." In the song about the slaying of the Soledad brother, Dylan spoke on several planes: "Sometimes I think this whole world is one big prison yard/Some of us are prisoners, the rest of us are guards . . ."[1] *Melody Maker* was moved enough by "George Jackson" to make their lead headline on November 27, 1971: DYLAN GETS BACK TO PROTEST. Chris Van Ness in *New Musical Express,* December 4, 1971: "The record makes the first time in about four years that Dylan has actually attempted to say something with a song." CBS Records, which promoted "the rock revolution" in the mid-1960s, chose as its promotional line: "Dylan's New Single Is a Political Act."

Dylan popped up on TV in November 1971, on a *Free Time* WNET-TV show with Ginsberg, Orlovsky, Gerard Malanga, and other poets, playing background guitar and singing along, unbilled, to the poets' strongly political material. But even Dylan's appearance on August 1, 1971, at the concerts for Bangladesh, before forty thousand people, wasn't enough for politicos. At a Carnegie Hall concert in autumn 1971, Joan Baez said she'd written a song for Dylan, whom she hadn't seen in four years. She launched into "To Bobby," which implored him to retrieve all his little lambs who'd lost their shepherd.

Dylan was one of many 1960s radicals who had moved into new lives. Jerry Rubin told the *San Francisco Chronicle* on October 31, 1973: " 'This is a growth period for everyone, including me. I'm . . . working on myself. I've gone very deep into the human potential movement . . . bioenergetics, Reichian therapy, gestalt therapy, Erhard Seminars . . . yoga, natural foods . . . the relationship between psychology and politics. . . . In the 1970's, people are more in touch with their bodies and souls and each other. Too much happened too fast in the 1960's, and people are repairing themselves.' "

On September 12, 1974, in *The Village Voice,* Carole Getzoff described "Tripping Out on Torah": "Former blue-jeaned freaks donning blue suits, replacing funky old cowboy hats with . . . yamulkas. . . . Former throwers of the *I Ching* diligently studying The Torah and The Talmud." From Berkeley came a report in *The Times* in late 1972 indicating that the campus had politically hibernated. Berkeley student leaders and Yippies could change, but Dylan was consistently berated for "selling out." Ira Mayer defended him in *The Village Voice* on December 2, 1971: "I don't understand why people continue to pester him about 'commitment.' Isn't music itself 'commitment' enough?" After Israel, 1971, Dylan joined Leon

Russell and The Tulsa Tops on a single, "Watching the River Flow," an energetic, funky-gospel rocker. The promotional photograph showed Dylan with a camera to his eye. At that point, he wanted to be just an observer:

> What's the matter with me,
> I don't have much to say . . .
> People disagreeing everywhere you look,
> Makes you wanna stop and read a book.
> Why only yesterday I saw somebody on the street
> That was really shook.
> But this ol' river keeps on rollin', though,
> No matter what gets in the way and which way the wind does blow,
> And as long as it does I'll just sit here
> And watch the river flow. . . .[2]

On May 9, 1974, an unbilled Dylan appeared in New York at a Felt Forum benefit for Chilean refugees from the junta that deposed Socialist president Salvador Allende. Hosts for this Friends of Chile concert were Phil Ochs and actor Dennis Hopper. Dylan jammed with Ochs, Van Ronk, Seeger, and Arlo Guthrie. He spent time then with Joan Jara, widow of Victor Jara, the Chilean folk singer whose fingers had been smashed with an ax before the junta executed him in Santiago's National Stadium. Joan Jara, reliving her loss at rallies around the world, was under great strain. Dylan asked if she could ever relax. " 'Come down and see some nice pictures,' Dylan said to me, 'Meet me at Fifth Avenue and Fifty-fourth Street tomorrow afternoon at three, and I'll take you to see some nice pictures.' I never imagined he would be there. But I showed up, and there he was, leaning against a lamppost. And he took me to the Museum of Modern Art and showed me around, said he was with us." He was difficult to talk to, Joan Jara said.

Gradually, Leftist critics realized Dylan was still on the side of the angels. Significantly, in 1975, although Dylan was the strongest voice speaking out for imprisoned boxer Rubin "Hurricane" Carter, Dylan's name never appeared on the list of Carter's patron-supporters. Still, the Left had its doubts. During Dylan's 1974 tour, rumors circulated that he was going to contribute some proceeds to Israel. Mimi Fariña told the *San Francisco Chronicle* that ticket purchasers should have the right to know that they were contributing to a nation at war. Jeremy Larner, Oscar-winning scriptwriter of *The Candidate* and former speechwriter for Eugene McCarthy, contested Mimi's view. Characteristically, Dylan stood silent. Meanwhile, as late as summer 1975, there were guns on the Right. South Africa's *Transvaal Educational News* ran a story headed: BOB DYLAN, "A VOICE FOR THE REDS," alleging that Dylan had become "the most successful proponent of communism's new class war, youth versus age" and had "become a millionaire while singing lyrics about the poor overthrowing the rich. . . ." And in September 1977, the *Soviet Literature Gazette* dismissed Dylan as "nothing more than a money-hungry capitalist now." Which side was he on?

The greater an artist's influence, the more various causes try to align him as a spokesman. Dylan turned political questions back to the questioners: Do it yourself; don't ask me or anyone else to do it for you. His message was consistently misunderstood and misapplied. Perhaps the reason he chose to go in and out of "political commitment," to pick the causes he chose to support, was that he simply didn't want to be tied to people who might speak for him without his permission.

DR. DYLAN TAKES HIS OWN PULSE

What was the greater surprise? That Princeton University offered Dylan an honorary doctorate of music, or that the antiacademic college dropout accepted it? Dylan arrived the night before the ceremony of June 9, 1970, with his wife, David Crosby, and Ben Saltzman, his music publisher's husband. Among the nine to be honored at Princeton's two hundred twenty-third graduation ceremonies was another writer, Walter Lippmann, and another singer, Coretta King, widow of the Reverend Dr. Martin Luther King, Jr. At first, like twenty-five of the twelve hundred graduating seniors, Bob refused to wear the traditional black robe, but he later put it on over his dark, pin-striped suit. He wore no tie or mortarboard. Like most of the graduates, he put on a white armband bearing a peace symbol. Dylan's escort was William H. Attwood, editor in chief of *Look,* a Princeton trustee, and a key man in the Cowles Communications empire.

Princeton's President Robert F. Goheen gave Dylan his D.Mus., writ in Latin on parchment. The more informal citation read: "As one of the most creative popular musicians of the last decade, he has based his techniques in the arts of the common people of our past and torn his appeals for human compassion from the experience of the dispossessed. Paradoxically, though known to millions, he shuns publicity and organizations, preferring the solidarity of his family and isolation from the world. Although he is now approaching the perilous age of 30, his music remains the authentic expression of the disturbed and concerned conscience of young America."

Ill at ease through most of the ceremony, Dylan smiled at "perilous age." On many American campuses, students had been prodding administrations for more substance, more relevance. By 1970, honorary degrees were going increasingly to women, unionists, blacks, and the young. Princeton attributed the choice of Dylan directly to two undergraduates on the nominating committee. A few months later, on the album *New Morning,* surfaced "Day of the Locusts."

I put down my robe, picked up my diploma,
Took hold of my sweetheart and away we did drive . . .
Sure was glad to get out of there alive. . . .[3]

The song's title brought to mind both the biblical plague on the pharaoh and Nathanael West's Hollywood-based novel, *The Day of the Locust.* In West's climax, a lower-middle-class mob who feel cheated unleash horrible violence.

As he was receiving his D.Mus., Dylan released the album *Self Portrait,* which remains his most contentious album. A *Rolling Stone* chorus of twelve writers voiced outrage. "What is this shit?" Greil Marcus challenged Dylan, warning, "Unless he returns to the marketplace, with a sense of vocation and the ambition to keep up with his own gifts," the music of 1965–66 would dominate his career. Charles Perry wrote: "We know Dylan was the Rimbaud of his generation; it seems he's found his Abyssinia." *Time:* "For a man who charged his way through the 1960's like an Orpheus in Hades," this Dylan is "astonishingly contemplative." *Record World:* "The revolution is over. Bob Dylan sings 'Blue Moon' to Mr. Jones."

Self Portrait contains twenty-four tracks, fourteen by Dylan. Three of these are primarily instrumentals, so many people felt overcharged for a double album. Four tracks come from the Isle of Wight sessions with The Band; the others were recorded in New York and Nashville. *Self Portrait,* an elaborate production job, had a cast of fifty supporting musicians and singers; strings, brasses, female vocal ensembles. Some called the resulting mélange "easy listening" or "middle of the road." Others thought the double album was a joke, a cynical cop-out, or Dylan's test of his power. It sold fabulously well, grossing three million dollars by the end of June 1970, jumping up the *Billboard* chart from two hundred to seven in one week, and to number one in *Record World* by August.

I told Dylan that *Self Portrait* confused me. Why had he recorded "Blue Moon"? He wouldn't be drawn out, although obviously he had been stung by the criticism. "It was an expression," he said. He indicated that if the album had come from Presley or The Everly Brothers, who veered toward the middle of the road, it wouldn't have shocked so many. (Wayne Stierle, in *New Musical Express,* November 7, 1970, saw Presley's influence in *Self Portrait.*) My initial reaction was negative, because *Self Portrait* sounded like somebody else, a self-portrait drawn from a cracked mirror, suggested by the cover of a hollow-eyed Roualt-Chagallesque clown looking at his reflection. Was Dylan trying to show us that he saw himself as made up of fragments of folk, country, and old pop songs, accompanied by a modern sound? Was the album an experiment that didn't work? Was he pulling our collective legs? My reaction has since mellowed, although I still place *Self Portrait* among my least favorite Dylan albums. *Self Portrait* was another step in Dylan's retreat from significance toward being the simple man, the country squire pictured inside the album jacket standing near a barn, talking to a chicken. Perhaps he figured that if *Nashville Skyline* had reached more listeners than any previous album, he should try a middle-of-the-road approach and touch even more people. Now I view *Self*

Portrait as an experiment in appealing to Middle America on its own terms. Dylan later said: "A lot of worse stuff was appearing on bootleg records." It was, "so to speak, my own bootleg record."

I think *Self Portrait* could have been one moderately good LP instead of a double album padded with material better left in the can. "In Search of Little Sadie" was an eccentric foray into modulation, yet the song works as excellent, cheery country. "Alberta 1" was mediocre, yet "Alberta 2," with its mournful mouth harp, was fine. Some of the material, like "I Forgot More Than You'll Ever Know" and "Take Me As I Am," are not my kind of gritty country songs, and I think Gordon Lightfoot's "Early Mornin' Rain" and "Let It Be Me" are pap. At least two jokes on the album simply don't work: "Blue Moon" à la Bing Crosby; and "The Boxer" by Paul Simon, in which, using overdubbing, Dylan seems to be sending up *both* Simon and Garfunkel. Quality gets rather lost amid such dross. "All the Tired Horses" and "Wigwam" are hard to forget. "Days of 49" is flavorful period Americana. "Woogie Boogie" is a superb instrumental, full of grinding Fats Domino–Johnny Otis echoes. "Living the Blues," "Gotta Travel On," and "It Hurts Me Too" have moments ranging from fine to excellent.

Self Portrait forced Dylan to show doubters that his inspiration still burned. His early return to the studios in autumn 1970 to tape the twelve songs of *New Morning* certainly seemed like a riposte. This album, and title song, recalled his line of 1964: "An I shall wake in the mornin and try t start/lovin again."[4] Many regarded *New Morning* as his best album since *Blonde on Blonde.* The new album was unpretentious, and had more cohesion and shape than *Self Portrait.* It contained Dylan's first prayer ("Father of Night"), first jazz song ("If Dogs Run Free"), first Hank Williams–style talking country song ("Three Angels"), and first *waltz* ("Winterlude"). Another innovation was Dylan gospel-style slow block-chording on piano. Altogether, an excellent collection of quiet gems.

Greil Marcus, in *The Sunday New York Times,* called it Dylan's "best album in years . . . an act of vitality. . . ." Ed Ward, in *Rolling Stone:* "One of the best albums of the year . . . perhaps his best." Ed Ochs, in *Billboard:* "Dylan is dancing, singing to the sun, you can really love him. Dylan's voice of the year runs free with fresh, determined blues rhythms. . . . Dylan lives!" Lucian Truscott, *The Village Voice:* " 'New Morning' is similar to the enlightened anachronism that was 'folk music' when Dylan took it to a pinnacle of visionary art. . . ."

Dylan was once again reflecting a social climate in America. He was presaging a shift away from "Too Much of Nothing." In *Rolling Stone,* Ralph Gleason could shout: "We've got Bob Dylan back again . . . the most reassuring thing . . . this year of the bombings. . . . This is a hopeful album, and, my God, how we need it." On February 22, 1971, a special *Time* section, "The Cooling of America," saw many of the extremes of the war-scarred 1960s starting a return to "a mood approaching quiet . . . the

calm ... suggests a complex of rather sober fear ... there is a chastened air
... such a weariness—and much more—accounts for the profound hiber-
nation of the radical movement in the U.S."

New Morning began the 1970s with a statement of serenity, even as Self
Portrait had ended the 1960s with nostalgic pastiche. Morning proclaimed
Emersonian "self-reliance," a frontier of personal freedom. Dylan asks: "If
dogs run free, then why not we ... ?"[5] This wistful contentment, free of
smugness, converges in "Sign on the Window":

> Build me a cabin in Utah,
> Marry me a wife, catch rainbow trout
> Have a bunch of kids who call me "Pa,"
> That must be what it's all about ...[6]

Dylan recorded "New Morning," "Time Passes Slowly," and "Father of
Night" for Archibald MacLeish's play The Devil and Daniel Webster. When
the producer didn't like "Father of Night," Dylan backed out of the production. He says he wrote "If Not for You" "thinking about my wife."

Dylan's response to public disappointment in Self Portrait was an affirmation of life and happiness. Even when he senses the locusts coming
along to snatch all Establishment-trained people after their graduation, he
doesn't sing of plague. As the drifter of John Wesley Harding discovered,
there is an escape route from the horror.

Late in 1969, Dylan escaped back to the Village, to an apartment house on
lower MacDougal Street, below Bleecker. For a time, he enjoyed the
anonymity that he lost in the country. But not for long could he dissolve
into city streets and live quietly behind closed doors. He surfaced in old
haunts, seeing what was left of his old Village gang. A decade had changed
the Kettle, Folk City, the Gaslight, the Bitter End.

New York's intrusions on Dylan's privacy reached their apogee in
spring 1971. Although he was in Israel, The Scavenger organized that
"antibirthday party" on Sunday, May 23, in front of Dylan's house. In
Washington Square Park, street singer David Peel recruited a crowd by
banging a cowbell with a drumstick. Peel blew his police whistle and proclaimed: "We're going to Dylan's house now. It's the rich house next to
the Hip Bagel. You know why it's next to the Hip Bagel? Because Dylan
made a pretzel out of you...." In front of Dylan's house, Weberman,
appropriately atop a garbage can, addressed about three hundred people.
Weberman shouted through a megaphone for Dylan to come out. No response, and The Scavenger said: "You see, Dylan doesn't care about people
anymore. Dylan doesn't care if you or I drop dead." A heckler: "Dylan
does care. He wants you to drop dead." The Demosthenes of the garbage
pail went into his litany: "Dylan's sold out, he's ripped you off.... Right

now I'm trying to approach him as another human being. I have to try to get him interested in life again. But if he doesn't shape up fast I'm going to read the riot act to him." In the crowd, some of Dylan's friends appeared, including Al Aronowitz, who shouted: "Free hot dogs down the block, that way." Unsigned handbills appeared announcing a party at Weberman's house that evening. Weberman was annoyed: "I was told there would be retaliation for this party."

The Scavenger unveiled a special birthday cake with large candles decorated like hypodermic needles. Peel began denouncing Herman's Hermits. The party began to break up. Two cops chased someone into the microphone car, handcuffed him, and carted him off. The crowd chanted: "Pigs! Pigs!" Weberman led his march, prudently, to the local police station to look after the welfare of the man arrested earlier, singing "Blowin' in the Wind" through his megaphone.

CONCERT FOR BANGLADESH

Another plague, in the real world. Early in 1971, during the war in Bangladesh, millions of starving refugees flooded from East Pakistan into India. The Indian army was mobilized to fight West Pakistan, and global help for the hapless refugees began. Ravi Shankar, Indian sitar master and raga interpreter, spoke to his pupil, George Harrison, who sprang into action. On August 1, 1971, two concerts at Madison Square Garden raised $250,000 in one day. A film and recording of the concerts raised more.

Star power attracted forty thousand people. Harrison and Ringo represented The Beatles. Guitar hero Eric Clapton came out of retirement. Along came Badfinger, Klaus Voorman, Billy Preston, Leon Russell, Jim Keltner, and others. Harrison enlisted Dylan with a phone call. Wrote Richard Williams in *The Times* of London: "The real coup, of course, was to persuade Dylan, rock's own Garbo, to leave his self-imposed seclusion and return to the concert stage. Dylan's set turned the concert into an historic event and allowed it to become ... a summary of the best things which happened to popular music in the 1960's."

Harrison simply said: "Another friend of mine ... someone we all know." Dylan walked on in a denim jacket, as though at a 1960s folk club. His "Hard Rain," which followed film clips of Bangladesh, stung. Ray Coleman, in *Melody Maker:* "Nobody sings Dylan like Dylan ... he demonstrated again in that hesitant, piercing voice that he is the ultimate solo artist in contemporary music. Dylan seemed to have come full circle and to have fallen in love again with his old songs." Dylan contributed some of his old songs, including "Love Minus Zero," "Just Like a Woman," "Train to Cry," "Blowin' in the Wind," and "Tambourine Man." He did "Hard Rain" and "Wind" solo, but on the other songs he was joined by Ringo on tambourine and Harrison and Russell on electric guitars. There was also vocal harmony on "Just Like a Woman."

Hassles followed for months between Apple, Capitol, and Columbia Records over the triple album. It was released in January 1972, became a worldwide best seller, and netted UNICEF almost four million dollars. The recording and film ultimately were responses to Shankar's declaration: "Through our music we would like you to feel that agony ... in Bangladesh." On brief notice, director Saul Swimmer made a ninety-minute documentary from forty hours of footage. Harrison didn't want the mood impaired by swarming cameramen, and no extra lights were used. Harrison and Dylan played a big hand in editing the film, which was shown in thirteen cities on 70-mm film with six-track sound and elsewhere in 35-mm film with four-track sound. At its New York premiere, on March 23, 1972, critics were sympathetic. Tom Costner, in *The Village Voice:* "Someone has written that audiences are feminine. If that's correct, Shankar embraced it, Harrison made love to it, and Dylan took it by force."

George Harrison said: "It's only through India, Hinduism, yogis, and meditation that I learned what Christ really stood for." By spring 1970, Harrison was preparing to break out as a solo performer, and became a solo star after his triple album, *All Things Must Pass,* co-produced with Phil Spector. *Time* wrote: "Dylan's influence can be felt everywhere." Dylan had written the lyrics for the first track, "I'd Have You Anytime." Also included, along with fifteen originals by George, was "If Not for You."

George told *New Musical Express,* on November 22, 1969, that Dylan was enduring a similar misunderstanding that had plagued The Beatles: " 'People don't realize that he has changed quietly. . . . So much attention and pressure have been put on him for the wrong reasons. . . . He didn't make himself into a cult—the Press did. . . . Now he can't understand why people want to ask him ... what to do about Vietnam. He just wants to write and sing songs. . . .' " As late as December 1974, when George played Toronto's Maple Leaf Gardens, Dylan was present. They jammed backstage, but Dylan stayed offstage. Harrison told Ray Coleman of *Melody Maker* on September 6, 1976: " 'Bob Dylan is still the most consistent artist there is. Even his stuff which people loathe, I like. There's always something in what he does, to my ears, because every single thing he does represents something that's him.' "

MAN ABOUT TOWN

After nearly three years of listening to the silence, Dylan started listening to old musician friends and new. He made tentative moves toward the folk movement—the Guthrie concerts of 1968, the *Sing Out!* interview later that year, a meeting with Pete Seeger, a visit to a Clancy Brothers concert on March 17, 1969. He revisited Village streets, clubs, and studios. Publicity agents for performers quickly parlayed any contact into accolade.

In September 1973, Dylan quietly blew into his mouth harp while John Prine sang at the Bitter End. After some sessions in 1971 with Leon Rus-

sell, Russell rumored that Dylan might tour England with him. He
dropped in on Roger McGuinn's Columbia sessions for a brief gig, and at
Bette Midler's Atlantic sessions, where she cut a remarkable "I Shall Be
Released"; he later sang with her on "Buckets of Rain." In February 1973,
he was reported to be at a Willie Nelson Atlantic session with Russell and
Kristofferson. He went backstage twice at New York's Fillmore East in
November 1970, to meet Elton John and Crosby, Stills, Nash and Young.
In 1971, he repeatedly visited the Bitter End to hear Tony Joe White,
Prine, and Steven Goodman. In October 1972, he went to Max's Kansas
City to see a nervous Loudon Wainwright III. August 1972: Dylan surfaced at the Mariposa Folk Festival in Toronto. The same month, The
Grateful Dead jammed for five hours at Jersey City's Roosevelt Stadium
while Dylan listened from the wings. October 1972: Sly Stone was rumored to be producer of the next Dylan album. October 1969: Dylan visited Dr. John at the Fillmore East and chatted backstage with John Mayall
at the Café Au Go Go. March 1971: An old sidekick, Bobby Neuwirth,
was at the Gaslight, and Bob visited. July 26, 1972: Mick Jagger turned
twenty-nine and threw a party at the St. Regis, where Dylan was photographed with Zsa Zsa Gabor. May 1971: Tito Burns said he was having
British tour talks with Dylan. Bob was reported to be writing a Broadway
musical. December 1971: *New Musical Express* carried an exclusive report
that Dylan, Lennon, and Phil Ochs were holding heavy political talks with
Bobby Seale and Jerry Rubin. Recurring reports of imminent tours, of
great new departures, of "returns," all proved erroneous.

Leon Russell, who produced two tracks on *More Greatest Hits* and taped
much Dylan material, tended to exploit Bob's neighborliness. Happy
Traum and Emmylou Harris take honors for not using Dylan to enhance
their careers. In London, in 1975–76, Emmylou did two major concerts
without making any reference to her appearance on *Desire*. She told me: "I
was just an eavesdropper at those sessions. Really! Some mutual friends
asked me to drop in, and I just did a bit of harmony singing."

Other studio sessions at which Dylan watched or jammed stirred interest. Dylan had started his pseudonym game when he dubbed himself Big
Joe's Buddy, Tedham Porterhouse, and Blind Boy Grunt. As early as 1965,
rumors began that Dylan was Roosevelt Gook, the piano player on Tom
Rush's Elektra album, *Take a Little Walk with Me*. Actually, Dylan had
just visited those sessions. He suggested that Al Kooper use that pseudonym, even though Kooper did take credit under his own name as electric guitarist and celesta player. Grunt made another surfacing, taped at
the same 1962 session, with the 1972 release of *Broadside Reunion, Volume 6*
(Broadside-Folkways BR 5315). His tracks were "Train A-Travelin',"
"Emmett Till," "Donald White," and "Dreadful Day." Also in 1972,
Dylan said a few words and jammed on a new version of "Nashville Skyline Rag" on *Earl Scruggs: His Family and Friends*, drawn from a late 1970
Channel 13 film.

One of the most elusive sessions took place with Allen Ginsberg on November 14 and 15, 1971. The album's working title was said to be *Holy
Roll Jellyroll*. The recording died a-borning. Allen sent out word that he
was recording in New York with Dylan, Happy Traum, David Amram,
and poets Andrei Voznesensky and Gregory Corso. Allen had evidently
put up ten thousand dollars of his own money. Earlier, Ginsberg had been
interested in Indian mantras, and, in 1968, had tried to set Blake's "Songs
of Innocence" and "Songs of Experience" to a chant. Not until he got
some instruction from Dylan could he play three chords! Aside from Indian music, Ginsberg was interested in calypso and blues. One country-
rock song concerned Kerouac and other beats. A ten-minute improvised
piece, "Jessore Road," compared East Pakistani refugees to the victims of
Vietnam. *Guardian* critic Robin Denselow called this "direct, vivid and
very angry. Well produced, it could be a remarkably strong song, but the
tape I heard was only distinctive for Dylan's rhythmic piano-playing."
Apple was interested enough to press disks and print covers. Dylan used
the pseudonym Egg O'Schmillson. But Lennon and Apple were having
troubles, and Warner Bros. supposedly rejected the tapes as "too dirty."
Ginsberg quoted a June 1973 letter from Dylan: "Don't worry, the energy
has gone, save your songs for friends and go on to do something else."

Conflicting reports described the spring 1971 sessions in New York that
Dylan held with Leon Russell, Claudia Lennear, and others. *New Musical
Express* heard that Dylan "had no song prepared when the recording
began. . . . Dylan and the band would jam for about 30 minutes. Then he
would sit down and start writing a song. After about 15 minutes, he
would have a song to fit the music they had been playing. And all the
songs were masterpieces!" Maybe so, but within days of those sessions,
Dylan was terribly critical of the fluency of songwriting. He told me:
"Until the accident, I was living music twenty-four hours a day . . . if I
wrote a song, it would take me two hours, or two days, maybe even two
weeks. Now, two lines . . ." He paused and grimaced. Near his Village
home, Dylan set up a private studio with first-rate acoustical equipment,
where he could get fresh ideas down on tape and jam with friends.

In November 1972, Dylan held very enjoyable sessions with Doug
Sahm, leader of the Sir Douglas Quintet. On *Doug Sahm and Band* (Atlantic SD 7254), released in late 1972, Dylan played his own waltzy "Wallflower" and "Blues Stay Away from Me" on guitar, and "Me and Paul" on
mouth harp. He joined Sahm singing "Is Anybody Going to San Antone"
and "Wallflower." Dylan appeared under his own name. Among the sidemen were Dr. John, Dave Bromberg, and David "Fathead" Newman.
After Dylan had told me of his interest in the Sir Douglas Quintet, I had
tracked Doug Sahm down in Monterey, California, in summer 1966.
Sahm, a hip cowboy, with a long, lean face and a black Stetson, is a Texan
who was into the special mix of Tex-Mex music, Chicano funk, Louisiana
cajun, western swing—call it swamp music—from the border country.

Sahm told me, in his drawl, he'd "run into Bob along the road, up there around San Francisco a while back [1965], and I shore hope things would get better for him and that one day I shore would like to work in a studio with Bahb Dylan. . . ." Sahm had a couple of hits on Mercury, notably "Mendocino" (1965) and "She's About a Mover" (1968), but then he languished until Jerry Wexler got him to Atlantic. Sahm had great influence on Creedence Clearwater Revival, who split up in October 1972 while Sahm was recording with Dylan. During three weeks, Dylan came in and out, playing some lead guitar, some piano, sitting in on organ, a lot of harp, and singing with Sahm.

In September 1972, just before the Sahm tapings, Dylan and David Bromberg dropped in on a Buddah session for singer-songwriter Steve Goodman, whose "City of New Orleans" had just been a hit for Arlo Guthrie. Goodman asked Bromberg if he could find him a piano player. Bromberg replied that he knew one who played pretty good "but was kinda undependable." The piano player showed up forty minutes late for work on the single, "Election Year Rag." Dylan, listed as Robert Milkwood Thomas, sat in on "Rag" and the title track of Goodman's second Buddah album, *Somebody Else's Troubles.* Dylan saw a good deal of Bromberg, who played lead guitar on nearly half of *Self Portrait* and came back for further work on *New Morning.* Journalist Al Aronowitz, later Bromberg's manager, introduced him to Dylan, who soon started to show at clubs when Bromberg was playing.

In October 1971, Dylan recorded three tracks with Happy Traum on bass, banjo, second guitar, and vocal harmony, for the release, on November 17, of *Greatest Hits, Volume II.* Happy had been with the New World Singers with Gil Turner, while his brother Artie, with Maria d'Amato and Marlena Tyree, was in a trio called the Poolnot Family, a name Dylan had suggested. Happy was the first of the two brothers to move to Woodstock, and as editor of *Sing Out!*, eased the magazine away from its doctrinaire past. At their Bitter End gig in December 1970, the Traums brought down music of other Woodstockers: "Movie Man," by John Herald, and "Going Down to See Bessie," by Danko and Robertson. Dylan tried taping with the Traums, playing organ. An engineer said: "Hey, buddy, would you give me more sound from that organ?" The session was scrapped after a couple of takes. Happy's three tracks for *Greatest Hits* were done in New York on the spur of the moment, mixed down from five choices of Dylan's.

In mid-summer, 1973, Dylan got together in Muscle Shoals, Alabama, with Barry Goldberg, for an album called *Barry Goldberg* (ATCO SD 7040). Goldberg had played piano at the famous 1965 Newport electric set. After teaming with Steve Miller in the Goldberg–Miller Blues Band, he joined Mike Bloomfield when he organized The Electric Flag in 1968. Later, Goldberg started writing songs, and began years of failed attempts to record. Even though he'd won the top-organist category in the *Playboy* jazz poll, dubious record companies asked him for a demo. After some songwriting collaboration with Gerry Goffin, Goldberg began to see Dylan again, and for two days running they jammed for hours. Later, Goldberg went to Dylan's place at Woodstock, jamming there with Doug Sahm and The Band. Goldberg got an offer to do a single for RCA, but Dylan told him to hold off. The next day, Dylan rang him and said: "I'm on the phone with Jerry Wexler from Atlantic Records and I think we can work out a deal, but I'm gonna have to produce you; that's cool, isn't it?" There were five days of sessions in Muscle Shoals with Dylan playing percussion on "It's Not the Spotlight" and singing on the chorus of "Stormy Weather Cowboy," "Silver Moon," "Minstrel Show," and "Big City Woman." Dylan also played harmonica for the 1973 *Chronicles* album on A & M of Booker T and Priscilla Jones and for "A Story of David Blue" on Asylum, 1975.

From 1967 onward, the so-called recluse cultivated new and old friends. He lent encouragement where he could, doing what came naturally to him, making music. Then he got a call from Kris Kristofferson about a movie he was making down in Mexico.

A MAN CALLED ALIAS

Pat Garrett and Billy the Kid seemed an ideal vehicle for Dylan's commercial film debut. The film dealt with one of his favorite themes—the embattled antihero. The filming, from late 1972 to early 1973, involved several superindividualists: Sam Peckinpah, the director, a great stylist; actor James Coburn, a senior Hollywood hipster; Kristofferson, singer turning actor; Rudy Wurlitzer, bright young novelist making his mark as a scriptwriter. Dylan quietly upstaged nearly everyone. Reporters buzzed around, asking Mexican extras about Dylan.

Pat Garrett was the violent story of cocky William Bonney, a kid drawn into the frontier life, working with his guns during the range wars. Death hangs over the film's sunset colors. *Pat Garrett* is a memorable western about the confrontation between Billy and his friend-turned-lawman, Pat Garrett. Peckinpah implies that on the pair's deep bond of affection balances the need to destroy or be destroyed. Dylan plays a modern Fool, a youngish printer's assistant who follows and helps Billy. In a somber film, Dylan provides wistful humor. "What's your name?" Garrett asks, and he replies: "That's a good question." Later, he says his name is Alias, "Alias anything you want."

Kristofferson had been a Rhodes scholar at Oxford, and tackled a dissertation on Blake. Kristofferson invited Dylan: "There's a lot of heavies down there . . . you can get paid for learning." Bob was cautious: "If I do it, then they *got* me, on film." Kris countered: "Hell, they already got you on records. Come on, we'll have a ball." Three months later, few regarded it as a ball. Peckinpah was a perfectionist. Before Dylan decided to go down to Durango, Mexico, with his family, he later told Chet Flippo of *Rolling Stone:* " 'I saw "The Wild Bunch" and "Straw Dogs" and "Cable Hogue" and liked them. The *best* one is "Ride the High Country." . . . I want now, to *make* movies. I've never been this close to movies before. I'll make a hell of a movie after this.' " Later Dylan said: "I was just one of Peckinpah's pawns. . . . There wasn't any dimension to my part and I was uncomfortable in this nonrole. . . ." Still, he admired the director and said it was Sam's lack of final artistic control that "was the problem."

On his second day on the set, Dylan picked and sang his title song, "Billy." Peckinpah offered him a part on the spot. Dylan moved his family down the last week in November, and stayed on in Durango working, writing songs, and talking very little to anyone. Durango, a city of 150,000 about 600 miles north of Mexico City, has long been used by Glenn Ford and Kirk Douglas. John Wayne had a production company there. The town, with Mexico's highest murder statistics, fringed by the Sierra Madre, was ideal for the last days of Billy the Kid. There wasn't much to do except drink tequila, eat tacos, sample the local weeds, and laze in the storied landscape.

His first day's shooting was challenging, for Bob hadn't done much riding. But the turkey-chase scene came off well. Kristofferson: "I couldn't believe it. He's got a presence on him like Charlie Chaplin . . . you see him on screen and all eyes are on him. There's something about him that's magnetic. He doesn't even have to move. He's a natural . . . he has to throw a knife. It's real difficult. After ten minutes or so, he could do it perfect. . . . He does things you never thought was in him. One night he was playing flamenco and his old lady, Sara, had never known him to do it at all before." Michael Watts of *Melody Maker* admitted he was frightened of Dylan. Kris: "Sheeit, man. You're scared! I'm scared, and I'm making a pitcher with him!"

Scriptwriter Rudy Wurlitzer thought Alias could have been enlarged considerably, but Dylan let it remain a cameo role. Kristofferson said Bob went for days without even talking to his wife. A publicist: "He's really shy and withdrawn, and it's genuine. Reporters . . . follow him around, and, of course, he won't even talk to them, so they end up interviewing everyone else about him." Dylan was upstaging even the director. Wurlitzer: "It's happening, man. Sam knows he's losing to Dylan." Peckinpah arranged a Durango screening of *The Getaway,* but the others decided to join Dylan for a Mexico City taping session.

In a barnlike studio, Dylan started laying down some tracks for *Billy* a little after eleven P.M. one Saturday night in January 1973. Trial and error, adding and cutting. Dylan was in charge in the studio, although the film producer, Gordon Carroll, hovered about. Dylan led Kris's band into "Will the Circle Be Unbroken," then more instrumental tracks. Kris, Rita Coolidge, and James Coburn joined in on vocals. At three A.M., Bob was still going strong, taping "Holly's Song." He called for his two Mexican trumpeters, cued them on "Pecos Blues." Some obvious tension between Dylan and the producer. Someone noticed that Dylan used Hollywood as a nine-letter swearword. By four in the morning, the co-stars and the scriptwriter had evaporated. Dylan was still energetic, taping other versions of "Billy." The producer seemed to be warming up to Bob's ideas, but Dylan twitted him: "I don't think. Usually, I don't think. I hold it all in and then . . . act." By seven in the morning, the studio technicians were exhausted, but Dylan was wide awake.

When the film opened in summer 1973, critical opinion was sharply divided. Calling the film "a slow and ritualistic explosion," David Robinson in *The Times* of London said Dylan "appears as a captivating little figure." The film became a cult movie, frequently revived at art houses. Dylan's sound-track album, a model of economy and another new departure, has been highly regarded. At times, engineering supplies a full and echoey sound. Dylan hand selected some ace sidemen, including Roger McGuinn and Bruce Langhorne. The film is almost a folk tale, overhung by imminent death. The score comprises ten related works. The main title theme of "Billy" reappears, as "Billy 1," "Billy 4," and "Billy 7." Dylan's vocals are yearning and keening. Some have attacked Peckinpah's Billy as an overromantic view of a nasty little gunman, but Dylan seems to share the director's view of the central character.

Two songs on the second side provide notable contrast: "Turkey Chase" is bright and jumpy, spurred by a soaring fiddle. Then comes the album's hit single, "Knockin' on Heaven's Door." Even as the old-time, frontier-period sound of the harmonium in "Heaven's Door" yields to the final theme, a stately, hymnlike quality continues. "Pilgrims toward death" are the protagonists of this frontier epic, and Dylan's music never forgets that the film is a tragedy.

Despite his impact in *Pat Garrett,* naysayers were again chanting that his career was finished. Columbia Records carved another epitaph with the album they rushed out just before Christmas, 1973. *Dylan* must stand as his worst, least-representative album, reflecting extreme record-company cynicism. Since Dylan had let his Columbia contract run out, they scraped together rejects, from the *Self Portrait* and *New Morning* period. Columbia probably managed to sell a few hundred thousand copies on Dylan's name alone. Critics described this album as "corporate dirty pool," an implicit threat to Dylan not to stray too far for fear of more official bootlegs. Clive Davis had left Columbia, and no one wanted to take credit for this album of nine tracks by other writers, not a few of which are almost laughable. In the long run, it probably harmed Columbia more than Dylan.

This dreadful album added to a growing feeling that Dylan's career was at ebb tide, like Sinatra's eclipse before his great film comeback in *From Here to Eternity.* Yet Dylan already had plans for a dramatic return to live performances. Dylan had often emphasized that some tours had been kill-

ers. In *New Musical Express* on May 13, 1972, Kristofferson said: " 'Basically, many of these people are not extroverts. For most of us, like Bob
Dylan and James Taylor, it's pretty hard to get up and perform before an
audience . . . that's when you're really naked, especially when you're doin'
all your own songs.' . . . From experience, Kristofferson is of the opinion
that a lot of people expect, nay, demand, that an artist should bleed on
stage. . . ." Knowing this feeling, Dylan was ready at the end of 1973 to
stand naked and let it bleed onstage again.

TOUR '74

January 3, 1974: Chicago can be as heartlessly cold as Hibbing. This time
Dylan didn't have to face the cold alone. He had five trusted musician
friends beside him and nearly twenty thousand people in the Chicago Stadium saying "Welcome back." Yet, as the moments elapsed before going
onstage, he was alone again. Some out there would have been as delighted
if he made a fool of himself as if he triumphed.

Dylan was dressed down in the same "poor boy" outfit he wore the first
time he hit Chicago. To relieve the stage's impersonality, he had approved
a little set, with a bunk bed, a sofa, a Tiffany lamp, a clotheshorse, and a
few candles. A few balloons floated through the smoke of cigarettes and
joints. The audience was tense and expectant. Then a blue spotlight sliced
a hole in the dark, and Dylan and The Band, like five picadors and a matador, ambled on: Dylan, unsmiling, looked casual. *The Guardian* reported,
"The sounds that broke with the light was like Chicago tearing in half . . .
a vast mush of swelling, cheering, stamping. . . . Dylan was on the road
again."

"One foot on the highway, and one foot in the grave . . ."[7] he sang. It
was "Hero Blues" from 1963, but he'd rewritten it. Then on through
nearly thirty songs, a career spectrum. The star who had generally avoided
live audiences for nearly seven and a half years put both feet on the highway. About three hundred reporters were present. This became one of the
New Year's big stories. There's been near-stampedes at post offices to mail
in ticket orders, even though Dylan had told the tour's producer, seasoned
Bay Area rock impresario Bill Graham, to "keep it low-key." Tour '74
turned into a media festival, a homecoming, a quasi-religius, demi-political
rally for new fans and old.

After intermission, Dylan did his solo acoustic set, the highlight of that
and the thirty-nine shows that followed in twenty-one cities for six weeks.
He and his guitar told again how the times were changing and how Hattie
Carroll died. Then, in "It's Alright, Ma," he came to the line about the
president having to stand naked; the link to Nixon and Watergate
touched the audience. Mick Watts of *Melody Maker* said Dylan "spat out
the phrase with a peculiar venom that . . . made it nigh transcendental. . . ." Dylan quit the stage leaving an uproar behind him. Matches

flickered in the dark. That gossip about his being finished was meaningless. His encore was "Like a Rolling Stone." *Time:* ". . . arms linked together, swaying in unison, chanting in time to the psychic current, a
generation's anthem . . . not finally understood until a period of adult crisis. . . ." Barbara Charone in *New Musical Express:* "Dylan gained a whole
new audience and another 10 years."

Dylan earned a standing, shouting, stamping, and cheering ovation. The
audience lit thousands of matches, cigarette lighters, and scraps of paper.
Dylan and The Band finished wth "Most Likely You Go Your Way (and
I'll Go Mine)," which had so much punch, they used it to start the other
concerts. Tour '74 caused audiences to review their last thirteen years, their
own successes and failures, their direction home, or away from home. Glen
Brunman wrote in *Good Times:* "Every time Dylan opens his mouth, he's
telling us how badly we blew it in the Sixties . . . he shows what we might
have had, what we let slip away, and maybe, just maybe, what we can still
achieve."

David Geffen, of Elektra/Asylum Records, and Bill Graham had some
astounding figures to feed the press. Although only about 650,000 seats
were available, some 5 million mail-order applications came in, a total of
$93 million. The tour's gross income was about $5 million. *Melody Maker*
called it: "The biggest financial response for any event in entertainment
history." *Time* said: "Never in the history of American rock has a tour
aroused so much public interest . . . it seemed a moment for a legend—and
an era—to live again."

Countless magazines and newspapers carried tour news and reviews on
page one. TV coverage was extensive. One reported offer of a three-million-dollar feature-film advance was turned down. Many book offers were
refused, although *Rolling Stone* produced a paperback for Pocket Books,
Knockin' on Dylan's Door, and Stephen Pickering wrote a book for McKay
as well as a self-published pamphlet. Dylan and The Band still couldn't
erase memories of the hooting of 1965–66. Dylan: "Being on tour is like
being in limbo. It's like going from nowhere to nowhere. But at least the
audiences are different . . . they have been very warm." He told John
Rockwell of *The New York Times:* " 'The last tour we did, in 1965–66, was
like a hurricane. This one is more like a hard rain. . . .' "

Dylan was to be less an enfant terrible with the press. He expressed interest in meeting Richard Goldstein of *New York* magazine. Goldstein recalled, "I have never felt so shy in my life, not in front of any doctor,
woman, or corpse. Probably I was supposed to squeeze in some devastating
question here, but all I really wanted to do was cry. . . ." In Boston, Dylan
talked to Tom Zito of *The Washington Post* about the contrast between
now and then:

" 'Back then it was the scene. Greenwich Village, Gerde's. There wasn't
any audience and performer. It was all one. I wasn't a hero. I wasn't giving
those young people anything to focus on back then. It was just something

I was articulating that a whole bunch of us felt. But now there's a lot of ambiguity out there in the audience ... the younger kids, just not sure why they're there. Maybe they're just curious ... the lid came off with drugs. ... Before that, people used to try to find out what they were all about. Drugs nipped a lot of that in the bud. ... Now a lot of people just accept things the way they are. ...' " Zito failed to get Dylan to talk politics: " 'I guess I just don't really believe in the Democrat/Republican system. I like monarchies. I go in more for kings and queens. ...' "

Despite Dylan's apparent bonhomie, he still used interviews to decry interviews. To *Time,* after sitting for a cover story at *Newsweek:* " 'All this publicity. Sometimes I think they're talking about somebody else. I take it as it comes, but I'm not certain it's beneficial to my life.' " Everyone, of course, was speculating about why Dylan had returned to the stage at this point. " 'I just let people know I was ready,' " he told *Rolling Stone.* Others thought he needed the money, while A. J. Weberman was convinced the tour was a Zionist plot. The response that seemed closest to the bone was that the current music scene was a desert. Dylan told *Newsweek:* " 'What I want to hear I can't hear, so I have to make it myself.' " While insisting that the show was "up-to-date," Dylan could venerate the past: " 'I just carry that other time around with me ... when music was at that root level—that for me is meaningful music. The singers and musicians I grew up with transcend nostalgia.' " But he began to talk about his parents: " 'My father had to sweat. ... In this earthly body he didn't transcend the pain. I've transcended ... the pain of material things. I'd be doing what I'm doing if I was a millionaire or not, whether I was getting paid for it or not. ...' "

Dylan told *Newsweek:* " 'I'm not standing at an altar, I'm working in the marketplace.' " Many tour critics referred to his nervousness onstage, but he radiated confidence to *Newsweek:* " 'I give out a hard dose—like penicillin. People don't have to worry if Dylan's conning them. If it works, it works. If they don't like it, they don't have to try the dose again ... a lot of nervousness has gone. I used to feel nervous all the time before I went onstage.' " Dylan's singing style for the tour revamped melodies, tempos, emphases. This conscious but unsettling change in delivery disorientated some, who ascribed it to concert nerves. There was another reason why critics and audiences held their breath pending Dylan's return. Summing up Lucian K. Truscott's *Village Voice* review of the Wednesday night Madison Square Garden concert: "Dylan was afraid, that was for sure. But 'Tom Thumb's Blues' showed he wasn't afraid of us, the audience. It was himself he feared—... going back over those songs which bore the pain of becoming Bob Dylan, the highs, the lows, all of that life which was *living on the edge* ... how desperately we want our heroes to be self-destructive, as if only by living recklessly can they show us their essential humanity, their impermanence and mortality. ..."

Rolling Stones pressed Dylan about rumors of his tour proceeds going to assist Israel. " 'I'm not sure what a Zionist really is,' " he parried, dismissing the rumors as " 'just gossip.' " What about those religious images in his music? " 'Religion to me is a fleeting thing. Can't nail it down. It's in me and out of me. It does give me, on the surface, some images, but I don't know to what degree.' " Dylan wasn't going to suggest that " 'God's will' " had sent him back to the road. " 'I saw daylight ... I just took off,' " he said. He hinted to *Rolling Stone* that his return then was partially astrological, and that Saturn had been an obstacle in his " 'system. It came into my chart a few years ago, and just flew off again a couple of months ago.' "

It may have also been that his children were old enough, plus restlessness. It's also what performers do—perform. While tour news leaked out in November 1973, prior to the official announcements in early December, talks had begun the previous summer. David Geffen had long hankered to manage Dylan, and had been trying to lure Robbie Robertson. Bill Graham had been making overtures for years. Originally, Dylan had thought of perhaps only a dozen cities and the very best halls. Graham persuaded him that a limited tour did not make economic sense, considering that the performers would need their own airplane, and many technicians.

An appearance The Band had made at Watkins Glen had persuaded them that not everyone wanted to watch Alice Cooper hang himself onstage. Lengthy planning took place in private; full-scale rehearsals began three months before Chicago. In one four-hour session, Dylan and The Band reportedly came up with eighty numbers as a basic tour repertory. Graham booked halls in twenty-one cities anonymously, "to avoid the hysteria. ..." The Kennedys and the Rockefellers wanted tickets, as did unknown fans who queued up at post offices around the country before the deadline hour. The *San Francisco Chronicle* estimated that the tour netted about half the gross of five million dollars. Graham and his FM Productions probably took half a million, while Dylan and The Band, according to John Wasserman, "will net close to two million dollars for their eighty to one hundred hours of work, not, of course, counting rehearsals." Expenses were high. Full-page ads, and a chartered airplane, The Starship I, a forty-seat 707, was refitted with all a rock troupe demanded, at five dollars a mile.

Dylan was determined his free time should be free of frenzy. He reminisced: "The last tour, we were going all the time, even when we weren't going. ... We were looking for Loch Ness monsters, staying up for four days running—and making all those eight o'clock curtains, besides. There won't be any of that on this tour—for me, anyway." Perhaps not, but the itinerary, interviews, and offstage activities seemed a staggering schedule for someone who'd long been off the road. The final itinerary, which included the cancellation of a Dayton concert to allow for a third concert at Madison Square Garden, added up to a total of forty concerts in six weeks, with two concerts on most days.

Dylan also made some forays to little folk clubs and to a Philadelphia ice-skating rink. He duly noted the presence in his audiences of such media gurus as Marshall McLuhan in Toronto and Mike Porco at Madison Square Garden. Two of his more colorful visitors were Ronnie Hawkins and then-Governor Jimmy Carter. Big, blowsy Hawkins was amazingly benign at the reunion, considering Dylan had abducted his Hawks. Hawkins was still holding forth in Toronto's Nickelodeon Club when Dylan, most of The Band, and Graham showed up, with bodyguards. Hawkins put on a special show for his thirty-ninth birthday, singing "One Too Many Mornings" and bits of "Hollis Brown."

In the presidential campaign of 1976, candidate Jimmy Carter repeatedly quoted Dylan, most notably in his nomination acceptance speech, "He not busy being born is busy dying."[8] Carter's link to Dylan goes back to Tour '74. In December 1973, in a handwritten note, he invited Dylan to his home. After the first of his two 1974 concerts in Atlanta, Dylan and aides arrived at the governor's mansion. One of Carter's sons, Chip, had gone to Woodstock in late 1968, and the invitation was apparently his idea. About thirty people gathered for some of the food Dylan had requested—down-home grits, ham and eggs. When Graham greeted Carter at the concert, Graham told him that Bob was "particularly impressed by the fact that you had gone to Israel." But at the party, Carter said: "When I mentioned Israel, Dylan changed the subject and said he and his wife had recently been to Mexico and had enjoyed that country too." Carter called Dylan "painfully timid." In 1976, *TV Guide* asked about Carter's quoting him. Dylan replied: " 'I don't know what to think about that. People have told me there was a man running for President and quoting me. I don't know if that's good or bad . . . but he's just another guy running for President. . . . I'd like to see Thomas Jefferson, Benjamin Franklin and a few of those other guys come back. If they did, I'd go out and vote. They knew what was happening.' "

By the time Dylan got to New York for two concerts at the Nassau Coliseum and three at Madison Square Garden, *The New York Times*'s John Rockwell, who'd been rather cool about the Chicago opening, gauged an audience mood that was "expectant, even exultant." The shock over Dylan's sharp change of delivery was over, and Rockwell could see that "It all came together: the husky, growling baritone, the emphatic delivery, and mocking, laughing distortions of the ends of phrases . . . totally convincing. . . ." *The New York Times* greeted Dylan with a January 28 editorial that paraphrased "Times Changing," concluding: "Every generation has its Dylan. The generation of the '60's was blessed with a singing poet to help fashion that mood. Some things went wrong, and change is always challenged by stagnation. But as long as Dylan sings, the spirit that moved the land a decade ago will be heard."

Ellen Willis, in *The New Yorker,* found that the "two evening performances were masterpieces of controlled intensity . . . a catharsis I hadn't even

known I needed . . . a celebration of the past and a going beyond. . . .
Dylan's earliest songs were not only still alive but resonant with new
meanings. . . ." Some tour-watchers thought the January 30 Garden mati-
nee was the high point. Wednesday night attracted musician friends and
Dick Cavett, Shirley MacLaine, and Jack Nicholson. A party followed at
the St. Moritz. By February 11, Dylan was back in the Bay Area. Finally,
Dylan and The Band wound up back where they'd started their rehearsals,
at the Inglewood Forum in Los Angeles.

The final concert ended, after Dylan had called Graham and his aide,
Barry Imhoff, onstage for bows, with "Blowin' in the Wind." There was a
party at the Forum, then another at the Beverly Wilshire Hotel for just a
few who were close to Dylan—David Blue, Bobby Neuwirth, Robbie
Robertson, and a Minnesota friend, Lou Kemp. Tour '74 was over, for the
performers and the crowds, but the impact continued. Geoffrey Stokes
wrote in *The Village Voice* of April 4, 1976, "Dylan is more than memories. The media event is over for now . . . we are still talking about the
concerts, still trying to figure out what they meant to us. . . . This was a
quintessential . . . American event. Confrontation is, after all, the heart of
our national myth . . . we were the lynch mob to Dylan's Marshal . . . the
nervousness apparently faded, and only the tension was left . . . driving
him through a brilliant performance." Dylan made a promise at the finale
of his New York concerts: "See ya next year."

BACK IN THE MARKETPLACE

Columbia Records had a litany for pop artists: Cut a record and tour to
promote it. Dylan had resisted the formula, but no sooner were plans set
for Tour '74 than he and The Band were in West Los Angeles's Village
Recorder studios on November 5, 6, and 9 recording *Planet Waves*. That
done, he concentrated on the tour. During six weeks, Dylan and The
Band performed fifty-three songs, only three of which came from *Planet
Waves*. Before the album's release in January, two alternate titles had been
bruited about: *Lovesongs,* and *Ceremonies of the Horseman,* a chess image
from "Love Minus Zero/No Limit." *Planet Waves* echoed a 1968 City
Lights anthology of Ginsberg poetry entitled *Planet News*.

The album's theme is the many faces of love—for wifely figures, for
children, for various female prototypes. Even "Dirge" counterposed a love
of life against death, a quality also reflected in "Going Going Gone."
Planet Waves marked a return to stinging, aphoristic expression, free-form
melodiousness, self-involvement. If considered part of a trilogy with the
two subsequent albums, *Blood on the Tracks* and *Desire,* the album marked
a new stylistic period.

The album jacket's stark, black-and-white graphics are reminiscent of
early bootleg albums. A Dylan drawing of three faces suggests any or all
may be his own. On the back, hand-lettered words, many misspelled, have
the rough rub of graffiti. His notes, ringing with beat poetics, evoke mem-

ories, from Duluth to the Place des Vosges in Paris. This is almost another draft of "My Life in a Stolen Moment," tough-guy prose-poetry, urgently scribbled. This was the first album without Dylan's name on the front, although in England a covering wrapper used it.

Planet Waves can be seen as Dylan's edging into a new assault on language. There is a hesitancy, even a bit of clumsiness, as in the "age of fiberglass" line,[9] which sounds like he's revving up his engine. The album is strongly autobiographical, especially when he tells us in "Dirge" that he's "paid the price of solitude/But at least I'm out of debt ..."[10] The apposition of "Dirge" and "Going Going Gone" to the life-impulse of "Wedding Song" displays Dylan's recurring theme that pain has to be endured along the way to pleasure, and that pleasure is, above all, transitory. Still, love drives the motor—not just the courtly love of angelic women, but a love, or a deep need, of such earth-mothers as "Tough Mama" and "Hazel." No album to date since *Blonde* has had such unity, which goes beyond the sense of lyrics, into a musical cohesiveness. The songs "speak to each other," and certain motifs—dreams, sea, waves, mountains, hills, edges, ledges, and lonely, high places—reappear.

"On a Night Like This" opens in bright and neighborly spirit, with commonplaces and clichés of the standard love song—it's cold outside and I'm all the warmer because I'm inside with you. The mood and content flow directly from the idealized life Dylan painted in "Sign on the Window," only now we're behind that cabin door. "Going Going Gone," resembling an auctioneer's chant, is pure blues in spirit. Robbie's shivering electric guitar menaces. Is the leave-taking death or the dangerous return from solitude? "Tough Mama" is a contemporary boogie urban-blues shuffle, dominated by plosive singing and Hudson's omnipresent organ. Though there are some audacious rhymes—"crotch," "watch," and "notch," for example—there is also the fine compression of "I ain't a-haulin'/Any of my lambs to the market place anymore."[11] "Hazel," melodious and appealing, reminds me of Echo, from the wrong side of the Hibbing tracks. The singer is still looking back in "Something There Is About You," which he singled out during Tour '74 as a favorite—an evocation of times past in Duluth, a name he finds of more poetic weight than Hibbing.

As he had hinted on *Self Portrait,* Dylan was developing the painter's fascination with different sketches of one motif. During Tour '74, he startled listeners with a catalog of old songs in new keys or tempos. Some had new melody lines, some a new lyric or two. By the time he released *Hard Rain* in September 1976, he was proving that reinterpretation had become his compelling interest. He was arriving at the composer's and jazzman's sense of the way improvisation and free-form variation on a theme can expand a repertoire. "Forever Young," in two different tempos and approaches, foreshadows Dylan's reworking of his old songs during Tour '74 and the Rolling Thunder Revue. The first version is invocational with a spirit, like "Father of Night," while the second is playful. Here there are echoes of the fascinating, unsettling rhythmic thrust of Joseph Spence, an underground folk-guitar hero of the 1960s, whom Sam Charters had recorded on a field trip to Andros in the Bahamas.

On "Dirge," Dylan at the piano carries simple, forceful keyboard figures. This is less a love song than an elliptical essay on morbid dependency. Is he talking about the Left, the city, the audience, drugs, a woman—all the things he once felt he needed? This dark lyric counterbalances solitude with wholeness, loneliness with communal completeness. Dylan reportedly wrote this and the album's other heavy track, "Wedding Song," in the studio. In between the two is a bit of confection, "You Angel You." "Never Say Goodbye" has interesting echoes, notably of "Baby Blue." His dreams of iron and steel call attention to the sly subtitle of the album, "Cast Iron Songs and Torch Ballads." "Wedding Song" is a total statement of redemption through love. Even as he talks of how love saved his life, weighted images of knives, blood, and killing show a desperation in love's intensity. As the song ends an important transitional album, it foreshadows *Blood on the Tracks*.

Critical reaction varied widely. Loraine Alterman in *The New York Times* faulted *Planet Waves* for its lack of polish, but *The Village Voice* music editor Robert Christgau defended Dylan's purposeful roughness. Derek Jewell in *The Sunday Times,* London, of February 3, 1974: "There's vitality, shot through with tenderness, irony and some anger. . . . Dylan's standing today is paradoxical. He rejects, yet is accepted by millions. And isn't he, despite his evolution, still a man of his age? There is an inward-turning mood today . . . characterized by noninvolvement, a search for privacy and a tendency to look backwards. 'Planet Waves' mirrors it in a definitive, disturbing and haunting collection of songs." A 1974 poll of twenty-four critics in *The Village Voice* ranked *Planet Waves* as number eighteen, with *Before the Flood* at six. In 1975, *Rolling Stone* picked both *Blood on the Tracks* and *The Basement Tapes* as albums of the year. Although most reviews were enthusiastic, Dylan wasn't pleased with *Planet Waves* sales in America on Asylum or in Britain on the Island imprint. Columbia took a renewed interest in their lost star, notwithstanding their recurrent threats to package at least eight Dylan albums from material they had in the can. Dylan negotiated his royalty for *Before the Flood* to new heights, but it was his last work for David Geffen. At the end of the summer of 1974, he returned to the Columbia fold, with many problems sorted out. (The two albums for Geffen were later reissued on CBS/Columbia.)

For those who wanted a souvenir from Tour '74, *Before the Flood,* a double album, was designed. It was full of new Dylan/Band interpretations. The title may have been inspired by the first of Rimbaud's *Illuminations* called "After the Flood." If Rimbaud's work is a parable of the birth trauma, the album is a parable of a performer's rebirth. The title also could refer to Columbia's threats to flood the market with old Dylan tapes. *Flood* was drawn from ten sessions dating from the middle to the close of the tour—three from Madison Square Garden, two each from Seattle and

Oakland, and the final three from Los Angeles. The dominant impression is energy, extroversion, audience excitement, and a novel approach to old songs. The master of surprise was at it again. How many performers and composers have been content to find a style and spend a lifetime developing it? Here was a brash declaration that he was of the here and now. Dylan profited from the Isle of Wight anticlimax of his introversion. His Tour '74 style didn't ask listeners to reach toward him. Songs they'd memorized in other forms could be reexperienced. Here Dylan almost sounds like 1974's heavy-metal rockers, without their theatricality or gimmickry.

Dylan took his live audiences and album listeners off guard with biting, punching, sometimes snarling interpretations. "Most Likely You Go Your Way" leaps out from an obscure back page of *Blonde*. "Lay, Lady, Lay" acquires a different profile. "It Ain't Me, Babe" becomes jumping soul à la Otis Redding. Frequently, Dylan seemed to be using a black soul voice, grainy but with new range and phrasing. "Mr. Jones" becomes "Mr. Jo-HONES." In "Just Like a Woman," "knows" becomes "No-HOSE." In "Don't Think Twice," the word "right" trails off with a wounded sound. Several of the songs have "wind-up" introductions, as if cranking up an old Ford that takes off like a Lamborghini. This slow smoldering works to optimum effect in "Like a Rolling Stone." There's a palpable frisson in the audience when Dylan demands to know how they "fee-heel."

Before the Flood was supervised by Phil Ramone, a taping wizard who had been a White House consultant (before Nixon) and had worked with The Band on *Rock of Ages*. He taped thirty-five hours live, using a crew that included two chief engineers, one spare mixer, three men in the recording booth, one man onstage, and another backing up. Ramone called it "the peak of my career." Working with him was Rob Fraboni, who had supervised the engineering of *Planet Waves*.

Critical disagreement raged in *The Village Voice,* in three separate reviews. The third, by Greil Marcus, explained Dylan's change from "generational symbol" into "American artist." " 'Before the Flood,' " he wrote, "offers not ideas but passions . . . the triumph of Dylan's new music is that Dylan seems to take the failures [he sees in American life] as his opportunity for freedom." Marcus drew exhilaration from "the feeling that an artist is working over his head, that you are over yours, that limits have been thrashed. Such freedom—when an artist liberates himself from his form, he makes *you* feel free. . . . There's a good bit of Whitman's YAWP in this music. . . . Once, Dylan cruised the strip with a cool eye, keeping his distance. Now, he's right in the middle, and so are we. That, of course, is the *burden* of joining a bigger, more mysterious America. . . ."

THE "NEW" DYLANS

After 1963, many in the music business started talking about "a new Bob Dylan." It was inexact shorthand for an acoustic songwriter with the touch of a poet. I dropped the phrase casually in print and the A & R men

and a lot of ambitious songwriters began using the concept with calcula-
tion. From Eric Andersen and Janis Ian right on up to Mark Knopfler in
the 1980s, the term was bandied about cavalierly, especially at moments
when the old Dylan was coasting or quiet.

David Blue, Phil Ochs, Donovan, Tom Paxton, and Pat Sky were
among the first new Dylans. Paul Simon, with his canny ear and indisput-
able talent, qualified as a suburban new Dylan. Ochs was so rigorously
Leftist, he could write the marching songs when Dylan drifted out of
overt political statements. Carly Simon told *New Musical Express* in 1971
that Grossman " 'was trying to make me into a female Bob Dylan and that
ended up in just demoralising me so much I thought I would never sing
again.' "

Columbia wanted John Hammond to find more Dylans. He signed
Bruce Murdoch, Loudon Wainwright III, and the ultimate new Dylan,
Bruce Springsteen. For a time, John Prine, with his denim motorcycle
style, was a nouveau Dylan to some. Another, James Taylor, made it to the
cover of *Time*. Paul Nelson, with the help of a *Rolling Stone* subeditor,
called Elliott Murphy "the best Dylan since 1968 . . . the new . . . upstarts
must be allowed the respectful and necessary dual ritual function of slaying the founding fathers while simultaneously carrying on the old tradition. . . . Murphy, Springsteen, Lou Reed and Mott The Hoople mine the
Dylan genre much as Dylan mined Guthrie's."

The new Dylanism was relatively benign until Springsteen, a magic performer, was hyped to hysteria peaks. Two years before the hype for Bruce
culminated in October 1975 with simultaneous covers on *Time* and *Newsweek,* Steve Turner had written in *NME* of Springsteen: ". . . the surest way
of killing a man . . . is to liken him to the late Bob . . . those boots didn't
fit. . . . The other fault with P.B.D.'s [Potential Bob Dylans] is that people choose them on looks and sound alone. . . . Dylan filled the psychological need of a generation. Where there isn't a psychological need, there'll be
no B.D. or, indeed, no P.B.D. . . ."

The old Dylan watched all this with bemusement, and one English
music paper playfully called Dylan "the old Springsteen." One of the palpable new Dylans was the Modigliani tomboy street urchin dressed like a
junkyard angel, Patti Smith. She had her feet in ballet slippers and her
head in the poetic landscape of Rimbaud, Artaud, Jim Morrison, and
Dylan. She was into page writing before beginning her mesmerizing rock
performances, which she called "dreaming onstage":

"I was about sixteen and saw *Illuminations* with Rimbaud's picture on
the cover," she told me. "He looked like my father and Dylan. My factory
supervisor saw it was a bilingual book and suspected I was a Communist. I
always carried *Illuminations* around. Sometimes I read the French. Even
though I couldn't understand it, I got the music. Then, *A Season in Hell*.
It was the same thing with 'Prufrock' and even 'Highway 61.' I wasn't
man or woman enough to understand it, but the music within it was

great! The most beautiful thing about rock 'n' roll is it's an open art that allows you to be a megaphone to the univrese. There's no place you can't communicate with rock."

Patti was discovered by Tony Glover and *Creem* magazine. A page-one *Village Voice* picture of Dylan embracing her on July 7, 1975, bore the heading: TARANTULA MEETS MUSTANG: BOB DYLAN GIVES HIS BLESSING TO PATTI SMITH. Recalled Patti:

"It was so intense, like, when you have a crush on a guy in high school and after a year he finally talks to you and you have nothing to say ... it was so adolescent . . . very sexy. Dylan loves Rimbaud too. He talked about being behind bars, like Artaud, and about being a prisoner in his skin. . . . He's a great singer who's trained his vocal chords for twenty years. What I've trained myself to do is to dip into my subconscious ... to dip into the sea of possibilities."

Patti found that she and Dylan were both working toward Rimbaud's "derangement of the senses," that knowledge that comes from pain, voyaging, searching. She concluded that something may have been escaping him: "He has levels completely untapped. . . . I know he can probably go farther than he does. He just needs someone to help him pierce his skin. . . . I'm committed to him and his songs. They can do no wrong for me, but I still feel he can do *righter*. . . . He's a great improviser. . . . He just needs to be sprung loose again. He's got all this stuff just waiting to come gushing out. . . . He's an incredible guy! The electricity coming from his face, his eyes, is real!"

Other contemporary poets have been strongly influenced. Ferlinghetti was shaken; Rexroth was impressed; Leonard Cohen learned to sing and write songs; Michael McClure fondled the Autoharp Dylan had given him; Allen Ginsberg became increasingly interested in exploring the musical side of oral poetry. In 1976, Ginsberg published *First Blues—Rags, Ballads & Harmonium Songs 1971-74,* dedicated "To Minstrel Guruji Bob Dylan." Ginsberg's introduction delineates his musical experiences from unsuccessful piano and violin lessons until 1963, when he heard chanting in India and Japan. He kept hearing "fragments of Blake's 'Grey Monk' moaning through my brain. . . . I experimented, improvising music in F chord to the 'Grey Monk' on a Uher tape machine given me as a Christmas present in 1965 in San Francisco by Bob Dylan, who suggested that I learn an instrument. . . ."

At a 1971 Ginsberg poetry reading at New York University, Dylan and David Amram attended. Dylan was impressed with Allen's ability to improvise words, and arranged the recording sessions of November 17 and 20, 1971. Soon Ginsberg was turning back to "modeling my first blues on Richard Rabbit Brown's 'James Alley Blues,'" one of Dylan's early models. Ginsberg's conclusion shows the lines converging anew:

". . . I'd sung ragged ditties & tocattas & fugues with Kerouac under Brooklyn Bridge in 1945-49 and listened with him and Neal Cassady to car radio Rhythm and Blues of Louis Jordan & Fats Domino, moans of Slim Gaillard & shrieks of Little Richard, so I had some kind of American Blues in my heart without knowing it—I could sing but didn't reckon it important poetically, until I met Krishna & remembered Ezra Pound's ken that poetry & music, song & chant (and dance) went together before the invention of the printing press and long after—forgotten by the same academies that forgot that the genre of American Black Blues & rags was as great a treasury of poetics as Bishop Percy's *Reliques* & Scottish Border Ballads & Elizabethan song books & Tom O'Bedlam folk treasuries. . . . The doggerel element in the poetry has to be dealt with—perceptive doggerel inexcusable & inevitable in the process of learning to sing and making up words on the spot. The ideal in Campion & Nashe is a series of swift images. Dylan's 'Chains of Flashing images.' . . ."[12]

BLOOD ON THE TRACKS

Talk of "new Dylans" faded in January 1975 with the appearance of *Blood on the Tracks,* Dylan's third album in a year. Here the renewed Dylan reached fresh heights. Critical reaction ran to superlatives, calling *Blood* the best Dylan work in seven or nine years, or even his best work *ever.* Dylan got this album just as he wanted it: He replaced some New York tapings from September 1974 with December tapes from Minneapolis. He scrapped an elegiac liner-note essay by Pete Hamill, which later won a Grammy award, in favor of an abstract drawing.

Blood on the Tracks bore out *Planet Waves*'s forecast in "Dirge" and "Wedding Song." The artist was in torment. The new album was the spiritual autobiography of a wounded sensibility, whether the pronouns were "I," "he," "she," or "you." One of his most listenable albums, musically lustrous and varied, it contains some of his most direct, rich, emotive, and supple vocalizing. Like the mid-1960s albums, *Tracks* shows what Wallace Fowlie called Rimbaud's "persistent theme of abandonment." *Blood* is about impermanence and fragmentation of remembrance and relationships. Greil Marcus called it, "At once, the tale of an adventurer's war with a woman and with himself, and a shattering attempt to force memory, fantasy and the terrors of love and death to serve an artistic impulse to redeem disaster by making beauty out of it . . . the odyssey of a mythical lover possessed by an affair he can never resolve. . . ."

These ten songs show high craftsmanship and control. Translucent surfaces reveal many layers beneath; abstract imagery is rendered into colloquialism. Basic elements—blood, pain, storm, and rain—assume dozens of patterns. There are images of conflict—blood and barbed wire; life is a battleground and so is memory. "Rain" falls and falls again, coming with waves, flood tides, hail—"hard rain." Jonathan Cott's essay, "Back Inside the Rain," in *Rolling Stone* (March 13, 1975), equates Dylan's rain with memory. Too easy. I see rain as a fluid image, like blood—nature's blood, bringing life to deserts—as well as flood, tears, pain, loneliness, sensation itself. *Blood on the Tracks,* with its tears, insights, and wit, spells an end to complacency and contentment. Dylan finally admitted that although "being settled" may result in personal happiness, the romantic agony of loss and search are goads to greater art, even if he had to turn his own life into discord. The songs:

"TANGLED UP IN BLUE": Although the second album printing reveals a mottle-hued Dylan contemplating a blood-red backdrop, the predominant color is blue. The blues can be sprightly, and the album takes off with a sense of motion. There is a wistful searching, the quest myth again, but perhaps he always looks for the same thing in a lot of people, and always ends up contemplating the mirror of his self. Dylan puns, as the "day the axe just fell"[13] in the woods; a phrase out of common parlance, "keep on keepin' on,"[14] is returned, renewed, to the language. The Dante allusion remains ambiguous. In the New York tape and the folio, the poet dates from the thirteenth century, while the record makes it the fifteenth. (Dante's work spanned the thirteenth and fourteenth centuries.) Literary expert Wallace Fowlie reportedly thinks Dylan echoes a poet friend of Dante, Guido Cavalcanti. A new sort of road song, in which a dried-out spirit, not dusty boots, recalls his long march. Did he take the right turns? Dylan prefers the *Real Live* version.

"SIMPLE TWIST OF FATE": In whispered understatement, the narrator's painful recall, in dreams and imagination, is of loneliness. "He woke up, the room was bare"[15] recalls "Baby Blue" and the lover who walked out the door with "all his blankets from the floor."[16] The singer remains in a dreamlike state of mordant remembrance until the third verse, when he chafes under the poet's "sin" of too much vision, too much feeling.

"YOU'RE A BIG GIRL NOW": A sequel to "Just Like a Woman." The phrase is ironically patronizing to anyone but a child. Rarely has his singing been more openly emotional. His stresses on the interjection "oh" remind me of the screaming mouth of the sufferer in Edvard Munch's painting. The narrator, "back in the rain,"[17] is singing through tears, and going out of his mind with "a corkscrew to my heart."[18] The irony is that the woman feels liberated while the narrator suffers. In the *Biograph* notes, Dylan rants at the suggestion this was about his wife. "I'm a mystery only to those who haven't felt the same things I have."

"IDIOT WIND": Generally acknowledged as the album's "big song." It has some of the sting of "Rolling Stone," much of the anguish of Ginsberg's "Howl." It could be a ranting truth attack, an expression of the narrator's personal disorder, ruefulness, and suspicion in an equally disturbed society in which people's spoken words are in apposition to their real emotions. This is also catharsis, a venting of personal anguish as well as a portrayal of a milieu where gossiping and backstabbing have replaced caring and believing. The ultimate horror is that the wheels have stopped;

the air is fetid, paralyzing the body, mind, and spirit. A man, or a couple, undergo harassment and collapse while Nixon and his family are under siege, in the denouement of the Watergate scandal.

Dylan insists we listen to a "primal scream," so that we will not be as naïve as he. This song changed tremendously from its New York version, which had a different melody and even more direct personal links, but an almost benign setting and gentler delivery. This version's relentless shout has the impact of Albee's *Who's Afraid of Virginia Woolf?*—too true to bear, too close to the bone to accept. Yet these truths have to be faced before one can go on. Dylan leaves this version as he does some of his pessimistic songs: The wheels will start to roll again, the winds of plague will blow away, the helpless will learn to feed themselves.

"YOU'RE GONNA MAKE ME LONESOME WHEN YOU GO": A delicate melody transports witty half-threats. The lover pleads that he never be abandoned, despite his fatalistic fear that he will be. "Situations have ended sad,/relationships have all been bad,/Mine've been like Verlaine's and Rimbaud."[19] This is the first time Dylan directly wrote of Rimbaud. Verlaine, the older, established poet, touted Rimbaud when he arrived in Paris. According to Wallace Fowlie: "The story of Verlaine and Rimbaud in London and Brussels is one of the literal epics of our age, in which the myth of the modern artist is related. It is the same story recast 50 years later by James Joyce in the Dublin odyssey of Leopold Bloom and Stephen Dedalus. The two men, one older than the other, are really one man, and the dual search for love and knowledge is one search. . . ."[20]

The earlier line about shooting in the dark fleshes out the story. Verlaine introduced Rimbaud to a skeptical coterie of Parisian writers, then left his wife to ramble with the seventeen-year-old newcomer. On July 10, 1873, after various emotional storms, Verlaine shot Rimbaud. One bullet ran wild and the other hit Rimbaud's left wrist. Rimbaud filed no complaint, but Verlaine was charged with attempted manslaughter and spent eighteen months in prison. Fowlie: "Evil is a way of knowledge. Extreme experiences of evil awaken in most men the deepest desire to understand what they are doing and suffering in order to transcend it. Those who practice evil as deliberately and knowingly as Rimbaud and Verlaine did turn themselves into Satanic theologians much more than mere lovers."[21]

Side II begins with some of the finest blues singing Dylan has ever done. In "MEET ME IN THE MORNING," the keening voice is arresting. A classic blues, "Morning" is rich in traditional idioms and images, with a few contemporary touches.

"LILY, ROSEMARY AND THE JACK OF HEARTS": One of Dylan's longest fables, played out like a card game. Lively action, mysterious death, and constant ambiguity. Vaguely reminiscent of "Frankie Lee and Judas Priest," it is a narrative ballad in the western tradition, which Dylan has turned into a fifteen-verse playlet (verse twelve in the folio is not sung) filled with whimsy and mystification. There was some Hollywood talk of turning the song into a screenplay, with speculation that Dylan would play the Jack.

"IF YOU SEE HER, SAY HELLO": This musical high spot has lusciously intimate singing and warm, massed, Mexican-style acoustic guitars. The narrator, a man trying to be cool about a wrenching separation from a woman, cannot keep his feelings from bursting out: "Either I'm too sensitive/Or else I'm gettin' soft."[22] This attempt to be casual in the face of emotional turmoil gives the text line a sea-wave rhythm. Dylan's phrasing recalls the voice of Tour '74 when he turns "chill" into "chi-i-u-ill," "stay" into "stay-hay-ay," and "town" into "town-ow-ow-un-un." Michael Gray considers this a rewrite of "Girl from the North Country."

"SHELTER FROM THE STORM": Dylan again uses natural elements to describe his tempest-tossed mood. The caressing melody explores a Yeatsian search for salvation through love. The poet found shelter, but the roof leaked and the rain came in. There are many rich lines, like: "In a world of steel-eyed death and men—who are fighting to be warm," and "nothing really matters much, it's doom alone that counts./And the one-eyed undertaker,/He blows a futile horn."[23]

Finally, the album's theme of lost and found, of a fruitless search that uncovers only impermanence, concludes with "BUCKETS OF RAIN." I hear echoes of Mississippi John Hurt's singsongy blues here, mournful one moment and playful the next, laughing to keep from crying. This is an album of echoes, of the singer's past work, of the poet's images, of intense love for a woman, many women, old friends, all distanced to avoid painful confrontation. The new stirrings in *Planet Waves* have turned into a tidal wave. There are echoes of *Les Illuminations,* particularly "Historic Evening." The idiot wind blows a hard rain down Desolation Row.

Taping for *Blood* began on September 10, 1974, at Columbia's Studio A in New York. Dylan summoned some familiar talents of the 1960s—Eric Weissberg and his band, Deliverance; Buddy Cage, the pedal-steel guitarist; Tony Braun, and Paul Griffin. Mick Jagger dropped in, and at one point considered sitting in on drums and doing background vocals. The chief Rolling Stone danced about, and helped quaff some bubbly. On the eve of release, Dylan raced off to Minneapolis, and on Friday, December 27, and Monday, December 30, got together with some new session men rounded up by his brother, David—Bill Peterson, bassist; Ken Odegard, guitarist; Bill Berg, drummer; Greg Inhoffer, keyboards; and Chris Weber, twelve-string guitar. They recut all but three of the original versions. Four of the final tracks seem to be from the New York sessions and six from Minneapolis. The absence of any musician credits on the revised jacket leaves a discographical muddle.

There was no muddle in reviewers' reactions, however. One English Dylan freak greeted the personal background to these sessions—Dylan's turbulent home life following Tour '74—with a perverse sort of joy:

"Well, now that Dylan and Sara are having problems, maybe he'll start writing some better songs." Dylan was hoist by his own petard—you can't write love songs for a woman for years and then write about a troubled period without inviting gossip, which appears in nearly every review of *Blood.* During a noticeably reticent radio interview with Dylan in spring 1975, Mary Travers told him how much she enjoyed the album. He snapped back at how people could "enjoy" what was obviously so painful for him.

In *Rolling Stone,* Jon Landau appealed to Dylan to take greater care with recording production. Landau later backtracked somewhat about Dylan's spontaneity: "He has transcended his limitations more successfully than anyone else in rock. . . . Dylan hasn't handled every role with equal skill. He was unconvincing as the happy homeowner. People . . . reacted to the fact that he couldn't make that experience as real as he could the emotions of anger, pain, hurt, fear, loneliness, aloneness and strength. Like James Dean and Marlon Brando, he was better at playing the rebel than the citizen, the outsider than the insider and the outlaw than the sheriff . . . in returning to his role as disturber of the peace, Dylan hasn't revived any specific phase from the past, only a style that lets his emotions speak more freely and the state of mind in which he no longer denies the fires that are still raging within him and us. . . ." On *Biograph* Dylan scoffs: "How many roles can I play? Fools, they limit you to their own unimaginative mentality."

Robert Christgau in *The Village Voice,* January 27, 1975, gave the album an "A": "Dylan's new stance is as disconcerting as all the previous ones, but the quickest and deepest surprise is in the music. . . . On the whole, this is the leader's most mature and assured record."

Paul Cowan's influential review of February 3, 1975, in *The Village Voice,* was kind to the artist, but not to the man: "The message is a bleak one. At 34, with his marriage on the rocks, he is an isolate, lonely drifter once again. . . . Dylan, trapped in the prison of himself, is Tiresias in his dugs. America is his wasteland . . . as in all Dylan's great albums, pain is the flip side of his legendary cruelty. . . . Sometime, probably as his marriage began to shatter, his selfishness must have curdled into self-hatred. . . . Dylan bears a very special kind of curse. He seems unable to establish warm, lasting relationships, but he's too eager for love to make the cold decision to sacrifice his private life to his art, as Joyce or even Mailer can. 'Blood' is a great album because he's writing into the headwinds of that curse. . . . The entire record is the excruciating cry of a man who is tormented by his own freedom. But it is also filled with religious imagery, with hints that the wounded, weary Dylan seeks 'shelter,' not as a woman's warm home, but as the peace of God. . . . For him, perhaps the faith he is seeking is the only escape from his swirling emotions, the only alternative to madness or suicide. . . ."

Cowan's psycho-critique misunderstood Dylan's role playing. Would he say Shakespeare was guilt-ridden because Lady Macbeth washed her hands, or that the bard was indecisive because Hamlet was conflicted? Even if *Blood on the Tracks* was literally confessional, Cowan is a less-than-humane witness to a catalog of remorse, self-doubt, and chagrin. Dylan has been a cruel, self-centered loner. After the accident, he tried to change his ways. After his move back to the Village in 1969, he was also trying to rekindle old friendships. From the summer of 1975 onward, Dylan made an even more concentrated effort to forge a community of singers. Dylan has wanted to be liked, but he tried to balance that need with trying to be true to his many embattled artistic selves. Years before Rolling Thunder, Dylan was pondering how to revive his old music community of the early 1960s. The opportunity presented itself after he had purged his feelings, and those of many others, with the brilliant catharsis of *Blood on the Tracks*.

AULD ACQUAINTANCE

In early 1975, Bill Graham found a rallying point. With a touch of social conscience, a dash of his own organization, and warm responses from stars, he soon had things rolling. San Francisco's beleaguered school system faced a three-million-dollar budget shortage, which would end all sorts of extracurricular activities. Graham formed SNACK (Students Need Athletics, Culture, and Kicks), reasoning: "We make our living from the youth of San Francisco. This is one way we hope to thank them." On February 4, only two weeks after his brainstorm, Graham announced that he'd signed, for the schools' benefit, Jefferson Starship, The Doobie Brothers, The Grateful Dead, Santana, Baez, Graham Central Station, and Tower of Power. Rumored to appear: Dylan and Brando (each had five children), Neil Young, and The Band. On March 23, 1975, some sixty thousand people, mostly teenagers, besieged Golden Gate Park's Kezar Stadium. Football and baseball stars, notably Gene Washington and Willie Mays, joined the rock constellation. Radio station K-101 broadcast that "a surprise guest ... the man from the Fairmont ..." was expected momentarily. When Brando took the stage, many thought he was the surprise guest. "The Godfather" spoke with passion:

"It's not my generation ... but your generation's gonna catch the shit that my generation and the people before me have laid down for you ... there are plenty of people ... hurting. The poor people, the Indians, the white people, the blacks, the Chicanos, everybody's that's been ripped off.... I'm gonna give five thousand bucks ... we gotta give and give ... we gotta give of our feelings....

Baez followed Brando. The man from the Fairmont Hotel was noticed backstage, heading into the tuning-up trailer. Graham announced a supersession: "On bass, Rick Danko; on keyboards, Garth Hudson; on drums, Levon Helm; on guitar, Tim Drummond; on pedal-steel, Ben Keith; on harmonica and guitar, Bob Dylan!" Roar followed roar when Graham also

announced Neil Young. Nearly everyone sprang to their feet to greet the
Dylan-Young-Band-Doobies set. From the wings, Baez smiled approvingly.

Dylan worked mostly on guitar and harmonica, but went to the piano
to accompany Young's "Lookin' for a Love." He sang lead on "I Want
You" and "Knockin' at the Dragon's Door" after several numbers by
Young. At stageside, Brando and Baez embraced. Other numbers were
"Are You Ready for the Country," "Darker Side of Me," 'Loving You,"
"The Weight," and "Helpless." The final encore was "Will the Circle Be
Unbroken." The concert raised two hundred thousand dollars. As the lis-
teners trekked home at six P.M., Dylan, Brando, and Graham went to din-
ner at the home of Francis Ford Coppola, director of *The Godfather.*

Todd Tolces in *Melody Maker:* "Simply . . . the most important musical
event San Francisco has ever seen." He epitomized the forty-five-minute
Dylan/Young set as "history." According to *After Dark,* it was ". . . a vast
efflorescence of counter-culture sentiment, a harking-back to times when
rock wasn't all hype and money and problems and slick showmanship. . . .
It was a great, great show, unique in many ways. The 'political' part of it is
purest romance. . . ."

Still, there was Dylan sharing a stage again with the obdurately political
Baez and Brando, and enjoying every minute. He was hinting that he
might become identified again with social action. In the early seventies,
despite his overt indifference, Dylan had been wrestling with his longing
for community. His own romantic rebelliousness and social passions were
cool to the point of cynicism: "The Dream is over, the Great American
Dream is over . . . there are guys in prison that just can't afford to get out,"
he told me. Perhaps he also meant the prison of his own solitude.

He wasn't ready then to envision his changes in the 1970s. "George
Jackson," "Bangladesh," and his appearance at the benefit for Chile in
1974 were isolated events. I don't think he had lost his social compassion;
he simply wanted to run free, to drift. By spring 1975, he was planning the
official release of his biggest "looking back" album, *The Basement Tapes.*
Tour '74 had put Dylan in touch with his old music, including the music
that spoke of a certain political mood. What the 1970s needed, Dylan saw,
was another shot of that singular 1960s zeal. Dylan has described the sixties as "like a flying saucer landed . . . that's what the sixties were like.
Everybody heard about it, but only a few really saw it."

After Tour '74, offers for more shows flooded in. In May 1974, Dylan
and The Band were offered a million-dollar guarantee for a one-day show.
Amid promoters' attempts to capitalize on Tour '74, Dylan simply went
visiting. He popped up in San Francisco, with Paul McCartney and The
Doobies, at the wedding of one Chick Edwards, drummer of the local
band Bittersweet. In September 1974, Dylan revisited Highway 61, touring the North Country with Lou Kemp, showing his oldest children
where he'd grown up. Rumors persisted that Bob was buying an apartment and other property outside Minneapolis.

He visited a concert of a band he'd befriended and strongly influenced—Crosby, Stills, Nash and Young. Stills dedicated a song: "This
one's for Bob." There was a CSN&Y party afterward, where Dylan played
some of his new *Blood on the Tracks* material. Dylan's Tour '74 had, in
Crosby's phrase, been "the ice-breaker" for the quality music his band was
making. Dylan also had visited CSN&Y at the Fillmore East in June 1972.

That summer he literally had gone on record in praise of his old blues
chum, Ric Von Schmidt. On his Poppy album, Dylan's message, printed
on a yellow sticker, read, in part: ". . . his record is . . . an invitation to join
the glad, sad, biting, exciting, frightening, crabby, happy, enlightening,
hugging, chugging world of Eric Von Schmidt . . . who can sing the bird
off the wire and the rubber off the tyre. He can separate the men from the
boys and the notes from the noise; the bridle from the saddle and the cow
from the cattle. He can play the tune off the moon. The why of the sky
and the commotion from the ocean. Yes he can . . ."[24]

At the release of *Blood,* he was socializing with people he might have
written off earlier, like Dana Gillespie, the baroness actress friend of Donovan's. Dylan once scoffed that she sang folk songs on water skis, but now
he sat listening to her at New York's Reno Sweeney, with Bette Midler
and David Bowie at his table. By the time he was getting *The Basement
Tapes* ready for official release (July 1975), Columbia Records was promoting its prodigal-son-returned. In March 1975, both *Greatest Hits*
albums had entered the lower end of the charts again and were rising fast.
Some nine years after its release, *Blonde on Blonde* reentered the album
charts. Barbara Charone commented in *Sounds:* "All of this is an impressive
testimony to the artistic power of 'Blood.' . . ." America, she wrote, "seems
caught in the middle of a Dylan renaissance," and she heard echoes of it in
Britain as well.

Dylan was ready to spend summer 1975 walking the streets of the Village, hanging out again. *The Village Voice* trumpeted a page-one headline
on July 14, 1975: JAMMING WITH DYLAN: WILL MACDOUGAL ST. RISE
AGAIN? Jerry Leichtling; "You can't spit out your window these days
without hitting Dylan. . . ." Over the July Fourth weekend, The Other
End on Bleecker Street became the site of "The First Annual Village Folk
Festival." With many regulars out of town, the audience was small. Wearing a black leather jacket, beige corduroy trousers, and a blue striped T-
shirt, he'd jammed with Muddy Waters at The Bottom Line on Monday.
Thursday, he'd joined Jack Elliott onstage at The Other End. Paul Colby
had reopened the former Bitter End in June, after a year's darkness. On
Saturday night, Dylan returned with Patti Smith, Tom Verlaine, and
Bobby Neuwirth. Jake and the Family Jewels was the lead act. Dylan
jammed backstage with Neuwirth, who announced "a surprise backup
guitarist" and dragged the reluctant guitar-picker onstage. Dylan played
nonelectric piano as the talented crew joined him on "Will the Circle Be
Unbroken." He remained at the keyboard while Patti Smith sang lead on
"Amazing Grace," "Banks of the Ohio," and "Good Night, Irene," the

old Leadbelly classic. It was like a 1961 hoot. Tastes were broader now, rock had brought riches to folk, and vice versa.

Bob came in nightly with his guitar case, piles of papers, and notebooks. Phil Ochs and Dave Van Ronk staggered by. The old hassles may not have been entirely forgotten, but Dylan was trying. The next night, Dylan backed Elliott on "Pretty Boy Floyd" and "How Long Blues." Neuwirth and Dylan sang a song Dylan had been working on only that afternoon. After the time-honored finale, "This Land Is Your Land," the group moved next door to the Dugout, where the theme became "this drink is your drink." To Patti Smith, Dylan seemed to be "exploding" with his new material for *Desire.* To Neuwirth, Dylan was "an audio voyeur, just listening to and watching people." A few female fans reportedly threw themselves at Dylan, but he brushed them aside.

Neuwirth sensed that Dylan's scene-making was not just a momentary whim. To keep up with the momentum, Neuwirth organized a house band. Other musicians dropped in: Sandy Bull, Eric Kaz, Loudon Wainwright III, Mick Ronson, and T-Bone Burnette. On Neuwirth's opening night, Dylan sat in with this band, trying out his new "Isis" and "Joey." A beaming Columbia Records man told a few people that Dylan had been down to Trenton State Prison to visit Hurricane Carter, the imprisoned boxer, and had written a song for him. The same unnamed Columbia man said Dylan was considering a Broadway show and possibly some TV work.

All of this made Dylan think about a tour of small clubs. Probably Jack Elliott suggested it, perhaps Patti Smith, perhaps Neuwirth. For a cover story in *People* on November 10, Dylan told Jim Jerome: " 'I didn't consciously pursue the Bob Dylan myth. It was given to me—by God. Inspiration is what we're looking for. You just have to be receptive to it.... I was locked into a certain generation. I still am. A certain area, a certain place in the universe at a certain time.... I'm not an activist. I am not politically inclined. I'm for people, people who are suffering.... Writing a song, it can drive you crazy. My head is so crammed full of things I tend to lose a lot of what I think are my best songs, and I don't carry around a tape-recorder.... We have to be able to hear that voice. I'm through listening to other people tell me how to live my life.... I'm just doing now what I feel is right for me.... For my own self....' "

September 10, 1975: Station WTTW's National Educational Television Studios in Chicago were taping a telecast for December 13, *The World of John Hammond.* (Hammond had told me in 1972 that they still got on well personally, that they'd recently gone to a baseball game together.) In a lecture at Hunter College just before his TV tribute was broadcast, Hammond said: "Dylan changed my life, I guess." The taping of the hour-long show, part of the second series of *Soundstage,* began at nine P.M., but Dylan didn't appear on camera until two A.M., before a thinned-out audience of 150 people. Despite four heart attacks, Hammond was looking well, delighted to be honored by so many of his associates and artists. Among them were Goddard Lieberson, Benny Goodman, Jerry Wexler, former Count Basie singer Helen Humes, gospel queen Marion Williams, Sonny Terry, Hammond's son, and jazz stars Teddy Wilson, Benny Carter, Jo Jones and Red Norvo.

Dylan was rubbing the sleep out of his eyes when he arrived onstage, backed by Howie Wyeth on drums, Rob Stoner on bass and backup vocals, and Scarlet Rivera, on violin. Dylan and combo sailed into "Hurricane," jolting the tired audience. After taping "Oh, Sister" and "Simple Twist of Fate," Dylan retaped "Hurricane," adding even more sting to his performance. His intense scowl heightened the song's anger. Before he sang "Oh, Sister," Dylan said, on camera: "I want to dedicate this to someone out there watching tonight I know. She knows who she is." To one reporter, Al Rudis, "there seemed to be blood flowing from psychic wounds throughout this short set."

Dylan left hurriedly after his set. Observers were fascinated with the violinist in a long dress, with dark gypsy eyes and flowing hair. Some believed her to be a real gypsy Dylan had discovered walking along Second Avenue with her violin case. Some Chicagoans recognized her as Donna Shea, who had been on their local rock scene in the late 1960s. In New York, Dylan later remarked: "For all John Hammond's done for me, it was worth staying late."

13

THUNDER, HURRICANE, AND HARD RAIN

"The difference between good actors and big stars is that good actors disclose everything; big stars are mysterious."

—DAVID LEAN, 1965

"A work is not a series of answers, it is a series of questions . . . it is not the answer that enlightens, but the question."

—EUGENE IONESCO

"I define nothing. Not beauty, not patriotism. I take each thing as it is, without prior rules about what it should be."

—DYLAN, 1965

"Definition destroys . . . there's nothing definite in this world. . . ."

—DYLAN, 1976

During those hot summer nights of 1975, the idea of a "different" tour took fire. Dylan put it this way: "We were all very close. We had this fire going ten years ago, and now we've got it burning again." Neuwirth: "It's

gonna be a new living room every night. This is the first existential tour
... it's a movie ... a closed set ... it's rock 'n' roll heaven and it's historical.... It's been Rambling Jack's dream for a long time ... he's the one
who taught us all, and the dream's coming true...."

Dylan was preparing to tape *Desire* and continuing to hang out with his
Village crowd. One night at The Other End, he asked Jack Elliott if he
wanted to tour with him, to "play for the people." Jack's response to the
buddy he'd not seen in seven years: "Let's go!" It took planning. First,
Dylan went west to see his family, then popped up in Minnesota before
taping the TV tribute to John Hammond, the record producer who first
recorded him. He returned to New York with ideas about a rambling,
tumbling tour of the Northeast, with film cameras capturing it all. It
wouldn't be announced, it would just "happen." Lou Kemp, the Alaska
"salmon king" from Duluth, was named tour manager, assisted by Barry
Imhoff and Shelly Finkel. Jacques Levy helped with stage direction. Rob
Stoner organized a backup band that included Howard Wyeth, Luther
Rix, Mick Ronson, Scarlet Rivera, T-Bone Burnette, and a nineteen-year-
old mandolin/Dobro wizard named David Mansfield. The lead singers
would be Dylan, Neuwirth, Ronee Blakley, Roger McGuinn, Elliott, and
Joan Baez. (Dylan phoned to ask what she was doing in November. She
had a tour of her own planned, but this one sounded more of a challenge.
She said it was "irresistible" and she'd make it. "Diamonds and Rust," you
know.) She later described the troupe as "an incredibly happy family."

One morning in October, about twenty musicians were jamming at The
Other End. More signed on: Allen Ginsberg joined the chorus, fellow-poet
Peter Orlovsky enlisted as a "baggage handler," David Blue and Denise
Mercedes as musicians, and security people, advance men, and lighting
technicians. What started as a troupe of seventy swelled to more than one
hundred by Toronto. On October 22, at The Other End, David Blue was
finishing his gig. Dylan sang duets with Ronee Blakley, the beauteous
country singer who starred in *Nashville.* Ginsberg sang to McGuinn's guitar. "Allen, you're the king," Dylan told him.

The following night, a little surprise for Mike Porco, who was turning
sixty-one. To Mike's astonishment, four film technicians showed up at
Folk City, mumbling "educational television." (Under the direction of
Dylan, Howard Alk, and Mel Howard, this began hundreds of hours of
shooting footage.) On hand were Phil Ochs, Patti Smith, Baez, Commander Cody members, Bette Midler, and Buzzy Linhart. A bit after one
A.M., Dylan's red Cadillac Eldorado cruised up to Folk City, and in loped
Bob, Kemp, and Neuwirth. Dylan, as "the greatest star of all," went to the
stage; he brought up Baez. They sang "Happy Birthday" and "One Too
Many Mornings." Mike Porco grinned from wall to wall. He'd been waiting for this a long time!

This was a dress rehearsal for the Rolling Thunder Revue, as performers
took to the little stage of Folk City. Hours later, a hoarse Phil Ochs did a
set of his own, some traditional songs and "Lay Down Your Weary

Tune." Everyone at Dylan's table stood gaping at Phil. Dylan praised Phil when he finished. (When thirty-five-year-old Ochs hanged himself on April 9, 1976, some said his exclusion from the RTR was the last in a long line of crushing events that gave him no way out. Ochs could not be signed on the tour because of his heavy drinking and unpredictability. His friend and eulogizer, Ed Sanders, has described Ochs's "final flameout" as a reaction to "the tyranny of booze, despair, and maddening mood swings.")

That week also saw Dylan in a Columbia studio, retaping "Hurricane." He told two top Columbia Records executives that he wanted it rush released. After the session, producer Don DeVito said of Dylan: "He's just totally unpredictable." All that week the troupe had been assembling at the Gramercy Park Hotel. Over that weekend there were intensive rehearsals at a midtown studio. Two advance men had hired the Plymouth (Massachusetts) Memorial Auditorium, despite the town fathers' reportedly asking Baez not to make any political statements from the stage. On October 27, the troupe took off in three buses and a few cars, most of the singers riding in a Greyhound nicknamed Phydeaux. In a few hours, they arrived at the beachside Seacrest Hotel in North Falmouth, Massachusetts, where rehearsals continued for a couple of days. That night, Dylan sang in the hotel dining room and Ginsberg recited "Kaddish."

With the pilgrims landing first in Plymouth, it seemed like the grand bicentennial gesture, leading to that gag: "The new sound is Plymouth rock." It was Halloween too, so there were masks and games. With cameras rolling, the games became cinema. The rhetoric was flowing like a rock riff. Elliott had once worked on the rigging of *The Mayflower* replica at Plymouth. This time, Jack climbed to the top of the mizzenmast and roared, "Ahoy!" He waved down to Dylan and Ginsberg. Allen duly proclaimed: "We have, once again, embarked on a voyage to reclaim America."

Why Rolling Thunder? Dylan said he simply looked up at the sky "and heard a boom. Then, boom, boom, boom, rolling from west to east. I figured that should be the name." He appeared pleased when someone told him that to American Indians, rolling thunder means speaking truth. Along the way, a Cherokee medicine man named Rolling Thunder joined the troupe. At Providence, he was onstage stroking a feather in time to the music. On November 5, at a beach in Newport, Dr. Rolling Thunder made some good medicine around a fire. He asked everyone to add private prayers. Ginsberg: "Thanks to those who brought us together, and remembrance for those who are not here." Elliott: "O pray that the spirit we've generated here extends to everyone we meet on our travels." Dylan reportedly mumbled: "I pray we realize soon we are all of one soul."

Kemp's advance men were booking halls at a prodigious speed, often so fast the musicians didn't know the next stop. Handbills alone told the story. The itinerary for the autumn segment of the Rolling Thunder

Revue was: Oct. 30 and 31, Plymouth Memorial Auditorium; Nov. 1, Southeastern Massachusetts University, North Dartmouth; Nov. 2, Lowell (Massachusetts) Technical University, Nov. 4, two shows, Providence Civic Center; Nov. 6, two shows, Springfield Civic Center; Nov. 8, University of Vermont, Burlington; Nov. 9, University of New Hampshire, Durham; Nov. 11, Waterbury (Connecticut) Palace Theater; Nov. 13, two shows, New Haven Veterans Memorial Coliseum; Nov. 15, two shows, Niagara Falls Convention Center; Nov. 17, two shows, Rochester War Memorial Coliseum; Nov. 19, Worcester (Massachusetts) Civic Auditorium; Nov. 20, Harvard Square Theater, Cambridge.

Afternoon and evening shows were held on November 21 at the Boston Music Hall. Then, evening concerts: November 22, Brandeis University; November 24, Hartford Civic Center Arena; November 26, Augusta (Maine) Civic Center; November 27, Bangor (Maine) Municipal Auditorium; November 29, Quebec Coliseum; December 1 and 2, Toronto Maple Leaf Gardens; December 4, Montreal Forum; December 7, Clinton (New Jersey) State Prison; December 8, Madison Square Garden, New York, "Night of the Hurricane I."

Dylan had rarely seemed more amiable, onstage and off. Sometimes he'd disappear into a room reserved for him in the name of "Keef Laundry." With such voluble sources as Baez, Neuwirth, and Ginsberg, Dylan was relieved of burdensome interviews. Jim Jerome of *People* quoted Dylan in *Creem:*

" 'It used to be my life was very simple. It consisted of hanging around with a certain crowd and writing songs. I always had a place to write. . . . I tried to get rid of the burden of the Bob Dylan myth for a long time, because it is a burden. Just ask anybody who is considered a star. There are certain advantages and rewards to it, but you're *thinking:* "Shit, man, I'm only me." You know, that's who I am. We are all the same. No one is on any higher level than anybody else. We've all got it within us, for whatever we want to grasp for.' "

Baez found Dylan easier to relate to than in the previous ten years. Musician Mick Ronson: "He's a superbeing, from somewhere else." Steve Soles: "Dylan is a psychic, he paraphrases things I've dreamed." One troupe member: "Those looks of his onstage—there were, like, five levels to them. All meant different things. . . . He is unbelievably subtle. There was very close physical communication between him and the musicians— like I've never seen in him before."

Grandiloquent Allen Ginsberg talked volubly to Nat Hentoff for *Rolling Stone,* to Jim Jerome, and most elegiacally, to Peter Chowka of *New Age Journal:* " '. . . I hadn't seen Dylan for four years. He just called me up at 4 A.M. and said: "What're you writing? Sing it to me on the telephone. . . . O.K., let's go out on the road." . . . Rolling Thunder will be one of the signal gestures characterizing the working cultural community that will make the Seventies . . . wishful thinking that is also prophesy . . .

the first gesture toward communalism . . . he brought his mother along . . . the 'mysterious' Dylan had a chicken-soup Yiddish mama, who even got on stage at one point—[Toronto] . . . Sara and his children came. Sara met Joan Baez and they all acted in the movie together and Baez brought her mother and children, and Jack Elliott had his daughter. So there was a lot of jumping family. . . . Dylan is now exploring his kingdom, with a new majesty about him. He alone has the clear, clean authoritative strength to take his own monumental images, unbuild and rebuild them. This is instant teaching to a younger generation. This means he has the power to re-create America, too. All the shit he has gone through—arguments with himself—he has turned to gold. He is more a citizen than ever. And in the Bi-Centennial tradition, that is political, to be a hardworking citizen. . . . There are very few moments in my experience where I have felt the heart of history touched. . . .' "

From the July Fourth weekend right on through the spring segment of Rolling Thunder, significant changes in Dylan were seen. Onstage he displayed great mobility, moving about like a cross between a seventies rocker and a football coach, driving his "team" onward. The man in motion was not afraid to change interpretations, lyrics, stage manner, appearance. Dylan had his face painted white with pancake makeup. He dressed in many-colored scarves and different hats. He called it all "commedia dell'arte." At the first show in Plymouth, the backup band's masks also recalled that sixteenth-century Italian theater form in which stock characters improvised freely. Those less historically minded saw Dylan's new face as theatrical rock à la Bowie or Peter Gabriel. (Dylan said the makeup helped people in the back rows to see his face.)

There was some critical backlash. When the tour moved toward large auditoriums, Dylan was attacked for having "sold out," again. The idea of the small-scale show got lost as the cast grew and filming expenses mounted. One estimate: The first thirteen shows of RTR attracted more than eighty-three thousand customers paying a gross ticket price of $640,000. *Variety,* always interested in money, asked: "Is Dylan Interested in Money?" Dylan riposted: "We've got seventy people . . . we gotta pay for. We're gonna play any place we can, but we also have a lot of expenses to meet. We're not gonna . . . play living rooms. It's not a nightclub show, you know." Baez was testier: "Oh, tell them to just shove it up their asses!"

Spontaneity dominated the tour, including itinerary changes, improvisation, and guest appearances. Mimi Baez, once so critical of Dylan over what she regarded as his pro-Zionism, showed up. Joni Mitchell did two New Haven shows and reappeared. Arlo Guthrie came along in Springfield. Old friends David Blue, Gordon Lightfoot, and Robbie Robertson popped up. Roberta Flack was at the prison and New York concerts. Joan said she'd never seen such a spirit. Even after arduous shows, the cast would sing their way along on the bus. Joan: "We all sing and sing and laugh until we pass out. For us, it makes no difference if we just play for fifteen people or fifteen thousand." Love and kisses onstage, as well, with songs dedicated to Hurricane Carter, Kerouac, Sam Peckinpah, and Gertrude Stein. Joan told Hentoff:

" '. . . The feeling is good, because everybody has some room on stage. . . . Bob has so powerful an effect on so many lives. . . . I'm still deeply affected by his songs . . . by that presence of his. I've seen nothing like it, except in Muhammad Ali, Marlon Brando and Stevie Wonder. Bob walks into a room and every eye in the place is on him. There are eyes on Bob even when he's hiding. . . . I used to be too hard on him [and] a lot of people. . . . I don't expect Bob to champion my causes anymore. I've learned he's not an activist, which does not mean he doesn't care about people. . . .' "

With Baez and Dylan doing eye-to-eye duets again onstage, some thought they were witnessing a romantic reunion. Dylan even asked her to sing "Diamonds and Rust," although, playfully, she wouldn't concede that it was about *him*. Her "O Brother" suggests she had learned Dylan's elliptical methods. Joan told *People:* " 'Dylan has been a big element in my life, and he always will be. But we are different things to each other at different times. So much for Bob.' "

Some of the most affecting moments of the autumn tour were visible only to the camera crew. Lowell, Massachusetts: By Jack Kerouac's grave, Dylan and Ginsberg improvised a scene. Allen leafed through Kerouac's *Mexico City Blues*. Dylan told him he'd first read it in Minneapolis. At the graveside, Dylan played harmonium or guitar while Allen improvised blues. Ginsberg:

". . . There's a giant statue of Christ described by Kerouac. Dylan got up near . . . the statue. . . and goes into this funny monologue, asking the man on the cross, 'How does it feel to be up there?' . . . everyone sees Dylan as a Christ-figure too, but he doesn't want to be crucified. He's too smart, in a way. . . . Dylan was almost mocking, like a good Jew might be to someone who insisted on being the Messiah, against the wisdom of the rabbis, and getting himself nailed up for it. Dylan . . . said: 'What can you do for somebody in that situation?' I think he quoted Christ, 'suffer little children,' and I quoted part of 'Forever Young,' which is Dylan's hip, Americanese paraphrase of Christ's 'Do unto others.'

"So there was this brilliant funny situation of Dylan . . . addressing this life-size statue of Christ, and allowing himself to be photographed with Christ. It was like Dylan humorously playing with the dreadful potential of his own mythological imagery, unafraid and confronting it, trying to deal with it in a sensible way. That seemed to be the characteristic of the tour: that Dylan was willing to shoulder the burden of the myth laid on him, or that he himself created, or the composite creation of himself and the nation, and use it as a workable situation. As Trungpa would say it: 'Alchemize it.' "

Alchemize: This metaphor of Dylan, the Alchemist, had nagged me for
ten years. *Alchemy* had been a secret and blasphemous science. Jung had
made a respectable term of what had once been scoffed at as a prescientific
superstition. The alchemists were not simply trying to turn base metals
into gold, but were also aiming at the perfecting of matter and of "man in
fulfilling the laws of God." Jung, according to Anthony Storr, "saw alchemy as a process of inner, psychological development in the alchemist
himself, and the chemical changes and new combinations as changes
within the personality.... Jung regarded [alchemy] as a gigantic Ror-
schach test ... the projection of the psychological process of the experi-
menter. The alchemists, like Jung and his patients, were engaged upon a
spiritual progress, search for integration and individuation...."[1]

Alchemy is also a metaphor for the poetic process. Balzac, in *The Human
Comedy*, wrote: "To make gold was their point of departure, but ... they
were looking for something better, they wanted to find the essential mole-
cule, they were looking for movement at its beginning...." Wallace Fowlie, discussing Mallarmé: "What the poet does ... is very close to a magical
creation. In a deliberate darkness he calls up an object that has been silenced, by means of words that are allusive ... what happens next is truly
magic. By the enchantment of letters ... the words begin to glow and
mean until the illusion they evoke is equivalent to what the eyes of a man
can see in the material world ... the occupation of the poet, quite in
keeping with the ancient occupation of the alchemist, is the measuring or
dosage of essences.... Only the magician or the alchemist was able to
apply the formula and concoct the potions...."[2]

The word *alchemy* has been traced back to Noah's son Shem, or Chem.
Medieval alchemists thought The Ark was the original laboratory. Rimbaud's "Alchemy of the Word" passage from *A Season in Hell* keeps the
circle unbroken:

> ... I dreamed of crusades, of unrecorded voyages of discovery, of repub-
> lics with no history, of hushed-up religious wars, revolution in customs,
> displacements of races and continents: I believed in every kind of
> witchcraft.... I wrote out silences and the nights. I recorded the inex-
> pressible. I described frenzies. . . . Poetic old-fashionedness figured
> largely in my alchemy of the word. I grew accustomed to pure halluci-
> nation: I saw quite frankly a mosque in place of a factory, a school of
> drummers made up of angels, carriages on roads in the sky, a parlor at
> the bottom of the lake; monsters, mysteries. The title of a vaudeville
> conjured up horrors before me. Then I explained my magic sophisms
> with the hallucinations of words! At the end I looked on the disorder of
> my mind as sacred....[3]

Back in the Rolling Thunder laboratory outside Falmouth, the two poets
were improvising another scene, Allen playing the Emperor and Dylan

playing the Alchemist. Ginsberg: "I enter the diner and say: 'I'm the emperor, I just woke up this morning and found out I inherited an empire, and it's bankrupt. I hear from the apothecary across the street that you're an alchemist. I need some help to straighten out karmic problems with my empire.... I just sent for a shipload of tears from Indochina, but it didn't seem to do any good. Can you help? Do you have any magic formulae for alchemizing the situation?' Dylan kept denying he was an alchemist. 'I can't help, what're you asking me for?' "

Allen continued to insist that Dylan was the alchemist who knew the secrets. Dylan had the waiter bring him crackers, ketchup, salt, pepper, sugar, milk, coffee, yogurt, and apple pie, all of which he dumped into a big aluminum pot. Allen had put down his calling card—an autumn leaf, "just like the one Dylan pocketed in the graveyard—the leaf which runs through many of the scenes in the movie, representing, like in Kerouac's work, transiency, poignancy, regret, acknowledgments of change, death. So I threw my calling-card leaf in the pot and Dylan threw in a piece of cardboard, and then he fished out the leaf, all muddy, and slapped it down on top of my notebook, where I was taking down all the magical ingredients in his alchemical mixture. Then I said: 'Oh, I see the secret of your alchemy: ordinary object.' 'Yes,' Dylan said, 'ordinary mind.' "

In his long interview with Peter Chowka for the April 1976 *New Age Journal,* Ginsberg spoke of the three marks of existence: change, suffering, and egolessness. " 'I don't know him because I don't think there is any him. I don't think he's got a self! Yes, he's ever-changing. He's said very beautiful, Buddha-like things.... I asked him whether he was having pleasure on the tour and he said: "Pleasure. Pleasure. What's that? I never touch the stuff." ... He went on to explain that at one time he had had a lot of pain and sought a lot of pleasure but found that there was a subtle relationship between pleasure and pain....' "

One conversation led Allen to write a song, on November 1, 1975, published in *First Blues.* In "Lay Down yr Mountain Lay Down God," Ginsberg calls Dylan an alchemist. Ginsberg recounted his version of Dylan's "spiritual conversation with God," and quoted Dylan: " 'Anybody that's busy making elephants and putting camels through needles' eyes is too busy to answer my questions, so I came down the mountain ...' "

In the valley below, the Rolling Thunder Revue gathered momentum. Jerry Leichtling of *The Village Voice* said of the opening Plymouth concert: "This is one of the greatest shows I've ever seen ... this tour is Dylan's masterpiece...." Fans, press, and participants dubbed it: minstrel show, medicine show, magical mystery tour, a floating musical crap game. Some were reminded of Joe Cocker's "Mad Dogs and Englishmen" tour, while some regarded it as a traveling electric hootenanny. Some heard echoes of Ken Kesey's Acid Test. Ginsberg told Nat Hentoff that " 'Dylan's getting all his mysteries unraveled,' " but Hentoff thought otherwise: "If he has a mania, it is for survival.... And part of the way of survival is keeping some of his mysteries damn well raveled." Jon Landau in *Rolling Stone,* January 15, 1976: ". . . From a myth-making point of view, this is all astonishingly effective stuff. Here a man does a limited tour . . . refusing to make known his itinerary, doesn't release an album, does no interviews, is actively hostile to what little press penetrates his defenses—and winds up with extraordinary amounts of acclaim and attention. This is one rock star who still knows the importance of mystery in creating art and in calling attention to the artist. . . ."

Dylan brought his troupe to halls where folk purists had once booed him. *The Worcester Gazette:* "He could do no wrong. He could have stood on stage for two hours tuning his guitar and reciting nursery rhymes and they would have loved every minute of it." (In the front row sat Joseph P. Kennedy III, son of the late Robert Kennedy, as Dylan said: "This song is called 'Hurricane.' If you've got any political pull at all, maybe you can help us get this man out of jail. . . ." He introduced the song at Springfield: "I hear Massachusetts is the only state that didn't vote for Nixon. Is that true?" When the listeners cheered assent, Bob replied: "Well, neither did we.") John Rockwell of *The New York Times* was amazed at the Plymouth finale's ten-minute cheering ovation. Rockwell saw RTR as a summation of all Dylan's musical influences plus "politics and ballads fused . . . into something higher and more personal. . . . Rolling Thunder . . . is Dylan's Bi-Centennial gesture to this country's true spirit."

Rolling Thunder pursued a grueling schedule of shows that were at least three and a half hours long. The first Toronto show ran four and a half hours. At the Montreal Forum, there were twenty thousand in the audience. *The Montreal Star* writer felt that "still, Dylan hasn't lost the sense of intimacy that seemed so important to him when the tour was conceived." There was some grumbling among the roadies and technical staff, and Baez tried to organize greater democracy within the troupe. There were problems too with the press and security. Only Ken Regan of Camera 5 and Dylan's film crew had "exclusive" photography rights. Ticket holders showed considerable irritation at being frisked by what *The Niagara Gazette* called "a goon squad." After incidents at the Niagara Convention Center, the deputy police chief conceded that the dozen Rolling Thunder security people were "rougher than necessary," but were within their legal bounds. Paul Colby to Toby Goldstein in *Modern Hi-Fi & Music:* " '. . . the last night Dylan played in the back room [of The Other End] he said he wanted to play onstage so bad he could taste it. But . . . he was afraid of tape recorders . . . in fact, there were two tape recorders, brought by the same guy. I spilled a glass of wine in that guy's face and threw him out. . . . It's one of the reasons he doesn't play more often. . . . He's leery of the public. . . .' "

On November 16, at the Tuscarora Indian Reservation, north of Buffalo, Chief Arnold Hewitt received a telephone call—could the Rolling Thunder troupe drop in for a visit? Without speakers or amplifiers, troupe musicians, including Joni Mitchell and Eric Andersen, showed up at the Indians' community house. Song-swapping between his troupe and the Indians reached some intense moments. Tuscaroras did traditional songs and dances to drumbeating. While Dylan sang, a few of the younger Indian children played tag around the community house. The Rolling Thunder people and their hosts then feasted on corn soup, corn bread, and venison.

All of this was filmed, including five complete concerts and assorted improvised scenes. Ginsberg saw the tour as a reaffirmation of what was actually achieved in the sixties. He also saw the film and tour as having a dominant theme of "respect for mother-goddess, eternal-woman, earth-woman principles." Dylan told him that the film's "thread" was simply "truth and beauty." As the massed voices of the Rolling Thunder Revue sang out "This Land Is Your Land," these pilgrims who started at Plymouth Rock had another mountain to scale, Madison Square Garden.

THE HURRICANE BEGINS

How well Rubin Carter's nickname, "Hurricane," blended into Dylan's lexicon. In 1963, he wrote:

> Oh the time will come up
> When the winds will stop
> And the breeze will cease to be breathin'.
> Like the stillness in the wind
> 'Fore the hurricane begins,
> The hour when the ship comes in. . . .[4]

Each of the two hundred male and female convicts who heard Dylan and the Rolling Thunder troupe on Sunday, December 7, 1975, was waiting for some ship to come in. These prisoners at the medium-security New Jersey State Prison at Clinton listened to Ginsberg chant poems, and to Joni Mitchell, Roberta Flack, and Dylan sing.

Among the convict-listeners was a former middleweight boxer who'd been inside for nine years on a life sentence for a triple murder in Paterson, New Jersey, in 1966. Early in the morning on June 17, 1966, two black men had shot up a white working-class bar, killing the bartender and two of the three customers. A witness described the getaway car, and Carter and John Artis were found in an allegedly similar vehicle. Four months later, two small-time thieves, Alfred Bello and Arthur Bradley, testified they'd seen Carter and Artis running out of the bar. Carter and Artis were charged with the murders. In 1974, a New Jersey investigator and a *New York Times* reporter heard the two white thieves say they'd lied in fingering the two black men because the police had offered help with cases pending against them.

Rubin Hurricane Carter had long insisted that he and his friend Artis were framed; a growing number of people believed him. In summer 1975, Carter had sent his autobiography, *The Sixteenth Round,* to Dylan. Bob's reaction: "I realized Hurricane and I were coming from the same place spiritually. He's a brilliant man, one of the most truthful I have ever met. He is a perfect citizen in every way. I love him as a brother. It just isn't fair. He must get out. *Today.*"

After Dylan wrote "Hurricane," collaborating on the lyrics with Jacques Levy, the boxer declared: "Words are about the most powerful drugs known to men. Bob Dylan came to prison to see me and I met a man that was for life and living, not for death and dying." In Carter, Dylan found a renewed focus for his involvement with victims and outsiders, especially black recipients of white "justice." Dylan: "I never doubted him for a moment. He's just not a killer, not that kind of man." "Hurricane" is Dylan's *J'accuse* of the American judicial system:

> How can the life of such a man
> Be in the palm of some fool's hand?
> To see him obviously framed
> Couldn't help but make me feel ashamed to live in a land
> Where justice is a game.
>
> Now all the criminals in their coats and their ties
> Are free to drink martinis and watch the sun rise
> While Rubin sits like Buddha in a ten-foot cell
> An innocent man in a living hell . . .[5]

Largely through the zeal of advertising executive George Lois, The Hurricane Trust Fund was formed, and soon attracted the support of celebrities. Although Dylan was never listed on the fund's letterhead, his song and presence at two benefits gave the Carter-Artis appeal its greatest impetus. George Lois originally had sought Dylan's help while Rolling Thunder was in New Haven. They planned a Madison Square Garden benefit, where a large cast of mostly black stars would support Dylan. When booking problems mounted, Dylan told Lois, "The hell with it. I'll come in with my whole revue!"

The night after the prison concert, "The Night of the Hurricane, I" went to Madison Square Garden, where there were as many notables in the capacity audience as onstage. First came an hour of music from Neuwirth, Blakley, Joni, and the Rolling Thunder Revue Band. Then, for twenty minutes, the Hurricane cause was expounded. Heavyweight Muhammad Ali told the largely white audience: "You've got the connections and the complexion to get the protection." Hurricane, listening to the concert by telephone, said: "I thank you from my heart. I love you all madly." Ali swaggered with his customary feints and punches: "I know you all came here to see me, because Bob Dylan just ain't that big. . . ." John Rockwell, *The Times:* "The Carter people's desire for publicity and the Dylan people's characteristic secretiveness, inspired by the singer himself, have caused some unusual clashes . . . the press rebuffed by one side even as it was being encouraged by the other."

Then followed nearly four hours of performances from Roberta Flack, Richie Havens, Joni and Joan, The Rolling Thunderers, and Dylan. Even *New York* magazine's Nik Cohn, usually cool toward Dylan, was impressed: "Dylan . . . in whiteface . . . vagabond clown. . . . In 10 years, I'd never seen him work with more intensity . . . no poetical postures . . . he rasped and roared, he burned. . . ." During instrumental breaks, "he caromed all over the stage, stomping, rocking, as if even a moment's silence or stillness would cause him to blow sky-high. . . ." The shortened single version of the song, even with one expletive deleted, had already made its mark. The *San Francisco Chronicle:* "One of the most convincing artistic statements of the year . . . will stand with Dylan's greatest work." The *Los Angeles Times* said Dylan had "rekindled his intensity and purpose . . . a return to leadership."

To the song's accompaniment, legal moves quickened. On November 6, the New Jersey Supreme Court announced it would review the appeal. A month later, Carter and Artis withdrew their application for pardon, seeking "complete vindication" in the courts and asking executive clemency pending a new trial. On January 12, 1976, the top Jersey court heard the appeal, and in March unanimously threw out the convictions, saying that a fair trial "was substantially prejudiced" because the prosecution, to bolster the reliability of its two principal witnesses, had failed to disclose evidence. Carter and Artis were freed on bail and promised a new trial.

Meanwhile, plans were afoot for a "Night of the Hurricane, II." First planned for the New Orleans Superdome in December, it was moved to the Houston Astrodome on January 25, 1976. This promised to be the biggest rock benefit ever, with Dylan's troupe joined by Stevie Wonder, Stephen Stills, Ringo Starr, Dr. John, Santana, Shawn Phillips, Isaac Hayes, and others. Because of strange machinations behind the promotion, this superconcert was a curious box-office fiasco, attended by thirty thousand, half as many as expected.

Then came the anticlimax. Just before Christmas, 1976, after the new trial's jurors had listened to seventy-six witnesses for thirty-one days, Carter and Artis were found guilty again. Bello recanted his recantation, avowing that investigator Fred Hogan and *Times* reporter Selwyn Raab had "offered him bribes to recant." Two former defense witnesses also testified that they were not with Carter at the time of the shooting. *Time,* January 3, 1977: "The judge allowed the State to argue that Carter and Artis had killed the three whites in order to avenge the murder six hours earlier of a black tavern owner whose stepson was a friend of Carter's." The new defense lawyer replied that such tactics were "a racial horror that feeds on the basest, most dirty part of all of us." Carter and Artis were led back to jail on December 21, 1976. On February 9, 1977, Carter received two consecutive and one concurrent life terms. Artis received three concurrent life terms.

The Hurricane Fund had broadened its slogan to "Freedom for All, Forever," and there were shifts in its leadership. Dylan's song continued to be played widely, rising to the Top Forty. The eyewitness named in the song, Patty Valentine, brought a suit against Dylan, Levy, Columbia Records, and Warner Bros. Publishing, charging them with invasion of privacy and with presenting her "in an unfavorable light." The suit asked for a "fair and equitable share" of all money earned from the song. Ed Silvers, president of Warner Bros. Publishing, described it as "a crank litigation." The melody and the malady that inspired "Hurricane" linger on. Even if Carter and Artis should ever win their freedom on appeal, "it won't be over till they clear his name/And give him the time he's done."[6]

In November 1985, Hurricane Carter was released on bail from Rahway State Prison. Federal Judge Lee Sarokin cited "grave constitutional violations" by prosecutors. He ruled that the 1976 convictions had been based on "an appeal to racism rather than reason, concealment rather than disclosure." But Carter's nineteen-year ordeal may not be over because a third trial might be sought by the prosecution.

THE WHITE GODDESS, DESIRE

Another word in the Dylan lexicon is *desire,* which he had invoked as early as 1964. In the eleventh of his "Outlined Epitaphs," he declared that after the storm, under a sky "constantly meanin' change," he would welcome Desire:

> *an' after it's desire*
> *returnin'*
> *returnin' with me underneath*
> *returnin' with it*
> *never fearful*
> *finally faithful*
> *it will guide me well ...*
> *never failin' ...*[7]

The album named *Desire,* released in January 1976, was an eclectic musical statement, a marriage of legendary themes and contemporary meaning. The new album initially struck me as spare, almost rudimentary. Yet beneath its simple surfaces, *Desire* has proved alive and deep, the culmination of the trilogy that began with *Planet Waves.* In some ways, this album is the real self-portrait. I began a dogged search for clues and allusions that became my voyage through the wild and unknown country of myths and dreams that have lured Dylan.

Desire was the name of a New Orleans streetcar and a western that starred Marlene Dietrich. But many poets have been lured by Desire. To Blake, it was man's ladder to the stars. In "The Question Answer'd," Blake made gratification of Desire the pivotal human impulse. Eliot's "Four Quartets" orchestrated themes that also intrigue Dylan—time, justice, roles, rebirth, redemption, and desire. Eliot wrote of "the inner freedom for the practical desire" and concluded that "only through time time is conquered. . . ." Blake illuminated his manuscripts. Eliot used footnotes. Dylan plays his cards more slyly. His brief liner notes and carefully positioned visual symbols on album jacket and songbook use the symbolism of tarot cards. Other clues lead to Robert Graves's *The White Goddess,* a complex *Historical Grammar of Poetic Myth.* Graves showed how the patriarchal structure of Judeo-Christian religion attempted to erase the ancient worship of the Goddess. Graves also maintained that Desire was crucial to poetry: "Poetry is rooted in love and love in desire, and desire in hope of continued existence." Graves advised the poet to "achieve social and spiritual independence at whatever cost," for the poet must "learn to think mythically as well as rationally. . . ."

Dylan had been "thinking mythically" since he was a boy at the movies. *Desire,* however, is a giant step forward in the breadth of his mythological thinking, moving toward a summation of themes that have long absorbed him: apocalypse, personal or societal; identity; the hero's quest for love, knowledge, redemption, liberation. He deals here with manifold myths— of justice and the outsider ("Hurricane" and "Joey"), of the woman who suffers love and offers renewal ("Isis" and "Oh, Sister"); and of life as a movie ("Romance in Durango" and "Black Diamond Bay"). Dylan has shuffled his tarot cards like a diviner, melded his old preoccupations with new, made the Egyptian oracular island of Pharos as contemporary as a TV show.

Two keynotes of the album lie in the lyrics of "Oh, Sister": "We died and were reborn and then Mysteriously saved" and "Time is an ocean but it ends at the shore./You may not see me/Tomorrow."[8] Death and rebirth, and time lost, stolen, or threatened, are the Faustian questions of the alchemist who seeks spiritual perfection and redemption. Let's try to "lift the veil of Isis": The Empress tarot card on the album jacket and two other cards displayed in the song folio, the Magician and Judgment, are from the so-called Rider pack of 1910, traditional emblems redesigned by A. E. Waite and drawn by Pamela Colman Smith. Waite wrote that the Empress, "the fruitful mother of thousands . . . has been correctly described as desired and the wings thereof. . . ." Alfred Douglas, a contemporary Jungian, wrote in *The Tarot* (1973) that the Empress symbolizes an earth-mother, "descendant of Demeter and Ishtar [the most popular Assyro-Babylonian goddess], patronesses of mystery cults . . . at which the sacred dramas of death and the renewal of life were played out." The tarot cards have positive and negative meanings. If upright, the Empress symbolizes growth; if reversed, domestic upheaval, psychic alienation, and poverty. Few myths are more pervasive than the search for the conquest of death. The Egyptian example of Isis and Osiris is invoked in the song "Isis," but resonates throughout the album.

Isis, one incarnation of the Empress, was a mother goddess, patroness of navigation, the sorrowing wife whose tears formed the Nile. She was also the redeemer whose magic mysteriously reconstituted and revived the body of her slain husband-brother, Osiris. A moon goddess identified by her heifer horns, Isis also instituted marriage. Osiris anointed her as queen of Egypt, leaving her to rule while he rambled throughout Asia to conquer without violence, disarming strange people with his gentleness, his songs, and his music-making. In Egyptian mythology, Osiris has scores of names and incarnations. One was Proteus, the oracular Old Man of the Sea, priest-king of the Pharos, gifted with the power to change his shape. Proteus, Graves tells us, married Sarah, the goddess mother of the tribe of Abraham that visited Egypt near the end of the Third Millennium. (Dylan joked on his Rolling Thunder tour of gentle conquest that "Sara" was not necessarily about his wife, perhaps about the biblical Sarah.) Pharos lore also invested the number five with magic powers, affecting festivals, architecture, even the calendar. Dylan opens "Isis" with a line about the fifth month of the year: "I married Isis on the fifth day of May,"[9] then tells a wondrous tale of a strange quest through ice-clad pyramids. But in the denouement, the poet's laconic return to the "mystical child," Isis is stranger still.

In *The White Goddess,* Graves finds the Isis-Osiris story deeply imbedded in many cultures: ". . . the sacred king as the moon-goddess's divine victim; holding that every muse-poet must, in a sense, die for the goddess whom he adores, just as the king died. . . ." Isis, sister and wife of Osiris, reconciles opposites in a "divine unity." Such relationships exist in the Finnish epic, "Kalevala," and in Scottish ballads like "The Bobby Hind" and "Sheath and Knife." Dylan had long been searching for his ideal "twin," which heightens the sister image. Baez only confused the allusiveness when she asked in her "O Brother" how *she* came to be his sister.

In "Baby Blue," Dylan had already shown awareness of the Jungian doctrine of synchronicity: "Take what you have gathered from coincidence."[10] It is scarcely coincidence that he placed on the song folio's contents page a reproduction of the 1910 tarot design of the Magician, which bears an uncanny resemblance to Dylan. The Magician card has also been called the Minstrel, the Conjurer, or the Cobbler. It once represented the traveling showman, a medicine man who told fortunes, sold quack remedies, and spread heretical ideas. Tarot expert Douglas's description of the Magician reveals a startling dual portrait of Dylan: "Half mountebank and half wise man. . . . The Magician is forceful and self-confident, and stands alone." He is related to Prometheus, Till Eulenspiegel, Hermes, or Coyote, the Indian folk hero. Douglas thought the Magician-Prometheus figure referred to the time "when man first attained self-consciousness, 'stealing' it from the unconscious." He thus takes divine attributes, "possession of the world, but has lost sight of his soul. . . . The Magician faces perils and temptations . . . on the long quest to rediscover what he has lost. His wand represents his flaming will." Above his head, a figure eight on its side stands for inspiration from "his own true Self, the spark of divinity within him." Upright, the Magician card stands for strong will, personal expansion, taking risks, initiative, adaptability, versatility, diplomacy, and self-confidence. Reversed, Douglas says, the Magician becomes the Juggler, the trickster who conjures with life, delighting to observe the effect his clever sleight of hand has on lesser mortals. Then he is questing for power, not wisdom. He becomes a wizard, "the instrument of those demonic powers he sought to control."

The Judgment card in the folio symbolizes rebirth, resurrection, and redemption, and has been called the card of eternal life. Douglas: "The psyche is released from the walls that imprison it, the Divine Child that rises from the tomb is the regenerated self." To alchemists this meant "the Philosopher's stone." The rising Divine Child on the Blakean Judgment card is considered "the god within," the goal of the heroic quest. That search is nearing fulfillment, and elements of the psyche have "reached full integration and are being reborn."

In a brief album-jacket poem, Dylan drops more clues. He is "On the heels of Rimbaud moving like a dancing bullet."[11] Cryptically, he writes: "Tolstoy was right."[12] In *Resurrection,* his great novel of 1899, Tolstoy advanced his belief in redemption through love. *Resurrection* is a scathing indictment of modern society in general, and the institutions of justice and the church in particular. The protagonist, Nekhlyudov, Tolstoy's alter ego, is driven by "a desire to elevate himself by joining forces with those who are most lowly." He follows a victimized prostitute to Siberia in his search for personal redemption. According to Troyat, Tolstoy's biographer: "It is not sentiment that gives rhythm and warmth to this couple's story but the denunciation of social injustice and the search for a remedy that will cure mankind's ills."

Dylan's search for redemption stretches back to *Blonde* and *John Wesley Harding.* In everyday language, redemption means deliverance, reclamation, or salvation; in Christian terms, it is deliverance through Christ's atonement. In his 1936 essay, "Ideas of Redemption in Alchemy," Jung declared: "After the resurrection man becomes stronger and younger than he was before"—echoed in Dylan's famous line, "I'm younger than that now."[13] Jung tied the alchemist's search to the Messianic element of Hebrew prophecy, and to the myth cycles of Osiris, Orpheus, Dionysus, and Hercules, who all died and were mysteriously saved or redeemed. Jung found the epitome of artistic alchemical thinking in Goethe's *Faust.* What would Jung have made of Dylan's "chain with the devil" from his early Hibbing days until his redemption through love and through battling social injustice? Dylan's long search for redemption through alchemical identification with mythic characters culminates in *Desire.*

He refers to "the songs of redemption," which Ginsberg's notes to *Desire* take as a title. Ginsberg's essay recalls that he and fellow 1950s beats dreamed of a quest for liberation, and of the marriage of poetry to music. He described *Desire* as "another great surge of prophetic feeling,"[14] hearing Hebraic cantillation in "One More Cup of Coffee." I hear Tex-Mex and *ranchero* music, and the mélange of flamenco and soul that Otis Redding and others explored and Van Morrison developed.

Another response to *Desire* came from W. T. Lhamon, Jr., in *The New Republic:* "... a State of the Disunion Message ... by a man of great power, if indirect, and greater integrity, certainly, than most of the people addressing us this year." John Rockwell said in *The Times:* "... some of the most wonderful music Dylan has ever made." Dave Marsh, in *Rolling Stone,* saw an important change in Dylan's attitude toward women. Jack McDonough has written that Dylan's "best poetry comes when ... modern fright and confusion and romantic questing for secret, elusive beauty meet...."

Dylan's melodic resources have full sway, from the declamatory, rallying verse of "Hurricane" to the playful tune of "Mozambique," from the keening of "Sara" to the otherworldly cast of "Valley Below." "Hurricane," the album's first track and best-known song, sets tone and texture, tolling again those freedom chimes, previewing some of the album's major themes. The Isis-Osiris relationship in "Isis," "Oh, Sister," and "Sara" continues *Desire*'s implicit struggle—against false "justice," against false love, against false labeling. Ginsberg calls them "cameo novels." Dylan's dramatic-cinematic vision was never stronger. In "Romance in Durango," with a simple chorus in Spanish, he establishes a sense of place, as he evokes palpable spacelessness in "Isis." "Durango" and "Valley Below" are of a piece, Brando-Eastwood-Dylan scripts for the man on the run.

"Joey" came in for stern criticism, which missed the point of Dylan's long fascination with the social pariah, the outsider, and the badman. Dylan can step aside and savor Joey Gallo's Cagney-like panache, reminding us that all the world's not only a stage but a screen as well. Gallo simmered up on the very streets of Little Italy that Dylan scuffed along. On the West Coast, Dylan had befriended Robert De Niro, another son of New York's mean streets. Although Gallo had read Nietzsche in stir, Dylan was probably more impressed with Gallo's being "Always on the outside/Of whatever side there was."[15] In jail, he was closest to black men:

> *'Cause they seemed to understand*
> *What it's like to be in society*
> *With a shackle on your hand ...*[16]

For all the mythical thinking on *Desire,* Dylan's old whimsy is not subdued. In "Isis," the stranger dies and the narrator hopes it isn't contagious.

After endless travail and searching, the narrator is reunited with Isis. The Hemingwayesque understatement of their colloquy borders on burlesque. More whimsy surfaces in the "Black Diamond Bay" scenario, where life is again reflected in a card game. Dylan has always loved the shaggy-dog story and the confrontations of the poker game. (Baudelaire, in "Spleen," locked the Jack of Hearts and Queen of Spades in dialogue.) All the bizarre things that happen in "Black Diamond Bay" suddenly appear through a different lens when the perspective shifts in the last verse. The song's minutely observed action is instantly reduced to a news item the narrator glimpses as he idly watches TV in L.A. Are we all global village idiots whom television has reduced to voyeurism, or has television so deadened us to catastrophe that we can't tell a real crisis from a fictional one?

Finally, in "Sara," Dylan *seems* to be making an unabashed confessional to his wife. A plea for forgiveness and understanding, its open nostalgia stands out joltingly among Dylan's many covert, ambiguous games. After all his charades, his theatrical masks, and hide-and-seek games, he *seems* to say that this "Scorpio Sphinx," this "mystical wife"[17] has an actual, as well as a mythical, identity. She is Desire incarnate. The melody and vocalizing are pained. This track became the album's most controversial. Some heard it heralding a "new Dylan" ready to stand naked, and some were just plain embarrassed by "too personal a tale."[18] Some found it riddled with banalities easy to parody, while others were touched by his naming his "Sad-Eyed Lady." On *Biograph,* Dylan declares: "I don't write confessional songs." But how can he say it in the face of "Sara" and "Abandoned Love," a "confessional song" left off *Desire?*

Desire is dominated by women deities and women colleagues. Scarlet Rivera's violin is a genuinely innovative sound, blending melancholy and exoticism. Emmylou Harris's harmony is also an important new element. (She was on the first version of "Hurricane," but Ronee Blakley sings harmony on the released version.) The women's voices against Dylan's are another experiment in texture. Although Harris is a perfectionist about intonation and polish, she acceded to Dylan's imperatives of spontaneity and urgency. Some rough-and-ready cuts were released. There is fine instrumental support from six others, most of whom were with the Rolling Thunder Revue. A very cohesive ensemble sound dominates.

Desire was unique in the presence of Jacques Levy as co-lyricist on all tracks except "Sara" and "Valley Below." Levy, a Ph.D. in psychology, is well imbued with Jungian thinking. He's also a theatrical handyman, director of "Oh, Calcutta," and a seasoned lyricist. He and Dylan met through Roger McGuinn, who had worked with Levy back in 1968 on a country-and-western musical. The two put together two dozen songs in three weeks, sixteen of which were recorded on McGuinn/Byrds albums, the best known being "Chestnut Mare." Dylan met Rambling Jacques on Bleecker Street after Tour '74. A year later, after another chance Bleecker Street encounter, Bob suggested they try to "write some stuff together."

Dylan had a verse of "Isis" already written. Laughing and rapping, they worked through the night on it. At more meetings in July, things progressed so well that they went out to a Long Island retreat for three weeks in August to bang out more lyrics together, for reportedly fourteen songs. Levy suggested Joey Gallo as a theme, for he had known Gallo well during 1969, the last year of his life. Levy said that Dylan dreamed up "Valley Below" while living with gypsies in Corsica. And "Sara" had long been on his mind. He also turned to Levy for ideas for Rolling Thunder. McGuinn has attested that Levy's encouraging manner and style bring out the best in his partners.

Before arriving at his final *Desire* team, Dylan experimented with Eric Clapton, Kokomo, and the Dave Mason Band, looking for a compatible combination. Then he ran into a Lower East Side bar band, Rob Stoner and The Rebels, with whom Mick Ronson often sat in. Here Dylan found sidemen for the Rolling Thunder Band and for the final *Desire* sessions. Some of the songs' aura of search and struggle went into finding the musicians, as the credit on the album slyly attests: "This record could have been produced by Don DeVito."

An English critic, Simon Frith, summarized Dylan's role: "When people dream about Dylan—and most people do—they dream of him not as a lover but as a friend. If one of his skills has been to make his private concerns public, without being mawkish or self-concerned, another has been to let us make his public world, all the songs, private, relevant to our individual concerns. . . . Dylan sounds like a nice guy again. Someone to talk to—about the world and about ourselves."

DISTANT THUNDER

Primarily to raise money to produce the film *Renaldo and Clara,* a second segment of Rolling Thunder was added in 1976. What I call Distant Thunder was more muted than the Northeastern tour, because the novelty and the gaze of the major media had left.

After the Night of the Hurricane II at the Houston Astrodome (January 25, 1976) there was a break. The tour resumed on April 18 at the Lakeland (Florida) Civic Center, first of eight concerts during the Easter college break. By then, the backing group was calling itself Guam. They opened with a dozen songs, followed generally by Dylan doing two acoustic selections, then a set backed by Guam. McGuinn and Baez had solo stints, then Bob and Joan sang together, ending with ten or so songs from Dylan/Guam.

At the Belleview Biltmore Hotel in Clearwater, Florida, Burt Sugarman, producer of many of the shows for NBC-TV's *The Midnight Special,* videotaped the concert. A few weeks later, Dylan rejected the tape. Instead, he gave his nod to a group of documentary-makers called Top Value Television. For their show, they filmed the May 23 concert at Hughes Stadium, at Fort Collins, Colorado. The filmed footage was broadcast on NBC-TV on September 10. That day also saw the live *Hard Rain* album released, with additional tapes from the Tarrant County Convention Center, Fort Worth, Texas.

The TV show was appropriately under raining, cloudy skies. Bob looked very tense, and what Joan later called "his viper eyes" were darting around a lot. It came to be called "an anti-special," with most mainstream TV critics panning it, as "painfuly artless," "a mess ... a debacle." The underground *Boston Phoenix* called it "perhaps the most extraordinary and moving film of a concert ever made." Between Florida and Fort Collins, Rolling Thunder played Mobile, Hattiesburg, three cities in Texas, and Oklahoma City. The second part of Rolling Thunder ended, after a concert in Wichita, on May 25 in Salt Lake City.

Warming up for what was to become his most sustained period of visibility in the American press, Dylan provided a cover story for the most widely circulated magazine in the United States, *TV Guide,* on September 11. He ducked questions about Jimmy Carter, praising instead Jefferson and Ben Franklin. Since the credits of the show thanked, among others, Herman Melville and Rimbaud, Dylan explained his debts to them and to Conrad, Joyce, and Ginsberg. Asked how he imagined God, Bob replied: " 'I can see God in a daisy ... in the wind and rain. I see creation just about everywhere. The highest form of song is prayer....' " (The daisy line pre-echoes his final song on *Shot of Love,* from Blake's "Auguries of Innocence": "To see a World in a Grain of Sand/And a Heaven in a Wild Flower.") Dylan had praise for The Beatles and The Stones. " 'And Joan Baez means more to me than 100 of these singers around today.' "

Back in L.A., Dylan began editing *Renaldo and Clara.* He finished a new song, "Sign Language," which Eric Clapton taped in September, for his album *No Reason to Cry.* Phil Spector finally talked Dylan into a studio, to join backup singers on the song by Leonard Cohen and Spector, "Don't Go Home With Your Hard-on."

Thanksgiving Day, 1976, was chosen as the day The Band would say farewell to touring, at San Francisco's Winterland Palace. The rising director Martin Scorsese decided to direct a major film of the event, which also spawned a boxed, three-LP set.

Some of The Band had followed Bob from Big Pink to Malibu, where Robbie had a house called Shangri-La. To close out their sixteen years of hard traveling, they planned perhaps their greatest performance. With a three-hundred-page shooting script, the director had a forty-five-member crew running seven cameras on the thirty-seven programmed songs.

The guest roster included Dr. John, Joni Mitchell, Neil Diamond, Van Morrison, Neil Young, and Dylan. For visual opulence, Bill Graham rented sets from the San Francisco Opera's *La Traviata.* The five thousand listeners not only heard a great concert but also consumed two hundred

turkeys and three hundred pounds of salmon. The Berkeley Promenade
Orchestra provided the waltzes, foreshadowing the New Romantics by ten
years. Ronnie Hawkins, who had organized them as The Crackers in 1960,
was there, and so were Bobby Charles, Paul Butterfield, Muddy Waters,
and Eric Clapton.

Emmett Grogan was the emcee for The Last Waltz. He brought on
some Coast poets at intermission: Sweet William, Leonore Kandel, Michael McClure, Diane di Prima, and the dean, Larry Ferlinghetti. Robbie
Robertson had only finished the signature tune, "The Last Waltz," that
morning. He brought "one more friend." Dylan plugged in for "Baby, Let
Me Follow You Down." Grogan said Dylan was hamming it up in a
high-crowned white hat, "swaggered his lyrics" in "Hazel," "I Don't Believe You," "Forever Young," and then repeated his opener.

He remained stage center for the grand finale of "I Shall Be Released,"
with even more stars, Ringo Starr and Ronnie Wood, joining in the jam.
Scorsese, who had been on the crew of the *Woodstock* film, managed to
make the film retain a dignity rare in rock. Wrote Terry Curtis Fox in
The Village Voice: "While ostensibly . . . about The Band, Scorsese's editing makes no bones about how much a Dylan event it became. . . . Everything else disappears behind his presence. Scorsese . . . does nothing to hide
or minimalize this effect. It is not merely the best rock-concert movie ever
made; it is as intensely personal as anything Scorsese has done."

RENALDO AND CLARA

Another film director spent most of 1977 on a film about aspects of the
music life that was to be even more personal. Dylan helped edit down
240,000 feet—some 100 hours—for his film, *Renaldo and Clara.* The finished film, running nearly four hours, became a candidate for commercial
suicide. It was a complex, often noncommunicative film that was triumphant musically but a dramatic failure.

Not since *Self Portrait* were critics able to have such a field day in turning the finger-pointing toward the finger-pointer. Dylan was most hurt by
the reaction from his old neighborhood paper, *The Village Voice.* "Did you
see the firing squad of critics they sent?" he asked me in summer 1978.

The Voice published seven reviews on January 30, 1978. Karen Durbin
called it "The coup de grâce in his de-adulation campaign," resenting his
comparisons of himself to Jesus. Referring to confused scenes among
Dylan, Baez, and Sara, she wrote: "Dylan could love no one like he loves
himself." Richard Goldstein, like most, preferred concert scenes to the
"clumsily improvised 'fictional' interludes." But he found ultimate balance, finding moments "in Altman almost as insufferable, and moments
[here] as moving as anything you're likely to experience in a rock-concert
film."

James Walcott said the film sank so many reputations, "it's like watch-

ing the defeat of the Spanish Armada," and considered it the spiteful revenge of "an artist on his groupies." That tough professional, Pauline
Kael, in *The New Yorker,* said that "despite all his masks and camouflage,"
he's "still the same surly, mystic tease . . . more tight close-ups than any
actor can have had in the whole history of movies. He's overpoweringly
present, yet he is never in direct contact with us . . . we are invited to stare
. . . to perceive the mystery of his elusiveness—his distance."

Reaction in Europe was generally more favorable. Dylan courted trouble
with the extensive interviews he did in the autumn and winter of 1977–78.
"I talked too much about that film," Dylan told me later, but he said it
was necessary to minimize advertising costs.

The film was very much a one-man operation. Dylan not only directed
but also wrote and starred in it. His Lombard Films made the work, and
his own Minneapolis-based Circuit Films, in association with his brother,
distributed it. Because the film was flawed, and because of years of Dylan's
self-righteousness toward human flaws, it provided the ideal time for many
to hit him back.

In a long interview with Jonathon Cott, who compared Dylan to Luis
Buñuel, Dylan waxed lyrical and recondite with such Gallic verbal castles
as: "Art is the perpetual motion of illusion. The highest purpose of art is
to inspire." He made it clear that he regarded the film as being about
"identity" in which "the mask is more important than the face . . . is about
naked alienation of the inner self against the outer self." Dylan defended
the work's integrity: "being faithful to the subconscious." He counterat-
tacked in advance: "We may be kicked right out of Hollywood after this
film is released. In India, they show 12-hour movies. Americans . . . expect
art to be like wallpaper with no effort. . . . I'm sure of my dream self. I live
in my dreams. I don't live in the actual world."

More variation on these themes to *Playboy* and *The New York Times.* To
Maclean's magazine, Toronto, he said: " 'There's no way I should or could
explain the movie . . . but I can't explain "Desolation Row" either. . . .
Sara and Joan Baez were the same woman . . . it's like a cubist painting. . . .
Maybe there are only two or three people in the universe who are going to
understand what it's about.' "

A two-hour version, which I never saw, brought forward the excellent
concert footage. In the full version, there were forty-seven songs on the
soundtrack, twenty-two by Dylan and one each by Beethoven and Chopin.
Some songs, like "Isis," "One More Cup of Coffee," and "Knockin' on
Heaven's Door," are nothing less than classic. Tracks by Ronee Blakley,
Baez, McGuinn, and Jack Elliott shine. David Blue reminiscing about
some early Village days over a pinball machine was charming. Street interviews about Hurricane Carter had immediacy. But many dramatic scenes,
especially those involving Dylan, Sara, and Joan, could readily lose the
viewer.

The single most affirmative review I've seen was by Nigel Andrews of *The Financial Times* in September 1978, after the London opening. "... The mysteries exert an authentic fascination. ... I shall go out on a nervous limb and say that 'Renaldo and Clara' is probably the most important film of the year." It sought, he wrote, "to define a new morality, a new religion; a new sense of direction for an age which has lost faith in doctrinal Christianity."

BITCHING

Not all the commentary on the Thunder/Renaldo experience came from the press. Some observations were made by the playwright Sam Shepard, by Joan Baez in song, and by Sara Dylan in a law court.

Shepard was already esteemed as a playwright when he joined the Renaldo crew to write some dialogue. Not much happened there, but in his *Rolling Thunder Logbook,* he had had much, positive and negative, to record. He felt himself "a collaborator in a whirlpool." He meets Dylan, finds him "all blues" and making surrealist talk about French films. When he watched Dylan at the piano playing "Simple Twist of Fate," Shepard was touched: "Here is where it's at. The Master Arsonist. The place is smoking within five minutes. ... This is Dylan's true magic. Leave aside his lyrical genius for a second and just watch this transformation of energy which he carries ... the kind that brings courage and hope and above all brings life pounding into the foreground ... it's no wonder he can rock the nation."

The playwright began to wonder what he was doing there as the film "falls into smithereens" of random energy. "Ideas flying every which way but no play." He succumbs to the "communal giving of spirit energy through music," and sees it as an antidote to the blind adulation of the rock scene. Calling Dylan a "true-life Medicine Man" whose "heroism transcends being a faddist phenomenon. ... Because his very identity is a mystery, he pushes the question of 'who' he is into 'what' he is." Like many others, Sam Shepard found that Dylan raised more questions than answers: "What is this strange, haunted environment he creates on stage, on record, on film, on everything he touches? What world is he drawing from and drawing us all into as a result? It's right there in front of us, but no one can touch it."[19]

In a provocative essay, "Changing Trains," in *The Threepenny Review,* Irene Oppenheim traced the curious pasts of Dylan and Shepard, using Camus's *The Myth of Sisyphus* as a guidepost on the question of how one lives without a knowledge of the meaning of existence. Camus hinted that the only stable component of the known world is an absurdist uncertainty, a dilemma that can be resolved only by one of two responses: either suicide and its metaphorical counterpart, "the deadening of consciousness, or the leap of faith"; or "remaining on that dizzying crest," balanced warily between faith and despair.

The essay found both writers sharing the self-wasting process by canni-balizing themselves for material. Right after Rolling Thunder, Shepard wrote *Suicide in Bb*, about the death and potential rebirth of an artist. The central character is a musician being driven mad by inner voices. Oppen-heim thinks both writers retreated from the crest in life-preserving moves. "Dylan, after a long flirtation, and pushed to the edge by bitter marital problems, has made a leap of faith." Shepard, "mercilessly tortured by his creative demons, has opined, in desperation for a kind of suicide. . . ." By 1984, Shepard was reborn as a writer and an actor, a Hollywood figure of stature.

Joan Baez told me that she was embarrassed by some of the footage that ended up in *Renaldo and Clara,* and yet this didn't basically change her warm feelings toward Dylan. She did a little bit of mimicry of how Bob had called her in Europe at three in the morning and got her approval to let it all go as he chose to. In three songs on her late 1976 album, "Winds of Change," "Time Is Passing Us By," and "Sweeter for Me," she sings some amazingly frank revelations of her feelings toward Dylan.

Sara had already had her say on the failing marriage with Dylan in the divorce action of 1977. How ironic that after the bitter marital strife should come the film, with Sara as another of Bob's dark-haired women. The woman had been so much a part of Dylan's life, of his retreat from stage life to be husband and father, of the shape of some of his work from *John Wesley Harding* to *Street-Legal.* The song "Abandoned Love," released officially on *Biograph* in 1985, speaks volumes about what I can only inter-pret as Dylan's deepest feelings of the time. By 1978, getting so deep into opening up for the press to push *Renaldo and Clara,* he opened up about marriage:

"Marriage was a failure. Husband and wife was a failure, but father and mother wasn't a failure. I wasn't a very good husband. . . . I don't know what a good husband is. I was good in some ways . . . and not so good in other ways. But I feel my true family relationship is up ahead of me some-where. I'd try again. Yeah, I like comin' home to the same woman. . . . If you fail at one job, and you pick up another job, which you like more, well then you can't consider what happened a failure. There aren't really any mistakes in life. They might seem to knock you out of proportion at the time, but if you have the courage and the ability and the confidence to go on, well, then . . . you can't look at it as a failure, you just have to look at it as a blessing in a way. . . ." He said that no one in his family gets di-vorced and that he "figured it would last forever. . . . Most people . . . keep some contact, which is great for the kids. But in my case, I first got really married, and then got really divorced. I believe in marriage. I know I don't believe in open marriage. Sexual freedom just leads to other kinds of free-dom. I think there should be a sanction against divorce. Why should peo-ple be allowed to get married and divorced so easily? . . . People fall in love with a person's body, with who they know, with the way they dress, with their scorecards. With everything but their real selves, which is what you need to love if you're to be happy together.

". . . I became disillusioned about finding 'the right girl'—or the right anything, for that matter. Women are sentimental. They get into that romantic thing more easily. But I see that as a prelude. Women use romance and passion to sweeten you up. A man is no more than a victim of that passion. You give me a woman that can cook and sew and I'll take that over passion any day. I'd like to find a mate. But I can't spend any time with a woman if we're not friends. If we're not friends, I don't want to get involved on a personal level."

How costly the marriage was emotionally comes through in the albums. How costly it was to prove financially became visible when Sara retained Marvin Mitchelson, the flamboyant Hollywood lawyer. He had been a specialist in representing the wives of movie stars, or their girlfriends, like that of Groucho Marx, and the famous "palimony" case against Lee Marvin. The lawyer then turned to rock stars' wives.

On March 1, 1977, Sara's divorce petition was filed in Superior Court in Santa Monica. She sought permanent custody of Maria, 15 (by her marriage to Victor Lownes), and her children by Dylan: Jesse, 11; Anna, 9; Samuel, 8; and Jacob, 6. She also sought child support, alimony, and court-supervised disposition of the couple's community property. Assets involved included real estate in four states, plus Dylan's holdings in publishing companies, recordings, and literary copyrights.

Dylan's lawyers won a ruling to have certain legal documents closed to the public. But the British press, perhaps tipped off by Mitchelson, who certainly likes publicity, made page-one news of the family squabbles. Must I record it here for posterity? Do you really want to know the personal details of an argument they had here or there, or of some hysterics on Sara's part, or who slapped whom? Anyone who has endured the breakup of a long relationship will know it is rarely serene.

Sara was granted temporary custody of the children and exclusive use of the Malibu house. The size of the settlement was among the documents hidden under the court's apron. But Mitchelson soon after was bruiting about a ten-million-dollar case he had recently won, and it was obvious that this was the case. In the opinion of some observers, Mitchelson's slice probably was between two and four million dollars.

Although use of the Malibu house reverted to Dylan, it was really more of a house than a home. The famed beach colony of the stars was known for the privacy it once afforded its residents, but as its glamour spiraled, it too became increasingly more of a fishbowl. It was there that F. Scott Fitzgerald once wrote in a cottage and came up with the French pun: "Honi soit qui Malibu." As the rock aristocracy succeeded the celluloid pantheon, Johnny Rivers took over the house where Greta Garbo once tried to be alone. In nearby Bel Air, the chief Beach Boy, Brian Wilson, lived in a spread that Tarzan profits had created for Edgar Rice Burroughs. Among the other rock stars who made Malibu their home were Neil Diamond, Linda Ronstadt, Mick Jagger, and Robbie Robertson.

Before the split, the Dylans had bought a relatively modest home on the Point Dome promontory from a *Los Angeles Times* columnist, on a three-acre site. In 1975, architect David Tobin undertook the remodeling, on which Dylan eventually spent more than two million dollars. Tobin said he "had to keep a straight face when Bob told him he wanted a living room he could ride a horse through." Neighbors took to calling it Dylan's Taj Mahal, because it was crowned with a huge onion-shaped copper dome, which cost sixteen thousand dollars.

There were frequent disagreements about the designs, and much revision work was done. Bob and Sara moved in in late 1976. One designer on the project called it "an eclectic version of an East Coast stick and shingle house, basically American Victorian and Mediterranean. Inside it's pure New Mexico." Some neighbors were intrigued by the large outdoor polymorphous pool, and took to calling it a lake. It was heated and nestled among boulders and shrubbery. If Bob had really wanted to keep it all quiet, he never should have done an interview with a woman reporter from *The Chicago Daily News* at the poolside.

More land was acquired for the old homestead, until the site could hold twenty houses. The construction team lived in wigwams while the work proceeded. There were many specially crafted items, like tiled floors made in kilns on the spot. In front of the huge fireplace was a twenty-foot whale in inlaid tile.

The designer said that in fifty to one hundred years, the house, "simply the nicest in Malibu, could be a historic landmark." As lavish as it was, the Malibu colony had homes that were bigger and more expensive. Dylan's comment: "One hundred years from now, I won't be judged for the house." Remarked *Time* magazine drily: "He is probably correct. One local geologist believes the mansion is already slipping into the ocean."

By the end of 1977, his family life in tatters, with various battles between Dylan and Sara over the children still unresolved, Dylan seemed at low ebb. He was about to launch a film he anticipated would be demolished by most critics, although he nourished the hope that the audience would still support it. He made plans to undertake a world tour and another recording. It was the beginning of the end of another phase, another life, another career. With the American audience's backlash at *Renaldo and Clara,* and with the rest of the world still enthusiastic about him, it looked as if, once more, there was, for this man, no direction home.

CODA

BUSY BEING BORN AGAIN

"He drew me up from the desolate pit,
    out of the miry bog,
and set my feet upon a rock,
    making my steps secure.
He put a new song in my mouth,
    a song of praise of our God.
Many will see and fear,
    and put their trust in the Lord."

—PSALMS 40:2–3

"For we are made a spectacle unto
the world, and to angels, and to man.
We are fools for Christ's sake."

—I CORINTHIANS IV: 9–10

"A portrait can never be finished;
it can only be abandoned."

—VARIOUSLY ATTRIBUTED TO CÉZANNE,
    FLAUBERT, AND GIACOMETTI

While Dylan scaled new heights around the world in 1978, he began to reach new depths with the American audience. In one year he played to 115 audiences in 10 countries, but encountered resistance only in his native land. As usual, some grumbles were to be heard everywhere: His look and new band suggested "the route to Las Vegas," the new album, *Street-Legal,* sharply divided opinions. And someone's catchphrase, "the alimony tour," was picked up pervasively. No matter how it tapered off in America as Dylan played while fighting a virus, the year still seemed a strong expression of will, stamina, and artistic growth.

By the end of 1977, Dylan had signed on as his business manager Jerry Weintraub of Management III. He had worked with John Denver, Frank Sinatra, Neil Diamond, and Tom Paxton to apparently good effect. Weintraub was known for noninterference, even nonattendance at his clients' concerts. "At the time I got Jerry to manage me, I almost didn't have a friend in the world. We were working on that movie. . . . I was being thrown out of my house. I was under a lot of pressure, so I figured I better get busy working," Dylan said.

Weintraub organized a flying squad of forty sound technicians, security people, and administrators. On the agenda were concerts in Japan, Australia, New Zealand, five countries of Western Europe, and, for the autumn, America and Canada. Dylan had recruited a new eight-piece backing band and a female gospel-style vocal trio, which yielded a radically new sound. They rehearsed seventy songs, many in startlingly new arrangements. When I asked Bob who had done the new charts, he said proudly: "There's nothing that band does that can't be worked out on my guitar. I started recruiting this band in January [1978]. It was difficult, hard. A lot of blood has gone into this band. They understand my songs. It doesn't matter if they understand me, or not."

The chief novelty was the presence of an edgy, mercurial *Blonde on Blonde* texture achieved partially by Steve Douglas on saxophone and flute. David Mansfield's manic mandolin and fiddle playing was a bubbly embellishment. He wanted others as backup singers. Dylan told me: "I was determined I was never gonna have the band sing anymore. It scatters their energy and they don't come up with the hard sound I want, if they also sing." Instead, a vocal trio, Helena Springs, Jo Ann Harris, and Carolyn Dennis, provided the gospel/soul backing voices. Although some saw this as commercialism, they simply weren't conversant with the black music style from which it came.

The troupe began with eleven concerts in Japan on February 20, 1978. In Tokyo and Osaka, more than one hundred thousand attended. Although it is the custom to react with polite restraint in the concert hall, the press reflected excitement. During two of the Tokyo gigs, Dylan recorded the *Live at Budokan* album, originally designed only for the Japanese market. The somewhat sterile sound didn't really reflect what the tour sound was to become, but because of its immaculate pressing, the album quickly became a collector's item. So many in Europe and America were buying *Budokan* at import prices of up to thirty-five dollars, it was decided to remaster it in the West, with some inevitable technical losses.

A dozen well-received Australian and New Zealand concerts followed, with some hints that a 1960s level of passion was being felt on both sides of the footlights. Dylan went into a Santa Monica studio for a week in April to tape *Street-Legal*. With the momentum of the world tour, the album did well around the world, but American critics admonished him to "get a producer."

Street-Legal is one of Dylan's most overtly autobiographical albums, telling of loss, searching, estrangement, and exile. It also clearly foreshadows the Christian conversion ahead, but who among us could perceive it at that time? It is peopled by a group of narrators who are oppressed, wandering, and lonely, traveling in a foreign country of the spirit. The tarot-card imagery of "Changing of the Guard" has confounded some of the shrewdest interpreters, but it is difficult not to ascribe it either to his years with Sara or with The Band, or both. I confess the song is still an enigma to me.

But the album is generally strong on communication, rather than on code. I call attention to two minor gems and a masterwork on the album, which have not fully been appreciated: "New Pony" has a scathing blues riff on which the women's voices drive home the repeated phrase "How much longer?" out of the Bible, yet in a song that seems to be pure sexuality. "Señor (Tales of Yankee Power)" is a strong and rueful political statement that finds American foreign policy confused and unjust. More biblical language is sandwiched in between American folk language with the reference to overturning the tables, from the passages describing Jesus and the money-changers.

I hear many echoes of Robert Johnson, the blues giant, especially on "Is Your Love in Vain?" but also later in the phrase about juice running down a leg. Powerful, raw stuff amid some tenderness in "Baby Stop Crying," "True Love Tends to Forget," and "We Better Talk This Over." I hear some fine Stevie Wonder echoes on the cataloging of "No Time to Think."

But the masterwork is the final song of anguish and prophecy, a song with the sweep of "Like a Rolling Stone," "Where Are You Tonight? (Journey Through Dark Heat)." Here we can discern the move toward Christianity, the foreshadowing of major changes after the hellish personal disorder that the narrator has gone through. This is catharsis and resolution as he steals off into a troubled night with such companions as St. John of the Book of Revelation. There are technical raw spots on the album, but Dylan clearly wanted to tape it red-hot and from the heart, and he had allowed himself only a week to do it before hitting the road again.

Dylan's return to Britain for six concerts at Earls Court, from June 15 to 20, really took the country by storm. The 100,000 tickets sold briskly, and it is not exaggeration to say that the whole town was talking. The method of sale had disturbed some, causing fans in London and some provincial towns to queue all day. Television and newspaper pictures of the weekend queues helped build the anticipation. Dylan's opening-night concert ranks in my memory as one of his greatest, a sentiment echoed in *The Daily Mail* by Ray Connolly, an often cynical commentator, who called it "the greatest concert I have ever seen."

Working with the CBS presswoman Ellie Smith, an American based in London, Dylan cordially greeted the press, by twos and threes, with a kind word for most, unless they happened to break protocol by taking notes on what was said informally. I received the royal summons the second night, and was sitting in the backstage area with Michael Gray and Gabrielle Goodchild, trying to hold a conversation with Jack Nicholson, then in London with Stanley Kubrick for the filming of *The Shining*. We saw Dylan poke his nose into the enclosure, then back away. Later he explained to me: "I saw you there, but it was too emotional a thing to go in there among all those people."

When the three of us went out to chat with Bob, he was standing beside Helena Springs, and he started to tell her about the old days at Folk City and the nearby Troubadour. Clearly sensing the triumph of the evening, Bob asked me whatever happened to the Greenbriar Boys, who had topped the bill with him at Gerde's. Gabrielle got into small talk with Bianca Jagger and Michael was doing his best to say something to his idol, Dylan. The idol indicated he was rushed that night and promised more time with me, so I raced off to find Ellie to make arrangements. Before I did, I told Bob the band was impressive, and asked where he had got them together. "It's about the only thing I have got together now," he said candidly.

The next night, backstage, Dylan was a bit more relaxed, and he told Gabrielle, me, and his old Woodstock friend, Happy Traum, about how England had once been so lavish with honors for Big Bill Broonzy and other black American bluesmen "when they were just working as janitors in the States." Seeing old friends in London after the post-divorce depression and the trashing of *Renaldo and Clara* by the American critics seemed to bring Bob great joy and relief. He suggested another night for supper and an interview, since he had to talk to a reporter from *L'Express,* Paris, which had a cover story planned.

We showed up at a smart Knightsbridge restaurant, San Lorenzo, where the concert promoter, Harvey Goldsmith, was hosting the crew and local staff with a dinner after the final concert. Gabrielle and I got there early, and I sized up the room. "I think he'll probably want to sit in a corner where he can watch the door," I remarked. A few minutes later, Bob walked in and headed straight for the corner table before he even saw us there. With him were singers from the gospel trio and Shusha, the Iranian-born singer-songwriter.

Dylan wanted to make it clear he was "subservient to those songs. I'm not out there as a performer underneath a dance team. The writing part is a very lonely experience, but there's strength in that loneliness. But I'm a performer too, and that's an outward thing. One is the opposite of the other, and it makes me crazy sometimes, because I can't write with the energy that I perform with. I can't perform off the energy that I write with. There just has to be time for both."

Bob nibbled at his food and kept working on the bottle of Courvoisier that was near him. He was better at small talk than I could ever remember, but he also wanted to get into the interview. "It's for your book, but you can do whatever you want to with it," he said. I teased him with his famous question, "How does it feel?" Dylan insisted that the ovations and rave reviews were for his work:

"It's not me. It's the songs. I'm just the postman. I deliver the songs. That's all I have in this world are those songs. That's what all the legend, all the myth is about—my songs. I started writing those songs before I could walk. George Harrison told me last night I'd be singing 'It's Alright, Ma' when I'm ninety. Nobody else gives those songs life. It's up to me to do it. . . . But those songs have a life of their own too. Jimi Hendrix sang them . . . Stevie Wonder, Van Morrison, and Elvis Presley have sung them." How did he take the news of Presley's death? "I broke down . . . One of the very few times. I went over my whole life. I went over my whole childhood. I didn't talk to anyone for a week after Elvis died. If it wasn't for Elvis and Hank Williams, I couldn't be doing what I do today."

At the final concert, Bob had told his audience, "I'm thinking about moving up to Liverpool." Would he consider living outside America? He told me about time spent in Corsica and France around *Blood on the Tracks* time, marvelous, haunting times, with and without Sara. Would he seriously consider the expatriate life? "Yes, I would. But creatively, I couldn't live anywhere but America, because I understand the tone behind the language there. I'd love to live somewhere else, but only for a while. I lived in Mexico for three months. I wrote my fourth album in Greece, but that was an American album." He spoke with animation about "two birthdays ago" of a gypsy festival at Stes.-Maries-de-la-Mer, France, with all the flamenco in the air, and the wildness of Corsica. But he always brought the raging beauty back home.

"I feel at home in America," Bob continued, "because, as primitive as it is, I still can create from America. All my feelings come out of America. When you leave, you get peace. America is a very violent place, so when you leave, you get that peace . . . to create. In America, everybody's got a gun. I've got a few of them!" It sounded like Dylan was loading up for some target practice, so I threw up the bull's-eye, the talk about "the alimony tour." Dylan replied: "The myth of the starving artist is just that—a myth!

"I earn everything I make! I'm not getting nothing for nothing. Reggie Jackson of the New York Yankees gets three million dollars a year, for striking out! For every dollar I make, there's a pool of sweat on the floor. I feel we are all underpaid—my band, my singers. I put in an eight-hour day in two hours onstage." Mentioning a few of the other rock veterans "who had come through," Dylan declared: "It's a question of how much of it you can stand. How much can you stick it out?"

Was he any more comfortable now being called a poet. "Very much so. I consider myself a poet first and a musician second." (In his first American interview of the autumn 1978 tour, he told a reporter: "I'm a musician first and a poet second.") Bob went on: "I live like a poet and I'll die like a poet. I've always liked my stuff. All you really have to please is yourself in any arena of life." I asked him if he were able to relax on the tour, and he downed another shot of Courvoisier. He had been going up each day to a pool in North London for a swim, and was not recognized there.

By July 15, Dylan had sung to more than 800,000 people in 50 concerts. The Continental leg of the 1978 tour took him to The Netherlands, West Germany, France, and Sweden.

Still, I saw some tension, some turbulence I couldn't identify under the surface. I urged him to expand on something he'd been saying for the past year or so: "No man can fight another like the man who fights himself. Who could be a stronger enemy?"

"It's true," Bob said, "that a man is his own worst enemy, just as he is his own best friend. If you deal with the enemy within, then no enemy without can stand a chance." What was his enemy within? "Suspicion," he replied, as if he could answer all those allegations of paranoia in one word. Could he put his finger on the enemy within? Dylan laughed at my question. He pointed his index finger toward his heart. Cautiously, he continued: "It's all in those two verses of that last song." He directed me toward the mortal battle with his alter ego in "Where Are You Tonight?"

Typical of his ambiguity, the twin Dylans have so many paired faces: the Gemini polarities of strength versus weakness, kindness versus cruelty, optimism versus pessimism, life versus death, suspicion versus friendliness. It has been said by psychologists in the 1980s that the forward motion of creative people uses wide mood changes as its motor. This dialectic of internal contradiction was really a pair of matched twins locked in struggle. If any word alone can be found to characterize the contradictions in Bob Dylan, it would have to be *ambivalence.* If you're not being born, you're dying. The old "vegetation myth" told us that the death of kings fertilizes the soil for future crops, yet the "twin myth" might take that a step further, actually within one artist. Leaving me to ponder this, Dylan was busy being a stage star again, and he was off to the Continent.

The first stop was a folk festival at Feijenood Stadium, Rotterdam, The Netherlands, for an audience of thirty thousand. Afterward, Dylan visited the home of Rembrandt, and then went to Anne Frank's house in Amsterdam. He played two concerts in Dortmund, West Germany, at the Westfalenhalle, and then sang at the Deutschlandhalle in West Berlin. Perhaps the most amazing venue of any tour was on July 1, when he played at the Zeppelinfeld, Nuremburg, West Germany, the huge open stadium where Hitler used to stage some of his most theatrical rallies. A plan to visit a former concentration-camp site in Germany had to be scrapped for lack of time.

He played five concerts at the Pavillon De Paris from July 3 to 8, one concert having been canceled. None of the problems of the 1966 Paris appearances were evident, and he was greeted with highly serious pieces in *Le Monde* and other quality French papers. After a brief interview for Danish TV at Kastrup Airport in Copenhagen, he did a pair of shows at the Scandinavium, Göteborg, Sweden. Along the way, he took in the sights and spent many evenings jamming with Eric Clapton and members of his band.

According to concert producer Harvey Goldsmith, Dylan had originally wanted only three or four large outdoor arenas for the whole European trip, but Harvey had talked him into the six nights at Earls Court. The advance ticket sales were so great that Goldsmith undertook to convert the old Blackbushe Aerodome an hour and a half south of London into a site for an audience of 100,000. When Saturday, July 15, burst fair, a lot of people who hadn't bought tickets decided to spend the day in the country listening to Dylan, Clapton, Joan Armatrading, and others. The official police figure was 200,000, but may have been even 20 percent higher than that. It was described as Britain's largest rock audience of all time, and even made news on American TV that night. Flushed with excitement, Dylan donned a top hat, which he wore throughout his three hours onstage, and sang thirty-three songs in a general mood of euphoria.

As throughout the tour, Dylan was mostly revamping many of his old hits into startling new arrangements. Many were finding new insight into the lyrics when, as in "Tangled Up in Blue," there was new emphasis and shape to songs long since taken for granted. As Russell Davies wrote in *The Sunday Times,* it was the best "creative re-vamping since Duke Ellington stopped coming round with savagely recycled oldies." Blackbushe soon entered the language of the British folk fan, as Woodstock had. It was more than a concert; a community, really.

This mood did not extend to the ambitious North American tour, which began on September 15 at the Augusta (Maine) Civic Center. The Continental triumph seemed a distant echo, and there was still resentment toward *Renaldo and Clara* and *Street-Legal.* But the chief problem in performance impact seemed to be that Dylan was ailing. On September 19, at the Montreal Forum in Quebec, he went onstage when he probably should have been resting in bed. Dylan recalled, in 1985: "The only time I've ever wanted to replay a show was in Montreal, 1978. I had a temperature of one hundred four, and couldn't even stand up. The promoter said, 'You've got to play the show,' and we played the show. And there was a response! You'd think the Pope was there!"

By the end of September, doing two concerts at Madison Square Garden in the same week that Neil Young had played there, *Time* and *The New York Times* critics compared the two. Wrote John Rockwell in *The Times:* "Mr. Young [despite an extremely variable performance] was 'the winner.' But Mr. Dylan's [performance] was downright terrible." He didn't like how Dylan dressed, or spoke and disdained the "fussing" with arrangements in versions that "sound uninteresting and inferior; the overall effect of the set was of a detached cynicism, with arrangements slick and turgid and the singing a petulant shout." America and the rest of the world were out of sync; the great divide was greater than ever. In October, he played twenty-one shows, including Toronto, and ended up in St. Paul, Minnesota. By November 23, he did another fifteen shows, including Vancouver.

During the later part of 1978, Dylan was using a powerful, brooding song no one could put a name to as a warm-up instrumental. It turned out to be "Slow Train Coming," the title track that would proclaim his involvement with Christianity in late 1979. The album was a shocker that made page-one news widely, for Dylan's conversion, and its musical expression, caught nearly everyone by total surprise. Dylan later explained how he had accepted Jesus in 1978 after "a vision and feeling" during which the room he was in actually moved:

"There was a presence in the room that couldn't have been anybody but Jesus," Bob said. Many believe, he continued, "Jesus comes into a person's life only when they are either down and out or are miserable or just old and withering away. That's not the way it was for me. I was doing fine. I had come a long way in that year on the road. I was relatively content, but a close friend of mine mentioned a couple of things to me, and one of them was Jesus. The whole idea of Jesus was foreign to me.... I trusted this person and I called back and said I was willing to listen about Jesus." This led to his visiting a born-again Christian community, The Vineyard Fellowship, not far from his Malibu home.

Dylan asked probing questions. He told a trusted reporter, Robert Hilburn of the *Los Angeles Times*, that he began accepting that "Jesus was real." The pastor of the Fellowship, Ken Gulliksen, said that in spring 1979, Dylan's girlfriend (Mary Alice Artes, an actress, although he didn't name her) attended morning service. She rededicated her life to the Lord, the pastor said, and asked if a couple of pastors might visit Bob. According to *Buzz*,[1] a British Christian monthly, Larry Myers and Paul Edmond went to Dylan's house "and ministered to him. He responded by saying yes, he did, in fact, want Christ in his life and he prayed that day and received the Lord."

Pastor Gulliksen indicated that many he knew had been praying for Dylan, and that when Bob was in Copenhagen, thousands across the road "spent 20 minutes in intercessory prayer for Bob.... So we had nothing to do with it compared with those people who prayed for him for such a long period. I just felt like he was being born and we kind of caught him as he was coming out." According to Gulliksen, Dylan spent five days a week for three and a half months attending his School of Discipleship, "learning the word, growing in the Lord."

Aware that they had sway over an extremely influential public figure, the pastor still denied that they had a hand in banning all secular songs from Dylan's concerts in 1979. *Slow Train Coming* had been taped in Muscle Shoals, Alabama, in May, produced by Jerry Wexler and Barry Beckett, with Mark Knopfler of Dire Straits and others. Background vocals were by Carolyn Dennis, Helena Springs, and Regina Havis. The album was released in August 1979, to wonderment, exclamations, and derision. Even those most reluctant to accept that it was anything more than still another exploration by Dylan—into gospel song—were shocked by its fundamentalist, conservative theology. The scoffers felt that Dylan had also abandoned the progressive, tolerant side of Christianity to espouse an uncompromising, unforgiving sort of gospel stance. Later asked if he was concerned about being lumped together with the ultra–right-wing Bible-thumpers, Dylan spoke about reactionary religions as something "to be careful about.... It's real dangerous. You can find anything you want in the Bible. You can twist it around and a lot of people do that. I just don't think you can legislate morality.... The basic thing, I feel, is to get in touch with Christ yourself. He will lead you. Any preacher who is a real preacher will tell you that: 'Don't follow me, follow Christ.' "

On October 20, 1979, Dylan went on network TV (*Saturday Night Live*) with three gospel songs. Singles released in September and November carried four tracks from the religious album. Perhaps most amazing, when Dylan was again ready to face live audiences, was that he had dropped all his old songs. He did fourteen concerts at the Fox Warfield Theatre in San Francisco that were jeered with requests for his old songs. Twelve more concerts, until December 9, at Santa Monica, San Diego, Tempe and Tucson, Arizona, and Albuquerque, New Mexico, similarly encountered walkouts and derision. In Tempe, he delivered a blast against homosexuality that startled many who knew him as a tolerant person. He seemed, to many, possessed, fuming about Iran and the end of the world. He continued to tour with a small band and singers until February 9, but it was clear that although many enjoyed the excitement and the passion he brought to the music, many more were not at home with the new Dylan.

What was baffling Dylan and some of his staunchest admirers was that he was making great gospel music. Some of the songs on *Slow Train Coming*—notably "Gotta Serve Somebody," "When You Gonna Wake Up," and the title song—were among the most powerful music he'd done since *Desire*. It was simply, I think, that people had trouble accepting the lyrical content from him, no matter how strong the music or performances. "Great gospel, poor Dylan," someone said. "I don't care what his religious beliefs are, but does he have to sing about it?" asked an English fan. Again, Dylan was swimming against the tide, and, I fear, mistaking his role of misunderstood combatant for past similar roles in which he was simply running too far ahead of the consciousness of his audiences. This time they never quite caught up. Until, that is, he was ready to mix the new material with the old and to make a consistent pattern of the whole body of his work.

The religious impetus throughout Dylan's work had been building for years. As early as 1962, in "Long Ago, Far Away," he'd talked about the Crucifixion. As long ago and far away as *The Basement Tapes,* he'd written "Sign on the Cross," indicating how worrying the Christian "question" could be. We've seen the slow buildup of born-again myth, and the equally strong content of Judeo-Christian morality, throughout his work. To believers, for a Jew to turn toward Christianity represents a form of "completion."

But these matters failed to persuade the large body of his old fans. Many felt the religious imagery in his work was even stronger before the conversion than after it, that his own lyrics were more powerful than any New Testament gospel echoes or even paraphrases. Yet, artistically, even if we didn't like the direction, Dylan was moving! He moved into the Muscle Shoals Sound Studio again in late February to work with those same Atlantic Records masters, Jerry Wexler and Barry Beckett, to put down nine tracks for a new album, *Saved.* Released in June 1980, the album continued the deeply religious vein, but there was a softening of the preacher's tone. Rather than spewing hellfire and damnation, this was an album of personal faith and resolution. Some have seen it as a great album musically, with some of the most fascinating modulations (as in "In the Garden" and "Covenant Woman") he'd ever written.

In 1980, it was estimated that there were fifty million American born-again Christians, and there was a believer in the White House. Ironically, Dylan won his first-ever Grammy Award for "Gotta Serve Somebody." When the award was presented on February 27, 1980, Dylan appeared in white-tied formal dinner wear! Sticking resolutely to only the new gospel songs, Dylan gave twelve concerts in April in Toronto, Quebec, Albany, and Buffalo. In May, he did eighteen more shows in seven states. There was still a clamor for the old songs, but he didn't accommodate his audiences until later in the year, when he did nineteen concerts, mostly in San Francisco, but also in the Pacific Northwest.

Explaining later why he had to stay with the songs of his religious vision, Dylan said, "I truly had a born-again experience. . . . I always knew there was a God or a creator of the universe and a creator of the mountains and the sea . . . but I wasn't conscious of Jesus and what that had to do with the supreme creator. I just sat up in bed at seven in the morning and I was compelled to get dressed and drive over to the Bible school. I couldn't believe I was there."

Dylan denied that his Christian experiences were part of a seeking for a religious answer that had taken him to Israel. And he didn't want what he'd been through to be dismissed as an aberration, like the Karma-Cola instant Indian mysticism so many had gone through. "This is no Maharishi trip with me. Jesus is definitely not that to me. When I walk around some of the towns we go to, however, I'm totally convinced people need Jesus. Look at the junkies and the winos and the troubled people. It's all a sickness which can be healed in an instant. The powers that be won't let that happen. The powers that be say it has to be healed politically."

The Vineyard Fellowship was fully aware of what a coup it had scored in winning Dylan. Someone there likened his conversion to that of Roman Emperor Constantine in A.D. 312! Gulliksen: "We did not anticipate his ministry would be so radical, probably the most far-reaching ministry of any of the rock generation people. Dylan is potentially able to reach more people with the Gospel than anybody in our generation because of his history. We strongly encouraged him that he had a platform that no one else had and that he should continue in that position. We told him to be open to God's leading if he felt he should do something else."

For the first time, during 1980, Dylan had among his road crew a padre. Gulliksen said: "Bob asked Pastor Larry Myers to come with the band on the road, so Larry would be there to lead in prayer and Bible study and to minister to him personally. He and Bob became very close and trusted each other. Larry was often the backboard for Bob to share the lyrics."

Part of the healing process between Dylan and his old fans began in the November 1980 concerts at the Fox Warfield Theatre in San Francisco, when about eight of a typical evening's twenty songs were older hits. The audiences began to settle down and even accept the power of the religious songs. It was when he sang "Solid Rock," with its words about the absolutely imperative importance to him of the rock of Jesus, that people began to see the whole Christian matter as an intense work of personal salvation. Dylan denied that he was the broken vessel that needed repairs, of which he sang. Take your choice. Dylan only knows whether it was crisis or culmination that brought him to Jesus.

With a final album in the trilogy, *Shot of Love,* Dylan appeared to have worked through his direct religious expression for the time being. The album was not totally in a gospel vein, but also had secular love songs, a paean to the avant-garde comedian Lenny Bruce, and, in "Every Grain of Sand," a remarkable Blakean wonderment at creation and all its infinite joys and mysteries.* By the time Dylan got to London in late June, he was ready to criticize his record company onstage for hassles over the delayed release of *Shot of Love.* (It apparently wasn't the content, but technical matters, and the masters are frequently rather rough.)

The six concerts set for Earls Court from June 26 to July 1, 1981, indicated that the religious phase of his career had done great damage to his following. Not only wasn't there a comparable stampede for tickets, there was some rather visible apathy. There were rumors that there might be

---

* The Greek-born singer Nana Mouskouri told my associate, Liz Thomson, in London in 1984: "Bob Dylan wrote 'Every Grain of Sand' for me, and I recorded it before he did. I met him in Los Angeles in 1975 or 1976 through mutual friends. He didn't know that I did a lot of his songs in French and German." See *Biograph* notes for a Dylan sermon on this song.

cancellations, but ultimately the tickets sold. Harvey Goldsmith hit back at those who said the series would be a fiasco, and claimed that one hundred thousand tickets sold. Dylan also did two concerts at the Birmingham National Exhibition Center, which were reportedly stronger than his opening night in London. Three nights earlier, Richard Williams in *The Times* offered a preview from the Stades Colombes in Paris, saying that the new mix of old and recent songs should not stir controversy. He found his singing style "a very conscious amalgamation of all the approaches he has ever tried," but found, compared to his youthful rawness, that "these songs now sound denatured and harmless." Except, Williams qualified, the religious songs, which took about one third of his program. The sacred songs "were delivered with a commitment I felt to be missing in the secular compositions."

A reasoned estimation of where Bob Dylan stood was written by Mick Brown in *The Guardian*. He found that in the light of the Christian revivalism sweeping America and Dylan's history of questing for answers, "Dylan's conversion does not seem so incongruous. . . . Dylan is being as true to the mood of his times and to himself as he was in the 1960's." Still, the opening night at Earls Court was a muted detached performance. Some who had only weeks before been caught up in the rampant energy that Bruce Springsteen brought to his show at Wembley were ready to write obituaries. But a positive approach came from Brown: "Rather than simply consolidating a safe position Dylan is obviously prepared to stand on his convictions and perform material which challenges his audience's expectations rather than appeasing them." He concluded: "Astonishingly, he was actually slow hand-clapped during a beautiful rendition of 'Abraham, Martin and John.' But not allowing himself to become a prisoner of his audience's expectations and still be able to sell out six nights at Earls Court and receive two standing ovations, has always been Dylan's particular talent."

Down the years, as rock-studio techniques became increasingly sophisticated, there had been a chorus of critical yelping about the production values of Dylan's music. In the first two Christian albums, production values were markedly more polished and controlled. For the big album of 1983, the album that was to proclaim a change from overt Christian statement, *Infidels,* Dylan took the greatest pains of any album he's recorded. Working with Mark Knopfler of Dire Straits as co-producer, weeks were spent to get things just as he wanted them.

CBS got behind this album as they hadn't in years, for they hoped it would signify a comeback. A photograph on the album shows Dylan touching soil on a mountaintop overlooking Jerusalem. Instantly, speculation began again that he was reexploring Jewish roots, although it might have been site inspection for Blake's New Jerusalem that was being pictured.

Dylan had been spending considerable time in 1983 at a Brooklyn center called Chabad Lubavitch, the Hasidic cult that puts music so centrally into its rituals and group life. At the Bar Mitzvah of his son Jesse, 16, he had been photographed in Jerusalem wearing a yamulke and prayer shawl. Dylan was ready to say at the release of *Infidels,* in November 1984, that "all these political and religious labels are irrelevant." He referred to that born-again period as "part of my experience. When I get involved in something, I get totally involved. I don't just play around." He had no visible regrets about that period of "telling people how to get their souls saved. Whoever was supposed to pick it up" did, he said. Now, he continued, "maybe the time for me to say that has come and gone. It's time for me to do something else. Sometimes those things appear quickly and disappear. Jesus himself only preached for three years."

Infidels was a social thermometer that found the spiritual health of America failing. *The New York Times* said its "incendiary political rants, quasi-Biblical tirades and surreal love songs capture the apocalyptic mood of the moment with shuddering immediacy." Many ranked it beside his strongest albums, but the British reception was cooler. The album gamboled up the charts, and it looked like it might reverse the Christian-induced disaffection.

One song that seemed especially strong and ironically self-revealing is "Jokerman." *Time* thought its "metaphorical protagonist" was "part salvation hunter, part satanic twister." Because of the rise of the rock video and his old interest in filmmaking, Dylan did a video of one love song, "Sweetheart Like You," which failed to bring the song or the screen to life. He tried again with "Jokerman," with the help of writer Larry Sloman and George Lois, the adman who helped enlist Dylan into the Hurricane Carter campaign. Lines of the poetic lyrics were used on top of paintings by Michelangelo, Bosch, Dürer, and Munch. *Rolling Stone* said the video made "most run-of-the-mill videos look like the glorified cola commercials they generally are." By 1985, Dylan disparaged the video cult as "all fake. Anybody can make a video; all you need is a camera. I don't care about being a video star or a movie star."

But no song as powerful or lilting as "Jokerman" and no technical video artistry could bring back the climate of the 1960s off which to spark. Dylan denied that "Neighborhood Bully" was a defense of Zionism and decried those who saw political content throughout *Infidels.* "Politics is an instrument of the Devil . . . politics is what kills . . . politics is corrupt," he said.

Dylan's pessimism—which he regarded only as realism—still saw us headin' for Armageddon. He defined peace sardonically as "the moment when you reload your rifle." And it wasn't until autumn 1985 that he brought out officially those five albums of older material that for years were rumored to be in preparation. By 1984 he was even saying that the marvelous *Basement Tapes* wouldn't have been released officially if he had been the only one to decide on it.

By summer 1984, Dylan was ready to surface again in Europe on an ambitious concert tour with Santana, produced by Bill Graham. At a press conference in Verona, Italy, in early June 1984, 150 European reporters and photographers turned out, although Dylan didn't have much to say to them and it ended in a customary shambles. But by the time he arrived in Madrid, he had some lucid views: "I don't think I'm gonna be really understood until maybe one hundred years from now. What I've done, what I'm doing, nobody else does or has done. When I'm dead and gone maybe people will realize that, and then figure it out. I don't think anything I've done has been even mildly hinted at."

From Rotterdam to Göteborg, from Berlin to Nice, from Barcelona to Newcastle to Dublin, Dylan performed to about three quarters of a million people. Joan Baez sang on the same bill with him and Santana at Hamburg, Munich, Offenbach, Berlin, Cologne, and Nice. But they actually sang together only at Hamburg and Munich. Joan told my journalist associate, Liz Thomson: "I sang with Dylan at two concerts. The press have blown it up. It really isn't the coming together of two myths. Dylan's doesn't consider the audience. I said, 'We owe it to them to sing together.' But the more insistent I got that it was expected, the less interested he became. In order to perform together professionally, you have to be asked." There were many other guest stars along the way who appeared either on the bill or with Dylan: Eric Clapton, Chrissie Hynde, and Van Morrison at Wembley, and Hugues Aufray in Paris, among them. While Dylan wasn't doing any preaching this time around, ironically his appearances followed European evangelizing tours of Luis Palau and Billy Graham.

Dylan still displayed antagonism toward the press. The West German weekly *Stern* was said to have offered him a front-cover story in exchange for a very brief visit, but Dylan said, *"Nein."* When a reporter at Verona asked about his current religious views, he was scornful. Why didn't people ask Billy Joel about his religious views? he asked, refusing to countenance how important he'd made religion in his music.

When Mick Brown, this time with *The* (London) *Sunday Times,* heard him at a Madrid football stadium, among twenty-five thousand others, he saw him looking like "some avenging backwoods preacher" and sounding like "an uncompromising moralist," despite the absence of Christian songs. Dylan denies this was a nostalgia tour: " '*A Tale of Two Cities* was written 100 years ago. Is that nostalgia? Just another label,' " he told Mick Brown.

Dylan recalled that the worst reaction toward the born-again Christian period (another label he couldn't tolerate) was in 1979 on university campuses where "the so-called intellectual students showed their true monstrous selves." (That was when stunned listeners had called out again, "We want the old Dylan," until the power of the gospel performances turned it all from disaster to triumph. That's when he had sung in Santa

Monica for World Vision, an international Christian group, to raise
money for Cambodia relief, and Dylan preached his way into songs as in
black churches: "Christ will return to set up His Kingdom in Jerusalem.... There really is a slow train coming and it is picking up speed....
Satan has been defeated by the Cross.")

Although he wasn't talking in those terms by 1984, he still was thinking about Apocalypse as forecast in the Book of Revelations, and still saw
the false gods of corporate Mammon all around. He remembered the 1960s
with warmth: "America is not like that anymore. But what happened,
happened so fast that people are still trying to figure it out. The TV media
wasn't so big then. Woodstock wasn't about anything, just a whole new
market for tie-dyed T-shirts. It was about clothes. All those people are in
computers now.... It seemed [then] there was room to be different.... I
came along at just the right time, and I understood the times I was in. If I
was starting out right now, I don't know where I'd get the inspiration
from, because you need to breathe the right air to make that creative process work.... There's never been any glory in it for me. For me, the fulfillment was always in just doing it. That's all that really matters."

What was remarkable about Dylan's 1984 visit to London, in contrast
with 1981, was the absence of much preconcert buildup in the press, but
still a turnout of one hundred thousand at Wembley Stadium. Only *The
Times* seemed to be regarding Dylan's visit as vital. The five pop weeklies
were not even publishing, because of industrial action. The audience I observed was made up of, say, 20 percent older people, "the wrinklies." The
bulk of those within my sight, and I moved around, seemed to be seven-
teen- to twenty-three-year-olds. And they were responsive to any intro that
signaled a familiar song. With such a huge turnout paying eleven pounds
for tickets, Dylan may have been making as much as ten thousand pounds
a song as he went through a retrospective of his songwriting career, with
nothing more religious than "Knockin' on Heaven's Door." But he had
already turned his back on more fortunes than most of us can ever hope to
see in a lifetime. The age of the audience proved that nothing he had done
could shatter himself as an idol and prevent vast numbers of fans in Europe from revering him and what he stood for. That still another generation had tuned in on him was visible in Europe in 1984. When Alan
Franks, *The Times* journalist who had written an appreciation of Dylan a
few weeks earlier, was later invited to talk about him to a sixth-form college (students from sixteen to eighteen), he concluded that youth interest
in Dylan may have become less frenzied, but that it was still keen.

As 1985 opened, Dylan remained very much the superindividualist.
Speaking about where he stood as he released a minor album of old songs
drawn from the 1984 tour, *Real Live,* Dylan was still the combatant. He
sorely missed such inner-directed men at his recording company as John
Hammond and Goddard Lieberson, who were willing to flout fashion and
sales for recordings they wanted to make.

Lamenting the technology that had seized power in modern recording studios, he hailed naturalness. He saw the ultimate folly of it in the replicating of human handclaps by machinery. Although he expressed greater personal contentment now, he confessed, "I don't know where I'm going as a person." He had been dividing his time recently between his farm outside St. Paul, Minnesota, and sharing a boat in the Caribbean on which he could cruise the islands and enjoy solitude, listening again to the silence.

He was older than all that now, and although 1984's European trip had meant a qualified return, he had not come back as we, or probably he, might have wanted. There were no doubt mistakes he'd made that he simply poured into the vat of his experience, things to be later understood, writers' raw material. All along, there were voices telling him what he should be doing at any given point, whether friends and associates or those who so cared about him that they were haunted by anything less than total mastery from him.

"There are always people trying to tell you how to do everything in your life," he said in 1985. "The easiest way to do something is just don't ask anyone's opinion . . . if you really believe in what you're doing." There was advice all around. As a hungry reader, he might have studied the experiences of Arthur Rimbaud or William Butler Yeats.

Just seventy years, to the month, before Dylan was born, the father of modern poetry, Arthur Rimbaud, wrote to his friend Paul Demeny: "For *I* is someone else. . . . If old imbeciles had not discovered only the false meaning of the Ego, we would not have to sweep away those millions of skeletons which, for time immemorial, have accumulated the results of their one-eyed intellects by claiming to be the authors!

". . . I say one must be a *seer,* make oneself a *seer.*

"The Poet makes himself a *seer* by a long, gigantic and rational *derangement* of all the senses. All forms of love, suffering, and madness. He searches himself. He exhausts all the poisons in himself and keeps only their quintessences. Unspeakable torture where he needs all his faith, all his superhuman strength, where he becomes among all men the great patient, the great criminal, the one accursed—and the supreme Scholar!— Because he reaches the *unknown*! Since he cultivated his soul, rich already, more than any man! He reaches the unknown, and when, bewildered, he ends by losing the intelligence of his visions, he has seen them. Let him die as he leaps through unheard of and unnamable things; other horrible workers will come; they will begin from the horizons where the other one collapsed!"[2]

Dylan was in a summing-up mood in early 1985: "I was never going to be anything else. Never. All I wanted to do was play my guitar. It was a way of gaining attention, and whatever. It starts out that way . . . but I didn't know where it was going to lead. Now that it's led me here I still don't know where it is. I don't know what's going to happen when I'm not around to sing anymore. I hope somebody else comes along, you

know, who could pick up with what I'm doing and learn exactly what it is
that makes it quite different. I keep looking for that somebody who's
going to pick up on that . . . to take it a step further. I've already taken it
as far as I can take it. Maybe I won't see that person. I don't know. I want
somebody, sometime to take it a step further. No one who I've seen has
taken what I've done any step further. I don't say that in a bragging sort of
way, it just hasn't gone any further, you know."

Dylan was not outlining another epitaph in 1985. He spoke of how he's
been on plateaus in his life before, but all that meant to him was further
effort to get off the plateau and start climbing the mountain again. He
hadn't painted his masterpiece yet, he said, "and I hope I never do." Some
possibilities lay in the lives of other songwriters, who have had longer
careers than rock performers, because the life is less wasting.

A songwriter like Yeats produced his greatest work from his fiftieth to
his seventy-fifth year. He had hit a high-water mark at fifty-eight, when he
won the Nobel Prize for Literature. Yet at that point, he was increasingly
disillusioned with what transpired in Ireland. At sixty-six, he fell under the
sway of an Indian swami, which affected his work thereafter. He wrote: "I
want to plunge myself into impersonal poetry, to get rid of the bitterness,
irritation and hatred my work in Ireland has brought into my soul. I want
to make a last song, sweet and exultant." At sixty-eight, he became involved with a group of Irish Fascists (the Falange blue shirts of General
O'Duffy) to the astonishment of all who had regarded Yeats as a rock-
hard liberal humanist.

By the age of seventy, Yeats refused to speak for or against any government. He would not budge even for the sake of a writer, Ossietsky, imprisoned by the Nazis. "Do not try to make a politician of me. I shall
never be that again. As my sense of reality deepens . . . my horror at the
cruelty of governments grows greater."[3] In one of his last great works,
Yeats declared politics were irrelevant.

Rimbaud, the poet of revolt, finished his major, influential writing between the ages of sixteen and nineteen. Dylan could have written not another line or song, or made another performance beyond 1966 or 1976, and
his reputation would have rested securely in any other world than that of
the rock star. Or he could find this last period of searching as a ground for
new creativity.

The mid-1985 album, *Empire Burlesque,* was stronger than any since *Slow
Train Coming. Time* ranked it beside *Blood on the Tracks.* Opinions tended
to split over the Atlantic, many Americans treating it as a comeback
album, many Britons less convinced. By any standards, it is a major album,
carefully produced, with free, excellent singing and an open expressionism
in the soul vein. It testifies that the grip of fundamentalism has been loos-
ened, allowing some old themes and concerns to resurface: fragile love,
moral balances, bruised idealism teetering on a razor's edge with rueful betrayal.

Contradictory moods again: A song of deep betrayal, "Seeing the Real You at Last," is followed by declared faith in a loved friend, "I'll Remember You." There is political-social fury in the sardonic "Clean-Cut Kid," which tells of the savaging of American youth by the Vietnam War. And there is the menace of imminent apocalypse in "When the Night Comes Falling from the Sky." Anger and love dance a tarantella together. "Dark Eyes" is solo acoustic, an affirmation of love's transcendence in a painful world. The emblematic song of the album, which sums up Dylan's attitude toward false or real gods, fake or true heroes, is "Trust Yourself." In the country whose motto "In God We Trust" appears on every copper penny, however devalued by maturing experience and cheapening inflation, Dylan posits an antihero's postconversion slogan in "Trust Yourself."

In a full-page review in *Time,* Jay Cocks was elegiac: "*Empire Burlesque* is full of turmoil and anger and mystery, an oblique diary ... It is also a record of survival and a tentative kind of triumph. ..." Tracing Dylan's tortuous journeys since *Blood on the Tracks,* he concedes the singer's excursions into "political conservatism and the rigors of religious conversion ... took their toll on his audience." Yet, to those who would dismiss Dylan as a marginal man of yesterday, *Time* concluded: "One playing of *Empire Burlesque* and all such questions become academic. Listen up. You too, Mr. Jones."

The dominant event of 1985, in world affairs as well as in popular music, was the famine in Africa. Borrowing a leaf from those causes, protests, and benefits of the past twenty-five years in which Dylan has been a central figure, the pop world lent its powerful voice in support. One afternoon in late January, a group of American rock stars gathered in the A & M studios on Hollywood's Sunset Boulevard. Harry Belafonte had organized the session in response to Bob Geldof's superstar record "Do They Know It's Christmas," by the British musicians' movement Band Aid, created to aid African famine victims.

Now, an American recording, "We Are the World," went on to raise even more money. Two dozen artists participated, among them Diana Ross, Tina Turner, Smokey Robinson, Bruce Springsteen, Ray Charles, Paul Simon, Michael Jackson, Waylon Jennings, Stevie Wonder, and Dylan. There was a spirit of unity and celebration in their powers with a vast audience. Dylan seemed to be hanging back from the fellowship. To some, he looked the outsider, the expatriate. He seemed to need coaching and confidence. At his piano, Stevie Wonder imitated Bob and got him to exaggerate his own style. Producer of the session Quincy Jones had hung a sign outside the studio reading: "Check your egos at the door." When Dylan finally got his solo recorded, Quincy Jones hugged him, and Bob broke into a wide, relieved smile.

By July 13, Geldof had organized the biggest international popular-music event of all time, the greatest single TV audience ever. From Europe and America, centered on stadiums in London and Philadelphia, the Live Aid show was broadcast for sixteen hours. Moving on precedents of the sixties, it became pop's finest hour. In America, Bob Dylan received the honored position of closing the international spectacular that raised some fifty million dollars for starving Africans.

Emotions had been peaking all day long. Sting, Bowie, Jagger, and Tina Turner had mesmerized the vast audience. Dylan's brief, closing set was an anticlimax. He appeared with Keith Richards and Ron Wood of the Rolling Stones, but the three acoustic guitars sounded muddy. After Jagger and Tina Turner, perhaps anything would have been an anticlimax, but many felt that Dylan and confreres just threw the conclusion away. Maybe they were telling us we should trust ourselves, not them.

The times had changed, yet they remained very much the same. There was suffering in the world, and the singers, black and white, used their art and star-power to help the charity. There was talk of a Nobel Prize or a knighthood for Bob Geldof. It was like the old days, and rock music was covered in honors from a society all too quick to dismiss it as a juvenile phenomenon. All this despite a drift toward the right in Reagan's America. A report to *The Times* (London) during the 1984 presidential election had found Ronald Reagan the new campus hero. The "counter-culture that spawned the activist Tom Hayden, the acid lyrics of Bob Dylan, and a generation of student liberals, is dead." I think the obituary is premature. In 1983, those lovable rebel rockers, The Rolling Stones, signed the richest deal in music history, with CBS Records, for seven million dollars an album for four albums! The continuing viability of rock and its place in society doesn't need a price tag, no matter how much America values everything by the price it commands.

It was an anticlimax to a day of international pride in the power of the rock community to show its own power and compassion. Actor Jack Nicholson had introduced Dylan: "Some artists' work speaks for their generation . . . one of America's great voices of freedom. It could only be one man—the transcendent Bob Dylan." The muddiness of his Live Aid set, he later said, was because of bad sound monitoring, and he repeated it on a visit to London on *The Old Grey Whistle Test* TV show at a session with Dave Stewart of Eurythmics (with whom he had made some videos from the *Empire Burlesque* album). But he did say at Live Aid that American farmers were also in need and suggested that some of the money coming in go to help American farmers with their onerous mortgage debts.

The suggestion seemed to take aback those concentrating on the African famine, but soon the wheels were in motion for a Farm Aid special benefit, produced by Willie Nelson, with the support of Neil Young and a huge cast of musicians. They gathered in a stadium in the heartland at the University of Illinois ("Proof positive," said *Rolling Stone,* "that when Bob Dylan mutters, the world still listens"). On Sunday, September 22, a fourteen-hour telethon rang out with many from the rock world and also many from America's country music scene, like Waylon Jennings, Johnny Cash,

Merle Haggard, Charley Pride, and Kenny Rogers. The audience was eighty thousand in Champaign, Illinois, and more than ten million dollars was pledged, with future recordings and videos expected to raise fifty million dollars.

Dylan appeared on the Sun City single, recorded on October 30, to help the battle against apartheid. Between Live Aid and Farm Aid, Dylan attended a poetry festival in Moscow, as a guest of Russian poet Yevgeny Yevtushenko. Although Dylan's appearance hadn't been trumpeted, a large, respectful crowd of young people showed up, many with old copies of his albums for him to sign.

By mid-November of a season that had also seen publication of *Lyrics, 1962–1985,* Dylan attended a party in his honor at Manhattan's Whitney Museum to mark the release of *Biograph.* This five-LP boxed set spanned his whole career. Pop musicians at the party spanned the years: Lou Reed, Roger McGuinn, Roy Orbison, and Rick Danko of the old guard were there. Dave Stewart and Billy Joel were among the crowd, which included filmmakers Paul Schraeder and Martin Scorcese. John Hammond, Sr., told a reporter about the "Hammond's Folly" days: "The first time I saw him on West Tenth Street, I knew he had it. He had that staying power. He had something to say and he was fearless."

Dylan did major interviews to stir interest in *Biograph.* Wrote Jay Cocks in *Time:* "Bob Dylan not only lived on the margin, he was the margin. Approach at your peril. Precious few have ever got near him, and no one has gone beyond." He found especial joy on the first release of "Caribbean Wind," left off the *Shot of Love* album. In the context of the fifty-three tracks, which included eighteen unreleased tracks, *Time* found: "In this context, the controversial and sometimes reviled religious rock that Dylan produced . . . makes better sense and seems even more powerful."

To another *Time* reporter, Dylan spoke lucidly, giving no clue that *Biograph* and its notes would one day help form a powerful treatment for a film biography of himself. He discounted that he had prepared the set for release. (Bruce Dickinson, Don DeVito and Jeff Jones were credited with that.) "This set could have been all unreleased songs. If it was worth my while, I could put together a ten-record set of unreleased songs, songs that have never gotten out and songs that have been bootlegged. Bootlegging is a big business. It's like the dope business. It's supposed to be illegal, but a lot of people make their livelihood off it. . . . My favorite songs of all time aren't anything I've written. I like stuff like 'Pastures of Plenty' and 'That's All,' and 'I Get a Kick Out of You.' "

Dylan continued: "I was the same twenty, thirty years ago that I am now. My values haven't changed. . . . In life, well, I mean I feel like I fall short in just about everything. In music I can do just about what I need to do. . . . If I review my situation at all, it always seems like I'm up there walking the plank. I'm probably a driven person. I never felt like I was searching for anything. I always felt that I've stumbled into things."

On the eve of the British release of *Biograph* in Britain, *New Musical*

Express named its Top 100 LPs of all time. In the top ten were *Highway 61 Revisited* (at number 3) and *Blonde on Blonde* (at 8), with *The Band* at number 7. When compiling its statistics, *NME* included seven Dylan albums, making him tied for fourth place. But in a compilation of points, Dylan came ahead of The Beatles and Marvin Gaye at top place!

Writing of *Biograph,* Richard Williams in *The Times* found "in the way it mirrors the inconsistency and contradictions of his extraordinary career, *Biograph* is the closest he has come to creating a full self-portrait.... All these combine to create the image of an enigmatic figure who did as much as anyone else to mould post-war Anglo-American popular music and the international youth culture which it was to inspire."

Threading through the *Biograph* interview (with screenwriter Cameron Crowe) are recurring themes and passions: the battle against cheapness, the supremacy of feeling over intellect, how time had indeed proved to be an enemy, the betrayal of youth with contrived consumerism, the duel with universities and commentary that robs art of its gut impact. Rock, Dylan charges, had become "a highly visible enterprise, big establishment thing. You know things go better with Coke because Aretha Franklin told you so and Maxwell House coffee must be OK because Ray Charles is singing about it. In the beginning ... it ... had nothing to do with panty-hose and perfume and barbecue sauce.... It's like Lyndon Johnson saying 'We shall overcome' to a nationwide audience, ridiculous.... There's an old saying, 'If you want to defeat your enemy, sing his song' and that's pretty much still true. I think it's happened and nobody knows the difference. In the old days, there's that phrase again, you paid the price to play.... The corporate world, when they figured out what it was and how to use it they snuffed the breath out of it and killed it.... Elvis, Little Richard, Chuck Berry ... they all struck fear into the heart. Now they got a purpose, sort of ... to sell soap, blue jeans, anything, it's become country club music ... it's all been neutralized ... nothing threatening, nothing magical ... nothing challenging. For me I hate to see it because it set me free, set the whole world on fire, there's a lot of us who still can remember, who've been there.... The same people who praise you when you're dead, when you were alive they wouldn't give you the time of day. I like to wonder about some of those people who elevated John Lennon to such a mega-god as if when he was alive they were always on his side.... The great folk music and the great rock 'n' roll you might not hear it again. Like the horse and buggy ..."

After a great evocation to those lone voices he loved, Jimmie Rodgers, Woody and Cisco, Robert Johnson, Judy Garland, Al Jolson: "I always thought that one man, the lone balladeer with the guitar could blow an entire army off the stage if he knew what he was doing.... I've seen it happen. It's important to stay away from the celebrity trip.... I think of a hero as someone who understands the degree of responsibility that comes with his freedom, someone who's not afraid to jump in front of a freight train to save a loved one's life. To draw a crowd with my guitar, that's about the most heroic thing that I can do.... You got to be strong and stay connected to what started it all, the inspiration behind the inspiration, to who you were when people didn't mind stepping on you.... As far as the sixties go, it wasn't any big deal. Time marches on. I mean if I had a choice I would rather have lived at the time of King David, when he was the high king of Israel. I'd love to have been riding with him or hiding in caves with him when he was a hunted outlaw ... or maybe at the time of Jesus and Mary Magdalene—that would have been interesting to really test your nerve ... or in the time of the Apostles when they were overturning the world.... I'm amazed that I've been around this long, never thought I would be. I try to learn from both the wise and the unwise, not pay attention to anybody, do what I want to do. I can't say I haven't done my share of playing the fool.... I was in the right place at the right time. People *dissect* my songs like rabbits but they all miss the point.... Sometimes I think I've been doing this too long. I can understand why Rimbaud quit writing poetry when he was nineteen.... How would I change my life? Yeah, well, sometimes I think that I get by on only fifty percent of what I got, sometimes even less. I'd like to change that I guess ... that's about all I can think of."

In a separate brochure with *Biograph,* Dylan (and Crowe) have a go at song commentary, not dissection, sometimes maddeningly spare, but often filled with insight. "You can't take my stuff and verbalize it, like I don't write confessional songs. Emotion's got nothing to do with it." In his extended comments on "Every Grain of Sand," Dylan defends the old biblical truths and disdains those who reject them simply because they are religious in tone: "People like to talk about the new image of America, but to me it's still the old one—Marlon Brando, James Dean, Marilyn Monroe. It's not computers, cocaine, and David Letterman.... I like to keep my values scripturally straight though—I like to stay a part of that stuff that don't change.... God is still the judge and the devil still rules the world, so what's different? No matter how big you think you are history is gonna roll over you. Sound like a preacher, don't I? To the aspiring songwriter and singer I say disregard all the current stuff, forget it, you're better off, read John Keats, Melville, listen to Robert Johnson and Woody Guthrie."

We can't put a price on those rhythms, cadences, and images from Bob Dylan that have reentered our everyday speech, from which he had mined, then refined them. We know Mister Jones as the arch-Philistine who is unaware that something is happening. Even though we're stuck inside Desolation Row, we keep on keeping on. There may be blood on those tracks and nothing is revealed, yet he's told us there must be some way out of here. There may be no direction home for him or a lot of us, but with one foot on the highway and the other in the grave, we try to get outside the empty cage that holds us. Desperation and hope fight in the captain's tower, a pair of warring twins. Although it's all over now, we renew ourselves by leaving the dead behind us. We're younger than all that now. Death and rebirth. For every seven people dyin' there's seven new one's busy being born. We forget where Dylan's lines end and our own begin.

Even though he denied being in "the teachin' business," there's a world to learn by following his road, of self-made culture, of self-education. When he hopped off the subway from America's heartland in Greenwich Village, we were all looking for answers, only he probed deepest, knowing the question itself might unlock the answer. We turned to him for his vision, wit, fresh ideas, but mostly for his daring to try what hadn't been tried. Find your own answers, man, and you'll value them more, he said to us, man and woman, time and again. Even when we insisted, he didn't want to play guru. He was too skinny then to carry a cross, and too wary to let his manager carry it for him.

"There's so many sides to Dylan, he's round," said a Woodstock friend. And he's been so many different people that this wasn't a biography of one man, but of several. "It's always lonely where I am," he said in 1966, but ten years later he said the only place he could find solitude was on a public stage. Long before Dylan met or read Robert Graves, he was following the old poet's admonition that a poet must think mythically as well as rationally. He's a disturber of the peace—ours as well as his own.

He may get off the plateau he's on, or he may not. The past could be prelude or postlude. He's already poured five lifetimes into one. He may follow Rimbaud's route, having articulated more of the language of revolt than the world was then ready for. Or he may follow Yeats's route of more seeking and more finding and even greater creativity toward old age. Knowing Dylan as much as the mystery of genius will reveal to us, he'll probably do it his own way. He always has.

ACKNOWLEDGMENTS

The author wishes to thank all copyright holders of Bob Dylan's songs and poems: Warner Bros. Inc., Ram's Horn Music, Big Sky Music, Dwarf Music, and Special Rider Music. Also, we acknowledge permission to quote from *Tarantula,* from Dylan and the Macmillan Publishing Company.

For permission to quote from various writings and lyrics of Woody Guthrie, our thanks to the Woody Guthrie Children's Trust Fund.

Because this book was always designed to reflect many voices commenting on the life and music of its subject, a vast number of people helped me to assemble it. Especial thanks to Liz Thomson, Gabrielle Goodchild, and Roger Ford for being the stalwart trio who helped me most directly.

A variety of doors were opened up to me at the Dylan Revisited conventions in Manchester in 1979 and 1980, for which I especially thank its chief organizer, Richard Goodall.

The collectors and/or discographers Steven Goldberg, Stephen Pickering, and Jacques von Son were especially helpful.

I actively corresponded with a dozen academics, mostly in America, who were carrying forward multidisciplinary "Dylan Studies" in their own classrooms and research. Among those who helped me the most were Eugene Stelzig, Louis Cantor, W. T. Lhamon, Jr., Bill King, Jack McDonough, Belle Levenson, Suzanne MacRae, Carolyn Jane Bliss, and Betsy Bowden.

I traveled many thousands of miles to research the work, and want to express my thanks for the help extended to me by the subject's mother and brother and late father. Tony Glover was especially conscientious in pulling together the chaotic, stimulating days in Minneapolis-St. Paul.

In New York, I was given detailed historical/emotional reconstructions by Suze Rotolo and her sister, Carla. Sis and Gordon Friesen were, as ever, generous with their recollections of the heady *Broadside* days.

Special thanks to the author of the first serious book on Dylan, Michael Gray, for strong support over a number of years, and for his work in assembling my material on The Band, the first Australian tour, and the thorny question of bootleg recordings.

For technical musical advice, thanks to the singer-guitarists Carol Crist and Barry Tomlinson.

Too many editors were all too fleetingly involved on this project—a total of eleven publishers' editors and my two personal editors, Gabrielle Goodchild and Liz Thomson. I want to offer a special toast to Diane Matthews and Maggie Pringle, formerly of Doubleday & Co., and to Simon Scott, formerly of New English Library, who kept the wheels turning at crucial times.

For endless rush deadlines on the manuscript typing, many thanks to Yvonne Hodson for her punctilious work. For typing and tape transcribing, Alice Robinson in Wadhurst and Emily de Souza in Hampstead.

A host of friends made the "siege of Sydenham" bearable, notably Meg and David Elliott, Michael Davies, Patrick Humphries, Wendy Robin, Cathy Lloyd, Jim, Niall and Heather, Ricky and Arthur. And many thanks also to Gillian Youngs, Claire Simpson, Alison Holt, Jackie Shepcott, Gaby Landau, and Ross MacPherson.

COPYRIGHT CITATIONS AND NOTES TO TEXT

EPIGRAPHS

1. "Open the Door, Homer," copyright © 1968, 1975 by Dwarf Music.
2. "Where Are You Tonight? (Journey Through Dark Heat)," copyright © 1978 by Special Rider Music.

CHAPTER ONE

1. Bob Dylan, *Tarantula* (New York: Macmillan, 1966, 1971), pp. 108–109.
2. "It's Alright, Ma (I'm Only Bleeding)," copyright © 1965 by Warner Bros. Inc.
3. "My Life in a Stolen Moment," copyright © 1973 by Special Rider Music.
4. *Joan Baez in Concert, Part 2* (jacket notes), copyright © 1973 by Special Rider Music.
5. "My Life in a Stolen Moment," copyright © 1973 by Special Rider Music.
6. *Ibid.*
7. "North Country Blues," copyright © 1963, 1964 by Warner Bros. Inc.
8. *Tarantula,* p. 109.
9. *Joan Baez in Concert, Part 2* (jacket notes), copyright © 1973 by Special Rider Music.

10. *Ibid.*
11. Pauline Kael article in *The Atlantic,* March 1966.
12. One Eyed Jacks by Bob Dylan. Unpublished, reprinted with permission of author.

CHAPTER TWO

1. "Like a Rolling Stone," copyright © 1965 by Warner Bros. Inc.
2. "My Life in a Stolen Moment," copyright © 1973 by Special Rider Music.
3. "11 Outlined Epitaphs" (liner notes), copyright © 1964 by Special Rider Music.
4. Woody Guthrie, *Born to Win* (New York: Macmillan, 1965), p. 223. copyright © 1965, The Guthrie Children's Trust Fund. Written December 3, 1944.
5. *Ibid.,* p. 81. Date written unknown.
6. *Ibid.,* pp. 18, 19. Written March 13, 1946.
7. "My Life in a Stolen Moment," copyright © 1973 by Special Rider Music.
8. *Ibid.*

CHAPTER THREE

1. Bob Dylan jacket notes to *Peter, Paul & Mary: In the Wind* (Warner Bros. Records 1507, 1963). Copyright © 1963, Special Rider Music.
2. "11 Outlined Epitaphs" (liner notes), copyright © 1964 by Special Rider Music.
3. *Ibid.*
4. *Ibid.*
5. Woody Guthrie. *Born to Win* (New York: Macmillan, 1965), p. 248. Copyright © 1965, The Guthrie Children's Trust Fund. Written November 1954.
6. "Talkin' Subway," Woody Guthrie TRO-© copyright 1960 by Ludlow Music, Inc., New York, N.Y. Used by permission.
7. "Pretty Boy Floyd," Woody Guthrie, copyright © 1958 by Sanga Music, Inc., New York.
8. "Man of Constant Sorrow," arrangement of music and new lyric by Bob Dylan, copyright © 1962, 1965 by Duchess Music Corporation.
9. "Pretty Peggy-O," arrangement of music and new lyric by Bob Dylan, copyright © 1962, 1965 by Duchess Music Corporation.
10. *Ibid.*

CHAPTER FOUR

1. "Tomorrow Is a Long Time," copyright © 1963 by Warner Bros. Inc.
2. "11 Outlined Epitaphs" (liner notes), copyright © 1964 by Special Rider Music.

3. *Ibid.*
4. "Outlaw Blues," copyright © 1965 by Warner Bros. Inc.
5. "Subterranean Homesick Blues," copyright © 1965 by Warner Bros. Inc.
6. Gil Turner, "The Great New York Newspaper Strike," copyright © 1963, as published in *Broadside* magazine number 20. Reprinted in *Broadside, Volume 1,* Oak Publications, p. 32. Copyright © 1964, *Broadside* magazine.
7. Josh Dunson brought together a lot of material on the new songwriters in his paperback book, *Freedom in the Air: Movements of the 60's.* New York: International Publishers, 1965.
8. "Mixed Up Confusion," copyright © 1962, 1968 by Warner Bros. Inc.
9. "Tangled Up in Blue," copyright © 1974, 1975 by Ram's Horn Music.

CHAPTER FIVE

1. From "A Message," Dylan's open letter to Emergency Civil Liberties Committee after his speech to them, autumn 1963.
2. "11 Outlined Epitaphs" (liner notes), copyright © 1964 by Special Rider Music.
3. Joan Baez, *Daybreak* (New York: Dial Press, 1968), p. 84.
4. Reprinted from *The Chicago Daily News,* November 1965.
5. Reprinted from *The Village Voice,* March 1965.
6. Dylan's comments to the Emergency Civil Liberties Committee were supplied to the author in a transcript the committee prepared, from its executive director, Edith Tiger.
7. From New Yorker profile of Dylan by Nat Hentoff, October 4, 1964, p. 64.
8. *Ibid.*

CHAPTER SIX

1. Ralph J. Gleason, ed., *Jam Session: An Anthology of Jazz,* from "Essay Toward a New Form: Jazz and Poetry," by Gleason (New York: G.P. Putnam's Sons, 1958), pp. 285–86.
2. *Ibid.,* p. 286.
3. Newport Folk Festival program book, July 1963.
4. *Ibid.*
5. *Ibid.*
6. *Ibid.*
7. *Ibid.*
8. *Ibid.*
9. *Hootenanny* magazine, column by Bob Dylan, September 1963.
10. *Ibid.*
11. *Hootenanny* magazine, column by Bob Dylan, November 1963.
12. *Ibid.*

13. *Ibid.*
14. "The Times They Are A-Changin'," copyright © 1963, 1964 by Warner Bros. Inc.
15. *Ibid.*
16. *Ibid.*
17. "Ballad of Hollis Brown," copyright © 1963 by Warner Bros. Inc.
18. *Ibid.*
19. "With God on Our Side," copyright © 1963 by Warner Bros. Inc.
20. "One Too Many Mornings," copyright © 1964, 1966 by Warner Bros. Inc.
21. *Ibid.*
22. "North Country Blues," copyright © 1963, 1964 by Warner Bros. Inc.
23. "Only a Pawn in Their Game," copyright © 1963, 1964 by Warner Bros. Inc.
24. "When the Ship Comes In," copyright © 1963, 1964 by Warner Bros. Inc.
25. *Ibid.*
26. "The Lonesome Death of Hattie Carroll," copyright © 1964, 1966 by Warner Bros. Inc.
27. "Restless Farewell," copyright © 1964, 1966 by Warner Bros. Inc.
28. *Ibid.*
29. "11 Outlined Epitaphs" (liner notes), copyright © 1964 by Special Rider Music.
30. From "Sweeney Agonistes" in *Collected Poems, 1909–1962,* by T. S. Eliot, copyright 1936 by Harcourt, Brace and Jovanovich, Inc.; copyright © 1963, 1964 by T. S. Eliot. Reprinted by permission of Harcourt, Brace and Jovanovich, Inc., and Faber and Faber Ltd., London.
31. to 57. "11 Outlined Epitaphs" (liner notes), copyright © 1964 by Special Rider Music.
58. "Chimes of Freedom," copyright © 1964 by Warner Bros. Inc.
59. *Ibid.*
60. *Ibid.*
61. *Ibid.*
62. "I Shall Be Free No. 10," copyright © 1971, 1973 by Special Rider Music.
63. "To Ramona," copyright © 1964 by Warner Bros. Inc.
64. *Ibid.*
65. *Ibid.*
66. *Ibid.*
67. "My Back Pages," copyright © 1964 by Warner Bros. Inc.
68. *Ibid.*
69. *Ibid.*
70. *Ibid.*
71. "I Don't Believe You (She Acts Like We Never Have Met)," copyright © 1964 by Warner Bros. Inc.
72. "Ballad in Plain D," copyright © 1964 by Warner Bros. Inc.

73. *Ibid.*
74. "Some Other Kinds of Songs . . ." (jacket notes), copyright © 1973 by Special Rider Music (Part 1).
75. *Ibid.*
76. *Ibid.* (Part 3.)
77. *Ibid.*
78. *Ibid.*
79. *Ibid.*
80. *Ibid.* (Part 5.)
81. *Ibid.*.
82. *Ibid.*
83. *Ibid.*
84. *Ibid.* (Part 9.)
85. *Ibid.* (Part 10.)
86. *Ibid.*
87. *Ibid.* (Part 11.)
88. *Ibid.*

CHAPTER SEVEN

1. "A Hard Rain's A-Gonna Fall," copyright © 1963 by Warner Bros. Inc.
2. "Bringing It All Back Home" (jacket notes), copyright © 1965 by Special Rider Music.
3. "Tombstone Blues," copyright © 1965 by Warner Bros. Inc.
4. "It Ain't Me, Babe," copyright © 1964 by Warner Bros. Inc.
5. "Advice for Geraldine on Her Miscellaneous Birthday," copyright © 1964 by Special Rider Music.

CHAPTER EIGHT

1. "Desolation Row," copyright © 1965 by Warner Bros. Inc.
2. "Like a Rolling Stone," copyright © 1965 by Warner Bros. Inc.
3. Wolfgang Kayser, *The Grotesque in Art and Literature* (New York: McGraw-Hill/Indiana University Press, 1963), pp. 184–88.
4. *The Reader's Encyclopedia,* edited by W. R. Benet, copyright © 1965 by Thomas Y. Crowell Company.
5. "Taking It Easy," words and music by Woody Guthrie and Paul Campbell (pseudonym of Pete Seeger), copyright © 1953 by Folkways Music Publishers, Inc. Published in *Woody Guthrie Folk Songs,* copyright © 1963 by Ludlow Music Inc.
6. "Subterranean Homesick Blues," copyright © 1965 by Warner Bros. Inc.
7. *Ibid.*
8. *Ibid.*
9. "She Belongs to Me," copyright © 1965 by Warner Bros. Inc.
10. "Love Minus Zero/No Limit," copyright © 1965 by Warner Bros. Inc.

11. *Ibid.*
12. "Outlaw Blues," copyright © 1965 Warner Bros. Inc.
13. "Mr. Tambourine Man," copyright © 1964, 1965 by Warner Bros. Inc.
14. *Ibid.*
15. *Ibid.*
16. A. Norman Jeffares, *Profiles in Literature: W. B. Yeats* (Boston: Routledge & Kegan Paul, 1971), p. 43.
17. Gwendolyn Bays, *The Orphic Vision* (Lincoln, Neb.: University of Nebraska Press, 1965), p. 212.
18. "Gates of Eden," copyright © 1965 by Warner Bros. Inc.
19. Carolyn Jane Bliss, *Younger Now: Bob Dylan's Changing World and Vision,* unpublished dissertation (see bibliography).
20. "Gates of Eden," copyright © 1965 by Warner Bros. Inc.
21. *Ibid.*
22. *Ibid.*
23. Bill King, *Bob Dylan: The Artist in the Marketplace,* unpublished dissertation (see bibliography).
24. "It's Alright, Ma (I'm Only Bleeding)," copyright © 1965 by Warner Bros. Inc.
25. *Ibid.*
26. *Ibid.*
27. "It's All Over Now, Baby Blue," copyright © 1965 by Warner Bros. Inc.
28. *Ibid.*
29. *Ibid.*
30. Carl G. Jung, foreword to the *I Ching,* or *Book of Changes* (New York: Pantheon Books, 1950), p. iv.
31. *Bringing It All Back Home* (jacket notes), copyright © 1965 by Special Rider Music.
32. *Ibid.*
33. "Tombstone Blues," copyright © 1965 by Warner Bros. Inc.
34. "Just Like Tom Thumb's Blues," copyright © 1965 by Warner Bros. Inc.
35. Arthur Rimbaud, "My Bohemian Life (Fantasy)," from *Rimbaud: Complete Works, Selected Letters,* trans., intro., and notes by Wallace Fowlie (Chicago: University of Chicago Press, 1966), p. 63.
36. "Outlaw Blues," copyright © 1965 by Warner Bros. Inc.
37. *Playboy* magazine interview with Dylan, March 1966.

CHAPTER NINE

1. Yevgeny Yevtushenko, *Stolen Apples* (New York: Doubleday, 1971 and London: W. H. Allen & Co., Inc., 1972), from Introduction, "Being Famous Isn't Pretty," p. xiii of British edition.

2. "When I Paint My Masterpiece," copyright © 1971, 1972 by Big Sky Music.
3. *Ibid.*
4. "Visions of Johanna, copyright © 1966 by Dwarf Music.
5. *Ibid.*
6. "Pledging My Time," copyright © 1966 by Dwarf Music.
7. *Ibid.*
8. "Visions of Johanna," copyright © 1966 by Dwarf Music.
9. "Just Like a Woman," copyright © 1966 by Dwarf Music.
10. "Temporary Like Achilles," copyright © 1966 by Dwarf Music.
11. "Absolutely Sweet Marie," copyright © 1966 by Dwarf Music.
12. "From a Buick 6," copyright © 1965 by Warner Bros. Inc.
13. "Love Minus Zero/No Limit," copyright © 1965 by Warner Bros. Inc.
14. Prefatory notes by Paul Nelson to songbook of *Blonde on Blonde,* published by Bob Dylan Words & Music Co., Inc., New York, p. 7.

CHAPTER ELEVEN

1. George Steiner excerpt from "Silence and the Poet" in *Language and Silence: Essays on Language, Literature and the Inhuman.* Copyright © 1963, 1967 George Steiner. Reprinted with the permission of Atheneum Publishers, Inc., and Faber and Faber Ltd., London.
2. Pete Hamill, from jacket notes to Bob Dylan's album *Blood on the Tracks.* Notes were deleted after first run of jacket printing, but were reprinted as foreword to the *Blood on the Tracks* songbook, published by EMI Music Publishing Ltd., London, 1975, p. 7.
3. Clive Davis with James Willwerth, *Clive: Inside the Record Business* (New York: William Morrow and Company, 1975), p. 65.
4. *Ibid.,* p. 72.
5. Dylan interview with John Cohen and Happy Traum in *Sing Out!* magazine, October/November 1968, p. 24.
6. *Ibid.*
7. Tony White (pseudonym of Michael Gray), *Let It Rock* magazine, November 1972, p. 28.
8. Gwendolyn Bays, *The Orphic Vision* (Lincoln, Neb.: University of Nebraska Press, 1964), p. 88.
9. "All Along the Watchtower," copyright © 1968 by Dwarf Music.
10. Dylan interview with John Cohen and Happy Traum in *Sing Out!* magazine, October/November 1968, p. 24.
11. "John Wesley Harding," copyright © 1968 by Dwarf Music.
12. "The Ballad of Frankie Lee and Judas Priest," copyright © 1968 by Dwarf Music.
13. "I Pity the Poor Immigrant," copyright © 1968 by Dwarf Music.
14. "I Threw It All Away," copyright © 1969 by Big Sky Music.
15. "Country Pie," copyright © 1969 by Big Sky Music.

CHAPTER TWELVE

1. "George Jackson," copyright © 1971 by Ram's Horn Music.
2. "Watching the River Flow," copyright © 1971 by Big Sky Music.
3. "Day of the Locusts," copyright © 1970 by Big Sky Music.
4. Dylan letter to *Broadside*, January 1964.
5. "If Dogs Run Free," copyright © 1970 by Big Sky Music.
6. "Sign on the Window," copyright © 1970 by Big Sky Music.
7. "Hero Blues," copyright © 1963 by Warner Bros. Inc.
8. "It's Alright, Ma (I'm Only Bleeding)," copyright © 1965 by Warner Bros. Inc.
9. "Dirge," copyright © 1973, 1974 by Ram's Horn Music.
10. *Ibid.*
11. "Tough Mama," copyright © 1973, 1974 by Ram's Horn Music.
12. Allen Ginsberg, *First Blues, Rags and Harmonium Songs* (New York: Full Court Press, 1975). Also, see *Allen Ginsberg Collected Poems, 1947-1980* (New York: Harper and Row, 1985).
13. "Tangled Up in Blue," copyright © 1974, 1975 by Ram's Horn Music.
14. *Ibid.*
15. "Simple Twist of Fate," copyright © 1974, 1975 by Ram's Horn Music.
16. "It's All Over Now, Baby Blue," copyright © 1965 by Warner Bros. Inc.
17. "You're a Big Girl Now," copyright © 1974, 1975 by Ram's Horn Music.
18. *Ibid.*
19. "You're Gonna Make Me Lonesome When You Go," copyright © 1974, 1975 by Ram's Horn Music.
20. Wallace Fowlie, *Rimbaud* (Chicago: University of Chicago Press, 1965), p. 127.
21. *Ibid.*
22. "If You See Her, Say Hello," copyright © 1974, 1975 by Ram's Horn Music.
23. "Shelter from the Storm," copyright © 1974, 1975 by Ram's Horn Music.
24. From Bob Dylan's jacket notes on *Poppy* album by Ric Von Schmidt.

CHAPTER THIRTEEN

1. Anthony Storr, *C. G. Jung* (London: Fontana), p. 93.
2. Gwendolyn Bays, *The Orphic Vision* (Lincoln, Neb.: University of Nebraska Press, 1964), p. 98.
3. *Rimbaud: Complete Works, Selected Letters,* trans., intro., and notes by Wallace Fowlie (Chicago: University of Chicago Press, 1966), pp. 193-95.

4. "When the Ship Comes In," copyright © 1963, 1964 by Warner Bros. Inc.

5. "Hurricane" (words written with Jacques Levy), copyright © 1975 by Ram's Horn Music.

6. *Ibid.*

7. "11 Outlined Epitaphs" (liner notes), copyright © 1964 by Special Rider Music.

8. "Oh, Sister" (words written with Jacques Levy), copyright © 1975, 1976 by Ram's Horn Music.

9. "Isis" (words written with Jacques Levy), copyright © 1975, 1976 by Ram's Horn Music.

10. "It's All Over Now, Baby Blue," copyright © 1965 by Warner Bros. Inc.

11. *Desire* (liner notes), copyright © 1975 by Ram's Horn Music.

12. *Ibid.*

13. "My Back Pages," copyright © 1964 by Warner Bros. Inc.

14. Allen Ginsberg, jacket notes to *Desire*.

15. "Joey" (words written with Jacques Levy), copyright © 1975, 1976 by Ram's Horn Music.

16. *Ibid.*

17. "Sara," copyright © 1975, 1976 by Ram's Horn Music.

18. "Chimes of Freedom," copyright © 1964 by Warner Bros. Inc.

CHAPTER FOURTEEN

1. *Buzz* magazine, a Christian monthly, is edited by Peter Meadows, from 51 Haydons Road, London, SW19 1HG, England.

2. *Rimbaud: Complete Works, Selected Letters,* trans., intro., and notes by Wallace Fowlie (Chicago: University of Chicago Press, 1966), p. 307.

3. A. Norman Jeffares, *Profiles in Literature: W. B. Yeats* (Boston: Routledge & Kegan Paul, 1971), p. 95.

SELECT BIBLIOGRAPHY

BY BOB DYLAN:

Tarantula. Copyright © 1966 by Bob Dylan. New York: Macmillan, 1971. New York: Bantam Books, 1972. London: MacGibbon & Kee, 1971. London: Panther Books, 1972; Penguin Books, 1977.
Translations: Copenhagen, Denmark: Lindhardt & Ringhof, 1972; Bussum, North Holland: 1972; Uitgeverj C. de Boer Jr., Oslo, Norway; Glydendal Norsk Forlag, 1972; Paris, France: Christian Bourgois Editeur, 1972; Milan, Italy: Arnoldo Mondadori Editore, 1973; Tokyo, Japan: Kadakowa Shoten, 1974; Buenos Aires, Argentina: Granica Editor, 1974; Barcelona, Spain: Producciones Editoriales S.A., 1976; Frankfurt-on-Main, Germany: Zweitausendeins, 1976.

Writings and Drawings by Bob Dylan. New York: Alfred A. Knopf, Inc., 1973. Toronto: Random House of Canada Ltd., 1973. London: Jonathan Cape Ltd., 1973. London: Panther Books, 1974.
Translations: Tokyo, Japan: Shobun Sha Publishers (two volumes), 1974; *Ecrits et Dessins.* Paris, France: Editions Seghers, 1975; *Escritos, Canciones y Dibujos* (two volumes). Madrid, Spain: Editorial R. Aguilera/Ediciones Castilla, 1975; *Texte Und Zeichnungen.* Frankfurt-on-Main, Germany: Zweitausendeins, 1975; Oslo, Norway: Den Norske Bokklubben, 1977.

The Songs of Bob Dylan from 1966 Through 1975. New York: Alfred A.
   Knopf, Inc., 1976.
Lyrics, 1962–1985. (Includes all of *Writings and Drawings* plus 120 new
   writings.) New York: Alfred A. Knopf, Inc., 1985. London: Jon-
   athan Cape, 1986.
Bob Dylan Songbook. New York: M. Witmark & Sons, 1965.
Bob Dylan. New York: Warner Bros. Inc., 1974.
   (Note: Individual songbooks have been published for each album, by
   Leeds Music, Warner Bros. Inc., Special Rider Music, and Big Sky
   Music. See Song Index, category 4.)

ABOUT BOB DYLAN:

BIOGRAPHICAL

Amendt, Gunter. *Reunion Sundown: Bob Dylan in Europa.* Munich: Hobo
   Press, 1985.
Davis, Clive, with Willwerth, James. *Clive: Inside the Record Business.* New
   York: William Morrow & Co., Inc., 1975.
Gross, Michael (produced by), and Alexander, Robert (text by). *Bob
   Dylan: An Illustrated History.* London: Elm Tree Books, 1978. *Bob
   Dylan: Une Histoire Illustrée.* Paris: Albin Michel, 1980. American edi-
   tion originally published by Grosset & Dunlap, revised and updated
   by Michael Gross. New York: Tempo Books, 1980.
Hammond, John, with Townsend, Irving. *John Hammond on Record.* New
   York: Ridge Press/Summit Books, 1977.
Kooper, Al. *Backstage Passes: Rock 'n' Roll Life in the Sixties.* New York:
   Stein & Day, 1977.
Miles, Barry (compiler). *Bob Dylan: In His Own Words.* London and New
   York: Omnibus Press, 1978.
Miles, Barry. *Bob Dylan.* London: Big O Publishing Ltd., 1978.
Pennebaker, D. A. *Bob Dylan: Don't Look Back.* New York: Ballantine
   Books, Inc., 1968.
Ribakove, Sy and Barbara. *Folk-Rock: The Bob Dylan Story.* New York: Dell
   Publishing Co., Inc. 1966.
Robinson, Earl (editor). *Young Folk Songbook.* New York: Simon &
   Schuster, 1963.
Rolling Stone magazine editors. *Knockin' on Dylan's Door: On the Road in '74.*
   New York: Pocket Books, 1974.
Scaduto, Anthony. *Bob Dylan: An Intimate Biography.* New York: Grosset
   & Dunlap, 1971. Updated in 1979 with a new afterword by Steven
   Gaines. New York: Signet/New American Library.
Schmidt, Eric von, and Rooney, Jim. *Baby Let Me Follow You Down: The
   Illustrated Story of the Cambridge Folk Years.* New York: Anchor
   Books, 1979.
Shepard, Sam. *Rolling Thunder Logbook.* New York: Viking Press, 1977.
   Penguin Books, 1978.

Sloman, Larry. *On the Road with Bob Dylan: Rolling with the Thunder.* New York: Bantam Books, Inc., 1978.

Thompson, Toby. *Positively Main Street: An Unorthodox View of Bob Dylan.* New York: Coward-McCann, 1971. London: New English Library, 1972.

Wurlitzer, Rudolph. *Pat Garrett and Billy the Kid.* New York: Signet Film Series (New American Library), 1973.

DISCOGRAPHICAL BOOKS:

Cable, Paul. *Bob Dylan: His Unreleased Recordings.* London: Scorpion Publications Ltd./Dark Star, 1978. New York: Schirmer Books, 1980.

Hoggard, Stuart, and Shields, Jim. *Bob Dylan: An Illustrated Discography.* Dumbarton, Scotland: Transmedia Express, 1979.

Krogsgaard, Michael. *Twenty Years of Recording: The Bob Dylan Reference Book.* Scandinavian Institute for Rock Research, 1981.

Roques, Dominique. *The Great White Answers: The Bob Dylan Bootleg Records.* Salindres, France: Southern Live Oak Productions, 1979.

COMMENTARY ON DYLAN'S WORK:

Anderson, Dennis. *The Hollow Horn: Bob Dylan's Reception in the United States and Germany.* Munich: Hobo Press, 1981.

Bauldie, John. *Bob Dylan and Desire.* Manchester, England: Wanted Man, 1984.

Bliss, Carolyn Jane. *Younger Now: Bob Dylan's Changing World and Vision.* Unpublished dissertation, 1976.

Bowden, Betsy. *Performed Literature: Words and Music by Bob Dylan.* Indiana University Press, 1982.

Cantor, Louis. *Bob Dylan and the Protest Movement of the 1960's: The Electronic Medium Is the Apocalyptic Message.* Unpublished essay.

Denisoff, Serge. *Great Day Coming: Folk Music and the American Left.* Urbana, Ill.: University of Illinois Press, 1972.

———. *Sing a Song of Social Significance.* Bowling Green, Kentucky: Bowling Green University Popular Press, 1972.

———, and Peterson, Richard (editors). *The Sounds of Social Change: Studies in Popular Culture.* Chicago: Rand McNally & Co., 1972.

Dergoth, Jonas (publisher). *Renaldo and Clara: A Concise Synopsis of Bob Dylan's Masterpiece.* Date and place of origin unknown.

Dickstein, Morris. *Gates of Eden: American Culture in the Sixties.* New York: Basic Books, Inc., 1977.

Diddle, Gavin. *Images and Assorted Facts: A Peek Behind the Picture Frame.* Manchester, England: The Print Centre, 1983.

Dowley, Tim, and Dunnage, Barry. *Bob Dylan: From a Hard Rain to a Slow Train.* Tunbridge Wells, England: Midas Books, 1982. New York: Hippocrene Books, Inc., 1982.

Ducray, F., Manoeuvre, P., Muller, H., and Vassal, J. *Dylan.* Paris: Albin Michel, 1975. (Revised 1978.)

Estrik, Robert van. *Bob Dylan: Concerted Efforts.* Privately published in the Netherlands, 1982.

Fong-Torres, Ben (editor). *What's That Sound? Readings in Contemporary Music.* New York: Anchor Books, 1976.

Frith, Simon. *The Sociology of Rock.* London: Constable and Co., Ltd., 1978.

Gans, Terry Alexander. *What's Real and What Is Not: Bob Dylan Through 1964: The Myth of Protest.* Munich: Hobo Press, 1983.

Goldstein, Richard. *The Poetry of Rock.* New York: Bantam Books, Inc., 1968, 1969.

———. *Goldstein's Greatest Hits: A Book Mostly About Rock 'n' Roll.* Englewood Cliffs, N.J.: Prentice-Hall, Inc., 1970.

Gray, Michael. *Song and Dance Man: The Art of Bob Dylan.* London: Hart-Davis, MacGibbon, 1972. New York: E. P. Dutton, Inc., 1973. London: Abacus (Sphere Books, Ltd.), 1973. Updated, Hamlyn, 1981.

Herdman, John. *Voice Without Restraint: Bob Dylan's Lyrics and Their Background.* Edinburgh, Scotland: Paul Harris Publishing, 1982.

Hetmann, Frederik. *Bob Dylan: Bericht Uber Einen Songpoeten.* Hamburg: Rowohlt Taschenbuch Verlag, 1976.

Karpel, Craig. *The Tarantula in Me: A Review of a Title.* San Francisco: KLONH, 1973.

King, Bill. *Bob Dylan: The Artist in the Marketplace.* Unpublished dissertation.

Levinson, Belle D. *The Deranged Seer: The Poetry of Arthur Rimbaud and Bob Dylan.* Unpublished essay.

Lhamon, W. T., Jr. "Poplore and Bob Dylan" and "Dada Punk." Two essays, dates unknown.

McDonough, Jack. *It Takes a Train to Cry.* Unpublished dissertation.

McGregor, Craig (editor). *Bob Dylan: A Retrospective.* New York: William Morrow & Co., Inc., 1972. Sydney: Angus & Robertson Pty., Ltd., 1973. London: Picador, 1975.

Marcus, Greil. *Mystery Train: Images of America in Rock 'n' Roll Music.* New York: E. P. Dutton, Inc., 1975.

———. *Stranded: Rock and Roll for a Desert Island.* New York: Alfred A. Knopf, Inc., 1979.

Mellers, Wilfrid. *A Darker Shade of Pale: A Backdrop to Bob Dylan.* London: Faber and Faber, Ltd., 1984.

Miller, Jim (editor). *The Rolling Stone Illustrated History of Rock and Roll.* New York: Random House, Inc., 1977.

Pichaske, David R. (editor). *Beowulf to Beatles: Approaches to Poetry.* New York: The Free Press, 1972.

———. *A Generation in Motion: Popular Music and Culture in the Sixties.* New York: Schirmer Books, 1979.

———. "Perspectives on the Self—The Art of Dylan's Middle Period." Unpublished essay from *Toward an Aesthetics of Rock.* Illinois English Bulletin, 1972.

Pickering, Stephen. *Bob Dylan Approximately: A Portrait of the Jewish Poet in Search of God: A Midrash.* New York: David McKay Co., Inc., 1975.

―――. *Bob Dylan Tour 1974.* Aptos, Calif.: Echo, Echo Ltd., 1973.

Poague, Leland A. *Performance Variables: Some Versions of "It Ain't Me, Babe."* Unpublished dissertation.

Remond, Alain. *Les Chémins de Bob Dylan.* Paris: Epi sa Editeurs, 1971.

Rodnitzky, Jerome L. *Minstrels of the Dawn: The Folk-Protest Singer as a Cultural Hero.* Chicago: Nelson-Hall, 1976.

Schmidt, Mathias R. *Bob Dylan's Message Songs der Sachziger Jahre.* Frankfurt-on-Main: Peter Lan GmbH, 1982.

Shelton, Robert (photographs by David Gahr). *The Face of Folk Music.* New York: Citadel Press, 1968.

Stelzig, Eugene. *Bob Dylan's Career as a Blakean Visionary and Romantic.* Unpublished dissertation, date unknown.

Thomson, Elizabeth M., ed. *Conclusions on the Wall: New Essays on Bob Dylan.* Manchester, England: Thin Man, Ltd., 1980.

Vassal, Jacques. *Electric Children: Roots and Branches of Modern Folk-Rock. New York: Taplinger Publishing Co., Inc., 1976.*

Williams, Don. Bob Dylan: The Man, the Music, the Message. New Jersey: Fleming H. Revell, 1985.

Williams, Paul. *Dylan—What Happened?* Glen Ellen, California: And/Entwhistle, 1980.

MAINLY PICTORIAL:

Brockum International, pubs. *Bob Dylan.* Programme book for 1978 European tour. Oxford, 1978.

Cott, Jonathon. *Dylan.* New York: Doubleday & Co., Inc., 1984. London: Vermilion & Co., 1984.

Kramer, Daniel. *Bob Dylan.* Secaucus, N.J.: Castle Books, 1967. New York: Pocket Books, 1968.

Landy, Elliot. *Woodstock Vision.* Hamburg: Rowohlt Verlag GmbH, 1984.

Rinzler, Alan. *Bob Dylan: The Illustrated Record.* New York: Harmony books, 1978. *Bob Dylan: Het Volledige Platenverhaal,* Amsterdam: H. J. W. Becht., 1980.

GENERAL BACKGROUND:

Allsop, Kenneth. *Hard Travellin': The Hobo and His History.* New York: New American Library, 1967. London: Hodder & Stoughton, 1968.

Baez, Joan. *Daybreak.* New York: Dial Press, 1968. London: Panther, 1971.

Bays, Gwendolyn. *The Orphic Vision: Seer Poets from Novalis to Rimbaud.* Lincoln, Neb.: University of Nebraska Press, 1964.

Bradshaw, Steve. *Cafe Society: Bohemian Life from Swift to Bob Dylan.* London: Weidenfeld and Nicholson, 1978.

Campbell, Joseph. *Myths to Live By.* London: Souvenir Press, 1972.

Dunaway, David King. *How Can I Keep from Singing: Pete Seeger.* New York: McGraw-Hill, Inc., 1981. London: Harrap, Ltd., 1985.

Dunson, Josh, *Freedom in the Air: Song Movements of the '60's.* New York: International Publishers Co., Inc., 1965.

Gillett, Charlie. *The Sound of the City.* London: Souvenir Press, Ltd., and Sphere Books, Ltd., 1970.

Graves, Robert. *The White Goddess: A Historical Grammar of Poetic Myth.* London: Faber and Faber, Ltd., 1961.

Guthrie, Woody. *Bound for Glory.* New York: E. P. Dutton, Inc., 1968.

Laing, Dave, Dallas, Karl, Denselow, Robin, and Shelton, Robert. *The Electric Muse; The Story of Folk Into Rock.* London: Eyre Methuen, 1975.

Martz, Louis L. *The Poetry of Meditation: A Study in English Religious Literature of the Seventeenth Century.* New Haven, Conn.: Yale University Press, 1954.

Nadeau, Maurice. *The History of Surrealism.* London: Jonathan Cape, 1968.

Newfield, Jack. *A Prophetic Minority: The American New Left.* London: Anthony Blond, 1967.

Oliver, Paul. *The Story of the Blues.* London: Penguin, 1972.

Plowman, Max. *An Introduction to the Study of Blake.* London: Frank Cass & Co., 1967 (second ed.).

Seeger, Pete (compiler and ed.). *Woody Guthrie Folk Songs.* New York: Ludlow Music Inc., 1963.

Wilson, Colin. *The Outsider.* London: Victor Gollancz, 1956. London: Pan Books, 1963.

BOOK AND INFORMATION SERVICES:

There are two principal clearinghouses for books and information and the publication of monographs on Dylan. One is The Telegraph/Wanted Man, c/o Bob Dylan Information Office, P.O. Box 18, Bury, Lancashire, BL9 OXJ England.

The other is Hobo Press, P.O. Box 19 00 62, 800 Munich 19, West Germany. Both of these services are run by ardent Dylan students and "fans" and can be relied upon to supply rare publications about Dylan and his music.

SONG INDEX

By S. J. Estes, edited and revised by Roger Ford

The Song Index is an alphabetical catalog of songs written or recorded by Bob Dylan. For each song it provides information, where applicable, in the following five categories:

CATEGORY 1: COPYRIGHT HOLDER AND DATE

The song's copyright holder (normally the publisher) and the date(s) of this copyright are given here for songs written partly or wholly by Dylan. If Dylan wrote the song in collaboration, then full details of authorship will be given in Category 5. If the song is not by Dylan, then Category 1 will be absent and Category 5 will state the author.

The earliest copyright date is usually a fair guide to when the song was written; if there is evidence to the contrary, this is indicated in Category 5. Later copyright dates are of no great interest, apparently relating, in most cases, to the publication of sheet music for the song.

CATEGORY 2: DYLAN'S RECORDING

If a recording of the song by Dylan has been officially released, it is indicated here; the record number and release date may be found in the Discography. If more than one Dylan recording has been released, then the "standard" (almost invariably the earliest) version is given here, and the others are listed under Category 5.

CATEGORY 3: RECORDING BY ANOTHER ARTIST

If Dylan has not released a recording of the song, or if his recording is not readily available, then a recording by another artist (if there is one) is indicated here. It is hoped that this information is fairly comprehensive, and that a useful number of the recordings are still available.

CATEGORY 4: WORDS AND MUSIC

This states where, if anywhere, to find printed words and music for the song if it is partly or wholly written by Dylan. If the song is in *Writings and Drawings by Bob Dylan* or *Lyrics, 1962–1985* (words only), this is indicated, but sheet music is given too, if available. A large number of songs appear in more than one songbook, a reference to only one of which is given for each song; these references have been selected so as to enable the reader to acquire sheet music with the minimum of duplication.

The Dylan songbooks referred to more than once are:

Writings and Drawings by Bob Dylan (Knopf)
Lyrics, 1962–1985 (Knopf; this includes all of *Writings and Drawings*)
Bob Dylan Himself (Leeds Music)
Bob Dylan (Warner Bros.)
Bob Dylan: A Retrospective (Warner Bros.)
The Songs of Bob Dylan from 1966 Through 1975 (Knopf)
Self Portrait (Big Sky Music)
Pat Garrett & Billy the Kid (Rolf Budde Musikverlag KG, Berlin)
Street-Legal (Special Rider Music)
Slow Train Coming (Special Rider Music)
Saved (Special Rider Music)
Shot of Love (Special Rider Music)
Infidels (Special Rider Music)

The words to a few otherwise unprinted Dylan songs have been published, with permission, in *The Telegraph,* the quarterly magazine of Wanted Man, a Dylan information service. Details of subscriptions and back issues are available from P.O. Box 18, Bury, Lancashire, BL9 OXJ, England.

All other sources of words and music are detailed fully under the entries for the songs concerned.

Songbooks are available for most of Dylan's albums individually, published by the copyright holder of the songs on the album.

CATEGORY 5: MISCELLANEOUS INFORMATION

This includes authorship details, further Dylan recordings, notes of concert or film performances of unrecorded songs, and other information thought to be significant.

CRITERIA FOR INCLUSION OF SONGS IN THE INDEX

The Index includes:

(a) Songs copyrighted as being partly or wholly written by Dylan and subsequently recorded by Dylan or other artists, performed by Dylan in public, on film, or on television, or published in print.

(b) Songs not written by Dylan but included in his own official recordings.

It excludes:

(a) Songs associated with Dylan only through illegally released or circulated recordings. These include only a handful of wholly original Dylan compositions, many of which are clearly unfinished. There are two personally lamented exclusions: "I'm Not There (1956)," a beautiful, though in many places incomprehensible, song sent out as a demonstration recording with much of the *Basement Tapes* material to Dylan's publishing company offices; and "Blind Willie McTell," a perfectly composed and magnificently performed lament which was recorded at the *Infidels* sessions but left off the album.

(b) Songs which Dylan's publishers have registered for copyright purposes, but which have not been made public in any way. Thirty to forty such songs are known to exist; there may be many more.

(c) Songs not written or recorded by Dylan but performed by him in public, on film, or on television. These are numerous, but are not felt to be as important as either those songs by others which he has chosen to record, or those of his own which he has performed but not recorded.

(d) Songs not written by Dylan but on which he makes a guest appearance on another artist's recording. The interpretations of these songs (which are detailed in Section 4 of the Discography) are essentially those of the artists concerned, Dylan's contributions being, as a rule, accordingly modest.

SONG TITLES

Many Dylan songs have appeared in different places under different titles. It is generally not possible to say which of the titles is "correct," so the following arbitrary rules have been applied in order to avoid duplicating song entries:

The nearest thing there is to a definitive collection of Dylan songs is *Lyrics, 1962-1985* (see Bibliography); this has been used as the principal source of titles.

For songs which are not in this anthology but which do appear in other Dylan songbooks, the titles are taken from there. This leaves (a) Dylan songs which have not appeared in print, for which the titles have been obtained from the publishers, and (b) songs not written by Dylan but which he sings on his records, for which the titles are taken from the record sleeves.

Cross-referenced entries for variant song titles are included in the Index where they are felt to be necessary.

ABBREVIATIONS USED IN THE INDEX

Freewheelin': The Freewheelin' Bob Dylan
Times Changing: The Times They Are A-Changin'
Another Side: Another Side of Bob Dylan
Back Home: Bringing It All Back Home
Highway 61: Highway 61 Revisited
Greatest Hits: Bob Dylan's Greatest Hits
Greatest Hits II: Bob Dylan's Greatest Hits, Vol. II
Pat Garrett: Pat Garrett & Billy the Kid
Basement Tapes: The Basement Tapes
Budokan: Bob Dylan at Budokan
Slow Train: Slow Train Coming
W & D: Writings and Drawings by Bob Dylan
L: Lyrics, 1962–1985
Songs of Bob Dylan: The Songs of Bob Dylan from 1966 Through 1975
A Retrospective: Bob Dylan: A Retrospective

ACKNOWLEDGMENTS

The format of the Song Index and the larger part of the information it contains are the result of many years' work by S. J. Estes. He wishes to thank the following for all their kind help: Duchess, Witmark, Dwarf, Big Sky, and Ram's Horn publishers, Columbia Records (especially John Hammond), the music press, House of Oldies, Music Inn, and Sam Goody's; and Robert Shelton, Michael Gray, Alan Goldberg, Elizabeth Mayers, Cali Hollander, Bob Stern, Bob Adams, Betty Prashker, Hugh O'Neill, and Diane Mathews.

For their invaluable assistance in my job of assembling the Discography and revising S. J. Estes's original compilation of songs, I would like to thank Diane Lapson and Naomi Saltzman at Special Rider, Sandy Gant, Rob Griffiths, Betsy Bowden, Stephen Pickering, Colin Traynor, Ian Woodward, Robert Shelton, Christopher Ricks, Kathleen Turtletaub, John Bauldie, and Clinton Heylin.

—ROGER FORD, MAY 1986

ABANDONED LOVE   1. Copyright © Ram's Horn Music 1975, 76; 2. *Biograph;* 4. *L; Songs of Bob Dylan.*

ABSOLUTELY SWEET MARIE   1. Copyright © Dwarf Music 1966; 2. *Blonde on Blonde;* 4. *W & D; Songs of Bob Dylan.*

AIN'T GONNA GO TO HELL FOR ANYBODY   1. Copyright © Special Rider Music 1980; 5. Performed in concert during 1980.

AIN'T GONNA GRIEVE   1. Copyright © Warner Bros. Inc. 1963, 68; 4. *W & D; Bob Dylan;* 5. First published in *Broadside,* August 1962, copyright © 1962 by Bob Dylan.

AIN'T NO MAN RIGHTEOUS, NO NOT ONE   1. Copyright © Special Rider Music 1981; 3. Jah Malla: *Jah Malla* (Modern MR38-135); 4. *L;* 5. Performed by Dylan in concert in late 1979.

ALBERTA #1 and ALBERTA #2   1. Copyright © Big Sky Music 1970; 2. *Self Portrait;* 4. *Self Portrait* (includes both versions); 5. Copyrights for these two versions of the same traditional song are based on Dylan's "Revised Melody and Arrangement" and "New Music," respectively.

ALL ALONG THE WATCHTOWER   1. Copyright © Dwarf Music 1968; 2. *John Wesley Harding;* 4. *W & D; Songs of Bob Dylan;* 5. Live recordings: (a) *Before the Flood,* recorded with The Band at L. A. Forum, afternoon of Feb. 14, 1974; (b) *Budokan,* recorded in Tokyo, March 1, 1978.

ALL I REALLY WANT TO DO   1. Copyright © Warner Bros. Inc. 1964; 2. *Another Side;* 4. *W & D; Bob Dylan;* 5. Live recording: *Budokan,* recorded in Tokyo, March 1, 1978.

ALL OVER YOU   1. Copyright © Warner Bros. Inc. 1968, 70; 3. Dave Van Ronk: *In The Tradition* (Prestige Folklore 14001), under the title "If I Had to Do It Again (All Over You)"; 4. *W & D;* 5. Performed by Dylan in concert in early 1963.

ALL THE TIRED HORSES   1. Copyright © Big Sky Music 1970; 2. *Self Portrait;* 4. *Songs of Bob Dylan.*

ANGEL FLYING TOO CLOSE TO THE GROUND   2. Single (B side of "Union Sundown"); 5. Written by Willie Nelson; recorded at the *Infidels* sessions.

ARE YOU READY   1. Copyright © Special Rider Music 1980; 2. *Saved;* 4. *L; Saved.*

AS I WENT OUT ONE MORNING   1. Copyright © Dwarf Music 1968; 2. *John Wesley Harding;* 4. *W & D; Songs of Bob Dylan.*

BABY, I'M IN THE MOOD FOR YOU   1. Copyright © Warner Bros. Inc. 1963, 1966; 2. *Biograph;* 4. *W & D; Bob Dylan;* 5. Recorded at one of the *Freewheelin'* sessions in mid-1962.

BABY, LET ME FOLLOW YOU DOWN   2. *Bob Dylan;* 5. On the above album, composition credited to Ric Von Schmidt. Live recording, with additional reprise, on *The Last Waltz* (see Discography, Section 4), recorded with The Band at Winterland, San Francisco, Nov. 25, 1976; in this version, composition attributed to Rev. Gary Davis.

BABY STOP CRYING 1. Copyright © Special Rider Music 1978; 2. *Street-Legal;* 4. *L; Street-Legal.*

BALLAD FOR A FRIEND 1. Copyright © Duchess Music Corp. 1962, 65; 4. *W & D; Bob Dylan Himself.*

BALLAD IN PLAIN D 1. Copyright © Warner Bros. Inc. 1964; 2. *Another Side;* 4. *W & D; Bob Dylan.*

BALLAD OF A THIN MAN 1. Copyright © Warner Bros. Inc. 1965; 2. *Highway 61;* 4. *W & D; Bob Dylan;* 5. Live recordings: (a) *Before the Flood,* recorded with The Band at L.A. Forum, afternoon of Feb. 14, 1974; (b) *Budokan,* recorded in Tokyo, March 1, 1978; (c) *Real Live,* recorded at Wembley Stadium, London, July 7, 1984.

BALLAD OF DONALD WHITE 1. Copyright © Special Rider Music 1962; 2. *Broadside Reunion* (see Discography, Section 3); 4. *W & D;* 5. The recording, which omits the second verse, was made in 1962 for a *Broadside* radio show that was never broadcast.

THE BALLAD OF EMMETT TILL (see THE DEATH OF EMMETT TILL)

THE BALLAD OF FRANKIE LEE AND JUDAS PRIEST 1. Copyright © Dwarf Music 1968; 2. *John Wesley Harding;* 4. *W & D; Songs of Bob Dylan.*

BALLAD OF HOLLIS BROWN 1. Copyright © Warner Bros. Inc. 1963; 2. *Times Changing;* 4. *W & D; Bob Dylan;* 5. Originally published in *Broadside* under the title "Rise and Fall of Hollis Brown," copyright © 1962 by Bob Dylan. An extra verse, between the second and third, appears in the songbook *Young Folk* (Simon & Schuster, 1963).

THE BALLAD OF IRA HAYES 2. *Dylan;* 5. Written by Peter La Farge.

BALLAD OF MEDGAR EVERS (see ONLY A PAWN IN THEIR GAME)

BAND OF THE HAND 1. Copyright © Special Rider Music 1986; 2. Single; 5. Recorded with Tom Petty's Heartbreakers for the film *Band of the Hand;* also to be included in the soundtrack album.

BELLE ISLE 1. Copyright © Big Sky Music 1970; 2. *Self Portrait;* 4. *Self Portrait;* 5. Copyright based on Dylan's "New Music"; the song is traditional.

BIG YELLOW TAXI 2. *Dylan;* 5. Written by Joni Mitchell.

BILLY 1. Copyright © Ram's Horn Music 1972, 73; 2. *Pat Garrett;* 4. *L; Songs of Bob Dylan;* 5. The album has three versions, entitled "Billy 1," "Billy 4," and "Billy 7." The printed version (just "Billy") does not correspond exactly to any of these, and has a verse of its own.

BILLY'S SURRENDER 1. Copyright © Ram's Horn Music 1973; 5. This instrumental is used in the soundtrack of *Pat Garrett & Billy the Kid* but does not appear on the album.

BLACK CROW BLUES 1. Copyright © Warner Bros. Inc. 1964; 2. *Another Side;* 4. *W & D; Bob Dylan.*

BLACK DIAMOND BAY 1. Copyright © Ram's Horn Music 1975, 76; 2. *Desire;* 4. *L; Songs of Bob Dylan;* 5. Words written with Jacques Levy.

BLESSED IS THE NAME   1. Copyright © Special Rider Music 1979; 5. Performed in concert in late 1979 and early 1980.

BLOWIN' IN THE WIND   1. Copyright © Warner Bros. Inc. 1962; 2. *Freewheelin'*; 4. *W & D; Bob Dylan;* 5. Live recordings: (a) *Evening Concerts at Newport, Vol. 1* (see Discography, Section 3), recorded at the Newport Folk Festival, July 26, 1963; (b) *The Concert for Bangladesh* (see Discography, Section 3), recorded at Madison Square Garden, evening of Aug. 1, 1971; (c) *Before the Flood,* recorded with The Band at L.A. Forum, Feb. 13 and evening of Feb. 14, 1974—the track is spliced; (d) *Budokan,* recorded in Tokyo, March 1, 1978. *W & D* and the sheet music both have the second and third verses reversed; Dylan is not known ever to have sung the verses in this order.

BLUE MOON   2. *Self Portrait;* 5. Written by Lorenz Hart and Richard Rodgers.

BOB DYLAN'S BLUES   1. Copyright © Warner Bros. Inc. 1963, 66; 2. *Freewheelin';* 4. *W & D; Bob Dylan: A Collection.*

BOB DYLAN'S DREAM   1. Copyright © Warner Bros. Inc. 1963, 64; 2. *Freewheelin';* 4. *W & D; A Retrospective.*

BOB DYLAN'S 115TH DREAM   1. Copyright © Warner Bros. Inc. 1965; 2. *Back Home;* 4. *W & D; A Retrospective.*

BOB DYLAN'S NEW ORLEANS RAG   1. Copyright © Warner Bros. Inc. 1970; 4. *W & D;* 5. Performed in concert in early 1963.

BOOTS OF SPANISH LEATHER   1. Copyright © Warner Bros. Inc. 1963, 64; 2. *Times Changing;* 4. *W & D; Bob Dylan.*

THE BOXER   2. *Self Portrait;* 5. Written by Paul Simon.

BUCKETS OF RAIN   1. Copyright © Ram's Horn Music 1974, 75; 2. *Blood on the Tracks;* 4. *L; Songs of Bob Dylan;* 5. Dylan sings a rather different version of this song with Bette Midler on her album *Songs for the New Depression* (see Discography, Section 4).

BUNKHOUSE THEME   1. Copyright © Ram's Horn Music 1973; 2. *Pat Garrett;* 4. *Pat Garrett;* 5. Instrumental.

CALIFORNIA   1. Copyright © Warner Bros. Inc. 1972, 85; 4. *W & D;* 5. Recorded at the *Another Side* sessions but not released. *W & D* states that this is an early version of "Outlaw Blues"; the songs have a verse in common.

CAN YOU PLEASE CRAWL OUT YOUR WINDOW?   1. Copyright © Warner Bros. Inc. 1965, 66; 2. Single; 4. *W & D;* 5. The single listed in the Discography, recorded with The Band, is also on *Masterpieces* and *Biograph.* An earlier version, recorded at the *Highway 61* sessions, was mistakenly released on the West Coast under the title "Positively 4th Street" when that single was first released in Sept. 1965; it was quickly replaced by the correct track.

CAN'T HELP FALLING IN LOVE   2. *Dylan;* 5. Written by G. Weiss, H. Peretti, and L. Creatore.

CANTINA THEME (WORKIN' FOR THE LAW)   1. Copyright © Ram's Horn Music 1973; 2. *Pat Garrett;* 4. *Pat Garrett;* 5. Instrumental.

CARIBBEAN WIND   1. Copyright © Special Rider Music 1985; 2. *Biograph;* 4. *L;* 5. Recorded at the *Shot of Love* sessions. Dylan performed an earlier version in concert in late 1980.

CATFISH   1. Copyright © Ram's Horn Music 1975, 76; 3. Joe Cocker: *Stingray* (A & M AM 4574); 4. *L; Songs of Bob Dylan;* 5. Words written with Jacques Levy.

CHAMPAIGN, ILLINOIS   1. Copyright © Cedarwood Publishing Co. Inc. 1969; 3. Carl Perkins: *On Top* (Columbia CS 9931); 4. *Country Song Hall of Fame No. 16: Bob Dylan* (Southern Music, England); 5. Written with Carl Perkins.

CHANGING OF THE GUARDS   1. Copyright © Special Rider Music 1978; 2. *Street-Legal;* 4. *L; Street-Legal.*

CHIMES OF FREEDOM   1. Copyright © Warner Bros. Inc. 1964; 2. *Another Side;* 4. *W & D; A Retrospective.*

CITY OF GOLD   1. Copyright © Special Rider Music 1980; 5. Performed in concert in late 1980 and 1981.

CLEAN CUT KID   1. Copyright © Special Rider Music 1984; 2. *Empire Burlesque;* 4. *L; Empire Burlesque;* 5. Originally recorded at the *Infidels* sessions but not released; re-recorded for *Empire Burlesque.*

CLOTHES LINE   1. Copyright © Dwarf Music 1969, 75; 2. *Basement Tapes;* 4. *W & D; Songs of Bob Dylan;* 5. Recorded in 1967. The title "Clothes Line Saga" is used on the record and in the sheet music.

COMING FROM THE HEART (THE ROAD IS LONG)   1. Copyright © Special Rider Music 1979; 3. The Searchers: *Searchers* (Sire SRK 6082: English); 4. *L;* 5. Written with Helena Springs. Performed by Dylan in concert in late 1978.

COPPER KETTLE   2. *Self Portrait;* 5. Traditional.

CORRINA, CORRINA   1. Copyright © Warner Bros. Inc. 1962, 66; 2. *Freewheelin';* 4. *W & D; Bob Dylan;* 5. The credit on the record label is "Adapted and arranged by B. Dylan": It is Dylan's reworking of a traditional song. A slightly different version, recorded at the same sessions, was released as the B side of "Mixed Up Confusion."

COUNTRY PIE   1. Copyright © Big Sky Music 1969; 2. *Nashville Skyline;* 4. *W & D; Songs of Bob Dylan.*

COVENANT WOMAN   1. Copyright © Special Rider Music 1980; 2. *Saved;* 4. *L; Saved;* 5. Performed in concert in late 1979.

COVER DOWN, BREAK THROUGH   1. Copyright © Special Rider Music 1980; 5. Performed in concert in early 1980.

CRASH ON THE LEVEE (see DOWN IN THE FLOOD)

DADDY, YOU BEEN ON MY MIND (see MAMA, YOU BEEN ON MY MIND)

DARK EYES   1. Copyright © Special Rider Music 1985; 2. *Empire Burlesque;* 4. *L; Empire Burlesque.*

DAY OF THE LOCUSTS   1. Copyright © Big Sky Music 1970; 2. *New Morning;* 4. *W & D; Songs of Bob Dylan.*

DAYS OF 49   2. *Self Portrait;* 5. Although the *Self Portrait* songbook credits Dylan with "Revised melody and new music," no copyright is held by Big Sky; the song is traditional.

DEAD MAN, DEAD MAN   1. Copyright © Special Rider Music 1981; 2. *Shot of Love;* 4. *L; Shot of Love.*

DEAR LANDLORD   1. Copyright © Dwarf Music 1968; 2. *John Wesley Harding;* 4. *W & D; Songs of Bob Dylan.*

DEAR MRS. ROOSEVELT   2. *A Tribute to Woody Guthrie, Part One* (see Discography, Section 3); 5. Written by Woody Guthrie. The recording was made with The Band at a Guthrie memorial concert, Carnegie Hall, Jan. 20, 1968.

THE DEATH OF EMMETT TILL   1. Copyright © Warner Bros. Inc. 1963, 68; 2. *Broadside Reunion* (see Discography, Section 3); 4. *W & D; Bob Dylan;* 5. The recording was made in 1962 for a *Broadside* radio show that was never broadcast. The words included with the album are copyright © 1962 by Bob Dylan; the title used is "The Ballad of Emmett Till."

DENISE   1. Copyright © Warner Bros. Inc. 1970; 4. *W & D; A Retrospective;* 5. Recorded at the *Another Side* sessions but not released.

DESOLATION ROW   1. Copyright © Warner Bros. Inc. 1965; 2. *Highway 61;* 4. *W & D; Bob Dylan.*

DIRGE   1. Copyright © Ram's Horn Music 1973, 74; 2. *Planet Waves;* 4. *L; Songs of Bob Dylan.*

DO RIGHT TO ME BABY (DO UNTO OTHERS)   1. Copyright © Special Rider Music 1979; 2. *Slow Train;* 4. *L; Slow Train.*

DON'T FALL APART ON ME TONIGHT   1. Copyright © Special Rider Music 1983; 2. *Infidels;* 4. *L; Infidels.*

DON'T THINK TWICE, IT'S ALL RIGHT   1. Copyright © Warner Bros. Inc. 1963; 2. *Freewheelin';* 4. *W & D; Bob Dylan;* 5. Live recordings: (a) *Before the Flood,* recorded at L.A. Forum, evening of Feb. 14, 1974; (b) *Budokan,* recorded in Tokyo, Feb. 28, 1978. Originally published in *Broadside* under the title "It's All Right."

DON'T YA TELL HENRY   1. Copyright © Dwarf Music 1971, 75; 3. The Band: *Basement Tapes* (see Discography, Section 1); 4. *W & D; Songs of Bob Dylan;* 5. Recorded in 1967.

DOWN ALONG THE COVE   1. Copyright © Dwarf Music 1968; 2. *John Wesley Harding;* 4. *W & D; Songs of Bob Dylan.*

DOWN IN THE FLOOD   1. Copyright © Dwarf Music 1967, 75; 2. *Basement Tapes;* 4. *W & D; Songs of Bob Dylan;* 5. The title used on the album and in the sheet music is "Crash on the Levee (Down in the Flood)." *Greatest Hits II* contains a later version, recorded in late 1971 with Happy Traum.

DOWN THE HIGHWAY   1. Copyright © Warner Bros. Inc. 1963, 67; 2. *Freewheelin';* 4. *W & D; Bob Dylan.*

DREADFUL DAY (see I'D HATE TO BE YOU ON THAT DREADFUL DAY)

DRIFTER'S ESCAPE   1. Copyright © Dwarf Music 1968; 2. *John Wesley Harding;* 4. *W & D; Songs of Bob Dylan.*

DUSTY OLD FAIRGROUNDS   1. Copyright © Warner Bros. Inc. 1973, 85; 3. Blue Ash: *No More, No Less* (Mercury SRM 1 666); 4. *L;* 5. Performed by Dylan in concert in 1963.

EARLY MORNIN' RAIN   2. *Self Portrait;* 5. Written by Gordon Lightfoot.

EMOTIONALLY YOURS   1. Copyright © Special Rider Music 1985; 2. *Empire Burlesque;* 4. *L; Empire Burlesque.*

ENOUGH IS ENOUGH   1. Copyright © Special Rider Music 1984; 5. Performed in concerts in Europe in 1984.

ETERNAL CIRCLE   1. Copyright © Warner Bros. Inc. 1963, 64; 3. Coulson, Dean, McGuinness and Flint: *Lo and Behold* (Sire SAS 7405); 4. *W & D; Bob Dylan.*

EVERY GRAIN OF SAND   1. Copyright © Special Rider Music 1981; 2. *Shot of Love;* 4. *L; Shot of Love;* 5. Written in 1980, or possibly earlier.

FAREWELL   1. Copyright © Warner Bros. Inc. 1963, 73; 3. Judy Collins: *Recollections* (Elektra EKS 74055); 4. *W & D; Bob Dylan;* 5. First published in *Broadside* under the title "Fare-Thee-Well."

FAREWELL ANGELINA   1. Copyright © Warner Bros. Inc. 1965, 66; 3. Joan Baez: *Farewell Angelina* (Vanguard VSD 79200); 4. *W & D; Bob Dylan.*

FATHER OF NIGHT   1. Copyright © Big Sky Music 1970; 2. *New Morning;* 4. *W & D; Songs of Bob Dylan.*

FINAL THEME   1. Copyright © Ram's Horn Music 1973; 2. *Pat Garrett;* 4. *Pat Garrett;* 5. Instrumental.

FIXIN' TO DIE   2. *Bob Dylan;* 5. Written by Bukka White.

A FOOL SUCH AS I   2. *Dylan;* 5. Written by Bill Trader.

FOREVER YOUNG   1. Copyright © Ram's Horn Music 1973, 74; 2. *Planet Waves;* 4. *L; Songs of Bob Dylan;* 5. *Planet Waves* has two versions of the song, and music for each of these is included in the songbook for the album; that in *Songs of Bob Dylan* is for the slower version. A rough demo version appears on *Biograph.* Live recordings: (a) *The Last Waltz* (see Discography, Section 4), recorded with The Band at Winterland, San Francisco, Nov. 25, 1976; (b) *Budokan,* recorded in Tokyo, Feb. 28, 1978.

FOURTH TIME AROUND   1. Copyright © Dwarf Music 1966; 2. *Blonde on Blonde;* 4. *W & D; Songs of Bob Dylan.*

FREIGHT TRAIN BLUES   1. Copyright © Leeds Music Corp. 1978; 2. *Bob Dylan;* 5. Copyright based on Dylan's arrangement; the song is traditional. Original unpublished copyright by Duchess, 1961.

FROM A BUICK 6   1. Copyright © Warner Bros. Inc. 1965; 2. *Highway 61;* 4. *W & D; Bob Dylan;* 5. A different recording from the same sessions, which appeared on some early U.S. copies of *Highway 61,* may currently be found on the Japanese edition of the album (CBS/Sony 25AP 273).

GAMBLIN' WILLIE (see RAMBLING, GAMBLING WILLIE)

GATES OF EDEN   1. Copyright © Warner Bros. Inc. 1965; 2. *Back Home;* 4. *W & D; A Retrospective.*

GEORGE JACKSON   1. Copyright © Ram's Horn Music 1971; 2. Single; 4. *L; Songs of Bob Dylan;* 5. The single comprises two versions, labeled "Big Band" and "Acoustic"; the former is also on *Masterpieces.* The sheet music is for the acoustic version.

GET YOUR ROCKS OFF!   1. Copyright © Dwarf Music 1968, 73; 3. Manfred Mann: *Get Your Rocks Off* (Polydor 5050); 4. *W & D; Songs of Bob Dylan.* 5. Recorded by Dylan at the *Basement Tapes* sessions but not released.

GIRL FROM THE NORTH COUNTRY   1. Copyright © Warner Bros. Inc. 1963; 2. *Freewheelin';* 4. *W & D; Bob Dylan;* 5. Dylan also sings this, with Johnny Cash, on *Nashville Skyline.* Live recording: *Real Live,* recorded at Slane Castle, near Dublin, July 8, 1984.

GO 'WAY LITTLE BOY   1. Copyright © Special Rider Music 1984; 3. Lone Justice: on B side of 12-ich single "Sweet, Sweet Baby (I'm Falling)" (Geffen); 5. Recorded by Dylan at one of the *Empire Burlesque* sessions but not released.

GOING, GOING, GONE   1. Copyright © Ram's Horn Music 1973, 74; 2. *Planet Waves;* 4. *L; Songs of Bob Dylan;* 5. Live recording: *Budokan,* recorded in Tokyo, March 1, 1978.

GOIN' TO ACAPULCO   1. Copyright © Dwarf Music 1975; 2. *Basement Tapes;* 4. *L; Songs of Bob Dylan;* 5. Recorded in 1967.

GOLDEN LOOM   1. Copyright © Ram's Horn Music 1975, 76; 3. Roger McGuinn: *Thunderbyrd* (Columbia PC 34656); 4. *L; Songs of Bob Dylan.*

GONNA CHANGE MY WAY OF THINKING   1. Copyright © Special Rider Music 1979; 2. *Slow Train;* 4. *L; Slow Train.*

GOSPEL PLOW   1. Copyright © Duchess Music 1962, 65; 2. *Bob Dylan;* 4. *Bob Dylan Himself;* 5. Copyright based on Dylan's "Music and New Lyric"; the song is traditional. The sheet music contains three verses Dylan does not sing on the recording.

GOTTA SERVE SOMEBODY   1. Copyright © Special Rider Music 1979; 2. *Slow Train;* 4. *L; Slow Train.*

GOTTA TRAVEL ON   2. *Self Portrait;* 5. Written by P. Clayton, L. Erlich, D. Lazar, and T. Six.

THE GRAND COULEE DAM   2. *A Tribute to Woody Guthrie, Part One* (see Discography, Section 3); 5. Written by Woody Guthrie. The recording was made with The Band at a Guthrie memorial concert at Carnegie Hall, Jan. 20, 1968.

THE GROOM'S STILL WAITING AT THE ALTAR   1. Copyright © Special Rider Music 1981; 2. Single (B side of U.S. issue of "Heart of Mine"); 4. *L;* 5. Recorded at the *Shot of Love* sessions; later included in *Biograph.* Dylan performed an earlier version at concerts in late 1980.

GUESS I'M DOIN' FINE   1. Copyright © Warner Bros. Inc. 1964, 66; 3. Hamilton Camp: *Paths of Victory* (Elektra EKS 7278); *W & D; Bob Dylan.*

GYPSY LOU   1. Copyright © Warner Bros. Inc. 1963, 66; 4. *W & D; Bob Dylan.*

A HARD RAIN'S A-GONNA FALL 1. Copyright © Warner Bros. Inc. 1963; 2. *Freewheelin'*; 4. *W & D; Bob Dylan*; 5. Live recording: *The Concert for Bangladesh* (see Discography, Section 3), recorded at Madison Square Garden, evening of Aug. 1, 1971.

HARD TIMES IN NEW YORK TOWN 1. Copyright © Duchess Music Corp. 1962, 65; 4. *W & D; Bob Dylan Himself.*

HAZEL 1. Copyright © Ram's Horn Music 1973, 74; 2. *Planet Waves;* 4. *L; Songs of Bob Dylan.*

HE WAS A FRIEND OF MINE 1. Copyright © Duchess Music Corp. 1962, 65; 3. Dave Van Ronk: *Dave Van Ronk, Folksinger* (Prestige International 13056); 4. *Bob Dylan Himself;* 5. Copyright based on Dylan's "Arrangement of Music and New Lyric"; it is an adaptation of a traditional song.

HEART OF MINE 1. Copyright © Special Rider Music 1981; 2. *Shot of Love;* 4. *L; Shot of Love;* 5. First released, in abridged form, as a single in Britain and Europe. Live recording: *Biograph,* recorded at Saenger Theater, New Orleans, Nov. 11, 1981.

HERO BLUES 1. Copyright © Warner Bros. Inc. 1963; 4. *W & D; Bob Dylan.*

HIGHWAY 51 2. *Bob Dylan;* 5. Written by Curtis Jones.

HIGHWAY 61 REVISITED 1. Copyright © Warner Bros. Inc. 1965; 2. *Highway 61;* 4. *W & D; Bob Dylan;* 5. Live recordings: (a) *Before the Flood,* recorded with The Band at L.A. Forum, evening of Feb. 14, 1974; (b) *Real Live,* recorded at Wembley Stadium, London, July 7, 1984.

HONEY, JUST ALLOW ME ONE MORE CHANCE 1. Copyright © Warner Bros. Inc. 1963, 66; 2. *Freewheelin';* 4. *W & D; Bob Dylan;* 5. This is Dylan's adaptation of a song by Henry Thomas, who receives joint credit on the album but not in the songbooks.

HOUSE OF THE RISIN' SUN 1. Copyright © Leeds Music Corp. 1978; 2. *Bob Dylan;* 5. Copyright based on Dylan's arrangement; the song is traditional. Original unpublished copyright by Duchess, 1961.

HURRICANE 1. Copyright © Ram's Horn Music 1975; 2. *Desire;* 4. *L; Songs of Bob Dylan;* 5. Words written with Jacques Levy.

I AIN'T GOT NO HOME 2. *A Tribute to Woody Guthrie, Part One* (see Discography, Section 3); 5. Written by Woody Guthrie.

I AM A LONESOME HOBO 1. Copyright © Dwarf Music 1968; 2. *John Wesley Harding;* 4. *W & D; Songs of Bob Dylan.*

I AND I 1. Copyright © Special Rider Music 1983; 2. *Infidels;* 4. *L; Infidels;* 5. Live recording: *Real Live,* recorded at Slane Castle, near Dublin, July 8, 1984.

I BELIEVE IN YOU 1. Copyright © Special Rider Music 1979; 2. *Slow Train;* 4. *L; Slow Train.*

I CAN'T LEAVE HER BEHIND 1. Copyright © Dwarf Music 1978; 5. *Eat the Document,* filmed in Europe in spring 1966, shows Dylan playing this song in a hotel room.

I DON'T BELIEVE YOU (SHE ACTS LIKE WE NEVER HAVE MET) 1. Copyright © Warner Bros. Inc. 1964; 2. *Another Side;* 4. *W & D; Bob Dylan;* 5. Live recordings: (a) *Biograph,* recorded with The Band at the ABC Cinema, Belfast, May 6, 1966; (b) *The Last Waltz,* recorded with The Band at Winterland, San Francisco, Nov. 25, 1976.

I DON'T WANT TO DO IT 1. Copyright © Big Sky Music 1984; 3. George Harrison: *Porky's Revenge* original soundtrack album (Columbia); 5. Probably written in 1969 or 1970.

I DREAMED I SAW ST. AUGUSTINE 1. Copyright © Dwarf Music 1968; 2. *John Wesley Harding;* 4. *W & D; Songs of Bob Dylan.*

I FORGOT MORE THAN YOU'LL EVER KNOW 2. *Self Portrait;* 5. Written by C. A. Null.

I MUST LOVE YOU TOO MUCH (see LOVE YOU TOO MUCH)

I NEED A WOMAN (see NEED A WOMAN)

I PITY THE POOR IMMIGRANT 1. Copyright © Dwarf Music 1968; 2. *John Wesley Harding;* 4. *W & D; Songs of Bob Dylan.*

I SHALL BE FREE 1. Copyright © Warner Bros. Inc. 1963, 67; 2. *Freewheelin';* 4. *W & D; Bob Dylan;* 5. The version in *W & D* is substantially revised.

I SHALL BE FREE NO. 10 1. Copyright © Special Rider Music 1971, 73; 2. *Another Side;* 4. *W & D.*

I SHALL BE RELEASED 1. Copyright © Dwarf Music 1967, 70; 2. *Greatest Hits II;* 4. *W & D; Songs of Bob Dylan;* 5. Originally recorded at the *Basement Tapes* sessions but not released; the *Greatest Hits II* recording, made in late 1971 with Happy Traum, omits the first verse. Live recordings: (a) *The Last Waltz* (see Discography, Section 4), recorded with The Band and others at Winterland, San Francisco, Nov. 25, 1976; (b) *Budokan,* recorded in Tokyo, March 1, 1978.

I THREW IT ALL AWAY 1. Copyright © Big Sky Music 1969; 2. *Nashville Skyline;* 4. *W & D; Songs of Bob Dylan;* 5. Live recording: *Hard Rain,* recorded with the Rolling Thunder Revue at Terrent County Convention Center, Fort Worth, Texas, May 16, 1976.

I WANNA BE YOUR LOVER 1. Copyright © Dwarf Music 1971, 76; 2. *Biograph;* 4. *W & D; Songs of Bob Dylan;* 5. Recorded with The Band in late 1965.

I WANT YOU 1. Copyright © Dwarf Music 1966; 2. *Blonde on Blonde;* 4. *W & D; Songs of Bob Dylan;* 5. Live recording: *Budokan,* recorded in Tokyo, March 1, 1978.

I WILL LOVE HIM 1. Copyright © Special Rider Music 1980; 5. Performed in concert in early 1980.

I WILL NOT GO DOWN UNDER THE GROUND (see LET ME DIE IN MY FOOTSTEPS)

I'D HATE TO BE YOU ON THAT DREADFUL DAY 1. Copyright © Warner Bros. Inc. 1964, 67; 2. *Broadside Reunion* (see Discography, Section 3); 4. *W & D; Bob Dylan;* 5. Earlier words, transcribed from the recording (only three verses, probably recorded in late 1962) are included with the album and are copyright © 1962 by Bob Dylan; the title used here is "Dreadful Day."

I'D HAVE YOU ANY TIME   1. Copyright © Big Sky Music and Harrisongs Music Ltd. 1970; 3. George Harrison: *All Things Must Pass* (Apple STCH 639); 4. *W & D; Songs of Bob Dylan;* 5. Written with George Harrison.

IDIOT WIND   1. Copyright © Ram's Horn Music 1974, 75; 2. *Blood on the Tracks;* 4. *L; Songs of Bob Dylan;* 5. Live recording: *Hard Rain,* recorded with the Rolling Thunder Revue at Hughes Stadium, Fort Collins, Colorado, May 23, 1976. An earlier, very different version of the song was included on promotional copies of *Blood on the Tracks;* the words to this version are printed in Betsy Bowden's *Performed Literature* (see Bibliography).

IF DOGS RUN FREE   1. Copyright © Big Sky Music 1970; 2. *New Morning;* 4. *W & D; Songs of Bob Dylan.*

IF I DON'T BE THERE BY MORNING   1. Copyright © Special Rider Music 1978; 3. Eric Clapton: *Backless* (RSO RS 1 3039); 4. *L;* Eric Clapton songbook *Backless* (Chappell Music); 5. Written with Helena Springs.

IF I HAD TO DO IT ALL OVER AGAIN (see ALL OVER YOU)

IF NOT FOR YOU   1. Copyright © Big Sky Music 1970; 2. *New Morning;* 4. *W & D; Songs of Bob Dylan.*

IF YOU GOTTA GO, GO NOW   1. Copyright © Warner Bros. Inc. 1965; 2. Single (only released in part of Europe); 3. Manfred Mann: *The Best of Manfred Mann* (Capitol M 11688); 4. *W & D;* 5. The single, though not released until 1967, was recorded at the *Back Home* sessions.

IF YOU SEE HER, SAY HELLO   1. Copyright © Ram's Horn Music 1974, 75; 2. *Blood on the Tracks;* 4. *L; Songs of Bob Dylan;* 5. An earlier version was included in promotional copies of the album.

I'LL BE YOUR BABY TONIGHT   1. Copyright © Dwarf Music 1968; 2. *John Wesley Harding;* 4. *W & D; Songs of Bob Dylan.*

I'LL KEEP IT WITH MINE   1. Copyright © Warner Bros. Inc. 1965, 68; 2. *Biograph;* 4. *W & D; Bob Dylan;* 5. Recorded at the *Back Home* sessions.

I'LL REMEMBER YOU   1. Copyright © Special Rider Music 1985; 2. *Empire Burlesque;* 4. *L; Empire Burlesque.*

IN MY TIME OF DYING   1. Copyright © Leeds Music Corp. 1978; 2. *Bob Dylan;* 5. Copyright based on Dylan's arrangement; the song is traditional. Original unpublished copyright by Duchess, 1961.

IN SEARCH OF LITTLE SADIE   (see LITTLE SADIE)

IN THE GARDEN   1. Copyright © Special Rider Music 1980; 2. *Saved;* 4. *L; Saved;* 5. Performed in concert in late 1979.

IN THE SUMMERTIME   1. Copyright © Special Rider Music 1981; 2. *Shot of Love;* 4. *L; Shot of Love.*

IS YOUR LOVE IN VAIN?   1. Copyright © Special Rider Music 1978;

2. *Street-Legal;* 4. *L; Street-Legal;* 5. Live recording: *Budokan,* recorded in Tokyo, March 1, 1978.

ISIS   1. Copyright © Ram's Horn Music 1975, 76; 2. *Desire;* 4. *L; Songs of Bob Dylan;* 5. Words written with Jacques Levy. Live recording: *Biograph,* recorded with the Rolling Thunder Revue at Montreal Forum, Dec. 4, 1975; this recording was originally released as the B side of "Heart of Mine" in the United States and parts of Europe.

IT AIN'T ME, BABE   1. Copyright © Warner Bros. Inc. 1964; 2. *Another Side;* 4. *W & D; Bob Dylan;* 5. Live recordings: (a) *Before the Flood,* recorded with The Band at L.A. Forum, evening of Feb. 14, 1974; (b) *Real Live,* recorded at Wembley Stadium, London, July 7, 1984.

IT HURTS ME TOO   1. Copyright © Big Sky Music 1970; 2. *Self Portrait;* 4. *Self Portrait;* 5. Copyright based on Dylan's "New Music"; the song is traditional.

IT TAKES A LOT TO LAUGH, IT TAKES A TRAIN TO CRY   1. Copyright © Warner Bros. Inc. 1965; 2. *Highway 61;* 4. *W & D; Bob Dylan;* 5. Live recording: *The Concert for Bangladesh* (see Discography, Section 3), recorded at Madison Square Garden, evening of August 1, 1971.

IT'S ALL OVER NOW, BABY BLUE   1. Copyright © Warner Bros. Inc. 1965; 2. *Back Home;* 4. *W & D; Bob Dylan;* 5. Live recording: *Biograph,* recorded at the Free Trades Hall, Manchester, May 17, 1966.

IT'S ALRIGHT, MA (I'M ONLY BLEEDING)   1. Copyright © Warner Bros. Inc. 1965; 2. *Back Home;* 4. *W & D; Bob Dylan;* 5. Live recordings: (a) *Before the Flood,* recorded at L.A. Forum, evening of Feb. 14, 1974; (b) *Budokan,* recorded in Tokyo, Feb. 28, 1978.

JACK O'DIAMONDS   1. Copyright © Special Rider Music 1973 (Some Other Kinds of Songs); 3. Fairport Convention: *Fairport Convention* (Cotillion SD 9024); 5. Credited to Dylan and Ben Carruthers. Carruthers adapted some of the words from Dylan's poem in "Some Other Kinds of Songs" (on the sleeve of *Another Side*) and set them to music that was not accepted by Dylan; he nevertheless recorded the song in 1965 with a British group, The Deep. Fairport Convention's recording of Carruthers's arrangement was also made without proper consent.

JESUS IS THE ONE   1. Copyright © Special Rider Music 1982; 5. Performed in concert during 1981.

JET PILOT   1. Copyright © Special Rider Music 1985; 2. *Biograph;* 5. Recorded in 1965, probably at the *Highway 61* sessions; originally entitled "Pilot Eyes."

JOEY   1. Copyright © Ram's Horn Music 1975, 76; 2. *Desire;* 4. *L; Songs of Bob Dylan;* 5. Words written with Jacques Levy.

JOHN BROWN   1. Copyright © Warner Bros. Inc. 1963, 68; 2. *Broadside Ballads, Vol. 1* (see Discography, Section 3); 4. *W & D; Bob Dylan;* 5. Words transcribed from the recording (probably made in late 1962) are included with the album and are copyright © 1962 by Bob Dylan.

JOHN WESLEY HARDING 1. Copyright © Dwarf Music 1968; 2. *John Wesley Harding;* 4. *W & D; Songs of Bob Dylan.*

JOKERMAN 1. Copyright © Special Rider Music 1983; 2. *Infidels;* 4. *L; Infidels.*

JUST ALLOW ME ONE MORE CHANCE (see HONEY, JUST ALLOW ME ONE MORE CHANCE)

JUST LIKE A WOMAN 1. Copyright © Dwarf Music 1966; 2. *Blonde on Blonde;* 4. *W & D; Songs of Bob Dylan;* 5. Live recordings: (a) *The Concert for Bangladesh* (see Discography, Section 3), recorded at Madison Square Garden, evening of Aug. 1, 1971; (b) *Before the Flood,* recorded at L.A. Forum, evening of Feb. 14, 1974; (c) *Budokan,* recorded in Tokyo, March 1, 1978.

JUST LIKE TOM THUMB'S BLUES 1. Copyright © Warner Bros. Inc. 1965; 2. *Highway 61;* 4. *W & D; Bob Dylan;* 5. Live recording: single (B side of "I Want You"), recorded with The Band at Liverpool Odeon, May 14, 1966; this version is also on *Masterpieces.*

KNOCKIN' ON HEAVEN'S DOOR 1. Copyright © Ram's Horn Music 1973, 74; 2. *Pat Garrett;* 4. *L; Songs of Bob Dylan;* 5. Live recordings: (a) *Before the Flood,* recorded with The Band at Madison Square Garden, afternoon of Jan. 31, 1974; (b) *Budokan,* recorded in Tokyo, March 1, 1978. Both of these versions contain an extra verse not included in the original recording or the sheet music.

LAY DOWN YOUR WEARY TUNE 1. Copyright © Warner Bros. Inc. 1964, 65; 2. *Biograph;* 4. *W & D; Bob Dylan;* 5. Recorded at the *Times* sessions.

LAY, LADY, LAY 1. Copyright © Big Sky Music 1969; 2. *Nashville Skyline;* 4. *W & D; Songs of Bob Dylan;* 5. Live recordings: (a) *Before the Flood,* recorded with The Band at L.A. Forum, Feb. 13, 1974; (b) *Hard Rain,* recorded with the Rolling Thunder Revue at Terrent County Convention Center, Forth Worth, Texas, May 16, 1976.

LEGIONNAIRES' DISEASE 1. Copyright © Special Rider Music 1981; 3. Delta Cross Band: *Up Front* (Medley MdLP 6065: Danish); 4. *L;* 5. Probably written in late 1978.

LENNY BRUCE 1. Copyright © Special Rider Music 1981; 2. *Shot of Love;* 4. *L; Shot of Love.*

LEOPARD-SKIN PILL-BOX HAT 1. Copyright © Dwarf Music 1966; 2. *Blonde on Blonde;* 4. *W & D; Songs of Bob Dylan.*

LET IT BE ME 2. *Self Portrait;* 5. Written by M. Curtis, G. Becaud, and P. Delano. A version recorded at the *Shot of Love* sessions was released in Britain and Europe as the B side of "Heart of Mine."

LET ME DIE IN MY FOOTSTEPS 1. Copyright © Warner Bros. Inc. 1963, 65; 3. Happy Traum: *Broadside Ballads, Vol. 1* (see Discography, Section 3); 4. *W & D; Bob Dylan;* 5. This song appeared on some very early copies of *Freewheelin'.* The *Broadside* album includes words and music for the song, under the title "I Will Not Go Down Under the

Ground"; this is a slightly different version of the song from that in *W & D,* etc., and is copyright © 1962 by Bob Dylan. Dylan is alleged to have sung harmony vocals on the Traum recording, but this appears to be undocumented.

LET'S KEEP IT BETWEEN US   1. Copyright © Special Rider Music 1982; 3. Bonnie Raitt: *Green Light* (Warner Bros.); 4. *L;* 5. Performed by Dylan in concert in late 1980, with words somewhat different from those printed.

LICENSE TO KILL   1. Copyright © Special Rider Music 1983; 2. *Infidels;* 4. *L; Infidels;* 5. Live recording: *Real Live,* recorded at St. James Park, Newcastle, July 5, 1984.

LIKE A ROLLING STONE   1. Copyright © Warner Bros. Inc. 1965; 2. *Highway 61;* 4. *W & D; Bob Dylan;* 5. First released as a single. Live recordings: (a) *Self Portrait,* recorded with The Band at the Isle of Wight Festival, Aug. 31, 1969; (b) *Before the Flood,* recorded with The Band at L.A. Forum, Feb. 13, 1974; (c) *Budokan,* recorded in Tokyo, March 1, 1978.

LILY OF THE WEST   2. *Dylan;* 5. Written by E. Davies and J. Peterson.

LILY, ROSEMARY AND THE JACK OF HEARTS   1. Copyright © Ram's Horn Music 1974, 75; 2. *Blood on the Tracks;* 4. *L; Songs of Bob Dylan;* 5. An earlier version was present on promotional copies of the album; this version includes the song's twelfth verse, which the released version omits.

LITTLE SADIE and IN SEARCH OF LITTLE SADIE   1. Copyright © Big Sky Music 1970; 2. *Self Portrait;* 4. *Self Portrait* (both versions); 5. Copyrights for these two versions of the same traditional song are based respectively on Dylan's "Revised Melody and New Music" and "New Music."

LIVING THE BLUES   1. Copyright © Big Sky Music 1969, 70; 2. *Self Portrait;* 4. *W & D; Songs of Bob Dylan.*

LO AND BEHOLD!   1. Copyright © Dwarf Music 1967, 75; 2. *Basement Tapes;* 4. *W & D; Songs of Bob Dylan.*

THE LONESOME DEATH OF HATTIE CARROLL   1. Copyright © Warner Bros. Inc. 1964, 66; 2. *Times Changing;* 4. *W & D; Bob Dylan.*

LONG AGO, FAR AWAY   1. Copyright © Warner Bros. Inc. 1962, 68; 3. Odetta: *Odetta Sings Dylan* (RCA Victor LSP 3324); 4. *W & D; Bob Dylan.*

LONG DISTANCE OPERATOR   1. Copyright © Dwarf Music 1971, 75; 3. The Band: *Basement Tapes* (see Discography, Section 1); 4. *W & D; Songs of Bob Dylan;* 5. Performed by Dylan in concert in late 1965.

LONG TIME GONE   1. Copyright © Warner Bros. Inc. 1963, 68; 3. Odetta: *Odetta Sings Dylan* (RCA Victor LSP 3324); 4. *W & D; Bob Dylan.*

LOVE IS JUST A FOUR-LETTER WORD   1. Copyright © Warner Bros. Inc. 1967; 3. Joan Baez: *Any Day Now* (Vanguard VSD 79306/7);

4. *W & D; Bob Dylan;* 5. The songbooks *Don't Look Back* (Witmark) and *Bob Dylan the Original* (Warner Bros.) contain an earlier, unfinished version of the song, apparently transcribed from Joan Baez's May 1965 hotel room performance, shown, in part, in *Don't Look Back.* The Baez recording of the finished song, made in 1968, includes an extra fifth verse which has not appeared in print.

LOVE MINUS ZERO/NO LIMIT   1. Copyright © Warner Bros. Inc. 1965; 2. *Back Home;* 4. *W & D; Bob Dylan;* 5. Live recording: *Budokan,* recorded in Tokyo, Feb. 28, 1978.

LOVE YOU TOO MUCH   1. Copyright © Special Rider Music 1979; 3. Greg Lake: *Greg* (Chrysalis); 4. *L;* 5. Originally written by Dylan and Helena Springs, and copyrighted under the title "I Must Love You Too Much"; the words to this version are printed in Issue 17 of *The Telegraph.* Greg Lake changed the words and added several new verses and recorded the song as "Love You Too Much"; this version is printed in *L,* and is credited to Dylan, Springs and Lake.

MAGGIE'S FARM   1. Copyright © Warner Bros. Inc. 1965; 2. *Back Home;* 4. *W & D; Bob Dylan;* 5. Live recordings: (a) *Hard Rain,* recorded with the Rolling Thunder Revue at Hughes Stadium, Fort Collins, Colorado, May 23, 1976; (b) *Budokan,* recorded in Tokyo, March 1, 1978; (c) *Real Live,* recorded at Wembley Stadium, London, July 7, 1984.

MAIN TITLE THEME   1. Copyright © Ram's Horn Music 1973; 2. *Pat Garrett;* 4. *Pat Garrett;* 5. Instrumental.

MAMA, YOU BEEN ON MY MIND   1. Copyright © Warner Bros. Inc. 1964, 67; 3. Joan Baez: *Farewell Angelina* (Vanguard VSD 79200) (under the title "Daddy, You Been on My Mind"); 4. *W & D; A Retrospective.*

MAN GAVE NAMES TO ALL THE ANIMALS   1. Copyright © Special Rider Music 1979; 2. *Slow Train;* 4. *L; Slow Train.*

THE MAN IN ME   1. Copyright © Big Sky Music 1970; 2. *New Morning;* 4. *W & D; Songs of Bob Dylan.*

MAN OF CONSTANT SORROW   1. Copyright © Duchess Music Corp. 1962, 65; 2. *Bob Dylan;* 4. *Bob Dylan Himself;* 5. Copyright based on Dylan's "Arrangement of Music and New Lyric"; the song is traditional. The sheet music contains two verses Dylan does not sing on the recording.

MAN OF PEACE   1. Copyright © Special Rider Music 1983; 2. *Infidels;* 4. *L; Infidels.*

MAN ON THE STREET   1. Copyright © Duchess Music Corp. 1962, 65; 3. Dave Van Ronk: *No Dirty Names* (Verve Forecast FT 3009), under the title "The Old Man"; 4. *W & D; Bob Dylan Himself.*

MARY ANN   2. *Dylan;* 5. Traditional.

MASTERS OF WAR   1. Copyright © Warner Bros. Inc. 1963; 2. *Freewheelin';* 4. *W & D; A Retrospective.* 5. Live recording: *Real Live,* recorded at Wembley Stadium, London, July 7, 1984.

MEET ME IN THE MORNING 1. Copyright © Ram's Horn Music 1974, 75; 2. *Blood on the Tracks;* 4. *L; Songs of Bob Dylan;* 5. The recording omits the song's fourth verse.

MEMPHIS BLUES AGAIN (see STUCK INSIDE OF MOBILE WITH THE MEMPHIS BLUES AGAIN)

THE MIGHTY QUINN (see QUINN THE ESKIMO)

MILLION DOLLAR BASH 1. Copyright © Dwarf Music 1967, 75; 2. *Basement Tapes;* 4. *W & D; Songs of Bob Dylan.*

MINSTREL BOY 1. Copyright © Big Sky Music 1970; 2. *Self Portrait;* 4. *W & D; Songs of Bob Dylan;* 5. Recorded with The Band at the Isle of Wight Festival, Aug. 31, 1969.

MIXED UP CONFUSION 1. Copyright © Warner Bros. Inc. 1962, 68; 2. Single; 4. *W & D; Bob Dylan;* 5. The single was released in very small quantities in December 1962 and withdrawn soon after; it was released again in 1966, but only in part of Europe. A different version, recorded at the same time, is on *Masterpieces* and, remixed, on *Biograph.*

MONEY BLUES 1. Copyright © Ram's Horn Music 1975, 76; 4. *L; Songs of Bob Dylan;* 5. Words written with Jacques Levy.

MOST LIKELY YOU GO YOUR WAY (AND I'LL GO MINE) 1. Copyright © Dwarf Music 1966; 2. *Blonde on Blonde;* 4. *W & D; Songs of Bob Dylan;* 5. Live recording: *Before the Flood,* recorded with The Band at L.A. Forum, evening of Feb. 14, 1974.

MOTORPSYCHO NIGHTMARE 1. Copyright © Warner Bros. Inc. 1964; 2. *Another Side;* 4. *W & D; Bob Dylan.*

MOZAMBIQUE 1. Copyright © Ram's Horn Music, 1975; 2. *Desire;* 4. *L; Songs of Bob Dylan;* 5. Words written with Jacques Levy.

MR. BOJANGLES 2. *Dylan;* 5. Written by Jerry Jeff Walker.

MR. TAMBOURINE MAN 1. Copyright © Warner Bros. Inc. 1964, 65; 2. *Back Home;* 4. *W & D; Bob Dylan;* 5. Live recordings: (a) *The Concert for Bangladesh* (see Discography, Section 3), recorded at Madison Square Garden, evening of Aug. 1, 1971; (b) *Budokan,* recorded in Tokyo, March 1, 1978.

MY BACK PAGES 1. Copyright © Warner Bros. Inc. 1964; 2. *Another Side;* 4. *W & D; A Retrospective.*

NASHVILLE SKYLINE RAG 1. Copyright © Big Sky Music 1969; 2. *Nashville Skyline;* 4. *Songs of Bob Dylan;* 5. Instrumental. A later recording, made with Earl Scruggs for his National Educational Television special, broadcast Jan. 1971, is on the album *Earl Scruggs: His Family and Friends* (see Discography, Section 4).

NEED A WOMAN 1. Copyright © Special Rider Music 1982; 3. Ry Cooder: *The Slide Area* (Warner Bros.); 4. *L;* 5. Cooder has said that he substantially altered Dylan's words for the song, and his version has little in common with that printed in *L;* however, Dylan is known to have rewritten the song several times himself.

NEIGHBORHOOD BULLY 1. Copyright © Special Rider Music 1983; 2. *Infidels;* 4. *L; Infidels.*

NEVER GONNA BE THE SAME AGAIN   1. Copyright © Special Rider Music 1985; 2. *Empire Burlesque;* 4. *L; Empire Burlesque.*

NEVER SAY GOODBYE   1. Copyright © Ram's Horn Music 1973, 74; 2. *Planet Waves;* 4. *Songs of Bob Dylan;* 5. The printed words differ noticeably from those used in the recording.

NEW MORNING   1. Copyright © Big Sky Music 1970; 2. *New Morning;* 4. *W & D; Songs of Bob Dylan.*

NEW PONY   1. Copyright © Special Rider Music 1978; 2. *Street-Legal;* 4. *L; Street-Legal;* 5. The recording omits the song's fourth verse.

NO TIME TO THINK   1. Copyright © Special Rider Music 1978; 2. *Street-Legal;* 4. *L; Street-Legal.*

NOBODY 'CEPT YOU   1. Copyright © Ram's Horn Music 1973, 76; 4. *L; Songs of Bob Dylan;* 5. Performed in concert in early 1974.

NORTH COUNTRY BLUES   1. Copyright © Warner Bros. Inc. 1963, 64; 2. *Times Changing;* 4. *W & D; A Retrospective.*

NOTHING WAS DELIVERED   1. Copyright © Dwarf Music 1968, 75; 2. *Basement Tapes;* 4. *W & D; Songs of Bob Dylan.*

OBVIOUSLY FIVE BELIEVERS   1. Copyright © Dwarf Music 1966; 2. *Blonde on Blonde;* 4. *W & D; Songs of Bob Dylan.*

ODDS AND ENDS   1. Copyright © Dwarf Music, 1969, 75; 2. *Basement Tapes;* 4. *W & D; Songs of Bob Dylan;* 5. Recorded in 1967.

OH, SISTER   1. Copyright © Ram's Horn Music 1975, 76; 2. *Desire;* 4. *L; Songs of Bob Dylan;* 5. Words written with Jacques Levy. Live recordings: (a) *Hard Rain,* recorded with the Rolling Thunder Revue at Terrent County Convention Center, Fort Worth, Texas, May 16, 1976; (b) *Budokan,* recorded in Tokyo, March 1, 1978.

THE OLD MAN   (see MAN ON THE STREET)

ON A NIGHT LIKE THIS   1. Copyright © Ram's Horn Music 1973, 74; 2. *Planet Waves;* 4. *L; Songs of Bob Dylan.*

ON A RAINY AFTERNOON   1. Copyright © Dwarf Music 1978; 5. Written with Robbie Robertson. *Eat the Document,* filmed in Europe in spring 1966, shows Dylan playing this song with Robertson in a hotel room.

ON THE ROAD AGAIN   1. Copyright © Warner Bros. Inc. 1965; 2. *Back Home;* 4. *W & D; A Retrospective.*

ONE MORE CUP OF COFFEE (VALLEY BELOW)   1. Copyright © Ram's Horn Music 1975, 76; 2. *Desire;* 4. *L; Songs of Bob Dylan;* 5. Live recording: *Budokan,* recorded in Tokyo, March 1, 1978.

ONE MORE NIGHT   1. Copyright © Big Sky Music 1969; 2. *Nashville Skyline;* 4. *W & D; Songs of Bob Dylan.*

ONE MORE WEEKEND   1. Copyright © Big Sky Music 1970; 2. *New Morning;* 4. *W & D; Songs of Bob Dylan.*

ONE OF US MUST KNOW (SOONER OR LATER)   1. Copyright © Dwarf Music 1966; 2. *Blonde on Blonde;* 4. *W & D; Songs of Bob Dylan;* 5. The recording, made with The Band, was originally released as a single.

ONE TOO MANY MORNINGS   1. Copyright © Warner Bros. Inc. 1964, 66; 2. *Times Changing;* 4. *W & D; A Retrospective;* 5. Live recording: *Hard Rain,* recorded with the Rolling Thunder Revue at Hughes Stadium, Fort Collins, Colorado, May 23, 1976.

ONLY A HOBO   1. Copyright © Warner Bros. Inc. 1963, 68; 2. *Broadside Ballads, Vol. 1* (see Discography, Section 3); 4. *W & D; Bob Dylan;* 5. Probably recorded in late 1962 or early 1963.

ONLY A PAWN IN THEIR GAME   1. Copyright © Warner Bros. Inc. 1963, 64; 2. *Times Changing;* 4. *W & D; A Retrospective;* 5. *We Shall Overcome* (see Discography, Section 3) includes an edited version of a recording made at the March on Washington, Aug. 28, 1963, under the title "Ballad of Medgar Evers" (misprinted on the record sleeve as "Ballad of Medgar Evans").

OPEN THE DOOR, HOMER   1. Copyright © Dwarf Music 1968, 75; 2. *Basement Tapes;* 4. *W & D; Songs of Bob Dylan.*

OUTLAW BLUES   1. Copyright © Warner Bros. Inc. 1965; 2. *Back Home;* 4. *W & D; A Retrospective.*

OXFORD TOWN   1. Copyright © Warner Bros. Inc. 1963; 2. *Freewheelin';* 4. *W & D; Bob Dylan.*

PATHS OF VICTORY   1. Copyright © Warner Bros. Inc. 1964; 3. The Broadside Singers: *The Broadside Singers* (Broadside/Folkways BR 303); 4. *W & D; Bob Dylan;* 5. The Broadside Singers' album includes words and music; this is a slightly different version from that in *W & D,* etc., and is copyright © 1962 by Bob Dylan.

PATTY'S GONE TO LAREDO   1. Copyright © Ram's Horn Music 1977, 78; 5. A recording, made in late 1975 with members of the Rolling Thunder Revue, is used in the soundtrack of *Renaldo and Clara.*

PEGGY DAY   1. Copyright © Big Sky Music 1969; 2. *Nashville Skyline;* 4. *W & D; Songs of Bob Dylan.*

PERCY'S SONG   1. Copyright © Warner Bros. Inc. 1964, 66; 2. *Biograph;* 4. *W & D; Bob Dylan;* 5. Recorded at the *Times* sessions.

PLAYBOYS AND PLAYGIRLS   1. Copyright © Warner Bros. Inc. 1964, 68; 2. *Newport Broadside (Topical Songs)* (see Discography, Section 3); 4. *W & D; Bob Dylan;* 5. Recorded with Pete Seeger at the Newport Folk Festival, July 28, 1963; the title used on the record is "Ye Playboys and Playgirls."

PLEASE, MRS. HENRY   1. Copyright © Dwarf Music 1967, 71; 2. *Basement Tapes;* 4. *W & D; Songs of Bob Dylan.*

PLEDGING MY TIME   1. Copyright © Dwarf Music 1966; 2. *Blonde on Blonde;* 4. *W & D; Songs of Bob Dylan;* 5. The recording was originally released, in edited form, as the B side of "Rainy Day Women # 12 & 35."

POOR BOY BLUES   1. Copyright © Duchess Music Corp. 1962, 65; 4. *W & D; Bob Dylan Himself.*

POSITIVELY 4TH STREET   1. Copyright © Warner Bros. Inc. 1965; 2.

Single; 4. *W & D; Bob Dylan;* 5. Recorded at the *Highway 61* sessions; later included in *Greatest Hits.*

PRECIOUS ANGEL   1. Copyright © Special Rider Music 1979; 2. *Slow Train;* 4. *L; Slow Train.*

PRESSING ON   1. Copyright © Special Rider Music 1980; 2. *Saved;* 4. *L; Saved;* 5. Performed in concert in late 1979.

PROPERTY OF JESUS   1. Copyright © Special Rider Music 1981; 2. *Shot of Love;* 4. *L; Shot of Love.*

QUEEN JANE APPROXIMATELY   1. Copyright © Warner Bros. Inc. 1965; 2. *Highway 61;* 4. *W & D; Bob Dylan.*

QUINN THE ESKIMO (THE MIGHTY QUINN)   1. Copyright © Dwarf Music 1968; 2. *Biograph;* 4. *W & D; Songs of Bob Dylan;* 5. Recorded at the *Basement Tapes* sessions in 1967. Live recording: *Self Portrait,* recorded with The Band at the Isle of Wight Festival, Aug. 31, 1969.

QUIT YOUR LOW DOWN WAYS   1. Copyright © Warner Bros. Inc. 1963, 64; 3. Peter, Paul and Mary: *In The Wind* (Warner Bros. S 1507); 4. *W & D; A Retrospective.*

RAINY DAY WOMEN # 12 & 35   1. Copyright © Dwarf Music 1966; 2. *Blonde on Blonde;* 4. *W & D; Songs of Bob Dylan;* 5. Live recording: *Before the Flood,* recorded with The Band at L.A. Forum, Feb. 13, 1974. The *Blonde on Blonde* version was originally released, in edited form, as a single.

RAMBLING, GAMBLING WILLIE   1. Copyright © Duchess Music Corp. 1962, 65; 4. *W & D; Bob Dylan Himself;* 5. This song appeared on some very early copies of *Freewheelin',* under the title "Gamblin' Willie"; on some promotional copies it was called "Gamblin' Willie's Dead Man's Hand."

RESTLESS FAREWELL   1. Copyright © Warner Bros. Inc. 1964, 66; 2. *Times Changing;* 4. *W & D; Bob Dylan.*

RITA MAY   1. Copyright © Ram's Horn Music 1975, 76; 2. Single (B side of "Stuck Inside of Mobile with the Memphis Blues Again"); 4. *L; Songs of Bob Dylan;* 5. Recorded at the *Desire* sessions. Also on *Masterpieces.*

RIVER THEME   1. Copyright © Ram's Horn Music 1973; 2. *Pat Garrett;* 4. *Pat Garrett;* 5. Instrumental.

ROCKS AND GRAVEL   1. Copyright © Warner Bros. Inc. 1963, 66; 4. *A Retrospective;* 5. Although Dylan is credited with full authorship, this is very similar to a traditional song of the same name. It appeared on some very early copies of *Freewheelin',* under the title "Solid Road," with backing similar to that on "Mixed Up Confusion."

ROMANCE IN DURANGO   1. Copyright © Ram's Horn Music 1975, 76; 2. *Desire;* 4. *L; Songs of Bob Dylan;* 5. Words written with Jacques Levy. Live recording: *Biograph,* recorded with the Rolling Thunder Revue at Montreal Forum, Dec. 4, 1975.

SAD-EYED LADY OF THE LOWLANDS 1. Copyright © Dwarf Music 1966; 2. *Blonde on Blonde;* 4. *W & D; Songs of Bob Dylan.*

SARA   1. Copyright © Ram's Horn Music 1975, 76; 2. *Desire;* 4. *L; Songs of Bob Dylan.*

SARAH JANE   1. Copyright © Big Sky Music 1974; 2. *Dylan;* 5. Copyright based on Dylan's arrangement of words and music; the song is traditional.

A SATISFIED MIND   2. *Saved;* 5. Written by Red Hayes and Jack Rhodes.

SAVED   1. Copyright © Special Rider Music 1980; 2. *Saved;* 4. *L; Saved;* 5. Written with Tim Drummond; performed in concert in late 1979.

SAVING GRACE   1. Copyright © Special Rider Music 1980; 2. *Saved;* 4. *L; Saved;* 5. Performed in concert in late 1979.

SEE THAT MY GRAVE IS KEPT CLEAN   2. *Bob Dylan;* 5. Written by Blind Lemon Jefferson.

SEEING THE REAL YOU AT LAST   1. Copyright © Special Rider Music 1985; 2. *Empire Burlesque;* 4. *L; Empire Burlesque.*

SEÑOR (TALES OF YANKEE POWER)   1. Copyright © Special Rider Music 1978; 2. *Street-Legal;* 4. *L; Street-Legal.*

SEVEN CURSES   1. Copyright © Warner Bros. Inc. 1963, 74; 4. *W & D; Bob Dylan.* 5. Performed in concert in 1963.

SEVEN DAYS   1. Copyright © Ram's Horn Music 1976, 79; 3. Ron Wood: *Gimme Some Neck* (Columbia JC 35702); 4. *L;* 5. Performed by Dylan in concert in early 1976 with various word changes; the printed words are copyright © 1979.

SHE BELONGS TO ME   1. Copyright © Warner Bros. Inc. 1965; 2. *Back Home;* 4. *W & D; Bob Dylan;* 5. Live recording: *Self Portrait,* recorded with The Band at the Isle of Wight Festival, Aug. 31, 1969.

SHELTER FROM THE STORM   1. Copyright © Ram's Horn Music 1974, 75; 2. *Blood on the Tracks;* 4. *L; Songs of Bob Dylan;* 5. Live recordings: (a) *Hard Rain,* recorded with the Rolling Thunder Revue at Hughes Stadium, Fort Collins, Colorado, May 23, 1976; (b) *Budokan,* recorded in Tokyo, Feb. 28, 1978.

SHE'S NO GOOD   (see YOU'RE NO GOOD)

SHE'S YOUR LOVER NOW   1. Copyright © Dwarf Music 1971, 76; 3. The Original Marauders: *Now Your Mouth Cries Wolf* (Rare Records 7902); 5. Recorded by Dylan in late 1965, with an extra fourth verse, under the title "Just a Little Glass of Water," but not released.

SHOT OF LOVE   1. Copyright © Special Rider Music 1981; 2. *Shot of Love;* 4. *L; Shot of Love.*

SIGN LANGUAGE   1. Copyright © Ram's Horn Music 1976; 2. See 5; 4. *L;* Eric Clapton songbook *No Reason to Cry* (Warner Bros.); 5. Dylan sings this with Eric Clapton on Clapton's album *No Reason to Cry* (see Discography, Section 4).

SIGN ON THE CROSS   1. Copyright © Dwarf Music 1971, 73; 3. Coulson, Dean, McGuinness and Flint: *Lo and Behold* (Sire SAS 7405); 4. *W & D;* 5. Recorded by Dylan at the *Basement Tapes* sessions, with words somewhat different from those in *W & D,* but not released.

SIGN ON THE WINDOW   1. Copyright © Big Sky Music 1970; 2. *New Morning;* 4. *W & D; Songs of Bob Dylan.*

SILENT WEEKEND   1. Copyright © Dwarf Music 1973, 76; 4. *L; Songs of Bob Dylan;* 5. Probably written in 1967.

SIMPLE TWIST OF FATE   1. Copyright © Ram's Horn Music 1974, 75; 2. *Blood on the Tracks;* 4. *L; Songs of Bob Dylan;* 5. Live recording: *Budokan,* recorded in Tokyo, Feb. 28, 1978.

SITTING ON A BARBED WIRE FENCE   1. Copyright © Warner Bros. Inc. 1970; 4. *W & D; Bob Dylan;* 5. Recorded at the *Highway 61* sessions, under the title "Over the Cliff," but not released.

SLOW TRAIN   1. Copyright © Special Rider Music 1979; 2. *Slow Train;* 4. *L; Slow Train.*

SOLID ROAD   (see ROCKS AND GRAVEL)

SOLID ROCK   1. Copyright © Special Rider Music 1980; 2. *Saved;* 4. *L; Saved;* 5. Performed in concert in late 1979.

SOMETHING THERE IS ABOUT YOU   1. Copyright © Ram's Horn Music 1973, 74; 2. *Planet Waves;* 4. *L; Songs of Bob Dylan.*

SOMETHING'S BURNING, BABY   1. Copyright © Special Rider Music 1984; 2. *Empire Burlesque;* 4. *L; Empire Burlesque.*

SONG TO WOODY   1. Copyright © Duchess Music Corp. 1962, 65; 2. *Bob Dylan;* 4. *W & D; Bob Dylan Himself;* 5. Printed in *Sing Out!* in late 1962, under the title "Letter to Woody."

SPANISH HARLEM INCIDENT   1. Copyright © Warner Bros. Inc. 1964; 2. *Another Side;* 4. *W & D; Bob Dylan.*

SPANISH IS THE LOVING TONGUE   1. Copyright © Big Sky Music 1978; 2. Single (B side of "Watching the River Flow"); 4. Words included with the Japanese edition of *Masterpieces;* 5. Traditional; the copyright is for Dylan's arrangement. A more elaborate version, recorded around the same time (mid-1970) was subsequently released on *Dylan. Masterpieces* contains the single version.

STANDING ON THE HIGHWAY   1. Copyright © Duchess Music Corp. 1962, 65; 4. *W & D; Bob Dylan Himself.*

STEPCHILD   1. Copyright © Special Rider Music 1978; 5. Written with Helena Springs. Performed in concert in late 1978.

STUCK INSIDE OF MOBILE WITH THE MEMPHIS BLUES AGAIN   1. Copyright © Dwarf Music 1966; 2. *Blonde on Blonde;* 4. *W & D; Songs of Bob Dylan;* 5. Live recording: *Hard Rain,* recorded with the Rolling Thunder Revue at Terrent County Convention Center, Fort Worth, Texas, May 16, 1976; the single listed in the Discography is an edited version of this recording. The song was apparently originally entitled "Stuck Inside of Mobile with The" (see *Blonde on Blonde* songbook), but on the album it was misnamed "Stuck Inside of Mobile with Thee" and, later, "Memphis Blues Again"; since *Greatest Hits II,* the full title has been used.

SUBTERRANEAN HOMESICK BLUES 1. Copyright © Warner Bros. Inc. 1965; 2. *Back Home;* 4. *W & D; Bob Dylan;* 5. A rough worksheet is reproduced in *W & D* alongside the finished song.

SWEETHEART LIKE YOU 1. Copyright © Special Rider Music 1983; 2. *Infidels;* 4. *L; Infidels.*

TAKE A MESSAGE TO MARY 2. *Self Portrait;* 5. Written by Boudleaux and Felice Bryant.

TAKE ME AS I AM 2. *Self Portrait;* 5. Attributed on the record label to Boudleaux Bryant, but in the *Self Portrait* songbook to George Thompson and Edgar Battle; the latter registered the song earlier.

TALKING BEAR MOUNTAIN PICNIC MASSACRE BLUES 1. Copyright © Duchess Music Corp. 1962, 65; 4. *W & D; Bob Dylan Himself.*

TALKING DEVIL 1. Copyright © Special Rider Music 1963; 2. *Broadside Ballads, Vol. 1* (see Discography, Section 3); 4. Words included with the album; 5. The album gives a copyright date of 1962.

TALKING FOLKLORE CENTER 1. Copyright © The Folklore Center 1962; 4. Songbook *The Best of All* (Music Sales Corp., 1970); 5. Words and music originally published by The Folklore Center, New York, as a song sheet in 1962.

TALKIN' HAVA NEGEILAH BLUES 1. Copyright © Warner Bros. Inc. 1963, 68; 4. *Bob Dylan.* 5. Recorded in 1962 but not released.

TALKIN' JOHN BIRCH PARANOID BLUES 1. Copyright © Special Rider Music 1970; 4. *W & D; Bob Dylan Collector Series* (Warner Bros.); 5. Words and music first published under the title "Talking John Birch" in *Broadside,* Feb. 1962. The song appeared on some very early copies of *Freewheelin',* under the title "Talkin' John Birch Society Blues."

TALKING NEW YORK 1. Copyright © Duchess Music Corp. 1962, 65; 2. *Bob Dylan;* 4. *W & D; Bob Dylan Himself.*

TALKIN' WORLD WAR III BLUES 1. Copyright © Warner Bros. Inc. 1963, 66; 2. *Freewheelin';* 4. *W & D; Bob Dylan.*

TANGLED UP IN BLUE 1. Copyright © Ram's Horn Music 1974, 75; 2. *Blood on the Tracks;* 4. *L; Songs of Bob Dylan;* 5. An earlier version was included in promotional copies of the album. Live recording: *Real Live,* recorded at Wembley Stadium, London, July 7, 1984; the words to this substantially rewritten version are included with the Japanese compact disc edition of the album and are also printed in Issue 21 of *The Telegraph.*

TEARS OF RAGE 1. Copyright © Dwarf Music 1968, 70; 2. *Basement Tapes;* 4. *W & D; Songs of Bob Dylan;* 5. Music written by Richard Manuel.

TELL ME, MOMMA 1. Copyright © Dwarf Music 1971, 73; 3. The

Original Marauders: *Now Your Mouth Cries Wolf* (Rare Records 7902); 4. *W & D; Songs of Bob Dylan;* 5. Performed by Dylan in concert, with considerably different words, in early 1966.

TELL ME THAT IT ISN'T TRUE   1. Copyright © Big Sky Music 1969; 2. *Nashville Skyline;* 4. *W & D; Songs of Bob Dylan.*

TEMPORARY LIKE ACHILLES   1. Copyright © Dwarf Music 1966; 2. *Blonde on Blonde;* 4. *W & D; Songs of Bob Dylan.*

THAT'S ALL RIGHT, MAMA   1. Copyright © Warner Bros. Inc. 1963, 66; 4. *Bob Dylan;* 5. Recorded in late 1962 but not released. The song is very similar to the Arthur Crudup song of the same name, recorded by Elvis Presley and others.

THIEF ON THE CROSS   1. Copyright © Special Rider Music 1982; 5. Performed in concert in late 1981.

THIS WHEEL'S ON FIRE   1. Copyright © Dwarf Music 1967, 70; 2. *Basement Tapes;* 4. *W & D; Songs of Bob Dylan;* 5. Music written by Rick Danko.

THREE ANGELS   1. Copyright © Big Sky Music 1970; 2. *New Morning;* 4. *W & D; Songs of Bob Dylan.*

TIGHT CONNECTION TO MY HEART (HAS ANYBODY SEEN MY LOVE)   1. Copyright © Special Rider Music 1985; 2. *Empire Burlesque;* 4. *L; Empire Burlesque;* 5. This is a reworking of "Someone's Got a Hold of My Heart," a song recorded at the *Infidels* sessions but not released.

TIME PASSES SLOWLY   1. Copyright © Big Sky Music 1970; 2. *New Morning;* 4. *W & D; Songs of Bob Dylan.*

THE TIMES THEY ARE A-CHANGIN'   1. Copyright © Warner Bros. Inc. 1963, 64; 2. *Times Changing;* 4. *W & D; Bob Dylan;* 5. Live recording: *Budokan,* recorded in Tokyo, Feb. 28, 1978.

TINY MONTGOMERY   1. Copyright © Dwarf Music 1967, 75; 2. *Basement Tapes;* 4. *W & D; Songs of Bob Dylan.*

TO BE ALONE WITH YOU   1. Copyright © Big Sky Music 1969; 2. *Nashville Skyline;* 4. *W & D; Songs of Bob Dylan.*

TO RAMONA   1. Copyright © Warner Bros. Inc. 1964; 2. *Another Side;* 4. *W & D; Bob Dylan.*

TOMBSTONE BLUES   1. Copyright © Warner Bros. Inc. 1965; 2. *Highway 61;* 4. *W & D; Bob Dylan.* 5. Live recording: *Real Live,* recorded at St. James Park, Newcastle, July 5, 1984.

TOMORROW IS A LONG TIME   1. Copyright © Warner Bros. Inc. 1963; 2. *Greatest Hits II;* 4. *W & D; Bob Dylan;* 5. Recorded at New York Town Hall, April 12, 1963.

TONIGHT I'LL BE STAYING HERE WITH YOU   1. Copyright © Big Sky Music 1969; 2. *Nashville Skyline;* 4. *W & D; Songs of Bob Dylan.*

TOO MUCH OF NOTHING   1. Copyright © Dwarf Music 1967, 70; 2. *Basement Tapes;* 4. *W & D; Songs of Bob Dylan.*

TOUGH MAMA   1. Copyright © Ram's Horn Music 1973, 74; 2. *Planet*

Waves; 4. *L; Songs of Bob Dylan.*

TRAIN A-TRAVELIN' 1. Copyright © Warner Bros. Inc. 1968; 2. *Broadside Reunion* (see Discography, Section 3); 4. *W & D; Bob Dylan;* 5. Words and music first published in *Broadside,* March 1963, with no copyright indicated; the words to the three verses Dylan sings in the recording are included with the album and are copyright © 1963 by Bob Dylan.

TROUBLE 1. Copyright © Special Rider Music 1981; 2. *Shot of Love;* 4. *L; Shot of Love.*

TROUBLE IN MIND 1. Copyright © Special Rider Music 1979; 2. Single (B side of "Gotta Serve Somebody"); 4. *L;* 5. The recording omits the song's last verse.

TRUE LOVE TENDS TO FORGET 1. Copyright © Special Rider Music 1978; 2. *Street-Legal;* 4. *L; Street-Legal.*

TRUST YOURSELF 1. Copyright © Special Rider Music 1985; 2. *Empire Burlesque;* 4. *L; Empire Burlesque.*

TURKEY CHASE 1. Copyright © Ram's Horn Music 1973; 2. *Pat Garrett;* 4. *Pat Garrett;* 5. Instrumental.

UNION SUNDOWN 1. Copyright © Special Rider Music 1983; 2. *Infidels;* 4. *L; Infidels.*

UP TO ME 1. Copyright © Ram's Horn Music 1974, 76; 2. *Biograph;* 4. *L; Songs of Bob Dylan;* 5. Recorded at the *Blood on the Tracks* sessions.

VISIONS OF JOHANNA 1. Copyright © Dwarf Music 1966; 2. *Blonde on Blonde;* 4. *W & D; Songs of Bob Dylan;* 5. First recorded and performed in late 1965 under the title "Freeze Out," and later, "Seems Like a Freeze Out." Live recording: *Biograph,* recorded at the Royal Albert Hall, London, May 26, 1966.

WALK OUT IN THE RAIN 1. Copyright © Special Rider Music 1978; 3. Eric Clapton: *Backless* (RSO RS 1 3039); 4. *L;* Eric Clapton songbook *Backless* (Chappell Music); 5. Written with Helena Springs.

WALKIN' DOWN THE LINE 1. Copyright © Warner Bros. Inc. 1963, 65; 3. Joan Baez: *Any Day Now* (Vanguard VSD 79306/7); 4. *W & D; A Retrospective.*

WALLFLOWER 1. Copyright © Ram's Horn Music 1971, 76; 2. See 5; 4. *L; Songs of Bob Dylan;* 5. Dylan sings this with Doug Sahm on *Doug Sahm and Band* (see Discography, Section 4).

WALLS OF RED WING 1. Copyright © Warner Bros. Inc. 1963; 3. Joan Baez: *Any Day Now* (Vanguard VSD 79306/7); 4. *W & D; Bob Dylan.*

WANTED MAN 1. Copyright © Big Sky Music 1969, 76; 3. Johnny Cash: *Johnny Cash at San Quentin* (Columbia CS 9827); 4. *W & D; Songs of Bob Dylan.*

WATCHING THE RIVER FLOW 1. Copyright © Big Sky Music 1971; 2. *Greatest Hits II;* 4. *W & D; Songs of Bob Dylan;* 5. Originally released as a single.

WATERED-DOWN LOVE 1. Copyright © Special Rider Music 1981; 2. *Shot of Love;* 4. *L; Shot of Love.*

WE BETTER TALK THIS OVER 1. Copyright © Special Rider Music 1978; 2. *Street-Legal;* 4. *L; Street-Legal.*

WEDDING SONG 1. Copyright © Ram's Horn Music 1973, 74; 2. *Planet Waves;* 4. *L; Songs of Bob Dylan.*

WENT TO SEE THE GYPSY 1. Copyright © Big Sky Music 1970; 2. *New Morning;* 4. *W & D; Songs of Bob Dylan.*

WHAT CAN I DO FOR YOU? 1. Copyright © Special Rider Music 1980; 2. *Saved;* 4. *L; Saved;* 5. Performed in concert in late 1979.

WHAT KIND OF FRIEND IS THIS? 1. Copyright © Dwarf Music 1978; 5. Apparently Dylan's adaptation of an old blues song. *Eat the Document,* filmed in Europe in spring 1966, shows Dylan playing it in a hotel room.

WHAT WILL YOU DO WHEN JESUS COMES? 1. Copyright © Ram's Horn Music 1977, 78; 5. A recording made in late 1975 with members of the Rolling Thunder Revue is used in the soundtrack of *Renaldo and Clara.*

WHATCHA GONNA DO 1. Copyright © Warner Bros. Inc. 1963, 66; 4. *W & D; Bob Dylan.*

WHEN I PAINT MY MASTERPIECE 1. Copyright © Big Sky Music 1971, 72; 2. *Greatest Hits II;* 4. *W & D; Songs of Bob Dylan.*

WHEN HE RETURNS 1. Copyright © Special Rider Music 1979; 2. *Slow Train;* 4. *L; Slow Train.*

WHEN THE NIGHT COMES FALLING FROM THE SKY 1. Copyright © Special Rider Music 1985; 2. *Empire Burlesque;* 4. *L; Empire Burlesque.*

WHEN THE SHIP COMES IN 1. Copyright © Warner Bros. Inc. 1963, 64; 2. *Times Changing;* 4. *W & D; Bob Dylan.*

WHEN YOU GONNA WAKE UP 1. Copyright © Special Rider Music 1979; 2. *Slow Train;* 4. *L; Slow Train.*

WHERE ARE YOU TONIGHT? (JOURNEY THROUGH DARK HEAT) 1. Copyright © Special Rider Music 1978; 2. *Street-Legal;* 4. *L; Street-Legal.*

WHO KILLED DAVEY MOORE? 1. Copyright © Warner Bros. Inc. 1964, 65; 3. Pete Seeger: *We Shall Overcome* (Columbia CS 8901); 4. *W & D; A Retrospective;* 5. Words and music first published in *Broadside,* July 1963.

THE WICKED MESSENGER 1. Copyright © Dwarf Music 1968; 2. *John Wesley Harding;* 4. *W & D; Songs of Bob Dylan.*

WIGWAM 1. Copyright © Big Sky Music 1970; 2. *Self Portrait;* 4. *Songs of Bob Dylan;* 5. Instrumental.

WINTERLUDE 1. Copyright © Big Sky Music 1970; 2. *New Morning;* 4. *W & D; Songs of Bob Dylan.*

WITH GOD ON OUR SIDE 1. Copyright © Warner Bros. Inc. 1963;

2. *Times Changing;* 4. *W & D; A Retrospective;* 5. Live recording: *Newport Broadside (Topical Songs)* (see Discography, Section 3), recorded with Joan Baez at the Newport Folk Festival, July 28, 1963.

WOOGIE BOOGIE   1. Copyright © Big Sky Music 1970; 2. *Self Portrait;* 4. *Songs of Bob Dylan;* 5. Instrumental.

YE PLAYBOYS AND PLAYGIRLS   (see PLAYBOYS AND PLAYGIRLS)

YOU AIN'T GOIN' NOWHERE   1. Copyright © Dwarf Music 1967, 72; 2. *Basement Tapes;* 4. *W & D; Songs of Bob Dylan;* 5. *Greatest Hits II* contains a later, rather different version, recorded in late 1971 with Happy Traum.

YOU ANGEL YOU   1. Copyright © Ram's Horn Music 1973, 74; 2. *Planet Waves;* 4. *L; Songs of Bob Dylan.*

YOU'RE A BIG GIRL NOW   1. Copyright © Ram's Horn Music 1974, 75; 2. *Blood on the Tracks;* 4. *L; Songs of Bob Dylan;* 5. Live recording: *Hard Rain,* recorded with the Rolling Thunder Revue at Hughes Stadium, Fort Collins, Colorado, May 23, 1976. An early version of the song was included in promotional copies of *Blood on the Tracks* and later released on *Biograph.*

YOU'RE GONNA MAKE ME LONESOME WHEN YOU GO   1. Copyright © Ram's Horn Music 1974, 75; 2. *Blood on the Tracks;* 4. *L; Songs of Bob Dylan.*

YOU'RE NO GOOD   2. *Bob Dylan;* 5. Written by Jesse Fuller. Usually mistitled "She's No Good" on the record label.

DISCOGRAPHY

Compiled by Roger Ford

This discography is intended to represent the body of Dylan's recorded work in the form in which it was released to the public, primarily in the United States. It is certainly not a catalog of all records bearing Dylan's name. Foreign releases are listed only if they contain material unavailable in the United States; and singles are included only if they contained new material at the time of their release.

Illegally released and circulated recordings are quite beyond the scope of this work; those interested should refer to the excellent books by Paul Cable, Michael Krogsgaard, and Dominique Roques listed in the Bibliography.

The records are listed in four categories:

1. Dylan albums
2. Dylan singles
3. Other albums including tracks by Dylan
4. Records including guest appearances by Dylan

Song titles are taken from the sleeves of albums and the labels of singles; these sometimes differ from those used in the Song Index.

SECTION 1: ALBUMS

BOB DYLAN (Columbia CL 1779/CS 8579, released March 1962)
SIDE 1: You're No Good; Talkin' New York; In My Time of Dyin'; Man of Constant Sorrow; Fixin' to Die; Pretty Peggy-O; Highway 51.
SIDE 2: Gospel Plow; Baby, Let Me Follow You Down; House of the Risin' Sun; Freight Train Blues; Song to Woody; See That My Grave Is Kept Clean

THE FREEWHEELIN' BOB DYLAN (Columbia CL 1986/CS 8786, released May 1963)

SIDE 1: Blowin' in the Wind; Girl from the North Country; Masters of War; Down the Highway; Bob Dylan's Blues; A Hard Rain's A-Gonna Fall
SIDE 2: Don't Think Twice, It's All Right; Bob Dylan's Dream; Oxford Town; Talkin' World War III Blues; Corrina, Corrina; Honey, Just Allow Me One More Chance; I Shall Be Free

THE TIMES THEY ARE A-CHANGIN' (Columbia CL 2105/CS 8905, released February 1964)
SIDE 1: The Times They Are A-Changin'; Ballad of Hollis Brown; With God on Our Side; One Too Many Mornings; North Country Blues
SIDE 2: Only a Pawn in Their Game; Boots of Spanish Leather; When the Ship Comes In; The Lonesome Death of Hattie Carroll; Restless Farewell

ANOTHER SIDE OF BOB DYLAN (Columbia CL 2193/CS 8993, released August 1964)
SIDE 1: All I Really Want to Do; Black Crow Blues; Spanish Harlem Incident; Chimes of Freedom; I Shall Be Free No. 10; To Ramona
SIDE 2: Motorpsycho Nitemare; My Back Pages; I Don't Believe You; Ballad in Plain D; It Ain't Me Babe

BRINGING IT ALL BACK HOME (Columbia CL 2328/CS 9128, released March 1965)
SIDE 1: Subterranean Homesick Blues; She Belongs to Me; Maggie's Farm; Love Minus Zero/No Limit; Outlaw Blues; On the Road Again; Bob Dylan's 115th Dream
SIDE 2: Mr. Tambourine Man; Gates of Eden; It's Alright, Ma (I'm Only Bleeding); It's All Over Now, Baby Blue

HIGHWAY 61 REVISITED (Columbia CL 2389/CS 9189, released August 1965)
SIDE 1: Like a Rolling Stone; Tombstone Blues; It Takes a Lot to Laugh, It Takes a Train to Cry; From a Buick 6; Ballad of a Thin Man
SIDE 2: Queen Jane Approximately; Highway 61 Revisited; Just Like Tom Thumb's Blues; Desolation Row

BLONDE ON BLONDE (Columbia C2L 41/C2S 841, released May 1966)
SIDE 1: Rainy Day Women #12 & 35; Pledging My Time; Visions of Johanna; One of Us Must Know
SIDE 2: I Want You; Memphis Blues Again; Leopard-Skin Pill-Box Hat; Just Like a Woman
SIDE 3: Most Likely You Go Your Way and I'll Go Mine; Temporary Like Achilles; Absolutely Sweet Marie; 4th Time Around; Obviously 5 Believers
SIDE 4: Sad Eyed Lady of the Lowlands

BOB DYLAN'S GREATEST HITS (Columbia KCL 2663/KCS 9463, re-leased March 1967)
SIDE 1: Rainy Day Women #12 & 35; Blowin' in the Wind; The Times They Are A-Changin'; It Ain't Me Babe; Like a Rolling Stone
SIDE 2: Mr. Tambourine Man; Subterranean Homesick Blues; I Want You; Positively 4th Street; Just Like a Woman

JOHN WESLEY HARDING (Columbia CL 2804/CS 9604, released January 1968)
SIDE 1: John Wesley Harding; As I Went Out One Morning; I Dreamed I Saw St. Augustine; All Along the Watchtower; The Ballad of Frankie Lee and Judas Priest; Drifter's Escape
SIDE 2: Dear Landlord; I Am a Lonesome Hobo; I Pity the Poor Immi-grant; The Wicked Messenger; Down Along the Cove; I'll Be Your Baby Tonight

NASHVILLE SKYLINE (Columbia KCS 9825, released April 1969)
SIDE 1: Girl from the North Country (with Johnny Cash); Nashville Sky-line Rag; To Be Alone with You; I Threw It All Away; Peggy Day
SIDE 2: Lay Lady Lay; One More Night; Tell Me That It Isn't True; Coun-try Pie; Tonight I'll Be Staying Here with You

SELF PORTRAIT (Columbia C2X 30050, released June 1970)
SIDE 1: All the Tired Horses; Alberta #1; I Forgot More Than You'll Ever Know; Days of 49; Early Morning Rain; In Search of Little Sadie
SIDE 2: Let It Be Me; Little Sadie; Woogie Boogie; Belle Isle; Living the Blues; Like a Rolling Stone
SIDE 3: Copper Kettle; Gotta Travel On; Blue Moon; The Boxer; The Mighty Quinn (Quinn the Eskimo); Take Me As I Am
SIDE 4: Take a Message to Mary; It Hurts Me Too; Minstrel Boy; She Be-longs to Me; Wigwam; Alberta #2

NEW MORNING (Columbia KC 30290, released October 1970)
SIDE 1: If Not for You; Day of the Locusts; Time Passes Slowly; Went to See the Gypsy; Winterlude; If Dogs Run Free
SIDE 2: New Morning; Sign on the Window; One More Weekend; The Man in Me; Three Angels; Father of Night.

BOB DYLAN'S GREATEST HITS VOL. II (Columbia KG 31120, re-leased November 1971)
SIDE 1: Watching the River Flow; Don't Think Twice, It's All Right; Lay Lady Lay; Stuck Inside of Mobile with the Memphis Blues Again
SIDE 2: I'll Be Your Baby Tonight; All I Really Want to Do; My Back Pages; Maggie's Farm; Tonight I'll Be Staying Here with You
SIDE 3: She Belongs to Me; All Along the Watchtower; The Mighty Quinn (Quinn the Eskimo); Just Like Tom Thumb's Blues; A Hard Rain's A-Gonna Fall
SIDE 4: If Not for You; It's All Over Now, Baby Blue; Tomorrow Is a

Long Time;* When I Paint My Masterpiece;* I Shall Be Released;*
You Ain't Goin' Nowhere;* Down in the Flood*
(* previously unreleased)

PAT GARRETT & BILLY THE KID (Original Soundtrack Recording) (Columbia KC 32460, released July 1973)

SIDE 1: Main Title Theme (Billy); Cantina Theme (Workin' for the Law);
Billy 1; Bunkhouse Theme; River Theme

SIDE 2: Turkey Chase; Knockin' on Heaven's Door; Final Theme; Billy 4;
Billy 7

DYLAN (Columbia PC 32747, released November 1973; recorded mid-1970)

SIDE 1: Lily of the West; Can't Help Falling in Love; Sarah Jane; The Ballad of Ira Hayes

SIDE 2: Mr. Bojangles; Mary Ann; Big Yellow Taxi; A Fool Such As I;
Spanish Is the Loving Tongue

PLANET WAVES (Asylum 7E 1003, released January 1974; reissued as Columbia PC 37637)

SIDE 1: On a Night Like This; Going Going Gone; Tough Mama; Hazel;
Something There Is About You; Forever Young

SIDE 2: Forever Young; Dirge; You Angel You; Never Say Goodbye;
Wedding Song

BEFORE THE FLOOD (Asylum AB 201, released June 1974; reissued as Columbia KC 377661; credited to Bob Dylan/The Band)

SIDE 1: Most Likely You Go Your Way (And I'll Go Mine); Lay Lady
Lay; Rainy Day Women #12 & 35; Knockin' on Heaven's Door; It
Ain't Me, Babe; Ballad of a Thin Man

SIDE 2: Up on Cripple Creek;* I Shall Be Released;* Endless Highway;*
The Night They Drove Old Dixie Down;* Stage Fright*

SIDE 3: Don't Think Twice, It's All Right; Just Like a Woman; It's
Alright, Ma (I'm Only Bleeding); The Shape I'm In;* When You
Awake;* The Weight*

SIDE 4: All Along the Watchtower; Highway 61 Revisited; Like a Rolling
Stone; Blowin' in the Wind
(* performed by The Band)

BLOOD ON THE TRACKS (Columbia PC 33235, released January 1975)

SIDE 1: Tangled Up in Blue; Simple Twist of Fate; You're a Big Girl Now;
Idiot Wind; You're Gonna Make Me Lonesome When You Go

SIDE 2: Meet Me in the Morning; Lily, Rosemary and the Jack of Hearts; If
You See Her, Say Hello; Shelter from the Storm; Buckets of Rain

THE BASEMENT TAPES (Columbia C2 33682, released July 1975; credited to Bob Dylan and The Band; recorded June–October, 1967)

SIDE 1: Odds and Ends; Orange Juice Blues (Blues for Breakfast);* Million Dollar Bash; Yazoo Street Scandal;* Goin' to Acapulco; Katie's Been Gone*

SIDE 2: Lo and Behold; Bessie Smith;* Clothes Line Saga; Apple Suckling Tree; Please Mrs. Henry; Tears of Rage

SIDE 3: Too Much of Nothing; Yea! Heavy and a Bottle of Bread; Ain't No More Cane;* Crash on the Levee (Down in the Flood); Ruben Remus;* Tiny Montgomery

SIDE 4: You Ain't Goin' Nowhere; Don't Ya Tell Henry;* Nothing Was Delivered; Open the Door, Homer; Long Distance Operator;* This Wheel's on Fire
(* performed by The Band)

DESIRE (Columbia PC 33893, released January 1976)
SIDE 1: Hurricane; Isis; Mozambique; One More Cup of Coffee; Oh, Sister
SIDE 2: Joey; Romance in Durango; Black Diamond Bay; Sara

HARD RAIN (Columbia PC 34349, released September 1976)
SIDE 1: Maggie's Farm; One Too Many Mornings; Stuck Inside of Mobile with the Memphis Blues Again; Oh, Sister; Lay, Lady, Lay
SIDE 2: Shelter from the Storm; You're a Big Girl Now; I Threw It All Away; Idiot Wind

MASTERPIECES (CBS/Sony 57AP-875/6/7, released March 1978 in Japan; also released in Australia and New Zealand: CBS S3BP 220502) Except where indicated, the tracks on this compilation are the "standard" recordings, as cited in Category 2 of each song's entry in the Song Index.
SIDE 1: Knockin' on Heaven's Door; Mr. Tambourine Man; Just Like a Woman; I Shall Be Released; Tears of Rage; All Along the Watchtower; One More Cup of Coffee

SIDE 2: Like a Rolling Stone (from *Self Portrait*); The Mighty Quinn (Quinn the Eskimo) (from *Self Portrait*); Tomorrow Is a Long Time; Lay, Lady, Lay (from *Hard Rain*); Idiot Wind (from *Hard Rain*)

SIDE 3: Mixed Up Confusion (previously unreleased version); Positively 4th Street; Can You Please Crawl Out Your Window?; Just Like Tom Thumb's Blues (from B side of "I Want You" single); Spanish Is the Loving Tongue; George Jackson (Big Band Version); Rita May

SIDE 4: Blowin' in the Wind; Hard Rain's A-Gonna Fall; The Times They Are A-Changin'; Masters of War; Hurricane

SIDE 5: Maggie's Farm (from *Hard Rain*); Subterranean Homesick Blues; Ballad of a Thin Man; Mozambique; This Wheel's on Fire; I Want You; Rainy Day Women #12 & 35

SIDE 6: Don't Think Twice, It's All Right; Song to Woody; It Ain't Me

Babe; Love Minus Zero/No Limit; I'll Be Your Baby Tonight; If Not for You; If You See Her, Say Hello; Sara

STREET-LEGAL (Columbia JC 35453, released June 1978)
SIDE 1: Changing of the Guard; New Pony; No Time to Think; Baby Stop Crying
SIDE 2: Is Your Love in Vain?; Señor (Tales of Yankee Power); True Love Tends to Forget; We Better Talk This Over; Where Are You Tonight? (Journey Through Dark Heat)

BOB DYLAN AT BUDOKAN (Columbia PC2-36067, released April 1979; recorded in Japan in February–March, 1978, and first released there in November 1978)
SIDE 1: Mr. Tambourine Man; Shelter from the Storm; Love Minus Zero/No Limit; Ballad of a Thin Man; Don't Think Twice, It's All Right
SIDE 2: Maggie's Farm; One More Cup of Coffee (Valley Below); Like a Rolling Stone; I Shall Be Released; Is Your Love in Vain?; Going, Going, Gone
SIDE 3: Blowin' in the Wind; Just Like a Woman; Oh, Sister; Simple Twist of Fate; All Along the Watchtower; I Want You
SIDE 4: All I Really Want to Do; Knockin' on Heaven's Door; It's Alright, Ma (I'm Only Bleeding); Forever Young; The Times They Are A-Changin'

SLOW TRAIN COMING (Columbia FC-36120, released August 1979)
SIDE 1: Gotta Serve Somebody; Precious Angel; I Believe in You; Slow Train
SIDE 2: Gonna Change My Way of Thinking; Do Right to Me Baby (Do Unto Others); When You Gonna Wake Up; Man Gave Names to All the Animals; When He Returns

SAVED (Columbia PC 36553, released June 1980)
SIDE 1: A Satisfied Mind; Saved; Covenant Woman; What Can I Do for You?; Solid Rock
SIDE 2: Pressing On; In the Garden; Saving Grace; Are You Ready

SHOT OF LOVE (Columbia TC-37496, released August 1981)
SIDE 1: Shot of Love; Heart of Mine; Property of Jesus; Lenny Bruce; Watered-Down Love
SIDE 2: Dead Man, Dead Man; In the Summertime; Trouble; Every Grain of Sand

INFIDELS (Columbia QC-38819, released November 1983)
SIDE 1: Jokerman; Sweetheart Like You; Neighborhood Bully; License to Kill
SIDE 2: Man of Peace; Union Sundown; I and I; Don't Fall Apart on Me Tonight

REAL LIVE (Columbia FC 39944, released December 1984)

SIDE 1: Highway 61 Revisited; Maggie's Farm; I and I; License to Kill; It Ain't Me, Babe

SIDE 2: Tangled Up in Blue; Masters of War; Ballad of a Thin Man; Girl from the North Country; Tombstone Blues

EMPIRE BURLESQUE (Columbia FC 40110, released June 1985)

SIDE 1: Tight Connection to My Heart (Has Anybody Seen My Love?); Seeing the Real You at Last; I'll Remember You; Clean Cut Kid; Never Gonna Be the Same Again

SIDE 2: Trust Yourself; Emotionally Yours; When the Night Comes Falling from the Sky; Something's Burning, Baby; Dark Eyes

BIOGRAPH (Columbia C5X 38830, released November 1985) Except where indicated, the tracks on this boxed compilation are the "standard" recordings, as cited in Category 2 of each song's entry in the Song Index.

SIDE 1: Lay Lady Lay; Baby, Let Me Follow You Down; If Not for You; I'll Be Your Baby Tonight; I'll Keep It with Mine (previously unreleased)

SIDE 2: The Times They Are A-Changin'; Blowin' in the Wind; Masters of War; Lonesome Death of Hattie Carroll; Percy's Song (previously unreleased)

SIDE 3: Mixed-Up Confusion (*not* the single, but a different mix of the version on *Masterpieces*); Tombstone Blues; Groom's Still Waiting at the Altar; Most Likely You Go Your Way (from *Before the Flood*); Like a Rolling Stone; Jet Pilot (previously unreleased)

SIDE 4: Lay Down Your Weary Tune (previously unreleased); Subterranean Homesick Blues; I Don't Believe You (She Acts Like We Never Have Met) (previously unreleased version); Visions of Johanna (previously unreleased version); Every Grain of Sand

SIDE 5: Quinn the Eskimo (previously unreleased version); Mr. Tambourine Man; Dear Landlord; It Ain't Me, Babe; You Angel You; Million Dollar Bash

SIDE 6: To Ramona; You're a Big Girl Now (previously unreleased version); Abandoned Love (previously unreleased); Tangled Up in Blue; It's All Over Now, Baby Blue (previously unreleased version)

SIDE 7: Can You Please Crawl Out Your Window?; Positively 4th Street; Isis (from B side of "Jokerman" single); Caribbean Wind (previously unreleased); Up to Me (previously unreleased)

SIDE 8: Baby, I'm in the Mood for You (previously unreleased); I Wanna Be Your Lover (previously unreleased); I Want You; Heart of Mine (previously unreleased version); On a Night Like This; Just Like a Woman

SIDE 9: Romance in Durango (previously unreleased version); Señor (Tales of Yankee Power); Gotta Serve Somebody; I Believe in You; Time Passes Slowly

SIDE 10: I Shall Be Released; Knockin' on Heaven's Door; All Along the Watchtower (from *Before the Flood*); Solid Rock; Forever Young (previously unreleased version)

SECTION 2: SINGLES

This list excludes the large number of singles of which both sides were taken from already released albums. An asterisk denotes a recording that has never been included in an album released in the United States.

Mixed Up Confusion*/Corrina, Corinna* (Columbia 3-42656, changed to 4-42656, released December 1962; also released in the Benelux countries, 1966: CBS 2476)

Like a Rolling Stone/Gates of Eden (Columbia 4-43346, released June 1965)

Positively 4th Street/From a Buick 6 (Columbia 4-43389, released September 1965)

Can You Please Crawl Out Your Window?/Highway 61 Revisited (Columbia 4-43477, released December 1965)

One of Us Must Know (Sooner or Later)/Queen Jane Approximately (Columbia 4-43541, released February 1966)

Rainy Day Women #12 & 35/Pledging My Time (Columbia 4-43592, released March 1966)

I Want You/Just Like Tom Thumb's Blues* (Columbia 4-43683, released June 1966)

If You Gotta Go, Go Now*/To Ramona (CBS 2921, released July 1967 in the Benelux countries only; "If You Gotta Go, Go Now" was recorded in early 1965)

Watching the River Flow/Spanish Is the Loving Tongue* (Columbia 4-45409, released June 1971)

George Jackson (Big Band Version)*/George Jackson (Acoustic Version)* (Columbia 4-45516, released November 1971)

Hurricane (Part 1)/Hurricane (Part II) (Columbia 3-10245, released November 1975)

Stuck Inside of Mobile with the Memphis Blues Again/Rita May* (Columbia 3-10454, released November 1976; "Rita May" was recorded in summer 1975)

Gotta Serve Somebody/Trouble in Mind* (Columbia 1-11072, released August 1979)

Heart of Mine/Let It Be Me* (CBS A-1406, released July 1981 in Britain and Europe only)

Heart of Mine/The Groom's Still Waiting at the Altar (Columbia 18-02510, released September 1981)

Union Sundown/Angel Flying Too Close to the Ground* (CBS A-3916, released October 1983 in Britain and some European countries only; the rest of Europe had "I and I" on the A side, catalog no. CBS A3904)

Jokerman/Isis (Live from the film *Renaldo and Clara*) (Columbia 38-04425, released April 1984)

Band of the Hand (MCA 52811, released April 1986; B side not by Dylan)

SECTION 3: OTHER ALBUMS INCLUDING TRACKS BY DYLAN

These albums all comprise tracks by various artists; only the Dylan tracks are listed.

BROADSIDE BALLADS, VOL. 1   (Broadside/Folkways BR 5301, released October 1963; Dylan appears under the pseudonym Blind Boy Grunt)
John Brown; Only a Hobo; Talking Devil

NEWPORT BROADSIDE (TOPICAL SONGS)   (Vanguard VSD 79144, released May 1964; the first song is credited to Bob Dylan and Pete Seeger and the second to Joan Baez and Bob Dylan; recorded at the Newport Folk Festival, July 1963)
Ye Playboys and Playgirls; With God on Our Side

EVENING CONCERTS AT NEWPORT, VOL. 1   (Vanguard VSD 79148, released May 1964; recorded at the Newport Folk Festival, July 1963)
Blowin' in the Wind

WE SHALL OVERCOME   (Broadside/Folkways BR 5592, released 1964; recorded at the Civil Rights March on Washington, August 1963)
Ballad of Medgar Evers

BROADSIDE REUNION   (Broadside/Folkways FR 5315, released November 1971; recorded in 1962 and 1963; Dylan is credited as Blind Boy Grunt)
Train A-Travelin'; Dreadful Day; The Ballad of Emmett Till; The Ballad of Donald White

THE CONCERT FOR BANGLADESH   (Apple STCX 3385, released December 1971)
A Hard Rain's A-Gonna Fall; It takes a Lot to Laugh, It Takes a Train to Cry; Blowin' in the Wind; Mr. Tambourine Man; Just Like a Woman

A TRIBUTE TO WOODY GUTHRIE, PART ONE   (Columbia KC

31171, released January 1972; recorded at a Woody Guthrie memorial concert, January 1968)

I Ain't Got No Home; Dear Mrs. Roosevelt; The Grand Coulee Dam

SECTION 4: RECORDS INCLUDING GUEST APPEARANCES BY DYLAN

MIDNIGHT SPECIAL   Harry Belafonte (RCA LSP 2449, released May 1962; recorded autumn 1961) Dylan plays harmonica on the title track.

CAROLYN HESTER   (Columbia CL 1796, released 1962; recorded September 1961) Dylan plays harmonica on "Come Back, Baby," "Swing and Turn Jubilee," and "I'll Fly Away."

THE BLUES PROJECT   Dave Van Ronk, John Koerner, and others (Elektra EKS 7264, released 1964; recorded mid-1963) Dylan, under the pseudonym Bob Landy, plays the lower piano part on "Downtown Blues."

JACK ELLIOTT   (Vanguard VSD 79151, released 1964; recorded mid-1963) Dylan plays harmonica on "Will the Circle Be Unbroken" under the pseudonym Tedham Porterhouse.

THREE KINGS AND THE QUEEN   Big Joe Williams, Roosevelt Sykes, Lonnie Johnson, and Victoria Spivey (Spivey LP 1004, released 1964; recorded October 1961) Dylan plays harmonica and sings behind Big Joe Williams on "Sitting on Top of the World," and plays harmonica on "Wichita."

DICK FARINA & ERIC VON SCHMIDT   (Folklore F-LEUT 7, released 1967 in U.K. only; recorded January 1963) Dylan, under the pseudonym Blind Boy Grunt, provides harmonica and backup vocals on "Glory, Glory," "Overseas Stomp," "You Can Always Tell," "Xmas Island," "Cocaine," and "London Waltz."

EARL SCRUGGS: HIS FAMILY AND FRIENDS   (Columbia KC 30584, released 1971) Dylan plays acoustic guitar on his own "Nashville Skyline Rag."

THREE KINGS AND THE QUEEN, VOL. 2   Big Joe Williams, Roosevelt Sykes, Lonnie Johnson, and Victoria Spivey (Spivey LP 1014, released 1972; recorded October 1961) Dylan plays harmonica on "Big Joe, Dylan And Victoria" and "It's Dangerous."

SOMEBODY ELSE'S TROUBLES   Steve Goodman (Buddah BDS 5121, released late 1972) Dylan, appearing as Robert Milkwood Thomas, provides piano and harmony vocals on "Somebody Else's Troubles." He also plays piano on "Election Year Rag," a single (Buddah BDA 326) recorded at the same time but omitted from the album; this was later included in *The Essential Steve Goodman* (Buddah BDS 5665 2).

ROGER MCGUINN   (Columbia KC 31946, released late 1972) Dylan plays harmonica on "I'm So Restless."

DOUG SAHM AND BAND   (Atlantic SD 7254, released late 1972) Dylan receives a general credit for vocals, harmony, guitar, harmonica, Hammond organ, and Vox organ. He is also specifically credited with shared vocals on "(Is Anybody Going to) San Antone," shared vocals and lead guitar on his own "Wallflower," shared vocals and guitar solo on "Blues Stay Away from Me," and harmonica on "Me and Paul."

CHRONICLES   Booker T and Priscilla Jones (A & M ST 4413, released 1973) Dylan plays harmonica on "The Crippled Crow."

DISCONNECTED   The Dial-A-Poem Poets (Giorno Poetry Systems GPS 003, released 1974; recorded November 1971) Dylan plays acoustic guitar on Allen Ginsberg's track, "Jimmy Berman."

BARRY GOLDBERG   (Atco SD 7040, released 1974) Dylan is credited with backup vocals on "Stormy Weather Cowboy," "Big City Woman," "Minstrel Show," and "Silver Moon," percussion on "It's Not the Spotlight," and shared production of the album.

COMIN' BACK FOR MORE   David Blue (Asylum 7E 1043, released 1975) Dylan plays harmonica on "Who Love."

SONGS FOR THE NEW DEPRESSION   Bette Midler (Atlantic SD 18155, released 1976; recorded late 1975) Dylan sings his own "Buckets of Rain" with Midler.

NO REASON TO CRY   Eric Clapton (RSO RS 1 3004, released 1976) Dylan sings his own "Sign Language" with Clapton.

DEATH OF A LADIES MAN   Leonard Cohen (Warner Bros. BS 3125, released 1977) Dylan provides backup vocals on "Don't Go Home With Your Hard-on."

THE LAST WALTZ   The Band (Warner Bros. 3WS 3146, released April 1978; recorded November 1976) Dylan contributes guitar and lead vocals on "Baby Let Me Follow You Down," "I Don't Believe You (She Acts Like We Never Have Met)," "Forever Young," "Baby Let Me Follow You Down (Reprise)," and "I Shall Be Released."

SO YOU WANNA GO BACK TO EGYPT . . .   Keith Green (Pretty Good Records PGR 1, released 1980) Dylan plays harmonica on "Pledge My Head to Heaven."

FIRST BLUES   Allen Ginsberg (John Hammond Records W2X 37673, released early 1973; recorded November 1971) Dylan appears on "Jimmy Berman (Gay Lib Rag)," "Vomit Express," and "Going to San Diego," playing guitar and organ. The first of these tracks was previously released on *Disconnected* (see above).

WE ARE THE WORLD   U.S.A. for Africa (Columbia, released March 1985) Dylan makes a vocal contribution on the title track, which was first released as a single.

LANGUAGE BARRIER   Sly and Robbie (Island, released August 1985) Dylan plays harmonica on "No Name on the Bullet."

SUN CITY   Artists United Against Apartheid (Manhattan, released December 1985) Dylan makes a vocal contribution on two versions of the title track.

INDEX

"Abandoned Love," 473
Abrams, Harvey, 68–69, 71, 75
"Absolutely Sweet Marie," 324
"Advice for Geraldine on Her Miscellane-
    ous Birthday," 264, 313
"Aesthetics of Silence, The" (Sontag), 374
Agnew, Spiro, 321
Agudath Achim Synagogue, 36
"Ain't Runnin' Any Race," 404
"Alberta 1," 419
"Alberta 2," 419
Ali, Muhammad, 460–461
Alk, Howard, 262, 366, 383
Alk, Jones, 262, 383
"All Along the Watchtower," 393
Allen, Steve, 167–168
"All I Really Want to Do," 219
"All the Tired Horses," 419
Almanac Singers, The, 78, 139
"Alternatives to College," 235
Altshuler, Bob, 298
Amram, David, 424, 439
Andersen, Eric, 257, 438, 459
Anderson, Bill, 297, 400
Andrews, Nigel, 471–472
Animals, The, 121, 123, 289, 294, 311
Another Side of Bob Dylan (album),
    219–225, 256, 262, 360
Anti-love songs, 272
"Apple Suckling Tree," 385
Armatrading, Joan, 482

Armstrong, Louis, 243
Aronowitz, Al, 217, 274, 421, 425
Artes, Mary Alice, 483
Artis, John, 459, 460, 461–462
"Artist in the Marketplace, The" (King),
    322
Asch, Moses, 78, 97, 141–149, 357
Ashby, Hal, 398
Ashford, Nicholas, 321
"As I Went Out One Morning," 392
Attwood, William H., 417
Auden, W. H., 228, 327
Augustine, Saint, 392
Avis, Bill, 329, 341, 361

"Baby, Let Me Follow You Down," 122
"Baby Stop Crying," 478
Baez, Joan, 52, 82, 92, 105, 121, 123, 124,
    128, 143, 159, 160, 167, 256, 257,
    261, 271, 289, 296, 297, 301,
    327–328, 353, 398, 404, 445, 446,
    461, 489
    Dylan and, 98, 170, 181, 183–190,
    250–251, 252, 264, 355, 415, 455,
    469
    concert appearances, 183–184, 263
    in *Renaldo and Clara*, 470, 471, 472, 473
    on the Rolling Thunder Revue tour,
    451, 452, 453, 454–455, 458, 468
Bailey, Mel and Lillian, 92, 95, 359
Baldwin, James, 200, 211

"Ballad in Plain D," 222, 241
"Ballad of a Thin Man, The," 280–281
"Ballad of Frankie Lee and Judas Priest,
     The," 393
"Ballad of Hollis Brown," 69, 152, 165,
     213
"Ballad of the Ox-Bow Incident," 126
Ballard, Hank, 18
Band, The, 286, 314–319, 320, 340, 341,
     361, 363, 365, 371, 385, 396, 406,
     429, 430, 432, 478
     "Last Waltz, The" (concert and film),
     318, 469–470
Bangladesh benefit concert, 421–422
Barron, Arthur, 167, 403
Basement Tapes, The (album), 317, 318,
     319, 383–385, 436, 446, 447, 485,
     488
Bays, Gwendolyn, 389
Beatles, The, 39, 53, 68, 144, 229, 230, 265,
     267, 288, 292, 294, 302, 308, 333,
     335, 366, 384, 469, 496
     Dylan on, 344, 358, 362
Beat poetry, 91, 138
     fusion with jazz of, 156, 210, 226
     reaction to Dylan by beat poets, 333
     Tarantula and, 236
     See also names of beat poets and writers
Beckett, Barry, 484, 485
Beecher, Bonny Jean, 79–80, 130
Before the Flood (album), 318, 378, 436–437
Behan, Dominic, 213
Belafonte, Harry, 93, 109, 116, 129, 153,
     493
Bennett, Tony, 179
Berry, Chuck, 226, 271, 280, 307, 338, 496
Berryman, John, 83, 231
Bibb, Leon, 93
Bikel, Theodore, 93, 109, 152, 170–179,
     181, 306
Billboard, 164, 264, 399, 400, 418
"Billy," 427, 428
Biograph (album), 441, 444, 467, 473,
     486n, 495–497
Bitter End, 93, 420
Blackbushe Aerodome concert (London),
     13, 482
"Black Cross," 81
"Black Crow Blues," 219–220
"Black Diamond," 463, 466
Blake, William, 218, 225, 231, 276, 463
Blakley, Ronee, 412, 451, 460, 471
Bliss, Carolyn, 214, 275, 392
Block, Bert, 379, 406
Blonde on Blonde (album), 63, 235, 317,
     318, 319–327, 360, 361, 384, 419,
     435, 447, 465, 496
Blood on the Tracks (album), 323, 384, 434,
     440–445, 492, 493
Bloomfield, Mike, 302, 315

"Blowin' in the Wind," 60, 140–141, 153,
     155, 157–158, 160–162, 167, 254,
     289, 310, 414, 421, 434
     as civil rights anthem, 164, 179, 268
Blue, David, see Cohen, David
Blue Angel, 93, 116
Bluegrass music, 312
Bob Dylan (album), 116–124
"Bob Dylan's Blues," 81, 155
"Bob Dylan's Dream," 156
"Bob Dylan's 115th Dream," 46, 83,
     273–274
Bob Dylan Words and Music (music-pub-
     lishing company), 379
Bogorad, Samuel, 227
Bolden, Buddy, 243
Bollard, Bob, 161
Bond, Julian, 170
Boone, Daniel, 35
"Boots of Spanish Leather," 214, 254
Born to Win (Guthrie), 79, 100–101, 336
Bouchillon, Chris, 119
Bound for Glory (film), 300, 398–399
Bound for Glory (Guthrie), 67, 74–75, 76,
     77, 78
Bowie, David, 447, 494
Boyles, Norman, 245–246
Brandeis University folk festival, 169
Brando, Marlon, 44–45, 53, 300, 358, 445,
     446, 497
Brassens, Georges, 369
Braun, Jonathan, 413–414
Braun, Tony, 443
Brecht, Bertolt, 145, 208, 391
Brel, Jacques, 210, 369
Brickman, Marshall, 112
Bringing It All Back Home (album), 267,
     270–277, 295, 320, 338, 360
Broadside, 129, 138–142, 149, 157, 158, 162,
     191, 260, 264, 314, 411
     Dylan's open letter to, 207–208
Broadside Ballads, Vol. I (album), 153,
     157–158
Bromberg, David, 425
Brooks, Harvey, 306
Brothers Four, The, 167
Brown, Hugh, 68, 71–72
Brown, Mick, 487, 489
Bruce, Lenny, 44, 82, 138, 268, 344
Brunman, Glen, 430
Buber, Martin, 195, 269
"Buckets of Rain," 443
Bucklen, John, 16, 43, 44, 45–46, 47, 49,
     51, 52, 53, 56, 61
Bucklen, Ruth, 46
Buckley, Lord, 82, 133, 282
Burdon, Eric, 293, 311
Burgess, Anthony, 229
Burns, Tito, 291–292, 423
Burroughs, William, 353

Butterfield, Paul, 315, 470
Buttrey, Kenneth, 320, 391, 403
Byrds, The, 121, 124, 147, 265, 274, 308–310

Café Espresso (Woodstock), 261–262
Café Wha? (New York City), 91, 93, 94
Caffè Lena (Saratoga Springs), 128–129
Cage, Buddy, 443
Camp, Hamilton, 146, 311
Campbell, Glen, 164, 311, 400
Camus, Albert, 269–270, 472
Canby, Vincent, 366
Cangacero music, 324
Cannon, Geoffrey, 399
"Can You Please Crawl Out Your Window," 331
Capitol Records, 317, 368
Carawan, Guy, 147, 170
Carlebach, Rabbi Shlomo, 413
Carradine, David, 105, 399
Carroll, Gordon, 427
Carruthers, Ben, 223
Carter, Chip, 433
Carter, Fred, 316
Carter, Jimmy, 433, 469
Carter, Rubin ("Hurricane"), 416, 448, 459–462
Carter, Sidney, 255–256
Carthy, Dorothy, 253, 255
Carthy, Martin, 155, 156, 251, 253, 255, 290
Cash, Johnny, 77, 218, 260–261, 263, 307, 494
  Dylan and, 400–404
Cash, June Carter, 402
Cassady, Neal, 439
Catcher in the Rye (Salinger), 147
Cavalier, 282–283, 286
Chabad Lubavitch (Hasidic center), 488
Chad Mitchell Trio, The, 160, 161, 165, 169
Champlin, Charles, 329
Chandler, Len, 93, 106, 141, 257
"Changing of the Guard," 478
"Changing Trains" (Oppenheim), 472–473
Chaplin, Charlie, 125
Charles, Bobby, 470
Charles, Ray, 321, 493
Charone, Barbara, 430, 447
Chartwell Artists, 379
Chelsea Hotel, 261
Chicago Daily News, The, 49, 195–196
Chicago Tribune, The, 374, 376
"Chimes of Freedom," 220, 241, 258, 259, 310
Chowka, Peter, 453, 457
Christgau, Robert, 383–384, 399, 415, 436, 444
Ciardi, John, 227

Citizen Kane (film), 14, 49
Civilization and Its Discontents (Freud), 410
Clancy, Pat, 106, 112
Clancy, Tom, 112, 143
Clancy Brothers, The, 93, 94, 101, 116, 422
Clapton, Eric, 421, 468, 469, 470, 482, 489
Clayton, Paul, 149, 156, 222, 240, 241, 242, 248, 249, 259–260, 263
"Clean-Cut Kid," 493
Cleave, Maureen, 290
Clive: Inside the Record Business (Davis), 377
"Clothes Line Saga," 385
Coburn, James, 426, 427
Cochran, Eddie, 307–308
Cocker, Joe, 407
Cocks, Jay, 493, 495
Coffeehouses of Greenwich Village, 88, 91–94
Cohen, David (David Blue), 257, 330, 331, 434, 451, 471
Cohen, John, 101, 300, 379
Cohen, Leonard, 156, 229, 230, 327, 439, 469
Colby, Paul, 458
Cole, Nat "King," 58, 121
Coleman, Ornette, 52
Coleman, Ray, 288–289, 366, 370, 421, 422
Collins, Judy, 64, 146, 155, 162, 168, 249, 262, 274, 311, 336, 395, 397
Columbia Records, 309
  Dylan and, 17, 107, 112, 115, 142, 147, 179–180, 376–377, 434, 436, 447, 487
Commons, The, 91, 92, 94, 105
Connolly, Ray, 405
Connors, Jerry, 85
Coolidge, Rita, 427
Coppola, Francis Ford, 446
CORE (Congress of Racial Equality), benefit concert for, 129
"Corrina, Corrina," 81, 153, 154, 157
Corso, Gregory, 52, 138, 368, 383, 424
Cosby, Bill, 282
Costner, Tom, 422
Cott, Jonathan, 440, 471
Country music, 15, 16, 39, 399–404
Country Music Story, The (Shelton), 400
"Country Pie," 404
Court, John, 153, 165, 190, 205, 262, 274, 298, 320
Cowan, Paul, 444
Craig, James, 295
Crawdaddy, 326, 327, 391
Creedence Clearwater Revival, 425
Cremer, Jan, 336
Crippa, Chet, 22, 37
Crosby, David, 308, 310, 417
Crosby, Stills, Nash and Young, 404, 423, 447
Crowe, Cameron, 496

Crump, Stuart, 197–198
Cuban Revolution, 69
cummings, e. e., 187

Dallas, Karl, 256, 407
Dandy, Jim, 46, 51, 56
Daniels, Charlie, 400, 403
Danko, Rick, 315, 317, 495
Darin, Bobby, 311
"Dark Eyes," 493
Darkness at Noon (Koestler), 276
Davis, Clive, 376–378, 400, 428
Davis, Reverend Gary, 95, 107, 122, 131,
    262
Davis, Miles, 211, 333
Daybreak (Baez), 188–189
"Day of the Locusts," 417–418
"Days of 49," 419
Dean, James, 22, 23–24, 44, 45, 53, 497
"Dear Landlord," 393–394
Decade of Dylan—1963 to 1974, A (bootleg
    album), 388
De Niro, Robert, 466
Denisoff, R. Serge, 316
Dennis, Carolyn, 477, 484
Desire (album), 235, 404, 434, 436, 462–468
"Desolation Row," 282–283, 306, 333, 370
DeVito, Don, 452, 495
Diamond, Neil, 469, 475
"Diamonds and Rust," 189–190
Dickens, Charles, 231
Dickinson, Bruce, 495
Dillion, James, 49
Dillon, Matt, 14, 35, 49
"Dink's Song," 109
"Dirge," 434, 435, 436, 440
Disc and Music Echo, 366, 367, 386
Donovan, 294–295, 297, 300, 311, 438
Don't Look Back (film), 61, 272, 289, 293,
    297–299, 366
"Don't Think Twice, It's All Right," 132,
    141, 156, 163, 182
Doobie Brothers, The, 445, 446
Doors of Perception, The (Huxley), 71
Douglas, Alfred, 463, 465
Douglas Sahm and Band (album), 424
"Down Along the Cove," 394, 395
"Down the Highway," 155
Drake, Pete, 391, 403, 404
"Drifter's Escape, The," 376, 393
Driscoll, Julie, 318
Dunson, Josh, 139–140, 313
Dupee, F. W., 229
Dylan (album), 428–429
Dylan, Anna, 474
Dylan, Bob
    albums recorded by, evaluation of
        Another Side of Bob Dylan, 219–225
        Basement Tapes, The, 383–385
        Before the Flood, 436–437

Belafonte album, 129, 153
Biograph, 495–497
Blonde on Blonde, 319–327
Blood on the Tracks, 440–445
Bob Dylan, 116–124
bootleg performance tapes, 385–388
Bringing It All Back Home, 270–277
Broadside Ballads, 153, 157–158
Desire, 462–468
Empire Burlesque, 492–493
Freewheelin' Bob Dylan, The, 153–157
Highway 61 Revisited, 277–283
Infidels, 487–488
John Wesley Harding, 389–395
Nashville Skyline, 399–404
New Morning, 419–420
Planet Waves, 434–437
religious conversion albums, 483, 484,
    485, 486
Self Portrait, 418–420
Street-Legal, 478
Times They Are A-Changin', The,
    212–215
ancestral background of, 27–28
Baez and, 98, 170, 181, 183–190,
    250–251, 252, 264, 355, 415, 455,
    469
    concert appearances, 183–184, 263
The Band and, 314–319, 320, 340, 341,
    361, 363, 365, 371, 385, 396, 406,
    429, 430, 432, 478
    "The Last Waltz" (concert and film),
        318, 469–470
on The Beatles, 344, 358, 362
Beecher and, 79–80, 130
on being accepted, 343–344
benefit concert appearances and record-
    ings of
    Bangladesh relief, 421–422
    Chile refugees, 416
    CORE, 129
    Farm Aid, 494–495
    Guthrie memorial, 395–398, 422
    Live Aid, 494
    "Night of the Hurricane, The,"
        460–461
    SNACK, 445–446
    "We Are the World" recording, 493
with Bobby Vee's band, 54–55, 63, 72
Broadside and, 139–142, 157, 158,
    207–208
brother and, 34, 35, 44, 59–60, 61, 471
Carter's 1976 presidential campaign and,
    433
Cash (Johnny) and, 400–404
childhood and adolescence in Hibbing
    of, 32–33, 38–52
civil rights movement and, 129, 135,
    149–150, 170–179, 203, 206, 214,
    247–248, 359

Columbia Records and, 17, 107, 112,
    115, 142, 147, 179-180, 376-377,
    434, 436, 447, 471, 487
concert performances in New York City
    of, 127-128, 152, 164-165, 193,
    198-199
concert tours of
    Australia, 362-365
    effect of religious conversion on,
        486-487, 489-490
    England, 252-254, 255-257, 288-299,
        370-371, 478-482, 490
    Europe, 365-371, 477, 481-482,
        489-490
    North America, 482-483, 484, 485,
        486
    Rolling Thunder Revue, 451-459,
        468-470
    Tour '74, 429-434
    U.S., 328-330, 332-335, 336-339,
        340-362
    world tour, 477-490
conversion to Christianity of, 74, 478,
    483-486
    effect on concert tours of, 486-487,
        489-490
critical reception for
    albums and music, 126, 153, 218-220,
        303, 307, 326, 383-384, 399, 418,
        419, 436, 440, 443-444, 466, 492,
        509
    films, 299-300, 366-367, 428, 470-471,
        472
    first solo concert, 164
    as folk singer (Folk City), 111-112
    Newport Folk Festival (1963),
        182-183
Dean and, 22, 23-24, 497
on death and suicide, 60, 126, 133-134
drawing and painting skills of, 148, 383
on drugs, 16-17
early Greenwich Village days of, 87-126
    coffeehouse performances, 91-94, 128,
        129
    first concert performance, 107
    at Folk City, 95-97, 98, 106, 107-113,
        116, 129
father and, 33-34, 37-38, 40, 41, 50, 55,
    56-61, 85
    effect of death on Dylan, 60-61
film appearances of
    Don't Look Back, 297-300
    Eat the Document, 366-367, 378-379
    Festival, 300-301
    Pat Garrett and Billy the Kid, 426-428
    Renaldo and Clara, 470-472
folk heroes of, 35, 44-45, 49, 59, 497
on folk music, 338, 356-357
folk-rock music and, 121, 153, 232,
    307-312

aesthetic and philosophical concepts
    expressed in, 267-271
    in Bringing It All Back Home and
        Highway 61 Revisited, 267
with The Golden Chords, 40-41, 42
Grossman and, 17, 42, 104, 115,
    142-147, 152, 153, 163, 167, 190,
    193, 254, 297, 298, 313, 325, 358,
    362, 369, 374, 379
    contract settlement, 379
    recording contract renewal, 376-
        377
    star-making strategy, 160-161,
        164-165, 169, 180, 182-183
Hammond (Sr.) and, 113-115, 116-117,
    118, 126, 142, 147, 153, 258, 490,
    495
Harrison and, 421, 422
Helstrom (Echo) and, 46-52, 53, 80
Hibbing's effect on, 24-25, 26, 27, 56,
    57-58, 61, 69, 71, 104, 214, 216
influence of films on, 22, 23-24, 126,
    149, 300, 358, 393, 497
influence on contemporary poets of,
    225-230, 333, 439-440
influence on young musicians of, 140,
    161-162, 437-440, 447, 480
Isle of Wight Festival and, 405-409
Israeli visit of, 16, 18, 412-414
Judaism of, 35-36, 37, 45, 391, 488
on marriage, 473-474
at Monterey Folk Festival, 169-170
mother and, 33, 34, 38, 41-42, 45, 55,
    57, 58, 61, 85
motorcycle accident and convalescence
    of, 371-372, 374-376
musical influences on, 38-41, 42, 53-55,
    55-56, 58, 64, 97-100, 102-104,
    125
    black musicians, 46, 92, 120, 124, 125,
        150-151, 234, 478, 496, 497
    Guthrie, 69, 74-77, 80, 82, 92,
        100-102, 118-119, 125, 164, 356,
        496, 497
musical self-training of, 36-37, 73
    guitar, 37, 40, 68, 115, 118, 120
    harmonica, 64, 115, 118, 125
name change by, 49-50, 68, 73
at Newport Folk Festivals
    1963, 180-181
    1964, 257-261
    1965, 301-304, 306
personal mythology of, 33, 68, 69, 71,
    92, 109-110, 125-126, 128
political interests of, 15, 69, 71, 72, 82,
    136, 191-193, 414-417, 446
press relations with, 147-148, 190-
    198, 199, 218, 283-288, 331-332,
    359, 363-365, 367, 369, 431-
    432

Dylan, Bob (*cont.*)
Newsweek cover story, 193–194, 198, 199, 215
New Yorker profile, 202–204
Princeton awards honorary doctorate to, 417–418
pseudonyms used by (when recording), 14, 423–426
receives Grammy Award, 485
"rediscovery of America" tour by (1964), 240–252
Rotolo (Suze) and, 52–53, 107, 116, 117, 126, 129, 130–136, 148, 152, 154, 164, 165, 169, 179, 182, 183, 185, 187, 192, 193, 206, 208, 213–214, 218, 222, 239, 251, 252, 274, 335, 355, 356–357, 362
The Scavenger's campaign against, 410–412, 420–421
summation of career, 491–492
teenage rebellion of, 38, 42–44
television appearances of, 166–168
Saturday Night Live, 484
World of John Hammond, The, 448–449, 451
the Tom Paine Award dinner and, 200–205, 239
at University of Minnesota, 55–56, 63, 65–67, 68
with the Dinkytown crowd, 66–72, 85–86
wife of, 18, 279, 398, 412, 417, 427, 478
divorce and settlement, 473, 474–475
family life, 383, 446
marital problems, 443, 444
marriage, 325
Woodstock as retreat for, 261–263, 265, 380–383
writings and song lyrics of, 41–42, 88–90, 234–235
academic studies of, 231–234
early dismissal as serious writer by establishment, 83–85
"11 Outlined Epitaphs," 212, 215–219
first poems, 34–35
as mass-media poet, 82, 83–84, 100, 210–212, 225–230, 353, 481
"Some Other Kinds of Songs," 223–225
Tarantula, 233, 234, 235–238
Writings and Drawings by Bob Dylan, 234–235
See also titles of songs written by
Dylan, Jacob, 474
Dylan, Jesse, 406, 474, 488
Dylan, Samuel, 474
Dylan, Sara, 14, 18, 279, 298, 375, 398, 412, 417, 427, 444, 478
divorce and settlement for, 473, 474–475
Don't Look Back and, 298

marital problems of, 443, 444
marriage of, 325
Renaldo and Clara and, 470, 471, 472, 473
on the Rolling Thunder Revue tour, 454
as the "Sad-Eyed Lady," 325–326
as "Sara," 467
Dylan: From Desolation Row to the Basement (bootleg album), 388
Dylan Liberation Front, 411
Dylan Live With The Band, Royal Albert Hall, 1966 (bootleg album), 388
Dylan Love Songs (bootleg album), 388
Dylan—The Very Early Years: My Back Pages (bootleg album), 388

"Ear Music" (Guthrie), 78
East of Eden (film), 44
Eat the Document (film), 300, 366–367, 378–379
Edelstein, Florence, 28
Ed Sullivan Show, The, 154, 166
Edwards, Chick, 446
Edwardson, Monte, 40, 41, 61, 64
Eldot, Walter, 56, 84
Electric Flag, The, 425
Elektra Records, 17, 114, 125, 309, 378
"11 Outlined Epitaphs," 91, 163, 192, 212, 215–219, 462
Eliot, T. S., 282, 463
Ellington, Duke, 164
Elliott, Jack, 73, 92, 98, 101–102, 107, 110, 112, 118, 123, 125, 128, 132, 395, 447, 451, 452, 454, 471
Emergency Civil Liberties Committee, 184, 200, 201, 202, 205
Empire Burlesque (album), 235, 492–493
English, Logan, 101, 112
Ephron, Nora, 283, 311, 325, 377
Epstein, Brian, 144, 308
Esquire, 199, 228
Evening Standard, The (London), 290, 376, 405
"Eve of Destruction," 308, 310
Everly Brothers, The, 53, 121, 418
Evers, Medgar, 179, 214
"Every Grain of Sand," 486
"Every Time I Hear the Spirit," 66
Existentialism in Dylan's folk-rock music, 269–270

Fabbro, Larry, 42, 43
Face in the Crowd, A (film), 149
Faithfull, Marianne, 292, 297
Fariña, Mimi Baez, 185, 230, 416, 454
Fariña, Richard, 105, 112, 114, 185, 187, 230, 250, 251, 254, 260, 296, 327, 372, 382
Farm Aid benefit concert, 494–495

"Father of Night," 419, 435–436
Fats Domino, 375, 440
Faulk, John Henry, 152, 153, 167, 184, 200
Faulkner, William, 247
Feinstein, Barry, 211, 248
Feliciano, José, 96
Ferlinghetti, Lawrence, 70, 138, 156, 209,
    226, 268, 333, 334, 337, 439, 470
Festival (film), 300–301
Financial Times, The (London), 472
First Annual Village Folk Festival, The
    (1975), 447–448
First Blues—Rags, Ballads & Harmonium
    Songs 1971-74 (Ginsberg), 439
Fitzgerald, F. Scott, 29–30, 319
"Fixin' to Die," 121
Flack, Roberta, 163, 340, 454, 459, 461
Folklore Center, 91, 94, 95, 127
Folk music, 18, 66, 73, 77–79, 82, 92–94
    beat poetry and, 91
    Columbia Records and, 115
    disdain among performers for media rec-
        ognition, 116, 129, 168–169
    Dylan on, 338, 356–357
    folk-rock and, 312–314
    freedom songs as, 161–162
    Greenwich Village 1960s boom in,
        87–90, 97–100
    Kennedy assassination and, 206
    Newport Folk Festivals and, 88, 92,
        180–183, 257–261, 301–304
    protest movement and, 137–138, 414–417
    song-writing tradition of, 163–164, 194
Folk-rock music, 121, 153, 232, 307–312
    aesthetic and philosophical concepts as
        expressed by Dylan in, 267–271
    in Bringing It All Back Home and High-
        way 61 Revisited albums, 267,
        271–283
    folk singers' attitude toward, 312–314
Folkways Records, 17, 97, 114, 125, 157
Fonda, Peter, 398
Foreman, Clark, 184, 200, 201, 204–205
Foreman, Geno, 105, 201, 259
Forest Hills Music Festival (1964), 263
Forest Hills Music Festival (1965), 306–307
"Forever Young," 435
Forman, James, 149, 170, 211, 217, 367
"Fourth Time Around," 324
Fowlie, Wallace, 440, 441, 442, 456
Franklin, Aretha, 163, 179, 359, 400
Freed, Alan, 38
Freedom Singers, The, 167, 170, 211
Freewheelin' Bob Dylan, The (album),
    153–157, 241
"Freight Train Blues," 123
Freud, Sigmund, 410
Friends of Chile benefit concert (1974), 416
Friesen, Gordon, 139, 140, 141, 155, 157,
    207, 314, 411

"From a Buick 6," 280
Fuller, Jesse, 64, 103, 110, 118, 125, 157,
    286

Gallo, Joey, 466, 467
Gardner, Susan, 124–125
Garland, Judy, 299, 496
Gaslight, 91, 94, 105–107, 420
"Gates of Eden," 275–276, 306
Gates of Paradise, The (Blake), 276
Gaye, Marvin, 496
Geer, Will, 77, 395, 397, 398
Geffen, David, 378, 430, 432, 436
Geldof, Bob, 493
Genet, Jean, 353
"George Jackson," 414, 415
Gerde's Folk City, 13, 18, 67, 70, 94–97,
    105–106, 108–112, 114, 116, 123,
    129, 150, 251, 420, 479
Giant (film), 22, 44
Gibran, Khalil, 390
Gibson, Bob, 93, 113, 143, 257
Gide, André, 104
Gilbert, Ronnie, 199, 258
Ginsberg, Allen, 52, 70, 71, 99, 138, 156,
    168, 226, 230, 268, 271, 277, 282,
    287, 297, 301, 332, 333, 336, 353,
    368, 375, 383, 398, 405, 414, 415,
    424, 434, 439–440, 466
    on the Rolling Thunder Revue tour,
        451, 452, 453–454, 455, 456–457,
        459
"Girl from the North Country," 79, 155,
    254, 403
Gleason, Ralph J., 170, 181, 190, 209,
    234–235, 250, 260, 272, 299, 332,
    333–334, 362, 419
Glover, Dave (Tony), 73, 75, 79, 80–81,
    82, 118, 210, 211, 258, 439
Goddard, Jack, 196–197
"Going Going Gone," 434, 435
"Goin' to Acapulco," 384, 385
Goldberg, Barry, 302, 425–426
Goldberg, Steven, 327, 389
Golden Chords, The, 40–41, 42
Goldsmith, Harvey, 395, 479, 482
Goldstein, Richard, 274, 299–300, 326, 327,
    380, 391, 395, 430, 458, 470
Goliards (singer-poets), 226
Goodchild, Gabrielle, 214, 220, 236–238,
    275, 393, 479
Gooding, Cynthia, 67, 109
Gospel music, 312, 484–485
"Gospel Plow," 121
"Gotta Serve Somebody," 484, 485
"Gotta Travel On," 419
Graalman, Bob, 233
Graham, Bill, 429, 430, 432, 433, 434, 445,
    446, 469, 489
Grammy Award, 485

Grapes of Wrath, The (Steinbeck), 51, 77
Grateful Dead, The, 423, 445
Graves, Robert, 226, 463, 464, 498
Gray, Michael, 319, 387–388, 479
Great White Wonder, The (bootleg album),
    386, 387
Greenbriar Boys, The, 106, 108, 111, 112,
    183, 194
Grossman, Albert B., 88, 106, 113, 301,
    330
  Bearsville home of, 261, 262, 382
  Dylan and, 17, 42, 104, 115, 142–147,
    152, 153, 163, 167, 190, 193, 254,
    297, 298, 313, 325, 358, 362, 369,
    374, 379
    contract settlement, 379
    record contract renewal, 376–377
    star-making strategy, 160–161,
      164–165, 169, 181, 182–183
Grotesque in Art and Literature, The
    (Kayser), 268–269
Grotesques in Dylan's folk-rock music,
    267–269
Guardian, The, 229, 292, 314, 399, 429, 487
Gulliksen, Ken, 483, 486
Guthrie, Arlo, 79, 101, 300, 395, 397, 416,
    425, 454
Guthrie, Jack, 77
Guthrie, Marjorie, 77, 78, 396, 397
Guthrie, Woody, 24, 60, 67, 68, 69, 71,
    74–79, 80, 82, 92, 110, 118–119,
    121, 123, 125, 143, 164, 219, 226,
    234, 336, 356, 496, 497
  death of, 395
  Dylan's meeting with, 100–102
  tributes to and benefit concerts for, 317,
    395–399, 422

Haden-Guest, Anthony, 407
Haggard, Merle, 495
Halloween Concert (1964), 263
Hamill, Pete, 373, 440
Hammond, John, Jr., 98, 106, 115,
    315–316, 449
Hammond, John, Sr., 108, 113–115,
    116–117, 124, 140, 438
  Dylan and, 113–115, 116–117, 118, 126,
    142, 147, 153, 258, 490, 495
  television tribute to, 448–449, 451
Hardin, Tim, 257, 260, 382
Hard Rain (album), 435, 469
"Hard Rain's A-Gonna Fall, A," 83, 100,
    140, 152, 156, 165, 181, 182
Harris, Emmylou, 404, 423, 467
Harrison, George, 366, 409, 421, 422, 479
Havens, Richie, 122, 395, 397, 406, 407,
    461
Hawkins, Ronnie, 315, 316, 433, 470
Hawks, The, *see* Band, The
Hayden, Tom, 248

Hayes, Isaac, 461
Hays, Lee, 78, 88
"Hazel," 435
Heller, Joseph, 281
Helm, Levon, 306, 315, 316, 408
Helstrom, Echo, *see* Shivers, Echo Helstrom
Helstrom, Martha, 47, 51, 52
Hemingway, Ernest, 327
Hendrix, Jimi, 480
Henske, Judy, 145, 251
Hentoff, Nat, 181, 202, 204, 221, 287, 313,
    453, 455, 457–458
Herald, John, 106, 132, 149, 325
"Hero Blues," 198
Hester, Carolyn, 93, 105, 112–113, 114,
    122, 167, 168
"He Was a Friend of Mine," 124
Hibbing, Minnesota, 16, 22–61
"Highway 51," 121
"Highway 61 Revisited," 281–282
Highway 61 Revisited (album), 267,
    277–283, 358, 360, 496
Hillman, Chris, 308, 309, 310
Hoffman, Abbie, 405, 413
Hoikkala, Le Roy, 40, 41
Holiday, Billie, 114
Holly, Charles Hardin "Buddy," 40, 53–55,
    58, 113, 338
Holmes, John Clellon, 227
"Honey, Just Allow Me One More
    Chance," 157
Hooker, John Lee, 95, 96
Hootenannies, 95, 123, 168–169, 180
Hootenanny (magazine), 206, 211–212
Hootenanny (TV show), 166, 168–169, 207
"House Carpenter, The," 123
House of Representatives Committee on
    Un-American Activities, 137
"House of the Rising Sun," 64, 110, 111,
    121, 122, 294
Houston, Cisco, 77, 78, 95, 101, 496
"Howl" (Ginsberg), 277, 282, 441
"How Much Longer?," 478
Hudson, Garth, 315, 316–317
"Hurricane," 449, 452, 458, 459–462, 467
Hurricane Trust Fund, The, 460, 462
Hynde, Chrissie, 489

Iachetta, Michael, 191, 375
"I Am a Lonesome Hobo," 394
Ian, Janis, 257, 311, 438
Ian and Sylvia, 146, 262
I Ching, 13, 15, 70
"Ideas of Redemption in Alchemy"
    (Jung), 465
"I'd Have You Anytime," 422
"Idiot Wind," 441–442
"I Don't Believe You," 222
"I Dreamed I Saw St. Augustine," 392–393
"If Dogs Run Free," 376, 419

"I Forgot More Than You'll Ever Know,"
    419
"If You Gotta Go," 295
"If You See Her, Say Hello," 443
"I'll Be Your Baby Tonight," 394–395
"I'll Remember You," 493
Illuminations, Les (Rimbaud), 436, 438, 443
"I'm Gonna Get You, Sally Gal," 108
Imhoff, Barry, 434, 451
Infidels (album), 487–488
In His Own Write (Lennon), 230
"In My Time of Dyin'," 120, 360
"In Search of Little Sadie," 417
"I Shall Be Free," 157
"I Shall Be Free No. 10," 220
"I Shall Be Released," 318, 376, 384, 385
"Isis," 463, 464, 466–467, 468
Isle of Wight Festival (1969), 14, 318,
    405–409, 437
Israel, 16, 18, 412–414
"Is Your Love in Vain?," 478
"It Ain't Me, Babe," 63, 222, 257
"It Hurts Me Too," 419
"It's All Over Now, Baby Blue," 277, 302,
    371, 472
"It's Alright, Ma (I'm Only Bleeding),"
    276–277
"It Takes a Lot to Laugh, It Takes a Train
    to Cry," 280, 302
Ives, Burl, 116
"I Want You," 323
"I Will Not Go Down Under the
    Ground," 141, 158

Jackson, Mahalia, 151–152, 243–244, 359
Jagger, Mick, 261, 423, 443, 475, 494
James, Billy, 147, 193, 194, 308, 329, 334
Jara, Joan and Victor, 416
Jefferson, Blind Lemon, 110, 123–124, 157,
    324
Jennings, Waylon, 493, 494
Jerome, Jim, 448, 453
Jewish Defense League, 412, 413
Joan Baez in Concert, Part 2, 24, 188
"Joey," 466
John, Elton, 423
John Birch Society, 137, 154, 166
"John Brown," 158
John Hammond on Record (Hammond), 146
Johnson, Bernice, 149–150, 211, 243, 359
Johnson, Lyndon, 308, 337
Johnson, Robert, 120, 121, 124, 234, 478,
    496, 497
Johnston, Bob, 278, 320
"John Wesley Harding," 391–392
John Wesley Harding (album), 59, 117, 314,
    315, 318, 377, 384, 389–395, 398,
    400, 465, 473
"Jokerman," 488
Jones, Jeffrey, 281, 495

Joplin, Janis, 143, 146, 195
Joseph, Anthea, 252–253, 255
Journal of Albion Moonlight, The (Patchen),
    236–237
Joyce, James, 29, 236
Jung, Carl, 13, 456, 465
"Just Like a Woman," 323, 421
"Just Like Tom Thumb's Blues," 282

"Kaddish" (Ginsberg), 333, 336, 338, 353
Kael, Pauline, 44–45, 471
Kafka, Franz, 390, 391
Karman, Pete, 240, 241, 242, 243, 244, 248,
    249, 250
Kayser, Wolfgang, 268–269
Kemp, Lou, 434, 446, 451, 452
Kennedy, John F., 18, 19, 199, 201, 206
Kerouac, Jack, 13, 70, 99, 138, 227, 236,
    237, 240, 439, 455
Kettle of Fish, 105, 294, 335, 420
King, Bill, 221, 222, 231, 273, 276, 322,
    323, 389
King, Coretta, 417
King, Martin Luther, Jr., 18, 149, 185
King Lear (Shakespeare), 385
Kingston Trio, The, 92–93, 113, 129
"Klan, The," 64, 68
Knockin' on Dylan's Door, 430
"Knockin' on Heaven's Door," 428, 490
Koerner, "Spider John," 66, 67, 73, 116,
    117
Koestler, Arthur, 276
Kooper, Al, 279, 302, 306, 307, 320
Kornfeld, Barry, 104, 195, 222, 251
Kramer, Daniel, 263, 271, 278, 330
Kristofferson, Kris, 320, 379, 426–429
Kweskin, Jim, 105, 149

LaFarge, Peter, 141, 257
Lampell, Millard, 78, 395, 396
Landau, Jon, 327, 384, 390–391, 458
Langhorne, Bruce, 115, 275, 428
"Last Waltz, The" (concert and film), 328,
    469–470
"Lay Down Your Weary Tune," 185, 186
"Lay, Lady, Lay," 94, 378, 404
Leadbelly, 56, 119, 125, 381
Lennon, John, 39, 230, 294, 324, 325, 362,
    398, 405, 409, 410, 423, 496
"Leopard-Skin Pill-Box Hat," 323
Lester, Julius, 139, 257
Leventhal, Harold, 79, 101, 142–143, 144,
    164, 199, 202, 300, 301, 395, 396,
    398
Levinson, Belle D., 220, 231
Levinson, Leonard L., 199
Levy, Jacques, 451, 460, 467–468
Lhamon, W. T., Jr., 231, 233, 466
Library of Congress's Archive of Folk Cul-
    ture, 77–78

Lieberson, Goddard, 117, 179–180, 376, 378, 449, 490
Life, 52, 259, 299
"Like a Rolling Stone," 83, 261, 278–279, 288, 302, 371
"Lily, Rosemary and the Jack of Hearts," 442–443
Little Richard, 22, 39, 40, 41, 53, 58, 125, 440, 496
Little Sandy Review, 73, 84, 153, 218–219
Live Aid benefit concert, 494
Live at Budokan (album), 477
"Living the Blues," 419
"Lo and Behold," 385
Lois, George, 460, 488
Lomax, Alan, 54, 73, 78, 122, 261, 301, 312, 398
Lomax, John, 55, 109
London Daily Sketch, The, 255, 406
"Lonesome Death of Hattie Carroll, The," 198, 212, 214–215
"Long Ago, Far Away," 485
"Long-Distance Operator," 384
"Long Time Coming, A," 81
"Love Minus Zero/No Limit," 272–273, 306, 421
Lowell, Robert, 231
Lownes, Victor, 325, 474
Lyrics, 1962–1985 (Dylan), 215, 235, 495

McCarthy, Joseph R., 137
McCartney, Paul, 39, 311–312, 325, 362, 445
McClure, Michael, 333, 336, 439
MacColl, Ewan, 296, 312, 313, 314
McCoy, Charlie, 320, 324, 391, 403
McDonough, Jack, 220, 221, 232, 273, 393, 394, 466
McGuinn, Roger, 308, 309, 310, 423, 428, 451, 467, 468, 471, 495
McGuire, Barry, 310, 311, 312
MacKenzie, Eve and Mac, 92, 95
McKuen, Rod, 229
McLuhan, Marshall, 433
"Maggie's Farm," 83, 163, 272, 300, 302, 306
"Maid of Constant Sorrow," 64, 73
Maier, Rabbi Reuben, 36
Mailer, Norman, 336
Maimudes, Victor, 228, 240, 247, 248, 249, 329, 338–339, 341, 361
Makem, Tommy, 93, 94, 101, 116
Making of a Counter Culture, The (Roszak), 308
Mann, Manfred, 146, 289, 294
"Man of Constant Sorrow," 120, 360
"Man on the Street," 124
Mansfield, David, 451, 477
Manuel, Richard, 315, 317
Marcus, Greil, 384, 405, 418, 419, 437, 440

Marsh, Dave, 371, 466
"Masters of War," 140, 141, 155
Mayer, Ira, 415–416
Meade, Marion, 323
"Meet Me in the Morning," 442
Mekas, Jonas, 366
Melody Maker, 199–200, 288, 292–294, 311, 325, 366, 371, 375, 384, 407, 408, 415, 421, 427, 430, 446
"Memphis Blues Again," 323, 327
Mercedes, Denise, 451
Mexico City Blues (Kerouac), 455
MGM Records, 146, 376, 377
Midler, Bette, 423, 447, 451
Midnight Cowboy (film), 93–94
Midnight Special (Belafonte album), 129, 153
Miller, Edwin, 147–148
Miller, Henry, 223
"Million Dollar Bash," 384
Minnesota, University of, 15, 50, 55, 63, 65
Minstrels of the Dawn: The Folk-Protest Singer as Cultural Hero (Rodnitzky), 233
"Mr. Tambourine Man," 83, 121, 254, 257, 274–275, 300, 302, 306, 308, 309, 421
Mitchell, Joni, 402, 454, 459, 460, 461, 469
"Mixed Up Confusion," 153, 154
Modern Language Association, 231
Mogull, Artie, 145–146, 160, 162, 379
Monroe, Marilyn, 497
Monterey Folk Festival (1963), 169–170
Morrison, Jim, 229, 230
Morrison, Van, 382, 469, 489
Morton, Dave, 62, 66, 69–70, 83
Morton, Jelly Roll, 125
"Most Likely You Go Your Way (and I'll Go Mine)," 323–324
"Motorpsycho Nightmare," 221
Mouskouri, Nana, 486n
"Mozambique," 466
Murdoch, Bruce, 438
Murphy, Elliott, 438
Musgrave, Lynn, 206, 325–326
Music from Big Pink (The Band album), 315, 317, 318
"My Back Pages," 221
Myers, Larry, 483, 486
"My Life in a Stolen Moment," 24, 65, 86, 360
Myth of Sisyphus, The (Camus), 472

Nashville Skyline (album), 16, 377, 399–404, 409, 418
"Nashville Skyline Rag," 403
National Guardian, 191–192
"Neighborhood Bully," 488
Nelson, Paul, 62, 73–74, 80, 81, 84, 118, 313, 324, 327, 438

Nelson, Willie, 423, 494
Neuwirth, Bob, 250, 325, 329, 335, 336,
    423, 434, 447, 448, 450, 452
"Never Say Goodbye," 436
Neville, Richard, 364
Newfield, Jack, 228–229
New Morning (album), 14, 235, 377, 417,
    419–420, 425, 428
New Musical Express, 278, 291, 292, 418,
    422, 429, 495–496
"New Pony," 478
Newport Folk Festival (1959), 88, 92
Newport Folk Festival (1963), 154, 160,
    180–183
Newport Folk Festival (1964), 257–261
Newport Folk Festival (1965), 301–304,
    306
Newsweek, 56, 104, 131, 162, 208, 215, 229,
    299, 311, 374, 376, 386, 390, 399,
    431, 438
    cover story on Dylan, 193–198, 199,
    215
    Dylan's reply to, 218
New York, 430
New York Daily News, 191, 375
New Yorker, The, 221, 326, 398, 433, 471
    Dylan profile in, 202–204
New York Herald Tribune, 330
New York Post, The, 166, 283, 311, 325,
    375, 377
New York Times, The, 68, 82, 96, 106, 107,
    124, 161, 164, 170, 215, 264, 299,
    306, 307, 313, 323, 366, 372, 378,
    398, 430, 433, 436, 458, 459, 461,
    471, 482, 488
    review of Dylan's Folk City performance,
    111–112
New York Times Magazine, The, 227–228
"New York Town," 119
Nicholson, Jack, 434, 479, 494
"Night of the Hurricane, The," benefit
    concerts, 460–461, 468
"North Country Blues," 24, 27, 104, 214
"Nothing Was Delivered," 384, 385
"No Time to Think," 494
Nyro, Laura, 229

"Obviously Five Believers," 324
Ochs, Phil, 100, 140, 141, 208, 230, 257,
    259, 260, 330, 331, 399, 416, 438,
    448, 451
"Odds and Ends," 385
Odetta, 66, 71, 93, 143, 146, 167, 254, 262,
    395, 396, 397
Ogilvy, Shelden, 182, 184
O'Hara, Frank, 327
"Oh, Sister," 463, 466
Okun, Milt, 155, 160–161, 235, 391
"On a Night Like This," 435
"One More Cup of Coffee," 466

"One More Night," 404
"One of Us Must Know (Sooner or
    Later)," 322
"One Too Many Mornings," 213–214
"Only a Hobo," 158
"Only a Pawn in Their Game," 82, 179,
    212, 214
Ono, Yoko, 325, 410
"Open Letter to Bob Dylan" (Silber),
    312–313
"Open the Door, Homer," 385
Oppenheim, Irene, 472–473
Oral literature, 225–230
"Orange Juice Blues," 385
Orlovsky, Peter, 415, 451
Orphic Vision, The (Bays), 389
Osborne, John, 138, 297
Oswald, Lee Harvey, 201, 203
"Outlaw Blues," 273
Ox-Bow Incident, The (film), 126, 393
"Oxford Town," 156, 198
OZ, 364, 386

Page, Gatemouth, 39, 48
Pankake, Jon, 73, 81, 84
Parables and Paradoxes (Kafka), 390
"Pastures of Plenty," 101
Patchen, Kenneth, 236–237
Pat Garrett and Billy the Kid (film), 300,
    378, 412, 426–428
Paturel, Bernard, 262, 379, 382, 383
Paturel, Mary Lou, 262
Paxton, Tom, 107, 141, 161, 163, 164,
    257, 262, 313, 314, 395, 397, 407,
    438
Peckinpah, Sam, 300, 426, 427, 428
Peel, David, 420, 421
Peel, John, 266, 386, 410
"Peggy Day," 404
Pennebaker, Donn, 297, 298, 366–367,
    375
People, 448, 453, 455
"People I Owe" (Guthrie), 79
Peter, Paul and Mary, 88, 96, 113, 143, 144,
    146, 153, 154, 155, 159, 160, 164,
    169, 182, 188, 300–301, 362, 414
    "Blowin' in the Wind" and, 161
Phillips, Shawn, 461
Pichaske, David R., 232, 389, 391
Pickering, Stephen, 237, 391, 412, 430
Planet News (Ginsberg), 434
Planet Waves (album), 318, 378, 413,
    434–437, 440
Playboy, 287, 471
"Playboys and Playgirls," 140, 141, 182
"Pledging My Time," 321, 322
Plimpton, George, 236
Poetry of Rock, The (Goldstein), 326
Popular culture, literary and sociologic
    studies of, 230–234

Popular Culture Association of the South, 233
Porco, John, 94
Porco, Mike, 18, 94, 108, 150, 168, 369, 433, 451
"Positively Fourth Street," 99, 264, 334
Potok, Chaim, 15–16
Prendergast, Tom, 94, 95
Presley, Elvis, 38, 39, 40, 44, 58, 98, 125, 356, 405, 418, 480, 496
"Pretty Boy Floyd," 119
"Pretty Peggo-O," 121
Pride, Charley, 495
Princeton University, 417
Prine, John, 422, 438
Protest songs, 139–142, 149–150, 157–158, 257, 259

"Queen Jane Approximately," 281
Quin, Mike, 77

Raines, Quinton, 136–137
"Rainy Day Women #12 & 35," 320, 321–322, 365, 371
"Ramblin' Blues," 124
Ramparts, 288
R & B (rhythm and blues) music, 39, 48, 82, 87
Ray, Dave, 80, 118
Ray, Johnny, 38
Reagon, Cordell, 150, 243, 359
Real Live (album), 490
Rebel Without a Cause (film), 44, 149
Record World, 418
Redding, Otis, 362
Reed, Lou, 438, 495
Renaldo and Clara (film), 189, 301, 331, 468, 469, 470–472, 473, 475, 479, 482
"Restless Farewell," 215
Resurrection (Tolstoy), 465
"Reuben James," 101
Rexroth, Kenneth, 156, 209, 226, 227, 439
Reynolds, Malvina, 141, 250, 257
Richards, Keith, 494
Richards, Roberta, 413
Ricks, Christopher, 214, 231, 273
Rimbaud, Arthur, 99–100, 156, 220, 282, 321, 326, 333, 338, 418, 436, 438, 439, 440, 442, 456, 469, 491, 492, 497, 498
Rivera, Scarlet, 449, 467
Robertson, Jeannie, 338
Robertson, Robbie, 306, 315, 316, 317, 320, 330, 361, 362, 376, 397, 432, 454, 470, 475
Robeson, Paul, 211
Robinson, Earl, 64, 398
Robinson, Smokey, 226, 493
"Rock 'n' Roll Is Here to Stay," 43

Rock 'n' roll music, 38, 40, 43, 68, 87
Rock poetry, 227, 229–230
Rock videos, 488
Rockwell, John, 383, 430, 433, 458, 461, 466, 482–483
Rodgers, Jimmie, 58, 104, 125, 496
Rodnitzky, Jerome L., 233
Rogers, Kenny, 495
Rolfsen, Bonn, 43, 56, 61
Rolling Stone, 94, 326, 336, 384, 403, 405, 411, 414–415, 418, 427, 431, 436, 440, 444, 453, 458, 466, 488
Rolling Stones, The, 39, 68, 292, 405, 469, 494
Rolling Thunder Logbook, 472
Rolling Thunder Revue, 15, 301, 310, 319, 376, 435, 445, 451–459, 468–470
"Romance in Durango," 463, 466
Rooney, Jim, 266, 303
Rosenzweig, Rabbi Yoso, 413
Roszak, Theodore, 308
Rothschild, Charlie, 95, 112, 144, 190, 306, 330, 375, 379
Rotolo, Carla, 107–108, 131, 134–135, 136, 179, 180, 192–193, 206, 222, 240, 251
Rotolo, Mary, 131, 132, 206
Rotolo, Suze, 52–53, 107, 116, 117, 126, 129, 130–136, 148, 152, 154, 164, 165, 169, 179, 182, 183, 185, 187, 192, 193, 206, 208, 213–214, 218, 222, 239, 251, 252, 274, 335, 355, 356–357, 362
Rubin, Barbara, 271, 335
Rubin, Jerry, 410, 415, 423
Russell, Leon, 309, 415–416, 422–423, 424
Rutgers University concert, 128
Ryan, Robert, 395, 396, 397, 398

Saal, Hubert, 195, 374
"Sad-Eyed Lady of the Lowlands," 320, 324–326, 362
Sahm, Doug, 424–425
Sainte-Marie, Buffy, 257, 311
Salinger, J. D., 147
Sandburg, Carl, 239, 242–243, 247
Sandperl, Ira, 187, 188
San Francisco Chronicle, 170, 334, 432
Santana, 445, 461, 489
"Sara," 325, 464, 466, 467, 468
Sartre, Jean-Paul, 269
Saturday Evening Post, The, 56, 376
Saturday Night Live, 484
Saturday Review, 227, 327, 390
Saved (album), 485
Saville, Philip, 252, 253, 254
Schaap, Dick, 193
Schatzberg, Jerry, 263
Scorsese, Martin, 469, 495
Scott, Molly, 94, 101, 107

Season in Hell, A (Rimbaud), 456
Sebastian, John, 52, 163
Seeger, Charles, 164
Seeger, Pete, 64, 66, 68, 77, 78, 79, 91, 92,
    121, 137, 138–139, 140, 144, 168,
    169, 179, 181, 182, 207, 216, 218,
    257, 296, 312, 314, 381, 395, 396,
    397, 399, 416, 422
"Seeing the Real You at Last," 493
"See That My Grave Is Kept Clean," 110,
    111, 123–124, 124, 125
Self Portrait (album), 16, 418–420, 425,
    428, 435
Sellers, Brother John, 97, 115
Senate Internal Security Sub-Committee,
    137
"Señor (Tales of Yankee Power)," 478
Sergeant Pepper, 384, 391
Shakespeare, William, 225, 231, 299, 385
Shankar, Ravi, 421, 422
Shapiro, Ben, 169, 170, 300
Shaw, George Bernard, 239, 344
"She Belongs to Me," 272, 306
"Shelter from the Storm," 443
Shepard, Sam, 472–473
Shivers, Echo Helstrom, 46–52, 53, 61, 79,
    80
Shot of Love (album), 486
"Sign Language," 469
"Sign on the Cross," 485
"Sign on the Window," 376, 420
Silber, Irwin, 97, 258, 259, 312–313, 314
Silver, Roy, 143, 160
Simon, Carly, 438
Simon, Paul, 163, 230, 251–252, 260, 438,
    493
Simon and Garfunkel, 96, 144, 155,
    251–252, 311, 378
"Simple Twist of Fate," 441
Sinatra, Frank, 362, 428
Singer, Isaac Bashevis, 15–16
Sing Out!, 67, 73, 84, 97, 123, 138, 139,
    191, 192, 211, 218, 253, 258, 264,
    303, 357, 378, 425
    attack on Dylan's folk-rock music by,
    312–313
    Dylan featured in, 152–153
Sir Douglas Quintet, 424
Sloan, P. F., 307, 310, 311
Slow Train Coming (album), 483, 484
Smith, Patti, 438–439, 447, 451
SNACK benefit concert, 445–446
"Solid Rock," 486
"Some Other Kinds of Songs ... Poems by
    Bob Dylan," 223–225
"Something There Is About You," 435
Song and Dance Man: The Art of Bob Dylan
    (Gray), 319, 387
*Songs of Bob Dylan from 1966 Through 1975,
    The*, 235

"Song to Woody," 82, 102, 109, 122, 163
Sonny and Cher, 307, 309, 310
Sontag, Susan, 328, 374
Sound of the City, The (Gillett), 294
Soviet Literature Gazette, 417
Spaniards in the Works (Lennon), 230
"Spanish Harlem Incident," 220
Spector, Phil, 206, 207, 308, 321, 334–335,
    359, 422
Spencer, Lena and Bill, 128
Spender, Stephen, 228
Spivey, Victoria, 107, 150
Spoelstra, Mark, 97–98, 106, 141
Springs, Helena, 477, 479, 484
Springsteen, Bruce, 438, 487, 493
Staples, Mavis, 211, 359
Staple Singers, The, 151, 167, 359
Starr, Ringo, 404, 421, 461, 470
Steinbeck, John, 51
Stelzig, Eugene, 221, 222, 232, 389–390
Stewart, Dave, 494, 495
Stills, Stephen, 461
Sting, 494
Stokes, Geoffrey, 434
Stone, Ben D., 27–28, 32
Stookey, Paul, 143, 144, 330
Street-Legal (album), 473, 477, 478, 482
Student Non-Violent Coordinating Com-
    mittee (SNICK), 149, 150,
    170–179, 243, 359
"Subterranean Homesick Blues," 271–272,
    297
Svedberg, Andrea, 193, 194
Swamp music, 424–425
"Sweetheart Like You," 488

"Take Me As I Am," 419
"Talkin' Devil," 158
"Talking Bear Mountain," 106, 109, 111
Talking blues, 119
"Talking New York," 87, 109, 111,
    118–119, 152
"Talking Subway Blues," 118–119
"Talkin' Hava Negilah Blues, 109, 111
"Talkin' John Birch Paranoid Blues," 140
"Talkin' John Birch Society Blues," 152,
    154, 166, 198
"Talkin' World War III Blues," 156–157
"Tangled Up in Blue," 441
Tarantula (Dylan), 16, 208, 212, 220, 224,
    233, 234, 341, 353, 361, 378, 384
    analysis of, 233–238
Tarot, The (Douglas), 463
Tate, Allen, 83
Taylor, James, 230, 429, 438
"Tears of Rage," 318, 384, 385
"Tell Me That It Isn't True," 404
"Temporary Like Achilles," 324
Tender Is the Night (Fitzgerald), 319
Terry, Sonny, 69, 94, 125, 449

Thal, Terri, 99, 142
"This Land Is Your Land," 79, 182
"This Life Is Killing Me," 108
"This Wheel's on Fire," 318–319, 384, 385
Thomas, Dylan, 14, 49–50, 99, 215, 230, 255, 256, 337
Thompson, Hank, 40, 400
Thomson, Liz, 486n, 489
"Three Angels," 419
Three Kings and a Queen (album), 150–151
Time, 22–23, 190–191, 195, 315, 321, 399, 405, 418, 419–420, 430, 431, 438, 461, 475, 492, 493, 495
"Time Passes Slowly," 420
Times, The (London), 15, 235, 255, 436, 490, 496
"Times They Are A-Changin', The," 212–213, 289, 301, 414
Times They Are A-Changin', The (album), 212–215, 241, 242
Tiny Tim, 80, 93
"To Be Alone with You," 403
Tolstoy, Leo, 305, 465
"Tombstone Blues," 279–280
"Tom Joad," 75
"Tomorrow Is a Long Time," 81, 133, 160
Tom Paine Award, 200–201
"Tonight I'll Be Staying Here with You," 404
"Too Much of Nothing," 375–376, 384, 385
Topical songs, 139–142, 149–150, 157–158, 257, 259
"To Ramona," 220–221
Toth, Emily, 231
"Tough Mama," 435
Tour '74, 13, 429–434, 437
"Train to Cry," 421
Transvaal Educational News, 416–417
Traum, Happy, 140, 158, 262, 383, 398, 423, 424, 479
Travers, Mary, 138, 144, 336, 376, 444
"Tribute to Woody Guthrie" concert (1968), 317
"True Love Tends to Forget," 478
Truscott, Lucian K., 419, 431
"Trust Yourself," 493
"Turkey Chase," 428
Turner, Gil, 135, 138, 139–140, 149, 153, 319, 425
Turner, Joe, 157
Turner, Tina, 334, 335, 493, 494
Turtles, The, 310, 313
Tuscarora Indian Reservation, 458–459
TV Guide, 413, 469

Uhler, Max, 71, 85

Valens, Ritchie, 54
Valentine, Patty, 462

"Valley Below," see "One More Cup of Coffee"
Vanguard Records, 17, 92, 114, 123, 125, 181
Van Ronk, David, 92, 98–100, 102, 105, 106, 107, 110, 112, 122, 125, 128, 183, 207, 328–329, 416, 448
Variety, 161, 199, 307, 310, 329, 399
Vee, Bobby, 54–55, 63, 72
Velvet Underground, The, 328, 336
Verlaine, Paul, 442
Vietnam War, 308, 328, 338, 493
Village Voice, The, 19, 72, 95, 153, 196–197, 228–229, 307, 326, 327, 368, 383–384, 391, 398, 399, 410, 415, 422, 431, 434, 436, 437, 439, 444, 447, 457, 470
Villon, François, 91, 99, 134, 215, 216
Vineyard Fellowship, The, 483, 486
"Visions of Johanna," 320, 322, 327
Von Schmidt, Eric, 98, 105, 122, 169, 182, 254, 447
Voznesensky, Andrei, 424

Wainwright, Loudon, III, 423, 438
Walcott, James, 470–471
"Walls of Red Wing," 84
Warhol, Andy, 169, 328, 336
Wasserman, John, 432
"Waste Land, The" (Eliot), 282
"Watching the River Flow," 376
Waters, Muddy, 53, 261, 447, 470
Watts, Michael, 427, 429
"We Are the World," 493–494
Weavers, The, 88, 93, 137, 169
Weber, Harry, 62, 66, 67–68, 69, 83
Weberman, Alan Jules (The Scavenger), 139, 410–412, 420–421, 431
"We Better Talk This Over," 478
"Wedding Song," 435, 436, 440
Wein, George, 88, 180, 181, 303
Weinberger, Sybil, 107–108, 135, 136
Weintraub, Fred, 93, 168
Weintraub, Jerry, 477
Weissberg, Eric, 112, 443
Wenner, Jann, 261
Wexler, Jerry, 425, 426, 449, 484, 485
Wharton, Joan, 194
Wheeler, Billy Edd, 257
"When I Paint My Masterpiece," 318, 319
"When the Night Comes Falling from the Sky," 493
"When the Ship Comes In," 214, 414
"When You Gonna Wake Up?," 484
"Where Are You Tonight? (Journey Through Dark Heat)," 478, 481
Whitaker, Dave, 69, 71, 72, 75
Whitaker, Gretel Hoffman, 54, 68, 72, 75, 80, 81, 82
White, Booker T. Washington, 121

White, Josh, 67, 93, 109, 120
White Goddess, The (Graves), 226, 463, 464
Whitehead, Ralph Radcliffe, 380–381
White Horse Tavern, 105, 131, 138
"Wicked Messenger, The," 394
"Wigwam," 419
Wild One, The (film), 44, 149
Williams, Big Joe, 92, 121, 124, 127, 150–151
Williams, Hiram "Hank," 39, 40, 45, 53, 58, 103, 125, 226, 389, 395, 480
Williams, Paul, 273, 326
Williams, Richard, 421, 487, 496
Williams, Tennessee, 247
Williams, William Carlos, 70
Willis, Ellen, 327, 374, 433–434
Wilson, Tom, 121, 154, 211, 219, 273, 277, 295
"Winterlude," 419
"With God on Our Side," 140, 179, 180, 182, 213, 258, 306
Wolfe, Paul, 208, 259
Wonder, Stevie, 164, 461, 480, 493
Wood, Ronnie, 470, 494
Woodstock, New York, 14, 165, 261–263, 265, 380–383
Woodstock Nation (1969 festival), 80, 180, 382, 383, 405
Woody Guthrie Children's Trust Society, 79
"Woogie Boogie," 419
World of John Hammond, The (TV special), 448–449, 451
World Vision, 490
Writings and Drawings (Dylan), 24, 222, 223, 234–235, 318, 319, 326

Wurlitzer, Rudy, 426, 427
Wyatt, Lorre, 162

Yardbirds, The, 39
Yarrow, Peter, 138, 144, 145, 160, 165–166, 262, 271, 302, 380, 382
"Yea! Heavy and a Bottle of Bread," 385
Yeats, William Butler, 491, 492, 498
Yediot Achronot (Israeli newspaper), 412
Yellin, Bob, 107, 112
Yevtushenko, Yevgeny, 305, 313, 495
"You Ain't Goin' Nowhere," 384
"You Angel You," 436
Young, Israel (Izzy), 94, 95, 102, 107, 112, 127–128, 129, 146, 313, 314
Young, Neil, 445, 446, 469, 482, 494
"You're a Big Girl Now," 441
"You're Gonna Make Me Lonesome When You Go," 442
"You're No Good," 118

Zappa, Frank, 145, 382
Zhito, Lee, 400
Zimmerman, Abe, 28–32, 33–34, 35, 37, 371–372
    death of, 59–61
    Dylan and, 33–34, 37–38, 40, 41, 50, 55, 56–61, 85
    importance of music to, 36
Zimmerman, Beatrice Stone, 28–32, 33–34
    Dylan and, 33, 34, 38, 41–42, 45, 55, 57, 58, 61, 85
Zimmerman, David, 31, 32, 35, 47, 56, 59
    Dylan and, 34, 35, 44, 59–60, 61, 471
Zimmerman, Maurice, 32
Zimmerman, Paul, 32
Zimmerman, Robert Allen, *see* Dylan, Bob
Zito, Tom, 430–431